THE JESUITS AND THE INDIAN WARS OF THE NORTHWEST

by *Robert Ignatius Burns, S.J.*

University of Idaho Press   Moscow, Idaho

University of Idaho Press
Box 3368, University Station
Moscow, Idaho 83843

Library of Congress catalog card number: 65-22314

PREFACE

THIS STUDY is the product of twenty years' intermittent research in American and European manuscript depositories. It began modestly enough as a project of editing source materials during a three-year tenure as assistant archivist at the Jesuit historical archives for the Pacific Northwest, one of the richest collections of manuscripts on the Indian. Over a six-year period I published in technical journals preliminary studies around the theme of Jesuit involvement in Indian-White troubles in the Northwest from 1840 to 1880. The search soon widened to include other American collections, and widened still further during a six-year residence in Europe. Eventually some fifty manuscript centers contributed to the making of the book.

The Jesuit materials deserve particular notice. They range from official records—such as reports to Rome and mission burial books—through house chronologies and amateur ethnological writings, to items as informal as a personal letter or a portfolio of paintings on Indian life. Non-Jesuit materials are equally necessary to the Jesuit-Indian theme. Archives like those of the War Department and the Indian Bureau are rich in unexploited documents. Lesser collections, like the Hudson's Bay Archives in London or the Coe and Miller manuscripts at Yale University, contribute vital information.

Many episodes of Pacific Northwest military and Indian history had never been explored in their manuscript sources—for example, the Kalispel Council of Stevens in 1856, the role of Agent Owens in the pacification of 1858–59, the dispositions of the Plateau tribes during the Nez Percé War, and the Wheaton Council of 1877. Many other episodes were known only in outline, or had important elements missing. Even the Stevens treaty tour needed to be recast, taking into account a wider documentation.

A theme as important as Jesuit peace services in the Northwest Indian troubles has not gone wholly unexplored. Preliminary work has appeared on several segments of the full story. Bischoff in his dissertation and articles goes into the Yakima War, biographers like Laveille and Donnelly touch on De Smet's 1859 peace tour, and biographers like Crosby and Weibel tell of Cataldo's 1877 rides for peace. There also exists a body of published Jesuit letters and communications, often scattered through old domestic journals.

Some encouragement toward a larger view can be drawn from general commentaries like Palladino's memoir on Montana Catholicism, Garraghan's chapters on the early Rocky Mountain missions under the jurisdiction of St. Louis, and Bischoff's history of the Oregon province.*

All this in turn has to be related to the numerous books and articles about Northwest history, and about church groups Protestant and Catholic there. Indian history poses a special problem; it is surprising how little has been done in depth. The Jesuit materials, combined with recent ethnological works on the several Interior tribes, bring this Indian world into focus. Thus the present work is part synthesis, part revision, and part contribution.

Some mechanical procedures require a word of explanation. The text displays those arbitrary choices of spelling (Okanogan, Charlo, Bitterroot, San Poils, MacDonald) and some mannerisms (capitalized White, retention of French names for only some Indians like Ignace, correction at times of Spokan or Colvile within quotes) which are the prerogative of every author. Nez Percé retains its accent, though this pedantic dictionary-usage is against local custom and encourages an incorrect, three-syllable pronunciation. On the other hand, Cœur d'Alêne is Americanized as Coeur d'Alene; and the Colvilles or Chaudières are simply Kettles.

Another problem of nomenclature, that of the upper and lower Spokanes, is treated in note 34 of Chapter 5. The missionaries' custom of maltranslating the more benevolent *sauvages* as the English "savages" is retained but should be noted. Military men generally bear their brevet or their formerly superior rank, even though serving actively in a lower rank; in the same fashion contemporaries often spoke of Colonel Steptoe and of Generals Wheaton and Gibbon. Lastly, Indian and White reminiscence is occasionally drawn upon, without apology but with caution; the reader may use or ignore it.

Footnotes, like a cavalry escort to a westering caravan, are a disturbing presence, obtrusive, noisy, and dusty. If there are too many of them, the diffident reader refuses to embark upon what promises to be arid and perilous pages. If there are too few, encouragement is given to tribes of implacable specialists who swarm out as one approaches their respective territories, eager to put an arrow into the unprotected author and his trusting reader. Our escort should be just enough to get us through. Though the notes bulk large, in fact they have been much cut back, often surviving only to locate quotations. Notes are frequently consolidated; where necessary, each element of such a note is related to its apposite textual matter by a clue-word in parenthesis.

Finally, I must acknowledge my debt to the many who have helped during the past two decades. This includes especially the officials at each of the manuscript depositories given in the bibliography; their aid was generous and

* See below, Bib.

their interest was often personal. In some places a special debt is owed. At Fribourg, for example, I had the full run of the manuscript stacks in the (Lyons) Propagation of the Faith archives for a year; at the central Jesuit archives in Rome all reserved categories were lifted; at the National Archives in Washington my importunities were answered with a cheerful and monumental service. In the final stages of the book's organizing, the University of San Francisco gave a faculty grant for a month's archival travel; and a Guggenheim Fellowship, though awarded in connection with an entirely different research project, allowed me to check a few last details in Europe.

For their encouragement and help I should like to single out R. Rahmann, S.V.D., of Université de Fribourg and the Anthropos-Institut, and especially William Lyle Davis, S.J., of Gonzaga University.

San Francisco   Robert Ignatius Burns, S.J.
May 1965

CONTENTS

ABBREVIATIONS

(See Bibliography for Full Citation)

ABFM	American Board of Foreign Missions, Archives, Houghton Library, Harvard University.
ACIM	*Annals of the Catholic Indian Missions of America.*
AFL	*Annales de l'association de la foi, Lyon.*
AFQ	*Annâles de la propagation de la foi pour la province de Québec.*
AGO	See under NA.
BAE	Bureau of American Ethnology, Smithsonian Institution.
BC	British Columbia, Province Archives, Victoria.
BJ	Archives de la province (jésuite) belge du nord, Brussels.
BL	Bancroft Library, University of California, MSS.
CD Docs.	Flathead Indians, *Our Friends the Coeur d'Aleine Indians.*
CF	Archives cantonales (Staatsarchiv), Fribourg.
CHSM	*Contributions to the Historical Society of Montana.*
CM	Bureau of Catholic Indian Missions, Washington, D.C., Archives.
CR	De Smet letters in *Life, Letters and Travels of Father Pierre-Jean De Smet, S.J.*, ed. H. M. Chittenden and A. T. Richardson.
DAB	*Dictionary of American Biography.*
EW	See under NA.
EWS	Eastern Washington State Historical Society, Spokane, MSS.
FL	Archives de la société pour la propagation de la foi de Lyon, Fribourg.
FP	Archives de la société pour la propagation de la foi de Paris.
HB	Archives of Hudson's Bay Company, London.
HED	U. S. Congress, *House Executive Documents.*
HL	Huntington Library, San Marino, California, MSS.
IA	See under NA.
IHS	Idaho Historical Society, Boise, MSS.
JMUS	G. G. Garraghan, S.J., *Jesuits of the Middle United States.*
LC	Division of MSS, Library of Congress.
LN	English Jesuits, *Letters and Notices.*
LPT	Turin Jesuits, *Lettere della provincia torinese.*
LR	See under NA.
LS	See under NA.

MC	*Missions catholiques*, Paris.
MD	Militia documents, Archives of the Military Dept., Washington State (Tacoma).
MHM	*Maryland Historical Magazine.*
MHS	Montana Historical Society, Helena, MSS.
MJ	Jesuit Historical Archives, Missouri Province, St. Louis.
MVHR	*Misssissippi Valley Historical Review.*
NA	National Archives, Washington, D.C.

	AGO	Adjutant General's Office
	EW	Early Wars Branch
	IA	Indian Affairs Office
	LR	Letters Received
	LS	Letters Sent

NYPL	New York Public Library, MSS.
OH	Oregon Historical Society, Portland, MSS.
OHQ	*Oregon Historical Quarterly.*
OJ	Jesuit Historical Archives, Oregon Province, Spokane.
OS	State Archives, Salem, Oreg.
OU	Library, University of Oregon, Eugene, MSS.
PA	Archdiocese of Portland, Archives.
PHR	*Pacific Historical Review.*
PNWQ	*Pacific Northwest Quarterly.*
RACHS	*Records of the American Catholic Historical Society.*
RBIC	Board of Indian Commissioners, annual *Report.*
RCIA	Commissioner of Indian Affairs, annual *Report.*
RJ	Archivum historicum societatis Jesu, Rome.
RO	Oblates of Mary Immaculate, Rome, Archives.
RR	I. I. Stevens, *Narrative and Final Report of Explorations for a Route for a Pacific Railroad.*
SA	Archdiocese of Seattle, Archives.
SED	U. S. Congress, *Senate Executive Documents.*
SF	University of San Francisco, Archives.
SI	Smithsonian Institution, Natural History, MSS.
SM	Archives du Collège Ste. Marie, Montreal.
SU	Library, St. Louis University, MSS.
TJ	Archivio della provincia torinese della compagnia di Gesù, Turin.
WHQ	*Washington Historical Quarterly.*
WL	American Jesuits, *Woodstock Letters.*
WL	State Library, Olympia, Wash., MSS.
WP	Library, Washington State College, Pullman, MSS.
WS	State Archives, Olympia, Wash.
WU	Library, University of Washington, Seattle, MSS.
YU	Western Americana MSS, Library, Yale University.

I. Two Worlds: Red Men and White (1840-1880)

WILDERNESS EMPIRE

AMERICA in the 1830s was an innocent and rural land. A strip of eastern seaboard served to house the larger part of her population. The North displayed a growing urbanization and primitive industry, the South a concentration on cotton. But to the west for decades the frontier had been surging forward erratically. From the Appalachians to the Mississippi this frontier was slowly filling up. Infrequent farms and hamlets dotted its expanse. Plantations were laid out in its south. Small cities stood in its older sections or materialized abruptly at unlikely points. Canals and steamboats multiplied, and from 1840 railroads.

This frontier area was not yet really broken to civilization. There was lawlessness and speculation and wild, empty country. But the Indian at least was disappearing. Tribe after tribe, bearing its bitter burden of hatred toward the Whites, was "removed" across the barrier of the Mississippi River. In 1836 the Senate committee for Indian Affairs could report that the Indians were finally and forever "on an *outside* of us." [1]

In the next decade, then, the wild frontier would lie across the Mississippi, in the incalculable space that stretched to the Pacific Ocean. Here was the Great American Desert, and here was the new Indian country, on the north-central steppes of the Louisiana Purchase. More important, here lay imperial domains ripe for the taking—like the Texas republic, New Mexico, California, Utah, and the Oregon country, each with its own history, geography, climate, and native population. The vision of a providential Manifest Destiny dazzled many an American. This was to be the decade of the war with Mexico, the Mormon settlement of Utah, the California gold rush, and the struggle for Oregon. Indian wars erupted over the West again and again. The

1. *Sen. Doc.*, 24 Cong., 1 Sess., 246 (1836); cf. doc. 228; 31,000 had gone and most of the remaining 72,000 had agreed by treaty to go soon. For antecedents and previous policy see below, Bib., under Harmon, Prucha.

population flow became a tumbling flood. Then suddenly, thirty or forty years later, the frontier was gone.

The sweep and proportions of this westward movement are dramatic, but what stuns the imagination is its pace. Individuals could and did live through the entire process. Immediately after the Louisiana Purchase in 1803, for example, the Lewis and Clark expedition had ventured into the unexplored Northwest regions. The last survivor of that expedition, born before the American Revolution, died in 1870. The Indian woman who had helped in it lived on bright and alert to 1884. A Flathead woman who saw its coming was alive as late as 1890.

In 1835 a young Indian named François Saxa accompanied his father from the Oregon Rockies to St. Louis as part of a "Flathead delegation" seeking priests. He lived to become a respected Montana cattleman, to watch the Northern Pacific Railway thunder by his house for four decades, and to die after World War I in 1919. Many of the Oregon Jesuit missionaries were born in the Napoleonic world or its aftermath and survived to see the end of the American Wild West. De Smet lived from 1801 to 1873, Joset from 1810 to 1900, Cataldo from 1837 to 1928. Accolti's span was from 1807 to 1878, Specht's from 1809 to 1884, Ravalli's from 1812 to 1884, Hoecken's from 1815 to 1897, Congiato's from 1816 to 1897, Palladino's from 1837 to 1927, and Caruana's from 1836 to 1913.

This rapidity of evolution is an essential element in the Indian story. It helped give an epic quality to the conquest of the Oregon country. It also made of it, from the Indian side, a tragedy. Had the settlement been less precipitate, and had Americans enjoyed sufficient time to adjust to circumstances, the bitter drama of Indian and White in the Pacific Northwest might have taken a different turn.

There is an equally imposing dimension of space. In 1830 the name "Oregon" could arouse fearsome specters in the mind of the hearer. The pioneer of the Mississippi Valley looked west toward Oregon over the Great American Desert, "an ocean between civilization and barbarism" which required months to cross.[2] At the end of such a journey he knew he would be confronted with Oregon's massive mountain barrier, the Rockies, which seemed like "the ruins of a whole world" tumbled down by a great convulsion of nature and covered with "eternal snow as with a shroud." [3] Beyond this threshold he could contemplate immensities that stretched far and away to the Pacific. Here were Bryant's "continuous woods, where rolls the mighty Oregon, and hears no sound save his own dashings." Dense forests of pine and fir swept awesomely down to an indeterminate boundary near Mexican Califor-

2. CR, *1*, 207–08, 391; *4*, 1402; but cf. below, Bib., Prucha.
3. CR, *1*, 215.

nia. Oregon's northern expanses rolled through tangled wilderness, through fields of snow and ice where its limits mingled with Russian claims.

The American Oregon country by itself comprised 285,000 square miles, about a tenth of the continental United States. It included the future states of Oregon, Washington, Idaho, and western Montana, a land area almost equaling France, Germany, Spain, and Italy combined. It held a falls higher than Niagara, a gorge deeper than the Grand Canyon, and a river outmatching the Missouri or the Nile. Small pockets are wonders today: the Craters of the Moon National Monument, or the Glacier National Park with its 60 glaciers, 100 peaks, 250 lakes, and 500 waterfalls. It was a land of silence, of soaring stone towers and columns of light, of desert plains, mountain ranges, and waterways rolling to the sea. When Father Joset arrived in 1845, into what is now Idaho, he wrote home to Switzerland that he was "at the end of the earth in the middle of a labyrinth of mountains, forests, lakes, and rivers." [4]

The reader may conveniently picture American Oregon in terms of its interior: a huge rectangle, much longer from west to east than it is from north to south. Down the left or western side run the Cascade Mountains. The Cascades isolate the main settlements of the Whites for most of our period; farms and unimpressive hamlets were tucked away in the coastal valleys of the western margin. Down the right or eastern side of the rectangle march the majestic Rocky Mountains, whose range upon range of imposing peaks comprise a physiographic province in themselves.

This interior may be divided into a lower region, which will not concern us so much, and an upper area, known as the Columbia Plateau. More properly, the upper region is a basin; and physiographically it is only half of the Canadian-American interior. This important area constitutes a square within the original rectangle. It is hemmed in on both sides by the Cascades and the Rockies. The Blue Mountains bound it on the south, below the Snake River. Along its north the Okanogan Highlands, an odd set of parallel north-south ranges, come down from the Canadian border to halt abruptly at the edge of the Plateau.

The Plateau embraces some 12,700 square miles, and deceptively resembles a plain. It includes fertile valleys and grassy plains, as well as 2,800 square miles of wrinkled scablands and 900 square miles of gravelly desert. Its main feature is the Columbia River, one of the great waterways of the world. This enters the square at the top center, soon turns west, and then drops down along the Cascades until it finds an opening to the sea at the lower left of the square. Near the top it receives the waters of the Spokane River; near the bottom it takes those of the Snake River.

In terms of human geography the Interior Plateau was preeminently the

4. *AFL*, *18* (1846), 504, Joset to Father Fouillet, S.J. (in French), 22 February 1845.

domain of the wild tribes. For practical purposes the Oregon pioneer reckoned it as including the world of the mountain Indians and even, on occasion,
the beginning of the Great Plains just beyond the Rockies. The ethnologist
might delimit the Interior one way, the physiographer another. At the risk of
some imprecision around the edges, the term may be accommodated slightly
to the needs of history.

The extent of this wilderness deserves to be meditated upon because it conditioned all human activity. For most of our period there were few roads or
bridges. Snow and flood were dire perils. Even to travel from one mission to
another, some 200 miles, could develop into a dangerous adventure. "In these
vast lands, occupied by numerous Indian tribes of a more or less nomadic nature," wrote the Jesuit general in Rome as late as 1869, the Jesuits carried on
their apostolate. Around the same time the general referred to "these missions, assuredly among the most difficult"; "they cover immense territories
which the missionaries must ceaselessly traverse on horseback." [5]

Under such conditions decisive military action against hostile Indians was
extremely difficult. Guerrilla warfare could continue indefinitely, to the advantage of the Indians, in a country where even the finding of those Indians
was a major project. The trader at the Hudson's Bay post of Fort Vancouver
underlined this in 1848 when writing of a war between the Whites of the Coast
and an Indian tribe situated relatively close to them in the Interior. "Hostilities have virtually ceased from the total exhaustion of resources on both
sides." [6] If a winter were severe, as it often enough was, all contact with the
Interior might be severed. [7]

THE INDIAN INTERIOR

At first sight the Oregon wilderness seemed empty. Deserts spread themselves naked before the eye. Hoofbeats of the solitary horseman echoed
lonely and unheard in the forested valley. Below this surface, however, life
stirred. This was an Indian world, nomadic and private, with its nations and
confederations and shifting alliances, its unmarked boundaries and traditional
enmities. Each of its tribes had its own history, its own hopes, terrors, heart-
breaks, and fierce joys. Here the Whites were like intruders from another
planet. The Jesuit missioners, like the soldiers and settlers, were to come upon
these Indians at a critical moment in their evolution. This must be under-

5. FP, I, 5, Peter Beckx to Association (in French), 16 April 1869 and 6 May
1865.

6. HB, Annals, *19*, under 1849, No. 101, Fort Vancouver, 1 October 1848.

7. As in 1857 (HB, D5, *43*, Simpson Correspondence inward, D. Mactavish to Simpson, Fort Vancouver, 22 January 1857).

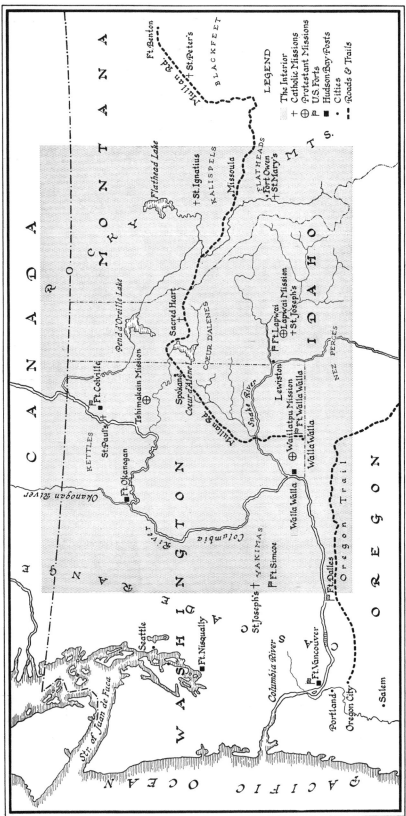

2. The "Interior," 1840–1880.

stood, if the Jesuit efforts in peace and in war are to fall into perspective.

The traveler hardy enough to traverse this Indian world at several points could not help being impressed by its variety. Few places on the continent ever held such a jumble of tribes, such a contradiction of cultures, and such a babble of separate tongues. The Indian population for both American and Canadian Oregon combined, according to Catholic and Protestant missionaries around 1840, was over 100,000. This figure is two to three times too large but probably represents the best estimate of the Hudson's Bay people. The Indians were divided into about 125 different tribes, with 56 mutually unintelligible languages. Still, this stir of life was sluggish. The human content was swallowed by the geographical dimension. Ten thousand Indians might cavort in war dances or scatter to dig for roots and go unnoticed. The wilderness absorbed them.

It is perhaps most convenient to approach these Indians by concentrating on the American Oregon country, dividing its tribes broadly into three categories: coastal, Interior, and Plains. The Plains Indians far to the east, such as the Blackfeet, Crows, and Sioux of Montana, belonged to the familiar culture of the buffalo-hunting horseman, with his tipi and war bonnet. They were not domiciled in the Oregon country itself. They were not included in the reckonings above either, nor will they enter the story very often until the final chapter. But they did live within the somewhat wider limits of the Pacific Northwest. They would also eventually be the concern of the Rocky Mountain Jesuits rather than of the missionaries of the Great Plains. As for the coastal Indians, they had their own distinctive culture, in forms more varied and numerous than those of the Interior. Below the Columbia River their way of life was somewhat assimilated to that of the Interior.

The tribes of the Interior comprised roughly all those between the Cascades and the Rocky Mountains. (Like the pioneer we broaden the term Interior to include the various tribes of the Rockies.) The Interior was relatively protected by its mountain barriers, though by no means insulated. The coastal culture had a strong formative influence—particularly in the western part, with Puget Sound Indians communicating through the mountain passes and the Chinooks controlling trade channels to the Interior from the mouth of the Columbia. The Plains Indians similarly influenced the Interior, their impact coming especially from the east and the southeast.

The Interior had its own culture and economy, which continued north uninterruptedly into Canada, though the artificial Canadian boundary of the Whites accidentally fell near a cultural cleavage, showing modifications both in social and in material culture. To the south, the Interior Plateau may be defined as stopping short at the Blue Mountains. Below this point tribes such as the Snakes and Bannocks in southern Idaho and southern Oregon belong to

a Great Basin subculture, akin to the Indians of Nevada and Utah. They are
in the same physiographic province nevertheless, and both Basin and Plateau
tribes tended to assimilate to a common Interior way of life. Thus they could
be called, not unjustly, Interior or Plateau tribes. We are not very interested
in this southern Interior sector, any more than we were in the northern or
Canadian Interior tribes. Our Indians are those in the central Interior zone.
To this, and its mountain hinterland, we confine the terms Interior and Plateau. The Protestant and Catholic missioners, though active elsewhere, went
especially to these central Indians.

Besides this cultural division for the Indian Interior, there was a basic division by languages. Oddly enough, these language boundaries do not correspond with the cultural divisions, even in a secondary way. Two major language families divide most of the American Interior, though they were not
confined there. Varieties of Salishan were spoken in the northern half among
the Flatheads, Coeur d'Alenes, Spokanes, Kettles, Okanogans, Kalispels, San
Poils, Columbias, and other tribes. The Sahaptin language controlled the
south among the Nez Percés, Palouses, Yakimas, Cayuses (formerly believed
to speak a separate language), Walla Wallas, Umatillas, and neighboring
tribes. On the eastern Plains fringing the Oregon country, Algonquian and
Sioux were dominant. Along the far south, tribes such as the Snakes and Bannocks spoke the Shoshonean tongues. Apart from all this, the Kutenais at the
Canadian border had a separate language. There was intercommunication by
sign language, by mastering other dialects or languages, and by the trade jargon known as Chinook.

These are schematizations. The subdivisions and dialect differences were
forbidding. A Salish-speaking Indian would understand the dialects in his
own subgroup. The Western Spokanes, San Poils, Southern Okanogans, and
Kettles, for example, fell into such a subgroup. The Eastern and Central Spokanes, with the Kalispels, could comprehend each other's tongues; but the
Coeur d'Alenes stood alone in their unique subgroup. Similarly, the Nez
Percés formed a special subgroup of the Sahaptin, unintelligible to the
other groupings of their own language. Language was not necessarily an important bond. The Southern Okanogans denied any identity with the Northern Okanogans though they spoke the same dialect. The Eastern Spokanes
were closely identified with the Coeur d'Alenes despite divergent dialects.
And the Flatheads were allies and trade partners with the Nez Percés, although their basic language families were different. Even so, most Salishan
speakers on the Plateau were friends, and language did tend to draw neighbors together.

For practical purposes the important distinction was not by culture or by
language family but by individual political units. And it was here that the

White man particularly failed to grasp the nature of the Indian world. He was used to the large, disciplined "tribes" with their dramatic tribal councils and powerful chiefs. This structure he innocently projected onto the Oregon scene. The misunderstanding had some foundation in reality. In parts of the Interior the tribe as a political entity was discernibly emerging. Even where the process of transformation had not begun, an observer might reasonably impose a certain unity among related collections of villages. The Indians themselves could not recognize some of these larger systems; where they did, they seldom gave them a name. It is important to dwell on the point, since this book will speak, as contemporaries spoke, of pseudo-tribes like the Spokanes, Kettles, Nez Percés, Okanogans, San Poils, or Coeur d'Alenes.

The basic political unit of the Interior was the village, often related with others into a band. The band might be a loose assortment of villages or a closely knit cluster operating together. It could even be a mobile small corps, perhaps long established or perhaps recently gathered around a war chief or attracted by some common enterprise. Any larger aggregation was usually nonpolitical, being socio-economic or linguistic or merely geographic. The village had its chief, or at least a headman, with an important chief for larger groupings and sometimes a head chief over all.

Each association had a range or recognized zone of territory. The component village, which generally stood upon a waterway of some kind, had a similar inner zone, which might grow vaguer as the distance increased from the environs of the village. Besides the villages there were many camping grounds, since the tribes frequently wandered elsewhere to hunt, fish, dig roots, or pick berries, for months at a time. Although there was a tendency to village autonomy, diverse bonds ensured continuing relations: habitat, customs, intermarriage, values, religion, a common hunting or berrying range, or a shared dialect. When these unifying forces combined in sufficient strength, even with little loss of autonomy, the result might be mistaken for a political "tribe."

Swanton's authoritative lexicon of Indian tribes lists well over a hundred such "tribes" for the American Oregon country.[8] It would be easy to analyze and arrange them into twice that number. The Plateau tribes that enter our story directly may be simplified into about fifteen natural and arbitrary groupings. Visualizing the Interior plateau and mountains as a square and consulting the attached map, the tribal groupings in the mid-nineteenth century may be simplified as follows.[9] The Flatheads occupy the Rockies along

8. *The Indian Tribes of North America*, comp. J. R. Swanton, BAE, Bull. 145 (Washington, D.C., 1952), sections on Oregon, Washington, Idaho, and Montana.

9. From V. R. Ray, *Cultural Relations in the Plateau of Northwestern America* (Los Angeles, 1939), p. 2. This is the tribal distribution around 1850 as revealed by his field

the eastern or right side. A tier of tribes—Kutenai, Kalispel with Pend d'Oreille, Coeur d'Alene, and Nez Percé—curves down the Flatheads' western flank, from north to south. Next, at the center of the square in a similar tier are the Lake, San Poil and Kettle, Spokane, Palouse, and Walla Walla with Cayuse tribes. To the west of them again runs another lateral tier, comprising Okanogan, Southern Okanogan, Columbia, Yakima, and Umatilla Indians. Along the foot of the Cascades a final tier involves about six tribes less important to us.

Four northern tribes of the Plateau represent only the American edge of very large Canadian tribes: the Thompsons, Okanogans, Lakes, and Kutenais. The Kalispels extend a short distance into Canada. Out on the Plains, the Blackfoot tribes (Piegans, Bloods, Blackfeet) stretch along the top of Montana, followed to the east by the Assiniboine branch of the Sioux, and finally by the Gros Ventre branch of the Arapahoes. The Crows held southeast Montana. Other tribes, such as the Snakes and the Bannocks of southern Idaho, bordered upon and influenced the Plateau Indians.

The Indians of the Interior were a strangely anarchistic yet peaceful lot. They had startlingly little in the way of political organization. Their allegiance to chiefs and subchiefs was at best informal. Under an unusual chief, government might become patriarchal. There was no strong leadership, no priesthood, no social stratification except in a minor way according to differences in wealth or prestige. Cooperation as a tribal unit was casual and passing. Unity, though sometimes strong, was highly informal. Apparent exceptions to this political structure were those tribes along the east and south of the Plateau. Associations such as the Flatheads and Nez Percés, with their tipis and fierce war complex, seemed to be like Plains tribes. This paradox, and indeed the many ambiguities of Plateau culture, is explained by a revolution that was still going forward when the White man arrived.

Spanish horses, handed up through Apache raiders to Shoshone traders, reached the Interior before 1725.[10] Soon they were being bred, and dispersed across the Rockies to the Plains tribes. Some Oregon chiefs held up to 5,000 head apiece. The horse brought greater mobility: swift travel, heavy trans-

researches. A somewhat different methodology and purpose are involved in the more local studies of Leslie Spier, *Tribal Distribution in Washington*, Amer. Anthrop. Assoc., Gen. Ser., 3 (Menasha, Wisc., 1936), and J. V. Berreman, *Tribal Distribution in Oregon*, Amer. Anthrop. Assoc., Memoirs, 47 (Menasha, Wisc., 1937). This part of our chapter is indebted not only to missionary manuscripts and such older investigators as Teit, but especially to the ethnological works of Ray on village and Plateau culture and on the San Poil-Nespelem tribes, of Liljeblad on the Idaho tribes, of Turney-High on the Flatheads and Kutenais, and Cline-Spier on the Southern Okanogans (see below. Bib.). The tribal lines on our map are adapted largely from Murdock (see below, Bib.).

10. F. G. Roe, *The Indian and the Horse* (Norman, Okla., 1955), p. 78; cf. p. 129.

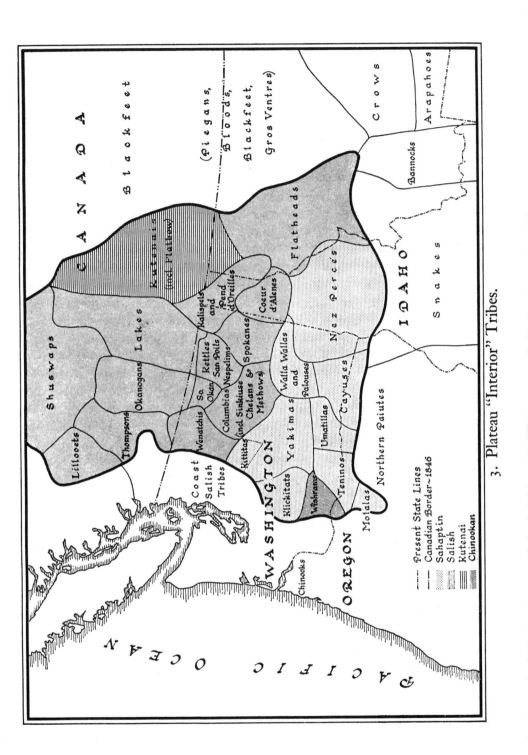

3. Plateau "Interior" Tribes.

PACIFIC OCEAN

CANADA

Blackfeet

(Piegans, Bloods, Blackfeet, Gros Ventres)

Crows

Arapahoes

Bannocks

Kutenais (incl. Flatbow)

Flatheads

IDAHO

Snakes

Shuswaps

Lakes

Okanogans

Pend d'Oreilles

Coeur d'Alenes

Nez Perces

Lillooets

Thompsons

Kalispels and San Poils

Spokanes

Sa. Okan. Kettles

Wenatchis

Columbias (incl. Sinkiuse Chelans & Methows)

Napelims

Walla Wallas and Palouses

Kittitas

Coast Salish Tribes

Klickitats

Wishrams

Teninos

Yakimas

Cayuses

Umatillas

Northern Paiutes

WASHINGTON

Molalas

OREGON

Chinooks

Present State Lines
Canadian Border ~1846
Sahaptin
Salish
Kutenai
Chinookan

port, and easy contact with tribes near and far. Food was more assured. The hunt and warfare became efficient and exciting. Greater leisure and sophistication resulted. Women's status rose. Village groups drifted to more open country. Some clans or individuals reorganized into larger bands. Intertribal communications, commercial rendezvous, and the whole pattern of trade improved. For tribes like the Southern Okanogan, river trade was now supplemented by an expanded range. In short, the horizon of the Indian widened, and his development intensified.

If the coming of the horse did not occasion the rise of a warrior culture, it facilitated it. The Plains influence seems to have come in a rush to the tribes on the eastern and southern borders of the Interior. They turned now to the portable skin tipi, tailored buckskin clothing, and elaborate ornament. Aggressive militarism developed. They "adopted a war complex virtually in its entirety." [11] War paint, war dances, and a new armory appeared. Young men of many tribes tended to ride with some redoubted leader on raids. No one was responsible for these brigand bands, which often broke up after the raid. An arbitrary hierarchy of war honors was elaborated. The Flatheads, Coeur d'Alenes, Kutenais, Nez Percés, and Umatillas had an exultant Scalp Dance. The war complex was borrowed "to the fullest" by the Flatheads, Kutenais, Nez Percés, Cayuses, and Umatillas, and to a considerable degree by the Coeur d'Alenes and others. Actual warfare "was greatly amplified in frequency and in skill." [12] It was a selective borrowing, however, and the combination of elements taken varied from tribe to tribe.

The further one traveled west, the weaker this Plains influence became. The Coeur d'Alenes had a substantial measure of it, the Western Spokanes far less, while the San Poils determinedly kept to primitive pacifism. Plains influence in general only superficially affected the central Salish, such as the Western Spokane, Kettle, San Poil, Southern Okanogan, and Columbia villages. Even where this influence was strongest, it left much of the older structure intact. Buffalo hunting did become more prominent. But the tribal economy still centered on the cycle of root digging, berrying, hunting deer or small game, and fishing at the great intertribal salmon centers.

The Kalispels would still break up their villages of rush huts and scatter in winter, in units of four to six lodges, to seek food. The Coeur d'Alenes were still located in some thirty permanent villages, from which they went away on long expeditions during a food-gathering cycle. Most of the Plateau tribes, though they adopted the tipi, retained some mat lodges also as permanent dwellings. The easy movement from tribe into tribe continued both by immigration and by intermarriage. A Flathead village might be largely Nez Percés, Spokanes, Kalispels, or mixed breeds, many of whom had assumed

11. Ray, *Cultural Relations,* p. 146; cf. pp. 14, 40.
12. Ibid., pp. 42, 14.

the new tribal affiliation. The arrival of the Plains culture had been too swift and violent to be properly assimilated.

This uneasy adjustment of an older culture to a superficial but permanent overlay is a key to understanding the Interior Indians. For example, where Plains influence developed a tribal structure one sees a kind of political specialization. The "tribe" would be evident in warfare, intervillage functions, and similar large affairs, while the village, under its village chief and council, controlled local or peacetime activities. The spirit was less that of a divided tribe than of an agglomeration of villages upward to form a tribe. Thus the Nez Percés had a tribal structure, yet they remained a congeries of several autonomous tribes, each composed of rather independent villages. Each village had its chief, and there was little political connection between villages in peacetime. The Flatheads were similarly organized, but placed more emphasis upon the role of the tribal chief. The Coeur d'Alenes were an ethnic and tribal grouping of three bands; village authority was strong, and the head chief weak.

The Spokanes, somewhat under Plains influence, were really three tribes; in each there was a pronounced village autonomy. The Lake Indians were fairly closed off from Plains influence, and unified by constant waterways communication. The Kutenais were a single grouping, yet decentralized into strong villages. The Southern Okonogans were four bands, each with its own territory and chief or rather administrative manager. Their unity was largely a matter of intermarriage and mingling. The San Poils had no tribal organization but were a series of neighboring, independent villages. Their sense of community owed much to a constant interchange of population.

Tribes under heavy Plains influence tended to maintain more rigid boundaries and to refuse the use of their lands to foreigners. They often chose their chiefs on grounds of achievement, especially in war. They tended to go to buffalo on the Great Plains, where their presence was violently resisted by tribes such as the Blackfeet and Sioux. Even the peaceful San Poils and Southern Okonogans would sometimes ride to buffalo. The Flatheads, Nez Percés, Cayuses, and Umatillas had permanent war chiefs. Such examples only introduce the problem of Plateau complexity and exceptions. The whole situation was fragmented, and the fragments were in movement and evolution. This evolution was to assume new scope with the coming of the missionaries, the wars with the Whites, and changes in economic life.

FORTS AND GODS OF THE WHITE MAN

Fifty years after the horse, White explorers intruded in force upon this changing scene. By the end of the century coastal tribes were accustomed to the casual but regular ships from many countries pausing to barter for furs. A trickle of White commodities was abroad. Between 1789 and 1843 in the Oregon country some fifty fur posts were to go up, if one counts rebuildings and forts of very brief life span.[13]

The important event for the Interior Indians was the penetration of their region by the British and Americans. In 1805 Lewis and Clark, the most famous of the land explorers here, made their way over the Rockies and down to the sea. Fur companies of both nations came hard upon their heels, inaugurating a brief era of cutthroat rivalry. After 1821 the Hudson's Bay Company by merger and maneuver became supreme; Americans continued to trade in the mountains, especially up to 1837. From Fort Vancouver, located at the mouth of the Columbia River, the Company began its quarter-century career as the major White presence in the Oregon country Interior.

The tiny posts of the Company were physically an insignificant addition in this vast region, but they were to mark the Indian way of life deeply. Firearms, blankets, fishhooks, tobacco, knives, utensils, cloth, and trade goods of all kinds now became common. The Company persuaded various bands to start vegetable plots, then taught them beekeeping, herding, and other elementary disciplines. The Indians, taking a giant stride away from their immemorial isolation, were excited by the ways of these fantastic strangers and were conditioned to accept the White presence. They soon came to respect the Company and prize its trade. The militaristic tribes among them were especially enthusiastic; they were desperate for guns, because their encroaching Plains enemies had them. They could now recover the offensive, and even indulge more effectively in intramural raiding. In a hunting economy the gun complemented the horse. Forty Flathead hunters, for instance, could bring down three hundred deer in a day.[14] Eventually this new efficiency was bound to diminish both game and furs, but for a blissful interim period cultural development accelerated.

Hudson's Bay employees, mostly French Canadians and Iroquois with Scots overseers, could travel anywhere in comparative safety. They married into the many tribes, subtly influencing tribal habits and psychology. By this time many of the nameless Interior "tribes" answered to French names, chosen by the traders for reasons trivial or fanciful or erroneous. These appellations the later Whites usually retained either in an English version (Snakes, Kettles, Flatheads) or in badly pronounced French (Nez Percés, Coeur d'Alenes).

The eventful years to about 1840 were generally happy for the Interior Indian. He hardly realized that a Pandora's box of trouble had been unlocked.

13. J. N. Barry, "Early Oregon Forts, a Chronological List," *OHQ*, 46 (1945), 99-133.
14. CR, 2, 467 (ca. 1845). On the Flathead trade see P. C. Phillips, *The Fur Trade*, 2 (2 vols. Norman, Okla., 1961), 258, 458.

Yet the White man's diseases were spreading recurrently through the tribes, taking a toll more terrible than any Black Death known to Europe's history. Over two-thirds of the Indians of the Pacific Northwest simply disappeared. In 1780 there were perhaps 75,000 in the future American portion of the Oregon country (exclusive of the Plains area); after 1830 there may have been less than 20,000. In 1782 it was smallpox, in 1831 fever and ague, in 1835 smallpox again, and so on. The smallpox of 1846, the measles of 1847, and the smallpox of 1852–53 were terrible killers in the Interior. Tuberculosis and venereal diseases ravaged the coastal Indians.[15]

On the Coast these disasters were compounded by another kind of plague. Tribal morals disintegrated under the impact of bad example; the Indian was fatally attracted to the worst elements of the frontier population. Wholesale prostitution and ruinous alcoholism were one stage of his descent into misery. So painful was the spectacle that some sympathetic Whites felt it a mercy when disease swept away almost whole tribes. Catholic missionaries were later to remark upon the rapid decline of the Indian character as White settlement increased.

Like the arrival of the first ants at a picnic, the trading ships and fur posts were only an advance guard. The White invasion had begun. Ironically, the coming of the first missionaries in 1834 was to swell the invasion to proportions that the Indians could no longer tolerate. The time was the period just before and after 1840. The crucial place was the final stretch along the Oregon Trail.

The weakest element in the culture of the Interior tribes had been religion. A simple animism sufficed. Irreverence was abhorrent to the Indian; blasphemy he had to learn from the Whites. Morals varied from tribe to tribe. There was neither cult nor priesthood, and only the beginnings of spiritual concepts. The outstanding feature of the native Interior religion was the Guardian Spirit idea, the quest for a personal vision or dream through which a spirit might direct one's career. This theological vacuum could not long survive the appearance of the more sophisticated Plains and White religions. Before 1830 both were already disturbing and altering the Interior religion.

The influences predisposing the Indians to receive White missionaries were varied and insistent. News of this religion had filtered into the Oregon country quite early. The Interior echoed with such news and rumors. Just as grass from the Rockies traveled through trade channels to the basketmakers on the coast, so religious information circulated. Movement was constant between the Nez Percé south, the Flathead east, and the Kettle north. Opportunities

15. L. M. Scott, "Indian Diseases as Aids to Pacific Northwest Settlement," *OHQ*, 29 (1928), 144–46, 149. Swanton, *Indian Tribes*, p. 413.

for observation and inquiry soon became frequent enough.[16] There had been brief contacts with Spanish missioners; and at least one Spokane woman seems to have visited the California missions. Protestant and Catholic traders could be seen at occasional Sunday devotions or burial services. Around 1810 in the remote Flathead region one is surprised to discover several men, of devout and even proselytizing temper, separately in touch with the Indians. At Fort Vancouver near the mouth of the Interior, the Hudson's Bay factor conducted regular forms of both Episcopalian and Catholic worship.

A direct and important source of Christian knowledge were the ubiquitous French Canadian voyageurs. Living among the tribes or settled in small communities, frequently attached to Indian women without benefit of clergy, they seem at first sight unlikely apostles. They were a wild and woolly lot, tolerant, and fairly heedless of religious obligations. Some were vicious and irreligious. Most were dismally ill-informed; but then the Indian himself was capable at first of receiving only the elementary ideas of Catholicism.

The first priests to work in this region, though they spoke candidly of the vicious element among the Canadians, acknowledged their debt to the rest. They described how the North West Company, even before the days of the Hudson's Bay dominance, "had employed only Canadians and Catholic Iroquois," thus contributing "powerfully" in planting the seeds of Christianity among the Indians. In the Hudson's Bay Company the bondsmen were "not very Christian," and were given to debauchery; the "majority" of the semi-free trappers contrasted with them by their basic attachment to religion. Archbishop Blanchet, in a memorandum presented to Rome in 1847 a decade after his arrival, went into the matter. Despite the drift to "religious indifference" and despite "the dissoluteness of many," the Canadians had "recalled with happiness the very powerful and sweet memories of religion" so that "they would speak with comfort to the Indians about their faith [and] their priests." Thus the welcome given by the tribes to the missionaries "had been prepared for a long time." [17]

Eugene Duflot de Mofras, an agent for France who was preparing a report on the prospects of the region in 1840–42, stressed the cultural foundations of this voyageur attachment. So fanatically French were they that it pained them to have overseers of another "race and religion." As soon as

16. A number of early influences and opportunities are gathered by T. C. Elliot in his "Religion Among the Flatheads," *OHQ*, 37 (1936), 1–8, and by Cyprian Bradley, O.S.B., and E. J. Kelly in their *History of the Diocese of Boise 1863–1952* (Boise, Idaho, 1953), pp. 50–58.

17. F. N. Blanchet, M. Demers, et al., *Notices and Voyages of the Famed Quebec Mission to the Pacific Northwest*, ed. Carl Landerholm (Portland, Oreg., 1956), pp. 217–18, 184–85, 228.

Blanchet arrived in 1838, wrote Duflot, his mission became their vital social center, so that they thrust upon him a "patriarchal" authority.[18] When an Episcopalian chaplain at Fort Vancouver previously had been baptizing and marrying some more tolerant bondsmen, and dreaming of conversions, Chief Factor McLoughlin sharply warned the Company of the explosive dangers involved.

Some Canadians in the Interior even assumed the active role of lay missioners. At Fort Okanogan in 1840 Father Demers found "unexpected help"; one Robillard "had taught the prayers to the natives" who therefore "eagerly awaited me." In the Flatbow country Father De Smet discovered the tribe already "in the best disposition to embrace the faith," due to the "instructions and counsels of Berland" who "for a long time has resided among them" as a trader. Berland had instructed them "in the principal mysteries of religion" and taught them "canticles in the French and Indian tongues." Pambrun, the commander of the Hudson's Bay post at Walla Walla, taught the Indians in his region the basic Christianity of the Creed and the Lord's Prayer. Again, De Smet found Prudhomme living among the Flatheads; the trader immediately became De Smet's factotum and interpreter.[19]

Canadians "had long spoken" of Blackrobes—the *Robes noires* of their homeland—to the Nez Percés, Cayuses, Lakes, Kettles, San Poils, Spokanes, Okanogans, Wenatchis, and "most of the Indians" of the Interior; the Nez Percés had even tried to purchase from them the services of a priest.[20] A Nez Percé chief was to greet the first Presbyterian minister with the information that "he had heard something of the worship of God from the traders but did not understand it." [21] Pambrun told the first Methodist minister in 1834 that his Indians already had received as much Christianity as they could assimilate. Reverend Samuel Parker found Nez Percés (or perhaps Spokanes) imitatively putting a cross on a grave; he indignantly destroyed it. It is

18. E. Duflot de Mofras, *Travels on the Pacific Coast*, ed. M. E. Wilbur, 2 (2 vols. Santa Ana, Cal., 1937), 100, 109–14; cf. "Extract from Exploration of the Oregon Territory," ed. N. B. Pipes, *OHQ*, 26 (1925), 169–70, 170–73.

19. *Quebec Mission*, p. 34 (Robillard). CR, 2, 490, 494 (1845, Berland), 677; 1, 292 (1841, Prudhomme). Bonneville, the Whitmans, and Pambrun's son testify to Pambrun's apostolic activities; Simpson, who disliked him, remarked his "considerable influence" over the Indians. Both Spier and Jessett today question his work—though not, I think, convincingly—each in arguing his own thesis. A brief biography is given in the *Dictionnaire historique des canadiens et des métis français de l'ouest*, ed. A. G. Morice, O.M.I. (Quebec, 1908), pp. 216–18.

20. *Quebec Mission*, pp. 21–22, 16–18, 17 n. Cf. CR, 1, 29, 327; 3, 991; and below, p. 213, n. 32.

21. F. G. Young, ed., "Journal and Report by Dr. Marcus Whitman of His Tour of Exploration with Reverend Samuel Parker in 1835 beyond the Rocky Mountains," *OHQ*, 28 (1927), 248.

not surprising to find Governor Simpson of the Hudson's Bay Company, in his trip in the Interior around 1825, receiving delegations from Nez Percé chiefs in the south and from the Thompson's River country far to the north, inquiring after the French Master of Life. Later, the chiefs of eight tribes at the heart of the Interior would express a similar interest.

But the most pervasive, lengthy, and intense influence was that of the Iroquois Indians. These were formidably Catholic, and were descendants of those converts who had moved up to the Canadian missions in large numbers to practice their faith freely. They were active in the Oregon fur trade from its beginnings. The Hudson's Bay Company especially employed them on short-term engagements, because they were at once expert canoemen and skillful trappers. They were also tough and independent. The Hudson's Bay trader Ross, writing before 1825, tells us that "they form nearly a third of the number of men" employed by the Company throughout the Oregon country. He describes them as "a set of civilized Indians from the neighborhood of Montreal," who were "chiefly of the Iroquois nation." Although Ross disliked them as treacherous and violent, he concedes that "they are brought up to religion, it is true, and sing hymns oftener than paddle-songs." [22]

Iroquois were resident among the Interior Kutenais before 1800. Others traveled here with David Thompson for the North West Company in 1810–13. Others again helped Donald McKenzie penetrate Idaho in 1818. Twenty-five of the latter remained to settle among the Snakes, seven of them permanently. At the building of Fort Nez Percé in 1818 there were thirty-eight Iroquois. A famous band of twenty-four under Ignace La Mousse left the Caughnawaga mission near Montreal around 1816 for the Oregon country. They soon settled permanently among the Flatheads and spoke insistently of religion.

Even in the ancient days before the horse, a messianic figure known as "Shining Shirt" had taught and prophesied among the Flatheads. Probably an Iroquois, he told how men with white skins and long black robes would one day teach them religion, give them new names, and change their lives radically both in spiritual and material ways. After the arrival of these Blackrobes all wars would cease. An irresistible flood of Whites, unfortunately, would soon follow. Shining Shirt's talisman was a piece of metal inscribed with a cross; before a critical battle he had each warrior kiss ("bite") this.[23]

A late but important influence were the Interior Indians sent back by Governor Simpson to receive an elementary Episcopalian education at the Red

22. Alexander Ross, *The Fur Traders of the Far West*, ed. K. A. Spaulding (Norman, Okla., 1956), pp. 194–95. Cf. below, p. 213, n. 32 and text.

23. H. H. Turney-High, *The Flathead Indians of Montana*, Amer. Anthrop. Assoc., Memoirs, 48 (Menasha, Wisc., 1937), pp. 41–43.

River settlement. Spokane Garry was the most noted of these. Upon his return in 1830 Garry built a church, where he held Episcopalian services and for a time read the Bible to the Indians of his neighborhood. He aroused interest especially among the Spokanes and Coeur d'Alenes.

A wider attraction was the exciting Prophet Dance. This was a strange amalgam of Christianity and pagan Prophet cult. It swept in a great wave over the Interior from about 1830. Among its doctrines it taught the imminent destruction and renewal of the world, and the resurrection of the dead. A ritual dance was to hasten the process. The Prophet religion seems first to have appeared among the Flatheads and neighboring tribes, then to have spread swiftly among their friends the Nez Percés in the south, dispersing to the Walla Wallas, Cayuses, and other tribes. It is possible that some apparent evidences of Christian ceremonial among the early Plateau Indians really derived from this ancestor of the later Ghost Dance.[24]

The upshot of all this ferment was the celebrated Flathead–Nez Percé "delegations" to St. Louis. That town, two thousand miles to the east, was the center of the American fur trade of the Rocky Mountains. It was also the residence of the superintendent of Indian Affairs, currently the Indians' friend, General Clark of the Lewis and Clark expedition. It was, besides, the center for the recently established Plains missions of the Jesuit Blackrobes. Since the Indians of the delegation spoke no language known at St. Louis, there can never be absolute certitude as to their exact purpose, tribal affiliation, or number. They did make the Catholic sign of the cross, and other signs which seemed to relate to baptism. Clark, an active Episcopalian, therefore sent them to the Catholic cathedral where they were baptized. When presented with the cross, they took it eagerly and repeatedly kissed it. Two of them soon died; the others seem to have disappeared on their return journey. Historians have elaborated upon these details with an exegetical superstructure of interpretation, conjecture, ambiguous allied information, and contradictory later testimony.

Though there are vigorous schools of dissent, the 1831 visit seems to be the first of those successive groups, mixed Flathead–Nez Percé in membership, who came seeking priests at St. Louis in 1835, 1837, and 1839. Led by French-speaking Iroquois, these subsequent delegations asked the Jesuits at St. Louis

24. On the prophet cult see Leslie Spier, *The Prophet Dance of the Northwest and Its Derivatives: The Source of the Ghost Dance*, Amer. Anthrop. Assoc., Gen. Ser., 1 (Menasha, Wisc., 1935), p. 20. T. E. Jessett, *Chief Spokan Garry, 1811–1892, Christian, Statesman, and Friend of the White Man* (Minneapolis, 1960), esp. pp. 34 ff., 66 ff. In his enthusiasm for Garry, Jessett allows himself to argue that there was a "religious vacuum" of information among the Indians until 1830, which Anglicanism then filled as the major preliminary Christian influence.

College to open a permanent mission for them. They told the priests that Indians of six other tribes besides the Flatheads wanted priests: Nez Percés, Pend d'Oreilles, Kutenais, Spokanes, Cayuses, and Kettles. The Iroquois proved well instructed in the Catholic catechism. Those of 1839 carried a book of Catholic hymns in Iroquois. A curious by-product of the first delegation was a widely printed fraud that the Indians had been searching for "the white man's Book of Heaven." Stirred by this plea, with its sorrowful "Indian Lament," Protestant missionaries became the first arrivals in the field, in 1834 and 1836. The Jesuits did not come until 1840. Independent of these delegations, an Episcopalian chaplain worked briefly at Fort Vancouver (1836–38), and Canadian priests organized a permanent mission for the French-speaking settlements and Indians (1838).

The 1840s were to be as much a turning point in the Interior Indians' history as the era following the acquisition of the horse had been, a century before. Protestant and Catholic missions were active there. Indian society was split into antagonistic levels—pagan and Christian, Protestant and Catholic, friends of the Americans and traditionalists. Some Indians would have nothing to do with the White man's religion. Others were attracted superficially, or were greedy for status or advantage, or simply curious. Conversions had the effect of slowly altering the folkways and Indian personality. And ominously, all this time, the great stream of American wagon trains kept rolling up the Oregon Trail and out to the Coast. The Indian looked upon the Trail's great swath with its litter and could hardly believe that any Whites were left in the East. Then, before 1850, political control of the whole Interior passed by treaty from the deft management of the Hudson's Bay traders into the brasher hands of American pioneers.

The general appearance of the country remained much the same. The timeless face of the Interior bore only the scar of the Oregon Trail. But many tribesmen could discern an oppressive change of atmosphere. The masters were arriving. These were not the "French" but the "Bostons," who mistrusted the inferior Indian, a multitudinous people who meant to settle everywhere and take over the land. Already the pelts and game were less plentiful. Already disease and liquor had worked their deadly ravages. Agitators, some of whom had been educated in White towns and shrewdly read the future, were stirring up the Interior tribes. Soon war parties began riding. Just before 1850 came the Whitman Massacre at the Presbyterian mission, with the concomitant Cayuse War. Protestant missionary work in the Interior ceased. Catholic work was disturbed for a decade.

There ensued a quarter century of Indian retreat. The government labored to immobilize the tribes, proposing separate treaties with them and relegating them to reservations. Government promises were broken again and again;

those fulfilled were capriciously timed. Indian affairs were now conducted by a civilian Indian bureau rather than by the army. Agents robbed the tribes. Towns came and the game fled. Out on the Plains the buffalo disappeared. Waves of miners took the Indian lands. Squatters interfered with the communal Indian fishing rights, and stripped Indian holdings of their timber. Despite the availability of better lands elsewhere, settlers hurried westward like lemmings.

Ugly incidents multiplied. Wars erupted and ran their course. Garrisons sprang up close at hand. The reservation Indian, deprived of his traditional economy, living in a tribal framework no longer very functional or meaningful, was a man exploited, insecure, and hopeless. Native apathy intensified to a maximum. By 1880 the Indian was a despised inferior in his own country, caught between two ways of life and thought. In the southwestern corner of the Interior, where this evolution began earlier, a Catholic missioner saw the process far advanced by 1862. The "Americanized Indians" on their "melancholy" reservations, he wrote sadly, were not the same kind of men he had encountered at his arrival fifteen years previously.[25]

In some ways the country still had not changed. The absolute number of Whites in the Interior was absurdly small. One might ride far without encountering a road or a house. But consider a chief just seventy-five years old, born at the time Lewis and Clark penetrated the Interior, already a young warrior when the Hudson's Bay Company built its first posts, a mature chief when the pioneer missionaries came, and a man of fifty years when government treaties were signed with the powerful Interior tribes. To such a chief these declining twenty-five years of his life had been the end of his world.

WESTWARD HO: WHITE MAPS AND JURISDICTIONS

For the White as for the Indian the 1840s were to be a turning point. Half a century of colorful incident preceded, in which the White had been little better than a transient. The map he superimposed on the country had almost no basis in reality. It was interesting in that it showed how the Russians had retreated from Oregon northward beyond 54°40′, and the Spanish southward into California. Britain and America remained in "joint occupancy." In actual fact it was an Indian world with a traders' world lightly superimposed. But now the Whites were to build their towns, divide the Oregon country into American and Canadian, and plot a shifting grid of territories and counties. The army would add its changing map of garrisons, the Indian Affairs people their reservations and agencies, the churches their several jurisdictions. Like a small but terrible cancer, the White man had fastened upon the Coast, in-

25. Mesplié Papers (PA), I, No. 42, 3 October 1862.

exorably creeping inland. Soon his map would be the only reality. It may be well to glance at the most important of these crisscrossing lines defining men's allegiances, natural and supernatural.

In 1840 the Hudson's Bay Company was king. It had "28 establishments west of the Rocky Mountains" in the Canadian and American fur trade.[26] Through them, over forty thousand beaver skins were still annually being taken from the western slope of the Rockies. The Interior posts lay along the Columbia River. Fort Colville stood somewhat below the river's point of entry into the Interior from modern Canada, Fort Okanogan where it looped abruptly toward the south along the western edge of the Interior, Fort Walla Walla at the bottom of its descent where it joined the Snake River, and Fort Vancouver, the main depot, near its mouth on the coast. A good distance to the southeast of these posts were Forts Hall and Boise on the Oregon Trail.

Every principal post was much like the others, consisting of a fortified stockade about fifteen feet high enclosing some two hundred square feet of space, with warehouses and shops, and sometimes with farms of ex-employees in its neighborhood. The headquarters at Fort Vancouver boasted a population of about four hundred, mostly Indians, and ten thousand head of stock. The focus of settlement was the Willamette Valley, running south across the river from Fort Vancouver. Here a handful of American families were installed along with French Canadian farmers. The lordly arbiter of all this domain for the British crown was Dr. John McLoughlin.

But Oregon Fever was burning in the United States. Expansionist congressmen, visionaries, chauvinistic religious groups, and harried farmers were speaking of the Willamette as a paradise. The covered wagons were already straggling up the Oregon Trail. By 1839 some 70 Americans were on the Coast. The number doubled by 1840, climbed to over 500 by 1842, then was reinforced by almost 1,000 people in the Great Emigration of '43. By the time the Oregon Problem threatened to cause war between England and America, there were some 5,000 Americans and 700 crown subjects on the Coast. The next year this American population doubled.

The Hudson's Bay Company, stripped of its power and monopoly south of the newly negotiated border, remained the major presence in the Interior except for the missionaries. Harassed by the jingoistic coastal Whites, the Company slowly declined and disappeared. Forts Hall, Boise, and Walla Walla were given up in 1855. Forts Okanogan and Vancouver were gone by 1860. Only Fort Colville, near the Jesuit mission chain in the mountains, survived for a few more years.

The slavery controversy delayed until 1848 the organization of the American Oregon country into Oregon Territory. Then in 1853 the Territory was

26. *Quebec Mission*, p. 15.

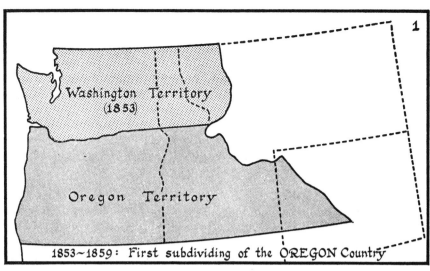

1

Washington Territory (1853)

Oregon Territory

1853~1859: First subdividing of the OREGON Country

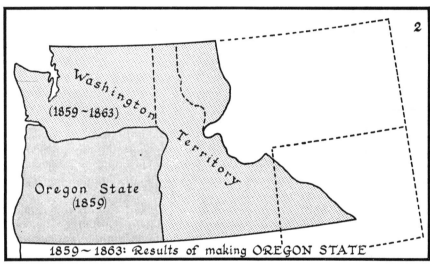

2

Washington (1859~1863) Territory

Oregon State (1859)

1859~1863: Results of making OREGON STATE

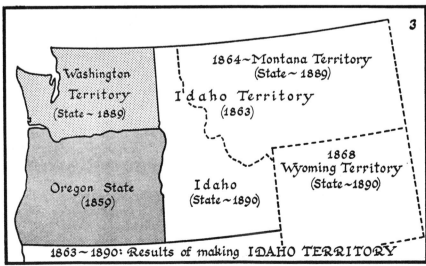

3

1864~Montana Territory (State~1889)

Washington Territory (State~1889)

Idaho Territory (1863)

1868 Wyoming Territory (State~1890)

Oregon State (1859)

Idaho (State~1890)

1863~1890: Results of making IDAHO TERRITORY

4. Pacific Northwest Territorial and State Boundaries, 1853–1890.

split. Its upper half from the ocean clear to the crest of the Rockies was now
called Washington Territory. In 1859, however, Washington Territory expanded to include most of the former American Oregon country; ironically
the name Oregon would henceforth be confined to a southwestern square of
land ranking as a state. In 1863 Washington similarly shrank, though still
only a territory, to an equivalent northwestern square. The eastern half of
the old Oregon country took the name of Idaho Territory, but it now included an even larger area out on the Great Plains. This huge entity very
soon diminished by the loss of Montana Territory (1864) and Wyoming
Territory (1868). All of these territories—except, of course, Oregon state—
became states themselves in 1888–90.

The Interior never ceased to be a natural unity. Indeed, as early as 1855 a
convention at The Dalles had projected a separate state made up of the inte-
riors of Washington and Oregon. In 1861 many Whites wanted a special Interior "Walla Walla Territory" separated from a coastal Washington Territory. In 1877 men spoke of carving a territory from the Cascades to the crest
of the Rockies. There would be a strong movement to connect the Idaho
panhandle with western Montana. In 1886 Congress did assign the Idaho panhandle to Washington, only to be frustrated by a presidential pocket veto
(perhaps related to anti-Mormonism). At first sight all this passion for re-
drawing maps and multiplying rural legislatures seems to have nothing to
do with the Interior Indian. His plains and forests were stubbornly remote no
matter what territorial image was superimposed.

In fact, the boundary lines related the Indian to a succession of governors
and policies. The tribes of the Jesuit missions were thus to fall under the settlers' provisional government, and then under the territories of Oregon
(1848), Washington (1853), Washington and Idaho (1863), and Wash-
ington-Idaho-Montana (1864). The Flathead tribe in modern Montana was
successively under five such separate jurisdictions within twenty years. The
artificial border of Canada meanwhile ran through such mission tribes as the
Okanogans, Lakes, Kalispels, and Kutenais. Until 1858 military policy for
the Interior was based upon its natural destiny as a huge Indian territory
closed to Whites, with the Cascades and Rockies serving as walls of separation between the two races. Nevertheless, a section of the Indian land in 1853
had been hopefully designated Walla Walla County; it measured 200 miles
by 450, comprising 90,000 square miles. In 1859 something called Spokane
County ran from the Cascades to the Rockies, and included most of modern
Washington, all of Idaho and Wyoming, and a good piece of Montana.

Mining changed this situation abruptly in the '60s. The summer of 1861
saw 2,500 miners and 5,000 other men in central Idaho. In Montana 670 peo-

ple arrived by 1863, over 18,000 by 1870, over 39,000 by 1880, and over 132,000 by 1890. Little towns made their appearance, such as Boise, Helena, and, on Nez Percé land, the bustling river port of Lewiston. Brief, dazzling strikes launched waves of miners onto the country of the Okanogans, the Kettles, the Kutenais, the Flatheads. The transcontinental railroad soon passed near the southeastern back door of the old Oregon country. Roads, farms, newspapers, churches, stage lines, and schools all appeared in the Interior with surprising promptness. Vigilante action flared luridly. The cattle industry started up on the open range. The Northern Pacific was about to cut straight across the Indian lands. In the space of a child's growing up, the Interior transformed itself into White man's land.

We have seen how the White man brought his religious organizations with him. In a sense the religious organizations brought the White man, since the first settlement had been in good part an evangelistic effort to hold the country against the presumably allied forces of Romanism and England. All through the first half of the century a strong missionary spirit had been stirring among European and American Protestants. From 1798 a series of separate projects was proposed for the conversion of the remote Oregon Indians. Even before this, the tradition of commitment to the conversion of the Indians was a feature of American Protestantism. Two missionary associations especially touch our region—the Methodist Missionary Society, begun in 1819, and the American Board in Boston, begun a decade earlier. The latter represented an alliance but was destined to be rather more Presybterian than Congregationalist in the Oregon country. Both organizations responded with enthusiasm to the "Flathead delegation."

The Methodists had a party of four in the field by 1834 under Jason Lee; reinforcements coming in 1837 and 1840 brought the total to 151 persons. Strangely enough, this group was immediately seized by the conviction that an evangelical colony in the Willamette Valley would best serve Protestant Christianity. They did essay several coastal missions, some apostolic journeying among the tribes, and a station briefly at the threshold of the Interior. But they were to be involved mostly in the religiocultural history of the coastal Whites.

The substantial Protestant effort came from the American Board. Dr. Marcus Whitman, courageous and kindly, established Waiilatpu among the Cayuses; its situation just east of Walla Walla on the Oregon Trail soon made it popular as a resting or wintering shelter. The Reverend Henry Spalding, a fiery and difficult personality, built Lapwai among the Nez Percés, sixty miles to the northeast. Their colleagues Eells and Walker traveled far north to open Tshimakain among the Spokanes. With their wives and assistants, these men labored for more than a decade in dedicated patience to win their respective tribes. There was some success, but mostly disappointment.

The work was already dissolving in failure and dissension when it was dramatically ended in 1847 by the Whitman Massacre and the rising of the Cayuses. If the Protestant missions were gone, however, they left a Christian presence behind. A core of Indians had been converted. Many others had been favorably affected to some degree. Others again came to realize how unselfish this missionary dedication had been. A foundation was left for the later Presbyterian return to the Nez Percés and Spokanes around 1870.

Two years after the American Board missionaries, Catholic priests reached the Oregon region. Since they provided the ecclesiastical framework in which the Jesuits were later to operate, some understanding of their activities will be useful. Francis Blanchet and Modeste Demers were French Canadians. They came in response to the petition of the Hudson's Bay settlers (1834), and as missionaries to the Indians. An immediate problem facing them was the jursidictional structure. Rome had given a vague responsibility for this "vast region of barbarians" [27] to the missionary bishop of the Red River vicariate (in modern Manitoba), who was subject in turn to the metropolitan of Quebec. In the ambiguous political situation, Quebec realized that a great part of Oregon belonged in fact to the Americans. The American ecclesiastical claimant, under the metropolitan of Baltimore, would be the bishop of St. Louis.

Roman authorities avoided a hasty solution by making all of Canadian and American Oregon a temporary entity in 1843. Called the vicariate apostolic of Oregon City, it was remotely controlled by the bishop at Red River but administered by Francis Blanchet as vicar apostolic. Because of the new district's inaccessibility (it was almost as easy to make the round trip to Rome as to Quebec or Baltimore), Bishop Blanchet persuaded the Holy See to approve a bizarre project. In 1846 the Oregon wilderness, with few Catholics and almost no clergy, was designated a separate metropolitan province of the United States, the only one in the country besides the all-embracing Baltimore province.

The subsequent mapping of dioceses and vicariates within the new province displays eccentricities not dissimilar to those of the territories. At first the main division was between coast and interior. But for most of the '50s and '60s American Oregon was split across. The archdiocese of Oregon City under Archbishop Francis Blanchet held all the bottom half from the ocean to the Rockies, while its northern suffragan Nesqually under his brother

27. Indult from the Holy See transcribed in Bradley and Kelly, *Diocese of Boise,* p. 17.

Augustine Blanchet covered the equivalent top half. Rapid shifts in population forced by 1868 a drastic revision. Oregon City and Nesqually diminished respectively to the modern area of Oregon and Washington states; all the rest became the Idaho vicariate under Oregon City.

Out on the Plains that same year, after an independent civil career as part of larger entities like Nebraska Territory, a Montana vicariate was devised. Only in 1883 would this be adjusted to include western Montana—the whole becoming at the same time subject to Oregon City. Archbishop Blanchet lived through all these changes to 1883; his brother, Bishop Augustine Blanchet, died in 1887. Like the civil divisions, these are confusing changes. But they show how careful one must be when placing a Jesuit mission at any given time in its proper relation to the non-Jesuit Catholic world. During a forty-five year period, for instance, the Flathead mission fell successively under St. Louis diocese (to 1843), Oregon City vicariate (to 1846), Walla Walla, the forerunner of Nesqually diocese (to 1850), Oregon City archdiocese as administrator of Walla Walla (to 1853), Nesqually (to 1868), Idaho vicariate (to 1883), Montana vicariate (to 1884), and the equivalent Helena diocese thereafter.

Jurisdictional confusion for the Jesuit missions was minimized by several factors. Conducted by an "exempt" Order responsible mostly to the pope, the Jesuit establishments were in many ways self-operative. The mission world itself was remote, insulated from many changes and necessarily rather self-sufficient. Above all, the infant dioceses and vicariates were preoccupied with their own frantic problems of subsistence and growth. Even in 1884, the Montana vicariate became Helena diocese while it had only four secular priests for fifteen thousand Catholics scattered over a diocese the size of France.

This diocesan background could occasionally assume closer relevance, as at an episcopal visitation or by the sudden drain of Jesuit personnel from Indian missions into diocesan work. Then again, diocesan clergy made apostolic excursions among the Indians when they could, and even had a few Indian missions. Priests like the Blanchets, Brouillet, and Mesplié ranged widely among certain tribes and had real influence. This is relevant in the larger Indian setting, though it directly affected the Interior mostly at its southwest corner.

The Oblates of Mary Immaculate, recently founded in Provence, had three missions among the Yakimas, located down near the southwestern corner of the Interior, as well as a fourth mission briefly among the neighboring Cayuses. The Oblates arrived just in time to have their work hindered by the Whitman Massacre and the Cayuse War. About five years later they were disturbed by the Yakima War. By 1860 they had abandoned American Oregon, except for a successful mission among the coastal Indians, where they continued another twenty years. Their work in the Interior, though it lasted for only one stormy decade, was important to these Indians.

INDIAN AGAINST WHITE

Here, then, were two separate worlds, a Red and a White. Neither of them was really homogeneous. Neither followed a simple pattern either within itself or in relating to its counterpart. Army policy was often opposed to territorial policy, and both were subject to large change. Some Indian agents were admirable, some venal. Some missionaries were hugely successful, others mediocre. Among settlers, trappers, and miners there were perceptive individuals who appreciated Indian virtues, and there were brutes who instinctively harmed any Indian. A man might be friendly with the local Indians or afraid or wary or truculent or contemptuous.

On the Indian side one encounters the same variety. There were Indians who hated the Whites. Others were indifferent and apathetic over their coming. Others again remained their fast friends or enthusiastic converts. And the attitude of some fluctuated according to circumstances, or even manifested a combination of discordant feelings. We have seen that even between Indian and Indian there were unexpected patterns of relating. Tribes would ally or be deadly enemies. They might split internally along religious lines, or largely ignore such differences on either a tribal or intertribal level. A certain caution should therefore preside over the following generalizations.

To most Whites one Indian was much like another. An associate judge of Oregon from 1850, who traveled with Indians "a great deal," confessed that the Westerners "hated an Indian as they do a rattlesnake." In time of peace they felt "a natural repugnance toward the filthy, dirty, lazy Indians; almost everybody does." [28] Of the seven Indian superintendents for Oregon personally known to one agent in the early days, only Palmer and Meacham had any faith that the Indians were worth much effort.[29] They shared the general feeling that failure was inevitable for anyone working in this field.

In time of war the image transformed itself into a merciless marauder who delighted in cruelty and in unprovoked attack. Sadistic tribes such as the Iroquois, Apache, southern Cheyenne, and Sioux had burned this terrible picture into the imagination of the intransigent Anglo-Saxon. The long history of Indian inhumanity to others was unjustly but understandably revisited upon the Oregon Indian. Yet the Plateau tribes were not vicious. Some were even pacifistic by tradition. Others were basically friendly and peaceful. Captives

28. W. D. Strong, ed., "Knickerbocker Views of the Oregon Country: Judge William Strong's Narrative," *OHQ*, *62* (1961), 76.
29. T. W. Davenport, "Recollections of an Indian Agent," *OHQ*, *8* (1907), 234.

from wars and other tribes might occasionally be submitted to days of ritual abuse amounting to mild torture before being adopted into some tribe. Yet burning at the stake was almost unheard of. They were of course primitives: unstable, ignorant, easily roused. Any of them could be goaded or frightened into outbursts like the Whitman Massacre.

Again, the Indian was conceived of as stoically impassive. He often appeared to the White as brutalized and degenerate, having no real domestic life, no finer feelings or true spirituality. Since he was unsympathetic to abstract thought, he was considered incapable of being profound. It was hard to imagine an Indian weeping, or loving his wife deeply, or seeking God determinedly. Some eastern sentimentalists could indeed imagine all this in the noble savage. But the humanitarian sentimentalists irritated the western settler, and justly. The humanitarian's Indian lacked the realistic elements of childishness and wildness. To see the Indian and see him whole, as truly human, though a different type of human, was not easy for either the humanitarian or the stiff-necked pioneer.

So the White entertained a curiously ambivalent attitude toward the Indian. He feared and hated him on the warpath, yet scorned him when peaceful. For decades the Nez Percés were contemned as tame Indians, underrated and even mistreated despite their unswerving friendship for the Whites. They won fame and respect only when they finally went to war. Thus the settler's feelings toward the Indian fluctuated between arrogance, fear, and righteous anger.

There were Indians enough—renegades, drunken Indians, or wild young bucks—who perpetuated the subhuman stereotype. Besides, the Plateau Indians had as neighbors some murderous and actively hostile tribes, like the fanatic Blackfeet on the Plains, the Snakes to the southeast, and the canoe Indians of the far northern Coast. Indians who had real grievance in defending their rights or lands were seldom distinguished from the rest. Not uncommonly both the Whites and the Indians avenged themselves upon some innocent but available member of the other people, a procedure that provoked ever widening circles of retaliation.

Nor did the Whites discern the internal structure of the tribe. This structure made it impossible for the chief to exercise real authority, for the peacetime chief to recall war parties, for a head chief to speak for all his bands, for a whole tribe to make peace or deliver up criminals, or for any Indian to look upon horse-stealing as a capital offense. The complexities of Indian political and property concepts, the courtesies and involvements of their own international law, the superstitions and oppressive fears assailing them, and even their strategy of fighting by constant retreat—all became occasions for further misunderstanding.

With the White mentality standing in such opposition to the Red, it was inevitable that the beleaguered Indian world would draw more closely together. Even where political or military solidarity could not be achieved, the Indian tended at least to sympathize with his own and give them his protection. The problem was thus compounded. When the White man did concentrate against a rebellious tribe, the other tribes could see their own future involved in the struggle. The White tended to create the very situation of intertribal identification that he had wanted to avoid. Then, when police action was indicated, he would angrily mount a full-scale war. Where firm justice was called for, he indulged in triumph. When a single tribe was involved, he could be fearfully sure that the whole country was aflame. Conversely he rode heedlessly into tense situations where a spark could ignite hostile tribes in all directions.

In 1856 a Hudson's Bay Company sympathizer feared that a "War of Races" was imminent, as American and Indian blocs grew ever more antagonistic. In his address to the legislature in 1862, Governor Pickering of Washington Territory echoed the fear of "an unfortunate war of the races." The Jesuit De Smet in 1858, though praising government policies, regretted the "insurmountable barrier between the two races," which disposed the settler relentlessly to pursue the weaker Indian.[30]

In his official capacity, the White man probably kept more promises than he broke. But he broke enough to make his moral position ambiguous. Bureaucratic government must process its promises through sluggish, convoluted channels, while events outrun good intentions. Too often negotiators made rash promises, settlers were greedy or impatient, Indian agents were corrupt, and courts were remiss. The fault here is diffused. Paradoxically the Indian-fighting army, less committed than were local interests, was often the Indians' only protection. This circumstance could strain relations between settlers and soldiers. It is sometimes difficult not to be overly harsh toward the settler. One tends to assign him the greater responsibility. He had the advantage of civilization and therefore the obligation of a trust. But he was no less human and fallible than ourselves.

Armored in righteousness, sometimes insulated by his consciousness of good will, the Oregon pioneer seldom reflected that he himself might be at fault. He was outraged and surprised when the Cayuses fought, when the Yakimas fought, when the Spokanes and Coeur d'Alenes fought, when the Nez Percés fought, when the Bannocks fought. He would have been equally surprised had the Flatheads fought. The pioneers were inept at judging Indian angers

30. BC, Record Office transcripts, F.O. 5, 617–63, 168. C. M. Gates, ed., *Messages of the Governors of the Territory of Washington to the Legislative Assembly, 1854–1889* (Seattle, 1940), p. 105. CR, 3, 1195. Cf. John Beeson, *A Plea for the Indians; with Facts and Features of the Late War in Oregon* (New York, 1858), pp. 25, 31, 108.

or capacities. All this hardly makes the average settler a monster or a fool. Nor does it absolve the Indian of his own full share of blame. Both were victims of their history and environment. The tragedy had to be played out.

From 1790 to 1879, some 275 clashes between Indian and White in the old Oregon country have been counted by one author who admits the list is not exhaustive.[31] There were coastal troubles such as the Modoc War, the Rogue River Wars, and the defense of Seattle. There were interior troubles not involving our Interior Plateau Indians such as the Bannock War, the series of Snake conflicts, and the brief Sheep Eater War. Wars of the Interior Plateau alone, within the space of less than thirty years, included the Cayuse War (1848), the Yakima War (1855–56), the Coeur d'Alene–Spokane War (1858–59), and the Nez Percé War (1877). If the harvest of troubles just beyond the Rockies were added, the list would include the complicated Blackfoot, Crow, and Sioux wars in Montana.

A drumfire of skirmishes and incidents continued between the more noticeable outbreaks. Settlers, miners, soldiers, and travelers were involved in vicious little fire-fights, in murders, or in raids. Sparks of trouble frequently flared, to be swiftly extinguished by negotiators or friends of the tribe concerned. Where no trouble existed, the wind of rumor could agitate Indian and White, bringing them to the brink of fighting. The expense of these wars was considerable. The Yakima War alone amounted to six million dollars in pre-Civil War money. When the federal government recoiled at the sum and opened an investigation of this "raid" on the national treasury, irate voters made the affair an issue in the local politics of 1859–60.[32]

Through all the troubles, with the smell of danger around them, a handful of Whites and Indians worked for peace. Some tried from the outside as representatives of official policy. This class includes the treaty makers, peace negotiators, Indian superintendents or agents, and the army itself. Their efforts were often compromised by their identification with American officialdom. Others however applied their efforts from within, or as independent of either party. Among these are the local Indian chief, the Hudson's Bay man, the occasional frontiersman or settler, and the missionary. Circumstances allowed some representatives of each class to make important or continuous efforts, while others were in a position to help only in one or another fortuitous episode.

Perhaps the most difficult contribution to assess is the diffused general influence of Protestant and Catholic Christianity in the Interior. Laymen and missioners of several denominations had a share in this. It was an operative motive with chiefs like Garry, Seltis, and Moses. And one cannot measure the

31. Scott, *OHQ*, 29, 145.
32. R. W. Johannsen, *Frontier Politics and the Sectional Conflict, the Pacific Northwest on the Eve of the Civil War* (Seattle, 1955), p. 144.

contributions to peace, or Indian character-formation, achieved by Protestant or Catholic clergy and by communities of teaching nuns, when their hidden labors never took a dramatic public turn.

Preservation of the peace was as vital a tradition among the diocesan clergy or any missionary group as it was with the Jesuits. Governor Simpson of the Hudson's Bay Company underlined the importance of such diocesan work in the Canadian West as early as 1818. "Indeed it is to the Catholic Mission we are alone indebted for the safety of the Company's establishment and the peace of the Colony" at Red River.[33] Jesuits were hardly alone therefore in their efforts to maintain or restore peace. In these pages we shall meet peacemaking officials like Governor Stevens and Generals Harney and Wheaton; Protestant missioners like Eells and Cowley; Oblates like Pandosy, Ricard, and Chirouse; diocesan priests like Brouillet, Mesplié, and Bishop O'Connor; Indian agents like Owen, Wilbur, and Ronan; frontiersmen like Craig; and Hudson's Bay men like Blenkinsop and MacDonald.

However, the Jesuits exercised a special control over the Indians directly under their care. These far-flung tribes formed a sizable bloc dominating the north and east of the Interior. They were relatively remote from other influences. Strategically located in the mountains, they were farthest too from the White bases of power. They included almost all the militarized groups of the Plateau except those on the southern edge. The influence of these tribes was spread even farther, due to socio-economic involvements like that of the Coeur d'Alenes with the Spokanes, and that of the Flatheads with the Nez Percés.

Jesuit influence was cast even more widely. There was a Catholic membership, sometimes substantial, in almost all the Plateau tribes. And the Blackrobe commanded wide respect among the pagan Indians. As the years went on the mission network and its outposts expanded greatly, and with it Jesuit ascendancy. Indeed, for half of our period the Jesuits were the only permanent missionary system in the Interior; the Protestant organizations withdrew from 1848 till almost 1870, the Oblates from 1856 and 1859, forever. Moreover, the Jesuits were a tightly organized group, intercommunicating, and sharing resources. They had closely identified themselves with Indian interests, lived much like their tribes, spoke the languages, knew the headmen, and as a group had formidable local experience. They were not burdened with families, individual property, or an American background. Among their own Indians, they enjoyed the authority and position accorded by Catholics only to their priests. None of these factors guaranteed success. But they placed the Jesuits in a particularly advantageous position for the work of peace.

33. J. P. Pritchett, *The Red River Valley 1811–1849, a Regional Study* (New Haven, 1942), p. 235.

2. The Jesuit and the Red Man

THE PLOT AGAINST THE WEST

To MANY a nineteenth-century American the word "Jesuit" had an ugly ring. A miasma of melodramatic myth hung about it. Men spoke darkly of disguised Jesuits, of Jesuit gold mines, Jesuit casuistry, and Jesuits plotting treason. Particularly damning were the implications of Jesuitical blind obedience, or mental reservation, or means justified by the end. The topic was not an esoteric one. Indeed it supported a popular horror literature of its own. Such urgent titles as *Jesuit Juggling, Intrigues of Jesuitism, Secret Instructions of the Jesuits,* and *Loyola or Jesuitism in Its Rudiments* catered to this taste. For less abstract patrons, who required entertainment as well as titillation, this art form was suitably broadened. There were, for example: *The Female Jesuit* (1851), *The Jesuit, a National Melodrama* (1851), *Helen Mulgrave or Jesuit Executorship* (1852), *Carlotina and the Sandfedisti or a Night with the Jesuits at Rome* (1853), *Carlington Castle, a Tale of the Jesuits* (1854), and *Stanhope Burleigh or the Jesuits in Our Homes* (1855).

The renewed activity of the Order in the early nineteenth century drew cries of apprehension from high places. In 1816 President Jefferson saw it as "a retrograde step from light toward darkness." Ex-President John Adams concurred, envisioning "swarms of them here in as many disguises as ever a King of the Gypsies" could assume. In some agitation he declared that "if ever any Congregation of Men could merit eternal Perdition on Earth and in Hell" it was the Jesuits.[1] The American Bible Society in 1829 divulged a Jesuit plot to drive the Bible from America. The *National Protestant* bravely assumed as its alternate title *The Anti-Jesuit.* When Boston Catholics began their paper *The Jesuit,* widespread anger forced a change in name. The populace in sober Maine enthusiastically tarred and feathered the good Swiss Jesuit Bapst. At the nation's capital in 1854 an Alabama legislator regaled the House of Representatives with an exposé of Jesuit spycraft and Jesuit projects for the conquest of America.

1. *The Adams-Jefferson Letters,* ed. L. J. Cappon, 2 (2 vols. Chapel Hill, 1959), 474, 486; cf. pp. 494, 484, 419–20.

All this was part of a larger anti-Catholic hysteria that afflicted the nation with particular virulence from 1830 until the Civil War. Its syndrome ranged from suspicious distrust of anything Catholic to active revulsion. Its severer visitations resulted in mob action akin to the race riots of the present era. The manic fringe of those stricken particularly relished setting churches afire, storming convents of nuns, or staging bloody street brawls. Sensational newspapers like the *Anti-Romanist* and the *Downfall of Babylon* fed extremist appetites. Hostility to Catholics also increased sharply in the conservative religious press. A political party briefly emerged to serve the cause, entrenching itself in some thirty-five state and territorial legislatures and sending seventy-five members to Congress. The roots of the movement were a tangle of social, economic, religious, and historical causes. Catholics were by no means without their share of responsibility for it, both in the intolerance and errors of their corporate past and in their present human defensive anger or arrogance.

The monumental credulity of the movement particularly centered upon a papal plot to seize the new American West. Jesuits were to be the controlling agents of this conspiracy. Among those alerting the Republic to its danger was the inventor of the telegraph, Samuel Morse. From 1835 to 1841 his book ran rapidly through five editions. His sequel enlarged on the Jesuit role, and his third book pursued the subject closely.

Assemblies of Protestant divines debated dispatching loyal missionaries to hold the West for America. Clarion calls were blown by the Boston Sunday School Union, the American Bible Society, the American Education Society, the British Reformation Society, and similar associations. Champions stood forth like Lyman Beecher, who toured the East with his "Plea for the West." Beecher even pondered moving out to the Mississippi Valley, the more adroitly to direct the great conflict. The *American Protestant Vindicator* felt constrained to caution its readers that "Jesuits are prowling about all parts of the United States in every possible disguise." Their focus, of course, was the West. "The western country swarms with them under the names of puppet show men, dancing masters, music teachers, peddlers of images and ornaments, barrel organ players, and similar practitioners." [2] More than one Conestoga wagon rolled westward as much to intercept the pope as to acquire prime farm lands.

Shrewder Americans, uninvolved in this rank undergrowth of fable, might nevertheless be sensible of an animus against the Order on more plausible grounds. They identified the Jesuit sometimes with reaction and dead tradition, sometimes with an unchristian liberalism and worldly compromise. Above all, they linked him with the deepest-dyed popery and Romanism, and

2. R. A. Billington, *The Protestant Crusade 1800–1860, a Study in the Origins of American Nativism* (New York, 1938), p. 120.

with an aggressive efficiency in warring against Reformation principles.

It is not easy to say how long the spirit against the Jesuits lasted, how deeply it penetrated, or how widely it extended. It betrays a fever chart of ups and downs, finally diminishing to almost nothing before the end of the century. Perhaps there was never a very large number of the credulous, even at the height of anti-Jesuitism. But probably the bigotry had touched a considerable percentage of Americans to some degree by mid-century.

Strangely enough, the better educated often found themselves simultaneously compelled to respect the Jesuit. So much obvious good emerged from the morass of Jesuitical evil that the mind boggled. This mystery had to be resolved, and the resolution by the intellectuals often proved to be as romantically and monstrously fascinating as that of the popular press. Parkman, in his great *Jesuits in North America* (1867), affords an amusing example of the fairminded man caught in this dilemma. He could only conclude that the Order was a "harmony of contradictions," a "moral Proteus" whose "virtues shine amidst the rubbish of error." No Order "has ever united in itself so much to be admired and so much to be detested." [3] Somehow the formidable Jesuit training managed to produce humane, intelligent, noble, cultivated men who were blind, cruel, unthinking fanatics.

The establishment of Jesuit missions in the Rocky Mountains in 1841, therefore, was no conventional item of religious news. To many it was the long-awaited invasion of the Oregon country. Some Oregonians called any priest or nun a Jesuit, but these agents were both foreign and genuinely, blatantly Jesuit.

Surely it would have shocked the Establishment in England to learn that they, by a bizarre quirk of logic, were considered the co-conspirators of the Jesuits here. This was particularly true of the Hudson's Bay Company. Many an Oregon farmer genuinely feared this combination of forces. Even in England, however, the religious advances of Romanism had been exposed. Herbert Beaver, after a stormy two years as chaplain at Fort Vancouver, had returned in 1838 to report Oregon as "the very stronghold of popery," where the population was "the prey of the kingdom of Anti-Christ." A certain confusion of metaphors attended Beaver's efforts to "take the papal bull by the horns" and expel "the hydra-headed monster from the northeastern shores of the Pacific." [4]

The Protestant missionaries in the Interior subscribed to the conspiracy theory. Even the good Whitman, premier missionary of the Interior, reported that Anglo-Roman plots had barely been impeded. With "the friends

3. New York, 1867, pp. 12–13.
4. R. C. Clark, ed., "Experiences of a Chaplain at Fort Vancouver, 1836–1838," *OHQ*, 39 (1938), 23, 37.

of the English interests," he wrote, "the Jesuit Papists would have been in quiet possession of this, the only spot in the western horizon of America not before their own." De Smet's diverting *Indian Sketches* revealed to Whitman anew "that the papal effort is designed to convey over the country to the English." Spalding, the second great figure of the Interior missions, had studied under Lyman Beecher and had been recommended for Indian work by him. Spalding's ferocity against the Jesuits came close to being an obsession. When his wife died in 1851, "a victim of the bloody harlot of Rome," he had her buried under a tombstone darkly inscribed: "She always felt that the Jesuit Missionaries were the leading cause of the [Whitman] massacre." [5]

The Jesuits were to be formally accused of instigating each of the Interior wars in turn—the Cayuse War, the Yakima War, the Coeur d'Alene–Spokane War, and even the Nez Percé War. An early pioneer demanded political action against the "Yesuit" Indian plots; "not a robbery has been committed" along the Oregon Trail "but was excited by Yesuits." In 1848 a bill for the forcible expulsion of all Jesuits was introduced into the territorial legislature but failed to pass. Both candidates for territorial delegate to Congress in 1849 gave space in their campaign for the issue of the Anglo-Jesuit conspiracy. The ex-revivalist Thurston carried the day, but his opponent also had promised to stop the Jesuits "who are pouring into Oregon for the entire destruction of all our liberties." A constituent soon informed him that Roman resources were not exhausted. Even now reinforcements were being rushed by the Hudson's Bay Company—six vessels bearing 150 priests and nuns for the Oregon country. In some quarters popular resentment ran high. Oregon would soon be "a sickly place for Yesuits," men said; "you will soon see hell kicked up." [6]

Without this background, one is unprepared for the difficulties and the episodes of hostility encountered in the story of the Jesuit as peacemaker in the Interior. On the other hand, it would be a serious mistake to see this as more than a fragment of the whole picture. Much animosity in the sources must be understood less from this absurd pattern than from the more normal religious passions, bluntly proclaimed by a blunt generation. Catholic and Protestant each saw the other in terms of a corruption and distortion of

5. *JMUS*, 2, 268; cf. the similar expression in ABFM, 18-3-1, 9, Whitman to Mission Board, 15 May 1845, No. 180. C. M. Drury, *Henry Harmon Spalding* (Caldwell, Idaho, 1936), p. 361; cf. G. P. Belknap, "*Authentic Account of the Murder of Dr. Whitman:* The History of a Pamphlet," *Papers of the Bibliographical Society of America*, 55 (1961), 319–46.

6. P. Knuth, "Nativism in Oregon," *Reed College Bulletin*, 24 (1946), 20, 15–16, 19–20, for quotations.

God's essential gift to man. Their feelings were thus in some measure a tribute to their genuine religious commitments. Each recalled the other also in terms of persecution; the ghosts of Torquemada and Oliver Cromwell stalked the Oregon forests.

The majority of settlers were saved from bigotry in any case by too many counterbalancing factors. There was the American tradition of religious liberty. Equally important, there was the generous good-fellowship, fair play, and common sense of the frontier. Often enough there was solid Christian charity, and of course the rising tide of tolerant secularism. Again, the alarming increase of Catholicism and foreign population in America, which had helped agitate the nativists, paradoxically also helped silence them. The growing numbers soon became too strong in many areas to be intimidated, and mingled too fluently into the human context of daily life to leave space for gross misunderstandings.

Responsible American Protestants had continued to work against fanaticism; by 1850 through legislative action they had removed the civil disabilities of Catholics in all states but one. Violence and calumny eventually alienated far more Protestants than they influenced. The American religious scene in the nineteenth century rarely displayed the widespread, uncompromisingly permanent bitterness that poisoned contemporary Europe. An air of tension persisted in certain places; the dramatic, stubbornly recurrent lightning might sometimes startle. Generally, however, pleasant relations existed between Oregon Protestants and Jesuits, especially after the first decade or so.

Even in the early days, the two opponents had made efforts to rise above bad feeling. The Reverend Mr. Spalding helped Father Joset and others at the founding of the Jesuit mission. Joset in turn was impressed by Spalding's sincerity, as well as by the dedication of his daily life. Father Nobili was equally edified by the charity and goodness of "the excellent Doctor Whitman," while Whitman on his part extended his hospitality to the Jesuits. Mengarini was received by a Protestant missioner "with great kindness and hospitality." Father Accolti's preaching was popular with many coastal Protestants. Joset's preaching, when the Colville area finally had a small town, drew "a good-sized congregation regardless of creed." In 1874 when a prejudiced agent at the Nez Percé reservation was trying to thwart Father Cataldo, Protestant townsmen rallied to his defense. Jesuits like De Smet, Ravalli, Joset, Giorda, and the rest enjoyed the best of relations with most Protestant settlers, officials, ministers, and transients. In his memoirs Bishop Tuttle of the Episcopalian church records his affection for Father Ravalli, "a dear friend." When Ravalli was dying, Tuttle came to say a final goodbye and to offer a prayer by his side. In 1848 and again in 1858, when anti-Jesuit feeling was being roused, the Jesuits could argue their case openly in Oregon and win what support they needed.[7]

Familiar, straightforward, clerical neighbors to some; master spies and even invaders to others; revered and simple Blackrobes, sly and furtive scoundrels—for many an uncomfortable enigma to be eyed warily; evil and holy; august, corrupt; direct yet devious; a menace, a friend! Surely this prodigy invites pause.

The Jesuit really *was* something different. Incarnate in each was a Jesuit esprit. Intrinsic to their Indian missions was a centuries-old Jesuit methodology and tradition. They were organized, with a chain of command mounting back to a general at Rome. They had not come haphazardly, but represented as it were one combat front of worldwide Jesuit missions, and an extension from existent missions to the Indians of America's Great Plains. As individuals these men were strikingly different from one another. As a group, common principles made them oddly alike. To understand them, and especially to appreciate what they were trying to do among the Oregon tribes, some note must be taken of the Jesuits' background. The Jesuit is in effect a man with an historical dimension to his personality. He is understandable only in the light of his history and heritage.

THE JESUIT ENIGMA: STRUCTURE, SPIRIT, AND TRADITION

The Jesuit spirit is the extension of one person, the Basque nobleman Ignatius Loyola, contemporary of Luther and Cortés. His formative environment was the courts and camps of Renaissance Spain. Neither a Spaniard in the modern sense of the word, nor really a soldier, he belonged to that class of warrior knights who lent color to Renaissance battlefields in the autumn of the age of chivalry. A modern officer might feel uncomfortable with him; Don Quixote would have recognized him at sight. The proud tradition of the knight, of the individualist dedicated to a larger cause, was reflected in the Order he founded. "The greater glory of God," the service most needed for Christendom at any given time, was its motto and object. Its men were to be mobile, and at the free disposal of the pope directly. The motive that existed as a living presence in the Jesuit's heart and work was a deep commitment to the person of Christ.

In a word, Loyola had joined to the mystique of the monk the parallel mystique of the Renaissance knight. What is unexpected and remarkable,

---

7. *JMUS*, 2, 344. G. Mengarini, S.J., "The Rocky Mountains, Memoirs of Fr. Gregory Mengarini," *WL, 18* (1889), 40. Thomas Graham, "Stevens County Fifty Years Ago," *Colville Examiner* (1928), clippings in WP. D.S. Tuttle, "Early History of the Episcopal Church in Montana," *CHSM, 5* (1904), 319.

then, is the hardheaded realism that distinguishes his rule, perhaps the most flexible and practical of the rules yet devised by a religious founder. As for Jesuit spirituality, it involved neither the withdrawal of the monk nor the alternate ministry and contemplation of the friar, but a concomitant fusing of the active and the mystical into one's work.

The eye is caught, of course, by the external structure. There was a general (no military connotation) at Rome, elected for life and possessed of sweeping control over the Order within the limits of its Constitution. There were provincials below him, with brief tenure over some large area. These in turn worked through temporary superiors of local residences. Visitation and ample correspondence from bottom to top served to keep the system supple. A training of many years provided a body of priests, aided by a body of lay brothers. No monastic or choir obligations impeded their mobility. No distinctive dress or peculiarity of daily order visibly set them apart from other clerics. No prelacy or honorific status was allowed to distract them, unless it was useful to their work. That work was generally undefined, though missions and education were favored. A cosmopolitanism and intellectual culture, originally that of the High Renaissance, was wedded to a Jesuit asceticism. Over this union presided the patristic tradition of the "spoils of the Egyptians" —human good was of God, destined to be incorporated by Christian ingenuity in evolving Christian civilizations.

The Order was to find itself at the head of battle in exceedingly bitter struggles. It had to set its face against some of the most powerful movements of modern times both inside and outside the Catholic church. One need only recall the Reformation, Gallicanism, the Jansenist tide, the Encyclopedist wing of the Enlightenment, continental Liberalism, and the acrimonious debates on theological doctrine or permissible missionary method. Meanwhile, human errors bedeviled the Order, as they do any institution. Logically enough, in view of its cosmic involvements, the Order's enemies became as legion and partisan as its friends.

Historians have been struck by the primacy of obedience in the Order, or by its discipline. Some see the Jesuit structure as rigid and military. Others have regretted the absence of democratic processes, which distinguished earlier Orders. A writer sympathetic to the Jesuit ideal would meet the complaint by indicating how individual initiative was vital to this tradition of obedience. And without generosity or dedication, the discipline would have remained sterile. The atmosphere of the barracks room, or the uniformity of the soldier, would necessarily be a distortion of the Jesuit ideal.

One cannot be so naïve as to imagine the naked ideal constituting the individual Jesuit. For one thing, each Jesuit was irreducibly the sum of his unique personality, reflecting his own environment, temperament, and limitations.

For another, the capacity to absorb this ideal varied with individuals. But by and large, the ideal was a constant factor, marking and coloring each Jesuit life. This ideal was inculcated in the long training, reaffirmed in the annual week's repetition of Loyola's Spiritual Exercises, and recalled daily in lesser ways. The ideal was to reach down through the centuries to influence the Oregon frontier. It was to be a vital force in Oregon Jesuit personalities as strikingly diverse as those of the romantic enthusiast De Smet; the tough, resilient Cataldo; the neurotic Point, given to melancholy; Imoda, methodical and contained; the facile and cordial Ravalli; and Congiato, a wry and careful soul.

But the Jesuits who came to the Oregon country brought something more than the organization, resources, experience, and distinctive spirit of their Order. They brought as well an unusual missionary tradition. It was rooted in the principle of accommodation, of assimilating one's life to one's immediate environment, so as to influence not only individuals but the environment itself. The Jesuit was to adopt the language and manner of life of the country to which he moved. His rule had built-in mechanisms for change and exception, for mobility and experimentation. Accommodation was inherent especially in the Jesuit's "incarnational" attitude—that all human good was potentially Christian. His humanist education buttressed this attitude, Renaissance classicism being to a large extent the successful adaptation to the Christian tradition of a pagan literature or cast of mind. The Jesuit did not claim that this principle of accommodation was original. Rather, he protested that it represented a patristic tradition that demanded re-emphasis. Nevertheless, few groups were as persistent and bold in its application.

In India Jesuits like de' Nobili transformed themselves into Brahmins. In China men like Schall acquired the status, skills, and appearance of Mandarins. These feats were slow and painful, the work of a lifetime. They shocked large segments of public opinion at home. In effect they comprise, aside from their missionary success, a memorable social experiment. By cultural transmigration into the dominating scholarly caste of a society, the Order hoped persuasively to modify and transmute its basis, naturalizing it to Christianity. Incidental to this labor, the Jesuit became the intermediary between East and West; Confucius, for example, thus became a common heritage. It is not to the point here to answer critics who feel that pure religion cannot be incarnated into the forms of the world without essential compromise. For such people, of course, Jesuit and perhaps even the wider Catholic missionary work must sometimes seem irrelevant to religion.

Even the sympathetic observer sees that the practice of adaptation has its perils. One might lose the Jesuit spirit or grow to neglect its essential rule. Naïveté might draw the unwary into purely political affairs or into irrelevant secular matters. Too human activity might plunge the impulsive into unnecessary, disconcerting change. Adaptation itself might devolve into compromise. Worse, accommodation might remain superficial, resulting in a facile, chameleon-like infiltration or a detached manipulation of alien values. The Jesuit savants, missionaries, and educators could avoid these dangers only by simultaneous commitment to Loyola's ideals and to whatever intellectual values or native culture occupied them.

Application of the principle of accommodation did not come easily. It was by no means always achieved. It represents rather an essential orientation, favored by strong tradition and a flexible Constitution. To see it pass from theory to action for a given area or problem, the Order had always to submit to the complicated process common to any human society, a dialogue between the emerging experience of conservatives and progressives, and between the enthusiasts and the prudent. When successful, it was only at the price of long suffering.

This principle is one reason why some have found it difficult to generalize about the Order. Even on a spatial plane, the Jesuits of England or Spain or Bohemia differed considerably in human accidentals. Similarly, they differed from age to age. The Jesuit was always in effect an integral man of his own time as well as place. There was a Jesuit pattern in the sixteenth century, another in the seventeenth; one of the eighteenth, and again of the nineteenth. Yet the Jesuit core remained—catholic and particular, ancient and modern, liberal yet in the service of tradition. These were the men who now came to Oregon. Their colleagues in past centuries had opened Tibet, cast cannon for the emperor of China, built a royal palace for the negus of Abyssinia, mapped the American Southwest, and founded solar physics. They were men who planned for a long future, and often for a very late harvest.

But not all cultures were as developed as those of China, Japan, Persia, or India. When the Jesuit worked among wilder peoples, some variant of the principle of accommodation had to be found. He still had to learn the language. He had to master the tribal eloquence. A sympathetic study was required into native customs and into the primitive concepts by which the society functioned. Niceties of native etiquette and taste had to be closely attended. All this made for only a good beginning. There was, besides, a parallel need to alter in some degree the very structure of the primitive society and economy. This task was both delicate and dangerous. In any case it would probably demand patient efforts over several generations. If it were to succeed, to be a living reorientation rather than a brutal end and beginning, it had to be done by a kind of inspired persuasion.

Such an exalted project implied piecemeal introduction of domestic over nomadic virtues, the eventual acquisition of agricultural techniques, and even the creation of a more serviceable political system so as to ensure minimum political and social stability. It involved protecting the tribe from slavery and from attacks by White settlers. The native must be interpreted to the White man. Peace must be created and preserved. If time ran out, as in Oregon, the effort changed into something of a race to elevate these people to a position of minimum parity with the aggressive Whites. Looking back today, with knowledge of the irresistible advance of the colonial tide over these lesser peoples, it is clear that sometimes the effort was almost hopeless.

The principle of adaptation was noticeable on the Oregon missions, though in the latter decades of the century the entire problem was thrown into a new perspective. Judge Strong, a Yale man who came to Oregon as associate judge in 1850 and who was no friend to Catholicism, blamed Jesuit success upon this principle. "They adapt themselves to the people they want to convert; if they should go to Lapland and find there the idea of a hot hell was rather agreeable than otherwise, they would immediately make one to suit the country." Mrs. Ronan, who resided with the Flatheads many years as the wife of their most successful agent, made a similar comment. "It was their custom to adapt whatever they could of the Indians' own to the observing and celebrating of religious rites." The same was true of retaining Indian social and political structure, dress, and mentality, where these represented no obstacle to Indian survival in the changing world or to Christian life.

On his 1853 tour through the Rocky Mountains, Dr. Suckley was impressed by this trait of accommodation to circumstances. It seemed to him to be a "lofty and common sense view of men and things, so utterly untrampled by narrow-minded notions as to be remarkable." Simply on the sociological level, this attitude distinguishes Jesuit methodology among the Interior Indians from that of the Protestant missionaries. The latter tended toward a more or less direct acculturation to a White, and presumably more Christian, way of life.[8]

It should not be necessary to insist that a spiritual goal underlay all such sociological exercises. Unless the reader bears in mind this side of the mission story, he will not be seeing it in depth. The conscious premise of the Jesuit approach to the savage was that soul and body were not entities but interlocking principles of an entity, and that improvement in the economic or social order was relevant to and necessary for optimum spiritual progress. The Jesuit approach would therefore consider mere humanitarian or sentimental motives sterile, perhaps even arrogant and harmful.

8. Strong, *OHQ*, *62*, 76. M. Ronan, ed., "Memoirs of a Frontierswoman," unpublished master's thesis (Montana State University, 1932), p. 312. SI, *Journal Containing the Daily Proceedings of the U.S. Exploring Expedition*, under 8 November. Cf. Beeson and Farnham on the Jesuits, in Beeson, *Plea for the Indians*, pp. 135–36 (1857); and on accommodation see also Peter Duignan, "Early Jesuit Missionaries: A Suggestion for Further Study," *American Anthropologist*, 60 (1958), 725–32. On acculturative tendencies in Northwest Protestantism, cf. below, p. 366, esp. nn. 15, 16.

The most brilliant example of such a primitive mission project was the Paraguay Reductions of the seventeenth and eighteenth centuries. This "forest utopia" or Jesuit Republic seized upon men's imaginations. To Voltaire the Reductions were "a triumph of humanity." To Montesquieu they proved for the first time "to the world that religion and humanity are compatible." To Chateaubriand they were "one of the most beautiful works ever accomplished by the hand of man." This subject is directly relevant to the Oregon missions.[9]

The Reductions were a confederation of autonomous native towns, which covered large parts of modern Paraguay, Argentina, Uruguay, Chile, Brazil, and Bolivia. They enjoyed a kind of independent dominion status under the Spanish crown. Europeans were excluded by law from the area. The Indians had been persuaded to settle here permanently and to submit voluntarily to a regime of work, games, and education. As many as a hundred Reductions were founded, though there were only about thirty to fifty at any given time in the century and a half of their existence. Each Reduction or town, carefully laid out on much the same pattern and holding from 350 to 7,000 souls, was self-contained. Each elected its own rulers and officials annually. Each centered on an ambitious church of some size and magnificence, surrounded by carefully laid out homes, workshops, hospital, school, and farms.

Music played an important role all through the day. Every town had its orchestra and choral group. The town also had its own police, and its courts enforced a mild penal law. A whipping or brief confinement were serious penalties; in place of capital punishment there was banishment. This progress had been bought at the price of unremitting patience and of martyrdom— some twenty-nine Jesuits killed. A native army, commanded by the Indians but trained by Spanish officers, defended the region. Every Reduction provided eight companies; the combined Reductions could field some thirty thousand troops. Between 1637 and 1753 this army took the field fifty times for the crown, proving itself in sustained combat. The Reductions made their own fortifications, cannon, small arms, and gunpowder.

The economy was communal, almost utopian. Some 4,000 boats operated in connection with it on the Uruguay and Paraná rivers. Tens of thousands of cattle and sheep grazed. Men and women put in an eight-hour working day and enjoyed a standard of living in some ways superior to that of the Spanish settlers. Their festivals, dances, theatricals, and devotions were on a generous

9. There is an extensive literature on the Paraguay missions. The standard work is Pablo Pastells, S.J., *Historia de la compañia de Jesús en la provincia de Paraguay* (5 vols. Madrid, 1912–33). Popular accounts in English include R. Cunninghame Graham, *Vanished Arcadia* (New York, 1924), and W. H. Koebel, *In Jesuit Land* (London, n.d.).

scale. Some have felt that the Indians allowed themselves to remain too long
under patriarchal tutelage; the point is moot and difficult to resolve. The entire system collapsed into irretrievable ruin when the Jesuit Order, its slow
work still in transition, was suddenly expelled by the crown.

In one sense the Reductions did not altogether die. They were to reappear
as the model for the Rocky Mountain missions. When a tiny nucleus of
twelve Jesuits first came from Maryland to St. Louis in 1823, it was with the
idea of starting an Indian state "something like in Paraguay" beyond the
Mississippi. In 1825 the Jesuit superior wrote to Rome of "the beginning of
another Paraguay." The Jesuit general in turn urged him to follow "as far as
possible" the Paraguay method, "tried and found most successful." By 1839
Father Christian Hoecken felt that the St. Louis mission "realizes the accounts" one reads of "in Paraguay." The theme of "Reductions" recurs in
these early trans-Mississippi missions.[10]

It is no surprise, then, to find Father De Smet carrying the specific idea of a
new Paraguay from St. Louis to Oregon. He made Muratori's history of the
Reductions "our *vade mecum*." His helper, Father Point, drafted the ground
and building plans for Oregon according to Muratori's information. The
methods and daily order were "to be executed in conformity with the
method formerly adopted in the missions of Paraguay." De Smet's letters pursue the theme in detail, touching on such practical items as land division, music, public worship, schools, and confraternities.[11]

Accolti, Ravalli, Point, and others were to return to this motif. The Hudson's Bay factor at nearby Fort Colville reported their arrival: "Paraguay is
fairly given up for the Flathead plains and the benefit of the hurricane Pieds
Noi[r]s."[12] In the crisis of the Oregon mission just a decade after its start,
the general would write from Rome that "the idea of renewing the miracles
of Paraguay amid those mountains" seemed hopeless. The land was "quite
different," Jesuit resources far less, the Indians too nomadic as yet, and the
Whites too free to settle there.[13]

JESUITS TO OREGON

The character and timing of the Oregon mission was determined by a cata-
clysm in 1773. Before that date the Jesuits had been no strangers to the Indi-

10. *JMUS*, *1*, 170, 171, 175; *2*, 193.

11. CR, *1*, 306, 327–30. L. A. Muratori (1672–1750), *Il Cristianesimo felice* (Venice,
1743), trans. as *A Relation of the Missions of Paraguay* (London, 1759); there are several printings in other languages.

12. P. C. Phillips, ed., "Family Letters of Two Oregon Fur Traders, 1828–1856,"
Frontier and Midland, 14 (1933), 72 (Archibald MacDonald to E. Ermatinger, 1842).

13. *JMUS*, *2*, 438.

ans of North America. They had set their missions on the banks of the Rio Grande and the Rappahannock, the Red River, the Missouri, and both sides of the Mississippi. Their labors had touched almost half of the present fifty states, from Arizona to Minnesota and from Florida to New York. They had explored Lower California and the Mississippi Valley, had passed the Yellowstone, and were the first to reach Hudson Bay. They had died under the tomahawk, and with sickening tortures at the stake. The tribes knew them well: Apache, Assiniboine, Abenaki, Choctaw, Huron, Illinois, Iroquois, Miami, Potomac, Shawnee, Sioux, Wyandot, Yazoo, and many more. French Canada had seen a mission chain rivaling Paraguay in fame, reaching from the mouth of the St. Lawrence to the Great Lakes, and probing toward the secret Oregon country beyond the Rockies.

In 1773 Pope Clement XIV suppressed the Jesuits, to preserve the peace of Christendom. Historians have quarreled passionately over this as they have over other facets of Jesuit history. Some see the suppression as a vindication of anti-Jesuit charges. Writers more sympathetic view it as a futile attempt to appease the secularist Enlightenment, with its threat of national churches. At any rate, some 23,000 Jesuits were affected in 670 colleges, 176 seminaries, 24 universities, and 273 mission areas. In South America alone 350,000 Indians lost their Jesuit guides.

A year later the Pope was dead. His successor desired the remnants of the Order to continue on in Germany and Russia. Shrunk to a tiny dimension, its organization and life barely intact, the Jesuit spirit flickered low for a quarter century. The next pope, in response to wide Catholic demand, restored the Order to its previous status by a series of steps from 1801 to 1814. Thus the American Jesuits were actually functioning in 1805, though the universal restoration came only in 1814. Surviving ex-Jesuits gathered to help restore and rebuild the shattered structure. They had lost all their property and resources, all their schools, libraries, and laboratories, all their missions, manpower, and training mechanisms. They were in effect a handful of survivors, a trickle of recruits. In America there were perhaps two dozen.

The Oregon missions were being organized therefore by a skeleton crew as part of a painful if enthusiastic wider movement. The intervening years, the era of the French Revolution and Napoleon, had swept away the old Europe. All the baggage of technique and mood, social structure, opportunities, and modes of thought and action had gone. Yet the Jesuit expansion in this new era was to be almost explosive. Again and again anticlerical governments were to confiscate their schools and exile whole provinces. The issues were now crystal clear to the Catholic community; again and again it forced a return of the Order. This too was to be part of the Oregon story. The talented exiles were rerouted often to the American West. Thus the Italian revolutions gave to the Northwest missions men like Congiato, Cataldo, and Diomedi.

Two generals directed the Order during the period of 1840–80. The Dutchman John Roothaan guided the Oregon development cannily from its inception until 1853. His major problem was to avoid overextension, channeling his few resources and energies into measured growth.[14] The Belgian Peter Beckx succeeded him from mid-century to 1883. Under him the Order mushroomed from ten to nineteen provinces, from five thousand to almost twelve thousand men. Both generalates coincided with the long pontificate of Pius IX (1846–78), the intransigent "prisoner of the Vatican." New religious congregations of priests and nuns proliferated; a number of these were to work in Oregon. Indian missions in Canada and America took on a new life from about 1830.

In 1833 the hierarchy of the United States assigned the "removed" tribes of the trans-Mississippi West especially to the Jesuits. Secretary of War John C. Calhoun had already made the suggestion in 1822 to Bishop Du Bourg of the Louisiana Purchase area. Du Bourg in turn had anticipated Calhoun by trying to secure Jesuits from Rome five times between their restoration as an Order and 1822. President Monroe had even given the bishop a subsidy toward this new Paraguay. President Jackson was also to give it his approval.

In 1823 two priests and ten other Jesuits left Maryland, flatboating down the Ohio to begin work among the Osages and Potawatomis. Settlement soon overtook the group. They found themselves involved in an extensive White apostolate, including two colleges, as well as in the Indian Reductions. One of their successful Indian missionaries, who had come from Maryland with the original dozen Jesuits, was the young Belgian Peter De Smet. Impulsive and openhearted, endowed with great physical strength, he was to be the founder of the Rocky Mountain mission.

De Smet is one of the more unusual figures in the history of the American West. No White man has ever come close to equaling his universal appeal to the Indian. For the majority of the tribes on the trans-Mississippi plains his name was one to conjure with. Kit Carson's autobiography remarks on De Smet's courage in handling them. Generals Sherman, Terry, Harney, Rosecrans, Sully, and others paid tribute to it. Many times the government would call for his help in pacifying the tribes. "No white man knows the Indians as Father De Smet," wrote Thurlow Weed in introducing him to President Lincoln, "nor has any man their confidence in the same degree." Senator Thomas Hart Benton, with the concurrence of the secretary of the Interior and the commissioner of Indian Affairs, wrote De Smet in 1851 of their conviction that he could do more toward pacifying the Indians, "keeping them in

14. Roothaan's relations to the Oregon missions in their world context are studied by J. A. Otto, S.J., *Gründung der neuen Jesuitenmission durch General Pater Johann Philipp Roothaan* (Freiburg, 1939), pp. 419–50.

peace and friendship with the United States," than an "army with banners." General Stanley in 1865 asserted that De Smet, "alone of the entire white race, could penetrate to these cruel savages at war and return safe and sound." This kind of praise was to become common for De Smet, from bishops and frontiersmen, political figures and generals.

Paradoxically, he was not really suited to the patient routine of the daily missionary, nor did he spend many years at such work. By temperament he tried to do too much, projecting dreams that had to be implemented in detail by others. He was at his worst as an administrator. A superior who knew him well says he was "thoroughly good but a little original" (odd); another friend characterizes him as "extremely impressionable." On the other hand, he proved to be eminently suited to systematic deskwork. Half the priestly life of this restless, visionary Jesuit was to be spent in the role of businessman and financier for his province. His Indian adventures, his many books, and his 180,000 miles of travel were mostly fitted into the interstices of this more prosaic life. His real talent was an intuitive flair for winning the Indian heart and reading the Indian mind. Allied to this were his services as publicist to Europe for the Indian world, his exploits as peacemaker, and his steady acquisition of men and money for the Indian missions.[15]

In answer to the Flathead delegations of the past decade, De Smet was sent out in 1840 to the Oregon country. His six years there combined reconnaissance and organization. His first trip turned into a triumphal tour. He preached to Cheyennes, Mandans, Kansas, various kinds of Sioux, Crows, Blackfeet, Snakes, Bannocks, Kalispels, Nez Percés, Flatheads, Kutenais, Coeur d'Alenes, and lesser tribes. Hundreds were baptized, and preparations were begun for the first Oregon Reduction. The original plans were impossibly grandiose. De Smet envisioned a proliferation of missions to all the tribes of the Oregon country. Joset, the next superior, hoped to bring the Snakes and Blackfeet to St. Ignatius mission and to start another mission among the Cayuses and Nez Percés. But the restored Order simply did not have the men; missions and ministries were devouring its slender resources all over the globe. As early as 1845 Mengarini deplored the fact that many Catholics among the Cayuses and Snakes could not be cared for.

There would therefore be Catholic Indians in many places where a mission or even a station could not be considered. In 1846 the general had advised that forces be concentrated near the point of origin, the Rocky Mountain country below the Canadian border. Existing missions were to be consolidated firmly, with an orderly rate of growth. The spacing of missions should take note of Hudson's Bay Company experience, so that some communica-

15. *Autobiography of Thurlow Weed, 1* (2 vols. Boston, 1884), 547–48. *JMUS, 3,* 68; *1,* 98; *2,* 431 (Jesuit quots.). CR, *4,* 1585.

tion and mutual support would effect a strong, interlocking network rather than completely isolated units.

The number of these units fluctuated to a confusing degree. When Joset succeeded De Smet as superior-general in 1846, he found four missions: St. Mary's among the Flatheads, Sacred Heart among the Coeur d'Alenes, St. Ignatius among the Kalispels, and St. Joseph's among the Okanogans. In 1847 Father De Vos listed the mountain missions with their attached stations as nine in all. In 1849 De Smet wrote that there were two priests among the Flatheads and their neighbors, two among the Coeur d'Alenes, two among the Kalispels and Kettles, two among the Okanogans and in British Columbia, and two on the coast, with an added total of twelve lay brothers. For 1863 De Smet enumerated eighteen missions or stations with chapels.

Such statistics are not altogether realistic. In 1869, for instance, Father General Beckx reported to Paris that fifteen priests and twelve lay brothers were "devoting themselves with zeal to all the fatigues of the apostolate." Yet at the same time Father Grassi, the local superior, was informing Lyons that all but about six of these were too old or ill for active work.[16] The crisis and contraction of the '50s were to be followed by several decades of ever-widening expansion over the Oregon and Plains country. But the waxing and waning fortunes of the network will fall naturally into subsequent, chronologically progressive chapters.

Each mission in the network was under its own superior. De Smet had been superior-general under the control of St. Louis. This connection with remote St. Louis soon became vague and impractical. Effective guidance came directly from Rome, overseas communication being more satisfactory; financial support came from continental alms deposited at the London headquarters of the Hudson's Bay Company. This situation was regularized in 1851, when the Oregon country formally was put under the direct governance of the general. From 1854, however, jurisdiction passed permanently to the province of Turin in Italy. This ensured a continuing supply of able and well educated Europeans for the Oregon frontier.

On the local scene, six missioners succeeded De Smet as superiors-general during our period.[17] Their headquarters were variously the Coast settlements, the mountains, or California. The addition of gold-rush California to the mission chain drew off major resources and precipitated a decade of contraction for the Oregon stations, counteracted somewhat in 1858 by the ap-

16. FP, I, 5, Beckx to Association (in French), 16 April; Grassi report, *AFL, 41* (1869), 384.

17. Joseph Joset (1846–50), Michael Accolti (1850–54), Nicholas Congiato (1854–62), Joseph Giorda (1862–66), Urban Grassi (1866–69), Giorda again (1869–77), and Joseph Cataldo (1877–93).

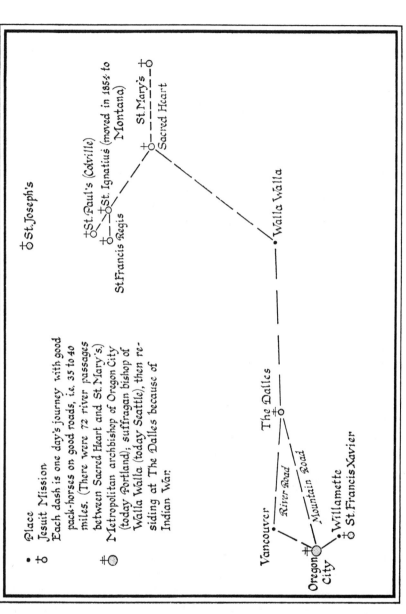

† St.Joseph's

†St.Paul's (Colville)

†St.Ignatius (moved in 1854: to Montana)

St.Mary's †

St.Francis Regis †

Sacred Heart †

• Walla Walla

Legend:
• Place
† Jesuit Mission
  Each dash is one day's journey with good pack-horses on good roads, i.e. 35 to 40 miles. (There were 72 river passages between Sacred Heart and St.Mary's.)
⚫︎† Metropolitan archbishop of Oregon City (today Portland), suffragan bishop of Walla Walla (today Seattle), then residing at The Dalles because of Indian War.

The Dalles †

Vancouver •

River Road

Mountain Road

Oregon City ⚫︎†

• Willamette
† St.Francis Xavier

5. Father Joset's Distance Map of the Early Mission Network, 1849.

pointment of separate superiors-general for California and Oregon. Both remained under Turin and to some extent shared the same men. Vanzina was
prefect at the San Francisco college before beginning his seventeen years on
the Oregon mission. Congiato and Mengarini came down from Oregon to
spend the last thirty years of their ministry in California. Men like Cataldo,
Palladino, Caruana, and Grassi taught at the Santa Clara or San Francisco colleges. The academic and primitive were never far apart.

Shape of an Indian Reduction

An individual mission was planted in the Oregon chain according to a program. At first the Indians would be visited for a time and won over. The missionary might find the tribe eager, ready to begin. Or he might have to visit
them for years before their dispositions proved satisfactory. An Indian's
fervor could pass as swiftly as it had come. Worse, it might be rooted in a
desire for the status or gifts a mission would bring. The novelty of Christianity, its connection with the remarkable White man, and its "magic" nature
facilitated initial success, if the missionary were unwary. The Blackfeet especially admired Jesuits as shamans who brought success in war. The Gros
Ventres brought Father Point their deformed people to be cured by miracles
—and blamed an earthquake on him.

Even when genuine interest was aroused, the psychological obstacles to
successful preparation were formidable. The old moral code had been a function of the social order. To give up polygamy, especially where children
by several women were involved, played havoc with family relations. Revenge
was almost instinctive to the Indian; he felt slights easily, treasured them long,
and could abandon his religion to avenge them. Excessive gambling and, for
many, liquor were neurotic compulsions. The concepts of the cross and
Christian self-sacrifice were hard even to understand, much less to practice.
In some tribes marriage customs deprived the bride of the Christian freedom
of consent; in others the marriage contract was considered at least termi-
nable.

Some tribes were possessed by arrogant pride, others lost in subhuman leth-
argy. The Indian's sloth, his aversion to abstract thought, his burden of
superstitions, his shallow, changeable personality—all made permanent conversion seem hopeless. To give him a White man's haircut and trousers, some
instruction in farming and reading, and a course of catechetics was to create a
dangerous cultural tension. The Jesuit Palladino cautioned the government
later that these generations would always remain Indians, and that their education must realistically be based on that fact. "All the millions in the United
States treasury" could not make the Indian into a White; "he will live more

or less according to his Indian nature." [18] In undertaking their work, the Jesuits knew both the problem and the obstacles. But then, "what were the Iroquois before their conversions, and what have they not since become?" [19]

Permanent, thorough conversion involved a lifetime of social and psychological formation. Even the converted Indian was unpredictable, had his own logic, could sulk or grow ominous, might yield to impulse, sink into a primitive apathy, or suddenly prove devious and rebellious. One had to think one's way slyly around the Indians, building upon their many real virtues, baptizing as it were their tribal code. Firmness, infinite tact, stubborn patience, some ingenuity, and above all love and liking were essential. On the other hand, the Indians delighted in the ceremonial and liturgical aspects of Catholicism. The spiritual drama of the Blackrobe's life (and that of the Lady Blackrobes or nuns) struck them deeply—people removed from the human concerns of family, country, and acquisition, to lose themselves in the Indian world. The Real Presence on the altar also had a stirring effect on the Indian.

When a large group of Indians had become enthusiastically committed to conversion, a site for the Reduction would be chosen. This was done with an eye to protection from White contacts, and for centrality to other tribes. A cross was raised with due solemnities. Plans were carefully drawn, trees felled, and roads opened. The Jesuits would survey, fence, and plant a farm. This was communal, though any Indian desiring his own farm might also have one. The farm was meant to furnish an alternate economy for the nomadic Indian. A temporary log chapel would go up, a rough residence for the missionaries, a barn, a gristmill or sawmill perhaps, a forge, and cabins for the few Indians preferring them. If necessary a stockade with blockhouses was thrown around the buildings.

A bewildering variety of materials had to be imported or contrived. Bells, statues, vestments, and all the ecclesiastical appurtenances were needed. Saws were devised from wagon tires, windows from scraped deerskin, rope from woven grass, and wheels from tree sections. Boards were cut, stone quarried, a clay mortar mixed, and millstones and millraces fashioned. A mission was soon able to produce its own bricks, candles, soap, smoking pipes, potato sugar, bronze crosses, chisels, bellows, grindstones, and the like. Cattle, poultry, pigs, seed, and agricultural implements had to be brought from the remote Coast.

The Fathers imposed a rigorous daily order from the very beginning. They balanced public devotions, work, games, instructions, and feasts. The Indians were kept busy and amused. The day began with morning Mass and

18. L. B. Palladino, S.J., *Indian and White in the Northwest; or, a History of Catholicity in Montana* (Baltimore, 1894), p. 114.

19. CR, *1*, 286.

instruction and ended with evening prayers and instruction. This obligation
was universal and permanent for those later remaining at the mission. An
hour's catechetical lesson was given the children in the afternoon. For this the
children divided into bands under "chiefs"; songs, recitation, certificates of
award, and other pedagogical devices came into play. At St. Mary's Brother
Savio gave marionette shows; Father Point painted the Indians' portraits.
When the tribe was fully prepared, mass baptisms took place. In an 1841 baptism no less than twenty-four tribes were represented among the neophytes.
Besides their Indian names Catholic Indians carried also a baptismal one. This
was sometimes French, usually mispronounced: Arlee for Henri, Mitt'ó for
Victor, Ameló for Ambroise, Eneas or Aeneas for Ignace.

An infirmary was part of the mission. The priest made daily rounds
among the sick, giving what medication he could. Where he could persuade
the Indians, he vaccinated them against smallpox and cholera. This was done
also among outlying tribes; thus Joset vaccinated the San Poils in 1853. Dr.
Suckley in that same year found smallpox already rare among the Pend
d'Oreilles and Kalispels because of Jesuit vaccination.[20] Ravalli was a particularly skilled medical amateur; Mengarini was selected by the Jesuit general
for his talents in music, languages, and medicine; Prando was to develop skill
in folk medicine and Indian herbalism.

A Reduction was also an educational establishment. Its pedagogical principles and techniques had developed from generations of experience among
many tribes. These involved emulation, rapid shifts of attention, formal assembly, and concentration upon influential individuals. A real school went up
as soon as it could be staffed. Nuns like the Ursulines and Sisters of Providence were brought in for the girls. Formal education involved a plain
drilling in the three R's, along with agricultural and manual training. The Indian had an abiding aversion to manual labor, and persuading him to industrious habits was always a problem.

On major feast days there were elaborate spiritual and secular festivities,
and the tribes gathered from hundreds of miles around. These occasions were
enlivened by gunfire, displays of Indian eloquence, and horse races. The devotional life, like education and the new customs, was assimilated through
tribal ways. Sermons followed Indian tastes in rhetoric, hymns were built from
ancient tribal chants; thus Mengarini turned a Flathead war song into a
funeral hymn. Since the Indians loved music, bands were organized. The
first Oregon mission soon had a band boasting a clarinet, flute, piccolo, tam-
bourine, two accordions, cymbals, and a bass drum.

Governor Stevens described the Coeur d'Alene mission in 1853, a decade after its opening. There was a "splendid church" fifty feet high, measuring

20. SI, Journal, in final summation.

forty feet by one hundred. Next to it were "a large barn, a horse-mill for flour, a small range of buildings" for the Jesuits, "a storeroom, a milk or dairy room, a cook-room and good arrangements for their pigs and cattle." "A new range of quarters" was going up. At the Reduction there were "hundreds of settled Indians"; twelve families lived in "comfortable log cabins." Two hundred acres were under cultivation. Thirty cows and one hundred pigs decorated the scene. The governor watched "some thirty or forty Indians" getting in the harvest, and others engaged in work like plowing or digging. The Flathead Reduction in 1841 had a chapel holding four to five hundred Indians, endowed with "pediment, colonnade and gallery, balustrade, choir, seats," lighting and an organ. By 1849 the first Kalispel mission had a church sixty-five feet by thirty-five, with walls twenty feet high; a barn measuring one hundred and four feet by twenty; a three-hundred-acre farm, thirty cattle, and hundreds of Indians more or less settled.[21]

There was no question of settling the many thousands of Catholic Indians at these missions. Only in later years would some success be achieved in this direction, especially among the Coeur d'Alenes. It was not easy to persuade an Indian to take up this toilsome and womanish economy and to persevere at it. Besides, if kept in one place for more than a few months, he became morose and melancholy. The most important reason, however, was that the Jesuits simply could not afford the necessary instructors or the expense. Farming in the mountains was a costly business. Efforts in this direction expanded only gradually. The Hudson's Bay governor pointed out the dilemma to Protestant missionaries planning work here: one could not follow the innumerable scattered families, yet gathering them in one place meant supporting them.[22]

The Jesuit general, Father Roothaan, believed that such stabilizing of the Indian society and economy was essential to further progress and must be achieved despite the cost in men and money.[23] A compromise eventually had to be accepted. The farming group was small and still had to supplement its income with game and roots. The other Indians had to be allowed, and for the time being helped, to maintain their old economy. The Jesuits were not in a position to stop the buffalo hunts on the Plains, even though these were an occasion for immorality and war. On the contrary, they went to great trouble to see that powder and shot were always available for the hunters. So well did they provide that their Hudson's Bay neighbors envied the Jesuit Indians their meat diet. "The Jesuits, though they do not intend it, injure us a great deal in the provision trade," by supplying free powder and shot brought up

21. *RR, 12*, i, 133. CR, *1*, 331. On Reduction education see below, p. 492, Gibson.
22. HB, D4, *52*, Simpson Corresp. out, to Rev. S. Grabau, 6 January 1857.
23. FP, I, 5, Roothaan to Association, 12 April 1845.

from the Coast; they kept the Indians in "meat in abundance, while we have to starve one half of the year for want of it." [24]

The mission was therefore seldom a true Reduction. Most of the tribes remained substantially nomadic from 1840 to 1880. But the mission was always their center. There was usually a fair number forming a nucleus around it, living permanently in cabins and tipis, and doing some farming. The rest of the families were scattered. They flocked to the church on feast days, or managed to visit it for confession and advice, or stayed for a season now and again. The priests also made circuits through their camps and appeared at their gatherings.

Each mission served a huge area beyond its own tribal range. As occasion offered, visits were made to the other tribes. Families from those tribes would drift in to settle for a time, or permanently, at the Reduction. Where an outlying situation seemed especially promising, a permanent station or sub-mission was erected. This might be anything from a chapel to an inchoate Reduction. It served as a rendezvous for public prayer, and for sporadic visitation from the central mission. In 1845 the station of St. Francis Regis cared for the band of Crees resident in the Rocky Mountains, Holy Heart of Mary was for the Kutenais, Assumption for the Flatbows or lower Kutenais, St. Francis Borgia for the Kalispels, and St. Peter's for the Lakes. In the same year a resident priest from St. Ignatius was serving a circuit that included such far-off tribes as the San Poils, Spokanes, and Okanogans. The Colville or Kettle mission in 1870 ministered to tribes at a distance of 50, 80, 100, 150, and even 350 miles. In 1872 St. Joseph's mission among the Yakimas served a central area of 200 by 60 miles, with 14 tribes.

This constant travel "was the most typical side of our lives." [25] Distances were great, but they were further compounded by difficulties of terrain. To cast off from the mission and venture into the mountain wilderness was a serious project. A half day's preparation was needed. The traveler slept on the ground, ate little and badly, put his life in his hands on mountain sides and river crossings, and easily became lost. Mishaps of all kinds marred such trips. One night a hungry animal made off with Menetrey's buckskin trousers. De Smet and Giorda narrowly escaped death by drowning. Nobili almost starved when lost in the woods.

The mountains were cut off from the outside world for much of the year by snow or thaw. It was difficult to know the day of the week; around 1870 the mission of St. Ignatius celebrated Easter on a weekday, a week or so late. Under such conditions the Fathers had to bring up provisions, maintain a siz-

24. A. J. Partoll, "Fort Connah: A Frontier Trading Post, 1847–1871," *PNWQ, 30* (1939), 401.
25. *JMUS*, 2, 319 (Joset, 1845).

able correspondence, serve their many stations, and set off instantly to the sick or dying. In 1862 one such call to a sick miner meant a round trip of 500 miles for Father Grassi. Some time later Father Kuppens, having missed an appointment at Fort Benton, put together a raft and floated 600 miles down river to remedy the defect. The health of more than one missionary broke under the strain. Others seemed to thrive on hardship and monotony. Father Grassi came to prefer a single diet of pancakes and bacon from one end of the year to the other. Father Cataldo, allowed to put in a few months on the missions before his imminent death, survived there another vigorous sixty years.

The problem of travel and communications eased considerably as the decades advanced. But as late as 1867 Palladino with three other Jesuits put in ten days of unremitting travel, under Indian guides, from Walla Walla to the first mountain mission, Sacred Heart. Even with the luxury of a stage line for the flatland part of the trip, it took eleven full days and nights from Walla Walla up to Fort Colville in 1866, with no accommodations en route. In 1863 the four nuns sent from Montreal to the Montana missions had to approach via Panama. Their trip from Walla Walla to Sacred Heart took seventeen days of constant movement; a full month passed before they arrived at St. Ignatius.

To get provisions at the main Hudson's Bay post at Vancouver involved a wilderness trip of not much less than a thousand miles. Mail was something of a nightmare. In 1844 it "ordinarily requires two years to get an answer, very often three or four years." [26] In 1849 two-way mail to the Coast was available twice a year. In 1850 an order from Rome required from one to two years en route, and even with duplicates sent by alternate mails it sometimes failed to arrive.

Poor soil, floods, enemy raids, or White encroachment easily conspired to force the removal of a whole mission establishment. New beginnings were particularly painful. Sacred Heart among the Coeur d'Alenes moved three times, as did St. Ignatius among the Kalispels; and St. Peter's among the Blackfeet moved four times in its first eight years. A Reduction might also be closed. This was a deliberate and successful technique designed to shock rebellious or backsliding Indians into repentance. Pressures built up within the Indians, as age-old habits and tribal structure were modified. At the moment of crisis the Fathers were always ready to go, thus forcing the Indian to make a voluntary choice between two painful losses. If Catholicity had struck its roots deeply enough, such a storm once weathered had permanent effect on tribal psychology. Often the mere threat of abandonment sufficed. Thus the Fathers twice threatened the Coeur d'Alenes with closure in 1843, again in 1847, very seriously in 1857 (for poor church attendance), and in 1858 for going to war against the Whites.

26. Ibid., p. 358, Father Van Assche to Roothaan.

St. Paul's among the Kettles was closed from 1859 to 1865; later it was to be abandoned for the more northerly St. Francis Regis. The Flatheads were temporarily abandoned in 1850; extrinsic circumstances stretched this closure into sixteen years. The Cheyenne mission closed after the Ghost Dance episode in 1888, the Blackfoot mission during the hostilities of the '60s, the Nez Percé mission briefly in 1870. The mission map was therefore confusingly fluid.

Not only did the missions move about or even close temporarily, but the Fathers themselves were reassigned from mission to mission. Menetrey was working on the Oregon coast in 1846, among the Coeur d'Alenes in 1848–54, among the Kalispels in 1854–57, with the Coeur d'Alenes again in 1857–59, back among the Kalispels in 1859–61, over to the Flatheads in 1862, up among the Kettles in 1863–67, on the coast managing the mission finances in 1867, back with the Kalispels in 1868, at a Helena parish for Whites during the late '70s, back to the Kalispels in 1880–84, in a Missoula parish 1884–89, and finally among the Kalispels in 1889–91. This is not atypical. Grassi worked among the Blackfeet, Gros Ventres, Kalispels, Okanogans, Chelans, Yakimas, and Umatillas. Joset had eight such successive careers on the mission chain; Ravalli, nine; Cataldo, ten; and Caruana, ten. Many Jesuits had checkered careers elsewhere before or after their stay on the Oregon missions. Workers were so few that a small crisis could set off a chain reaction of fitting new faces into jobs suited to their capacities. At a given mission this meant a steady turnover in personnel.

What were these people like? Few of them were brilliantly gifted in personality, talent, intellect or practical competence. Most were very ordinary beings, with human failings. Some were really unfit for mission life. A few were problems. But most seemed to share a capacity for rising above themselves when crises came. Most of them also had in common an ability to focus their sympathies and selves upon the tribes which was sometimes passionate. A surprising number were erudite and have left useful memoirs, treatises, and dictionaries.

A gallery of their faces in ancient photographs provides an interesting study. There are earthy, peasant faces and finely drawn aristocratic faces. There are faces somber and faces twinkling; faces withdrawn, deeply carved, and faces happily alert; faces intellectualized, and practical, no-nonsense faces; faces ill and faces hearty, faces confident or diffident, stern or gentle, open or closed. In brief, they reflect a generous range of personality. Most of them bear the stamp of character or self-reliance which can be observed, sometimes about the eyes or the set of the head, but most often around the mouth and chin.

The mission personnel was international, with an increasing number of

Italians after the adoption by Turin in 1854. The Indians were thus happily spared the experience of receiving Catholicism at the start in any single ethnic psychology—an Irish, French, Italian, or German Catholicism. (However, the fact that the Jesuits were foreigners for a while made them objects of suspicion to the local authorities.) [27] The original Oregon founders consisted of three Belgians, a German, an Italian, and a Frenchman. These were soon joined by a Dutchman, an Irishman, a Swiss, a Maltese, two Belgians, three Italians, and a Frenchman. In 1859 among the thirteen Jesuits in the missions there were three Italians, three Belgians, two Swiss, two Dutch, a German, a Maltese, and an Irishman. Even after the Italians began coming in waves during the 1860s and later, other countries continued to send their representatives.

The missionaries had a sound academic background. It was the ordinary education of the better classes in Europe, with extra philosophical and theological training. Although by present standards this education had serious defects, in mid-nineteenth-century America, and especially on the frontier, it was impressive. Most of the Jesuits had had some experience as teachers in secondary schools. The artist Point had studied in France, Switzerland, Spain, and America, and had founded St. Charles' College in Louisiana. Congiato had been vice-president of the College of Nobles in Italy, of the College of Fribourg in Switzerland, and president of the small Jesuit college at Bardstown in Kentucky; after his Indian career he was to be president of the San Francisco college.

Joset taught at the Fribourg college; Giorda at an Italian seminary; Canestrelli at the Gregorian University in Rome. Diomedi was a tutor at the Roman College. Imoda taught at the College of Nobles in Naples. D'Aste was sent by his superiors, after his theological studies, to pursue mathematics at the University of Paris. La Motte also attended the University of Paris. Cataldo studied in Sicily and Belgium; Prando at Rome and Monaco; Rappagliosi in Italy, France, and Belgium; and Palladino in Italy, Austria, and France. Such a background of teaching and travel was not irrelevant in handling the childlike Indian character.

TOMAHAWKS INTO PLOWSHARES

The dream of an Oregon Paraguay was to be a failure. There really had been little hope for it from the beginning. There never were enough men, nor was there sufficient money, to do the job properly. Still, by sheer courage and perseverance it might have been achieved after all if there had been enough

27. MJ, IX, AA, Joset to De Smet, 26 February 1857.

time. The latter decades of the century did witness an autumnal achievement. Missions then extended from the Yakimas, Umatillas, and Nez Percés over to the Cheyennes, Assiniboines, and Crows. Schools and churches became large, modern buildings. Farms were often Indian-operated and self-supporting. By 1890 in Montana alone there were "nine Indian missions counting dependencies, and nine [Indian] schools including the kindergarten, an aggregate of some 7000 Catholic Indians," out of a census of 10,000.[28] One thousand of these were in school, half of them boys and half girls. These Montana Indians were served by eighteen priests, eight scholastics, twelve lay brothers, fourteen Sisters of Providence, and sixty Ursulines.

Then everything seemed to degenerate and decline. Father George de La Motte, the son of a French army officer, was profoundly discouraged as superior-general in 1906. "What a fiasco our work [at St. Ignatius] has been; 50 years of work and this is the result." He saw "superstitious practices on the increase." The Indians were "lazy, uncivilized," and "doomed to a speedy, wretched end." The wife of the Indian agent Ronan, who had lived with the Flatheads through the Indian troubles of 1877, recalled those times so "different from the present situation," when the mission Indians had lived in good houses and farms and were thrifty and well-off.[29]

But if there had been no Paraguay here, there was such a substantial measure of achievement that other men called it success. In 1883 the United States Senate appointed Senator George Vest of Missouri to investigate the Indian schools. After a trip through the Northwest, Vest reported that the Jesuit system was the "one ray of light." The Senator was careful to state that he had grown up considering Jesuits "as very much akin to the devil." He was "a Protestant, born one, educated one, and expect to die one, but I say now that the system adopted by the Jesuits is the only practical system for the education of the Indian, and the only one that has resulted in anything at all."

General Alfred Sully, special Indian commissioner, had written almost identical words to De Smet when asking him to open missions in the Dakota Territory in 1866. "As I do not profess myself to be a Catholic, I can speak of the great good they have done without fear of being accused of prejudice; in fact I can say that the priests are the only missionaries I have ever seen who have been successful in improving the condition of the Indians to any great extent and I have had many opportunities of judging, not only in this country and California, but in Mexico and in parts of South America."[30]

28. Palladino, *Indian and White*, p. 234.

29. W. N. Bischoff, S.J., *The Jesuits in Old Oregon* . . . *1840–1940* (Caldwell, Idaho, 1945), p. 82. Ronan, "Memoirs," p. 245.

30. Bischoff, pp. 76–77. *JMUS*, 2, 481.

Similar statements came from Colonel Cumming, head of the western superintendency of Indian Affairs, from the secretary of War at mid-century, and from various congressmen and soldiers near its end. Historians have been equally generous. Perhaps the most impressive of the tributes were those paid over the decades by travelers, explorers, journalists, soldiers, and casual visitors, most of them neither Catholics nor particularly religious.

Many thousands of Indians lived a Catholic life between 1840 and 1880. To what depth did their faith penetrate? For Red men or White the question is more easily posed than answered. One is faced with such a spectrum of Indian reactions to the challenge of Christianity, such conflicting motivations and contradictory actions, that great caution is necessary in judging. Reports of missionaries vary from ecstatic to despairing. Again, much depends upon the particular tribe, and upon the exact time. The historian unfamiliar with religious psychology easily misconstrues the evidence. Judgments by the resolutely pious or the doctrinaire secularist tend to emerge as a few confident simplicities. Certainly the Oregon tribes can display examples of Christian life to equal the best of the Whites. And just as certainly there were more than a few spectacular failures. At all times the going was difficult.

A fever chart of the moral ups and downs would probably be dramatic enough, although without paying careful attention to the basic or residual commitments, this perhaps would not be very helpful. Reality never approached the idyllic situation depicted by the edifying letters in the mission magazines. But the community of Catholic Indians did seem to inhabit a respectably elevated plateau of moral action. From it they could easily tumble or be jostled to the depths. By and large, however, they clung there at least until the Whites arrived in some numbers. This psychological factor is as important a background to the Interior story as the geographical or cultural.

From their first appearance until 1880 the Jesuits had to work for peace. The Indian world was violent and warlike. It is not generally realized how true this was of the mission area. Intertribal raids and wars were a constant element in the lives of such Indians as the Flatheads and Kalispels against Blackfeet, Sioux, Bannocks, and other tribes. The Montana plains were dotted with their battlefields. The Blackfeet regularly carried the war directly into the mountains. There were numerous buffalo-hunting warriors among Interior tribes like the Coeur d'Alenes or Kettles. The Plains tribes, whom the Jesuits were reaching by the '60s, made such warfare "the main business of their lives." [31] The ferocity with which they dedicated themselves to war, as Father Grassi noted, threatened to result in mutual annihilation.

Such a "passion for war, rooted in the soul of the Indian," could not be

31. *LN, 3* (1865–66), 16, De Smet letter.

checked in a few years.[32] It was a particularly difficult problem because the roots were not only psychological but economic. Not even biological warfare was excluded. Father Hoecken tells how in 1858 some Nez Percés tried to spread the dreaded smallpox among the Flatheads by throwing infected clothing into the camp and rubbing infectious matter on lodge doors. Father Giorda, in order to put his message to the Gros Ventres in terms they could grasp, represented them as making war against God, giving himself the role of ambassador arranging a peace treaty.

Thus the problem of direct pacification was always a part of the Oregon missionary's life. Within the tribe itself trouble was never far away. Time and again ugly fissures appeared in the surface of the Oregon utopia, betraying the inner restlessness, confusion, and lack of self-discipline that bedeviled the poor Indian. With never-ending patience the Jesuits would manage to close the surface cracks and would continue the task of transforming the inner character and motivation of their people. In many ways this daily peacemaking between tribe and tribe, individual and individual, and parties of Indians and parties of Whites is the most interesting part of the story, but there is no space for it here.

Creating, preserving, and restoring the peace had always been part of the Jesuit mission tradition. In seventeenth-century Canada, Baron Lahontan had reported that the governor-general "cannot be without the services of the Jesuits in making treaties with the governors of New England and New York as well as with the Iroquois." In South America a similar service was offered. Father Joseph Anchieta even surrendered his person to Indians on the warpath against the Whites in sixteenth-century Brazil, as a hostage against European injustice. The great fur trade of North America owed much to the Jesuits' "strong influence" for peace among the trading tribes. Phillips' monumental *Fur Trade* records how the Jesuits "were of immense service in developing the fur trade of New France."

This Jesuit tradition of successful pacification was known to Calhoun, the American secretary of War. Writing in 1823 to General Clark, superintendent of the Indian West after his return from the Lewis and Clark expedition, Calhoun expressed himself in favor of Jesuit work in the new trans-Mississippi west. Not only would the Jesuits effect "ultimate civilization" among the Indians, but they would be "useful in preventing the commission of outrages and preserving peace with the tribes." In a similar vein Colonel Alfred Vaughan, agent for the Blackfeet in 1859, asking De Smet for a Jesuit mission, declared that his fifteen years' experience convinced him this was the best path to civilization and to peace for this fierce tribe.[33]

32. U. Grassi, "Montagnes rocheuses," *AFL*, 41 (1869), 382.
33. *JMUS*, 3, 66; 1, 50. Phillips, *Fur Trade*, 1, 92, 105.

The motive for this dangerous work was not pacifism. The Jesuits would have regarded such use of the doctrines of the King of Peace as a betrayal of their Indians. When the Jesuit Indians were unjustly attacked, it was assumed that they would defend themselves. When their European country was at war with another, it had been expected often that Indians should fight along with other citizens. The Indian armies of Paraguay had their counterparts, less well organized. In Canada the Reductions had to be frequently fortified and defended under Jesuit guidance against hostile Indians. Christian tribes fought for New France in the Seven Years' War. Among the Abenakis, Father Rasle had refused to interfere in the desperate Indian defense against the English colonists and their Indian allies; the result was vilification and his eventual murder by the colonists. In the American Civil War numbers of Jesuit Osages were to fight for the Union forces when they could not remain neutral.

Unless one understands this, the efforts for peace by Oregon Jesuits must seem like a kind of complicity in the White seizure of Indian lands. The Jesuit, like every White man, could see how completely hopeless the Indian military situation was in nineteenth-century America. Tribes might coalesce briefly, ambush a few troops, and especially drive out the settlers. But in terms of manpower, resources, discipline, and determination the White world was incalculably stronger. There was no question of self-defense in the military way. Any effort in this direction was suicide. The legal situation was similar. There was no Indian "country," no right to armed defense more than other Americans had. If anything at all was to be made of the Oregon Indian, he had to be kept at all costs from war against the Whites.

This was reversed in intertribal war. The Jesuits made sure their Indians had a continuing supply of powder for defense against Plains enemies. The lay brothers of the first St. Mary's carried rifles to work, and a wooden cannon was mounted on the mission palisades. Tribesmen were taught to pray before battle, to refrain from scalping and from emotion-raising war dances, and not to take prisoners or be cruel. When possible, they were to avoid fighting on Sundays. The Flatheads even showed such improvement in battle after becoming Christians that the Blackfeet superstitiously asked for a Jesuit medicine man for their own tribe. The Jesuits worked for peace, then, but according to a complicated pattern.

The missionaries were forever handling small but explosive incidents between Red men and White, or making peace and reducing tensions between the tribes, or quelling outbursts and riots within a given tribe. Attention will have to be confined to the violence of real magnitude, centering especially upon three episodes: the treaty troubles of 1855, the war of 1858, and the war of 1877. Each episode emphasizes a different aspect of the Jesuits' work for peace—in preventing war, in terminating a major war, and in limiting the scope of a war beyond their control.

By the end of our period the possibility of a rising was becoming ever dimmer. Two significant actions in the years 1890–91 reflect the White supremacy. At that time twenty-eight military forts in the West were abandoned by the army. And at that time the superintendent of the census announced that a real frontier could hardly be said to exist any more. The Wild West had gone.

3. The White Man Makes a Treaty

WARS AND RUMORS OF WARS

EARLY in July 1855 twelve hundred mountain Indians converged on a rendezvous in western Montana. They came to hold council with Governor Isaac Ingalls Stevens of Washington Territory. Some were returning from hunting on the far Plains; others emerged from deep folds in their native mountains. As befitted the occasion, the warriors were in a festive mood, with all the usual drumming and chanting, visiting, pony racing, and endless talk. The rendezvous, according to a sketch by the soldier Gustavus Sohon, who was present, lay along the flats of a wide, swift river, in a pleasant mountain prairie at the mouth of a forty-mile-long canyon. It was a biannual battleground of Blackfeet against mountain Indians, a notorious passageway through the Rockies aptly called the Gate of Hell.

There, under a clear sky and ringed by mountains, the Flatheads, Kutenais, and Pend d'Oreilles fought a stubborn diplomatic battle for their ancestral lands. These stormy eight days at the river bank are known to history as the Flathead Council, and the agreement that was concluded is called the Hell Gate Treaty. This episode is a microcosm of the clash between Red man and White; there are no heroes and no villains, a pavement of good intentions but a singular absence of communication. Studying such a meeting closely, one realizes how unjust the White men were—yet, considering their horizons then, how inevitably and innocently unjust.[1]

In 1855 the American Northwest was almost a decade old. It had been a

1. No serious studies of this council or treaty have previously been attempted. A. J. Partoll published an incomplete version of the official minutes as "The Flathead Indian Treaty Council of 1855," *PNWQ*, 29 (1938), 283–314. My own edition of the pertinent sections of Father Hoecken's diary, "A Jesuit at the Hell Gate Treaty of 1855," is in *Mid-America*, 34 (1952), 87–114. J. C. Ewers supplies an informal narrative of the council from Partoll's text as background to his monograph on *Gustavus Sohon's Portraits of Flathead and Pend d'Oreille Indians 1854*, Smithsonian Misc. Colls., 110, No. 7 (Washington, D.C., 1948). Hazard Stevens has a short section in his *Life of Isaac Ingalls Stevens by His Son*, 2 (2 vols. New York, 1901), 81–91; it is largely a brief paraphrase of the official proceedings, though Hazard was himself present.

decade of agitation and painful adjustment. For two years after the boundary settlement of 1846, the region had limped along under an improvised farmers' government. Organization as a territory came only in 1848. Even this proved unwieldy for the coastal settlements because of difficulties in communication. In 1853 Congress therefore broke off the northern half from the sea to the Rockies, and called it Washington Territory. The new territory was mostly a vacant land. Its census counted less than four thousand Whites, located almost exclusively on the Coast.

Indian problems had bedeviled the decade. The 1846 treaty was followed promptly by the Cayuse War. This war could be seen coming a long way off, advancing like some ominous thunderhead. When the Great Emigration of 1843 disgorged almost a thousand Whites in the Oregon country, only the protection of the Hudson's Bay Company and the decisive intercession of its chief representative, Dr. McLoughlin, prevented open trouble. Diseases like the Black Measles rode with these caravans, spreading fatally among the Indians. Generally the Whites recovered, but the Indians died. Indian outrages flared along the line of march from the Blue Mountains to The Dalles. Thefts and "incidents" became common; blood was spilled. The fate of the Indians on the Coast was not to be meekly accepted by their free-riding brothers in the Interior. Fiercely, the spirit of unrest blew back and forth along the Trail. A year after America entered into her Oregon heritage, war erupted. It appeared to involve only those Indians around the Presbyterian mission, which had become a wintering spot for the Oregon immigrants. Actually, the Cayuse War was far more serious.

Late in 1847 the Indians treacherously massacred a dozen people at the mission, bearing off some fifty women and children into temporary captivity. The settlers on the Coast were stunned. They were too distant and feeble to mount effective retaliation. There were no troops, and ammunition was scarce. The treasury held $43 and owed a debt of $4,000. There was no communication with the outside world.

Militia bands were hastily recruited and haphazardly equipped. With a brave display of military titles and jargon, they marched off to engage in a series of desultory, ineffectual skirmishes. As the amateur army groped about in the lower Interior, a frustrated peace commission accomplished little. Long before the year was out, actual campaigning ended. In this period of open fighting, both sides had their dead to mourn. Of particular regret was the demise of the White commander Cornelius Gilliam—ex-preacher, ex-sheriff, ex-Missouri legislator, ex-Mormon fighter and Indian fighter, one of those fiery "Oliver Cromwells of the frontier states." In a careless moment he had discharged a rifle into his body.[2]

2. F. F. Victor, *The Early Indian Wars of Oregon Compiled from the Oregon Archives and Other Original Sources, with Muster Rolls* (Salem, 1894), p. 159. On the

So isolated was the whole Oregon country at this time that the outside world knew nothing of the confused fighting until the late spring of 1848. The news was discovered, ironically enough, only through a naval transport sent to Oregon to gather recruits for the war with Mexico. Oregon was soon given territorial status, and a rifle regiment as token garrison. Meanwhile, the Cayuse outbreak had triggered open attacks and outrages by Klamaths, Klickitats, Snoqualmies, Molalas, Calapooyas, Tilamooks, and the Rogue River tribes.

The Cayuses on their part (only a hundred warriors in all) had been unable to rally the Indian world to united action. Even among themselves they were divided, with thirty lodges remaining stubbornly against war. Dispirited and confused, the Cayuses lost interest. Soon the Whites were "masters of the Cayuse country without having to fight for it." [3] To resolve the matter, the tribe persuaded five braves, accused by the Americans in connection with the massacre, to act as scapegoats. The five were promptly tried and hanged in June 1850. All died Catholics; they asked for a priest, who baptized and instructed them and walked with them to the scaffold. [4]

The Interior was now practically closed to settlement, until some disposition could be made of all tribes by treaty. Father De Smet foresaw the sequel, as the Indians themselves surely could. In 1851 he wrote how the pressure of population occasioned "pretexts for dispossessing the Indian." Already "the drama of population reaches its last scene at the east and west bases of the Rocky Mountains." Soon the Indian "will live only in history." [5]

The Cayuse trouble touched the far-off mission network of the Jesuits. It represented in fact a serious crisis throughout the whole Interior. Every tribe here housed its faction favoring war against the Americans and its faction counseling peace. [6] Torn by fears, jealousies, and hopes, troubled and divided, the tribes let their opportunity for action drift away. It was at this time that the Flatheads, for the first and only time in their mission history, became rebellious and unmanageable. The Jesuits themselves had no direct connection with the Cayuse hostilities. In its overt manifestations the war seemed to be an affair rather among the Protestant and pagan Indians.

---

peace commission see D. O. Johansen, ed., *Robert Newell's Memoranda . . . Travle to the Kayuse War* (Portland, Oreg., 1959), second treatise.

3. The diocesan priest Father Brouillet quoted in W. L. Davis, S.J., "Mission St. Anne of the Cayuse Indians 1847–1848," unpublished doctoral dissertation (University of California, 1943), p. 212. The massacre itself is extensively treated in C. M. Drury, *Marcus Whitman Pioneer and Martyr* (Caldwell, Idaho, 1937), chap. 19.

4. *AFQ* (March 1851), p. 65, letter of priest "F.J.C."

5. CR, *3*, 1198, 1203, 1208–09.

6. J. A. Teit, "The Salishan Tribes of the Western Plateaus," ed. Franz Boas, BAE *Annual Report, 45* (1927–28), 367–68.

Any number of people worked for peace. The diocesan clergy and the Oblates, as well as the Hudson's Bay traders, displayed coolness in their efforts to control the war. Bishop Augustine Blanchet worked hard among the Cayuses, even hammering out a peace agreement which proved abortive. The Oblates induced the Yakima Indians to declare their neutrality. The mountain man William Craig labored to keep the Nez Percés quiet, and was named agent here. Men like Father Brouillet and the Hudson's Bay factor Ogden, as well as Nez Percé friends of the Protestant mission, contributed to the effort.[7] Up in the north, where the Fort Colville trading post was mounting guards around the clock and where even the pacifist San Poils almost took the warpath, friendly Spokanes protected the Protestant missionaries. The Reverend Cushing Eells bravely clung to his post as long as he dared; before he left, he rode widely in the region around the fort to counsel peace.[8]

Both Protestant and Catholic missioners were ordered out of the Interior. The absence of a steady Protestant mission in the Interior from that time on may be partially responsible for the increasing hostility among the lower Indians. Even the controversial agent Dr. Elijah White, formerly a Methodist missionary, had done much in 1842 and 1843 "to prevent an outbreak on the part of the Cayuse and Nez Percé Indians."[9] And Dr. Whitman in discouragement, two years before his murder, had felt that his labors were justified at least by his having restrained the Indians from seeking revenge to their own ultimate hurt.[10]

The Catholic clergy protested against their own removal, being "convinced that the Catholic Missionaries risk no danger among the Indians."[11] Several of them soon returned. In the summer of 1848 the Oblate mission was

7. Davis, "Mission St. Anne," pp. 203–06. Cf. NYPL, Fort Nisqually journals in photostat, four Yakimas transmitting information from Blanchet later, 23 February 1848. See also *AFQ* (March 1851), p. 41, Brouillet letter; and, in general, H. H. Bancroft, *History of Oregon, 1834–1888, 1,* in *Works, 29–30* (2 vols. San Francisco, 1886–88), esp. 691, 709.

8. Myron Eells, *History of Indian Missions on the Pacific Coast; Oregon, Washington and Idaho* (Philadelphia, 1882), p. 234. C. M. Drury, *Elkanah and Mary Walker, Pioneers among the Spokanes* (Caldwell, Idaho, 1940), pp. 214–15; cf. p. 209. J. L. Lewes Letters (YU), Chief Factor Lewes to Rev. Mr. Walker, 12 February (San Poils). Cf. Mary Walker's diary on this period, in Narcissa Whitman et al., *First White Women over the Rockies, Diaries, Letters, and Biographical Sketches,* ed. C. M. Drury, 2 (2 vols. Glendale, Cal., 1963), 328–43.

9. A. W. Hoopes, *Indian Affairs and Their Administration with Special Reference to the Far West, 1849–1860* (Philadelphia, 1932), p. 70 and refs. For his further services to peace see Victor, *Early Wars,* chap. 3; Francis Haines, *The Nez Percés, Tribesmen of the Columbia Plateau* (Norman, Okla., 1955), chap. 10; cf. p. 100.

10. ABFM, 18, 3, 1, 9, No. 186, Whitman to Greene, 15 May 1846.

11. NA, IA, Oreg. Sup., LR, F. N. Blanchet to Gov. Lane, 9 March 1849.

re-established. The Jesuits were allowed to remain, since their distant tribes seemed uninvolved. These circumstances looked sinister to many a coastal nativist. Equally sinister had been the ability of all priests to wander among the non-Catholic or Catholic tribesmen at will, holding councils and converse. The Presbyterian minister Henry Spalding devoted considerable energy throughout the remainder of his life to propagating his conviction that Catholic priests in league with the Hudson's Bay men had engineered the war. And many volunteer soldiers were as angry at the priest as at the Indians. Some had even marched to the wars with the promise of a bullet for the bishop and his clergy. At the height of this excitement the coastal churches were in danger of being burned. Indian reports also worked upon the general credulity. The chief of the Dalles Indians told the Whites, for example, how the priests had made magic shields for the Cayuses, who thought themselves invulnerable.

The absurd conviction that priests had started the war was to survive for decades among a fair number of otherwise sensible people on the Coast. As late as 1869 a ministerial body publicly affirmed Catholic guilt "from personal knowledge and overwhelming testimony now before us." The priests had provoked "the reluctant Cayuse to butcher the Protestants, arranging the tomahawks and striking the first blow with one of their own hands." [12] But perhaps most settlers were indifferent to these religious passions. The archbishop of Oregon City in his statistical report of 1854 confessed himself unable to assign any particular religion to the majority of settlers on this frontier, "since most of them are Christians only in name." [13]

The Jesuits could not hope to escape the attention of the nativists. Even a sensible man like the Reverend Mr. Atkinson on the Coast was temporarily carried away by the rumors, confiding to his diary in June 1848 that "the Jesuit is hand in glove" with the priests involved in the Cayuse War.[14] In August 1848 the *Oregon American* revealed to the public the "clock work of Jesuitical machinery" by which the pope had simultaneously directed "his forces from the four winds to bear on a point even on the opposite side of the globe"; the massacre had then been plotted "to rid the Interior of Americans that the Jesuits might monopolize it to their own enterprises."

Suspicion of the Jesuits acquired powerful impetus from an incident in mid-

12. ABFM, 18, 4, 1, 2, No. 129, 1869 manifesto. Cf. Bancroft, *Oregon*, 1, 697, 613. On the prevalence of such beliefs "almost uncontradicted" to the end of the century, see Victor, *Early Wars*, pp. 126, 221; as an example see Eells' *History* of 1882, p. 231. Cf. Beeson, *Plea*, p. 31 (1855).

13. FL, *1856*, Répartition (in French) 12 July 1855. Of the 21,500 Whites in this southern diocese, only 1,500 were Catholic (1854 Répartition, 16 January 1854).

14. E. Ruth Rockwood, ed., "Diary of Rev. George H. Atkinson D.D., 1847–1858," *OHQ, 40* (1939), 182 (June 1848).

1848. As a war measure, the legislature had banned distribution of ammunition to the Interior. Father Joset traveled down the Coast to plead for an exception in favor of the mountain Indians. The latter could not live without their hunting equipment, nor could they drive off the ever-present Blackfeet. The Jesuit argument was favorably received. The Hudson's Bay Company was also protesting this blanket prohibition as dangerous, and Americans in the Vancouver area added their voices. Since Joset anticipated favorable legislation shortly, and since the law forbade distribution rather than the preliminary transportation, he ordered the two years' supply forwarded up the Columbia.

At this moment circumstances conspired to focus anti-Catholic feeling upon the issue. The principal chief of the Des Chutes tribe told Lieutenant Rodgers that the Jesuits meant to supply the Cayuses with ammunition for war. Rodgers, already under the influence of nativist propaganda, intercepted in July this shipment of 1,000 pounds of powder, 1,500 pounds of balls, 300 pounds of buckshot, and 36 guns. At that time the Oregon militia had been able to acquire only 500 pounds of powder. Rodgers firmly believed the Jesuits meant the material for the Cayuses. Quartermaster Johnson "swore" that it had to be so. Shades of the Gunpowder Plot and St. Bartholomew's Day were evoked. Anti-Jesuit angers flared. In December a bill was introduced into the Oregon legislature to expel the Catholic clergy.[15]

Before the end of 1848 the California gold rush distracted Oregon minds from their Jesuit preoccupations. But the mission Indians still required ammunition, and the superior-general wrote to Governor Lane in March 1849 that the tribes "cannot sufficiently provide for themselves by their agriculture" and were without the salmon fisheries of the other tribes. "To refuse them powder is to starve them," for "powder is to them what money is to us." They would have to leave the civilizing influence of the missions if ammunition could not be supplied. The enemy Blackfeet were well equipped from transmontane traders and "incessantly" prowled the mission lands.[16] Not long after this appeal the Jesuit Indians got their ammunition. The bigotry that had flared seems to have rebounded on the nativists and may have been an element in their defeat in the 1855 elections.

Ironically, the really serious crisis for the Jesuits in this decade was of domestic origin. The superior-general from 1850 was Michael Accolti—described by Father General Beckx as "not a good superior, but otherwise a good man." Accolti reserved his enthusiasm for newly acquired California,

15. *Oregon American*, esp. 23 May (Rodger's letter) and 1 March 1849. SA, Bishop A. Blanchet on seizure to Msgr. I. Bourget, 31 January 1849. *JMUS*, 2, 380; cf. pp. 375–87. Bancroft, *Oregon*, *1*, 681, 743. Victor, *Early Wars*, pp. 153, 155 n., 219–22.

16. NA, IA, Oreg. Sup., LR, Accolti to Gov. Lane, 7 March 1849.

diverting resources and manpower to the more promising opportunities opening there. The many tribes in the Interior were now served from only three stations, each with two priests and two brothers. Worse than the contraction of the mission effort was the closing of the pride of the Jesuit network, St. Mary's among the Flatheads.

The alienation of the Flatheads puzzled the resident Jesuits. The change of heart occurred quite suddenly, quite completely, during the fall hunt of 1846 on the Great Plains. A spiritual recovery for about eight months in 1848–49 was followed by a second lapse in 1850. Each Jesuit sought reasons to explain the mystery. After first suggesting that De Smet had promised the tribe too much, Ravalli soon shifted the blame to White and Indian intruders who had sowed discord. Mengarini stressed the antimissionary activities of a Flathead who harbored personal grievances against the priests. Both men felt that the terrible loss of life in tribal war, especially among the best Christians, had unsettled the Indians. Perhaps, as Congiato thought, in the final analysis their temporary abandonment was an unnecessarily severe expedient. Nevertheless, the disturbed Flatheads had left the missionaries exposed to Blackfoot attacks and had to be disciplined.

The Flathead troubles have been depicted as a rejection of White innovations by the underlying Indian culture, a return to native economy, social order, and even religion.[17] A case may be made out in support of this view, but it is at best a partial explanation. It seems clear that the troubles were only a part of the general revulsion agitating the Indian world from the time the Americans formerly supplanted the British. The Flathead unrest is thus related directly to the Cayuse War. Had a strong Blackfoot attack on the Jesuits not complicated the situation, time and patience would probably have allowed the priests to ride out the storm here as at the other missions.

THE GOVERNOR TAKES COMMAND

Such was the general situation by 1853, when the presidential appointee Isaac Ingalls Stevens came west to take office as first territorial governor of Washington. By far the larger part of his population was Indian. Stevens was to assess their number at seven to eight thousand on the Coast and six to seven thousand in the Interior. This was of particular importance because he was also ex officio federal superintendent of Indian Affairs in his territory. Along with these duties he sought and won command of explorations investigating a northern route for the transcontinental railroad, a project connected with American concern for Pacific ports and an easier China trade. The Governor was further interested in the possibility of a great overland

17. See below, p. 83, text to nn. 51, 52.

wagon road. As governor he was responsible to the secretary of State, as superintendent he answered to the secretary of the Interior, and as an explorer he obeyed the secretary of War. Any one of these jobs would have taxed all the energies of an able man.

In one way these functions mutually supported each other. The railroad surveys kept Stevens roaming the Interior, mapping, recording, and observing, during many months of 1853 and 1855. As superintendent, his Indian responsibilities made him sensitive to the human problems involved when the tribes felt threatened by the railroad line and by the prospect of heavy White immigration. And his office of governor assured him a hearty welcome from the tribes. The Indians neither understood nor respected an abstract American government. A live governor, with gifts and promises, was more acceptable.[18]

But the triple office brought with it also an implicit conflict of interests. Stevens was expected to advance the interests of the Whites while guarding the welfare and rights of the Red man. "More often than not these two aims were mutually irreconcilable." Above all, the hope of satisfying the land-hungry immigrants and the desperately land-loving Indians was "an impossible task." [19] In the event, settlement would receive priority. Still, the Governor did organize a skeletal Indian service as he surveyed west for a railroad; and he garnered all the information he could about the tribes. In his territory he created three agencies and two subagencies. The Interior itself he divided between agencies centering in the Flathead and Yakima regions, with a subagency in the Spokane country.

Hopeless though his task was, no man was better suited for the attempt than young Major Stevens. He had the imposing head and dramatically handsome countenance of a story-book leader, with an underlying aristocratic look, something finely drawn, untroubled yet alert. Stevens had graduated from West Point at the head of his class in 1839 and had served with the elite corps of engineers on the New England coast. His war record as a staff officer in Mexico was admirable. He had been severely wounded in battle and had written a book entitled *Campaigns of the Rio Grande and of Mexico*. As executive assistant to the federal coast survey from 1849, he demonstrated some agile political footwork and energetic administrative ability.

Stevens' intellect was keen and cultivated, his manners practiced and somewhat flamboyant in the nineteeth-century style. But not too far beneath

18. NA, IA, Special Cases, "Report on the Condition of the Indian Reservations in the Territories of Oregon and Washington," November 1857.

19. W. N. Neil, "The Territorial Governor as Indian Superintendent in the Trans-Mississippi West," *MVHR*, *43* (1956–57), 236 (first quot.). C. F. Coan, "The Adoption of the Reservation Policy in the Pacific Northwest, 1853–1855," *OHQ*, *23* (1922), 11.

his urbanity was an iron will impatient of opposition. His contemporary, Judge Strong, remembered him as possessing "a great deal of self-confidence and self-will." A Hudson's Bay administrator, professionally inimical, sent to London the caustic appraisal: "Stevens is a humbug." One colleague of his explorations found him "a smart, active, ubiquitous little man, very come-at-able." He was also "a very ambitious man," who "knows very well that his political fortunes are wrapt up" with the success of the railroad venture. He would eventually stir "the greatest amount of disaffection" among the members of his exploring company, "amounting almost to open mutiny," with violence and arrests.[20]

Not a hint of such problems intruded into Stevens' voluminous, hearty reports. His explorations and his treaties were prepared with meticulous attention to detail. He was gifted with the soldier's bold view, the optimistic swiftness of decision and the stubborn perseverance in attack. These are not the best qualities in a negotiator; praise and abuse swirled about his head. Both have continued in our own day.

Stevens' surveying trip, as he made his way west toward his new governorship in 1853, was no casual undertaking. Of the several railroad explorations then jointly going forward, his was the most elaborately equipped.[21] There were four branches in his party. He himself led the main effort, westward through the Rockies. Captain McClellan, the future commander of the Union armies in the Civil War, worked inland from the ocean over the Cascades to join Stevens in the Spokane country. Lieutenant Saxton led a reconnaissance up from Walla Walla to the Bitterroot Valley in the Flathead country, where he established a supply depot. A final party operated from the mouth of the Missouri to the mouth of the Yellowstone, uniting there with Stevens. Some 250 men connected with this enterprise ranged over the Indian Interior including soldiers, artists, topographers, engineers, and scientists. No detail was overlooked—meteorological, astronomical, magnetic, commercial, ethnological. The multivolume compilation of information resulting from all this remains an impressive monument even today.

Small wonder, then, that the tribes were upset. As the surveying branches converged on the Interior, panicky rumors flew. In the east the Assiniboines had already protested to Stevens against his "great road," which "will drive away the buffalo." In the west Lieutenant Saxton's commissary detachment

---

20. Strong, *OHQ*, *62*, *85*. HB, D5, *43*, Simpson Corresp. in, from Dugald Mactavish, 21 January 1857. Suckley Papers (YU), Nos. 4 and 6, 20 June, 9 December 1853.

21. G. L. Albright, *Official Explorations for Pacific Railroads* [*1853–1855*], Univ. of Cal. Pubs. in History, 11 (Berkeley, 1921), p. 44. For the project's wider context, see W. H. Goetzman, *Army Exploration in the American West, 1803–1863* (New Haven, 1959), esp. chaps. 7, 8.

of eighteen soldiers from the Fourth Infantry raised a fever of suspicion. They had to reassure the Walla Wallas that they had no "hostile intentions." Later they were stopped by "a delegation of Cayuse braves" who had heard the soldiers "were coming to make war upon them." Later still a large delegation of fifty excited Nez Percé and Palouse warriors "in full costume" confronted them, and had to be pacified in a "grand 'war talk.'"

Alarm continued to attend the party's progress. Like the Palouses, the Spokanes had understood from fur traders that Lieutenant Saxton was marching against the Indians. Even after the initial fears had been allayed, the tribes were not happy. The Coeur d'Alenes proved to be unhelpful to the survey party of Lieutenant Mullan. Some told him his route was extremely difficult, others that it was quite easy, others again "that it was and had been their hunting ground for years, which they did not want disturbed." They "threw no direct impediment" in his way, yet "with one accord seemed unwilling to point out the route or show any friendly signs to have their country explored, or willing disposition to have their country traveled over by the Whites." [22]

The Jesuits were to be of great help to the expedition. Even before starting, Stevens derived "much information" from De Smet's *Oregon Missions.* He wrote the priest to ask further information on the geography, the trading posts, and the nature and disposition of the tribes. He also sent Lieutenant Saxton to him at St. Louis for suggestions on "transportation etc.," and followed with a visit of his own. Unable to persuade De Smet to accompany him, on the eve of departure Stevens sent a last desperate telegram. "Is it an absolute impossibility for you to go with my expedition?" De Smet would "render great service" both to the tribes and to America. The Governor wanted a reply "immediately," for which he would pay. Though De Smet did not go, Stevens later felt himself "fortunate" in at least having the Jesuit's book to consult on his explorations. He seems to have borrowed a copy again later when preparing his report for publication. Meanwhile, Father Accolti had drawn up a letter of introduction in French and in English for McClellan's branch, commending it to the Jesuit missionaries in the Interior. Later, in his instructions to Lieutenant Mullan about the Flathead country, Stevens advised him to "dwell on the good Father" De Smet when talking to the Indians. He was to assure them that the Jesuit's words "have reached the Great Father at Washington" and "made all good men their friend." [23]

22. *RR*, *12*, i, 74; *1*, ii, 29, 253–56, 528.
23. CR, *4*, 1568–69 (April 1853). *RR*, *12*, i, 86; cf. pp. 128, 171, 201. Stevens Papers (WU), No. 7, to C. Billinghurst, 12 February 1858. McClellan Papers (LC), *5;* cf. P. H. Overmeyer, "George B. McClellan and the Pacific Northwest," *PNWQ*, *32* (1941), 19 (9 July 1853). *RR*, *1*, ii, 35.

Dr. George Suckley, the Governor's surgeon and naturalist on this trip, recorded that "the missions (all Roman Catholic) were visited and material sufficient to fill a volume obtained." The elaborate written reports bear him out. Gibbs, an amateur student who was to prepare the Indian memoir, "interested the priests at the Missions in his work and from them he has obtained much valuable assistance." Suckley received "much valuable information" about the Coeur d'Alene country from Father Joset, and "much important information as to the country and its inhabitants" from the priests in general. Mullan "interrogated the missionaries as to their knowledge of the character of that region and the feasibility" of transport routes, and pooled his observations "together with the information I obtained from the Rev. Fathers Hoecken and Joset, and others." Information on minerals was drawn from several sources but "especially from the testimony of the Jesuit fathers."

Stevens had the missioners working on a set of grammars and vocabularies for the languages of the tribes under their control; he intended to publish these, "credited of course to yourselves." The mission network acted as a message center, conveyed Indians news, and furnished hospitality and supplies. It was not without reason that the Jesuit general wrote, after Stevens' passage, that in Oregon "the works of our missions are esteemed by the government officials." In the lower country the Oblates too were "of great benefit." They "furnished all the information in their power respecting the country, secured good guides to the parties, and acted as interpreters." Father Pandosy made an extended loan of his manuscripts on the Yakima language to Gibbs. At one time, the report acknowledges, the Oblates "probably prevented trouble" with the Indians for McClellan.[24]

In Indian matters Stevens was to stand in particular need of Jesuit information and advice. He had begun his trip determined "to give great attention to the Indian tribes, as their friendship was important to be secured"; they might easily endanger both the railroad project "and the safety of my party." [25] This concern had deeper implications. The national commissioner of Indian Affairs had given him explicit instructions. Washington Territory, the commissioner confessed, "comprises within its limits a large extent of country in which but little progress has been made towards the adoption of suitable measures for placing the Department in the possession of full and satisfactory

24. Suckley Papers (YU), No. 6. *RR*, *12*, i, 146; cf. *1*, ii, 413, 415 (Gibbs), 299, with *12*, i, 162 (Suckley); *1*, ii, 258, 300 (Mullan); *12*, i, 254 (minerals), 134, 146, 161, 201; and *1*, ii, 70, 368, 528 (misc.). FP, I, 5, 24 April 1854 (in French). *RR*, *1*, ii, 409–11, 518, 630; *12*, i, 139, 152; cf. Overmeyer, *PNWQ*, *32*, 19–20. NA, IA, LS, Wash. Sup., 1853–56, Stevens to Hoecken, 10 November 1855 (grammars). W. N. Bischoff, S.J., "The Yakima Indian War: 1855–1856," unpublished doctoral dissertation (Loyola University of Chicago, 1950), p. 189 (Pandosy MS).

25. *RR*, *12*, i, 31.

information in regard to the condition of Indian affairs." Translated, this meant that the commissioner knew almost nothing about the Interior tribes, and had reason to worry about them. He therefore required the names and size of each tribe and of each internal division of the tribe. He wanted Stevens to report on the current mood of the Indians, and to urge them not to cross the international line. The Hudson's Bay influence had to be countered, but with the "utmost prudence and discretion" lest the Indians be disturbed. Stevens was encouraged to negotiate treaties of peace and friendship within his territory.[26]

What was the Governor's attitude toward the Jesuits? He was "much struck with the comparative civilized condition" of the Jesuit tribes and the "indefatigable labors" of the missionaries. He felt their work to be an illustration of De Smet's enthusiastic books about the Indian missions. Unfortunately, Stevens recommended encouragement of the missions as a way of preparing the area for White settlement. In a small manuscript essay on Indian policy at this time, he notes that "the success of the Missions among the Pend d'Oreille and Coeur d'Alene Indians" demonstrates what can be done toward civilizing the Indian.[27] On this trip, too, he seems to have been drawn especially to Father Ravalli, a jovial, outgoing man as energetic as the Governor himself. Stevens was to make regular use of the Jesuit in the coming treaties and war. Yet it seems to have been on this trip that Stevens also acquired that odd and contradictory prejudice against Jesuit influence over the Indians which flared in his subsequent dealings with the Fathers.

His views may partly be explained by his intense opposition to any influence on the Indians independent of his own, such as that of the Hudson's Bay Company. He was explicit in his determination to have the Indians "rely for counsel" as well as protection "on us alone." [28] Perhaps the Governor's Jesuit prejudices were due in great part to conflict of purpose, in that he was working to open the area to White settlement by railroad and road as soon as possible. He realized that the missioners feared this. Being unacquainted with their tradition and philosophy of mission work, and perhaps also being the man he was, he interpreted this opposition as a kind of spiritual imperialism, a lust for sole domination and power over the Indians. He also suspected that missionaries would use underhanded means to discourage his projects. Thus he cautioned one of his explorers to mistrust information from the

26. NA, IA, Wash. Sup., LR, Manypenny to Stevens, 9 May 1853.
27. Ibid., LR (from Wash. Sup.), Stevens to Manypenny, 6 and 29 December 1853. Field Records (Wash.), LS, 1853–56, "Indian Policy."
28. Overmeyer, *PNWQ, 32,* 14. Cf. instructions, commissioner to Stevens in NA, Wash. Sup., LR, 9 May 1853.

Oblate missions, since "it is believed here" that they "are in the habit of representing the country and the climate in the worst possible light, in order to discourage settlements." [29]

His geologist, George Gibbs, put the matter quite candidly into the Stevens report of 1853. Gibbs was a Harvard-trained lawyer with a respectable legal and scholarly career behind him and a distinguished one ahead, including later fame as a founder of the Smithsonian Institution's greatness in Indian research. In 1853 he wrote that "it is probably an object with the missionaries to discourage secular residents, who might divide their own influence over the natives." He returns to this charge later in the same treatise. Gibbs also believed that the Catholic missions, though making the Indian prayerful, had essentially failed in accomplishing "any great and lasting improvement." In context, he equates ethical practice with Christianity, and judges the Indian according to the White man's indices of character. He concludes that "the objects of these gentlemen are inconsistent with the settlement of the country." He thinks that the Jesuits have probably discouraged settlement "in the knowledge that their influence must infallibly be shaken" by it.

Still, Stevens could say to the Indians: "I am glad to see you and find that you are under such good direction . . . listen to the good father and to the good brothers who labor for your good." [30] These sentiments were undoubtedly genuine, if politic. But they expressed less than his whole attitude as it was revealed in the coming treaty tour.

Installed as governor on the Coast, Stevens faced a formidable Indian problem. For one thing, as he reminded the national authorities, his territory alone "embraces eleven degrees of longitude by six in latitude," with distant tribes falling under the direct care of an already busy executive. The federal Donation Act was encouraging haphazard settlement in coastal areas admittedly still belonging to the Indians. [31] Federal authorities upon assuming control of Indian affairs four years previously, had broached the grand "removal" of all Indians from the Coast to the Interior. This prospect had alarmed both coastal and inland Indians. A compromise was worked out, and nineteen treaties were signed involving a loss of six million acres to the tribes. The project collapsed when Congress refused to ratify it. Another policy, designed to extinguish Indian title by treaty while allowing the tribesmen to wander freely like gypsies, also proved impracticable. These fiascos had hardly increased the respect of the Indians for the government. Meanwhile, Whites were encroach-

29. *RR, 1*, ii, 617.
30. Ibid., pp. 422, 410; *12, i*, 134.
31. *RR, 1*, ii, 425, 422.

ing on lands guaranteed by treaty, others were cruelly pauperizing the Indians, and some were deliberately provoking them to violence. Little provocation was needed.

Joel Palmer, who became Indian superintendent for Oregon Territory at about the same time Stevens took office, found that "a general feeling of anxiety and mistrust pervades the tribes and bands from the sea-board to the Rocky Mountains." A "want of confidence" in the government "extends through the entire country." [32] Violence was increasing. Indians were openly resisting settlement on the southern coast of Oregon, in the Klamath Lake area, and in the upper Rogue River Valley. Fire-fights broke out in 1851 and in the winter of 1853. Rogue River Indians abused miners in 1850, attacked American regulars in 1851, remained troublesome in 1852, and struck the Valley settlements hard in 1853. A serious campaign subdued them, but the troubles recurred in 1854. Indeed the latter year saw more widespread violence than any previous year.

The Interior tribes were especially restless. By 1854 the Indians at the threshold had grown ugly. Five men were killed at The Dalles, and Major Rains feared a combined uprising from the Cascades to The Dalles. Throughout the year, Whites continued to take Indian lands and sell liquor. The Indians robbed and harassed immigrants on the Oregon Trail. Just east of Fort Boise, the savage Snakes massacred all but two of the Ward wagon train, brutally torturing the women and roasting their babies before their eyes. Even the indomitable Hudson's Bay Company traders reported to London that their activities in the Interior were curtailed "by the disturbed state of affairs." As early as 1853 a Jesuit lay brother in the Interior warned the government explorers of "plots among all the Indians of Oregon and Washington Territories." In April of that year the Oblate priest Pandosy wrote a letter on the danger of a great combination of all the Interior tribes. The diocesan missioner at The Dalles, Father Mesplié, communicated this to Captain Alvord, who translated and forwarded it. The Oblates felt at this time in fact that they were accomplishing among the Yakimas "little except as peacemakers." [33]

The very arrival of troops in the Oregon country seems to have upset the tribes. On the other hand, there were not enough soldiers really to impress or subdue them. The result amounted to a threat incapable of implementation. The coming of troops had been delayed until 1846 for lack of a treaty with

32. NA, IA, LR, Oreg. Sup., Palmer to Com. Manypenny, 8 October 1853. Coan, *OHQ*, 23, 3, 29.

33. HB, A11, 71, London Correspondence outward, D. Mactavish to A. Barclay, 4 November 1854. *RR*, 1, ii, 563 (Jesuit). Bradley-Kelly, *Boise Diocese*, p. 99 (diocesan miss.); H. Stevens, *Stevens*, 2, 25–26. *RR*, 1, ii, 409.

England, and then until about 1850 by the Mexican War and the slavery controversy. After that a handful of men was available, to be increased in time of war from departmental headquarters in California. Among the little forts thrown up were several lining the road approaching the Interior: Fort Vancouver, Fort Cascades and, at the very threshold, Fort Dalles. The Interior Indians were much concerned over this creeping advance of the military.

Both army and Indian Affairs officials filed reports with national authorities concerning the many incidents between Red men and White. In almost every case they placed the blame squarely on the Whites. Palmer, for example, attributed the general bad feeling of the Indians more "to the conduct of evil-minded whites toward them than to any desire on their part to annoy or injure the whites." [34] The settlers, of course, felt otherwise, with some good reason. Angry tension from now on strained the relations between the settlers and the officials of both army and Indian Affairs. In this tension Governor Stevens vigorously championed the side of the settlers.

EXILE TO THE RESERVATION

Stevens arrived in the West just as the reservation theory was being adumbrated. Some twenty treaties had already aborted, by the mischances of politics. There was no longer an unwanted area sufficiently ample to hold all the tribes. Let them be confined to reasonable preserves, then, protected, and educated to become citizen-farmers. Compensate their loss of land by annuities in goods. Under this policy in the space of less than three years, beginning in 1853, over fifty treaties were to be signed involving nearly a hundred tribes in western America. Thus in one sweep the Whites confiscated 174 million acres. Never in our history, reported the Indian commissioner complacently, had so many treaties been concluded or so much land acquired.[35]

Stevens saw eye to eye with Palmer on the manner of implementing this general policy of reservations in the Northwest. He followed Palmer's ideas in detail in his own territory, and cooperated with him for Indians residing on territorial borders. His problem was more difficult than Palmer's, in that the Washington Indians were more powerful and the Whites fewer. At his capital town of Olympia, "a small collection of houses, stumps, and mud," [36] Stevens vigorously outlined a magisterial Indian plan. Washington Territory suddenly found itself possessed of an organized Indian service, a policy, a congressional appropriation, and a determined leader prepared to fore-

---

34. NA, IA, LR (from Oreg. Sup.), 8 October 1853. Coan, *OHQ*, *23*, 2, 29.
35. *RCIA* (1856), pp. 20–21, 264–67.
36. Suckley Papers (YU), No. 8 (19 December 1853).

stall wars by an inclusive series of treaties. Agent Bolon was appointed to the Interior and supplied with vigorous, detailed directions.[37]

The Governor's instructions seem somehow unreal. Did Stevens actually believe the human situation would yield so readily to a military blueprint? Was he deceived by his own confidence, or was he attempting to impress higher politicians with his leadership? Did circumstances force his hand? Or can he be pitied as a product of the national Indian policy, fettered by his instructions from the national commissioner? At any rate he had been on the Coast less than five months when he left for Washington, D.C. There he spent eight months, the larger part of 1854, winning support for his Indian and railroad policies. On his return he and Palmer negotiated fifteen treaties in slightly more than one year, from the end of 1854 to the beginning of 1856. When ratified, these would clear the Northwest of Indian ownership, except for the few areas as yet untreated, like those of the Spokanes, the Coeur d'Alenes, and the Snakes.

Each treaty ceded the land to the Whites, set aside a reservation, provided annuities in goods, and promised buildings and White instructors. Each involved submission to federal jurisdiction rather than to tribal. Enough land was allowed so that every head of a family might eventually have a homestead. Stevens hoped that his agents could handle each tribe through one chief "strengthened" by special attentions. On the Coast he had pushed through seven such treaties by mid-1855. In June of that year three more would be signed at the lower Interior in the great Walla Walla Council.

The Governor's project in its broader outlines was neither unjust nor unwise. Perhaps it was as good as any of the practical alternatives facing the Whites. The Jesuits themselves could foresee the future direction of settlement, with its debauching effect on their charges, and they were therefore in principle not averse to a reservation policy. Hoecken and De Smet were each to propose one of his own. The danger or injustice lay rather in the amounts and quality of land taken, the guarantees for the remainder, honest payment of the promised compensation, tact in negotiation, and respect for the Indian's attachment to his own country. Whatever its substance, the treaty project was delicate and dangerous, demanding discretion rather than a whirlwind treaty tour. It also demanded proper timing. Even the colleague of the Governor, the Oregon superintendent Palmer, considered the Interior phase of the project premature and ill-advised.

Had everything gone according to plan, Stevens would have dealt with all the tribes of the Interior in one grand circuit. After finishing with the tribes of the southwest Interior at Walla Walla, he meant to journey diagonally into the extreme northeast for a treaty with the Flatheads and their neigh-

37. NA, IA, Field Records, Wash. Sup., Stevens to Bolon, 23 March 1854.

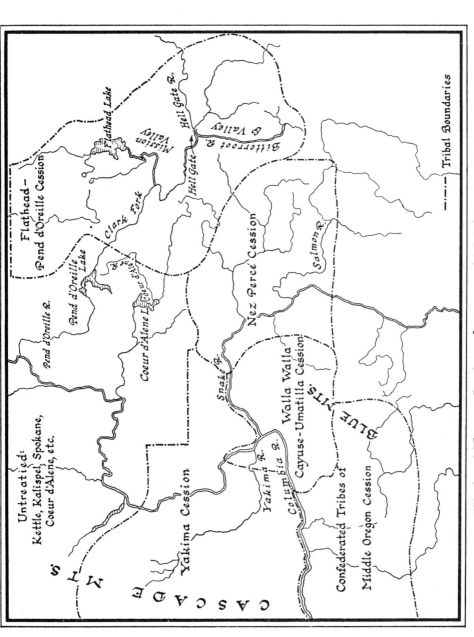

6. Flathead Treaty Cession of 1855, and Neighboring Cessions.

bors, then detour out onto the Plains to make peace between the Blackfoot raiders and the mountain Indians. On his return across the top of the Interior he planned to negotiate first with the Kalispels and then with the Coeur d'Alenes, "at their respective missions." Next there would be a treaty council on the Spokane River for the Kettles, Okanogans, and Spokanes. And finally he could dispose of the "remaining small tribes."

His timetable was kept flexible. Actually he was to be out in the Interior for over seven months before war interrupted the project at about its half-way mark. The way ahead was busily prepared by couriers, supply managers, liaison officers to the tribes, and the like. Moreover, treaties were not the only business on this tour. It was at the same time a final exploration for his railroad survey, "simply a continuation" of the 1853 trip.[38] In his deliberate, careful way Stevens assessed the importance of the Jesuits and included them in his treaty plans. On coming into the territory he noted (with exaggeration) that "nearly all the Indians east of the Cascades are sincere Christians, mostly Catholics, but the Spokanes and a part of the Nez Percés are Protestants." It was also remarked how "the only missions now" in the Interior "are those of the Jesuits and Oblat[e]s." [39]

When he entered the Interior for the treaties of 1855, there were two Oblate and three Jesuit missions, each of the five served by two priests. Doty, the Governor's advance agent for the treaty talks, kept in touch with the missionaries during the months of preparation, sending expresses to Colville and the Bitterroot. In the lower Interior Father Pandosy was Doty's consistent helper, though the Oblates remained determinedly neutral on the question of the Indians' selling their lands.

The Walla Walla Council progressed slowly in sweltering heat from May 24 to June 11. The weather was showery and the atmosphere electric with tension. Some five thousand Nez Percés, Yakimas, Cayuses, Walla Wallas, Umatillas, and other tribesmen camped in the valley. Their spokesmen resisted Stevens stubbornly. Most of the Palouses would not even come. Many Indians present refused to accept tobacco. Observers from other tribes were present, including a Flathead delegation, Spokanes, Kettles, and Coeur d'Alenes.[40] The northern Indians were concerned not only because their

38. Ibid., LR (from Wash. Sup.), 30 August 1855; this is the final, adjusted timetable. *RR*, *12*, i, 189.

39. *RR*, *1*, ii, 147, 422 (Gibbs).

40. Doty, Journal (NA, IA, Negots. Rat. Treaties), p. 1, expects these, with Pend d'Oreilles for Flatheads. The official transcript for the Flathead Council (cited below, p. 89; p. 285 in Partoll edn.) refers back to Flathead participation. The Journal refers back to Coeur d'Alenes present (p. 32) and to a Kettle chief (pp. 13–14). Standard treatments of the council include the eyewitness memoirs by Kip (see below, Bib.) and

turn was next but also because Stevens planned to move the Okanogans and Kettles onto his southwest reserve. None of the tribesmen was impressed by the Governor's small escort of forty-seven dragoons. During the council, conspiracies were secretly afoot, looking to a general war. A plot to assassinate the commissioners seems to have been foiled by some pro-American Nez Percés.

Then abruptly all opposition appeared to collapse. In return for three reservations the chiefs signed away a vast expanse of over 45,000 square miles. In fact, the Indians were using the treaties in the same way they believed the Whites used them—as an instrument of deception. "The chiefs agreed to a mock treaty," comments Father Joset, "in order to gain time and prepare for war." They meant to store up supplies, and begin hostilities in the winter. As the Yakima Chief Owhi admitted a few months afterward, "the war commenced from that moment." [41]

At the later council on the Spokane River a friend of the Americans, the Spokane chief Big Star, would boldly reproach Stevens: "the Indians say you are the cause of the war." Even the Governor's staunch friend Garry of the Spokanes admitted afterward that his loyalty wavered during the Walla Walla Council. He was to chide Stevens for having taken too much land for what he gave, and for having struck the Indian "to the heart." [42] The Oblate priests Pandosy of the Yakimas and Chirouse of the Cayuses, present "by invitation," signed the treaties as observers. They soon became troubled at the sequel. Pandosy reported to the diocesan priest Mesplié at The Dalles that, from the time the Walla Walla Council had ended, war against the Whites was the main subject of discussion. [43] Among the coastal Whites a topic of conversation was the announcement by Stevens and Palmer in newspapers, twelve days after the council, describing their acquisition of lands and (prematurely) inviting settlement there.

Jesuit participation in the council had been slight. Ravalli had arrived on May 7, bringing news of the Indians in the Jesuit mission region. At the request of the Stevens party, he wrote to the Coeur d'Alene mission to secure an Indian guide for their coming trip to the upper country. The priest had ap-

---

H. Stevens (*Stevens, 2, 29*), and the Indian side by A. J. Splawn, *Ka-Mi-Akin, the Last Hero of the Yakimas* (Portland, Oreg., 1917 [Yakima, 1958]), chap. 4.

41. Joset Narrative (OJ). W. N. Bischoff, S.J., "Documents: Yakima Campaign," *Mid-America, 31* (1949), 188. On this treaty as the cause of the war see also CR, *2,* 748; Teit, BAE *Annual Report, 45,* 369.

42. Doty, Journal, p. 61. Cf. below, p. 140, n. 49 and text.

43. NA, IA, Negots. Rat. Treaties, Stevens to Manypenny, June 14; cf. Doty letter of 20 May on preparation for the council at the mission on 1 April. HED, 35 Cong., 1 sess., 38 (1857), p. 10 (for Mesplié).

parently come to bring back a supply train of twenty-two pack animals, and does not seem to have attended the council. Father Menetrey, leaving St. Ignatius on April 10, was passing by on the fourth day of the council; he brought along the Coeur d'Alene guide Joseph, a large, fine-looking man, in answer to Ravalli's (and Doty's) request. He did not mean to stop but seems to have been invited to do so immediately. Stevens' secretary records his presence the next day, May 28, at the dealings with the Cayuses and Walla Wallas. He remarks that the Jesuit "speaks English fluently and is an agreeable gentleman." [44] Perhaps Ravalli had brought down the Coeur d'Alene observers, and Menetrey the Flatheads.

Stevens had hoped to be with the Coeur d'Alenes by June 15. However it wasn't until the 16th that he was able to leave Walla Walla and head into the wilderness north. There were five in the party besides his thirteen-year-old son Hazard, plus sixteen others listed as laborers, including the Coeur d'Alene guide. There were also forty horses and forty-one pack animals, ten of which were loaded with Indian goods. It was a clear, sunny day as the party single-filed north from the deserted council grounds. Behind them the Indians began to lay in food supplies and to rally help, looking to a war as soon as winter made travel difficult for the Whites. Just as the Stevens party set out and as Palmer was making other treaties to the south, a White man named John Edwards was exhorting the Indians at The Dalles not to sell their lands, telling them it was robbery. He was arrested for disturbing the peace and endangering the Whites' treaty plans.[45]

To the north, the Jesuits awaiting Stevens' coming were in no enviable position. Active peacemaking was a less ambiguous activity than participation in a Stevens treaty council. The priests felt constrained in all loyalty to introduce him and his policies to their Indians, and even to help supply his party and store his treaty goods. They could interpret for him when necessary or gather the Indians for a council. To a surprising extent they were willing to argue his case with the Indians. But there was a limit. They had serious obligations and responsibilities to the Indians themselves, and there was a line beyond which in conscience they could not cross. Some of their letters intimate as much to Stevens when they warn that they can go only so far without becoming compromised as tools of the government.

In 1859 when the Oblates abandoned their Interior missions forever, they offered this same reason. The Americans had wanted them to be "agents" who would "keep the tribes in submission and dispose them to accept all the whims of the government." Government officials "oblige us to speak for

44. NA, IA, Misc. Recd., May 27; Doty, Journal, pp. 12, 17–18 (May 28).

45. NA, IA, Negots. Rat. Treaties, Palmer to Dalles commander, 21 June. Doty, Journal, pp. 25–26.

them, to accompany them, and even to serve as their interpreters." This caused the Indians to hear the politicians' words "with the greatest respect because it is the priest who is speaking to them." The Oblates felt their ministry would be hopelessly compromised by this factor until the period of wars and treaties should have passed.[46]

Yet the Governor was suspicious and angry if he detected in any missionary a slackening of cooperation, lack of enthusiasm, or shade of neutrality. Stevens was never one to admit nuances of loyalty. In his military-minded programs no one was permitted to be neutral or to intrude substantial modifications into the settled plan of attack. He could not ignore the missioners, and he refers often to their great influence; but he was not really able to use them as tools, and so from time to time he petulantly saw their influence as baneful. He was capable of reporting, after the second Walla Walla Council the following year: "so great has been their desire for peace that they have overlooked all right [and] propriety" so that "the Indians seeing that the missionaries are on their side are fortified in the belief they are fighting in a holy cause."[47]

Thus Joset was to write during the coming war: "we find ourselves in a very difficult position; the Americans fancy that the priest completely controls the spirit and heart of the natives, and I think that the natives suspect the priest of leaning to the side of the Americans." The views of Stevens' colleague Gibbs are relevant. "There can be no doubt" that the missionaries were "to a certain extent beneficial in preserving peace among the tribes, as well as in settling private quarrels." Except for "a very small number," however, "their control over individuals is limited."[48] This is precisely what Father Joset is saying in another way. The secularist mind could conceive of immense influence only in terms of absolute power. It was not prepared to examine the love and respect of a free mind working in ambiguous areas partly obscure, partly free, and partly subject to freely given religious obedience.

After nine days of travel the treaty party reached the Coeur d'Alene mission. Men like Crosbie and McKenzie were already in the upper country, preparing the way. Governor Stevens was able to converse en route with groups of Nez Percés, Palouses, and Coeur d'Alenes with whom preliminary contact had already been made. Father Ravalli welcomed the party "in the most cordial and hospitable manner." One of the group, Landsdale, was

46. G. M. Waggett, O.M.I., "Oblates of Mary Immaculate in the Pacific Northwest, 1847–1878," *RACHS*, *64* (1953), 93.

47. H. Stevens, *Stevens*, *2*, 228–29.

48. MJ, II, AA, Joset to De Smet (in French), 26 February 1857. *RR*, *1*, ii, 422 (Gibbs).

somewhat overwhelmed by the missioners. "My blessing on the 'fathers,'" he wrote in his diary; "they are laborious, self denying, and zealous, and are deserving of all praise." The superior, Father Ravalli, was "accomplished and kind, and highly regarded by white and Red." [49]

A preliminary council was gathered at the mission, involving some thirty of the principal Coeur d'Alenes, including the three main chiefs. Stevens wanted a delegation to go to the Blackfoot Council, but the chiefs refused. He promised to come back in mid-September to hold a combined council for the Coeur d'Alenes, Spokanes, Kettles, and Okanogans, by which they would all sell their lands and go on reservations. Unwisely, he promised that it would be just like the Walla Walla Council. He assured the tribe: "we wish you to have your Missionaries; the President likes to have Missionaries among you who will do their duty." [50]

The Governor's aide, Henry Crosbie, had previously been dispatched to Colville for a similar preliminary meeting with the Kettles. The Jesuits at the Kettle mission were asked for help there. While the Governor was at the Coeur d'Alene mission, he administered the naturalization oath to the priests and brothers. Ravalli furnished the expedition with some supplies and with another Coeur d'Alene guide for the trip ahead. Stevens then set out for the Flathead country and the fateful Hell Gate Treaty. He floundered grimly through tangled forests and over cedar swamps and rain-swollen rivers. The timber-choked path was progressively cleared by a wood-cutting party in his van.

Far behind him, Indian runners were slipping from tribe to tribe, unleashing waves of unrest from the Cascades to the Rockies. Yakima runners from the hostile Chief Kamiakin arrived on the Spokane to harangue an Indian council. Meanwhile, Stevens received word from a passing Flathead, and later from a Coeur d'Alene messenger, that all preparations had been made for the Flathead Council and that the Indians anticipated his arrival.

THE FLATHEAD CONFEDERACY IN 1855

The section of the Rockies lying within Montana is imposing. With its spurs it embraces an area some 300 miles long by 200 wide. This tumble of mountains is divided into great ranges, favoring a northwesterly slant. The ranges make basins, and these divide into valleys. There are over fifty mountain ridges here, varying from 25 to 100 miles in length and from 5 to 25 in width. They rise regularly to 9,000 feet above sea level, sometimes to 12,000 feet. A cap of eternal snow gave them their first name, The Shining Moun-

49. Smaller Lansdale Diary (YU), June 25. *RR, 12,* i, 201.
50. Doty, *Journal,* p. 32. "Will" is crossed out but may be significant.

tains. The highest and most easterly of the ranges is the Bitterroot. Here the Jesuits had set their first mission in 1841: St. Mary's among the Flatheads. We have seen how they abandoned it at the end of 1850, and how circumstances conspired to keep them from returning.

The sociological tension that led to the abandonment had by no means destroyed the attachment of the majority of Flatheads to Catholicism nor the ascendancy of the Jesuits over them. This point is important, bearing as it does on the Flathead attitudes during the coming council. The Flathead revolt is open to many interpretations. There probably was a group within the Flatheads seriously opposed to mission establishments. But "the indifference and hostility of the Flatheads to religion" can easily be exaggerated. Again, it is misleading to view the Flatheads' persistence in hunting as a rejection of the mission life, or as an inability to "adjust" to a life of farming. The assumption here is that the farmers were nonhunters, or that the hunters preferred excitement to farming, or were "economic conservatives," or that the Jesuits had erroneously thought the Flatheads "aspired to a civilization after the European pattern." The Flatheads, the Jesuits, and the other mission tribes had no choice as to this element of the economy from the very beginning until the final disappearance of the buffalo.[51]

The theory that the Flatheads underwent a great spiritual revulsion, reverting again to their tribal patterns and away from the mission influence, is fair enough but does not come to grips with the problem. It misses the underlying permanent commitment and therefore the harrowing struggle within the Catholic Flathead. Nor does it reckon with all the causes. Above all, it misinterprets the Jesuit methodology, which had not issued in 1849 in a "thin veneer of white culture." [52] A similar theory is that the Flatheads embraced the Christian religion as a powerful war medicine; when it ceased to be effective and military catastrophes multiplied, they turned from it in disillusionment. This idea rests upon a misinterpretation of De Smet's comments about Blackfoot attitudes. The Blackfeet saw Christianity as a war medicine only; the Flatheads knew the relation between aggressively defensive warfare and Christian prayer. There is not much reason for believing with Ewers that

51. Ewers, *Sohon's Portraits*, pp. 32, 36, 46, 50, 26. See also S. Dunbar and P. C. Phillips, eds., *The Journals and Letters of Major John Owen, Pioneer of the Northwest 1850–1871*, 1 (2 vols. Helena, Mont., 1927), 6 n. ("indifference"). And see Richard Forbis, "The Flathead Apostasy, an Interpretation," *Montana, The Magazine of Western History*, 1, no. 4 (1951), 35–40.

52. This is the thesis especially of Claude Schaeffer, "The First Jesuit Mission to the Flatheads, 1840–1850, a Study in Culture Conflicts," *PNWQ, 28* (1937), 227–50, an otherwise able contribution to the problem. Authors like Ewers and Spier follow and cite him, as do some general works like R. M. Underhill, *Red Man's America, a History of Indians in the United States* (Chicago, 1953), p. 258 and n.

"the power of the Prince of Peace was strangely interpreted" among the Flat-heads.[53]

Catholic roots had gone deeply; despite the brief revolt, the work of the 1840s never really had to be done again. When Lieutenant Mullan visited the Flatheads during the explorations of 1853, he could report back to the Governor that the Jesuits had "laid among them a foundation [for civilization] upon a better and firmer basis than has ever been laid among any Indian tribe either east or west of the mountains." He felt that the government could now build upon this foundation an "ornament" to the region and "to our whole nation." Dr. Suckley at this time noted how the Flatheads "preserved some of the outward forms" of the Catholic faith; this, of course, is about all one might expect Catholic Indians to display to non-Catholics in the absence of a resident priest. Some Flatheads remembered to offer grace before meals. They kept up the forms of Catholic burial with crosses. The Angelus was rung three times daily. And the Sunday rest was observed. Many continued to "assemble morning and evening for prayers." Governor Stevens was impressed by this public prayerfulness.[54]

Much of the religious orientation was owing to the remarkable loyalty of the chiefs. Victor, Ambrose, Moses, and Adolph "never deviated" from the daily pattern of mission devotions and boldly used "all their influence" to redress the moral lapses of their people. These were precisely the chiefs with whom the Governor was soon to be negotiating. Their unusually dedicated example, however, should not be cited as proof that the rest of the Flatheads had fallen back into paganism.[55] The first band contacted for the Governor by Mullan "astonished him by having prayers upon his arrival" both morning and evening, "the whole tribe being assembled in the chief's lodge." The main encampment of fifty lodges, "plainly showing the good influence of the missionary instruction," sent a delegation of four headmen to confer with the Governor. These four were "devout"; they "never eat anything without a blessing, and never rise without praying." [56]

This does not mean that only piety prevailed. When Father Menetrey returned to evangelize the tribe two years after the Flathead Council, he found the external morality "deplorable," especially in sexual sins and gambling. Yet he was surprised to discover, as he reported to Rome, that "never even in their worst excesses have the Flatheads ceased to regret the departure of their mis-

53. J. C. Ewers, *The Blackfeet, Raiders on the Northwestern Plains* (Norman, Okla., 1958), p. 186.
54. Suckley Papers (SI), Journal, 29 September; his limitation ("some") is owing to others having kept more of their traditional ways. *RR*, *1*, ii, 439. CR, *2*, 765.
55. Ewers, *Portraits*, p. 43; Menetrey, 1857 letter, *JMUS*, *2*, 388.
56. *RR*, *12*, i, 124–25; cf. *1*, ii, 308, 311.

sionaries and to sigh for their return." No sooner had the Jesuits gone than the Flatheads wanted them back. A little over a year after the last Jesuit had left, they sent off a message to De Smet at St. Louis. The superior-general, Father Accolti, refused to accede to De Smet's plea to reopen the mission; Accolti argued that the Flatheads if sincere would have gone to see a local Jesuit. When the exploring party came, three years after the closure, the Flatheads petitioned Lieutenant Mullan to see that a Blackrobe was sent. Shortly afterward, a delegation of Flatheads traveled all the way to California to ask Father Mengarini to return.[57]

The index of the Flathead commitment is the instant success of Menetrey during his visit in mid-1857. The entire tribe gave up gambling, canceled debts, straightened out irregular marriages, and went to confession in a body. All three hundred adults confessed to Menetrey "with a piety and sorrow of which I should not have believed Indians capable." Morning and evening prayers by the whole tribe resumed. Bad habits abruptly stopped. Menetrey could only explain the change as "miraculous."[58] But it was simply the external manifestation of attitudes discernible during the previous years of abandonment. This change proved to be permanent. The Flatheads remained strong in their faith for another decade, served occasionally from St. Ignatius. In 1859 De Smet announced to the tribe the decision of the Jesuit general at Rome to reopen St. Mary's; it was fully re-established in 1866.

In 1855 one obstacle to Flathead re-establishment was about to disappear through administrative reorganization. The four years before the treaty had been the most critical and discouraging in the history of the mission network. Accolti, the superior-general, had continued to view skeptically the whole future of Oregon as opposed to California. But in 1853 he left for the East; soon he was to go to Europe to arrange for the formation of separate California and Oregon missions, each to be placed under the European province of Turin. The other major obstacle to re-establishment, "the proximity of the Blackfeet," was sufficiently diminished through the Blackfoot treaty of 1855 and the subsequent Jesuit missionary work among that tribe.[59]

Just a year before the council of 1855, another mission had been deliberately moved into the vicinity of the Flatheads. Numbers of them came to live here. This was St. Ignatius among the Kalispels, formerly well established but

57. Docs. in *JMUS*, 2, 386–88. Palladino, *Indian and White*, p. 52. J. Mooney, "Mengarini," *Catholic Encyclopedia*, 10, 188–89. W. P. Schoenberg, S.J., *Jesuits in Montana* (Portland, Oreg., 1960), p. 19.

58. *JMUS*, 2, 389.

59. FL, *1853*, Etats Unis, 28 January 1853, as the only obstacle. Gibbs also understood this to be the main reason for abandonment (*RR*, *1*, ii, 422). The Turin relation with our mission from here on is covered in Alessandro Monti, S.J., *La Compagnia di Gesù nel territorio della provincia torinese*, 5 (5 vols. Chieri, Italy, 1914–20), 572–602.

on poor soil some two hundred miles to the northwest. Before a year had
passed at the new mission, the Jesuits could see "a notable amelioration in the
whole nation" of the Flatheads in the valley below them. Menetrey and
Hoecken made pastoral visits down there.[60]

The new site for St. Ignatius was on Kalispel land just below the forty-mile-
long Flathead Lake, in a huge mountain valley only fifty miles north of the
abandoned Flathead mission. It was better for farming, more central to a
number of mission tribes, and remote from settlement. Even Fort Colville was
600 miles distant to the west, and the similar post of Fort Benton 400 miles to
the east—hard traveling in either direction. There was a Hudson's Bay *pied-
à-terre* called Fort Connah, served by one man, six miles above St. Ignatius.
In the Bitterroot Valley below, an independent trader named John Owen had
built a post on the Jesuit ruins; occasional drifters and mountain men tended
to gravitate to this wilderness oasis. The mission nearest to St. Ignatius was in
Coeur d'Alene land, 200 miles to the west when the paths were open.

When Governor Stevens began his treaty tour in 1855, the new St.
Ignatius, hardly more than six months old, was already a relatively imposing
cluster of farm buildings, residences, and a church. The archbishop of Oregon City wrote happily in that year of "the handsome, large new mission
which the Jesuit Fathers have succeeded in establishing by uniting at an
agreed locality the missions of the Flatheads, Pend d'Oreilles and Kutenais." [61]
Contemporary sketches of its prairie site, with mountains looming on the
near horizon and tipis dotting the tall grass, have been preserved in the Jesuit
archives at St. Louis and Rome. The originals of the figures who people these
sketches were as international in character as the Jesuit community here. By
the first week of April 1855, just before the treaty tour began, over a thousand Indians had gone to make their permanent home at this new site, with
its "pleasing variety of woodland and prairie, lake and river—the whole
crowned in the distance by the white summit of the mountains." [62]

The resident missioner counted Blackfeet, Spokanes, Kettles, Coeur
d'Alenes, Nez Percés, Crees, and Iroquois among those living there. One is
not surprised to discover also an occasional Sioux, Delaware, or Shawnee.
The main population, however, was drawn from the complex of tribes
shortly to be designated by the government as the Flathead Confederacy. Ranging over a far-flung mountain territory, most of them Catholics,
they numbered 2,000 Indians of four major tribes: Flatheads, Kutenais, Pend

60. CR, *4*, 1239–40.
61. FL, *1855*, Etats Unis, 15 January (in French). See also FL, *1856*, Rome (divers),
Jesuit general to Association, 10 May 1856: "environ 2,000 chrétiens se trouvent réunis"
here.
62. Sketch in RJ, MSax., II, 12, No. 1. Mullan published it in black and white, but
apparently presented this colored original to the missionaries. CR, *4*, 1232.

d'Oreilles, and Kalispels. These tribes "use[d] much to intermarry, for they use[d] to meet together very often for buffalo hunting." [63]

The Kutenais, a thousand tribesmen sharing a language unique to themselves, enjoyed a tribal range 200 miles wide and 250 miles long. Most of this fell within Canada. The American portion, with a stable population of about 400, ran along the northern edge of what is today Washington, Idaho, and Montana. The Kutenais were far advanced in the tribal and war culture of the Plains; paradoxically they clung also to the old decentralized village system. Economically they were split into the upper Kutenais of the east who were primarily hunters, and the lower Kutenais or Flatbows of the west who were fishermen. The tribe as a whole comprised a number of politically independent bands strongly united by cultural and emotional ties.

The 1855 treaty troubles will concern mostly the Tobacco Plains group, the mother band. Against universal opposition its chief, Michael, firmly insisted he was also head chief. Michael's band centered upon "a vast and beautiful amphitheatre" measuring some fifty by fifteen miles, in a bowl of mountains.[64] The band ranged also to Flathead Lake and rode to buffalo on the Plains. Theirs was a thickly timbered country of moose and elk, beaver, deer, and fish, traditionally coveted by the Kalispels, Coeur d'Alenes, and neighboring tribes. They possessed a cabin church, visited once or twice a year by a Jesuit until the removal to St. Ignatius late in 1854. A short, stocky people, they were known as busy hunters, inveterate traders, industrious but poor, scrupulously honest, and responsive to the Jesuit teachings. In later years the reservation group was to have a bad reputation among Americans and agency officials as lazy troublemakers. Kutenai warfare with the Blackfeet was continual and enthusiastic. Though nomads, they were relatively sedentary. Lack of funds had prevented the missioners from developing them in farming.

63. Joset Papers (OJ), No. 29. CR, *4*, 1246–47; Creeks here must be Crees (see above, p. 52). These tribes are described from the ethnologists cited above in Chap. 1, ns. 8, 9, 23, from Jesuit materials in CR and OJ (see esp. fonds St. Ignatius, St. Mary's), and from writers like Ronan and O'Connor given in Bibliography, below. Exact numbers are hard to come by. Stevens gives 450 Flatheads, 600 Pend d'Oreilles, and 350 American Kutenais, but omits Kalispels and the more numerous Canadian Kutenais as not being in the treaty. Even this total of 1,400 for the three treaty tribes may fall short by 300, he concedes, because it was "better to be a little below than above the mark"; later he says these totals are "believed to be rather under the actual numbers." (In NA, IA, Negots. Rat. Treaties, e.g. Stevens to Manypenny, 22 October, and Blackfoot Council "Official Proceedings," p. 48). Cf. H. Stevens, *Stevens, 2,* 503, and comparative statistics 1806–53 in RR, *1,* ii, 417–18. Agents seem to have copied these figures and one another's.

64. CR, *3,* 958. On the 1855 Kutenais see also Carling Malouf, "Early Kutenai History," *Montana, The Magazine of Western History, 2,* no. 2 (1952), 5–9.

Chief Michael's people were to be the only Kutenais involved in the Flathead treaty.

An ethnologist might see the Pend d'Oreilles and Kalispels as a single grouping or tribe. De Smet reported both together as "like the Flatheads in body, character, disposition, manners, customs and language," so that in practice "they form with them only one and the same people." [65] Like the Spokane and Columbia tribes, however, they were much less affected by the war complex. Politically they ran to local village autonomy, with a slight tribal tendency. Together they numbered a thousand or more. In practice they formed two separate groups, though the Pend d'Oreilles were sometimes known as upper Kalispels and the Kalispels as lower Pend d'Oreilles. Missionaries working among them, though conscious of their kinship, dealt with them as two tribes. From their extensive use of the bark canoe the Pend d'Oreilles were called in sign language the Lake Paddlers, while the Kalispels were called the River Paddlers. Dr. Suckley, who stayed a while at the mission during the 1853 explorations, was moved by their "fervor and earnestness," and felt that "surely some great cause has produced this change." He recorded that they were honest and brave, and "devoted to religion so far as external forms go and to the extent that their present understanding will admit." [66] Father Joset characterized them as proud and disorderly.

The Pend d'Oreilles (Earrings) centered upon the site chosen for the new St. Ignatius just below Flathead Lake. They ranged over the mountainous lake-and-forest country of northwest Montana. The five or six Pend d'Oreille bands were controlled by Head Chief Alexander or No Horses (a name paradoxically meant to denote its opposite, great wealth in horses), together with a subchief and four lesser chiefs. Alexander was to be the most important Indian at the council, after Victor, the Flathead. Like many Interior Indians Alexander was a tribal mixture, half Pend d'Oreille and half Snake. About 45 years old, he had been chief for about seven years. In appearance he was somber and thin-faced; in character he was straightforward, fearless, and implacably honest. An old traveling companion of Father De Smet's, he was a strong friend of the Jesuits.

Lieutenant Saxton's section of the 1853 expedition had met "a party numbering at least a hundred" Pend d'Oreilles returning from their buffalo hunt on the Great Plains, all "mounted on fine horses." They were "perfectly civil, and seemed to feel proud, rich, and independent." By that time Blackfoot wars had ravaged them so regularly that "all the principal chiefs" of the preceding decade had been killed.[67] Like the Kalispels, the Pend d'Oreilles were

65. CR, *3*, 992–93 (1840).
66. Suckley Papers (SI), Journal, 29 September, 15 October. *RR, 1,* ii, 298.
67. CR, *2,* 470; *RR, 1,* ii, 257. Teit, BAE *Annual Report, 45,* 379 (No Horses).

much attached to the Jesuits. Alexander himself had chosen the present site of the new St. Ignatius.

The Kalispels were to the west or northwest of the Pend d'Oreilles, in a long line across what is now Idaho and Washington, with a central point of reference at Pend d'Oreille Lake. They were an amalgam of Spokanes, Flatheads, Kalispels proper, and the like, who had gravitated not long before into a single group and way of life. Alexander of the Pend d'Oreilles claimed jurisdiction over them. They rejected the claim, and Stevens did not allow it in the 1855 council. The Kalispels did not take part in the Flathead Council; they were to have their own a few months later. Because they did not participate in the Flathead treaty, they were technically not part of what was to be called the Flathead Confederacy. In reality they were as close allies as the Pend d'Oreilles, and Stevens recognized the fact. In the opening session of the council he included them with the other three "all as one nation." [68]

Their head chief, Loyola or Standing Grizzly, had died the previous April. Elected in his place was the generous and extremely popular Victor, or Happy Man, not to be confused with the patriarchal Head Chief Victor of the Flatheads. Victor Happy Man was described by Dr. Suckley in 1853 as "a small man, young, and of good countenance, but so good and amiable in his disposition that he is scarcely able to maintain his authority over the tribe." Hoecken qualifies him as "a brave hunter," who was "remarkable for the generosity of his disposition." [69]

The Flatheads themselves, numbering less than five hundred Indians, were the most remarkable of all the mountain tribes. Frontiersmen, trappers, explorers, missionaries, and travelers disconcertingly agree that they were paragons: honest, open, reserved but not hostile; generous, industrious, and of indomitable bravery. The Gibbs memoir on the tribes during the 1853 expedition speaks of them as an "exception among the Indians of Oregon." Their "heroism in battle" and virtues in general have been "the theme of praise both from priest and laymen." Bancroft sums up these contemporary opinions in his statement that the Flatheads and Kutenais, with their friends the Nez Percés, "probably come as near as it is permitted to flesh-and-blood savages to the traditional noble red man" of fiction. Lieutenant Mullan had reported to Stevens that "the Flatheads as a nation have more reason to complain of a want of attention and care on the part of the government than any other

---

68. NA, IA, Negots. Rat. Treaties, Flathead Council "Official Proceedings." Cf. NA, IA, LR (from Wash.), Stevens to Manypenny, 5 May. Having neglected to write into his prepared treaty this idea of a Flathead Nation or Confederacy, Stevens supplied it at the council grounds by an insertion, along with a similar provision that other tribes could be "consolidated" into this nation later (cf. original treaty, NA, IA, Negots. Rat. Treaties).

69. *RR*, *1*, ii, 297. CR, *4*, 1230.

tribe of Indians probably in North America." [70] He seems not to have realized that this in itself may have been a blessing.

Their tribal range covered a huge expanse of western Montana, roughly halved by the Great Divide. Their home base was the Bitterroot Valley. But the several bands enjoyed local habitats as well, probably one near what is now Butte, one east of it, another near Helena, one in the Big Hole Valley, and so on. They were equally a Plains people. In the winter they migrated onto the Great Plains for an extensive buffalo hunt of many months. Their favorite spots were along the Musselshell and in the Yellowstone Valley, though they often worked along the edges of the Missouri. In the summer they made a briefer foray, largely for hides.

Their head chief, Victor, was a remarkable man, already known through De Smet's books to a wide audience in Europe and America. He lived with ten lodges in the valley, housed partly "in comfortable log cabins," supplementing the hunting with cultivation of "wheat, potatoes, and other vegetables." Father Accolti's claim in 1852 that he had lost control of the tribe by turning the other cheek when struck appears to be suspect, not so much because it is based upon hearsay but because it forms part of Accolti's very partisan argument for opposing the mission. [71]

The warrior complex and tribal evolution was far advanced among the Flatheads. They had an elaborate system of grading coups, a liking for scalps, an unusual intelligence system, and a stubborn constancy in war. The head chieftainship was hereditary and authoritative, though the tribe was comprised of semi-autonomous bands. A kind of general staff of subchiefs attended the head chief. The most able warrior acted as a permanent war chief. While the lesser chiefs administered their bands, several to each band, the head chief enjoyed special powers, notably in making war or peace.

The major sport of adult Flathead males was war. Their source of trade commodities and of the very staff of life was the biannual buffalo hunt. This too meant war, the hunts being serious military expeditions. One result was that many of their lodges "are only inhabited by women and their daughters." Another was that "very few" of the Indians were of purely Flathead origin. Neither of these phenomena is isolated, the first being common to the warrior nations, and the second to the tribes of the Interior. Another factor in the mixing process, especially from the time the Whites began to come, was the nature of the country; mountainous and relatively remote, it became "a haven" for Indian badmen, refugees, and drifters. The Jesuits had initiated them in agriculture; but the program had been relatively limited, and when

70. *RR, 1,* ii, 416, 437. H. H. Bancroft, *The Native Races of the Pacific States, 1,* in *Works, 1–5* (5 vols. San Francisco, 1874–83), 291.

71. *JMUS, 2,* 386 (Accolti). *RR, 1,* ii, 365 (quot.).

Jesuit direction was withdrawn, the system collapsed. The tribe did continue to maintain the Jesuit herd of a thousand cattle.[72]

FATHER HOECKEN IS SUMMONED

St. Ignatius was just emerging from the chaos of its new beginnings as Governor Stevens prepared his treaty tour. Construction had been going on apace for several months; fields were plowed and sown; and plans had been evolved to purchase equipment from St. Louis via Fort Benton. A major event this summer was to be the visit of Bishop Augustine Blanchet, who would conduct colorful confirmation ceremonies; on his last visit, before the mission was moved, he had confirmed six hundred Indians amid public festivity. The preliminary invitation to the council disturbed these plans, especially the project of sending a guard of honor two hundred miles west to receive the bishop. This first invitation from Stevens also had to follow Father Adrian Hoecken to the more westerly missions, where he was visiting his Jesuit colleagues.

At the moment when Stevens came up from Walla Walla, the mission was giving hospitality to Accolti's successor as superior, Nicholas Congiato. Congiato was just completing a three-month tour of inspection of the mission network and was about to return to California. Impressed by the progress at St. Ignatius, he reported that all was "going on wonderfully well." Father Hoecken "has succeeded in uniting three nations and a part of the Flatheads to live together under his spiritual direction." De Smet tells us that during this year conversions were "numerous," and requests for missions were "repeatedly" coming in from such distant tribes as the Blackfeet, Crows, Assiniboines, and Sioux.[73] Since the province of Turin had assumed control of the California and Oregon missions, a new spirit of optimism and expansion was abroad, unknown since the Cayuse troubles.

The mission remained badly understaffed and very remote from civilization. The general of the Order at Rome could furnish almost no information when requested to do so in 1854: "I have not had for a long time details concerning the work of our Fathers at this mission." He remarked that they ought to concentrate on the "preservation of progress already made, inasmuch as I am not able to increase the number of missionaries there."[74]

72. Turney-High, *Flatheads*, p. 116 (war). *RR*, *1*, ii, 150 (women), 415; cf. pp. 279, 397, and *12*, i, 169 (cattle). Teit, BAE *Annual Report*, 45, 323 (haven). Wissler classified the Flatheads as a Plains tribe; Kroeber in 1923 began the present practice of making them a Plateau tribe, but he later changed his views and gave them an intermediate status.
73. CR, *4*, 1234, 1237, 1278.
74. FL, *1854*, Rome (divers), report of Jesuit general (in French), 24 April.

The mission staff at St. Ignatius was as international as the Indian community. Each of the two priests and four brothers represented a different nation. Father Hoecken, the superior, was Dutch. Father Menetrey, in charge of temporalities, was Swiss. Brother Peter McGean, the farm manager, was Irish. Brother Joseph Specht, blacksmith, baker, and gardener, was German. Brother Vincent Magri, infirmarian, carpenter, and miller, was Italian. And Brother Francis Huysbrecht, carpenter and sacristan, was Belgian. At the time of the council, though Stevens invited both "the priests and the brothers," Hoecken was the only priest available. The brothers traditionally refrained from these civil involvements. Menetrey and a brother had left to guide Congiato out of the Indian country; Stevens was to meet and converse with the party eighty-six miles west of the mission. Throughout the council Menetrey remained away, attending a conference of delegates from the Oregon Jesuit missions.[75]

At the mission itself a cholera outbreak was causing anxiety. Late 1853 had been the frightful "cholera year" on the Great Plains, when "thousands" of Sioux and other tribesmen had died.[76] Perhaps the present scourge, less than two years later, was an echo. Hoecken and the brothers were laboring to keep it within bounds.

Thus, in the Flathead Council, Hoecken was the only Jesuit directly involved. Since our interpretation of the council leans heavily upon his personal observations, a closer look at the man is necessary. Adrian Hoecken had been born at Tilburg in Holland two days before Napoleon re-entered Paris to begin his triumphant Hundred Days' progress to Waterloo. Ordained deacon as a diocesan seminarian twenty-four years later, he left to enter the Jesuit Order on the American frontier. A priest in 1842, he traveled west as part of the famous emigration of '43 and with De Smet founded the Kalispel mission.

Father Hoecken worked with the Kalispels and their neighbors for the next fifteen years, founding the new mission in 1854. For six of those years he never saw another White man besides his lay brother companion. For a long time he knew nothing of such happenings as the Mexican War, or the accession of Pope Pius IX. After several years spent in establishing the Blackfoot mission on the Plains, broken health occasioned his recall to civilization in 1861, where he was to gain some fame as a pioneer worker among the American Negroes. His older brother, Christian, more widely known than Adrian for his exploits as a Jesuit missionary in the trans-Mississippi west,

75. Hoecken Diary (OJ). H. Stevens, *Stevens*, 2, 75. On Menetrey see *DAB*, 12, 534–35.
76. CR, 4, 1235, 1283. Cf. Mesplié Papers, I, 9, 4 June 1853, where 112 of Mesplié's Indians died in ten days.

had died in 1851 of the same cholera that now engaged Adrian's attention.

Those who knew Hoecken remarked upon his keen eye for natural beauty. They commented, too, on his close identification with Indian ways, which persisted in his mannerisms even after his removal to the East. A reticent man, he left no memoirs. There are some letters and an invaluable manuscript diary or jotting-book. Something of his nature emerges from a perusal of this small book. Its flavor and honesty are caught, for example, in this petulant Anglo-French entry: "Un fall out at breakfast Against me by R[ev.] P[ère] Menetrey for the horse given to the chief; my prodigality makes others suffer; I am not master of the property, etc., etc." [77] His thrifty business sense emerges too, and a meticulousness in details.

Dr. Suckley in 1853 reported "the truly benevolent and pleasing manner" with which Hoecken received him, and the priest's "cordiality and kindness of a Christian and a gentleman." Suckley confesses himself "not a religious person," though respecting Christianity. But during his stay here he could see that the Indians "look up to the Father, and love him; they say that if the Father should go away they should die." In short he was their "kind missionary and friend, the much loved." Stevens himself was impressed with Hoecken's work. In his report of 1855 the Governor commented that "it would be difficult to find a more beautiful example of successful missionary labors." [78]

Father De Smet valued Hoecken's hard work and his capacity for producing "the most plentiful results." Congiato strikes the same note, after his official visit in 1855, noting that Hoecken "does the work of several men." Later in the century, some seven years before Hoecken's death, Bancroft described him as being "nearly as indefatigable as De Smet." [79] Hoecken had not always been successful. The Coeur d'Alenes had proved too much for him in 1844, and he had been removed from their mission. The trouble centered around two incidents small enough in themselves, in which Hoecken was technically in the right; but his manner of handling them was apparently impatient and headstrong. A Dutch stubbornness and lack of flexibility seem to lie behind all this.

His later photo suggests a slight man and probably a small man. Large childlike eyes are shadowed and somewhat recessed by the ill health that removed

77. Hoecken Diary. For Christian see *DAB*, 9, 106–07. On Hoecken see items below, n. 79.

78. Suckley Papers (YU), No. 16, to uncle, 20 May 1854. *RR*, *12*, i, 161–62. Cf. Suckley Papers (SI), Journal, 15 October. *HED*, 33 Cong., 1 sess., 129 (1853-54), p. 278.

79. H. H. Bancroft, *History of Washington, Idaho, and Montana, 1845–1889*, in *Works, 31* (San Francisco, 1890), p. 604 n. See documentation in *JMUS*, *2*, 305–13, and obituary biography by W. H. Hill, *WL*, *26* (1897), 364–68. CR, *4*, 1228, 1277.

him from the mission. The mouth is wide and pleasant; on closer look it is very determined. A large nose threatens to upset the unity of the features; but a bald dome framed in sparse white locks draws them together and lends an odd distinction. The whole reflects a combined quality of gentleness and vigor.

For the treaty Governor Stevens had commissioned Thomas Adams, his assistant topographer and special temporary agent for the Flatheads, to gather the tribe and make all formal announcements. Adams had been in the Bitterroot Valley for some time now in this connection, keeping in touch with the Governor by courier. The formal invitation to Hoecken came at an inopportune moment. He disliked leaving his cholera patients. Inconveniently, too, the place chosen for the council was not the mission but Hell Gate "some thirty miles off," about seven miles northwest of modern Missoula.[80]

Father Hoecken with Brother McGean as companion set out almost immediately. The Indians were probably there already. At Hell Gate, however, there was no governor. The two Jesuits camped overnight, persisted through the following day, and again stayed overnight. No sign of Stevens or further message from him materialized. The priest was understandably annoyed, "since quite a few of our youngsters were dying or extremely ill." Moreover, he could not appreciate the Governor's insistence upon his attending this civil function.

Stevens had been delayed. He had planned to open the council on July 4, but travel conditions were bad. At one point a summer storm kept him in camp for two days. He had to ford the Coeur d'Alene River at sixteen different places in one day, and the Regis at thirty-nine another day. Thirteen to eighteen miles a day was as fast a pace as he cared to make. He was cutting his way through these forested mountains, and making scientific observations along the way. The day the Jesuits rode to the council grounds, July 4, Stevens spent floundering 150 yards across the swollen Bitterroot River. A nearby Flathead band with their lodges and families embarrassed the Whites by crossing the stream in an hour. While the Jesuits waited impatiently at Hell Gate next day, Stevens delayed until almost noon before breaking camp; then he progressed eighteen miles upriver. Since "time was too precious to waste," the two Jesuits went home to their sick Indians.

Indian runners had kept the Governor somewhat in contact with Adams in the Bitterroot Valley. Thus Adams could inform Stevens on July 1 through a Coeur d'Alene that "the Indians are all ready to assemble" and that a camp would be ready six miles below Hell Gate. Again on July 6 a Flathead arrived with Adams' note "saying that the Indians were patiently waiting." The as-

80. NA, IA, Negots. Rat. Treaties, Doty to Stevens, n.d.; Hoecken Diary; CR, 4, 1234.

sembled tribesmen must have presented an imposing and colorful spectacle. A census report a few months later recorded that "at the Flathead Council 1,200 persons were actually present" from the three tribes.

Early on the 7th, Adams met the little party of twenty-one and conducted them to the council grounds. A welcoming party of three hundred chiefs and warriors trotted out to greet them with a din of musketry "in the most cordial manner." Stevens spent some time in friendly conversation at their tents, then moved on to his own camp. At an informal conference on the afternoon of his arrival he was host to the three head chiefs and a retinue of lesser chiefs. After the usual prolonged puffing of tobacco to signify mutual friendship, Stevens outlined his plan for a reservation and formally invited the chiefs to the council.[81]

Some Nez Percés and Flatheads had come up with the Governor's party after attending the Walla Walla Council. Stevens now told the Flatheads that he meant to make the same kind of treaty here, and invited them to consult privately with these two groups. Many more Nez Percés were on their way, "a proper delegation" for the Blackfoot Council; they would be available for consultation during the latter half of the Flathead Council.[82] But the presence of disenchanted Indians from the Walla Walla meeting was a sinister circumstance.

In this first meeting Stevens solemnly promised the Flatheads that the proposed treaty with the Blackfeet, which he had promised two years ago during his explorations, would keep that tribe "out of this valley; and if that will not do it, we will then have soldiers who will." Chief Victor of the Flatheads announced that Stevens' preliminary measures for inhibiting Blackfoot aggression had failed. Twelve of the chief's peaceful hunters had been killed by the Blackfeet recently. Seven raiding parties had stolen Flathead horses. "I would have had my revenge ere this," he protested, had it not been for fear of White soldiers.

Chief Victor was to be the major figure in this council. He was beyond doubt the greatest in the long line of Flathead chiefs. At his death in 1870 Captain Mullan proposed that the government raise a monument to him. Yet Governor Stevens seems to have underrated him. When Stevens had first talked at length with the chief two years earlier, he had assessed him as "simple minded but rather wanting in energy, which might however be developed in an emergency." During the council Stevens treated him rather shabbily.[83]

---

81. Hoecken quots. from Diary; Adams-Stevens, in *RR*, *12*, i, 203, 207, 209. Census, in Blackfoot Council "Official Proceedings," p. 48.

82. Doty, Journal, p. 25.

83. Flathead Council "Official Proceedings" (NA, IA, Negots. Rat. Treaties); cf. above, p. 61, n. 1. Stevens on Victor in *RR*, *12*, i, 127–28.

Throughout the council one great obstacle stood in the Governor's path: the Indian's love for his own territory. A tribe might just possibly be cajoled into signing away most of its land; even so, it would wish to remain in the country of its fathers. The Governor, on the other hand, wanted to choose one place clearly within either the Flathead or the Pend d'Oreille region, and force the other tribes onto alien ground. He was to get it firmly into his head that the Pend d'Oreilles would not move south from their mission because of restraining Jesuit influence. The Flatheads, for their part, would not move north, he was convinced, because they disliked Jesuit control. Unprepared for serious delays or opposition at his council, he indulged in bizarre speculation as to their possible source. This in turn prevented him from confronting the real problem. His thirteen-year-old son Hazard, who was present, recalled the council as "unexpectedly difficult and protracted." [84]

The Council at Hell Gate

Sunday was a day of rest. On Monday, July 9, at 1:30 in the afternoon, Stevens and his six assistants met the assembled braves to open the council. The day was clear and "quite hot." Sohon's drawing shows the White men sitting at a rough table, shaded by a canopy of boughs supported on poles. Stevens stands in front with two chiefs. Though the Indian camp is some distance away, at least one Indian tipi is in evidence, together with the smaller tents of the Whites. The Indians, their buffalo robes negligently about their hips on this warm day, are massed in front of the table and to some extent around it. An American flag flaps above the scene in a cloudless sky. [85]

The first session ran through two and a half hours, the official record obviously abridging the proceedings. Stevens boldly outlined his plans to the Indians. They were to transfer to the Great Father in Washington all their lands. In his correspondence Stevens measured this home range at 23,000 square miles. The area was twice as large as Belgium, the Netherlands, or Maryland; three times as large as Massachusetts or Vermont; two thirds the size of Ireland or Portugal; half the area of states like New York and Louisiana; and many times the size of smaller states like Connecticut. Agent Ronan was to describe the cession later as "extending from near the forty-second parallel to the British line, and with an average breadth of nearly two degrees of latitude." [86]

84. H. Stevens, *Stevens*, 2, 81.
85. Smaller Lansdale Diary. Council details in Flathead Council "Official Proceedings."
86. Peter Ronan, *Historical Sketch of the Flathead Nation from the Year 1813 to 1890* (Helena, Mont., 1890), p. 56. See also the description in Art. I of the original treaty.

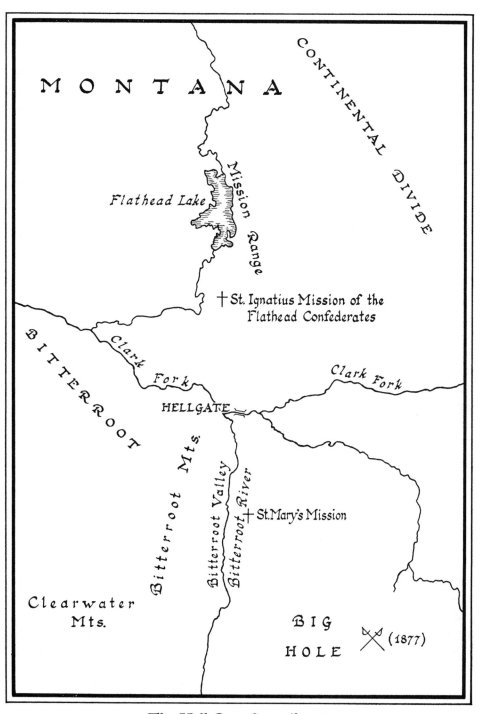

MONTANA

CONTINENTAL DIVIDE

Flathead Lake

Mission Range

† St. Ignatius Mission of the
Flathead Confederates

BITTERROOT

Clark Fork

Clark Fork

HELLGATE

Bitterroot Mts.

Bitterroot Valley

Bitterroot River

† St. Mary's Mission

Clearwater
Mts.

BIG
HOLE ✕ (1877)

7. The Hell Gate Council, 1855.

Moreover, this territory amounted to most of western Montana, a rich, dramatic, and beautiful sector of the present state, whose mountains, lakes, forests, and high prairies lent it infinite variety. If the Nez Percés at Walla Walla had been concerned over the loss of lands "well described as poor and barren," the sentiments of the Flathead tribes may well be imagined.[87] In return the Whites offered a single reservation of only 2,000 square miles which would have to accommodate not only these tribes but eventually such peoples as the Kalispels and Coeur d'Alenes.

The reservation was to center upon one of two valleys in question—probably the most beautiful in the region. The Bitterroot, about 5 miles in width and 80 in length, was well timbered and protected, with striking scenery and rich soil. A "valley of perpetual spring," its river banks were lined with tall pines. It was a valley "by far the most beautiful and productive in Montana." Mission Valley was equally magnificent and fertile. At first the Governor was partial to the Bitterroot because Adams had recommended it and perhaps also because the Jesuit influence might be less there.[88]

The Whites also offered a hospital with a resident physician, and for the next twenty years a farmer, a blacksmith, a wheelwright, a sawmill, a gristmill, and a school. Each Indian was to receive "a large amount" of "everything to start your farms," with more of each necessary item yearly for twenty years. The tribal law was to be respected. The Blackrobes were mentioned, not without implied criticism. "We look with favor on the missionaries that come amongst the Indians where they desire them," Stevens declared; "and I think their coming may do them good." He insisted, however, that "the priest will be your friend, but he will *not* have control whatever over your affairs." The Governor's resentment over what he conceived to be Jesuit influence emerged: "the priest will advise you in your spiritual affairs —that which relates to God, but he will have no control over your temporal affairs, your own laws; that you will manage yourself." [89]

Head Chief Alexander of the Pend d'Oreilles in his reply showed more tact. He touched briefly but boldly on hell, God, man's final purpose, and his people's undisciplined character. Perhaps, he surmised, fear of the Whites would succeed where priestly exhortations failed. "The priest instructs me and these people here," Alexander concluded; "I am very well content with the priest and am very well satisfied with you." Stevens had been put firmly in his place. He would never forgive Alexander for this and subsequent penetrating remarks. The council cannot be said to have opened on a genial note.

A certain logic commends the Governor's position to the secularist mind.

87. NA, IA, Negots. Rat. Treaties, Stevens to Palmer, June 1855.
88. *RR, 12*, i, 169; P. Ronan, p. 57. Hoecken Diary (Adams).
89. Flathead Council "Official Proceedings."

But its underlying assumptions are naïve. The Jesuits' control did not derive primarily from their role as economic and cultural guide, except to some extent in the opening stages of a mission. The relation was generally in diametric opposition. A process of partial acculturation became possible only insofar as a spiritual conquest first captured the Indian. Even then, the Jesuit stood usually above and outside tribal mechanisms. Where the Jesuit's influence was strong, it was tied in with a fierce personal loyalty and commitment on the part of the Indians to him as a disinterested and somewhat patriarchal figure. Many qualities converged to create such a figure, but the irreplaceable quality was his priestliness.

Head Chief Victor was the strongest and subtlest chief at the council. The official proceedings do not seem to have caught his speech well; in substance it was noncommittal and pathetic. It embodies fear of White power, conventional praises of the White man, concern that his tribe "may save their soul," and a protestation that he could not give the Whites a large piece of land because he had so little. Isaac or Red Wolf, a Flathead chief whose father was a Kutenai, complained that all this talk of one nation where before there had been three was confusing. And how was it that "my ground is all cut up in little pieces?" The talks between the Indians, he said, convinced him that each tribe had its own country. More talk was needed; Indians were poor; perhaps we can agree on something later. Stevens soon dismissed the lot, affecting to believe or believing that they simply needed more consultation among themselves. Again he cited the fatal Walla Walla precedent.[90]

Governor Stevens' speeches must have rung rather hollowly, because many of the things he promised had already been given to the Indians by their Blackrobes. At the Kalispel mission in 1853 Dr. Suckley had listed pigs, poultry, cattle, agricultural implements, tools, a windmill, both a blacksmith shop and a carpenter shop manned by lay brothers, barns, cow sheds, a central farm of 160 acres, and houses for the Indians. Stevens had asked Alexander "if he would like a flour mill, a sawmill, a blacksmith, a schoolteacher." To each question the chief answered no, "considering that they already possessed all these." [91]

The following afternoon the session was longer, running through three and a half hours. These meetings were slow, painful labor, since every idea had to pass through an interpreter and receive its comment back through him. In a Stevens council, the more formal negotiations of these public meetings were generally supplemented by private conversations and by further explanations from the interpreters.

In this second session Chief Big Canoe delivered the opening talk, one of

90. Ibid.
91. Hoecken Diary.

the longest and most poignant of the council. Doty gives it lengthy coverage. And Lansdale remarks upon it in his diary: "very long speech from Big Canoe." [92] Big Canoe was second in rank among the Pend d'Oreille chiefs. Born in 1799, he was now 56 and would live on until 1882. A staunch friend of the Whites, he was one of the greatest war chiefs the tribe ever had. As befitted a warrior, he spoke openly and candidly. In private council with the Indians, he declared, he had upbraided them for their fear of the Governor's power: "you tremble, ashamed of yourself; are you afraid of him?" He recognized that Stevens was "a very smart chief." The other Indians chiefs might be fearful or confused, he said, but he at least meant to speak out.

He could not understand the need for a treaty, for there had been no war. His people had never spilled a drop of White blood. "Where did I kill you? Where did you kill me? What is the reason we are talking about treaties?" At great cost to his tribe he had humored the Whites by calling back war parties who wished revenge against the Blackfeet. "I am quiet and sit down on my land," he said; "I thought nobody would talk about land, would trouble me." For his part he would never go to the White man's country and impose on them in this way. "Go back to your land"; we Indians here "are all one, close together." This is his country; he grew up here; he is poor and wants to keep his land. The White men talk "so smoothly, so well." They "just talk as they please" to the poor Indian. The White men have papers and notes open, "lying all over the table," while the Indian must rely on his wits. "Perhaps you will put me in a trap."

Some Indians, Big Canoe observed, felt that if they pleaded poverty and asked for help, the White man would not covet their holdings. Big Canoe himself must speak openly. "It is our land," he cried. "If you make a farm, I would not go there and pull up your crops. I would not drive you away from it. If I were to go to your country and say 'give me a little piece,' I wonder would you say 'here, take it.'" He protested that "this is all the small piece I have got; I am not going to let it go." He assured Stevens he did not mean to be impertinent. He had believed in the Governor, and had come to hear him. Both Stevens and the priest believe the Blackfeet will make a real peace. Big Canoe doubts it, but he desires to hear the Governor's message. [93]

Big Canoe's argument made a deep impression upon the Indians. Long after the council, they liked to repeat his words, holding out their hands in pantomime to indicate that they had never stained them with blood in a war against the Whites. [94] In this speech, for one brilliant moment, the Red man fired thunderbolts at his White manipulators. It was the kind of speech Stevens

92. Smaller Lansdale Diary, 10 July.
93. Flathead Council "Official Proceedings."
94. Hoecken Diary.

himself, properly roused, might have delivered. But it was not the kind of thing he was prepared to tolerate from someone else.

Determined to have his way, the Governor summarized Big Canoe's speech, framing it to his own purposes and boldly concluding that the chief favored the reservation scheme. Big Canoe protested: "I do not understand you right." Ignoring him, Stevens turned to the head chiefs. Each cannily conceded the general principle of a reservation but would not hear of leaving his own home territory. Since the Kutenai chief apparently indicated he would be willing to join the Pend d'Oreilles, Stevens waxed enthusiastic over the virtues of the upper or Mission Valley. He emphasized the alternatives— Mission Valley or the northern part of Bitterroot Valley. He painted a dark picture of the difficulties involved in supplying two reservations, and promised each chief a busy and important future as well as a furnished home and $500 a year for twenty years. He spoke, too, of each chief's prowess. The flattery here is laid on rather thickly. Tomorrow, concluded the Governor, the treaty would be made.

An intriguing entry went into the Landsdale diary for this second day. "It is evident there are two parties among these people; though all are Catholics and religious, however, many of them do not like the strictness of the fathers" at the mission. As a result, the Flatheads "want a reservation" in the Bitterroot, while "the other party want the common reservation to include the Mission." [95] This comment tells several things. First, it took the Whites two days to become really aware there were two opposed parties, a Pend d'Oreille–Kutenai and a Flathead. Secondly, the Whites ascribed this to a pro- and anti-mission feeling. It is just possible that these were secondary motivations for the two parties. But circumstances indicate that such an opposition reflects only the subjective conviction of Governor Stevens.

The official report cannot disguise the clumsiness of the Governor as a negotiator nor his insensitivity to the Indians' rights. He betrays a patronizing impatience for this lesser race whose problems intruded upon his policies and career. Stevens was particularly ill-served by his lack of sympathy for the realities of the religious situation, dominated as he was by a kind of cheerful secularism. Eventually he realized that these qualities were not advancing his cause. He then attempted to reassure the Indians. "You will have your priest with you, whether you go to the mission or Fort Owen; and here I would say those who want the priest can have him. The Great Father means that each one shall do as he pleases in reference to receiving the instructions of the priest." As concessions go, it was not much. It was at this time that Stevens again sent for Father Hoecken. The priest meanwhile had kept "a horse in

95. Smaller Diary, 10 July.

readiness for two nights" at the mission, hoping to leave as soon as the cholera allowed.[96]

The Wednesday afternoon convocation was the longest yet, lasting four and a half hours. Again the weather was hot.[97] Since Victor clung to his valley, Stevens reversed himself and exerted every effort to persuade Alexander to join the Flathead chief in the Bitterroot. He elaborated upon its advantages, as he had done the day before for the Mission Valley. But Alexander held fast to his own land. The priest was there, the berries and roots were there, it was the only place large enough. Through all the chief's arguments runs a stubborn determination not to leave his homeland and somehow to find reasons for this course which could sway the White man. In debater fashion Stevens badgered the chief, denying his arguments, alleging the superiority of White knowledge.

When the Pend d'Oreille chief evaded the Governor's attacks, Stevens turned to the Kutenai chief. As yet there had been almost no contribution from the Kutenais. An illuminating answer now came from Head Chief Michael: the other three tribes of the region spoke one language; the Kutenais were another people. The Kutenais were only here to observe, and "that is why I don't talk." Again Stevens manipulated the answer. He proclaimed that the Kutenai chief was ready to "stand by whatever" the Flathead and Pend d'Oreille chiefs agreed on. (Later the Kutenais refused to attend the Blackfoot Council, and the Governor again had it written into the records that Chief Michael was willing to let Victor and Alexander speak for him!)[98]

During an informal two-hour recess the Governor argued with Victor and Alexander. Alexander agreed to accept Stevens' favored spot, the Bitterroot Valley, only if the importunate Governor "would say he could not go to heaven at his own place." Stevens ignored the irony and took refuge in piety, admonishing the chiefs that they would go to heaven "if you do right." He returned to this theme when dismissing the Indians for the day. After delivering again the ultimatum of two choices, he referred to Alexander's desire to go to heaven, reproachfully asking, "can he and Victor live together in the next world if they cannot in this?" Then "in the name of God, live together here." In subsequent sessions it is a relief to find Stevens abandoning devout irrelevancies.

Clearly an impasse had been reached. With singular lack of common sense the Governor ascribed the result of his labors to the adverse influence of the Jesuits. "It being obvious that no progress would be made by continuing the council today, and that an influence was being exerted by the mission which might be adverse to the views of the government," he adjourned the council

96. Flathead Council "Official Proceedings"; Hoecken Diary (last quot.).
97. Smaller Lansdale Diary, 11 July.
98. Blackfoot Council "Official Proceedings," p. 48 bis.

until Friday and dispatched a messenger yet again for Father Hoecken. This time he sent "a formal command" to the priest. Whatever its legality, the command left no room for refusal. Did Stevens simply wish the priest to remove any obstacle he might have been intruding? Or did he want a great deal more, namely that Hoecken use his priestly influence in the promotion of Stevens' reservation plan? Hoecken suspected the latter. Support for his suspicion appears in the diary of Landsdale, whose entry observes that the tribes were "divided," and that the Governor could not make them "consent to one reservation." "And so," he adds, "he has sent for the father to try what he can do." [99] During the intervening recess, the Indians were given a feast and encouraged to hold discussions among themselves.

A recent historian suggests that many of Victor's tribe "were still hostile to the mission and might refuse to follow him if he agreed to move to a reservation near St. Ignatius." [1] There is no evidence for the premise. The conclusion may be true, though the speech of the Flathead chief Red Wolf at the council rather argues against it. Red Wolf believed that "if Victor goes there, though his people will not like to follow him, he cannot take it back and his people will have to go." This may or may not have been so. A number of Flatheads had already abandoned their home to live at St. Ignatius. Most of them would be hostile to such a movement for the same reason that they were hostile to the Governor's plans—not because of the mission, but because they could not bear to leave their land.

Friday was another hot day. "The father arrived this a.m.," Lansdale jotted in his diary. In place of council sessions "there is much consultation with the priest and others" on the subject of reservations. On the last day of the council Stevens wrote to the commissioner of Indian Affairs: "I carefully explained the whole matter to Father Hoecken, the Jesuit Missionary, whose presence I had required at the Treaty Ground, and whose influence over these Indians is almost unbounded." The Governor's change of heart after his talk with Hoecken is evident in his further statement to the commissioner. "Father Hoecken has labored faithfully among the Indian tribes for the last ten years, and has gained his influence by energy, devotion and the natural ascendancy of a patient and indomitable will." Is Stevens projecting something of himself here? The Governor adds that "he has promised to interpose no obstacle whatever to the views of the government, and I have confidence in his singleness of purpose." [2]

Father Hoecken's absence had undoubtedly annoyed Stevens as much as

99. Flathead Council "Official Proceedings"; Hoecken Diary (command); Smaller Lansdale Diary, 11 June.

1. Ewers, *Sohon's Portraits*, p. 31; cf. p. 48.

2. Smaller Lansdale Diary, 12 July; Flathead Council "Official Proceedings"; NA, IA, Negots. Rat. Treaties, Stevens to Manypenny, 16 July.

Stevens' absence had annoyed Hoecken on July 5. Stevens was to labor under
the delusion that Hoecken now "highly approved the treaty," an impression
belied by the Jesuit's writings.[3] Apparently the Governor characteristically assumed that Hoecken, since he was not working against Stevens,
must be on his side. But Hoecken's personal views were against any return to
the dangerous Bitterroot Valley. On yet another count he was not a disinterested spectator, because any move from Pend d'Oreille territory would be
"the end of St. Ignatius mission" and would mean painful new beginnings.
Nor did Jesuit thinking at this time run to bringing the Flatheads north en
masse. But all of this was a civil affair, out of Hoecken's hands. As he confided six months later to his superior in California: "I do not understand why
he summoned me; the treaty was none of my affair."[4] There is no evidence that the priest consciously used any influence on this point with the
Pend d'Oreilles or Flatheads. He seems to have stayed carefully neutral up to
the signing of the treaty.

Throughout the council Stevens spoke too self-confidently, too bluntly to
the chiefs. The Jesuit missionaries could have informed him that the Flatheads and Pend d'Oreilles, unlike the Kettles or Coeur d'Alenes, were of
"haughty character" and had "to be treated with gentleness"; hence "one
gains nothing by being brusque."[5]

The situation from now on deteriorated. Diplomatic smiles on both sides of
the council fire were slipping. Tempers flared during the Friday assembly.
The talks lengthened, this time to five hours. Stevens began the discussion by
congratulating the chiefs upon having almost reached agreement. Actually
the situation was exactly as it had been: the Pend d'Oreilles and Kutenais
holding fast for their upper country, the Flatheads for their lower region.

Stevens forged ahead, repeating his promises of money, houses, farms, and an
agent. "Are you ready to sign the treaty?" One is reminded of the complaint
of a Spokane chief to Stevens a few months later concerning the Walla Walla
Council: "you alone arranged the Indian's land; the Indians did not speak";
and again: "they who owned the land did not speak, and yet you divided
their land." On that same occasion Stevens' friend, Chief Garry, reproached
him for dealing with the Indians as inferiors: "since we have been speaking, it
is as if we had been talking for nothing." Garry urged the Governor: "if you
take those Indians for men, treat them so now; the Indians are proud, they are
not poor."[6]

Alexander was in no mood to be hurried into a treaty. He accused Stevens

3. H. Stevens, *Stevens*, 2, 85, 90.
4. Hoecken Diary.
5. *JMUS*, 2, 385.
6. Flathead Council "Official Proceedings"; Journal, pp. 67–68.

of concealing the small size of the proposed reservation on his lands. The chief had believed, or affected now to believe, that if the four tribes came to his upper country, the larger part of that region would remain as a reservation. "You never showed me the limits," Alexander protested. "When you first talked, you talked good, now you talk sharp, you talk like a Blackfoot." Assuming Alexander was speaking honestly, it is clear why the Kutenais held their peace during the council; the upper area thus conceived would have included enough of their own land. Further light on the Kutenai attitude came from a later speech by Alexander; Chief Michael had told him that if the Pend d'Oreilles moved down to join the Flatheads, "I won't go." Alexander observed that he, too, was tied to his own land.

Stevens taxed Alexander with contradicting himself. He emphasized also the temporary rights of pasture retained by the Indians on the lands to be taken by the government. "I am ashamed of you Alexander," the Governor chided; "talk straight and then we will agree." Perhaps neither chief nor governor fully understood the other. This painful dialogue continued for a while, each staying with his own theme. Stevens was speaking now as though the rejection of the Bitterroot Valley were already agreed upon, and that only the size of the more northerly reserve remained in question. Suddenly Victor interjected plaintively: "where is my country; I want to speak." Stevens tried to silence him: "when I call upon you to sign the treaty, you can make your objections." Then the Governor tactlessly brushed Victor aside: Alexander had agreed, and he was now speaking with Alexander. Little progress was made beyond this point.

The Governor managed to alienate Head Chief Victor, calling him "an old woman and a dog." Hoecken writes that the whole council was a "comedy" but that this last episode was a "tragedy." [7] Victor withdrew to his tent. The official transcript misses this drama. Stevens construed the chief's departure as a need for private meditation: "Victor is now thinking and studying over this matter." During the Friday session Chief Ambrose or Five Crows had taken a lively part, perhaps hoping to extricate his chief from the pressures of the discussion. The official record, despite Stevens' attempts to turn the phrases to his advantage and despite the obscurity of transcription, strongly suggests this. Ambrose was a very important chief, and in 1868 was to succeed Moses as aide to the head chief. He was a courageous warrior, holding top-honors coup from the Blackfoot wars.

The Governor's position at the end of this session was: "it seems that many of the Flatheads are ready to go to the mission" if their chief says so. Lansdale's diary laconically sums up the day: "no agreement."

7. Hoecken Diary; cf. Flathead Council "Official Proceedings."

THE FLATHEADS SIGN A TREATY

Victor refused to appear on Saturday, and no session took place. Alexander sent word to Victor that he could be head chief of the whole confederacy if he would consent to move north. The weather, too, offered some relief, the day being "very windy." In an optimistic mood Lansdale records that "all agreed to go to a reservation including the mission, except Victor of the Flatheads, who has held back till today, but who has at last agreed to go there also." [8] The events of the final session do not seem to bear out that happy impression.

The last conference, held on Monday, July 16, was lengthier than all its predecessors, an uncomfortable six hours. Neither Alexander nor Victor would hear of moving. Insofar as the transcript of proceedings is a reliable guide on such points, it would seem that Thursday's private conferences between the chiefs had produced some small result. Alexander admits he had offered to come to Victor's valley, but Victor had refused. Victor himself may have wavered in his reluctance to leaving his lands. And a group of Flatheads seems to have inclined toward going to the Pend d'Oreille valley. But these were probably mere momentary positions, diplomatic maneuvers designed for effect. As Red Wolf put it: "I know that if Alexander should come" to the Bitterroot, "his people would not follow him." Alexander may possibly have been magnanimous in offering to bring his tribe south, and later in offering the title of head chief of the confederacy should Victor go north. On the other hand, Victor and his people had previously given Alexander solid evidence that they did not mean to give in on either point. Alexander's generosity then seems a stratagem to throw the burden of decision upon Victor. Victor was to think a long time before emerging with a satisfactory counterploy. In any case, both chiefs were now intransigent and their head men with them.

Stevens steered a skillful course through the opposition, grasping at polite or conventional or deprecatory forms of speech in order to make it seem that an agreement was only inches away. His arguments took a peculiarly infelicitous turn when he held up as good examples the Yakima Chiefs Kamiakin and Owhi (who had just signed at Walla Walla to gain time for war). But the Flathead council had failed. There was not even to be a pretense of signing. Nothing was left for Stevens except to strike his tents, load his pack animals, and be off with what grace he could muster. It was at this point of desperation that Victor made an ambiguous and fatal remark. Let the Great Father come from Washington to see for himself whether the Bitterroot wasn't the better site. He would abide by the personal decision of the president. Thus "the treaty was only saved," Stevens' son recalls, "by Governor Stevens' per-

8. Smaller Diary, 14 July.

sistence and astuteness in accepting an alternative proposition offered by Victor at the last moment." [9]

Both Stevens and Hoecken understood Victor to have made a genuine compromise offer to submit the problem to higher authority in Washington. That Victor meant it differently, as a plaintive invitation to the president to see for himself how unreasonable Stevens was being, is indicated by the subsequent claims and attitude of the Flatheads. The tribe remained thoroughly, consistently convinced that this very proposal by Victor had cleverly guaranteed to them in writing the Bitterroot Valley. Stevens had therefore made a treaty hinging entirely on a compromise that was ambiguous at best. Moreover, the compromise was explicitly rejected by the other head chiefs.

The Pend d'Oreille and Kutenai peoples were assured a reservation in the Mission Valley. In a letter to the Indian commissioner on the same day, Stevens remarked that if the upper valley were chosen no further difficulties could ensue, since the two recusant chiefs would have no problem, while Victor would be bound by his promise to move. But if the Bitterroot were chosen, he pointed out, the treaty would need to be renegotiated.[10] Some months afterward, Stevens assured Father Ravalli "that St. Ignatius mission is on the reservation." [11] Joset reported the decision to Rome early in August.

There was to be no presidential survey. Stevens would merely have a member of his party examine the two sites. Then he was to recommend the upper valley to the Indian commissioner, thus effectively incorporating it into the annual recommendations. An administrative dodge thus solved the Governor's problem. Did Stevens prejudge the choice of valleys for the Flatheads? Such an action does not fit the character of either Stevens or the man he chose eventually to conduct his "presidential" survey. Stevens' limitations and flaws did not include conscious underhandedness. Lansdale's diary for the last day of the council indicates Stevens' thinking clearly enough. "The reservation includes [the] Catholic Mission, and perhaps there will be a 2d reservation at" the Bitterroot Valley.[12]

Stevens hastily accepted Victor's conditions. Eighteen chiefs and headmen from the three tribes each put his mark on the revised document. The coming war was to delay congressional ratification for almost four years. Father Hoecken signed the treaty as a witness, his signature appearing sixth below the Governor's. One of the three official drafts was given to Victor, and was later deposited with the Jesuits.[13] Gifts for the Indians were now produced.

9. H. Stevens, *Stevens*, 2, 80.

10. NA, IA, Negots. Rat. Treaties, Stevens to Manypenny, 16 July.

11. Hoecken Diary. RJ, MSax., II, 1: "retinent ea loca quae circa Missionem sunt."

12. Smaller Diary, 16 July.

13. NA, IA Negots. Rat. Treaties. The ambiguous Article XI is added below Article XII (old XI with an extra stroke) in the space remaining. Victor's copy is in OJ; there

They seem to have been purchased through Owen's trading post and not to have been very impressive. There is no record of a goods wagon having been brought, as was done at the more accessible Walla Walla and Spokane council grounds. Owen's ledgers show an entry of $172.50 for ammunition, flints, and the like, paid for by the Indian Bureau, without indicating whether these are gifts or expenses of the treaty party.[14]

Before the gifts were distributed and the council formally closed, the powerful Flathead subchief Moses or Bravest of the Brave contributed a pathetic and significant speech. Moses was second in the Flathead political hierarchy. He had remained a fervent Catholic even in the depth of the troubles, and now had a farm at St. Ignatius mission in the upper valley, as did Chief Insula and others. Like the other Flatheads, however, he still considered the Bitterroot his home and would continue to hunt on the Great Plains. He was "distinguished by his superior skill in horsemanship," had made himself an adopted Indian brother of Father De Smet, and was the "handsomest Indian warrior" of De Smet's long experience in the West.[15] He refused to sign the treaty.

"My brother is buried there," he told the assemblage of Indians and Whites. "I did not think you would take the only piece of ground I had." He indicated his unhappiness over Stevens' deliberate policy of exaggerating the power of the head chiefs: "here are three fellows, they say get on your horse and go." He protested, too, against the sweeping scale of land confiscation: "if you would give us a large place I would not talk foolish; if I go in your country and say give me this, will you give it to me?" The Indians wanted only what was theirs; "they have only one piece of ground." The Governor had presented himself to them under false colors during his explorations, as their protector against the Blackfeet. "Last year when you were talking about the Blackfeet you were joking"; the problem of the Blackfeet was really "the reason we all came together" to this council. Sadly he accused the Governor: "you have pulled all my wings off." Stevens challenged him, and a sharp interchange ensued. Moses was told he could indeed go into the Whites' country and take White land, "as much as you choose to buy." The chief subsided, with a noncommittal "now I understand." The record

is also an original of President Buchanan's ratified version, but without the Jesuit's name. Has this circumstance any significance? The published version in NA, IA, retains his name, but with "Sp" for "S.J." Ratified on 8 March and proclaimed on 18 April 1859, it appeared as *Senate Doc.*, 58 Cong., 2 sess., No. 319, serial 4624, and is in C. J. Kappler, ed., *Indian Affairs, Laws and Treaties*, 2 (5 vols. Washington, D.C., 1904–41), 722–25.

14. G. F. Weisel, ed., *Men and Trade on the Northwest Frontier, as Shown by the Fort Owen Ledger*, Montana State Univ. Studies, No. 2 (Missoula, 1955), p. 108.

15. CR, *1*, 305; *2*, 472, 576, 766; *4*, 1225, 1240. RR, *1*, ii, 325.

therefore put him down as adhering "to the treaty though still refusing to sign." [16] His name was added to the published document!

A final comment on the failure of the council was to come from the Kutenais. During the various sessions Head Chief Michael had said little, and most of that negative. His anger at Stevens and the Americans because of this treaty was to grow until he took his band bodily across the border into Canada where their descendants today are the Windermere band.

Father Hoecken returned to his mission that same Monday, anxious to begin the construction of a barn. Though he must have offered Mass each morning of his stay at the council, the previous Sunday services probably were particularly impressive. In the coast treaty with Chief Seattle, just before the signing, "the Indians sung a Mass after the Roman Catholic form and recited a prayer." [17] The Flathead confederates may have done the same this Monday morning. Before Father Hoecken left the council ground, the Governor in an aside to him made his final contribution to the council. "Father, your influence with the Indians is very strong; it is on account of you that the savages cling to their lands." He was referring to the Pend d'Oreilles and Kutenais, who "do not want to come onto the Flathead reservation." [18]

From the council grounds the Governor wrote to Fathers Ravalli and Gazzoli at the Coeur d'Alene mission: "we have been favored with the presence of Father Ho[e]cken." At the same time he reported his success to the Indian commissioner. Though "the Fathers at the mission show the most excellent disposition" and simply want whatever will help the Indians most, there had been many difficulties at the council "in consequence of the dislike of the Flatheads to Mission establishments." At the end of the century Hazard Stevens was to paraphrase this statement in the standard life of his father, thus giving the prejudice wide circulation.[19]

The obsession with Jesuit intrigue, or at least with their neutralizing influence, continued to haunt Stevens. Almost four months later, distracted by news of war all about him and with his life in danger, Stevens spared the time to write to Agent Lansdale to beware of Head Chief Alexander, "a man of grasping and overbearing disposition" who would use "every exertion to secure unusual and improper concessions to the injury of the Flatheads." Stevens declared that he feared "the Missionary fathers will use an active influence in his behalf, as it is also to be feared they will in regard to all their especial retainers." [20]

16. Flathead Council "Official Proceedings."

17. H. Stevens, *Stevens*, 2, 465.

18. Hoecken Diary.

19. NA, IA, Wash. Sup., LR, to Ravalli-Gazzoli, 17 July. LR (from Wash. Sup.), 16 July. Partoll, *PNWQ*, 29, 312–14. H. Stevens, *Stevens*, 2, 90.

20. NA, IA, Wash. Sup., LR, 10 November.

Had it not been for these preconceptions, Stevens might have made use of Father Hoecken's experience and skill. "You love your priests," the Governor had told Alexander; "that is why you won't give in." Understandably vexed, the chief had spelled out the basic source of disagreement and sought to disabuse Stevens of his *idée fixe:* "I love my lands, I do not love the Fathers." [21] Hoecken could have told the Governor the same thing, had his advice been asked. When the Jesuits previously had made efforts to move the Pend d'Oreilles to the Coeur d'Alene region or to the Camas and Horse Plains, the Indians had steadfastly refused. "This is our country," they had replied. "Here we were born, and here are the graves of our forefathers; we do not want to leave." Stevens had incorporated this incident into his own report of 1853; he should have pursued the topic more closely. Even after the Kalispels had settled permanently at the new St. Ignatius, they kept their lands at the older mission. The Flatheads at the new mission did the same. Alexander also stressed this point in telling Stevens: "years ago when the priests were at [the Flathead] St. Mary's, I lived on my own [Pend d'Oreille] lands." [22]

Stevens should likewise have informed himself more accurately as to the limited extent of power accorded to chiefs in the political hierarchy of the Flatheads. He neglected to address himself to the really influential warriors when they were not chiefs. Thus Iroquois Peter, who was noncommittal in council, had privately swayed the northern group strongly against the location chosen by Adams.[23] But even a chief as great as Michael Insula or Red Feather was not mentioned in the transcript. De Smet considered him the most influential of the Flathead chiefs. A battle-scarred veteran, he had refused the Nez Percé tribe's invitation to become their head chief. He was surely at the council (he had his portrait done by Sohon in 1854).

The same may be said of Fidelis or Thunder, one of the bravest. Then there was Chief Palchina, a man of sound common sense, who held high war honors, and whose brother had been killed while on the third Flathead delegation to St. Louis seeking Blackrobes. Similar figures silent at the council were the minor Flathead chief Michael, a friend of the Jesuits, later to become head chief; and Adolph or Red Feather, an outstanding Catholic and war chief of high rank, who for decades to come was to be one of the two intransigent leaders of the Flatheads opposed to moving from the Bitterroot.

Though an undercurrent of antagonism toward the mission had run through the negotiations, Hoecken could say that religion was never dis-

21. Hoecken Diary.
22. Ibid.; CR, *4,* 1241 (graves). Suckley, Journal (SI), 8 November; cf. *RR, 1,* ii, 298; *RCIA* (1854), p. 421.
23. Hoecken Diary.

cussed "by either side." [24] This was true enough, inasmuch as Stevens had deliberately segregated all moral, religious, and socioreligious considerations from the problem of land transfer. The shape of the Governor's mind was such, however, that he could only explain the rejection of his program by referring to religion. But Hoecken is unfair to Stevens in telling Joset: "one can easily see and understand that he is not a friend of the Catholics." The Governor's passions and bias took no particular religious direction. The one thing he seemed to require from Hoecken was impossible—"that I should side with him" in persuading the Pend d'Oreilles to come to the Bitterroot. "It would have been against my conscience." The Jesuit believed the Bitterroot at present "was suitable neither to the Flatheads and certainly not" to the Pend d'Oreilles.[25]

Was there any possibility that individual chiefs had asked Hoecken outright, as a matter of conscience, concerning their duty, and had thus been influenced by the priest? There is no way of excluding such a possibility. Its very nature precludes documentation. Certainly the Indians relied for all kinds of advice on Father Hoecken. For example, when Stevens first appeared in 1853, sending Mullan to announce the news of a possible peace treaty with the Blackfeet, Head Chief Alexander of the Pend d'Oreilles advised the Flathead chiefs to go to the mission, "see the Father, listen to what he has to say, and return and tell me." [26] Still, the Indians told Stevens this themselves and quite openly, whereas in the case of the reservation they denied it. Had the priest been so consulted, as a good confessor he ought at most to have expounded the principles involved but ultimately have left freedom of application. As a consultant or adviser, of course, he could be as specific as he wished. The question therefore has no easy a priori answer. The priest's own reactions, even to his fellow Jesuits in his letters, make it reasonably clear that he did not consciously use his influence. The whole tone of his diary casts him in the role of observer of a free contest. If Stevens detected a *sub rosa* opposition, it may well have had its origin in the guests he unwisely imported from the Walla Walla Council.

Even in the simple matter of interpreting for either side, the priest's skill could have been invaluable. Indeed, Hoecken considered incompetent translating to have been the deciding factor in the failure of the council. It precluded all chance of approaching an agreement by negotiation. Stevens had appointed two loyal men for the job. One was the German immigrant Sohon, a man particularly ill qualified. While a soldier with the 1853 exploration parties, Sohon had compiled little word lists and the like. At Walla Walla in

24. Ibid.
25. Ibid.
26. *RR, 12,* i, 125.

1855 he had interpreted for the Salish-speaking Spokane observers, and presumably for the Flathead and Kettle observers as well. In selecting him, Stevens had in effect put an international conference into the hands of a tourist. Sohon sensibly seems to have refrained from serious participation, and Hoecken does not mention his work.

The burden of translating fell upon Benjamin Kiser, a half-breed Shawnee living with the Flatheads. Kiser had worked for the trader Owen in 1851 and served as guide to Lieutenant Mullan in the 1853 exploration. He interpreted for both the Flathead and Blackfoot councils and later became a trader and rancher in western Montana. Kiser was a poor linguist, though he had the kind of working knowledge of Flathead that serves to keep foreigners afloat in an alien environment. Hoecken wrote to Joset just after the council that Kiser "speaks Flathead very badly and is no better at translating into English." Neither side was ever quite sure of the other's drift. "Not a tenth" of the negotiations "was actually understood by either party." [27] The Indians understood enough to alarm them, the Governor enough to irritate him. Each side supposed it had outwitted the other.

No hint of this ineptitude appears in subsequent historical discussion of the council.[28] Yet Hoecken did not make his statement lightly. He was a close and experienced observer, and had worked for over a decade among the Flathead confederates alone. There is no question of an attempt on his part to invalidate the final act of the council, since Hoecken, like Stevens, took Victor's proposal of a presidential survey at its face value. Nevertheless, because of the problems in interpretation, Hoecken does see the whole course of negotiation and the treaty itself as dubious. Even today one must use every clue as a guide to the real intent of the key speeches.

Once this question has been opened, it appears decidedly odd that Stevens appointed interpreters so incompetent as Sohon and so unprofessional as Kiser. An explanation may be found in Doty's complaint to Stevens in 1853 that "good interpreters for the government are very difficult to procure," because the available interpreters were hired by traders at higher wages than the government could afford. Suspicion that Stevens had trouble with his interpreters during the treaties also arises from the caution issued some thirty years later to the governor of Washington by A. J. Cain with regard to Indian trouble in the Interior. Cain had been secretary to Stevens and had served as Indian agent for the lower Interior. Later he was prominent as

27. Hoecken Diary. The Doty Journal lists Sohon officially as both "Interpreter and Artist" (p. 25). The Flathead treaty carries his signature as "Flathead Interpreter," but not Kiser's.

28. Partoll does question the "translation or recording" of some of Big Canoe's speech (*PNWQ*, *29*, 291 n.).

prosecuting attorney for the Walla Walla district and as the founder of three pioneer newspapers. He was not present at the Flathead Council itself. Remarking that his experience in handling Indians dated back to his days as aide to Stevens in the Interior in 1855, he warned that "many unfortunate and serious mistakes occur in dealing with Indians, from improper interpreting." He advises "great care in this respect." [29]

It is possible that the Jesuits, perhaps Stevens' friend Father Ravalli, also raised this difficulty just a month after the Flathead Council, at the next council among neighboring Salish Indians. Doty's journal will then reflect a concern about interpretation. William Peon acted "as Interpreter, and others [including Fathers Joset and Ravalli] were present who understood well the Salish language, and were requested to observe that the speeches on either side were correctly reported; this will be the mode of proceeding with all the 'talks' with these Indians."

An echo of the problem seems to sound in the pages of Stevens' later published report on his 1855 trip. Introducing his interpreter Kiser to his readers, Stevens uncompromisingly declares (a propos of nothing in particular in the context) that the Shawnee spoke English "quite well" and was "exceedingly reliable" as an interpreter.[30] But the problem recurs in subsequent Kutenai negotiations. Here the Flathead interpreter Michael Revais was "far from bilingual in Salishan and Kutenaian"; as a result "he led the chiefs to subscribe to treaties whose texts neither they nor Revais understood." [31]

The official transcript of the Flathead Council therefore must be read with a sharp eye. Certainly it omits a great deal, perhaps the most essential, of what the various Indians had to say. Its disjointed nature may have been even more incoherent in the original notes, with Doty reorganizing them as intelligibly as circumstances allowed. Doty, the son of a former governor of Wisconsin, deserved a better task. In the war that followed, he was to be rewarded with the inflated militia title of lieutenant colonel. But he would soon be curtly "dismissed from the public service" by an outraged Governor Stevens for being ingloriously drunk for four consecutive days. Some months later he put a bullet in his head.[32]

As far as Stevens was concerned, the council had terminated "successfully and happily," with "every man pleased and every man satisfied." The grate-

29. WS, Cain to Ferry, 29 July 1877. Doty, in *RR, 1*, ii, 442.

30 Doty, Journal, pp. 44–45. *RR, 12*, i, 221.

31. P. E. Baker, *The Forgotten Kutenai, a Study of the Kutenai Indians, Bonner's Ferry, Idaho, Creston, British Columbia, Canada, and Other Areas Where the Kutenai Are Located* (Boise, Idaho, 1955), p. 17.

32. V. F. Field, ed., *The Official History of the Washington National Guard, 2* (mimeographed collection, 4 vols. to date, Camp Murray, 1961 et seq.), 67; MD, Stevens to Doty, 8 March 1856.

ful savage had welcomed a treaty "remarkably liberal in its terms to the Indians." To one of his special agents at Olympia Stevens wrote from the council grounds that "we are succeeding grandly with our Indian business thus far," and have just "made a treaty yesterday with the Flatheads, Kootenays, and Upper Pend d'Oreilles numbering some 1,400 souls." [33] In this lyrical frame of mind the Governor broke camp on Wednesday, July 18. A Pend d'Oreille guide supplied by Chief Alexander conveyed the little party on their leisurely five-day trip to Fort Benton on the Plains.

THE WHITE MAN BREAKS HIS WORD

The Jesuit contribution to the Flathead Council may seem at first to have been incidental and negative. But Hoecken's refusal to commend the Governor's plans to the Indians and to betray their interests, was a positive action with far-reaching effects. On the part of the Indians in turn, it was no small thing to feel that the whole world was not against them, and that they had in their camp a White man of integrity and influence whom they could trust as a father. It would be to Hoecken that they would go when the council was over, to unburden themselves of the complaints and arguments to which the American officials had not cared to listen.

Neither the Indians nor Father Hoecken believed a definitive treaty had been made: it had included a protest to higher authority. "None of the Indians would hear of selling their lands." [34] Yet all knew that an ultimatum had been delivered. Even if a portion of each tribal homeland could be saved, the bulk of confederate land was now at the disposition of the White government. This explains the paradox of rejecting the treaty while expecting the government to keep some of its promises of compensatory payment. In the event, Hoecken complains, the Whites paid "not a farthing." [35]

Some trivia did arrive. An agent appointed to the Flatheads in 1863 because of their increasing hostility toward the government was to inform his superiors that articles totaling $24,000 had been sent. Most of them were "unfit" for Indian needs and many of them were "frivolous." Of this material, the tribes had actually received perhaps half. The trader Owen, serving *faute de mieux* as agent since the departure of Lansdale, had taken the rest and sold it to himself under the guise of reimbursement for freight charges.[36] Owen had given nothing to the Kutenais and almost nothing to the Pend d'Oreilles or to the Flatheads living at the mission. It is hard to blame him. He had heavy expenses and precious little income. Some of the government gifts are

33. Stevens Collection (WU), to Col. M. T. Simmons, 17 July 1855. H. Stevens, *Stevens*, 2, 89–90; cf. *RR, 1*, ii, 209.
34. Hoecken Diary.
35. CR, *4*, 1245–46, Hoecken to De Smet, 15 April 1857.
36. *RCIA* (1863), pp. 452–53.

recorded in his store ledger. But one detects slyness in the fact that most of the available supplies had gone to his neighbors and customers, the smaller group of Flatheads in the lower valley.

An examination of Owen's ledgers does not help much. It is difficult to distinguish purchases made by Indians in the beaver and buffalo trade from gifts or annuities; there is the problem of entries representing Indian Bureau allowances to Owen for expenses or salary. Owen did list items such as $266 in sundries to the Flathead tribe for 1859–60, and $500 to Lansdale's account in 1856. These are inconsequential trifles. The annual cost of running the Flathead agency at this date should have come to a minimum of $5,600. Meat purchased with goods from Indian hunters would alone come to $500, while provisions and gifts for hospitality to visiting Indians would reach $1,000. This is merely support for maintaining an agent and his establishment. Beyond this there were the annuities and promises of the treaty. When Owen took over from Lansdale, he found neither annuities nor even the necessary agency funds.[37]

"Substantially," the 1863 agent affirmed, "all that was stipulated by the Stevens treaty of 1855 is yet unfulfilled." Consequently, the nontreaty tribes like the Coeur d'Alenes, Kettles, Kalispels, and Spokanes "sneer" at the Flatheads. They "twittingly" invite them "to show their farms and agricultural implements, clothing, schools, and other fine promises made by Governor Stevens." "These things," the new agent cautioned, "are heartfelt with these Indians." Singularly enough, the agency itself continued to expand busily, and a respectable amount of money was acquired from the national government just to prop up its existence. The first agent, Landsdale, hired no fewer than eleven helpers, including a cook, two herders, and (at $500 a year) an interpreter. Owen soon secured the appointment of an auxiliary subagent for the Kutenais and Pend d'Oreilles at $1,000 a year.[38]

The authorities were to suggest that the Jesuits themselves undertake treaty obligations. The normal routine of the mission forestalled the request. The missioners had continued to bring in agricultural implements and raise buildings. Father Hoecken began his new barn immediately upon his return from the council, and was planning a better church. Nine months after the Hell Gate assembly, he could write proudly to De Smet that "here in our missions we already observe all the conditions stipulated in the treaty concluded last year by Governor Stevens." [39]

37. Weisel, *Fort Owen Ledger,* pp. 108–09, 112, 210. Detailed estimates for a Flathead agency, made for Stevens by Mullan in 1854, are in *RR, 1,* ii, 440–41.

38. *RCIA,* 1863 report. Weisel, pp. 140, 111.

39. CR, *4,* 1245 (15 April 1857). Palladino, *Indian and White,* p. 73. On 10 October 1864 a lack of funds ended a plan by which Father Grassi was to be the teacher promised by the treaty (Agent Hutchins to U. Grassi, S.J., MHS).

In his letter he cites examples: "Our brothers assist the Indians and teach them how to cultivate the ground; they distribute the fields and the seeds for sowing and planting, as well as the plows and other agricultural instruments." Then again, "our blacksmith works for them, he repairs their guns, their axes, their knives; the carpenter renders them great assistance in constructing their houses." For grinding their grain "our little mill is daily in use." For the welfare of the Indians "all we have and all we are" was available. "The savings that our religious economy enables us to make," Hoecken adds, "is theirs."

It was in this same letter that Hoecken proposed an idea for a reservation which he felt to be more feasible and magnanimous than the government's. "Were I authorized to suggest a plan," he said, "I would propose to have all the upper lands evacuated by the whites." At this time the latter amounted only to transient gold miners and a negligible scattering of settlers. Hoecken would then "form of it a territory exclusively of Indians." He would "lead there all the Indians" living to the south and west, "such as the Nez Percés, the Cayuses, the Yakimas, the Coeur d'Alènes, and the Spokanes." This was choice country, of vast extent, and fairly remote from White intrusion.

Could the southern tribes be persuaded to make such a transfer? One has doubts. But perhaps it would have had some appeal to the more southerly tribes if presented as an alternative to the government's harsh confiscation. Hoecken, who had some experience with that problem, was inclined to believe "that this plan, with such superior advantages, might be effected by means of missions in the space of two or three years." Hoecken may have been far too sanguine in his judgment. He was also obviously influenced by the present location of the Jesuit missions. Still, the principle involved was more just and effective than Stevens' own.

Hoecken and his colleagues continued to give the Indians of the mission network something to live for. A dozen years after the treaty, another Flathead agent reported very much along the lines of his predecessor how the Jesuits, "poor and unaided," had developed their Reduction, established their "church and school, and maintained themselves solely by their own exertion." With help from the Sisters of Charity they "educate, clothe and feed the orphans of these tribes without fee or reward." They "have been at the same time, priest, physician, and benefactor to these tribes." He declared that "without their aid and influence, the wrongs inflicted upon these people would long ago have driven them to war." Thus, though the missioners had several times helped Stevens during his treaty tour, their substantial contribution to the cause of peace was to come after the council fires had been scattered and the White men had gone home.[40]

40. CR, 4, 1245; Agent M. McCauley, *RCIA* (1869), p. 294.

4. War on the Empty Plains

THE BLACKFOOT PEACE TREATY

THE BLACKFOOT COUNCIL on the Great Plains was to be an affair of some magnitude, directly affecting at least sixteen thousand Indians of many tribes. It was a peace treaty, not a land treaty. It achieved its purpose, nevertheless, precisely by dividing and limiting the great hunting ranges. The Blackfoot "nation"—Bloods, Piegans, Blackfeet, and allied Gros Ventres—were implacably bloodthirsty. Their wars with the mountain Indians and other neighbors were unrelenting. It was no accident that the Oregon Trail ran far to the south of them, or that they were the last of the Plains Indians with whom the government was able to negotiate a treaty.

The Blackfeet lay outside Governor Stevens' Indian jurisdiction; but the Blackfoot problem involved his own tribes. Stevens had devoted great effort to securing government sanction and funds, together with his own appointment to be one of the three commissioners, for a Blackfoot treaty. As long before as September 1853, during his railroad explorations, he had convoked a preliminary meeting with thirty chiefs from the three Blackfoot tribes. He then left Doty to explore and observe in their country for many months. Stevens had hoped to hold the great council in the summer of 1854. In early 1855 he was asking General Wool for an escort of troops for his Blackfoot Council scheduled in July. His eventual date of mid-August 1855 now had to be postponed until late October.

Commissioner Cumming, designated to share authority with Stevens in holding this council (Palmer of Oregon did not come), was only slowly making his way up the Missouri, treating with various tribes as he came. Keelboats bearing the treaty goods had been stalled by bad planning and low water on the Missouri. At the last moment the council site would have to be moved east, a hundred miles down the Missouri, just below the mouth of the Judith River. The preliminary task of contacting the many scattered tribes and making arrangements for the council itself was time-consuming. Even after the tribes were collected in the vicinity and alerted, it was "as though one in New York without telegraphs, railroads or mails, had to regulate by pony express the movements of bands of Indians at Boston, Portland, Montreal, Buffalo, and Washington." [1]

Needing food, the Flatheads spent their time hunting along the Judith River, taking Adams along. The Pend d'Oreilles hunted on Smith's Fork of the Missouri, the Nez Percés on the Yellowstone. The Blackfeet were getting in as much buffalo as possible, north of the Missouri. Meanwhile the Whites pursued their railroad observations as well as their interminable preparations for bringing together the various bands. The commissary officer, Crosbie, was off arranging for the November treaties at the Coeur d'Alene and Pend d'Oreille missions. Subagent Bolon was expected to come up to the Spokane River to help make preparations for the treaties with the Kettles, Spokanes, and Okanogans. [2]

Stevens commissioned Lansdale to survey the alternative Flathead reservations. Dr. Lansdale, a veteran of the Mexican War and the California gold rush, and then briefly a medical practitioner, spent the better part of September at this task. He first examined the Bitterroot Valley in the south because of its previous status as Stevens' provisional reservation. His diary records the condition of the former Reduction at St. Mary's—"the fields abandoned," everything wearing "the aspect of neglect and decay," yet with magnificent scenery "in the midst of God's everlasting hills." In his official report of October 2 he puts the only traces of civilization as "a small private trading post" under Owen's supervision, plus one field and one garden.

His examination of the upper or Mission Valley was similarly careful. Soil, timber, water, available building sites, and even beauty of landscape were seriously considered. Lansdale was struck by the attractions of the new "Mission, with its houses, and fields, and herds." He remained several days as the guest of Father Menetrey, conversing with the Jesuits. A devout Methodist, he spent Sunday largely "in reading the Bible and trying to pray and meditate." Menetrey's religious services for the Indians at morning, noon, and night were in Flathead, so Lansdale learned to avoid them. Eventually he became convinced that the Mission Valley had more advantages by far, the most important being the mission establishment "in successful operation" with its cultivated fields, houses, mill, shops, and homesteads. Then, too, a far larger number of Indians were involved with the progress of this upper valley.

1. Doty, Journal, and Stevens correspondence, passim, for Stevens' progress. Blackfoot Council "Official Proceedings," recorded by Doty; A. J. Partoll, ed., "The Blackfoot Indian Peace Council," *Frontier and Midland*, 17 (1937), 199–207. Cf. also *RR*, 12, i, chap. 12; H. Stevens, *Stevens*, 2, chap. 33 (p. 111 for quot.). There is background information for our chapter in A. McDonnell and J. B. Ritch, eds., "The Fort Benton Journal, 1854–1856," *CHSM*, 10 (1940), 1–99; and in J. Bradley, "Affairs at Fort Benton from 1831 to 1869 from Lieutenant Bradley's Journal," *CHSM*, 3 (1900), 201–87.

2. NA, IA, LR (from Wash. Sup.), Stevens to Manypenny, 30 August. Doty, Journal; *RR*, 12, i, 220–21.

Material reasons were not the only considerations. The mission afforded the only available instruction in arts, morals, and religion. "And however much a protestant people and government might desire another system of religious training," Lansdale advised Stevens, "yet it is the choice of those most immediately concerned, and they should not be arbitrarily deprived of its blessings." He concluded by recommending "that the provisional reservation be not confirmed," because "the only desirable home" for an Indian wanting some taste of agriculture was the Jesuit mission. Lansdale in fact would begin to erect agency buildings not far from the mission. Stevens' own recommendation to the Indian commissioner, he assured Lansdale, would follow these views.[3]

Lansdale may have made further arrangements with the Jesuits for the Kalispel Council. He almost certainly conveyed again Stevens' plea for supplies. Neither the treaty party nor Fort Benton had victuals sufficient to meet the unexpected delay on the Plains. Menetrey promised to send what farm supplies he could. A poor crop had left little to spare and the seed was promised away to all Indians "who would make a field next spring." One might think that Father Hoecken was by now persona non grata to the Governor. Far from it. In August Stevens advised the priest that the Blackfoot Council would have to be postponed a bit. He suggested that the Jesuits supply the proposed Flathead agency with such necessaries as "plows and vegetables." Supplies for his own party on the Plains also "would be very desirable." Stevens gave notice of his "desire to hold a treaty" with the Kalispels at the mission in November. Would Hoecken kindly advise him on this treaty, "if opportunity" offered? At the Blackfoot Council too, the Governor hoped to see either Menetrey or Hoecken.

Another letter asked Hoecken to furnish information about the Kalispels to Crosbie, on the basis of which the latter would make certain decisions as to their council. Stevens had previously written twice to Sacred Heart mission, to have the Jesuits prepare for a Coeur d'Alene council soon. Now he wrote Ravalli that Crosbie would be asking information concerning the Coeur d'Alenes. Stevens told Crosbie, "you will concur with Father Raval[l]i for my meeting with the Coeur d'Alenes at the mission."[4]

"At the express request of Governor Stevens" Hoecken again had to leave

3. Smaller Lansdale Diary, 29 July. NA, IA, LR (Wash. Sup.), report and letters of 1 December, 1 January. Negots. Rat. Treaties, Lansdale's Report of Operations. Wash. Sup., LR, Stevens to L., 10 November.

4. NA, IA, Wash. Sup., Misc. Recd., Menetrey to Stevens, 25 September, with ref. to Stevens letter to Menetrey, 27 August; Ravalli to Stevens, 21 September, with ref. to Stevens letters of 17 July, 29 August. See Wash. Sup., LR, "Differences on Settlement of the Account of I. I. Stevens," item 35, where Stevens' offering becomes a purchase "overcharged" by Ravalli (cf. *RR, 12,* i, 134). See also Wash. Sup., LS, Field Records, Stevens to Hoecken and to Crosbie, both 28 August.

his mission, this time to help with the Blackfoot Council. The Jesuit had been away in mid-August visiting the Kettle mission. Since the cholera was finally under control, he had ridden down to enter upon the annual eight days of silence and prayer required by his Rule. He returned by way of Ravalli's mission to pick up supplies just in from the lower country. He then headed out onto the Plains in October. From St. Ignatius he took two Indians and a visitor, Father James Croke.

Croke was a young priest from County Cork, serving the archdiocese of Oregon City as a kind of itinerant apostle and as pastor of the Portland church. It is difficult to say what he was doing out of his archdiocese, even outside his ecclesiastical province. This was the low point in the history of the southern diocese, with the clergy diminished from nineteen to seven and the archbishop away touring South America for funds to meet his heavy debts. Croke would return to St. Ignatius as a guest, baptizing seventeen half-breed children at Fort Benton along the way. He would then leave permanently and rather cavalierly for San Francisco, where he was to enjoy a new career as vicar general for thirty years. His presence in Montana at this time has puzzled historians. His connection with the Blackfoot Council was accidental and unimportant.[5]

The business of organizing the council was enlivened by a running feud between Governor Stevens and his colleague Colonel Cumming. Both were men conscious of their own importance, petulant, and jealous of their personal authority. Alfred Cumming, the senior commissioner at the council, was a man of resolution and character, portly and somewhat pompous. Born into a prominent southern family, he had won a reputation for courage as mayor of Augusta during the Yellow Fever epidemic, had served as sutler to Scott in the Mexican War, and had already distinguished himself as superintendent of Indian Affairs for much of the trans-Mississippi west. His subsequent career was not so happy. Two years later President Buchanan named him to replace Brigham Young as governor of Utah, in time to become involved in the partisan wranglings of the Mormon War.

At the Blackfoot Council not only did the two men quarrel as to who was in command, but they found themselves in fundamental disagreement on policy. Cumming was convinced that the Blackfoot country was not rich enough to allow any considerable White immigration without economic loss; Stevens held that it was "fine grazing country whose capabilities no emigra-

5. CR, 4, 1276 (1856). Hoecken's movements from his diary and Ravalli letter to Stevens, NA, IA, Oreg. Sup., LR, 15 September. The larger Lansdale Diary (YU) notes his presence (p. 23). Croke, in Hoecken Diary; NA, IA, Oreg. Sup., LR, Ravalli letter of 21 September. The Croke Papers at All Hallows in Dublin and those at the University of Oregon shed no further light on this episode (see below, Bib.).

tion could exhaust." Cumming saw the Blackfeet as fierce, primitive savages, requiring delicate handling by the government; Stevens firmly believed them to be essentially friendly, desirous of farms and schools, a nation who "will in an extraordinary degree yield to any agencies which the government may put in operation" to civilize them. Bad feeling and wrangling between the two men persisted. During the council each ostentatiously kept separate quarters. Indeed, they would have been well advised to preface the council with a personal treaty of their own.[6]

The treaty was to be especially between the Blackfeet (Piegans, Bloods, and Blackfeet) and, on the other hand, the Nez Percés and the Flathead confederates (Flatheads, Pend d'Oreilles, Kutenais, and Kalispels). The Coeur d'Alenes refused to participate; so did the Kutenais, but they were reckoned as present. Included within Flathead Confederates and Nez Percés, by a kind of legal fiction, were any Interior tribes who might later be added to their respective reservations. The treaty also provided that the mountain Indians were not to wage war against the Crows, Assiniboines, Snakes, Crees, Sioux, or neighboring tribes. The Blackfeet were similarly to live in peace with their neighbors. In its most important features, it may be summed up as a perpetual treaty of amity between the Indians of the Plains and the Indians of the Interior.

At the council ground some 3,300 to 3,500 Indians were actually present. Some 5,400 others remained by Stevens' request on the Marias, Teton, and Milk rivers. More than a thousand Nez Percés had to absent themselves for hunting but were represented "through the delegated chiefs." Thus, though Stevens speaks of ten thousand Indians "actually participating," only a third of that number were on hand, mostly Blackfeet and Flathead confederates.[7] Thousands of other absent Indians were considered to be involved in the proceedings. Adams, for instance, had contacted the Snakes; and Doty had secured a promise from 57 Piegan lodges binding them to whatever agreement was reached.

In all, 59 prominent Indians from 10 different tribes, including 27 chiefs from west of the Rockies, sat in the first rows of that meeting under the lofty cottonwoods. Measles had scattered the Crow contingents, and most of the Snakes had gone beyond reach. In Sohon's drawing of the council, the trees stand leafless and bleak against a winter sky. Father Hoecken lived at the Flathead–Pend d'Oreille camp, located a mile from the council grounds and containing about 750 souls in something over a hundred lodges.

6. NA, IA, Negots. Rat. Treaties, e.g. Cumming report, 14 February 1856; Stevens to Manypenny, 27 October 1855; Blackfoot Council "Official Proceedings," passim.

7. Ibid., to Manypenny, 22 October. Statistics in Blackfoot Council "Official Proceedings"; see accompanying docs., passim.

The council itself was remarkably brief. Opening on Tuesday afternoon, it ran through most of the negotiations and the signing of the treaty itself by Wednesday the seventeenth. This left three more days for distributing gifts. The Indians "were indeed much disappointed at not finding" Father De Smet at the council. Cumming had tried to secure his services, but the priest was unable to come. Hoecken filled some 25 pages of his diary with minute script about the council and his trip. We need not delay over the details. It was a simple peace conference and an agreement to open the country to White settlement and passage, to agencies, forts, roads, and the like, with compensation and annuities for the Blackfeet.

It is not quite accurate to say that no land cessions were involved. The Flathead range on the Plains was curtailed drastically, with no recompense and little courtesy. The country north of the Missouri was reserved for the Blackfeet. Head Chief Alexander objected to having "only a narrow ridge" for hunting. It seemed odd to him that, while he could hunt widely when an enemy, he was now to be restricted as a friend. Stevens chided him for this reluctance to lose his hunting grounds, because his tribe already had the "farms and cattle" at the Jesuit mission.[8] Big Canoe predictably spoke out against the restriction.

The general approach of the council continued along the legalistic and paternalistic tone of its predecessors. It did not rest very firmly on a knowledge of the tangled tribal rights over the hunting areas. Congress hastened to ratify it within six months. Two circumstances doomed it from the start. The gradual diminution of game eroded the principles upon which it stood. Also, since a large number of Blackfeet took no part in the treaty, and especially since most of those who did failed to keep the peace afterward, the situation soon deteriorated to the status quo ante.

Both Fathers Croke and Hoecken signed the treaty. Victor, Alexander, Moses, Big Canoe, Ambrose, Fidelis, Palchina, and eight other mission Indians also signed. Hoecken wrote on October 18 to De Smet in St. Louis, from "the united camp of the Flatheads and Pend d'Oreilles." From the tone of De Smet's reply we gather that Hoecken was pleased with the council. Hoecken's private assessment of Stevens is surprisingly generous. The Governor "has always shown himself a real father and well affected towards our Indians," and he "has expressed a determination to do all in his power to forward the success of the missions." [9]

After next winter's hunt, Hoecken was to write: "may God bless the Gov-

8. Blackfoot Council "Official Proceedings," esp. p. 57. CR, *4*, 1253, 1276. The Bradley journal speaks loosely of the council lasting ten days (p. 274).

9. NA, IA, Negots. Rat. Treaties, for treaty; Hoecken's name on the first published version comes out "Hoeekeorsg." CR, *4*, 1235 (1855).

ernment for establishing peace among the Blackfeet!" All last winter "a good understanding prevailed" with these old enemies. Lansdale notes in his diary at this time that the Flatheads seemed quite pleased with the Blackfoot treaty. Little Dog, soon to be head chief of the Piegans, brought his friendly band to reside a while at the mission, entering with much formality "to martial music." Little Dog himself privately complained to Hoecken that the Whites had "never treated" of religion with them, "this so important affair" to the Blackfoot mind. Later the Jesuit took the Blackfoot chief to visit Agent Lansdale.[10] At the same time all was not quiet on the tomahawk front. The Flatheads killed two Crows and lost a man to the Bannocks and another to the Gros Ventres. The Coeur d'Alenes and Spokanes brought down six Bannocks, losing five Spokanes in the process. Ten days after the treaty the Bloods went to war against the Crows.[11]

Hoecken from the start was very much afraid "that the quiet will not be of very long duration." He hoped that the Jesuits themselves "will one day effect a more enduring peace" through the instrumentality of a mission. This was "the best and indeed the only means" to persuade the Blackfeet to "observe the treaty of peace which has just been concluded." A Blackfoot mission was "absolutely necessary" not only "for their own sake" but for "the peace of our converted Indians" in the mountains. He planned to visit the Blackfeet from time to time, making preparations for the day when a permanent establishment could be arranged. Hoecken also joined the trader Owen in assisting the authorities to find a good site for the Blackfoot agency.[12]

It is significant that Colonel Alfred Vaughan, the experienced and able agent for the Blackfeet, arrived independently at the same conclusion as Father Hoecken. A Jesuit mission "would advance the interests of the Government and those of the Indians at the same time," he felt, "civilizing and pacifying them" and "controlling their brutal outbreaks." Though a Protestant, he was to approach the Jesuits in May 1857 to secure such a mission for his Blackfeet. It is perhaps equally significant to discover Stevens several times asserting that the aim of the government itself was "to civilize and christianize" the Blackfeet. Insofar as his meaning can be discerned, he sees religion as a direct responsibility of the government, and a means to full acculturation. In its own way, the phrase adds point to Hoecken's observations.[13]

10. Larger Lansdale Diary, April and 5 September 1856. Hoecken Diary, 1 April (Latin). CR, 4, 1247–48 (1857).

11. CR, 4, 1248; Bancroft, *Washington*, p. 691.

12. Ewers, *Blackfeet*, p. 231; CR, 4, 1235 (1855), 1247 (1857), Hoecken quotes.

13. NA, IA, Negots. Rat. Treaties, Stevens to Manypenny, 28 September 1855. CR, 4, 1317 (20 May 1857).

"BATTLES, MURDERS, PLUNDERINGS, BURNINGS"

In early August the Jesuits sent a long report on the Flathead Council to Rome.[14] They also kept the civil authorities informed. Meanwhile, they worked unceasingly to dissuade the Indians from violence. On August 1, a few days after Stevens reached Fort Benton on his way to the Blackfoot Council, Joset wrote to Rome from his Kettle mission: "I can foresee nothing as to the future of this mission; the feelings [of the Indians] are thoroughly aroused, because the government has proposed to buy their country and to give them a piece of it in which they might live separate from the whites." He continues with the same neutrality already displayed by Hoecken: "soon a council will be held, at which this question will be fought out between the two parties." Joset is aware of the war fever sweeping the Indian world. "There are some who are stirring up the Indians, by spreading false rumors; they openly solicit our Christians to join in the war." But he tells his Indians "clearly that unless they conduct themselves peaceably the missionaries will leave them." [15] This threat of abandonment, never used lightly, indicates how seriously the Jesuits viewed the crisis.

By July, then, there was a somewhat organized movement afoot to unite the Interior Indians for war. This agrees with what the Oblates had said about the 1,500 Yakimas to the south. At the root of the war lay the seizure of Indian domains. The Oblate superior in Oregon would write to Europe on October 2 that "the savages seem resolved to maintain the struggle to the death, convinced that the treaties of the government for the purchase of their land are nothing but frauds." Stevens' colleague Gibbs saw the war as "the natural struggle between the hostile races for the sovereignty of the soil; the land is at the root of the war." The treaties had put the torch to the powder keg and had made war inevitable.[16]

A sudden influx of gold miners contributed to the disaster. The coming of these adventurers seems to have forced the Indians' hand and advanced their

14. RJ, MSax., II, 1 (in Latin).

15. Ibid., separate letter (in Latin). The 1855 or Yakima War is discussed in Bancroft, *Washington*, Bk. 1, chaps. 4–5; Victor, *Early Indian Wars*, pp. 423–500; C. H. Carey, *History of Oregon* (Portland, Oreg., 1922), chaps. 33–34; G. W. Fuller, *A History of the Pacific Northwest* (New York, 1938), chap. 13; H. Stevens, *Stevens, 2,* chaps. 36–40; and from the Indian side by Splawn, *Ka-Mi-Akin.* The best treatment is the Bischoff doctoral dissertation "The Yakima War" (see above, p. 71, n. 24); see also his "Yakima Indian War 1855–1856, a Problem in Research," *PNWQ, 41* (1950), 162–69; his "Yakima Campaign of 1856," *Mid-America, 31* (1949), 163–69; and his "Documents: Yakima Campaign," ibid., pp. 170–208.

16. Waggett, *RACHS, 64,* 82. Coan, *OHQ, 23,* 26–27.

timetable; there was neither patience nor time now for gathering more food in preparation for the winter attack. Gold discoveries in the Yakima Valley by McClellan's branch of the railroad survey even in 1853 had "caused considerable excitement" among his men. (At that moment the future war leader Owhi, the brother of Kamiakin, was camped nearby, "the most good natured Indian yet seen in the country.") A particular preoccupation of Stevens and Mullan in 1853 had been the "very good specimens of gold" in the Flatheads' own Bitterroot Valley. Again, when Stevens arrived at the Coeur d'Alene mission in 1855 on his way to the Flathead Council, he was greeted with news of a gold strike by two half-breeds in the Pend d'Oreille country. The Governor included in his official report an enthusiastic estimate as to the rich gold deposits of the Interior all the way to the Rockies.[17]

Even while Stevens was urging peace on the Blackfeet, gangs of miners were feverishly at work on a Colville strike. Others were hopefully roaming the neighboring regions of the Interior, and more were on their way. Colville was the "Eldorado of the North," where miners made "from 5 to 15 Dollars Per Day all winter" during 1855. Governor Stevens found difficulty restraining his escort from deserting. Besides the miners, some sixty White settlers had already overflowed along the Walla Walla and Umatilla rivers (not counting the more tolerable French Canadians) down at the southwest doorway to the Interior.[18]

Out on the Coast the Nesqually chief, Leschi, was making a tour of the tribes, organizing them for a general rising. He warned that reservations were a clever prelude to complete annihilation. The Nesquallies were particularly unhappy about their reservation. As far south as the Rogue River tribes, killings and reprisals were common in 1855; by September the local agent could report the month as one continued series of aggressions. In the Puget Sound area the Oblates got many tribesmen to promise "they will not take part in the war"; others, however, were "trying to procure a lot of ammunition." [19]

In the Interior the Klickitats considered themselves already at war with the Whites. They would easily merge with the larger war when it broke. Major Haller had just returned triumphantly from an Indian-hanging expedition to the Boise Valley. But at Fort Hall the Indian agent felt so insecure that he

17. *RR, 12,* i, 140–41, 201, 254, 257; *1,* ii, 56.
18. Wallace Indian War Papers (WU), No. 16, W. H. Wallace to J. Barron, 7 April 1856. HB, Simpson Correspondence, outward and inward, has a number of letters relating to the problem of the gold discoveries. Bancroft, *Washington,* pp. 108 n., 139 n. W. J. Trimble, *The Mining Advance into the Inland Empire, a Comparative Study of the Beginnings of the Mining Industry* (Madison, Wisc., 1914), pp. 15–16.
19. Waggett, *RACHS, 64,* 82.

refused to remain during the fall. Down along the Oregon Trail conditions were as dangerous as always. Even the Hudson's Bay people were in trouble; their trader Tolmie was upset to find the Yakimas preparing to waylay a brigade carrying valuable goods and ammunition.[20] In fact this war would see the abandonment of three important Hudson's Bay posts in the Interior along the emigrant trail: Fort Walla Walla, Fort Boise, and Fort Hall.

Rumor spoke of a great war council of all the Interior Indians in the Grande Ronde country southeast of Fort Walla Walla. The head chief of bands as far north as the Coeur d'Alenes and Kettles were supposed to have attended. The council proposed a united front against the White treaty makers, designating tribal holdings meticulously after the White manner, so that no areas could lie unclaimed as a temptation to the enemy. Both Chief Lawyer of the Nez Percés and Kamiakin's disreputable brother Skloom spoke to Agent Bolon of this meeting. Skloom even said that the priests were responsible for Indian distrust of the Whites, something he shrewdly realized Bolon wanted to hear. But Father D'Herbomez of the Yakima mission in an indignant rebuttal charged that the council story was "a pure lie."

In September four Sinkiuse-Columbias (Isle des Pierres) killed a miner named Henry Mattice; Chirouse says this was because he had assaulted the daughter of Yakima Chief Teias. Shortly afterward the Yakimas killed some seven other miners. The total soon ran up to twenty, and troops were ordered onto the route. Fears were expressed for Governor Stevens' safety; Acting Governor Charles Mason suggested that Major Rains detach a body of soldiers into the Spokane country to escort him.

Agent Bolon, on his way to join Stevens in the upper country, heard of the killings from Chief Garry. An energetic man with a flamboyant shock of red hair and beard, Bolon rode into the Yakima region to investigate. He spent two hours at the Oblate mission; in leaving he asked the priests to contact Chief Owhi for him. No one is really sure what happened to him afterward. He seems to have fallen in with an Indian party, to have conducted himself boldly, and to have voiced imprudent threats. For his pains, the Indians cut his throat on September 20. At this very time the Yakima missionary, Father Pandosy, on his way to beg the government to take the situation seriously, had almost reached Olympia. Here he spent four days discussing the dangerous situation with the authorities.

Stevens later described the 1855 war as beginning in early October among the Yakimas and Klickitats, extending to the Tyigh, Des Chutes, John Day, and Umatilla tribes of Oregon, then to the Cayuses and Walla Wallas, on to the Palouses of the Interior and to the Puget Sound tribes on the Coast, and thereafter widening. It was no easier for an Indian to remain neutral now

20. Huggins Papers (WU), H873w, f. 2.

than it was for a White. And the hostiles secured forced enlistment by threats of death. "Docile to the opinions of our Fathers, the Christian savages long for peace," the Oblate superior wrote; but the war party persecutes them and talks of killing the priests as being "in league with the foreigners." [21]

The Jesuit mission tribes were part of this agitation. On August 1, just after the Flathead treaty, Chief Peter John of the Kettles closed his country to all Whites. Some of the Southern Okanogans were eventually brought to the point of joining the war. We have seen Joset's pessimism as he tried to counter the war propaganda. Ravalli reported to the wandering Stevens about Coeur d'Alene dispositions; this was on the day after Bolon's death, an event of which both men would remain ignorant for some time to come. "Though for my part I have done all in my power to bend their savage wills to your desires," the main effect seems to be that Ravalli himself has "become an object of suspicion to them as a partisan of the government." [22]

In a previous letter the Governor had been determined that the Coeur d'Alenes "will go on" a reservation along with the Kalispels. He politely insisted that Ravalli and Gazzoli use "your good offices with the Coeur d'Alenes." He proposed to "treat with them at your mission on my return, if they like the arrangements." Subsequent letters elaborated on the total abdication of the Coeur d'Alene lands. Ravalli told Stevens bluntly: "I am of the opinion that they will not consent to change their place." He did feel that they might be induced to accept a reservation on their own Coeur d'Alene lands. This was precisely what Stevens had just refused to Victor's Flatheads; it serves to illuminate the Flathead mentality on this point. At the moment, observed Ravalli, the Coeur d'Alenes were angry because they feared Stevens meant to "wrest from them by force the peaceful possession of their forests." The priest promised to have a council soon, so as to be able to return some definite answer. He sent Stevens his "warmest wishes for the success of your benevolent designs for the amelioration of the Indians." [23]

The mood of the coastal settlers at this time is seen in a letter from the son of Lincoln's law partner, a substantial Illinois lawyer named Logan who had been driven by drink to emigrate to Oregon, where he eventually became mayor of Portland. The war was "raging," he informed his Springfield correspondent extravagantly, "simultaneous from the British possessions to the

21. Stevens, in *RCIA* (1856), p. 185. Waggett, p. 82. Bischoff, "Yakima War," pp. 62, 64–65, 79 (good on Bolon, Pandosy, Mesplié), 68 ff.

22. NA, IA, Wash. Sup., Misc. Recd., Ravalli to Stevens, 21 September. Bancroft, *Washington*, p. 109, erroneously calling the chief Pierre Jerome. Teit, BAE *Annual Report*, 45, 259. Walter Cline et al., *The Sinkaietk or Southern Okanagon of Washington*, ed. Leslie Spier, Amer. Anthrop. Assoc., Gen. Ser., 2 (Menasha, Wisc., 1938), p. 83.

23. NA, IA, Wash. Sup., LS, Stevens to Ravalli, 17 July; Misc. Recd., Ravalli to Stevens, 21 September.

Sacramento valley; the Jesuit Priests are with the Indians furnishing powder, Guns, etc." A subsequent letter, after the White failures in the field, finds his estimate radically deflated. He now reports a war maintained by "a few lean, ragged Locofocos in pursuit of glory (that is, office) by murdering the Scabby flat head Indians." [24]

In all the Northwest there were only about 350 regulars. But coastal authorities deemed it prudent to make some show of force. At the beginning of October Major Granville Haller of the Fourth Infantry, a veteran of the Seminole and Mexican fighting, took 102 men north, deep into a Yakima ambush of a thousand Indians. Surrounded, cut off from wood and water, and sixty miles removed from the last outpost, he sent a desperate message for help. In three days of steady fighting, partly by the grace of Indian overconfidence, the major managed to extricate his command. This he achieved at the expense of his horses, his cattle herd, his howitzer, his provisions, and his pride. A small supporting column of forty men on the north rapidly retreated to the Coast; the relieving force from the south prudently discontinued its aggressive plans. The Whites suffered a total of twenty-one casualties in killed and wounded, the Indians perhaps forty.

Panicky confusion assailed the coastal settlements. Any number of citizens with eyes in their heads could see what machinery lay behind these troubles. There was heady talk of hanging the Oblate priests. The Hudson's Bay Company was also assailed. "The cry of the present day" is that the company too was "supplying the Indians with arms and ammunition." [25] The Oblate superior felt it necessary early in October to apply to Acting Governor Mason for a public statement recognizing the Oblates' stand against the hostiles. He reminded Mason that the priests had notified civilian authorities whenever "danger of some kind threatened the security of the citizens." Mason brushed aside the necessity for such rebuttals but did deliver himself of an oral announcement to the effect "that the authorities had received from the priests every information that could be expected or desired." [26]

The settlements hastily recruited their amateur militia, detailing one company to rescue the Stevens party. They also demanded 4,000 soldiers. Major Gabriel Rains did manage to collect 334 regulars, largely by stripping the coast defenses. Accompanied by an independent force of 500 mounted militia, from both Oregon and Washington settlements, he penetrated the Interior. Young Phil Sheridan, later of Civil War fame, led the advance guard.

24. H. E. Pratt, ed., "22 Letters of David Logan, Pioneer Oregon Lawyer," *OHQ, 44* (1943), 268 (28 November), 271 (27 January 1856).

25. BC, Record Office transcripts, F.O. 5, 617–63, —— to T. Banister, recd. 28 January 1856, from San Francisco. Haller's own account of his fight is in BL, MS P-b 60.

26. Mason Correspondence (YU), Ricard to Mason, 1 December, referring to 12 October letter.

A curtain of charity may be drawn over the subsequent campaign. It was not without its excitement, chases, skirmishes, and incident, but it was badly conceived and fruitless. Hundreds of Indians enjoyed themselves in martial uproar, dispersing when pursued. Sheridan's cavalrymen gave prolonged chase to an ominous dust cloud, which eventually proved to contain frightened militia horsemen. The White man's howitzers made a particularly satisfactory bang, though it must be confessed that they hit nothing. It was all good exercise for man and horse alike. Had the rest of the war been as bloodless, both sides might well have congratulated themselves. Angry charges of incompetence were soon brought against the leader; they came to nothing, on the technicality that there were not enough appropriately ranking officers in the Northwest for a court-martial. The upshot of the campaign thus far was that two soldiers had contrived to drown themselves crossing the Yakima River.

Stevens was shortly to demand from the national authorities an investigation of the commander of the Department of the Pacific, General Wool. Wool had come up to Vancouver from Benicia near San Francisco, and departed showering rebukes upon Rains, Haller, the militia, and assorted targets. His brief appearance does not do him justice. The old general was an experienced, temperate man of common sense. Already famed as the defender of the Cherokees, and for his role as field commander and civil administrator in the Mexican War, he had a distinguished career still ahead of him. He might have brought the Indian troubles to an end here, had circumstances in his larger jurisdiction allowed him the leisure.

In the 1856 fighting Wool was at odds with Governor Stevens. This was due not merely to personal tensions in the past but, more especially, to differences over the origin and nature of the war, jurisdiction and strategy in the campaign, the usefulness of the militia forces, and feasible ways of establishing a firm peace. Upon his own safe return, Governor Stevens bombarded the old general with Olympian reproaches; Wool retorted that Stevens was crazy. It was like a re-enactment of the Cumming-Stevens feud, and was neither the first nor last such eruption in the latter's life. In a sense, this was one more episode in the long antagonism between settler and soldier in the trans-Mississippi west. Historians to this day tend to march under the banner of either Stevens or Wool, though an occasional recusant like Splawn indifferently damns them both.

A discreditable episode at this time was the destruction of the Oblates' Yakima mission. Finding that the priests had buried a half keg of powder, the troops on November 14 illogically but enthusiastically burned the mission buildings to the ground. Two days of intense looting yielded two wagonloads of goods, including devotional objects. Officers and officials protested their own innocence of this affair; Phil Sheridan thought it "disgraceful." Fortunately the Yakimas, after a preliminary rifling of the mission, had carried off the Oblate missionaries, so they were out of harm's way. Pandosy was still actively working for peace in his semicaptivity; he had elicited from the hostiles a set of compromise proposals, including surrender of part of their country.

The Oblate superior now pleaded again with Acting Governor Mason to speak out, calling his attention to bad feeling broadcast by some newspapers. Even a man of Joel Palmer's stature was resentful that Pandosy "still remains secure in the heart of the enemy country." Mason stiffly retorted that it was no part of his duty to publish anything concerning any "class or sect." He felt he had done enough in his earlier verbal statement, which he had the grace to repeat again and confirm.[27]

But Colonel James Nesmith, commanding the Oregon militia, had been brewing up a storm with Pandosy's account book. Essentially a genial and kindly man, Nesmith indulged himself in strong animosities. He took a dim view of Indian missionary work in the Northwest, whether Catholic or Protestant. To Nesmith, Pandosy's account book "clearly demonstrates the indisputable fact that he has furnished the Indians with large quantities of ammunition, and leaving it a matter of uncertainty whether *Gospel* or *Gunpowder* was his principal stock in trade." Major Rains read excerpts from the account book to his officers around the campfire. Only an investigation by the federal government in 1857 would cause these exuberant accusations to abate. Meanwhile, on January 18, 1856, a bill was introduced into the territorial legislature "to prevent Aliens" acting as missionaries to the Indians of Washington: history shows that such alien missioners have done "much mischief." The bill was debated but at the roll call overwhelmingly defeated.[28]

The Jesuit missioners at Colville understood that the Yakima Oblates had "been massacred." But after watching from a distance as the Americans

27. Mason Corresp., M. to Ricard, 4 December. See also Victor, *Early Wars,* for Pandosy's message for Kamiakin, looking to a settlement of the war, and Rains' answer, pp. 429–31. On Oblate movements see Bischoff, "Yakima War," pp. 90–92, 319–20, 97. Military dispositions, personnel, strength, and forts at this time are given in detail by Colonel Joseph K. Mansfield (chief engineer to General Taylor in the Mexican War), *Mansfield on the Condition of the Western Forts 1853–54,* ed. R. W. Frazer (Norman, Okla., 1963); sec. 2 covers the Department of the Pacific, including the Northwest; on Fort Vancouver see pp. 114–17, 170–74, and on Fort Dalles, pp. 116–17, 175–79, with plates 23, 24; on our Indians see esp. pp. 100–01 n., 104; on arms and personnel see tabular appendixes.

28. Nesmith Papers (OH), 979.107N, Report of 19 November to Gov. Curry. The Pandosy account book is among the Wool Papers in Albany, New York (cf. Bischoff, *PNWQ, 41,* 168–69; and his "Yakima War," pp. 23 ff., for an analysis, with pp. 134–35 on the legislative debate). On Nesmith's views of Protestant missions see Waggett, *RACHS, 64,* 73–74.

wildly burned their mission, the Oblates moved northward, slipped away from the Indians, and a week later took refuge with the Jesuits at the Kettle mission. "We were able to offer refuge" to them, the Jesuit general wrote, from hostile Indians and Americans alike. Here they would stay through the following spring. The whole war was a heartbreak for Father Pandosy. He had warned the Whites, yet he could not really blame his Indians. When Kamiakan had asked his advice in mid-1854, the Oblate honestly predicted the course of White settlement and refused to take sides. "I have learned to love you," he told Kamiakin; "I cannot advise you or help you; I wish I could." [29]

Father Chirouse remained at the Umatilla mission, working for peace, very unsure of his safety, and hearing "only of battles, murders, plunderings, burnings." Shortly after Governor Stevens made his way to Olympia, Gibbs would inform him that the friendly Indians were upset over militia provocations, but that "Chirouse is exerting himself to keep the Indians quiet" at his mission. There, though many were kept out of the war, the mission itself was burned, this time by the Indian combatants. Eventually even Chirouse and his colleague Ricard were ordered out of the area. They, too, went to the Kettle country, to the Jesuit mission.[30]

RESTRAINING THE COEUR D'ALENES AND THEIR NEIGHBORS

This background helps explain a letter Father Joset now sent to Stevens.[31] Neither the Jesuits nor Stevens nor any White men in the upper country knew of the open fighting so far below. The Indians certainly knew. The information in Joset's letter should be correlated with the military movements. On October 4, the first day of battle for Haller's ambushed command, some Nez Percés brought the Coeur d'Alenes word that the Americans in the south had killed not only Stevens' courier Pearson but also his Indian guide, Joseph Stellam, son of the Coeur d'Alene head chief. This news perturbed the Coeur d'Alenes. A similar case, involving the murder of the son of the Walla Walla chief, had helped precipitate the Cayuse War in 1847. Other Indians reported that the Yakimas had accidentally killed the two men, believing both to be Americans.

29. CR, 4, 1277. FL, *1857*, Rome (divers), 29 April 1857. Cf. FP, I, 5, general's letter of same date. Waggett, pp. 80–81, 84–85.

30. NA, IA, Wash. Sup., Misc. Recd., 7 January 1856 (Gibbs), Waggett, p. 84 (Chirouse, 18 November 1855). Cf. *RCIA* (1856), pp. 193–95 (Chirouse letter of 15 January, with Palmer letter of 27 January); Waggett, pp. 89–90.

31. NA, IA, Wash. Sup., Misc. Recd., Joset to Stevens, 14 October. In Mason correspondence, cf. Pandosy letter of same date (15 October), on the dispositions of the lower Indians.

Three days later, when Haller's beaten men were at bay on a lonely emi-
nence in the Yakima country, a significant attack occurred among the Coeur
d'Alene tribe gathered out on Coeur d'Alene Prairie some distance southwest
of the mission. "A lot of the Coeurs d'Alene with the old Stellam rushed armed
to the wagons" which held Stevens' supplies for the coming council. These
desirable articles—flannel shirts and other goods supplied by the Indian
Bureau—had been freighted here by Coeur d'Alenes employed under the
direction of Agent Bolon.[32] The attackers, firing as they came, drove off the
Indian guards protecting the depot. Fortunately, the respected half-breed
Antoine Plante came with his Indian relatives to the defense of the guards.
Chief Stellam therefore gave the order "don't kill." Some Spokanes under
Chief Garry also intervened.

Stellam was an old rascal who was gradually being supplanted in the head
chieftainship through the influence of the Jesuits. He may have been head of
the war party that existed in the tribe; it was apparently Indians from this
war group who spread the false report among the Nez Percés that Governor
Stevens was fighting the mountain Indians. On his way to the Flathead
Council, Stevens had met Stellam; the chief was then in the company of a
Palouse chief who had refused to sign the Walla Walla treaty and had left
that council in umbrage. Stellam now insisted on forcing the two wagons off
to his own camp. Most of the people took no part in the disturbance; but so
disturbed were the rioters that the chiefs "were unable to stop the first excitement." Seltis, a vigorous subchief already beginning to make his tentative bid
for head chieftainship, was especially embarrassed by the outburst. He had
been "recently elected by his people, and could not yet sufficiently establish
his authority." [33]

The Jesuits immediately learned of the robbery. "As soon as we heard of it
we hurried here." Ravalli rode over from Sacred Heart, and Joset journeyed
down all the way from his Colville post. "I arrived the last," says Joset, "and
found here the Coeurs d'Alene chiefs, some of whom had been accomplices to
the attack." Fortunately, the priests could refute the murder charge. A lay
brother just back from The Dalles had seen both putative victims in good
health. "So the anger of the Indians subsided, and the chiefs recovered their
authority." Their reaction had been so violent, however, that Governor Stevens was to return to the incident more than once during the coming
Spokane–Kettle–Coeur d'Alene Council.

Father Joset gave his Indians a vigorous scolding, painting for them the

32. Larger Lansdale Diary has the June freighting of these presents by Coeur d'Alenes
(n.p.). Doty, *Journal,* describes the organizing and routing of the wagons (pp. 25, 35,
and passim). Quotations from Joset letter.
33. Doty, *Journal,* pp. 32 (meeting), 91 (rumor). Joset letter.

probable consequences of their deed. "They felt it," he grimly remarks. Stellam still argued for keeping at least one wagon, deducting it from his expected share of gifts at the council. But all the wagons were retrieved and this time moved to Antoine Plante's cabin for close guarding. One revolver was missing, as well as a pound of powder and some fifteen pounds of shot. Father Joset felt it improbable that these items could ever be recovered.

Chief Stellam decided that he had merely wanted to protect the wagons from Nez Percé raiders. There seems to be a germ of truth in that. Some Spokanes disclosed to Joset that Nez Percés in the vicinity, apparently emboldened by Haller's defeat, had been about to seize these White riches. Perhaps Stellam was greedily forestalling them by staging his own robbery. Joset feared that Stevens would be angry with the whole Coeur d'Alene tribe on account of the insolence of one faction; this explains his letter. At the same time the priest realized that something deeper than a raid was afoot. He could get no further information on the Nez Percé story. He did feel constrained to give the Governor this solemn warning. "A great deal of irritation prevails amongst the Indians all over the country, and [I] would advise not to trust to[o] much the peaceable show, for Indians naturally dissimulate [and] will make a secret of their feelings." Joset's exact evidence was fragmentary. "But I heard enough to be able to say with certainty: a great deal of irritation prevails." [34]

Stevens should have expected all this. He was no man's fool, yet for the first and only time in his life he managed to make himself look fatuous. His treaty dispatches glow with mounting optimism. No doubt or qualifications shadow the complacent reports of his Indian dealings. At the Coeur d'Alene camp even the Palouses had expressed "satisfaction" with their treaty. At the mission conference everything "was entirely satisfactory to all parties." After the Flathead Council every man was "pleased and every man satisfied." Everywhere the Governor went, with each treaty and conference, he blithely recorded nothing but happy Indians.

Even afterward, though taught by war, he was to protest in his railroad reports that the Interior treaties were "the most extensive operations ever undertaken and carried out in these latter days of our history"; that the Walla Walla council "had a potential influence in preserving the peace of the country"; and that "I shall be able to vindicate" the treaties, and "show that they were wise and proper and that they accomplished a great end." Perhaps the simple truth is that Stevens had undertaken an impossible job. And even under happier circumstances, or at a more leisurely pace, it was not precisely the job indicated by his talents. Moreover, politically he could not afford to fail at this juncture, or admit failure. Later he would continue to insist "that the

34. Joset letter.

government made no mistake in the man whom it placed in the great field of duty as its commissioner to make treaties with the Indian tribes." [35]

On the evening before Rains' large force moved into the Interior, the Governor's bubble burst. It cannot have been such a complete surprise. Even before Pearson rode back from the Coast with his terrible news of war, Stevens was aware "from the letters of the Jesuit Missionaries and Angus M[a]cDonald, Esq." that the tribes with which he yet meant to treaty "were in an excitable state, and that a little matter might cause them to join in the general combination." [36] The Governor's decisive actions during the following weeks redeemed the complacent incompetence of his treaty tour. His courage, intelligence, and leadership shone brightly in this dark moment.

The party's sole contact with the lower country and the Coast had been through the courier William Pearson, a small, wiry man of pleasant aspect and great endurance. Because of the distances involved, young Pearson was more often in the saddle than at either terminus of his run. He had taken the reports of the Walla Walla Council out to Olympia when the Governor headed into the upper country; he then managed to rejoin the party among the Flatheads. Soon Pearson was carrying the news of the Flathead Council to Olympia, riding back all the way to Fort Benton, a remarkable round trip of 1,750 miles, in fewer than twenty-eight days. He accomplished a similar trip shortly afterward, intercepting Stevens two days west of Fort Benton. Stevens had bid Cumming good riddance and had turned himself west toward a Coeur d'Alene council. His party was warming itself at the campfire when a "haggard" Pearson "staggered in" out of the frosty twilight to disclose "the startling intelligence of a spreading war." [37]

There was no longer any question of sparing troops to rescue Stevens. His only chance, the coastal officials warned, was to retreat down the Missouri and sail from New York to Oregon. Instead, Stevens sent to Fort Benton for ammunition and fresh horses, then hurried on to the Bitterroot Valley. Here he conferred with "the Jesuit missionaries" and many Flatheads.[38] Here, too, he wrung a promise of protection from fourteen Nez Percés returning from the recent council. Stevens knew that the Nez Percé country harbored a hostile faction and would be dangerous. He knew also that the Yakimas had a war party out to cut off his retreat.

Since Lansdale was still in the Flathead country, Stevens left him there, on November 10 officially appointing him agent to the Flathead nation. In his instructions Stevens cautioned Lansdale that Jesuit influence among the Indi-

35. *RR, 12,* i, 197, 200, 202, 209.

36. NA, IA, LR (from Wash. Sup.), Stevens to Com. Manypenny, 22 December.

37. Doty, Journal, p. 36. H. Stevens, *Stevens,* 2, 101–02, 120–21.

38. *RR, 12,* i, 223. H. Stevens, *Stevens,* 2, 125–27. McDonnell and Ritch, *CHSM, 10,* 30 October.

ans was strong. "This influence must be discountenanced," he instructed. Any interference by the priests with the agent's work would be met by countermeasures from the government. The letter manifests again the Governor's preoccupation with a presumably unfriendly, or at any rate not governmentally controlled, Jesuit influence.[39]

Actually Lansdale was to get along well with the missionaries. Each spoke well of the other. Father Hoecken assisted the agent through the long months required to build and supply the agency. He ground tools, loaned axes, and furnished what aid he could. The Jesuit described Lansdale in a letter to De Smet as "a very just and upright man," adding that "we gave him all the assistance of which we were capable." There was cordial visiting to the mission, and return visits by Hoecken and the chiefs. When the agent traveled down to the Coast, the Jesuits supplied Indian guides.

Lansdale does not seem to have accomplished much in his capacity as agent. In fact he left the following fall, returning briefly for a few months late in 1857. During that trip he held a brief council at the Coeur d'Alene mission, while visiting with the Jesuits.[40] As for Special Agent Adams, who had gathered the Flathead tribes for the treaty, he knew a good thing when he saw it; he remained behind and settled in the Bitterroot Valley.

At the Governor's Hell Gate camp there occurred a trivial but revealing episode. Its details are known only from a letter that Stevens angrily fired off on November 10 to Hoecken.[41] The Jesuit had sent a message the previous day by Indian runner to Stevens' camp. It was meant for his aide Doty; the bearer had been instructed not to surrender it to the Governor. Stevens could not resist intercepting and opening it nevertheless, "as was my right and duty," an action he defended somewhat too strenuously: "To guard against any caviling as to my course today, a letter addressed to Mr. Doty as Secretary of the Commission is a letter addressed to me; it belongs to my files, and requires action from me so far as it is of a public character."

Hoecken's letter consisted of a "public part," complaining about the horses and mules left with the Kutenais by the treaty party, and a "private part" which Stevens leaves to Doty to answer. Stevens apologizes for the trouble to which the Indians and the mission were put; he assures a proper recompense. As for the more important and mysterious "private part," he says he himself told Hoecken of the matter about which the priest complained. "And courtesy required that the complaint should be addressed to me"—the word "per-

39. NA, IA, LR (from Wash.), Cf. 11 August 1854 appointment in Wash. Sup. (from Com.). Reconfirmed as agent 4 September 1858 (ibid.).

40. Larger Lansdale Diary, November–December, 3, 20–21 August (council, with Joset and Pandosy present). CR, *4*, 1241.

41. NA, IA, Wash. Sup., LR.

sonally" is superscribed—"and not to one of my subordinates" (for "subordinates" the Governor substitutes in his own copy: "one of my officers"). Stevens feels "called upon to observe that the marked discourtesy you have shown me in this matter is not calculated to promote that spirit of harmony in our mutual efforts to advance the welfare of the Indians, which is essential to promoting their greatest good."

What stands behind this outburst? Hoecken neglects to say anything about it elsewhere, nor do the voluminous remnants of the Stevens "files," public or private, yield further clues. The matter complained of may have been trivial in itself. The episode does show that Hoecken felt sufficiently constrained or diffident in his relations with Stevens to take some pains to make his needs or complaints known indirectly via the Governor's secretary. More significant is what it implies about Stevens' attitude toward Hoecken. A personal letter, deliberately meant to be concealed from his eyes, proved a bait too strong to resist. Had the Governor at least uncovered some evidence of intrigue, his petty deed would have been justified to himself and others. His reaction indicates rather annoyed embarrassment that he should so publicly and irredeemably have revealed his suspicions of the Jesuit's doings.

More important crises were afoot. Stevens planned to thrust himself suddenly into the midst of the nearest tribes, surprising them boldly into neutrality. He executed a stealthy, ten-day passage into the Coeur d'Alene territory, utilizing a snow-blocked, and therefore unguarded, pass. With six men of his advance guard he was able to dash into the mission settlement at sunset on November 24, prepared if necessary to open fire on the Indians and to make a stand in the mission church until the body of his party could arrive. His appearance so late in the season took the "Coeur d'Alenes entirely by surprise." The Yakima war party searching for the treaty makers had left only five days earlier. The tribe was very excited, balanced on the brink of war, with wild rumors abroad of Indian victories.

Stevens realized that "a chance word might turn them either way." He ordered his men to keep the Indians bemused with talk of the Blackfoot peace. He himself "held several talks with the Coeur d'Alenes" at the mission. He also picked up some useful information. "Rumors of all kinds met us here." It was said that the Yakimas were being driven back upon the Spokanes and that a part of the Nez Percé tribe had gone over to the hostiles. One could be sure of this at least, "that several of the tribes below were in arms, blocking our road, and had threatened to cut off our party in any event." [42]

One cannot say when the Jesuits had learned about the war, except that it

42. Doty, Journal, p. 35; cf. also NA, IA, LR (from Wash. Sup.), Stevens to Manypenny, 22 December 1855. Stevens Correspondence (YU), to Jeff. Davis, 19 February 1856. *RR, 12,* i, 223–24, is bowdlerized.

appears to have been antecedent to Pearson's arrival in the upper country. It would seem that for some time the Indians concealed any intelligence of the war from the Jesuits. Otherwise it is difficult to explain why the mission had not passed on the information to Stevens. By about November 22 the two Oblate war refugees had arrived at the Kettle mission. Stevens was to converse with them on his way through that country and have an opportunity to learn much about the recent fighting.

Down in California, Congiato wrote De Smet on November 29 about "the latest tidings" from the Interior Jesuits. The first reaction of the mission Indians had been "horror for the excesses committed below." The tribes "show no disposition to join them in the war." De Smet himself was convinced that the Indians "will doubtless follow the advice of their missionaries, who will divert them from such a great danger or so sad a misfortune." [43] This picture contradicts the one drawn by Stevens and by the missioners themselves. Perhaps it was compiled for publication during the war and therefore deliberately took a sunny view of things; perhaps it was simply a nervously voiced hope. It seems more probable, however, that it represents the initial reactions of the Indians, before the propaganda of the now victorious Yakimas began to increase the influence of the war faction. War fever seems to have risen rapidly thereafter, although it was temporarily lulled by Stevens' sudden appearance.

There was no question now of a land treaty with the Coeur d'Alenes. During a preliminary council at the mission they were persuaded to come down in a few days to a single, multitribal conference on the Spokane River. The tribesmen would have been considerably less favorable to the Governor's words had they been able to see his letter of two weeks previous to Agent Lansdale, where he reiterated his determination to move them from their own lands.

Stevens arrived at the mission on November 25, stayed the following day, and made a difficult nineteen miles to the west the next day. This hurried pace was due to "the excitement" which the Spokanes and Kettles ahead "were said to entertain." [44] Common sense also dictated that the party should strengthen itself by consolidating with fifteen miners who had fled as far as Plante's and were afraid to venture further. The day after leaving the mission Stevens penned a fervent letter of thanks for the "repeated good offices" of Fathers Joset and Ravalli. "I shall bear testimony to the efficient Services you have rendered in the cause of humanity." [45]

43. CR, 4, 1277. Bischoff, "Yakima War," pp. 75–77.
44. Doty, Journal, p. 39.
45. Joset Papers, No. 54, 28 November. Copied also into Joset's Latin report to Rome, RJ, MSax., II, 1, No. 14, 7 May 1856.

War on the Empty Plains

The three-day multitribal meeting at the Spokane River, Stevens tells us, proved to be "one of the most stormy councils" that had "ever occurred in my whole Indian experience." He had traveled down out of the mountains rapidly, took a Spokane encampment by surprise before they could be hostile, and arrived at Plante's place "at sundown", November 28. Plante, a quarter-blood Blackfoot and retired trapper, was the first settler in this area. His ferry service was a landmark. During the 1853 explorations he had served as a guide. He had been a restraining influence during the recent wagon seizure by the Coeur d'Alenes. His solidly constructed cabin of squared logs near the site of present-day Trentwood was to be the scene of the council.

Just three hours before Stevens' arrival, the Spokane Indians heard that he had detoured to the settlements via New York. Consequently they were "even more surprised than the Coeur d'Alenes at seeing us." They admitted to "no reliable news" about either troops or hostiles. The Governor "immediately" sent Indian messengers north to Colville for the Jesuit missioners, the main Kettle chiefs, and the Hudson's Bay factor Angus MacDonald. The next day, November 29, Father Ravalli arrived from the east with the Coeur d'Alene delegation.

Chief Garry of the Spokanes "was sent for," and had a "conference" with the Governor. While waiting for the other tribes to come in, preparations went forward for the trip south. The fugitive miners were organized into two militia groups. Stevens himself was uneasy. He approached the Indian talks "with the most anxious desire to prevent their entering into the war." He had sent all but three of the Nez Percés to prepare a way through their own people. During the council he learned that one of the remaining Nez Percés, Chief Looking Glass, was plotting with Spokane Garry to betray and kidnap him in the lower country.

Father Joset and Angus MacDonald arrived together at the camp on Monday, December 3. They brought a group of anxious settlers from Colville, as well as the chiefs and important men of the Kettle area. It snowed all day, discouraging any formal meeting. Snow fell heavily the next day, too. But since Garry had finally come back and other Spokanes had put in an appearance during the day, the council opened in the late afternoon. Delegates of the Coeur d'Alenes, the Kettles, the three Spokane tribes, and the San Poils attended, "all highly excited." The Okanogans would not come in.

The Indians were particularly determined to have a commitment that American troops never cross the Snake River. "Of course the Governor could promise no such thing," Father Joset commented afterward, "he evaded the question." The Kettles and the Spokanes evinced "extreme hostility" to the Whites. They "would make no promises to remain neutral." In fact if the fighting should gravitate in their direction, "probably many of the

Spokanes would join" the hostiles. A number of the Spokanes may already have been in the enemy camp. The territory between the Snake and Spokane rivers, said the Indians, "is our garden." [46]

Stevens tells us he "sought to raise a wall of adamant against the extension of hostilities." He really had little left to bargain with—aside from his forceful personality, which was almost enough. The qualities that had betrayed him with the Flatheads at Hell Gate now rescued him on the Spokane. Father Ravalli wrote the Governor some months later that "despite the general repugnance" of the Indians toward Americans, Stevens had personally "won their hearts" at this time.[47] Presumably the Jesuits and MacDonald exerted some influence to mitigate the hostility. Eventually the tribes seem to have been induced to promise neutrality. But before another month passed, Stevens would realize that these various tribes "have been much shaken" by further efforts to involve them; there was "great danger" again that they would fight.[48]

On the first day of the council Stevens labored to persuade the Indians he was not about to take their lands. "I have said to all the Indians, 'it is for you to say whether you will sell your lands and what you will have for them.'" If the Indians did not want to sell at all, that "is also good." The Governor was there simply as a friend and protector. In fact, "I do not think this is a proper time to talk about the land." The Indians, however, were very worried about the Governor's treaty policy.

Even Garry pronounced the Americans "equally guilty" with the Yakimas for the war. He was particularly upset that the American government was collecting depositions from French Canadian settlers on his lands in order to give them legal title under the Donation Act. Garry was angry too at White arrogance. "Do you think they are poor when you look at them that way? When you look at those Red men you think you have more heart, more sense than those poor Indians." The White man should not think he was "higher or better."

Stevens elaborated on the theme of his status as father. The Indians were being bad sons to him. He denied he had stolen Indian lands at the Walla Walla and Flathead councils. On the second day ex-Head Chief Stellam of

46. Council details from Doty, Journal, pp. 39–67; Joset Narrative; Stevens to Davis, as above, n. 42; *RCIA* (1856), pp. 186–89; *RR, 12,* i, 224–25. NA, cartographic division, J. Alden sketches, shows the site and raft-ferry in color. See also H. Stevens, *Stevens, 2,* chap. 35. The assumptions behind Jessett's odd interpretation of this council (*Spokan Garry,* pp. 129–31) will be touched on below, Chap. 5.

47. NA, IA, Wash. Sup., Misc. Recd., 2 August 1856.

48. Stevens to Gen. Wool, 28 December 1855, in *Message of the Governor of Washington Territory, also the Correspondence* (Olympia, 1857), p. 133. To avoid confusion with the very different book of nearly the same name edited by Gates (see above, p. 28, n. 30), this will be cited as *Message and Correspondence.*

the Coeur d'Alenes resisted this approach. "All the Indians are not yet your children; you have not yet made friendship." A chief of the lower Spokanes reiterated the plaint that "what has troubled the Indians was hearing that you would move the Coeur d'Alenes and Spokanes to the Nez Percé country." He considered the prohibition on ammunition sales recently, as well as the smallpox brought by the Whites, to be contributing causes to the Indian unrest.

A Spokane chief challenged Stevens: "when we see the soldiers don't cross the Columbia we shall believe you will take us for your friends." Head Chief Peter John of the Kettles also brought up the subject of the ammunition stoppage. Stevens handled the questions cleverly but with a sly indirection. His former ally Garry scolded him again, but finally extricated him from the situation. The chief suggested that the matter be tied up like a bundle and saved until later, since the Governor was now in a hurry. The Coeur d'Alene and Kettle chiefs acquiesced.[49]

On December 6 Stevens, with an escort of some fifty men under the imposing title of the Spokane Invincibles and the Stevens Guards, began his perilous dash southward through persistently miserable weather. Deep anxiety for his safety was felt down there. Acting Governor Mason declared the Interior a military district under martial law, the hostiles being unsubdued and the other tribes "being in an excited state." Militia moved forward to contact the Governor. A White victory of sorts by Kelly's volunteers, and the active loyalty of a portion of the Nez Percés, contributed to ensure his safety. By January 19 he was home in Olympia. Here "my time is completely occupied in making necessary arrangements for carrying on the Indian War."[50]

What was the role of Angus MacDonald in the council on the Spokane? He was no friend of Americans, either personally or in his official capacity as Hudson's Bay chief trader for the Columbia district. It seems unlikely that he would have contributed much to alleviate the discomfiture of Stevens, who was a leader in the movement to strangle Hudson's Bay trade. Humanitarian and even some commercial factors may have induced him, however, to help calm the Indians. At the time of the council MacDonald was a friend of the Jesuits, though not a Catholic. In 1854 Father Joset had regularized the trader's long-standing marriage to a Catholic Nez Percé, and later MacDonald was to send his children to the Flathead mission school.

That there was cooperation between Stevens and the trader is indicated both by the letter sent to the Governor after the Blackfoot Council and by another soon to be sent down to Olympia through Plante. In this second letter MacDonald passed on to Stevens the information that apparently no Spo-

49. Doty, Journal, for speeches.

50. NA, IA, Negots. Rat. Treaties, Stevens to Manypenny, 23 February. MD, Mason's proclamation and roster of Stevens' escort, December 1855; in Field, *National Guard*, 2, 55, 129.

kanes had joined Kamiakin. "On the nose of the New Year," he reported, the British, Indians, and Americans at Colville had danced Scottish strathspeys together. The Colville area was tense, and he urged the Governor not to risk the consequences of denying ammunition to the Indians there. "The most unrelenting barbarities are told here of your volunteers"; it was said they had murdered the chief of the Walla Wallas, "scalped and skinned him," used the skin for razor strops, and cut off his ears and put them in liquor which later an American officer drank.[51] The scalping and removal of ears had indeed taken place that December, causing a military scandal.

MacDonald seems to answer a query of the Governor's when he adds: "P.S. I question very much if the Coeur d'Alene priests would move to Antoine's even in the event of a war; perhaps I am mistaken." On the Coast at this time no international strathspeys were being danced. By the end of the year Governor Simpson of the Hudson's Bay Company was indignantly recording that Stevens "charges the Company with an active part in the war on the side of the Indians." [52]

AN ARMY WITH BANNERS

There had been clashes between troops and Indians on the coast by mid-November, as well as a sufficient number of bloody incidents to send half the territory's able-bodied men into homemade fortifications. In view of the scarcity of Whites in Washington, settlers and militia alike threw up over sixty defensive blockhouses, largely on the Coast. Governor Stevens envisioned that "the war will be emphatically a war of blockhouses. . . . Wherever 4 families are, they will build a blockhouse."

Arms, soldiers, and supplies were hurriedly ferried up from California. "A general distrust of all Indians pervades the public mind," the Governor reported to the national capital. "In short, this whole country is a frontier, within a few hours of the camps of the hostile Indians, and with four thousand friendly Indians in our midst of whose faith we cannot be certain." The matted, evergreen forests of the coast hemmed in the isolated settlements and obstructed movement. Communication with the outside world was still slow and painful. Many Whites would have abandoned the country altogether, except for their "absolute inability to get away." [53] It was to be a war of fear, and of aggressiveness inspired by this helpless fear.

51. NA, IA, Wash. Sup., LR, 27 January. MacDonald communicated to Stevens information on the Walla Wallas and Snakes next spring (H. Stevens, *Stevens*, 2, 198).

52. HB, D4, *52*, Simpson Corresp. in, 15 December 1856; cf. *53*, Simpson to Tolmie, 16 September 1857: "I have no doubt Stevens will give us any trouble he can at Washington"; and HB, A11, *71*, London Corresp. out, 1854 letters.

53. MD, Stevens to Jeff. Davis, 9 and 21 March 1856; in Field, *National Guard*, 2, 68, 76. H. Stevens, *Stevens*, 2, 157 (last quot.).

Though Indian depredations continued, the Whites could do nothing in the Interior during the winter. Along the Coast there was brisk action. The American navy found it necessary to adopt an Indian-fighting posture. When a large force of coastal and Interior Indians attacked tiny Seattle and destroyed part of it, the navy's sloop-of-war *Decatur* helped beat them back. Settlers in league with army and sea forces frustrated other attacks. There had been a massacre of settlers near Puget Sound in October of the previous year (and a more terrible massacre of Indians by militia in Oregon the same month). Now in February 1856 the massacre of 26 Oregon settlers together with a thirty-five day siege of the survivors further alarmed the Whites. Indian signal fires flickering on the Coast and Cascade ranges increased the tension. In some places great war canoes of northern coast Indians, bearing up to 75 men each, slipped through the high seas to strike isolated targets. The coastal campaigns of the Whites were fairly intense, reducing the hostiles to guerrilla warfare.

Colonel George Wright, a veteran of the Seminole and Mexican wars, brought up eight companies of the recently organized Ninth Infantry regiment from San Francisco in January and drilled them for a spring campaign in the Interior. Smartly turned out in pomponned kepis, full-skirted coats, and epaulettes, the elite Ninth proudly answered to bugle calls rather than to the usual infantry drum. A militia force in the Interior wintered in the field, mounting occasional sorties. This militia, reinforced to a total of 600 men, set out early in March on a grim search across the lower Interior for an Indian foe. The Indians of course avoided them. The only palpable result of this campaign was the loss of half the horses, due to lack of forage and to the cruel necessity of dining on them.

Colonel Wright's regulars, after much dithering, were at length prepared to sally forth into the wider Interior. When his 250 soldiers were suitably distant, the Klickitat, Yakima, and Cascade Indians descended far at his rear to hit the Cascades bottleneck. This Cascades Massacre proved to be one of the nastier sieges in Northwest warfare. Only nine soldiers were posted near the settlements there. In the ensuing action, twenty Whites were killed and twenty wounded. The troops, both regular and militia, arrived in time to save the beleaguered civilians. Phil Sheridan's dragoons almost managed by a clever attack to salvage some face for the Whites; but an injudicious bugler blared a timely warning, scattering the enemy.

The Cascades diversion over, Colonel Wright took the field late in April, this time to face a nightmare obstacle of streams risen to spring flood. The subsequent campaign was bizarre. With a command soon numbering 500 regulars, the Colonel walked his men fatuously over empty, endless landscapes. As a modern authority puts it: "more walking, talking, and less fighting transpired in the next weeks than in any frontier campaign" in our Indian fighting history. Wright's clumsy efforts amused his junior officer, Captain Archer; it was all "a bit funny," reminding Archer "of some of my early efforts to catch robins with fresh salt." George Gibbs thought the whole thing "a perfect farce." [54] Wright was prepared for a modern war but entirely unequal to this kind of Indian fighting. The enemy refused to accommodate him and determinedly kept their distance. Tentative contacts were made with Indian leaders, in line with Wool's conciliatory policy. To Wright's south, a great force of amateur militia operated with similar futility. A serious brush there with the enemy was interpreted by the Whites as a victory. But the Indians were more impressed by their own later capture of a government pack train.

As he trailed the Indians from place to place, Colonel Wright issued reports on his progress. In one he proclaimed that he had "determined to assume toward these Chiefs a tone of high authority and Power." In another he was plaintively "at a loss to know" why the Indian negotiators who had contacted him never returned. In yet another, "I do not despair" of having the Indians sue humbly for peace. The Colonel wrote a good deal about the Indians being frightened, of their being unable to elude him forever, of their being forced at some future time to surrender unconditionally.

Wright faced two embarrassing alternatives. He might be able to provoke the tribes into one or more pitched battles, to be followed by a never-ending guerrilla war. Or he might proffer a compromise peace settlement, which the Indians at this time would undoubtedly attribute to weakness. The Colonel himself saw a way out of the impasse. Governor Stevens' treaties were untenable and "ought not to be insisted upon." Wright recommended that the whole Interior be given back to the Indians. Stevens' anguish at this prospect may well be imagined; he communicated with the secretary of War, defiantly rejecting such a course.[55]

Many of the Indians were pacific at heart or were tiring of the war, and were not averse to a just settlement. On receipt of Wright's message of peace the Yakimas sent to the Jesuit mission among the Kettles, to obtain the advice of Father Pandosy. The Oblate sent them to the Colonel with a letter. Wright then sent for Pandosy himself, to act as interpreter and aide. The priest came down in a hard-riding rush, entering the Yakima war camp in time to interrupt preparations for a battle. As yet there had been no real fighting. The Indians had deployed at a distance, breaking and scattering when the Whites charged. They had feinted, fired the prairie, left ubiquitous and dis-

54. Archer Correspondence (Maryland Historical Society), to mother, 4 July 1856; Cascades fight in letter of 30 March. Cf. Bischoff, *Mid-America*, 31, 169; "Yakima War," pp. 197, 210.
55. Quotations in Bischoff, *Mid-America*, 31, 187–89. MD, Stevens to Jeff. Davis, 21 November (in Field, p. 126).

quieting traces, outrun all furious pursuit, and once had paraded in the distance so elegantly that some soldiers thought they were army reinforcements.

The Fabian retreats by Kamiakin were dimming his influence somewhat, and Father Pandosy took advantage of this. The priest gathered sixty of the peace party and took them to Wright under a flag of truce. Kamiakin's threats deterred more from participating. Later on, Pandosy again took the chiefs to see the Colonel. Wright's gratitude was expressed in his published report. "In all my operations recently the aid I have received from Father Pandosy has essentially contributed to our success." The priest "has great influence with these Indians, and has exerted himself both night and day in bringing matters to their present state." [56]

At this time the other Oblates seem to have been working to quiet such tribes as the Wenatchis and the Okanogans. By the end of July Wright was convinced that the Indians were in general becoming peaceful, so long as they were not disturbed in their Interior domain. Pandosy had persuaded 600 of them to move far from the influence of the hostile chiefs, Colonel Wright undertaking to protect them from the militia and to feed them. On these terms the war in effect was over, as far as the army was concerned. Governor Stevens, in the latter part of May, ruefully confessed: "it is not to be disguised that the tribes east of the mountains thus far consider themselves the victors." The Spokanes were harboring hostile Cayuses; Kamiakin was personally attempting to persuade the Spokanes to take up the war. "Not a White man now is to be found from the Dalles to Walla Walla." Congress was sufficiently disturbed to pass a special appropriation of $300,000 for the Indian Bureau, "on account of the state of Indian matters in Oregon and Washington," and for "restoring and maintaining the peaceable dispositions of the Indian tribes on the Pacific." [57]

To Governor Stevens the only alternatives remained either the old treaty terms or war to the bitter end. Perhaps he was genuinely convinced these terms afforded an opening to peace. Perhaps he couldn't afford to admit to himself the role of the treaties in the current war. Up in the Flathead country, in fact, Agent Lansdale had been instructed to proceed with the negotiation of yet another treaty. This was to be with the Kalispels, on terms similar to those imposed upon the other Flathead groups.

During the week before Christmas 1855, the agent invited Father Hoecken, Head Chief Victor Happy Man, and some principal men of the

56. Bischoff, *Mid-America, 31,* 192 (Wright report of 1 July); cf. p. 195 for July 7 visit. Waggett, *RACHS, 64,* 85–86.

57. MD, Stevens to Jeff. Davis, 24 May (cf. 7 July) (in Field, pp. 87, 97). NA, IA, Wash. Sup. (from Com.), 18 April (last quot.).

tribe to visit him, "intending to open the subject of a treaty with the Kalispelms." Hoecken discreetly refused the invitation. The chief and a dozen men arrived. As the conversation developed, Lansdale judged it prudent to avoid the subject of a treaty. Another attempt was made on December 27, Hoecken coming over to interpret for the meeting. The actual treaty council, after all these preliminaries, was held at the mission on Monday, March 24, of the following year. The interpreters were the Flathead tribesman Michael Revais "and others," apparently including Father Hoecken. Michael or Man-Who-Walks-Alone was a close friend of the Jesuits; his grandfather had come among the Salish as a member of the Lewis and Clark expedition.[58]

The discussion proceeded through the same wrangling stages as its predecessor but never resulted in a signed treaty. Chief Victor would agree to give up no more than half of his tribe's lands. Like the Pend d'Oreilles, Kutenais, and Flatheads before him, he absolutely refused to move away from his own country. He insisted that he needed at least a piece of his own territory. Lansdale was equally bound to take all the tribe's lands and to move them onto a reservation in Pend d'Oreille country. He was in no position to modify these drastic terms, being merely a spokesman for the absent Governor.

At the Flathead Council Alexander had predicted that the Kalispels too would refuse to move when asked, because they "have no horses, they have only canoes"—that is, a different way of life. Now Simon, brother of the Kalispel Head Chief Victor, pleaded for the Americans to show "pity on us, to give us a small spot" of Kalispel land, which was still so free from Indian and White intruders. That night the tribe talked the matter over by themselves. The majority voted against the American terms. The deadlock was absolute. Lansdale finally had to dismiss the council.

The talks had served no purpose except to upset the Kalispels and make them suspicious of the government. The documentation and proceedings of this abortive effort went off to the national capital. But Lansdale, once free of Stevens' rigid and military approach, adopted an entirely different approach to the problem. He sought the counsel of the missionaries, Fathers Hoecken and Menetrey. With their help he persuaded the tribe at least to agree in principle to move their center of actual residence to the new reservation area, without signing away any of their land. This was in itself no small victory. It was more than Stevens had yet accomplished anywhere in the Interior, except

58. Larger Lansdale Diary, 20 and 27 December (preliminary meetings). NA, IA, Wash. Sup., Treaty Records, Lansdale Report. Cf. proceedings of 24 March, appended to September 2 report of Stevens to Manypenny. Revais' picture is on file in BAE, photo section, from the 1884 Flathead delegation to Washington, D.C.

perhaps with the Nez Percés. Lansdale acknowledges in his report that "indeed this has been essentially accomplished under the advice and assistance of the Catholic Missionaries."

The Jesuits and the Second Walla Walla Council

There was to be yet another treaty council in the lower Interior, eventuating in another fiasco. Stevens was receiving disquieting news concerning the Indians in the upper country. None of these tribes were precisely hostile, but all were in a confused ferment and might easily plunge into war. Dangerous rumors and counter-rumors flew around both Red and White camps. In the Interior, "it is astonishing to know the rapidity with which intelligence is carried from one extreme of the country to another," so that "the commission of outrages (of which there have been many) by our people against an Indian is heralded forth by the hostile parties, augmented, and used as evidence of the necessity for *all* to unite in war against us." [59]

In fact, the agent at The Dalles was reporting how the settlers there favored massacring the peaceful Indians, children and all, as a measure of preventive war; they were restrained only by the coming of troops. Joset wrote to Rome in May, perhaps at Congiato's urging, frankly stating that "feelings of fear and hatred against Americans are shown by almost all the Indians." He added: "up to now we have restrained our own." [60]

Stevens expected little from the maneuverings of Colonel Wright's infantry; the Governor felt he would have to fight his own war and make his own treaties. But when he tried to buy powder at San Francisco in July for his campaign, General Wool warned the merchants that there was no war now in Washington Territory. Stevens could not allow this to be the end of all his previous treaty projects. As early as spring of 1856 he had turned his frustrated energies against the coastal Canadian squawmen suspected of sympathizing with the Indians, or at least of harboring feelings of neutrality. His summary arrests and subsequent attempts to foil habeas corpus proceedings resulted in a situation deliciously farcical. The federal judge ordered his arrest; he in turn, under martial law, arrested and incarcerated the chief justice, Edward Lander. Public opinion divided on the issue. For the rest of the year the factions wrangled violently, amid a flurry of writs and technicalities. Citizens and army officers, lawyers and public officials threw themselves into the fray—up to and including the President of the United States. Stevens was in his element.

59. *RCIA* (1856), p. 200, Stevens to Manypenny, 8 March.
60. RJ, MSax., II, 1, No. 14, May 7. *RCIA* (1856), p. 207, Thompson to Palmer, 31 March 1856.

Meanwhile, he was receiving news from the upper Interior through a kind of courier service. He had installed Craig as special agent in the Nez Percé country with instructions to communicate from time to time northward "with the settlers and Indians on the Spokane." Craig, a former trapper with the great Sublette, had married a Nez Percé and had long been homesteading in Nez Percé country. His information was to be relayed out through Shaw to Olympia. The most difficult part of this system of course was the upper country. Friendly Nez Percés and others could act as runners. Men like Plante and MacDonald would give help as occasion offered. The Governor's official functionary in the upper country was the French Canadian settler George Montour, ironically enough a British subject. But more important than Montour was Stevens' most valued correspondent and assistant, Father Ravalli.[61]

The news brought out continued to be depressing. Word came that even Chief Lawyer of the Nez Percés "considers the greater part of his tribe unreliable." Craig was convinced "there is no doubt but the Spokanes, or at least a part, have joined the war party." Warrior bands from the Cayuses, Palouses, Spokanes, Okanogans, Coeur d'Alenes, Kettles, and even Snakes—according to Craig—were already gathering south of the Spokane prairie. They boasted that the Red men had chased the Whites from their land. One mixed group of seventy had been in the Nez Percé country recently, talking "very saucy." Stevens summed up the situation in mid-1856: "the whole Interior is ripe for war." The Spokanes, Coeur d'Alenes, Kettles, and Okanogans "have accepted horses as the price of their services"; the Governor was sure "the general Indian war, of which I have been apprehensive, is about to burst upon us."

Despite reassurances from men like Montour, Stevens saw evidences that the Spokanes "are ready to join in the war." A letter from Joset to De Smet in 1855, forwarded to Rome, recounted the attempts of a Spokane chief to raise the Northwest tribes in war.[62] More than once Chief Garry advised Stevens that unless troops could be positioned as a buffer between his tribe and the hostiles, the retreat of the latter northward would involve the Spokanes also in the war. By now Stevens mistrusted Garry himself.

The mission tribes were equally perturbed. After hostilities had ceased and the Jesuit general could speak freely, he wrote to the mission aid society, the Propagation of the Faith at Lyons: "if it had continued longer, it would not perhaps have been possible to keep our Christians from taking part, for their

61. Doty, Journal, pp. 112, 103 (Craig). Wool incident above from Bischoff, "Yakima War," pp. 255–56.

62. RJ, MSax., II, 1, Joset to De Smet. Previous quotations in *RCIA* (1856), pp. 190–91 (Craig to Stevens, 27 May; Stevens to Manypenny, 5, 4 June).

minds were beginning to become agitated." The Coeur d'Alenes particularly were on the point of breaking out. Agent Lansdale became friendly with many of this tribe just after the war; from his experience he reported that Coeur d'Alene dispositions "were justly more than suspected during the late hostilities." [63] Joset told Rome in May 1856 of the disaffection of a party of Coeur d'Alenes who wished to join the war, which at the time was running in favor of the Indians; his letter reveals something of the Jesuit efforts for peace. Father Gazzoli was to send a similar report early in 1857. Fifteen years later Joset would commend the strong personal influence of the Kettle and Coeur d'Alene chiefs in 1856 who helped to restrain their respective tribes. [64]

As Ravalli told Stevens now, "a little thing may precipitate all the remaining tribes" except perhaps the Nez Percés into the war. This general unrest in the Interior induced the Governor to assemble another Walla Walla council. As early as January 24, 1856, Ravalli commented on the project. He was responding to a request from Craig concerning the dispositions of the tribes in the upper Interior. "It seems to me too much improbable," the Jesuit confessed, "that our Indians should remain in their own way inactive, having before them the example of the neighboring tribes."

In particular he listed four reasons: the tribes felt a sense of union "with the red people" and a kind of empathy toward the hostile cause; they believed their own turn would come next, with the Whites changing from friend to oppressor in the upper Interior as they had in the lower; the Colville miners would increase in number that spring, and then "the least occasion will be the beginning of massacre and war"; and finally, "Stevens with his determination of coming this spring for the treaty, and with competent force," will seem to be coming "for deceiving and killing the Indians, and I shall not be astonished if his arrival is the signal of hostility." Prescient words! [65]

A set of letters came down to Olympia that January, through Montour and Father Ravalli. In these, Garry of the Spokanes and Seltis of the Coeur d'Alenes sent messages of peace. The important Spokane chief Sgalgalt had called an informal meeting of the chiefs from both tribes; through Sgalgalt they too reaffirmed their promises of peace. Ravalli must have translated and written out Seltis' message at least, as the Jesuits invariably did. Later in the month a similar set of letters, in French, was dispatched. Communications from the Kettles and others followed.

In April 1856, when Stevens requested a military escort for his council, he

63. FL, *1857*, Rome (divers), 29 April; see also FP, I, 5, same date (in French). Lansdale Report, *RCIA* (1857), p. 377.

64. RJ, MSax., II, 1, Joset to general, 7 May 1856; fasc. 12, Gazzoli to same, 10 February 1857. BJ, Coll. 1ac–4ac, under 3ac, Joset to De Smet, 29 May 1871.

65. Bischoff, "Yakima War," pp. 330–31.

was projecting a grand meeting of all the chiefs from the Columbia to the Bitterroot, and from the Blue Mountains to the Canadian border. The hostiles were welcome; perhaps at least the wavering neutral tribes could be influenced. Stevens communicated with Ravalli, probably in July, to ask his services on a monumental scale. The Jesuit acknowledged this letter on August 2. He was already among the Spokanes with Montour; he assured the Governor he would help Montour interpret Stevens' message to the Indians. The priest enclosed a number of lengthy notes in French from four Spokane chiefs, five Coeur d'Alene chiefs, and one Pend d'Oreille. He then embarked on a great tour lasting some twenty days, in which he negotiated with chiefs over a wide range. Stevens was to tell the naval commander at Puget Sound that he received from the priest letters "from every chief of the friendly tribes to the northward, and between the main Columbia and the Bitter Root Mountains." These "letters are unquestionably the true dictations of the Indians, as they are written by Father Ravalli." [66]

In the latter part of August, Stevens again sent word to the Interior chiefs —Nez Percés, Spokanes, Coeur d'Alenes, and Kettles. He invited them to a council soon, hoping to cool the rising war fever among the uncommitted tribes. Much of the preparatory work among the Indians for this council would be done by Father Ravalli. Whatever the Governor's estimate of Jesuits as a whole, he looked upon Ravalli as "a gentleman of great worth and intelligence." In Ravalli's word "I can place implicit confidence." Ravalli indeed seems to have been the kind of person it would be difficult not to like. "A man of fine physique, tall, portly, and of commanding presence," with "a broad forehead, a true Roman nose, and finely-cut features," he was sociable and "merry." He was also "witty, very quick at repartee, and had a wonderful fund of anecdote at his command." In any company "he was at home, the most noticeable figure in it and the center of attraction." His major virtues were kindness and readiness to help with his mechanical, medical, and spiritual skills. He was later to be a favorite with miners of all creeds; the settlers in Montana would name Ravalli County after him. His defects were a lack of firmness and, oddly, a weak grasp of the Indian languages. Later, Congiato was to consider him a poor missioner at Colville and move him; nor was he successful with the Coeur d'Alenes. [67]

66. NA, IA, Wash. Sup., Misc. Recd., 30 January and 2 August. The latter include Polatkin, Sgalgalt, Garry's brother Tlimikun, and Quaqualise; the Coeur d'Alenes Vincent, Peter, Stellam, Melkapsi, and John Peter; and Kamistan. Both quotations from *Message and Correspondence*, p. 122.

67. *Message and Correspondence*, p. 122. I. M. Leo, "Father Ravalli, Missionary, Pioneer, Teacher," *Winston's Weekly* (repr. in *Daily Missoulian*, 8 March 1904); cf. also *JMUS*, 2, 455–56; the biography by Palladino in Bib., below; L. W. Reilly, "Father Ravalli, Pioneer Indian Missionary," *Catholic World*, 125 (1927), 67–73.

The Jesuit accepted the Governor's commission, sending an Indian runner to the Coast to say that he "would visit in person the several tribes, convey anew to them" the Governor's summons, and encourage delegations to the council from both neutral and hostile tribes. Stevens tells the commissioner of Indian Affairs on August 31 that "the good father will be here in person in some few days," bearing detailed information. Ravalli at first was inclined to believe that both the hostiles and friendlies could be induced to come. In a council there was a chance that the road to peace would be opened for the former, while the restlessness of the latter could be eased. It was at this time that Ravalli rode so widely among the Cayuses, Yakimas, Palouses, and other hostile groups, the service for which he has been most remembered.[68]

He held conversations especially with war leaders like Kamiakin, Skloom, Owhi, and Qualchin. None of them could be induced to appear at the council. Looking Glass of the Nez Percés took a dim view of the Governor's proceedings, and told Ravalli he would not be present. The idea of another council with Stevens, especially at ill-omened Walla Walla, seems to have been repugnant to almost all the Indians. Ravalli could not persuade the Spokanes to come. Garry sought to soften the blow with a letter pleading that his tribe would be too busy gathering salmon. Ravalli's own Coeur d'Alenes were out hunting buffalo on the Plains in order to keep them from Kamiakin's influence. "From Father Ravalli's report," Stevens realized "that all the Indians in the upper country, if not openly hostile, were yet far from entertaining a disposition of friendship to be relied upon." It was disconcerting to learn that Kamiakin had "personally visited most of the tribes" and been "universally credited by the Indians." [69]

The council was a dismal failure. Negotiations lasted from September 11 to 17. The Cayuses and some smaller tribes arrived in a state of open hostility, firing the grass as they approached. Kamiakin and other war chiefs hovered in the near vicinity. Craig was on hand from the Nez Percé country, Montour and Plante from the Spokane, with Lansdale representing the Flatheads. Fortune had even stationed a protective detachment of regulars four miles below the council grounds. To consolidate its peace, the army planned to occupy the Walla Walla Valley with a rudimentary fort; Colonel Steptoe and four infantry companies had just come out to choose a site.

Father Ravalli arrived on the evening of the eighth. Father Joset also seems to have participated; a letter from him at The Dalles places him close by. There were chiefs from the Nez Percés, Walla Wallas, Umatillas, Cayuses,

68. *RCIA* (1856), p. 192. Fuller, *Pacific Northwest*, p. 239. Bancroft, *Washington*, p. 169. "His influence was largely instrumental in holding the northern tribes quiet" ("Ravalli," *Catholic Encyclopedia*, *12*, 662). Similar comment in "Ravalli," *DAB*, *15*, 393–94.
69. Doc. in H. Stevens, *Stevens*, *2*, 210–11.

Tyighs, Palouses, John Days, and Des Chutes. Weapons were obviously being concealed by many braves. Even the friendly bloc among the Nez Percés joined the evening war dances. In the conferences the Governor was not prepared to move an inch from his previous treaty decisions. The Indians, casting the Whites in the role of defeated aggressors, refused to treat except upon the basis of keeping their own lands.

By the thirteenth "so alarming was the condition of affairs" that Stevens moved his camp close to the troops, advising the commander that all the Indians were hostile except about half the Nez Percés, and even they had warned that Craig's life could no longer be protected in the Nez Percé country. The Governor finally adjourned the council, having offered the tribes no compromise beyond "unconditional submission to the justice and mercy of the government."

He was retiring from the council grounds when the attack came. He had to fight his way free vigorously in order to effect a junction with the military. Rescued by the regulars of Steptoe, he then beat an inglorious retreat. In his report to the secretary of War in Washington, Stevens estimated that half the Nez Percé braves took part in the attack, together with 200 Yakimas and Palouses, "the great bulk of the Cayuses and Umatillas," and about 70 Walla Wallas and others. The war was spreading. "The least thing," he wrote nervously, "may cause the Spokanes, Coeur d'Alenes, Colvilles and Okinakanes to join them." He attached special blame to Wright's military cooperation, "so feeble, so procrastinating, so entirely unequal to the emergency."

In his October 22 reports to the superintendent of Indian Affairs and the secretary of War, Stevens pours out the vials of his wrath upon the military, upon the Hudson's Bay Company, and upon the Jesuit missionaries in the north. The Governor was particularly angry, Father Ricard revealed to his Oblate superior in France, at what he considered Ravalli's failure to swing the tribes over to his position. Much can be forgiven Stevens, since his career was at stake; two months later his political enemies would contrive to have him censured publicly by the territorial legislature. Whatever the justice of such moves, the gubernatorial barque was heading into dark waters. In his reports indignant phrases tumble out: "disgraceful to the government," "the most bitter consequences," demands to be "inflexibly insisted upon"; the Indians "should have been struck in battle and severely chastised." He wants to see "vigorous military operations—the whipping of hostile Indians into absolute submission."

What is *outré* is the blame he visits upon the Jesuits. Announcing that he is "determined to have no agent on the Spokane" because of the Jesuits' adverse influence, he particularly denounces their neutral position. "Siding with the Indians, siding with the Americans, but advising the latter particularly to agree to all demands of the former," the Jesuit counsel is for "murderers to go free, treaties to be abrogated, whites to retire to the settlements." This is "a position which cannot be filled on earth—a position between the hostiles and the Americans." He did not hesitate to "state on my official responsibility that the influence of the Catholic missionaries in the upper country has latterly been most baneful and pernicious."

Nor is this anger brief. In his November report to Commissioner Manypenny, the Governor drives the thing home. The Jesuit and Oblate influence "has of late been pernicious; for from the fear of their lives, from their seclusion from all civilized society and for other reasons, the Indians have had as much control over the minds of the missionaries as the missionaries over the minds of the Indians." The Catholic missionaries, "though not a word is said, encourage the Indians to resistance or to the making of impracticable demands." Through the Stevens end of the telescope the view is not without its own logic. Still, can this be the same Stevens recently so fervid in his praise of Ravalli? Blessed, but not by everybody, are the peacemakers.[70]

PRIESTS BEHIND THE SCENES

Ravalli stands out in these episodes more boldly than his colleagues; his services were official and consequently well documented. But one sees enough to realize that all the Jesuits were busy. At the time of the second Walla Walla Council Father Joset, in answer to a query from Rome, assured the general that "indeed we have left nothing undone which might help us to restrain our Indians from taking up arms." He was able to add that "thus far they have preserved a perfect neutrality." The details of his own work among the Kettles are shadowy, but like Menetrey among the Kalispels he is obviously at work. We glimpsed Joset at the Spokane River and second Walla Walla councils, as adviser to Hoecken before the Blackfoot Council, at the Coeur d'Alene troubles concerning Stevens' wagons, and as the recipient of Stevens' thanks for his many services. Father Caruana, who came to the missions five years after the war, was to write that Joset made "every effort to prevent the Indians from clashing with the whites."[71]

70. Archer Corresp., 3 October 1856. Ricard on Ravalli, in Bischoff, "Yakima War," p. 295. MD, Stevens report to Sec. of War Jefferson Davis, 22 October; in Field, *National Guard*, 2, 119–23; cf. H. Stevens, *Stevens*, 2, 227–30, report to Commissioner Manypenny, October 22. NA, IA, Wash. Sup., Stevens to Manypenny, 1 November 1856, as in J. P. Donnelly, S.J., "The Liquor Traffic among the Aborigines of the New Northwest, 1800–1860," unpublished doctoral dissertation (St. Louis University, 1940), p. 244.

71. RJ, MSax., II, 1, No. 15, 6 September 1856 (in Latin). Caruana memoir in *LPT* (1904), p. 108: "faceva ogni sforza"; the context of the chief's life being discussed shows that this cannot refer to his 1858 services.

His companion among the Kettles, Father Vercruysse, probably did rather little with the Indians. This is less because he was subordinate to Father Joset than because he was a far less able man. Popular with the French Canadian settlers, he was not too successful in Indian work. He tended to be sharp and overbearing, and was given to fierce, though effective, sermons. Stevens found him "to be a simple minded, good man." But plagued by an irritable and tactlessly imperious character, Vercruysse eventually had to be sent away from the missions altogether.

The last of the six Jesuit priests in the Interior is Gregory Gazzoli. Urbane and talented, he belonged to a noble family of Rome; his uncle was a cardinal, and he himself had been baptized by Pope Pius VII. He had been with the Coeur d'Alenes since 1850. During most of this time, as during the war itself, he was the superior of the Coeur d'Alene mission. Stevens speaks of him in 1853, as receiving "me with the most pleasing hospitality." [72] He knew Gazzoli was Ravalli's superior, and asked both for their help during his treaty tour. Why then is Ravalli more prominent in services to peace? Perhaps because Stevens took a special liking to him, and because Gazzoli spared him from the usual work of the mission to pursue this more dramatic course. In any event, it is unlikely that Father Gazzoli himself was inactive in restraining the Coeur d'Alenes.

In a letter to De Smet a year later, Hoecken particularizes on Ravalli's field of action. "Father Ravalli has worked as hard as he was able to pacify the tribes who live more to the west, that is to say, the Cayuses, Yakimas, Palouses, etc." Since Ravalli had sent his own Coeur d'Alenes onto the Plains for buffalo hunting in the winter of 1856–57, perhaps it was he who induced Garry and the Spokanes to do the same later that winter and again the next winter. The two tribes were partners in food-gathering, and a number of Catholic Spokanes lived at the mission establishments in 1856. At least one of Father Ravalli's tours, according to Stevens, centered upon "all the friendly tribes on and in the neighborhood of the Spokane" river.[73]

At the time of the second Walla Walla Council, when the Jesuits were visiting widely among the tribes, Joset sought to allay the anxieties of the general at Rome. "I see you are worried about the war; I think there is no danger for our men." The Indians "all have heard enough about the Blackrobes so that they mean no harm to us; at present they show themselves more friendly than ever, even the Protestants who had seemed to avoid us before." The Americans too "publicly give us signs of their esteem; the governor himself

72. NA, IA, LR (from Wash. Sup.), Stevens to Com. Manypenny, 6 December 1853; *JMUS*, 2, 385, 337. *RR*, 12, i, 133–34.

73. RJ, MSax., II, 11, Hoecken to De Smet (in French), 15 April 1857; cf. CR, 4, 1240. *RCIA* (1856), p. 192, Stevens to Manypenny, 31 August 1856.

put in writing that he owes us much on account of what we are doing in the cause of peace." Hoecken similarly writes back to De Smet that among the Indians "no one is ignorant that the Black-gowns are not enemies." [74]

Surprisingly, the complex of Flathead tribes, for all their professional militarism and interrelation with the Interior Indians, remained the most stable. They were still smarting from the 1855 attempt to seize their land, and their anger would grow as every Stevens promise proved false. There was overt provocation as well. Numbers of Nez Percés and Spokanes, hostile now to the Americans, "endeavored to communicate their hatred" to the Flathead tribes. Hoecken counterbalanced their influence, however. The chiefs connected with the mission were "firm" and repulsed the overtures.[75]

A helpful circumstance was the orientation of the Flathead tribes as much toward the Plains as to the west. The war, even as late as the spring of 1857, "took away all hope of procuring" supplies from the west; but shipments up the Missouri to Fort Benton sufficed in those years. The Blackfoot peace was in its flower, and the Flatheads were in any case on the Plains for well over half of each year. Was the cholera, which was abroad again among the confederates in both valleys, a deterring factor? Agent Lansdale managed a few reports from the Flathead country, sent west via Colville. But they only said he had no information about the war. Even about the Flatheads he knew little, because they were all away hunting. Later in the year he removed to the Coast, where he praised the Flathead confederates for their friendship and steadiness. Cumming similarly wrote to the commissioner from the Plains next month, commenting on the restraint of the Flatheads, "who have been so long fostered and instructed by the self-sacrificing Jesuits on the western slope of the mountains." [76]

Two other clerical peacemakers deserve some notice for their work in the Interior. It seems probable that the diocesan priest John Brouillet played some role. In a general way he had been "charged with the inspection of the Indian missions" by the bishop; and he was experienced in handling troublesome Indians. At the time of Agent Bolon's murder Brouillet was temporarily helping at one of the Oblate missions. He warned Agent Olney at The Dalles of the murderous temper of the Indians. General Wool had great confidence in Brouillet's ability to effect pacification. He served notice that it would be "exceedingly gratifying" if the priest would go into the Interior as guide and interpreter to his own expedition, "knowing that you can do much, if needed,

74. RJ, MSax., II, 1, No. 15, 6 September; ibid., Hoecken letter, above, n. 73.

75. Ibid., Hoecken letter, above, n. 73. NA, IA, Wash. Sup., Misc. LR, Ravalli to Stevens, 3 May 1857.

76. NA, IA, LR (from Wash. Sup.), 1 February. *RCIA* (1856), p. 193, 31 August; p. 66, 25 September. Cf. Lansdale's "decided" praise of Jesuit influence, *RCIA* (1857), p. 377, 22 September. CR, 4, 1228, 1239 (supplies, cholera).

to bring about a general peace." [77] Wool's expedition never took place, and Brouillet may have done little in the Interior.

Less obscure is the role of the diocesan priest Toussaint Mesplié. He was present at Palmer's treaty with the Wascos and certain bands of the Walla Wallas, on June 25 as Stevens was traveling to the Flathead country. Mesplié had been pastor of St. Peter's church at The Dalles from 1851. In the spring of 1855 his parish held only 117 Whites but 300 Indians; of the 500 people baptized up to that date most were Indians. When Captain Archer paid a tourist's visit to his church in March 1856, "to see the converted Indians at their devotions," the sermon and hymns were in the trade dialect Chinook. Mesplié had worked extensively out among the Wasco, Wishram, Des Chutes, Dog River, and other tribes. He paid irregular visits to the Yakimas, Klickitats, Cayuses, Wallulas, and Walla Wallas. We are told that during the war he "prevented many Indians from taking the war path." He is particularly credited with having prevailed upon the Wascos to refrain from war. Where it served the cause of peace, he also kept the government informed of the dispositions of the tribes around him.

His post was so situated that all missionaries and Catholic messengers coming down from the Interior passed near it. Thus he was in an excellent position for gathering information. Before the war, in fact, Mesplié complained that this central position tended to "exhaust" his resources; Oblates and Jesuits, with their Indian companions, would stop over during their long trips, making disconcerting inroads into the foodstuffs. On more than one occasion in his apostolic journeyings during the war years, Father Mesplié is said to have protected White travelers from unfriendly Indians. At the time of the Cascades massacre his influence seems to have restrained any number of Indians in that area. [78]

Mercifully, the war languished and subsided. After the disaster of the second Walla Walla Council, Colonel Wright soothed the tribesmen with promises that Whites would not settle the Interior until ratification of the treaties. This effected an uneasy truce. The departmental commander, General Wool, ordered a small outpost thrown up just to the northwest of Fort Dalles; his declared object in selecting this spot for Fort Simcoe was "that the troops might be in communication with Father Pandosy" nearby. Wool further ordered his post commanders to show kindness to Pandosy "and keep alive in

77. Sister Marian Josephine Thomas, S.H.N., "Abbé Jean Baptiste Abraham Brouillet, First Vicar General of the Diocese of Seattle," unpublished master's thesis (Seattle University, 1950), pp. 32–33, 122.

78. Mesplié Papers, No. 11, 18 August 1853 (visitors). In NA, IA, Negots. Rat. Treaties, cf. treaty for his presence. Bradley-Kelly, *Boise Diocese,* has a documented biography as chap. 2; cf. p. 99. Archer Corresp., to mother, 16 March 1856.

him those dispositions by which we have so much profited in information."

Kamiakin's recalcitrants planned a Christmas-week attack on the site of Fort Simcoe, but instead ran off the fort's herd of horses; did Father Pandosy's warning to the fort help here or (as Captain Archer believed) did Kamiakin deliberately leak the information to Pandosy's Indians as a feint, to distract military attention from the horses? At any rate, the military considered the war to be over in July (though Captain Archer, for one, thought this attitude "strange") or at least by December 1856.

Open skirmishing by a few tribes had given way to a diffused and general malaise over both Oregon and Washington territories. Contact was slowly reestablished between White and Red. One agent on the Coast wrote that he had been out of touch with his Salish tribe, the Nooksacks, throughout the war; "in fact I could not see any of them, nor could I get them to come down until the Jesuit [Oblate?] priests came here" in the fall of 1856.[79] The Jesuit general was relieved to hear the war was over. In April 1857 he wrote to Lyons that "the fears inspired by the Indian war against the Americans would seem to be dissipated, now that peace has been concluded." [80]

Numbers of Indian leaders were righteously hanged by the authorities as opportunity offered, or betrayed and assassinated by individuals. The army opposed this policy of petty retribution. When Chief Leschi was to be hanged, feeling ran high between the coastal settlers and the military. A few hours before the scheduled execution, the soldiers arrested both the sheriff and his deputy, using the federal charge of selling whiskey to the Indians. Thus they were able to spirit away both the officials and their death warrant. The action precipitated angry public demonstrations, a hanging in effigy of the local military commander, an extraordinary session of the legislature, a busy repealing of old laws and confecting of new, and special sittings of the supreme and district courts.

It had been "an expensive and disastrous war, from the effects of which the territories will suffer for many a year." War claims against the federal gov-

---

79. Archer Corresp., to mother, 31 July 1856, and to sister, 14 December, continued 5 January, 1856. H. D. Guie, *Bugles in the Valley* (Yakima, 1956), Wool order on Pandosy. *RCIA* (1857), p. 326, E. C. Fitzhugh to Nesmith, 18 June. These must be Oblates. Even Bancroft as late as 1884 will describe Blanchet, Demers, and Rosati as "Jesuits," in *History of the Northwest Coast, 2,* in *Works, 27–28* (2 vols. San Francisco, 1884), 536–37. The Oblates D'Herbomez and Chirouse were having "a very good effect" on the Puget Sound Indians from the time of their arrival in October 1856 (Agent Paige, in Waggett, *RACHS, 64,* 91).

80. FL, *1857,* Rome (divers), 29 April 1857. FP, I, 5, same date. Urban Grassi, S.J., has an account of the war in *MC, 13* (1880), 14–16; he was stationed in California during the war, and with the Indians from 1861. Two Catholic Indians, he says, conducted negotiations at Olympia preliminary to peace.

ernment, amounting to six million dollars, were carried East in the form of massive documentation in 1857 and presented to a reluctant Congress. Many easterners shared Horace Greeley's scorn for this "little bill for scalping Indians and violating squaws." But one can hardly blame the settlers for the temper of their feelings. America had owned Oregon now for only a decade, yet Bancroft estimates the number of dead from Indian attack in the southern or Oregon territory alone at nearly 700, plus 140 wounded, few of these in actual battle.[81]

81. J. Ross Browne Report, in *HED*, 35 Cong., 1 sess., 38 (1857), p. 2. Bancroft, *Washington*, pp. 175 n., 176 and n.

5. The Shadow of War

THE LITTLE GARRISONS

THE NEXT WAR arrived with shocking abruptness. Colonel Steptoe had been leading 157 troops on a routine march into the upper Interior. Rolling Palouse lands swelled and dipped around them, for all the world like an ocean frozen in action. The Sunday morning air breathed a peace proper to early spring on the Interior plains. Then, without premonition or prospect of trouble, the tiny command discovered itself "suddenly in the presence of ten or twelve hundred Indians of various tribes—all armed, painted and defiant." [1] The subsequent running battle culminated in a desperate stand on a lonely ridge in the Indian country. This Steptoe Disaster provoked the "War against the Northern Indians," a grim punitive campaign which stalked the hostiles that fall. The Northwest was suffering its third Indian war in less than a decade. And this time in the very storm center stood the Jesuit mission tribes and their allies.

The previous war had simply settled into a condition of permanent tension, a cold war. The elements of this tension were differently mingled in different parts of the Indian world. The Whites themselves were still of two minds. The larger number of settlers were determined to throw open the whole territory immediately; to this faction the only source of Indian trouble was the refusal of Congress to ratify the treaties of 1855. The army regarded the settlers as greedy, aggressive, and irresponsible. To the military men, dispassionate observers in all parts of the West, the situation seemed as familiar as it was unnecessary.

The American army in those days was an absurdly small affair, seldom reaching a total of 11,000 men before 1855 and not much over 15,000 thereafter. Behind a paper strength of 17,000 in 1858, there were only 11,000 men available for field service. This whole army would scarcely have amounted to two weeks' casualties in Grant's final battles of the approaching Civil War. During the period just before the Civil War nearly three-fourths of the army

1. NA, EW, Army Commands, Dept. Pacific, Fort Walla Walla Letterbook, Steptoe Report, 23 May 1858; also in *SED*, 35 Cong., 2 sess., 1 (1858), p. 346.

was holding the far West. Very few of the men available were posted to our Pacific Northwest—none at all until 1849—a total of 329 in 1854 which rose to 750 and then doubled in the war crisis of 1855–56. Under the circumstances, there was little room for grand strategy. Behind a protective screen of forts, thrown up in patterns dictated by immediate necessity and available resources, troops were shunted about to meet emerging crises.

Essentially these troops comprised a tightly knit family of professional officers supervising an unruly body of men often foreign in origin. An artillery captain named Phelps (later to be a Civil War general and candidate for the presidency) remarked upon the foreign complexion of the army of the West during the 1857–58 Mormon War. Since so many Mormons were also foreigners, he wrote with some exaggeration, "we exhibit to the sun the ridiculous spectacle of an army of foreigners led by American officers going to attack a set of foreigners on American soil." [2] Many soldiers were part of the exodus consequent upon the Irish potato famine, and De Smet always visited these Catholic contingents at the forts during his coming peace mission in the Northwest. Two years after the war Father Joset would act as informal chaplain to a garrison of these Irish soldiers at Fort Colville.

Sudden acquisition of a Far West empire had forced an administrative reorganization upon the army in the 1850s. In 1858 the isolated Oregon country was a segment of the far-flung Department of the Pacific. At departmental headquarters in San Francisco, just a year before the Steptoe war erupted, General Newman S. Clarke had replaced the strong-minded Wool as commander. Reception of this news on the Northwest Coast occasioned revelry and merry gunfire.

The Pacific department was responsible for 718,367 square miles of territory, almost all of it wild country. In our northern section of the command, eleven strategically placed little stockades held a scattered force of less than 1,600 men. Six of these forts were off on the Coast. Five lined the entry to the Interior: Fort Cascades at a supply portage, Fort Dalles as headquarters of the Ninth Infantry and watchdog at the Interior threshold, the hopeless new outpost Fort Simcoe just to its north in the Yakima country near Haller's battleground, and little Fort Walla Walla just being built, a perilous thirty miles out in the southwest corner of the Interior. The unevenly distributed garrisons were just about sufficient for their own defense. They were mostly in-

2. "Diary of Captain Phelps," in L. R. and A. W. Hafen, eds., *The Utah Expedition, 1857–1858, a Documentary Account*, Far West and Rockies Ser., No. 8 (Glendale, Cal., 1958), p. 115. General and local army background in SED, 36 Cong., 1 sess., 2 (1858–59), p. 576; 35 Cong., 2 sess., 1 (1858), p. 3; supplemented by military survey of Captain T. J. Cram, the department's chief topographical engineer (Cram Report, in HED, 35 Cong., 2 sess., 114 [1855], pp. 1–126); cf. below, Bib., under Bandel, Beers, Clark, Ledbetter, Prosch, Mansfield, and Prucha, and above, p. 130, n. 27.

fantry, though Walla Walla, for example, boasted a small representation of mounted dragoons. There were no further defenses in the Interior; even the Hudson's Bay post of Fort Colville had dismantled its palisade.

In short, the Northwest country was "in an almost wholly defenceless condition," at the very time when a general Indian rising was most feared "both east and west of the Cascades." For this reason one local commander refrained from making any arrests which might possibly cause Indian trouble. General Clarke's headquarters approved this discretion and urged that it be continued, because "there are no troops disposable at present by which you can be reinforced." [3] If one extends his horizons further to the east or north, the Rocky Mountain country, the Plains beyond, and of course the Canadian wilderness were even more in Indian hands.

Military communications were a desperate problem. An infantry force was like a large and ailing dinosaur. In Indian warfare it was also a half-blind dinosaur, fighting gnats. It could be pushed into the wilderness only for short distances and for short periods. It easily died of hunger or grew exhausted and demoralized. To forward its supplies even the short distance from Fort Dalles to Fort Walla Walla in 1858 required ten days. Yet its source of energy and of life reached all the way back to San Francisco, so that it drew up its men and materiel sluggishly at formidable expense over ocean, river, and wasteland.

The most ambitious of the projects afoot to improve the transportation network began this very year. The army proposed to cut a crude wilderness trace six hundred miles through the heart of the Indian Interior, roughly from Walla Walla to the fur post Fort Benton out on the Plains, linking the Columbia River to the headwaters of the Missouri. This would provide, at least during the dry months, a continuous though difficult boat-and-wagon route from the Atlantic to the Pacific. It was an ancient dream, but the War Department was particularly anxious to hurry it into being now; otherwise the threatening Indian troubles in the far Northwest could find the army unable to shuttle its men swiftly, while prospects of war with England made the alternate sea route unreliable.

The right man was at hand to volunteer for the job. Lieutenant John Mullan, a young West Point engineer with experience in the Seminole Indian wars, became fired with an almost visionary enthusiasm for the road during his service with Stevens' railroad surveys. He received much help from the Jesuits in planning and executing his project; "I ever found them my staunchest and most reliable friends." By mid-May Mullan had his official party in the

3. Contemporary report in C. M. Gates, ed., "Defending Puget Sound," *PNWQ, 36* (1945), 74, 76 ("defenceless"). NA, IA, Oreg. Sup., LR (January–December 1858), Clarke to commander at Fort Hoskins ("no troops").

field, working out of Fort Dalles on the preliminary task of clearing and grading. As guide and interpreter he had Sohon, the artist of the Flathead Council. Indian eyes watched their every move.[4]

GOLD RUSH: A SECOND FRONT AGAINST THE INDIANS

Mullan's was not the only penetration of the restless Interior Indian domain. In the spring of 1858 another survey party was at last about to run the boundary line between America and Canada. This tardy project, attended by loud quarrels between the principals, was well known to the Interior tribes. Men like Stevens had emphasized its significance in conversations with the Indians; and in Canada the possibility was being mooted of using Indian labor almost exclusively. In an 1858 council a Spokane chief gave voice to tribal discontent over the boundary. "One man comes with a party from the cold side of heaven and says this is my line," while another "with his party from the warm side says the land on this side is mine; and so they settle it, and we the poor Indian have nothing to say about it."

Meanwhile a rabble of miners had never ceased probing the upper country. In March 1857, for example, "parties are fitting out at The Dalles to explore that region." Now, at this most inopportune moment in Indian history, news came of a great gold strike in the Interior just over the Canadian border. The excitement was "intense." Places of business closed, soldiers deserted, and miners fought at San Francisco for places on northbound ships.[5]

At least 23,000 Californians hurried by boat and 8,000 more overland during the turning of spring into early summer. Reports were published on gold takings of fifty to two hundred dollars a day. *Harper's Weekly* ran a breathless story about "the New Eldorado in British America," thoughtfully providing their readers with a full-page map and later a page of cartoons. Even during the coming Indian war, miners were to jostle troops on the steamers going north. Oregon and Washington newspapers touted their respective

4. Early Mullan Road Report, in *HED*, 36 Cong., 2 sess., 29 (1860), p. 5 ("friends"). Trimble, *Mining Advance*, p. 39. M. G. Burlingame, "The Influence of the Military in the Building of Montana," *PNWQ*, 29 (1938), 137. *DAB*, *13*, 319–26. O. O. Winther, *The Old Oregon Country, a History of Frontier Trade, Transportation and Travel* (Stanford, 1950), chap. 14.

5. Owen, *Journals and Letters*, *2*, 177, letter to Nesmith, 11 July 1858 (council). HB, D5, *43*, Simpson Corresp. in, from Grahame, 9 March 1857 (miners). BC, Record Office transcripts, C.O. 60, *1*, Pt. 1, Douglas to Secretary of State for Colonial Dept., 8 May 1858 ("intense"). Cf. Archer Corresp., to mother, 16 May and 19 June 1857, on military escort leaving to escort boundary commission. Chief Factor James A. Grahame is commonly spelled Graham in American military correspondence (see *SED*, serial 975, passim).

areas as jumping-off places for the Interior. The *Weekly Oregonian* especially recommended passing via Fort Dalles up through the Yakima country, or pursuing a parallel route toward the east. As early as May 8 Governor Douglas in Canada informed London that all available small craft were "pouring their cargoes of human beings into Fraser's River." By summer parties from the East Coast were coming overland, and ships lay in the harbors of Boston and New York announcing passage to the mines. Almost on the very day of the Steptoe defeat, Stevens gleefully wrote from the nation's capital that the gold rush rivaled California "in her palmiest days." [6]

The British government became alarmed. This was not the first time their thoughts had turned to a possible American "filibustering descent" upon their defenseless western province. The Americans were said to be designedly intimidating or overawing the Canadians. The Hudson's Bay Company had previously encouraged London's nervousness concerning American dragoon movements near the border; they had warned that a chain of American forts was about to appear along the international line. A power of English troops had then been sent to the Red River. The rush of American miners now transformed this vague concern into a real crisis.

Local authorities warned London on May 19 that "on all sides the Americans are striving to force a passage into the Gold District through their own territories." If this continues, Canadian Oregon "will soon be overrun and occupied." Governor Douglas feared that "if the majority of the immigrants be American, there will always be a hankering in their minds after annexation to the United States, and with the aid of their countrymen in Oregon or California at hand they will never cordially submit to British rule nor possess the loyal feelings of British subjects." He therefore requested "a small naval or military force."

Two months later the British representative held talks with the American president; the president dispatched an official "to the Pacific Frontier for the purpose of advising and controlling the population who were pouring" into western Canada. In August the British government snatched their western territory from the Hudson's Bay Company and hastily constructed the crown colony of British Columbia to include all the mainland from the ocean to the Rockies, with Governor Douglas in almost dictatorial control. A picked detachment of 160 volunteers from the royal armed forces appeared

6. BC, Record Office transcripts, C.O. 60, *1*, Pt. 1, Douglas, May 8 letter; ibid., H.B.C., F.O., *735–36*, 186, Stevens to Lewis Cass, 18 May. Stevens Papers, to Yantis, 3 August; also in Ronald Todd, ed., "Letters of Governor Isaac I. Stevens, 1857–1858," *PNWQ, 31* (1940), 445. *Harper's Weekly,* 17, 24 July 1858. *Oregonian,* 24 April, 1 May 1858. Trimble, *Mining Advance,* chap. 2.

on the Oregon scene. They promptly and efficiently quelled a small American outbreak.[7]

California elements were prominent at the mines, and the Interior Indians knew how they had tried to exterminate the California Indians in one of the most brutal pages in the history of the trans-Mississippi west. Captain Cram, chief topographer for the Department of the Pacific, had reported that the miners in the upper Interior in 1856–57 were "Anglo-Saxon devils in human shape" whose crimes against Indians make one's blood boil. But if the miners added to the Indian unrest on both sides of the border, they also occasioned a firm British counterreaction which reassured the Canadian tribes and thus helped to limit the coming war.

The tribes tended to ignore Canadian and American claims to jurisdiction. They continued to live as though the boundary did not exist. An expressed reason for setting an army post at Colville as late as 1859 would be to control this free wandering across the line. Indeed Lieutenant Mullan, in his official report on the 1858 Interior war, would blame the Colville troubles which occasioned it on Canadian Indians, "many of whom come from British territory for the purpose of aggression and plunder." [8]

In the north, then, the Colville and Fraser mines were soon prolific centers of trouble between Red men and White. To the south, the Indians observed with darkening fear the creeping advance of the military forts, and the threat of the great road. The Interior Indians, especially those in the Jesuit country, had a double frontier of Whites closing in upon them.

THE MORMON FRIGHT AND THE INDIANS

In the distracted view of the White settlers, an allied problem loomed to their immediate south: the Mormons. Mormons were a less accessible bugaboo than were Catholics, but for that very reason all the more suspect. Who

7. BC, Record Office transcripts, F.O. 5, *617–63*, 168, —— to Th. Banister, San Francisco, 1855. *Copies of Despatches from the Secretary of State for the Colonies to the Governor of British Columbia*, in Papers Relative to the Affairs of British Columbia (London, 1859), Pt. 1, doc. 1, 19 May 1858. Douglas, May 8 letter, above, n. 5. Record Office transcripts, H.B.C., F.O., *735–36*, Napier to Earl of Malmesbury, 29 July (president). H. J. Deutsch, "The Evolution of the International Boundary the Inland Empire of the Pacific Northwest," *PNWQ*, *51* (1960), 75. A. C. Glueck, "Imperial Protection for the Trading Interests of the Hudson's Bay Company 1857–1861," *Canadian Historical Review*, 37 (1956), 121, 126–27, and passim. M. A. Ormsby, *British Columbia: A History* (Vancouver, 1959), chap. 6.

8. Trimble, *Mining Advance*, p. 18, citing reports (Cal. miners). John Mullan, *Topographical Memoir of Colonel Wright's Campaign*, in *SED*, 35 Cong., 2 sess., 32 (1859), p. 71. Cram Report, *HED*, p. 86; cf. p. 75.

knew what dark thoughts were harbored by this remote, secretive people, or what delicious scandals attended their polygamous doings? And since Oregon Whites reacted so predictably and satisfactorily to anti-Mormon rumors, wily Indians did not hesitate to furnish a suitable supply. The Oregon people had blamed Indian depredations on the Mormons from as early as the latter's arrival a decade ago; two circumstances now elevated their suspicions to certainty. A tiny Mormon settlement had been pushed north into what is now Idaho, not far below the Flatheads' Bitterroot Valley. Mormon traders were active in the Bitterroot itself, as we see in Hoecken's diary and from other Jesuit writings as well as from Owen's journal entries. On the heels of this activity came the Mormon War.

In 1857 President Buchanan executed a clumsy maneuver intended to upset Mormon control in Utah. He marched 2,500 troops overland, ostensibly as part of a military reorganization; a new panel of civilian officials was simultaneously to be introduced into the territory. The air of mystery enveloping this sly attempt, together with the memory of past persecutions, as well as loose talk by the troops, led the Mormons to anticipate an attack upon their liberties. Thus the Northwest was provided in the winter of 1857–58 with a "Mormon rebellion" on its southern flank. It was to prove a bloodless affair of talk, winter quarters, flight, more talk, and eventual agreement. But it could easily have exploded into violence several times during 1858 and 1859.

The Mormon troubles created serious tension in the Oregon Indian country. When the army gave thought to marching troops out of Fort Vancouver and down past Fort Walla Walla to Utah, the fear of an Indian uprising in the Interior discouraged them. Conversely, the troubles pinned down a considerable percentage of the American army when they were badly needed in the Interior Indian war. By the spring of 1858, 4,000 troops were committed to the Mormon project, some 2,500 of whom would be in Utah by summer. Contracts were let out for a hundred trains of twenty-six wagons each; preparations were afoot to carry sixteen million pounds of freight, in an effort involving 4,000 teamsters and 40,000 oxen.

Up in the Bitterroot Valley the trader Owen, acting as Indian agent, was frightened. He feared the Mormons were planning mischief with the Indians, possibly even a seizure of the valley's "locality and resources." In January 1858 he notified the Indian superintendent that the Mormons might soon attack. Against later war claims, he devoted "a week of unceasing labor" to prudently listing and certifying all his trading properties. In a separate letter to the superintendent again the same day, he recounted how "the whole country has been thrown into a state of alarm" by Brigham Young's declaration of martial law. "In fact the Country is filled with all kinds of reports sufficient in themselves to alarm most anyone." The Flatheads were already restive.

Owen announced to the Walla Walla commandant, Colonel Steptoe, his intention of leaving "for the East" immediately via Fort Benton on vague "business of a serious nature." He realized that "it may appear as if I had abandoned my post in the hour of peril"; but to offset this he had ordered his assistant to remain bravely with the store until violence forced him away. Ten days later Owen dropped the pretense of a business trip. Now he intended to drive his stock to Walla Walla as "a place of greater security" than the Bitterroot. He meant to go down as soon as the way was open in spring. A month later, on February 19, the Indian Bureau renewed his appointment as special agent. On March 19 he got out of the Bitterroot and headed for Walla Walla, a month before the Indian war finally broke.[9]

Lansdale, still technically Flathead agent but now resident on the Coast, recorded in his diary that the Mormon settlers in Nez Percé country had invited into alliance "all the Indians willing to fight" the Americans. Kamiakin's brother, the malicious gossiper Skloom, told the commandant of Fort Simcoe that the Mormons had twice sent emissaries around the Interior tribes to raise them against the government. Steptoe, at Fort Walla Walla, believed that the Indians considered using the Mormon revolt to cover their own rising; should the Mormons win or even hold on, Indian trouble could be expected in the Interior.[10]

The Colonel was particularly sensitive to this Mormon-Indian problem. His reconnaissance for a road west from Salt Lake City in 1854 had embroiled him briefly in Utah politics; for a time it had seemed certain that he would be appointed territorial governor there. Street brawls were an almost daily occurrence between his men and the Mormons that winter. Ordered at the time to investigate an Indian ambush, Steptoe became convinced that the Mormons were implicated; he had urged strong action against them. After his coming defeat in the 1858 Interior war, he would write into his report his suspicions that the Mormons supplied ammunition.[11]

9. NA, IA, Wash. Sup., LR, from employees in Flathead and Blackfoot agencies, Owen to Nesmith, 9 January 1858. Different letter of same day to Nesmith on property in Owen, *Journals and Letters*, 2, 170; same day to Steptoe, ibid., p. 171; 20 January, to Nesmith, ibid., pp. 172–73, and in NA. NA, IA, LR (from Oreg. Sup.), Nesmith to Commissioner Mix (relaying the January 20 information and requesting status), 1 April 1858; cf. next letter to Mix, 24 April, copy in Owen, *Journals*, 2, 173–74; cf. Fort Owen diary for 1858, ibid., *1*, 195–97.

10. Larger Lansdale Diary, p. 178, January 1858. *SED* military correspondence 1858; here, from NA, EW, Army Commands, Dept. Pacific, LR, from Major Garnett at Fort Simcoe, 30 January. Ibid., Major Grier to asst. adj. genl., 16 May 1858.

11. N. F. Furniss, *The Mormon Conflict 1850–1859* (New Haven, 1960), pp. 40–44, 162–63, 170, with evidence of some small Mormon involvement. The author does not give attention to our area, but see B. D. Madsen, *The Bannock of Idaho* (Caldwell,

Others took up the theme. The Oregon legislature memorialized Congress concerning the Interior Indian troubles, adding as special reason for concern "the present hostile and treasonable attitude assumed by the fanatical inhabitants of Utah." The Mormons were "in a position to exercise a powerful influence over the great interior tribes East of the Cascade Mountains"; they "are already reported to have seduced many bands to join them by offers to supply them with arms and ammunition." In January 1858 one prominent settler wrote east: "we expect a Mormon and Indian war; if Uncle Sam wants Oregon soldiers, he must pay us the five million expended in the last war that he yet owes us." General Clarke and Colonel Wright were both to believe the Mormons responsible for the 1858 Indian war, but they could not discover any real evidence.

Relayed to the national capital, these fears reinforced an already flourishing suspicion. Indian Commissioner Denver published his opinion that a "large portion" of the Indians would help the Mormons; he had ordered Agent Twiss in the winter of 1857 to visit the tribes all along the eastern edge of the Rockies to counteract Mormon influence. President Buchanan in his first annual message that December accused the Mormons of "tampering with the Indian tribes."

But the tiny Mormon settlement in the Interior, huddled within its palisades against the hostile Indian world about it, was making pathetic efforts to pacify the tribes. In 1857 the Mormons wrote to Owen, requesting him to induce the Pend d'Oreilles to make peace with the nearby Bannocks. Again, when the Snakes and Bannocks threatened war against the Nez Percés, the settlers tried to dissuade them with a feast. By early 1858 the Indian threat around the Mormon village had come to the point of open war. The mountain man John Powell, unable to dissuade the Indians, warned the settlers. On February 25 the battle came, leaving two Mormons killed and five wounded. In March 1858 the settlement was withdrawn. It had lived only long enough to set free a hornet's nest in the Oregon imagination. Alarums offstage to the south were therefore to attend the coming Indian war. And the fearful Whites were to be more than usually unreceptive to words of moderation and peace.[12]

Idaho, 1958), chap. 4. On Flathead trading in Utah and Mormon traders in the Bitterroot from 1850, see *JMUS*, 2, 383, 390 (letters of Accolti and Vercruysse); Stevens to Nesmith, 25 July 1857 (WU, and Todd, *PNWQ, 31*, 417). Cf. also W. B. Smart, "Oregon and the Mormon Problem," *Reed College Bulletin, 26* (1948), 53–56.

12. Logan, *OHQ, 44*, to sister in Springfield, Portland, 14 January 1858. For Oregon legislature quotations, see OS, Papers of Territorial Government, Nos. 8899, 8894, memorial to U.S. Senate and House, 25–27 January 1858. Trimble, *Mining Advance*, pp. 94–99. Furniss, pp. 159–60.

COLVILLE AND THE COLD WAR

In a determined attempt to appease the Indians, the army closed the whole Interior. They forcibly removed all except miners, missionaries, the few remaining Hudson's Bay workers or ex-workers, and the handful of settlers already holding land under the Donation Act. Post commanders were to inform the tribes that the Stevens treaties were neither ratified nor binding, so that no rights had been lost. Commanders should be firm in a friendly way, encourage all chiefs "without exception" to visit the local post, should redress all grievances, and hunt down the liquor sellers. The Cascades, Wool announced, were to form "a most valuable wall of separation between two races always at war when in contact." The Interior ought to remain inviolate, the end of the frontier, a "natural reserve" for the Red man.[13]

But Stevens set his face against this. Having weathered both a legislative and a presidential reprimand, he had resigned his governorship in the spring of 1857 to begin a new career as territorial delegate in Congress. He worked valiantly for treaty ratification, payment of Indian war debts, and complete opening of the Interior. The army declined to take a strong stand in Washington, D.C. Stevens determined to smoke them out. He was particularly anxious to hang the Yakima "murderers." He soon brought the secretary of War to authorize their arrest, though matters eventually came to a head before these Indians could be taken.[14]

A partisan of Stevens remaining on the local scene was J. W. Nesmith, the fire-eating militia leader who had charged the Catholic priests with deliberately instigating the recent war. As luck would have it, the Department of the Interior had just consolidated the entire Northwest Indian service as an economy measure, under a single supervisor far down at Salem. The supervisor was Nesmith.

Both Stevens and Nesmith were keenly alive to the imminence of war. Delegate Stevens wrote in frustration to the national commissioner early in 1857, quoting his agent Craig: "things are just as far from being settled as they were last summer." Rumor had it that a common war chief was soon to be chosen. Reports from the Interior "are of a serious character, going to show the determination on the part of the Indians to renew the war in the spring to be general." And Superintendent Nesmith warned Washington of "many indications" that the Indians would resume hostilities. A report arriv-

13. OH, 970.5, Special Orders No. 87, 29 June 1857. This reiterates the previous closure of 1855. H. Stevens, *Stevens*, 2, 226, for last two quotations by Wool in November 1855.
14. Stevens Papers, to Nesmith, 2 December 1857; also in Todd, *PNWQ*, *31*, 421.

ing from the Northwest in October viewed the situation as "daily growing worse"; it foresaw a general Indian war, involving the tribes east and west of the Cascades with many of the powerful Canadian tribes as allies. An elaborate report in November made the point that "even to Walla Walla a military escort is now necessary." Distance simply insulated the Interior tribes from any control or even cognizance by the superintendent. Nesmith complained that he would have had to travel 900 miles to reach the farther Rocky Mountain region, 160 to The Dalles, 550 to the Pend d'Oreille tribe, and so on.

Throughout 1857 a slow, burning desperation mounted throughout the Indian country. A band of renegade Yakimas was said to have "seized and whipped" Father Pandosy; he fled north once more to the asylum of the Coeur d'Alene mission, prophesying a general war. Out on the Coast numbers of settlers still refused to return to their farms. War canoes of the Canadian Indians "are all around us and gathering nearer every day." The federal customs collector for the Puget Sound district had his head detached and carried off. Stevens urged Captain David Farragut (of later "Damn the Torpedoes" fame) at San Francisco Bay to send naval help. The Governor also proposed that the chiefs of the Northwest be sent on a junket to the national capital, to overawe and subdue them. He estimated that thirty thousand dollars would suffice for this project. But even in making the suggestion, he suspected that it came too late.[15]

From San Francisco, General Clarke was anxiously penning official apprehensions to the War Department: "in Oregon and Washington territories, east of the Cascade range, I consider it unsafe to remove a man for service elsewhere." The secretary of War entertained the project of making "a great Cavalry depot" at Walla Walla, concentrating there "the whole" of the first dragoons—half of the army's most effective Indian-fighting arm.[16] At Fort Walla Walla in January 1858, Colonel Steptoe wrote San Francisco about a "meditated outbreak." He especially mistrusted the Snakes, Cayuses, Walla Wallas, Palouses, Yakimas, and Spokanes. In fact "there has never been a

15. NA, IA, LR (from Wash. Sup.), 13 February; Stevens to Manypenny, 6 March 1857 (cf. Chirouse letter in *AFQ*, March 1861, p. 163); Agent Robie to Stevens, April 1857. LR (from Oreg. Sup.), Nesmith to Commissioner Denver, 1 September 1857; Pandosy to Mesplié, 1 January 1858, but probably sent 17 April 1857. Special Cases, Report on Oregon-Washington, 1857 (distances). October report in "Defending Puget Sound," p. 75. Stevens Papers: E. C. Fitzhugh to Stevens, Bellingham Bay, W.T., 5 April 1857; Stevens to commander of Pacific Squadron through D. G. Farragut, Olympia, 26 August 1857; Stevens to Acting Commissioner Mix, Washington, D.C., 17 February 1858, on Indian delegation (Todd, *PNWQ*, *31*, 406, 420, 430).

16. Clarke Report, 1 January 1858, in *SED*, 35 Cong., 2 sess., 1 (1858), p. 336. Stevens Papers, to Nesmith, Washington, D.C., 29 December 1857 (also in Todd, *PNWQ*, *31*, 426–27).

doubt on my mind, that very slight encouragement would at any time suffice to revive their late hostile feelings." And "at this moment there is much restlessness among the Indians, which I have vainly tried to remove and now only await a fuller manifestation of it in some decided act of hostility"; the Indians are in constant debate over going to war. He worried about the Nez Percés; they were still receiving contradictory assurances on the question of treaty ratification. Even in the past summer he had felt "little doubt that it will all result in a collision before the summer is over." [17]

Similar unease prevailed in January among the new White settlers in the neighborhood of Fort Walla Walla. The Walla Walla Indians had ordered them from the valley, and the more diffident settlers had already taken refuge at the post. "The state of the Indians is alarming," reflected Flathead Agent Lansdale in the coastal Oregon City, "or at least uncertain all round." Later he writes that the Indians in the lower Interior *"wish* to be friendly," but if settlers or miners come up the military trails *"they will kill them."* He cautioned his Yakima and other Indian visitors against violence. Special Agent Owen reported in January that Indian outlaws were poisoning the minds of the Flatheads. Even the legislature of Oregon put on record its fear of an explosion in the Interior.[18]

The Jesuits were particularly in touch with this agitation and particularly concerned. At the beginning of May 1858 the Jesuit general in Rome was explaining to the mission aid society, the Propagation of the Faith at Paris, the fears that the Interior Indians had of losing their country and being forced onto reservations. The general told how the mission Indians here knew about the government and settlers seizing Indian lands on the Plains. Now they feared their own turn had come. Joset was sensible of the feelings among his remote Coeur d'Alenes. During the whole winter of 1857–58 "a great preoccupation prevailed" among them. Their nervousness and susceptibility to wild rumors caused him grievous worry.[19]

Joset wrote to De Smet in February 1857. "The hearts of our poor people are upset; within two years, what a change! They have become deaf to good advice." Even now they "expect at every moment to see their lands invaded." During the 1847 war, they had not really wanted to side with the disaffected

17. NA, EW, Army Commands, Dept. Pacific, Fort Walla Walla Letterbook, Steptoe Report, 29 January; NA, EW, Army Commands, Dept. Pacific, LR, Steptoe Report, 3 June 1857. Contrast the sunnier reports from the Fort Simcoe area in Archer Corresp., 16 July and 14 September 1857, 8 and 15 June 1858.

18. Larger Lansdale Diary, pp. 178–79, January 1858. Owen, *Journals*, 2, 170–71 (to Nesmith, 9 January). OS, memorial, 25–27 January 1858, as above, n. 12. Cf. NA, IA, LR (from Oreg. Sup.), Jos. Lane to Mix, 12 March 1858.

19. FP, I, 5, general to Association (in French), 2 May 1858. Joset Narrative (this citation explained below, p. 247, n. 11).

tribes. But now "we are afraid lest some violence on the part of the miners push them over the edge; all are like mice keeping watch on the movements of the cat; they appear to mistrust all whites."

Especially do the tribes "fear a treaty; in any event they protest they will yield only a part of their lands; poor people." The authorities "tell them one thing and have them sign something different." Blunt words indeed! "For all the treaties concluded, though two years have passed, there is not an Indian who imagines that they have ceded the totality of their lands; they think that the government has acquired no title to their country." In April, Hoecken told De Smet of the "great antipathy" abroad among the tribes. And Ravalli was predicting "a general rising" of the mission Indians by spring of 1858. The only note of optimism, oddly enough, came from an answer by Ravalli to a query from Stevens shortly before. He put the Spokanes and Coeur d'Alenes "in perfect tranquillity" toward the Whites; they were at that moment occupied in preparing a war against the Snakes, to "revenge the death of Garry's brother." [20]

The various Interior tribes, after their hunt on the Great Plains, usually gravitated to a common rendezvous for a week or two of conviviality and converse. This seems to have been in the Sun River Valley west of the Great Falls of the Missouri. This year all their talk was of war. The wife of one of the four autonomous chiefs of the Southern Okanogans later described this meeting. There was agreement that a united front was desirable: "we talk different and we cannot understand one another, but we have the same ways and the same kind of skin, therefore we should not fight among ourselves." At the time of the 1855 treaty also, the Blackfeet suggested to the Flathead confederacy an alliance against the Whites. "Until now we have quarreled about one [buffalo] cow, but now we are surprised by a third [party]," they told the mission Indians; "we will unite ourselves against him; if the Americans attack you, I will aid you; if they attack me, you will aid me." [21]

There were fewer restraining influences than ever in the Interior. The Protestant missioners had long been gone. The Oblates had left recently for good. Pandosy seems to have hung on in the Kettle-Okanogan area during the coming war. His decades of work from 1859 at a new mission on the east shore of Lake Okanagan in Canada, and the Oblate mission among the Puget Sound Indians during and after the war, are not irrelevant to the Interior story. But the direct Oblate impact here was finished. On June 6, 1858, the

20. MJ, IX, AA, Joset to De Smet (in French), 26 February 1857; RJ, MSax., II, 11, Hoecken to De Smet (in French), 15 April 1857; cf. CR, 4, 1240. MJ, Ravalli to Joset, quoted in Hoecken to De Smet, 2 April 1857, and Ravalli to De Smet, 16 February 1858 (all in French). NA, IA, Wash. Sup., Misc. LR, Ravalli to Stevens, 3 May 1857.

21. Cline, *Southern Okanagon*, p. 76 (the Kartar chief); on the probable place see Haines, *Nez Percés*, pp. 56–57. Joset Narrative.

bishop of Nesqually would number his total personnel, from the Pacific Ocean over through the Rockies, at two diocesan priests, six Oblates, and five Jesuits.[22]

As for the Hudson's Bay presence, it was strictly circumscribed and hard pressed by American policy. The Company's trade advantages and influence were diminished. Thus the Flathead trade was largely closed to them; Owen was not only agent for the tribes from 1857–60 but also licenced with a near monopoly of the region's trade, to the detriment of the Flathead economy. With Walla Walla and the other forts gone, Colville was the last trading post of importance remaining to the Hudson's Bay Company in the American Northwest. Yet if one had to choose a probable focus for the outbreak of war, the most likely was the Company's own Fort Colville area. And the most likely tribe would be the Jesuits' Kettles. The Colville Valley, over fifty miles long, varying from one to three miles wide, ran northwest to southeast near the Canadian border. There had always been a straggle of settlement here, but these had been sympathetic ex-employees, married to squaws and forming almost a part of the Indian world. These forty half-breed families were likewise under the spiritual care of the Jesuit missionaries. Now, however, there were miners and whiskey.

Early in 1857 the Company's people at Vancouver informed Montreal that at Colville the Indians "for the last two or three years have been very troublesome and unmanageable." They have at Vancouver "no intelligence of a reliable nature from the interior, but some queer stories are current here, about Indian Movements." Another Vancouver official later reported that "the Indians about Colville are in a very unsettled state and Mr. MacDonald anticipates trouble with them; they are not near so friendly with the Company's people as they have been, and evidently there is something brewing among them." Governor Simpson told his officials that "we must exercise great Caution and Vigilance in that quarter, as I fear there is likely to be trouble between the gold diggers and the natives." He urged his men to remain "friendly" with the Indians but not to "connive at or assist their acts of Violence towards the whites who wish to embark in the gold washing business" at Colville.

This was particularly disturbing because the Kettles were as numerous as tribes like the Flatheads, Coeur d'Alenes, or Spokanes. The Indian memoir in Stevens' report of 1853 describes them as "one of the largest of the Selish."

22. FL, *1858*, Répartition, 6 June (in French); same document in Bishop Blanchet Papers (SA) and in Blanchet Letterbooks (PA), II, 48–49. See also Mesplié Papers, folder 1, to archbishop, 22 October 1858; and Sr. M. C. Morrow, "Bishop A. M. A. Blanchet and the Oblates of Mary Immaculate," unpublished master's thesis (Seattle University, 1956), doc. app. B.

Joset, their resident missionary in 1853, reckoned them at between five and six hundred. The great Wheaton Council of 1877 counts them as 680. Other Catholic Indians were associated with the mission, bringing the total to about a thousand.[23]

To assess this Colville situation, Stevens sent a special agent to the area in the spring of 1857, "a prudent and reliable man" named Benjamin Franklin Yantis. He was instructed to contact the Jesuit missionary there. A Kentuckian about fifty years old, Yantis had a distinguished career ahead of him in Washington and Idaho politics. He found Father Joset "a most agreeable and devoted friend to yourself as well as the Indians." For his part the priest greeted the agent with a fervent "thank God." He assured him, as did "several of the most reliable" Canadian settlers here, "that it had been with great difficulty that the Indians have been kept down for some months past."

Joset arranged for a council with five of the main Kettle chiefs. "We had quite an interesting night of it," Yantis wrote. The basic cause of the difficulties, all agreed, was drunkenness. Twice the Indians themselves had assembled in a mob to beat the liquor seller, and twice the chiefs managed to dissuade them. Even while Yantis was investigating, a shipment of sixteen kegs of whiskey arrived; the agent confiscated it and secured a unanimous petition from the settlers approving his action. During the war itself, over eight hundred gallons would be imported into the valley in a single month and "every drop of it sold immediately." A modern student of the liquor traffic in the Pacific Northwest asserts that "probably during no single year were more complaints registered by Indian Agents and missionaries" about illegal liquor sales to the Indians than in 1857. Father Joset told Yantis it was "high time" to put the federal laws on this into execution; most of the Indians themselves, he said, hoped for this. But the whiskey traffic in the Northwest was well-organized. Nesmith and others despaired of controlling it.

Nothing lasting could be accomplished through a single visit by a special agent. Yantis had to report again in June "quite an unsettled feeling amongst the Indians." He felt that a permanent agent "is indispensable for the peace and safety of the inhabitants." In November the unhappy settlers met in a local store both to organize and to petition the army for a garrison.[24]

23. Partoll, *PNWQ*, *30*, 407. FP, May 2 letter, for Indian and half-breed numbers. HB, D4, *48*, Simpson Corresp. in, Mactavish to Hudson's Bay House, 23 February 1857; D5, *43*, Grahame to Simpson, 25 March 1857; Simpson Corresp. out, Ser. 1, to Mactavish, 14 October 1857. *RR*, *1*, ii, 413 (incl. Joset). On Wheaton Council, see below, p. 417.

24. Stevens Papers, Stevens to Nesmith, Olympia, 25 July 1857; Washington, D.C., 16 November 1858; Yantis to Stevens, Fort Colville, 27 May, 2 June; Colville Valley, 17 June 1857; also in Todd, *PNWQ*, *31*, 412, 414, 417, 457. MJ, IX, AA, Congiato to De Smet, 2 September 1858 (gallons). Yantis returned to Salem 22 October 1857 (Owen, *Journals*, *1*, 181). Modern student is Donnelly, "Liquor Traffic," p. 245, with last Joset to Yantis quotation (21 May) on p. 246.

THE AMERICAN AND FRENCH RELIGIONS: THE NEZ PERCÉS

The thousands upon thousands of Interior Indians—Kalispels, Lakes, Pend d'Oreilles, Flatheads, Kutenais, Coeur d'Alenes, Kettles, Spokanes, San Poils, Okanogans, Wenatchis, Sinkiuse-Columbias, Nez Percés, Cayuses, Palouses, Walla Wallas, Yakimas, and the lesser tribes—were alienated and aggrieved. So fragmented were these tribal groupings, so little used to cooperation among themselves, that there seemed small likelihood of their uniting against the common foe. Nor was this necessary for an Indian war. Multitribal Indian wars did not demand such union nor even collaboration. When neighboring tribes were simultaneously hostile to the Whites, it usually meant that the army had a long, desperate war on its hands. If these tribes joined in some kind of union, the war became that much more sustained and terrible. Confusion, anger, and fear were beginning now to effect such a common front. The major exceptions were the small pro-White nucleus among the Nez Percés and the similar but less enthusiastic faction within the Eastern Spokanes.

The Americans had encountered precious few allies in the Interior. On the Coast they enrolled some for the 1856 war: a company of Cowlitz, one of mixed Cowlitz and Chehalis, a scouting company of Squaxons, and Chief Patkanim's ambiguous alliance of eighty Snoqualmies and Snohomish. It was a different story among the free-riding Interior tribes. The American presence, which had persisted from the fur-trading days in the Rockies, diminished steadily after the 1837 panic. The "Bostons" had never enjoyed the organization, traditions, finesse, and status of the "Frenchmen" or "King George's men." In view of the Oregonian distaste for Indians and squawmen, their casual assumption of superiority and ownership, and their hurry to supplant the Indian on the choicest bits of tribal domain, it is hard to understand how the Americans acquired any Indian allies at all. Having done so among factions in two Interior tribes, they proceeded to misunderstand and exaggerate this influence beyond its true value and to lionize its leaders.

The Americans believed, as one of Colonel Wright's officers put it in 1858, that Hudson's Bay officials "inculcate" in the Indians a "reverence" for their own officials "and a proportionate contempt for the Americans." Lieutenant Saxton, reporting in 1854 on his exploratory march from Walla Walla to Fort Benton, complained of the Interior tribes "looking to United States officials as intruders and owning, as many do, England as their natural guardian." In the event of war between England and America, he feared therefore that "the powerful tribes might be made the instruments of incalculable injury to our frontier settlements." [25] Certainly the French Canadian squawmen and

25. Lawrence Kip, *Army Life on the Pacific: A Journal of the Expedition against the Northern Indians, the Tribes of the Coeur d'Alenes, Spokans, and Pelouzes, in the*

half-breeds, even aside from their affinity with the Company and the economy of the fur trade, had witnessed too much American injustice to their Indian friends elsewhere on the frontier.

This division unfortunately acquired a strongly religious dimension. Long ago the Episcopalian Simpson, the Hudson's Bay governor in charge of the Oregon country, had foreseen the tribal disruptions resulting from tension between Protestants and Catholics in a tribe. He had opposed the sending of Catholic missionaries. Later, impressed with the influence of Catholicism and its "imposing ceremonies," he urged that more priests be sent.[26] Catholicism, of course, was the religion of most Hudson's Bay workers; thus it enjoyed among the Indians the status and protective coloring of the resident "French."

When Protestant missionaries came up the Oregon Trail, with their English speech and acculturative hopes, they became in turn the "American" religion—a view the Oregon nativist himself shared. The federal investigator J. Ross Browne, in his report on the 1855 war, severely blames both Catholics and Protestants for the effect their mutual hostility exercised upon the Interior Indians. Some French Canadians and Iroquois used ridicule among the Indians to discredit Protestant ministers in the Interior, even calling them "the Brothers of the Long Knives" or dragoons. (Father Point comments wryly that these Catholics were not "actuated by higher motives.")[27]

What of the Jesuit missionaries? Though foreigners, they soon sought naturalization. They were not French like the Oregon diocesan clergy or the Oblates, and their personal sympathies lay enthusiastically with the Americans against the British and the Hudson's Bay Company. Still, they felt responsible for their Indian charges, and there would have been a certain identification with their French Canadian co-religionists. Their attitude must necessarily have been somewhat complicated.

Among the Nez Percés, a faction allied with the Americans in the coming war. Fifty years before this war, the Nez Percé tribe had been a collection of some seventy independent and fairly sedentary communities, sharing only language, culture, and locale. A Protestant minister in 1839 was dismayed to find them scattered into tiny bands of from ten to 100, no band exceeding 150 souls; each band lived from five to thirty miles from its neighbors, and there seemed to be "no form of government and no law." Their sudden transition to a semi-nomadic, tent-dwelling life, along the lines of the warlike

Summer of 1858 (New York, 1859), p. 12. *RR, 1,* ii, 268; Gibbs refused to believe that the Company tried to prejudice the tribes.

26. E. E. Rich, *The Hudson's Bay Company, 2,* Pubs. of the Hudson's Bay Record Society, 22 (3 vols. London, 1958–1961), 682–83.

27. N. Point, S.J., "Recollections of the Rocky Mountains," *WL, 11* (1882), 311. J. Ross Browne Report, in *SED,* 35 Cong., 1 sess., 40 (1857), p. 3.

Plains peoples, shook up their whole social structure. The breeding and sale of horses to the Hudson's Bay post at Walla Walla added a larger commercial dimension to their existence. The Oregon Trail ran closely enough to be of commercial advantage without despoiling or antagonizing them. And the Americans coming up the Trail were natural allies against their hereditary enemy the Snakes. In 1853 the Indian commissioner proposed hiring them for this reason, to guard a nasty stretch of the Trail.

The expansion of trade seems to have emphasized a growing split between the remaining hundreds of conservative, sedentary tribesmen and the more numerous and wilder buffalo hunters among the Nez Percés. The Hudson's Bay people, if they did not originate the split, deepened it by their presence. Indian Agent Cain declared that when he first arrived in the Nez Percé region he could hardly find a member of the conservative group familiar with the trade language called Chinook, whereas the buffalo group boasted "any number" who could. It is significant that the one mountain man who settled among the Nez Percés and influenced them, William Craig, was an American veteran of the trade wars against the Hudson's Bay Company in the Rockies.[28]

The American missionaries settled among the Nez Percés and allied Cayuses, with a third base in the Spokane country. Their Nez Percé converts tended, not unreasonably, to be drawn from the more traditional, rather sedentary party. Thus religion, like commerce, defined and aggravated the tribal tradition. A modern authority has suggested that this group paradoxically first welcomed Christianity to preserve the old tribal ways.[29] If true, this implies a further cultural tension. The Protestant missionaries tended toward a program of rather direct acculturation, thinking it un-Christian to leave the Indian in his primitive state. It was not possible to carry such an ideal into immediate action; but the spirit was there and reinforced in its own way the previous tribal division.

The conservative group now inclined to admire things American, as they had formerly inclined to reject the Hudson's Bay Company. Some wavered between the two. A later leader of the anti-Whites complained that "I have been talked to by the French and by the Americans, and one says to me go

28. ABFM, ABC 18, 5, 5, 2, Smith, "Journal Across the Rocky Mountains." NA, IA, LR (from Idaho Sup.), A. J. Cain to Howard, Dayton, W. T., 5 May 1877 (a rather formal report on his experience as agent); Cain, son of John Cain the agent for the lower Columbia Indians, was an agent on the Coast and, from January 1859, successor to Craig as agent for the Nez Percés, Cayuses, Spokanes, and others. On general background see Haines, *Nez Percés*, e.g. pp. 36, 39, 149; also Spinden and Drury works, below, Bib. The ample history of the Nez Percés by A. Josephy, soon to be published by Yale University Press, will not be ready in time for use here.

29. Haines, p. 77.

this way, and the other says go another way, and that is the reason I am lost between them." Significantly, a Presbyterian chief, Lawyer, was the leading figure of the pro-Whites; a pagan chief, Eagle From the Light, associate of the buffalo-hunting Flatheads, was his counterpart among the anti-Whites.

None of this invalidates the sincere religious commitments of the Indians, any more than politicocultural factors do in the case of Ulstermen and southern Irish. Protestant prayer-life survived the loss of the mission and demonstrated the personal commitment of the Nez Percé Protestant to his faith. Year after year these Nez Percés would send to Spalding, asking for his return. But the anti-Whites continued to be adamant trouble-makers. The Oblate Chirouse, who found Indians in general corrupt and treacherous, in 1849 considered the body of Nez Percés and their allied Palouses the most troublesome of all the neighboring tribes, "the most wicked of all." [30]

Nor was religion the only element around which the factions would polarize. Treaty and nontreaty became a rallying standard, as did other quarrels. The cultural antagonism was reflected in yet another religious contrariety— between Protestant and Catholic *within* the Nez Percé tribe. Agent Cain was to remark of the later evangelization by the Catholics: "the dif[f]erence in religious sentiments—Catholicism and Protestantism—follows this old division" of buffalo and conservative "to a considerable extent." [31] In 1858 there were probably less than a hundred Catholic Nez Percés; De Smet speaks of eighty such converts in 1841, and of some hundred other Nez Percés attending Catholic devotions regularly in 1842 out of curiosity. These early Nez Percé converts probably tended to drift up into the mission orbit of the northern Indians. Only in retrospect does this Catholic-buffalo nexus shed light on the 1858 problem within the Nez Percé tribe.

The religious identification could run deep. Chief Joseph, one of the first Nez Percé converts to Protestantism and an ally in the military camp of the Whites, would angrily give expression to his political realignment in 1863 by destroying his treasured New Testament, forever abandoning both the Americans' religion and their ways. Perhaps the same factors were involved in a reverse way at this very time on the eastern Plains. There, in a dramatic scene of mass hangings by the government, thirty-two of the thirty-eight Sioux about to die requested baptism from the Catholic priest. Similarly during the 1855 war Father Joset noticed a relaxation of Protestant Indians' hostility in the Interior as they discovered the Jesuits' cultural neutrality.[32]

30. ABFM, ABC 18, 5, 5, *1*, Spalding to Board, October 1857. H. Stevens, *Stevens, 2*, 49 (leader). Bischoff, "Yakima War," p. 16 (Chirouse); cf. p. 14.

31. Cain to Howard, 5 May 1877, above, n. 28.

32. Haines, *Nez Percés*, p. 149 (Joseph). CR, *1*, 339–40 (early Catholic Nez Percés); *2*, 785 (Sioux).

The Nez Percé political structure had been altered by the Americans. The creation of an intervillage group at the mission and the concomitant rise to prominence of convert chiefs favored by the ministers led first to disorders and then to a formal reorganization. In 1842 an ex-missionary agent persuaded the tribe to adopt a centralized structure with a head chief and a code of laws. Beneath it, the fragmented authority of the village chiefs persisted as before. Then, when the Nez Percés declined to join the Cayuses in the 1847 war, the Whites regarded them with an ever more favorable eye.

Thus Governor Stevens found, ready to hand, at least a small make-weight to counterbalance Hudson's Bay influence. Lawyer, active leader of the Protestant group and official head chief of the nation, was the Governor's friend and collaborator. He became even more so after the treaty of 1855 left him with the territory of his personal band intact, and with the lion's share of benefits. To this day his admirers see him as a man of foresight and sagacity, while more skeptical historians suggest that he was a sly opportunist who betrayed his people in order to be on the winning side. Still another view emphasizes his role as leader in a transitional tribe; his primary obligations were to his own group, not to the unsubstantial office of head chief.

Such are the broad outlines of the Nez Percé schism. Many of these lines crossed: for example, the mission party and Craig's adherents were sometimes inimical, and numbers of buffalo Indians were Protestant. The main body of the tribe seems to have belonged in detail to neither party but rather to have run a gamut of complex patterns, inclining toward one faction or the other but also swayed by immediate considerations. Some hundred Nez Percé warriors protect Stevens in 1855; a little over the same number attack him in 1856. Craig reports that two-thirds of the tribe made up the hostile faction that summer; by the end of the year Stevens estimates the Nez Percés about equally divided into pro- and antitreaty factions. Craig gives the same assessment for 1857. Most leading chiefs inclined to the Americans. The buffalo faction, Cain says, contributed hostiles successively in each war against the Whites.

The tribe would seem to have been equally divided on the eve of the 1858 war. Probably the erection of Fort Walla Walla, combined with Colonel Wright's policy of conciliation, had neutralized a good deal of the active hostility among the antitreaty Indians. Thirty-five Nez Percés were to take service with the American troops in 1858 against their Red brothers. On the other hand, as the Whites noticed, "the discontented portion of the Nez Percés had joined the enemy and were engaged in the two fights against us." Cain in his 1859 report admits to only "some few" Nez Percés taking part in the recent war. In 1860 he thinks the Nez Percé war faction had encouraged the war, although it had not actively engaged in all the hostilities.

Agent Owen complains shortly after the 1858 treaties: "I would like the attention of Agent Cain called to that portion of the Nez Percés tribe known as the Buffalo Indians; they number about one hundred lodges." They usually winter in the Flatheads' Bitterroot Valley, "and I do assure you they are the source of great annoyance." Mullan is more specific. "The mountain Nez Percés number from one hundred to two hundred, live and hunt with the Flatheads, and are an annoyance both to them and the whites." He says "they are generally disaffected, and cause much trouble and disturbance in the country." After the coming war these "Buffalo Nez Percés" will flee onto the Plains for a season, and for some time shelter Kamiakin. Lieutenant Kip, after his postwar investigations at the mission, says this leader group fought in both major battles. He estimates their number at forty lodges, or something between two and three hundred Indians. The Jesuits had some little influence over them.[33]

Split Loyalty: The Spokane Tribes

Among the other Interior tribes the only considerable figure who associated himself with the White man's culture and government was Spokane Garry. The association was not very steadfast, since Garry had also to maintain face among his tribesmen; besides, his own grievances rankled bitterly. Alongside the White myth of a Nez Percé Christian tribe under Lawyer, staunchly faithful to their White brothers, a companion myth would evolve portraying Garry as the devout and powerful arbiter of the north, altruistically holding the tribes to a policy of peace. The myth was to appeal to churchly people because of Garry's importance to the religious history of the upper country; it appealed also to the municipal chauvinist after the town of Spokane sprang up on Garry's territory and became the metropolis of the Interior.[34]

33. Kip, *Expedition*, p. 88; our total assumes seven souls per lodge as e.g. with Kalispels in *RR*, *1*, ii, 149. Gibbs gives a tribal total of 1,880 (*RR*, *1*, ii, 416; cf. figure 1,700 in 1853, p. 150). Cain estimate in *SED*, 36 Cong., 1 sess., 2 (1859), p. 384; see 2 sess., 1 (1860), p. 433; Cain to Howard, above, n. 28. Mullan 1860 Road Report, *HED*, p. 50. *SED*, 36 Cong., 1 sess., 2 (1859), p. 792, Owen letter, 31 May.

34. Our treatment diverges considerably here as elsewhere from that of Jessett, *Spokan Garry*. It follows Ray's divisions and ethnological findings; Teit is used only with caution. Since the names upper, middle, and lower Spokanes mean something different to Teit and Ray, a more direct terminology is adapted here to the latter's tribes wherever feasible. But some source materials are so involved with an older division of upper and lower Spokanes that it is best to leave their usage intact occasionally. See the maps and discussions in V. F. Ray, "Native Villages and Groupings of the Columbia Basin," *PNWQ*, 27 (1936), 103, 107–08, 116, 133–37, and esp. 121–22; and the charts and treatment, passim, in his *Cultural Relations in the Plateau*. OJ MSS are are also drawn upon here, esp. from the Joset Papers and Cataldo Papers.

The word Spokane conveyed nothing to the Indian world except the place where one small band lived. But the Whites gave the name to any of the bands living along the Spokane River. These may be grouped into three rough agglomerations, which can then be treated as though they were tribes. The Spokane River runs east to west across the upper central face of the Interior plains; the three groupings or tribes may be positioned on it as three boards of a fence. Each up-and-down rectangle of land runs north and south on either side of the river. Farthest downriver, at its mouth and juncture with the Columbia, were the Western Spokanes. With a dialect unintelligible to the others, they were culturally related to the Colville, San Poil, Southern Okanogan, and Columbia tribes. The Central Spokanes occupied the middle oblong. Here the Presbyterian mission had stood briefly. At the farthest extreme upriver and neighbors of the Coeur d'Alenes were the Eastern Spokanes. Both Central and Eastern tribes were dialectically akin to the Kalispels and economically allied to their Coeur d'Alene neighbors.

Everywhere the old system of village autonomy prevailed under independent village chiefs. The little villages clustered on the river and its adjacent waterways, with the inhabitants wandering seasonally to temporary campsites. Plains influence intruded only mildly, not as intensely as with the Nez Percés and Flatheads nor even as strongly as with the Coeur d'Alenes. Salmon was the staple, though many went to hunt buffalo with their eastern neighbors. In Indian sign language the name for all these villages was Salmon Eaters. Their local autonomy was offset by a kind of sociality within each of the three groupings, some common customs, sporadic cooperation, and geographic unity. Principal chiefs tended to emerge in the different regions, but there were no head chiefs. Nor were there formal war honors or a permanent, public war chief as there were among the Nez Percés and Flatheads, or a badge of authority as among the Coeur d'Alenes.

Official enumeration of the Spokanes varied widely from 250 to 1,250. It was not easy to determine which groups to classify as "Spokanes." It was even harder to estimate numbers in the far-flung, partly nomadic villages. De Smet in 1840 assesses them at "nearly 800"—but at the same time he overestimates the Coeur d'Alenes at 700. In 1853 Stevens' assistant Gibbs lists the Spokanes in seven major groups totaling 450. Agent Cain reports the various Spokanes at 600 in 1859, emphasizing that they are much reduced in numbers by famine and disease "within the last few years." Lieutenant Mullan, who was familiar with them from his road explorations, sets them at "about five hundred" at this period. Agent Paige later gives the number 1,000, then corrects it to 1,200. Agent Winans, in 1870, brings the figure down to 716. Lieutenant Boyle, in 1876, reckons them at 725.

The commissioner of Indian Affairs, in arranging for reservations in 1872, lists 725 Spokanes, 700 Coeur d'Alenes, and 631 Kettles—figures undoubtedly

involving some division and consolidation; 180 Eastern Spokanes are designated for the Spokane reserve, 145 for the Coeur d'Alene reserve; the Central
and Western Spokanes here total 367. At the Wheaton Council of 1877
Garry represents 160 Spokanes, Sgalgalt and Baptiste Peone 383 more, while
the Western Spokanes number 318. Thus it may be fair to estimate the whole
cumulus of tribes, including the more ambiguous Western Spokanes, at some
700 in our time.[35]

The Spokanes, beginning to drift from a pure village autonomy toward
transitional tribal groupings, were caught like the Nez Percés in religious and
cultural crosscurrents. Out of this confused situation emerged the importance
of Spokane Garry. He was a solidly built man, short in the legs and uncommonly bowlegged. Like most influential chiefs he possessed a talent and taste
for rhetoric. For a while after his return from Episcopalian catechetical training at Red River, he enjoyed a vogue as preacher among the Spokanes and
even briefly among the Coeur d'Alenes, Kettles, and Flatheads. Ridicule soon
led him to abandon the apostolate on a public scale, even among his own people. He reverted to the Indian way of dress and life, and took a second wife.

But he had helped form a pro-American, pro-Protestant faction among his
portion of Eastern Spokanes. His status as principal chief of the largest
Spokane fragment was greatly exalted by the attention focused upon him as a
religious teacher and by his acquisition of the American language and ways.
The Presbyterian mission working for a decade among the neighboring Central Spokanes probably reinforced the religious and cultural tendencies
introduced among the Easterners by Garry, despite its having gained no
converts. Soon "many" Spokanes had the habit of traveling down to the coast
settlements in winter, to take employment from Whites at a money wage.[36]

Garry had seen what the Whites expected in the way of a chief; he
shrewdly projected the image of himself as a full head chief. He went out of
his way to welcome every American official in these parts as a potential ally
against the overwhelming "French" influence around him. He impressed
Gibbs in 1853: Garry "is what he claims to be and what few are among their
tribes, a *chief*" among the numerous Spokane "petty chiefs." Stevens at first
found Garry "not frank, and I do not understand" the man; soon, however,
he became enthusiastic about this "man of education, of strict probity, and
great influence over his tribe." Stevens' party were pleased to find that Garry
"speaks English fluently" (or as Lieutenant Kip put it five years later, toler-

35. *RR, 1*, ii, 414 (Gibbs; two sub-tribes doubtful). *HED*, 36 Cong., 2 sess., 29 (1860),
p. 49. CR, *3*, 991. *RCIA* (1865), pp. 99, 101, 22. NA, IA, LR (from Wash. Sup.), Fort
Colville, 3 June 1876. Wheaton Council statistics below, p. 417.

36. *RR, 1*, ii, 424 ("many"). Drury, *Walker*, pp. 194, 215 (convert problem). Typescript copy of Mengarini "Memorie" (SF, in Italian) of 1848 (Flathead faction).

ably well). More impressive still, he and his family "were dressed in the costume of the whites, which in fact now prevails over their own." Garry raised his own wheat, and could offer White visitors "a cup of tea or coffee and bread." In short, the Governor considered him in 1856 "a white man in education and views of life." [37]

Garry convinced Stevens that the Spokanes were both a tribe and a potential ally. The Governor in turn deliberately promoted Garry's influence, and singled him out for special attention at councils or meetings. Stevens entertained the chief as a house guest in his quarters at Olympia "for weeks," corresponded with him, and praised him in reports. He went so far as to appoint Garry to the federal Indian service as interpreter for all the Salish tribes at an annual salary of $500. Even after Stevens' enthusiasm for him dimmed, the chief continued to draw his salary.[38]

The other Spokanes neither resisted nor acquiesced in Garry's pretensions. When it seemed useful in White dealings, they were content to let him speak for them. Since circumstances of Indian-White conflict did create a power vacuum, Garry frequently became the logical man to fill it. Thus the pose tended to assume some reality in the years after our war. The Whites seldom grasped the nature of Garry's earlier influence. Outside of his own group among the Eastern Spokanes it was not political or jurisdictional, nor was it precisely the power of a dominating personality. It was rather a prestige which fluctuated in the jumble of shifting rivalries, jealousies, and alliances. It was based largely upon his acceptance by the Whites, together with the important leverage afforded by his being the head chief of the largest single group, and spokesman for a religious party. These gave him an advantageous position from which he could present his personal views for consideration to village and regional chiefs of the whole Spokane area.

Eight years after the war, baffled Indian officials were to caution that "Spokane Garry is not understood to be the acknowledged chief of the tribe; he is so considered by the whites on account of his ability to talk English and read a little, but is not the equal of his brother in power and influence over the tribe." Five years later Agent Winans notes that Garry "has but little influence" outside his own immediate band. Even in the 1858 war General Harney, in commending some of Garry's suggestions to military superiors, assessed him as "one of the principal chiefs of the Spokan[e] Indians." De Smet, friendly with him in 1859, refers to him both as "one of the Spokan[e] chiefs" and as head chief or "great chief of the Spokan[e]s."

37. *RR*, *1*, ii, 57, 414; *12*, i, 136. Kip, *Expedition*, p. 67. H. Stevens, *Stevens*, *2*, 181 (Stevens to Wool, 20 March 1856).

38. Doty, Journal, p. 52 ("weeks"). NA, IA, Wash. Sup., LS, Stevens to Spokane Garry, Olympia, 24 March 1854.

The Protestant Agent Winans thought Garry "cunning and suspicious," with a "reputation of being treacherous and keeping a smart lookout for the main chance." But by that time Garry had become increasingly disenchanted with the Whites. A few years later the resident Protestant minister Cowley became involved in quarrels with the chief and described him as "of a suspicious, deceitful and unstable character"; he estimated that Garry was "held in very slight esteem, and has but little weight or authority with his people," his position as head chief resting "upon little else than a tolerable ability to read and speak English." [39]

If having a foot in both worlds conferred influence, it also conferred anguish. Despite all his efforts, Garry was still treated as an Indian, not really as an equal to the American. He reveals something of this in his complaints at the Spokane River Council of 1855. Perhaps it had something to do also with his lifelong problem, common to so many Indians, of alcoholism. He used his influence in favor of peace, as a chief was expected to do in Interior Indian society; but it remained a suspect and ambiguous influence by reason of this identification with the Whites. In 1855 "my mind was divided." In 1856 his "bad heart was a little larger than the good." When war broke out, as in 1858, Garry had to walk most softly lest he draw his people's anger on his head. Nor did Stevens fully trust him after Garry "seemed bent" upon joining an 1855 plot to seize the Governor's person. In mid-1857 Agent Yantis records that Garry was holding back hotheads in his tribe, though the Spokanes as a whole had "greatly retrograded." Yantis feels that in the work of pacification on the eve of the 1858 war the chief "can be of no avail to me." Pearson and Owen, however, give evidence of Garry's attempts to dissuade his people from violence in the 1858 troubles. [40]

Against Garry was arrayed a formidable opposition in the upper country. The majority of Spokanes at this time remained pagan. The Jesuit mission establishments surrounded Garry on two sides: among the Kalispels, the Kettles, and the Coeur d'Alenes. An increasing number of Spokanes hunted buffalo with their Catholic allies; a small number had even been converted and had removed to the Jesuit country. Then there were the French settlers,

39. *RCIA* (1866), p. 192; (1870), p. 22. M. W. Avery, "The W. Park Winans Manuscripts," *PNWQ*, 47 (1956), 17. C. M. Drury, *A Tepee in His Front Yard, a Biography of H. T. Cowley* (Portland, Oreg., 1949), p. 138. NA, EW, AGO, 48–0, from Harney, 28 March 1859. CR, *3*, 969; *2*, 766.

40. Doty, Journal, pp. 48, 50 (Garry: 1855, 1856). H. Stevens, *Stevens*, *2*, 136 (plot). Alcoholism incidents e.g. in C. M. Drury, *Walker*, p. 101 (1841); H. S. Brode, ed., "Diary of Dr. Augustine J. Thibodo of the Northwest Exploring Expedition, 1859," *PNWQ*, *31* (1940), 329 (November 1859); *RCIA* (1870), p. 23. Yantis quote in NA, IA, Wash. Sup., Colville letters, 1854–74, Yantis to Nesmith, 20 July 1857. Stevens Papers, Yantis to Stevens, 17 June (Todd, *PNWQ*, *31*, 415); Garry here is still on government payroll.

especially near Colville, and the traders. "The Indians and French about here are always telling lies about Garry," the chief protested in the 1855 Spokane council.[41] Worse, the French settlers were legalizing their farm holdings under the congressional donation act; these were the "Americans" against whom Garry in early 1855 was "exciting the hostility" of his Indians.[42]

This struggle to maintain influence, heavily colored by religious passions on both sides, may help explain Garry's insistence upon Catholic intolerance. In 1873 an inspector of Indian Affairs, himself an Episcopalian and an admirer of Garry, wrote that the chief "is distinguished, among other peculiarities, by a hatred of the Romish religion." This was not a late development. Even before the Jesuits arrived in the Rockies, Father Mengarini records in 1858, Garry had preached bitterly against Catholicism and priests to the Flatheads. He never lost this sustained animus.

Garry early discovered American susceptibility to the theme of intolerance, and consistently exploited it. During the 1853 railroad explorations he unburdened himself to McClellan: "there was bad feeling" between his tribe and its neighbors since the priests had come, because they said that "the American Religion of the Spokanes was bad, false, worthless, etc." To Gibbs, Garry "narrated to us the evils arising" from Catholic intolerance, "with a forbearance and Christian spirit of toleration which would have honored anyone." Garry said the Spokanes were "Protestants or of the 'American religion'" and that the Coeur d'Alenes "taunt" them "as heretics whose faith is worthless."[43]

After his own conversations with Garry, Governor Stevens stiffly reproached the Jesuits: "the liberal and enlightened principles of tolerance and kindness toward all denominations of Christians which you so warmly expressed to me induce me to rely fully upon your efforts to cultivate among your people a reciprocal feeling." During the postwar expansion of Catholicism, Garry was to go so far as to communicate to Agent Winans his apprehensions of bloodshed; he accused the Catholics of avoiding the Protestants lest "all go to hell together." Oddly enough, none of this prevented amicable personal relations between the Jesuits and Garry.[44]

The precise numerical strength of the Spokane Protestant group, and the extent to which it was inclined to be sympathetic to the American Whites,

41. Doty, Journal, p. 50.

42. *RR*, *1*, ii, 563 (misprint as Geny).

43. T. E. Jessett, "Anglicanism among the Indians of Washington Territory," *PNWQ*, *42* (1951), 238 (doc.; 1873). Overmeyer, *PNWQ*, *32*, 46. Gibbs, in *RR*, *1*, ii, 414; cf. p. 422. Typescript copy of Mengarini "Memorie."

44. Winans Collection (WP), Journal, p. 120; cf. p. 122. NA, IA, Wash. Sup., LS, Stevens to Jesuits, Spokane River, 1853; cf. NA, IA, LR, Stevens to commissioner, 6 December 1853.

are among the more difficult questions about the Interior Indian culture at this period. The problem is complicated by the fact that the acculturation involved was minimal, since this group was forged by an Indian in a relatively remote region. It is perhaps not wise to press the analogy with the Nez Percé situation too closely. Some attempt must be made, however, to assess the pro-American party among this critical tribe, and religious evidences are our best surviving approach.

During the buffalo hunt of 1853, the Stevens party encountered well over a hundred Spokanes engaged in a form of Protestant or Episcopal service. As the party continued downriver they met "band after band," who "invariably" displayed "the same regard for religious services." Numbers of Spokanes going to the Coast requested that a Protestant mission be sent to them.[45] Perhaps at this time the larger number of Garry's own band were committed to his form of Christianity. Yet, when the Jesuits inaugurated their Spokane ministry in the months just after the 1858 war, it was precisely among Garry's people that they had their striking success. Does this reveal a latent cultural opposition, crystallized by the anti-White angers?

Perhaps a clue may be found in the Catholic experience with them before and after the war of 1858. De Smet had been well received by some Spokanes; there were a number of Spokane converts also in the first years of the Jesuit mission. In 1847 Joset says that Spokane requests for a Jesuit mission of their own had already come "more than once." There were, of course, no Jesuits to dispatch. Joset was impressed with the "gentle" character of "such as have become baptized" by that year. In an 1849 report to Rome, Hoecken estimated that half of the Spokanes inclined to Catholicism and half to Protestantism. Not long afterward, Garry resumed the role of religious leader in an active way, seeking also Presbyterian and Episcopalian help to strengthen his own movement. This probably changed the balance strongly, creating the situation Stevens found in 1853. In his reservation plans of 1855 Governor Stevens acted on the assumption that the Spokanes were Protestant. Hoecken and the Jesuits at the time considered the Governor's position naïve, but it may have reflected the prevailing balance fairly enough.

The 1858 war seems to have swung the balance to favor the Catholics. The first formal missionary excursion by a Jesuit was well received in February 1859. Sporadic visits continued, especially after 1862. Within less than a decade after the war, a hundred of Garry's own band had been gathered around a Spokane Catholic mission with no great effort.[46] Garry's sister and other

45. *RR, 12*, i, 134. Drury, *Walker*, pp. 229–30 (1850–51). Yantis to Nesmith, 20 July, above, n. 40.

46. CR, *1*, 318, 379, 390; *3*, 801. *JMUS, 2*, 340 (Joset, Hoecken). On the 1859 trip see below, Chap. 8; on subsequent work see Bischoff, *Jesuits in Old Oregon*, pp. 168–69.

members of his family became Catholics. In answer to the challenge, a Presbyterian minister appeared and soon claimed over 300 adherents. (The Jesuits disputed the number, conceding only 100, but they are not impartial witnesses here.) Later, the permanent minister was to claim 321 as Protestants, with the majority of the tribe inclining also in that direction; he was working to prevent the Spokanes from falling under the Catholic Colville agency, so the figures are probably maximized. By this time the Jesuits (also exaggerating?) counted as their own 300 out of an estimated 600 Spokanes.[47]

Perhaps the least suspect estimate came thirteen years after the war, from the report of Agent Winans, a Presbyterian. It confirmed what we have already seen. "The tribe is about equally divided on the religious question, and as an Indian cannot be conservative and is from nature a fanatic, the feeling between the two factions is as bitter as between Orangemen and Hibernians." [48] By this time the pro-White link had been greatly weakened by unfortunate incidents attending the American settlement of the area, and Winans noted that the Spokane political sympathies did not parallel the religious divisions. Garry's own sympathies for everything White may have been at their lowest ebb during the months immediately after the 1858 war; Father De Smet traveled with him at this time and was under the impression that he was now a "pagan." [49]

PÈRE JOSET'S COEUR D'ALENES

The outstanding peacemaker in the 1858 war was Joset. To assess his letters and reports, and to give him some dimension, we must take a closer look at the man. He was born in 1810 at Courfaivre, a little hamlet tucked away in a green fold of mountain country to the north of the present canton of Berne, in Switzerland. A large and pious family (of four brothers, one would become a Capuchin friar, another a Jesuit lay-brother in New York, a third the prefect apostolic of Hong Kong) together with an "exceedingly inferior" schooling at his parish and at nearby Delemont comprise the known elements of his boyhood. The defect of schooling was remedied by four years at the Jesuit college of St. Michael in Fribourg, and by studies following his entry in 1830 into the newly re-established Order.

During the thirteen years of Jesuit training in Europe he seems to have prefected boarders, acted as librarian, and taught Latin, mathematics, French, and a little Hebrew. He experienced some difficulty with his health and had

47. CR, *4,* 1307 (300 Spokane Catholics; 1871). L. Van Ree, S.J., "The Spokane Indians, Sketch of the Work of Our Fathers," *WL, 18* (1889), 357. Drury, *Cowley,* pp. 106, 129.

48. *RCIA* (1871), p. 294.

49. CR, *2,* 766.

to be relieved from his teaching duties to recuperate at Lake Geneva. This episode contrasts with the robustness and capacity for hardship that distinguishes his long career among the Indians.[50]

During the cloistered quiet of his post-ordination ascetical year in France he made known to Rome his desire to be a missionary. Father General Roothaan, impressed with young Joset, suggested that the local superiors sacrifice him from his province for this greater good. By ocean packet and wagon train he arrived in 1844 into that part of the Oregon country where "the Indian was absolute master." Here he was to spend half a century in missionary work. Of physical hardship in these early years there was an abundance; on one occasion he was reduced by starvation to eating moss. He commented many years later: "it was no easy task."[51]

When De Smet set out in 1845 to negotiate a peace with the Blackfeet, he left the young priest in charge of all the houses of the network. When annual floods on the St. Joe River flats forced the removal of the Coeur d'Alene mission, Joset was commissioned to choose a new site and to direct the migration. Visiting St. Louis in 1846, De Smet again left Joset as substitute superior. The Jesuit general made the substitution permanent, until 1850. Joset established the Coeur d'Alene mission so solidly that it became with St. Ignatius "always the two principal centers" of the network.[52]

But this is to be a portrait. What features stand out in the man—personal appearance, traits of character, defects? His only surviving photograph has caught a homely but appealing countenance, with steady eyes and a happy smile. The picture reflects a spirit controlled, reserved, of deep piety. In later years a reporter from the *Coeur d'Alene Sun*, questioning Joset's choice of life, found his answer in that face. The passport of the young Joset preserves for posterity nine *signes particuliers:* blue eyes, black-gray hair, sharp nose, black eyebrows, large mouth, round chin, high forehead, light brown beard (later shaved), and full face. To these details the police bureau adds: thirty-four and a half years of age, five feet three inches in height.[53]

50. Joset Papers. See my "Descriptive Calendar of the Joset Papers," *PNWQ, 38* (1947), 307–14. These 103 items include everything from certificates of baptism, ordination, and citizenship to personal and official correspondence and ethnological writings. Other sources of information on Joset include family papers in Courfaivre, Switzerland (some copies or information in SF); correspondence in FL, MJ, RJ, CR, *AFL;* obituary articles by Barnum in *WL, 29* (1901), 202–14, and anon. in *LPT*, n.v. (1901), p. 187; (1902), p. 242; and province catalogues. The CF manuscripts have background material for his academic life. See also *JMUS, 2,* 290–300, 345–46, 394–95, 430–33; Otto Pfülf, S.J., *Die Anfänge der deutschen Provinz der neu erstandenen Gesellschaft Jesu und ihr Wirken in der Schweiz 1805–1847* (Freiburg, 1922), esp. p. 221.
51. Joset Papers, No. 34.
52. FP, I, 5, Jesuit general to Association, 18 April 1861.
53. Joset Papers, passport and No. 103 (clippings).

Cataldo, for fifteen years superior of the missions, felt that in all his ninety-year-long life, of the "many holy and eminent missionaries" he had known, "Father Joset was one of the three outstanding." Others note his "Swiss simplicity," his sense of the spiritual, his energy. Congiato, his superior in 1858, characterizes him as "an excellent missionary, a good religious, but odd and highly imaginative." A letter from Father Vercruysse to Rome records Joset's "unquiet, indecisive, precipitate character, which makes him do everything in a hurry"; he adds that "this excellent religious and indefatigable missionary recognizes his faults, acknowledges them, is humbled and distressed on their account." An obituary manuscript puts as a characteristic virtue his avoidance of eccentricity in devotion or daily life.

Despite his power of leadership, he lacked administrative talent. Father Gazzoli thought him "without a sense of the practical." Father General Roothaan wrote, "poor Father Joset, he has no head." He seemed unable to cope with the Kalispel or Flathead Indians, and was accused by other missioners of favoritism to the Coeur d'Alenes. The impressions of two non-Catholics are especially interesting. Dr. Suckley, in his 1853 report to Stevens, depicted the missionary as "very kind . . . a Swiss, and very gentlemanly and agreeable in his manners." Captain Keyes, on Colonel Wright's staff during the 1858 campaign, found Joset "a cultivated gentleman in the prime of life, fit to adorn the most polished society in the world." William Tecumseh Sherman, commander of America's armies, passed this way with his son Tom during the 1877 Nez Percé war. The non-Catholic Sherman praised Joset, but his young son was even more struck by him. Tom, for whom his father had ambitions in the legal profession, later became a Jesuit himself; he would rather be a Joset, he told his heartbroken father, than supreme justice of the United States.[54]

Joset's opinions of his co-workers reflect a native gentleness. His practicality in things ascetic is limned in the list of extra penances he allowed his Indians: "keep his tongue when angry," "not to swallow one drop," "every Saturday to keep her tongue," "every Friday not to speak bad," "not offend my husband—every Saturday." Cataldo remembers his "great genius" for things mechanical, and his grasp of Indian linguistics ("he composed a very learned comparative grammar"). To his other duties he added many amateur ethnological writings. Through him we have a window on the Indian world of 1858, especially on his own tribe, the Coeur d'Alenes, so central to the story of the war.[55]

The Coeur d'Alenes centered upon Lake Coeur d'Alene in the panhandle of

54. Ibid., No. 6, Cataldo on Joset; see also papers of other contemporaries such as Giorda *JMUS*, 2, 431. *RR*, *1*, ii, 299. For Keyes quotation see below, p. 307.
55. Joset Papers, No. 50, penance lists; Cataldo in No. 6.

present northern Idaho. The Kalispels were neighbors along their north, the Eastern Spokanes along their west; these three were associated in close cooperation and cultural intermixture. East of the Coeur d'Alenes were the Flatheads, to the south the Nez Percés. The Coeur d'Alene country ran about a hundred miles from north to south and an equal distance from east to west. Along the western margin it held a segment of the open Spokane plains. In general, however, the "surface is mountainous throughout"—an important factor in their military situation.[56]

It was a panorama of mountain ranges and intersecting valleys, of brooding evergreen forests and dashing mountain streams, varied by small open meadows or valleys. Stands of spruce and maple, cedars, some to two hundred feet, pine, poplar, and other trees were all linked and tangled by a formidable, choking undergrowth. "The vast solitude of the Coeur d'Alene mountains covered with heavy forest trees," Governor Stevens wrote in his 1853 report, together with the Rockies to the east and the Kutenai mountains to the north, "formed a *coup d'oeil* imposing and magnificent." Lazily rising belts of mist betrayed to the eye the courses of the many lakes and streams.

Lieutenant Kip on the 1858 campaign saw the Coeur d'Alene country as "very grand, the densely covered hills, interspersed with lakes, rolling as far as the eye could reach, to the horizon." As a military man he was particularly struck by its dark and "impenetrable" nature. Father Joset compared the region to the beautiful Swiss canton of Jura: "the same climate, the same display of large and small valleys, hills, and mountains covered with fine forests." In 1859 Father De Smet, who traveled the West as had only a few explorers or mountain men, confided how he treasured as a favored bit of scenery these "primeval forests" of the Coeur d'Alenes, dotted here and there with "lovely little lakes" three to six miles in circumference. General Sherman was so taken by this Coeur d'Alene country that he remembered it in his later letters as an Eden, a refuge from life.

This was not only a beautiful but also a savage land. Men could become desperately lost in its depths. And "during four months of the year the coun-

56. Teit devotes to them a section of his "Salishan Tribes" (BAE *Annual Report, 45,* 37-197); he is useful only if read with great caution, and his history is particularly defective. Gladys Reichard has published fine works on the language and myths. An able but unpublished book by Sven Liljeblad is available for study at IHS: "Indian Peoples in Idaho" (1957), with a revised version "The Indians of Idaho in Transition" (1960). Ray has valuable comments on the tribe throughout his *Cultural Relations* and in the maps and lists of his "Native Villages" (*PNWQ, 27*). See also *Notizie storiche e descrittive delle missioni della provincia torinese della Compagnia di Gesù nell' America del Nord, 2* (2 vols. Turin, 1898), 8-34; and *JMUS, 2,* 313 ff. Valuable unexploited source materials exist not only in OJ (esp. Joset Papers) but also, for example, in RJ, MJ, BJ, FL, CR, *RR,* and *AFL.* Quotation from De Smet, CR, *2,* 756.

try presents merely the aspect of a desert covered with deep snow," negotiable only on snowshoes. Just after the war Lieutenant Mullan described the horrors of snowblindness in this country, and how one of his road workers had to have both legs amputated after his feet froze; Mullan left the poor man with the Jesuits.[57]

Set like an emerald in all this splendor was Lake Coeur d'Alene, a sheet of water stretching thirty miles from north to south. The geographical memoir from the Stevens 1853 survey lets slip its mask of impersonal objectivity to describe it in lyric terms. It lay "embosomed in the midst of gently sloping hills covered with a dense forest growth," so that "the irregularity of its form and the changing aspect of the scenery about it makes it one of the most picturesque objects in the interior." Out of its top the Spokane River flows west to fall into the Columbia; down toward the bottom of its right side two large rivers feed into the lake, the Coeur d'Alene and below it the St. Joe.

At first sight the several hundred Coeur d'Alenes seemed hopelessly scattered along these three main rivers near the lake. Father Point, facing the problem of uniting the tribe into a Reduction, found them residing "in twenty-seven different localities." Their seasonal sites, if added, increased this number considerably. In 1858 about forty Indians lived at the mission itself. The largest settlement, of over a hundred Indians, stood at the northern end of the lake; a similar large group was on the St. Joe River fourteen miles southeast of the mission. There was a village of eighty Indians and another of sixty, but most ran from fifteen to twenty-five or even fewer.[58]

Upon closer observation, the Coeur d'Alene villages fell into three groupings or tribes, well defined by geographical location: the people of the mountains, of the lake, and of the prairie. Father Point used to refer to the mountaineers as *Bas Bretons* (the Celtic-speaking natives of western Brittany), and to the lake and prairie people as Parisians. The mountaineers were "simple and upright," relatively candid, and unselfish. The other bands were cunning and deceitful. Head Chief Vincent, the leader during the war of 1858, was himself a lake man; in his opinion, "in the mountains there is faith, at the lake it is half and half, in the prairie it is superstition." The "Parisians" dominated the mountaineers before the Jesuits' arrival, Joset tells us; subsequently in order "not to lose all their ascendancy, [they] were compelled to study religion more than otherwise perhaps they would have done." After the mission had begun, the prairie folk caused the Jesuits the most trouble. Their

57. *RR*, *1*, ii, 56, 560–61; *12*, i, 202; CR, *2*, 756–57; cf. pp. 562, 568, 759, and *1*, 377–78. Kip, *Expedition*, p. 78.
58. *RR*, *12*, i, 253 (1853 report). Point, *WL*, *12* (1883), 149. Ray, *PNWQ*, 27, 113 (village numbers). Kip, *Expedition*, p. 79 (forty at mission).

bad disposition may have derived partly from contact with the Colville trappers.[59]

The trappers apparently gave them their name (Awl-Hearts, perhaps Mean Hearts), "very likely out of spite for not being able to manage them as they did other tribes." There really was no tribal name. Skitswish or Schizu-e was simply the name of one spot, perhaps meaning "foundling." The Yakimas called them Camas People, because they came out onto the Interior plateau to gather the camas root. In sign language they were known as Wide Bows. The Plains Indians knew them as Bow and Arrow People from the Sunset, because they were among the last of the buffalo hunters from beyond the Rockies to secure guns.

From 1805 disease swept their numbers down from the 2,000 reported by Lewis and Clark. A trader listed them just before the Jesuit arrival at "157 men, 112 women, 60 boys, 75 girls." Before 1858 they had stabilized at some 500. In 1853 these were divided among 70 lodges, involving a little over 100 families. Although they managed to communicate with other Salish, they were the only tribe of the Interior Salish confined by a unique subgroup dialect not readily intelligible to some linguistic neighbors. This was a barrier in dealings with Whites. Some boasted a bit of broken French. But when Joset tried to teach two chiefs English, they protested that it would never be useful in such a far region.[60]

Particularly significant is their transitional economy. Because they were a buffalo tribe used to war, the 1858 outbreak came; because they were still also a food-gathering tribe, it came how and when it did. They hunted bear, rabbit, squirrel, elk, and especially deer. They had trout and other fish, but not the salmon of the lazier tribes to the west. With the Spokanes, Kettles, Nez Percés, and others, they jointly exploited the root meadows. By 1858 the bulk of the tribe annually went to hunt buffalo on the Plains, some time between August and the following April. De Smet's first Coeur d'Alene converts were buffalo hunters on the Missouri. Stevens met sixty of them on their way to the buffalo hunt in 1853 with 200 horses; he reports that the tribe had been "long at war" with the Blackfeet. Point traveled with their annual hunt in the early '40s, and Ravalli sent them away early one year to keep

59. Joset Papers, No. 48. Teit divides them simply by the three rivers and the lake, allowing for a possible identification of the lake and Spokane River bands. Ray has a triple division agreeing with this latter alternative.

60. Ibid., esp. No. 35 (on names); foreigners' names for tribe in Teit, BAE *Annual Report*, 45, 144. On numbers see OJ, Hudson's Bay transcript (figure of 1830s); *RR*, 1, 149 (500 in 70 lodges); cf. p. 151; *AFL*, 18 (1846), 496 (De Smet, over a hundred families); Barnum's obituary of Joset puts them at 320 when Joset arrived (p. 208); Grassi gives them as 400 even in 1869 (*AFL*, 41 [1869], 376); De Smet has 500 and 700 very early (CR, 2, 464; 3, 992, 997).

them out of mischief. In 1858 Mullan reports them as living "mostly" in portable buffalo-skin tipis rather than in lodges.[61]

Politically, the Coeur d'Alenes had moved farther than Palouses, Yakimas, or Spokanes into a prototribal organization. But authority in peacetime still tended to rest upon the individual village headman. Joset stresses the vestigial anarchy in saying that each Coeur d'Alene band seemed to be independent of the other, each family independent of the village chief, and each child as independent as was possible of its parents! All chiefs were elected, generally from a few families, and could easily be deposed or ignored. By 1858 the three band chiefs had become two: a head chief and a subchief.[62]

The Coeur d'Alenes were a solidly built people, heavier than the Spokanes for example, rather serious of aspect, and of middling height. The early traveler Cox thought them "more savage than their neighbours." After a decade of Jesuit work among them, Governor Stevens was impressed by their relatively civilized status; in 1853 he wrote that they "are underestimated by all the authorities." During the coming war, Lieutenant Kip would find the Indians of the upper Interior generally "splendid specimens of humanity," who "almost live on horseback" and are "skillful in the use of arms"; he adds that "no Indians with whom we have met have impressed us so favorably" as the Coeur d'Alenes.[63]

Joset considers that they "have always been of a character quite different from their neighbors." "Turbulent," flaring into anger and as quickly subsiding, they were the "least sociable" of all the Rocky Mountain tribes. Unlike their neighbors, "they never trusted much the whites," and proved themselves "generally troublesome" to the few Hudson's Bay traders who dared try to approach them. Even some of the Jesuits looked at them askance. Yet they were also "very sensitive and affectionate." In 1858 they had only a few pagans. Joset admits that "some I never see and do not know." Mullan records that even these individuals respected Joset; for them, too, he was the tribe's "father."[64]

61. On buffalo hunt see: Teit, pp. 96–97, 115, 319 (from 1800); MJ, IX, AA, p. 355, Joset to Fouillot (in French), 28 February 1845; *JMUS, 2,* 323 (1845); CR, *3,* 1143 (De Smet); Point, *WL, 11* (1882), 304. *RR, 12,* i, 131; *1,* ii, 365 (Stevens). On housing see: CR, *2,* 760 (lodges for some, 1858); *3,* 997 (wigwams for the tribe, 1845); cf. *3,* 1165; *RR, 1,* ii, 562 (bark lodges for a few oldsters); Point, *WL, 12* (1883), 148 (huts) with *13* (1884), 9 (wigwams); Mullan 1860 Road Report, in *HED,* p. 49

62. Ray, *Cultural Relations,* p.11; cf. pp. 51–52, 46. Joset Papers, ethnological essays, passim. Cf. Teit on chiefs, p. 153.

63. Teit, p. 39. Bancroft, *Native Races, 1,* 290 n. *RR, 1,* ii, 149. Kip, *Expedition,* pp. 11, 79.

64. Joset Papers, passim. Cf. *JMUS, 2,* 322–23. Mullan, *Topographical Memoir,* p. 38.

The Mission: Alarums and Excursions

In 1858 the focus of Coeur d'Alene life was the mission. Here the tribe gathered regularly for the great feast days. Here each tribesman was baptized, confirmed, absolved, married, and buried. Here he secured medical and economic help, or advice of all kinds. Here the councils with White men were held. And here the chiefs came to confer with the missioners on important policies. Of all the mission chain, Sacred Heart had remained the most isolated from White contact. Gazzoli indeed considered this its greatest advantage.[65] Roads and bridges did not exist. Colville was six days' toilsome journey to the northwest. A southwest trek to the bare beginnings of civilization involved six days and two hundred miles, much of it over arid semidesert; this still left the traveler at Fort Walla Walla, four days short of the doorway toward the Coast, The Dalles. Even the Bitterroot Valley to the east of the mission was six days' hard travel away. The infrequent White traveler found Sacred Heart an oasis of civilization; Mullan calls it "a St. Bernard in the Coeur d'Alene mountains."

The setting was idyllic. On the green north bank of the Coeur d'Alene River, about ten miles upstream, rose a two-hundred-foot pedestal or ridge. Dominating this podium stood an unlikely baroque structure ninety feet long and sixty feet high. This was Father Ravalli's famous church, built of hewn timber, completely without nails, by Indians using improvised mechanisms. A range of buildings flanked it: a "large and new" barn, stables, bakery, smithy, priests' residence, mill, and storeroom. Though the mission as a whole was poor and struggling, it did manage to keep ninety pigs, twenty cows, and sixteen oxen.

Below the church, on the flats and slopes leading toward the cottonwood groves of the riverbank, were the collected lodges, cabins, and tipis of those Coeur d'Alenes in permanent residence. This amounted to "quite a village"; it normally consisted of some forty people plus transient families. There was ample space for the wigwams of all the tribe when assembled for the great feasts. To the west and east stretched "extensive," rolling meadows. Some hundred acres of this eastern land was kept fenced and under cultivation by the Indians here. Scattered elsewhere were smaller fields. Lifting up around and behind the mission in its river valley were imposing ranges of successively higher hills and then mountains, dark, silent, and forest-carpeted.[66]

65. *JMUS*, 2, 318; similarly Archbishop Blanchet in PA Letterbooks, fol. 273, January 1852: Coeur d'Alene mission "va assez bien, c'est qu'elle est plus eloignée des communications des Blancs." Mullan 1860 Road Report, *HED*, p. 52. See brief treatments of mission in Bischoff, Garraghan, Cody, below, Bib.

66. *RR*, *12*, i, 133; cf. p. 366; *1*, ii, 561. Cf. CR, *2*, 760. On this church see W. B. Robinson, "Frontier Architecture," *Idaho Yesterdays, 3*, no. 4 (1959), 2–6.

For fifteen years the Coeur d'Alene mission had prospered and grown in strength. To be sure, it was understaffed. At the moment only Joset was on hand, with two ancient lay brothers. Menetrey should have been here, since Gazzoli had gone to St. Ignatius to change places with him. But Menetrey is nowhere in sight during the coming crisis; perhaps he was ill at St. Ignatius or off on a missionary excursion. The Piedmontese Jesuit, Father Tadini, was somewhere in the neighborhood, though out of touch and unavailable at the time of the first battle.[67]

Progress at Sacred Heart had not been uninterrupted. Stormy episodes had several times shaken the mission fabric; on each occasion it had emerged with renewed strength. The most recent of these domestic crises had just subsided by the spring of 1858. Frightened at the prospect of losing their lands to the Whites, and unsettled by the war on their southern borders, the Coeur d'Alenes had grown slack in religious practices. Father Ravalli had not been the man to keep them in hand. For one thing, he experienced some difficulty with all the Indian languages and particular difficulty with the unique Coeur d'Alene dialect.[68] His catechetical instructions in that tongue were not effective. Besides, no one except Father Joset ever had an easy time with this tribe. In 1857 this latest confusion and laxity had culminated in a decision to close the mission; too many tribes with better dispositions were begging for Blackrobes.

Joset rushed to their defense. He persuaded his superior, Congiato, to let him try his hand there again. Somehow he suited this cross-grained tribe. With a clear eye for all their faults, he loved them above other Indians. Even as superior-general he had remained among them, using their mission as his headquarters. Perhaps it was owing to this fierce attachment, which other Jesuits complained of as hurting their own Indians, that he had been reassigned from 1851 to 1856 up among the Kettle tribe. Now, having changed places with Ravalli, he inaugurated a religious renascence among the Coeur d'Alenes. They crowded into lengthy instruction classes, climaxing their de-

67. The *Catalogus provinciae taurinensis dispersae* (Rome, 1858) gives only Joset (house superior), Menetrey (*operarius* or available for general miscellany), and Brother McGean. The 1859 volume repeats this. The 1860 edition, perhaps reflecting belatedly some of the 1858 scene, adds Brothers Huysbrecht and de Kock, and Fathers Gazzoli, Vercruysse, and Imoda. In OJ, catalogues add Tadini for the earlier half of 1858, Gazzoli for the latter; a Cataldo commentary on the catalogues has McGean arrive in April. In the mission's "Liber baptizatorum" there are Tadini entries for February, March, May (16, 20, 21), and July 1858, and entries by Menetrey in mid-July and late September. But some baptisms may have occurred away from the mission and have been added after the precise weeks of trouble. The Joset narrative has himself alone with Brother McGean and Huysbrecht at least during the critical opening weeks of the war.

68. OJ, Diomedi, "The Year 57–58."

votions with a solemn coronation of the Blessed Virgin. Thus, at Sacred Heart the year 1858 opened with the promise of a bright future. Joset enters all this into the house chronology as the year of the "Great Catechizing." He would soon add the further sad rubric: "the Coeur d'Alenes make war with the troops." [69]

All that winter he had noticed a "great preoccupation" among his tribe. Soon he was to learn that Kamiakin of the lower Yakimas, leader of the last war, "has particularly tried to gain over the Coeur d'Alenes." Kamiakin had worked at this all winter, actually residing on Coeur d'Alene lands. He and the Palouse Tilcoax "tried every means" to sway the tribe. This concentration of energy was due to the fact that the Coeur d'Alenes "are more prompt and are better armed than the fisher Indians" such as the Spokanes. That "horrible Indian" especially insisted that the priest was, in the last analysis, White, with a White heart and a White man's ignominious treatment of young Coeur d'Alene warriors as though they were workmen or prairie wolves. The priests are "like the Americans," he said; "they all have one heart." Eventually Kamiakin "had won over the richest of the Coeur d'Alenes." These few influential tribesmen in turn were secretly unsettling the Indian mind. Several of the tribe mentioned to Joset that they "were tired of Kamiakin's doings." [70]

Despite all provocation, the Coeur d'Alenes remained steady. Jesuit influence foiled Kamiakin's machinations. He won none of the Coeur d'Alene chiefs, nor any open proselytes. The contest of nerves even threatened to go against the war party. In the face of the propaganda from Chief Tilcoax's Palouses and their Yakima guests, Head Chief Vincent confided to Joset: "it may very well happen that we shall have to fight the Palouses who are very sore against us *because we will not declare against the Americans.*" Vincent told this to the priest in April, three weeks before the first battle.[71]

How does this picture harmonize with De Smet's later talk of a union of nine tribes to resist the Whites? Such a defensive tribal union in the upper Interior seems certainly to have existed. The Indians felt that Stevens had pledged himself not to take their lands, nor to cross troops beyond the Snake without notifying them or treating with them. With all the rumors afloat about invasion and road building, they would naturally have reached some defensive understanding. De Smet's observation that "bands were quickly formed in various places," so that "in a few days a body of 800 to 1000 warriors was organized," belongs to this movement of alliance. It is significant that

69. Ibid.; Joset Papers, esp. chronologies and No. 79, "Return of Joset to Sacred Heart."

70. Joset Narrative; CR, 2, 748–49 (De Smet report but reductively Joset). On Kamiakin see below, Chap. 8.

71. CR, 2, 749 (De Smet's italics).

the union included Kutenais and Flatheads who in the event refrained from war, while it excluded the actively aggressive parties under Kamiakin, like Palouses, Yakimas, the Nez Percé war faction, and Walla Wallas.[72]

The Jesuit correspondence of these months betrays a keen awareness of the disturbed feeling among the tribes. Rumors of a troop movement were particularly insistent. But surely no expedition would advance to Colville, or the gold regions, without first warning the friendly tribes. The chiefs of the upper country had solemnly protested against any such venture during the council on the Spokane. All had agreed on this point, realizing that they could not restrain their tribes if the Snake were crossed. Several times that spring, when asked whether troops would march into the region, Joset could "imagine no cause" for this. "I told them always that I considered it an idle tale." An Indian from another tribe warned Joset that "should the soldiers come, even if they were only going to Colville, the people will be awfully mad."

Though the priest had their love, he was a White man. "The Indians mistrust me when I come to speak in favor of the Americans." Judicious questioning as to whether anyone would warn the Blackrobe if a plot were brewing elicited the laconic reply "no one." One of Joset's most loyal helpers during the coming war, young Bonaventure, asked him at this time "do you think that if we thought to kill the Americans we would come tell you so?"[73]

One of the most difficult factors to convey in the story of Indian-White relations is this limitation on Joset's influence. Joset himself was to protest, after the coming battle, that Indians consult their priest "about the affairs of their conscience, but as to the rest they consult us but little." Here he is desperately cutting away false impressions to expose a central truth; in the very act he is oversimplifying. Joset enjoyed a complicated sum of influences, some broad and some slight, some in his official capacity as priest, others as a person who loved his Indians and lived close to their consciences and family lives for so many years. His dynamic and resourceful personality favored him, as did his very person, being a bridge to the White world. Finally he was influential as a patriarchal community or Reduction leader. Because each phase of this multifaceted influence had its limitations and needed to be used with discretion, Joset was always annoyed at the Whites blaming the missionaries for not having knowledge, or not using influence, which they could not really count on as a regular thing.

Joset knew that the tribe was being hard pushed "by the false reports of the hostile Indians." He also kept hearing that various White men were

72. Ibid., p. 731.
73. Joset Narrative; MJ, IX, 10, Joset to De Smet, 6 September 1858 (crossing Snake).

frightening them with stories of troop concentrations for invasion. Did these tales derive from some bluff by frightened miners, or from the well-meant warnings of French Canadians in the Interior familiar with the ambitions of the coastal Whites, or were they malicious fabrications by Kamiakin?

An American in the Nez Percé country at this time (apparently Governor Stevens' former express carrier, Pearson) likewise encountered this fear. Pearson was able somewhat to reassure the Nez Percés. Soon afterward, a Coeur d'Alene friend came to him with the same worry. This Coeur d'Alene had once saved his life and was now engaged in recovering all the horses of Pearson's traveling party. The White told his Indian friend that perhaps a march might be made to the trouble spot of Colville. The Coeur d'Alene quoted Kamiakin and others as warning that more and more soldiers were about to come north unless the very first invading troops were repelled. Pearson sent this story out to the Coast. He added that "Father Joset of Coeur de'Laine mission has done a great deal to prevent a hostile feeling towards *los Americanos*." [74]

Joset was worried. The rumors were insistent, and he had no way of checking on them. "The very sight of an armed force would be enough to make all the Indians of the country take up arms." That such a military expedition would occur appeared "improbable." But the American commander had a right to know of the ugly rumors and hostile dispositions. Contact with the White soldiers by mail was unsafe. In any case, Joset could find no Indian willing to carry the message. "Under pretence of b[u]ying the ordinary supplies," he would have to go down to Fort Walla Walla himself. He meant to wait a short while until "the season should permit" travel. His hand was soon forced. In April news flew abroad that a Nez Percé had assassinated an American. On the heels of this, rumor had troops actually massing to strike across the Snake.

The Coeur d'Alenes were almost all off on the plains southwest of the mission, digging camas roots. Joset had tried to keep several Indians at the mission to aid him in his contemplated journey. But the families of these chosen men feared to entrust their heirs to the perils of the disturbed Palouse country below. Eventually Joset found three who would help. The chief of the mission area, Peter Paulinus, tried to dissuade him, thinking it better to wait for developments; but Joset felt he could not delay. Toward the end of April the four horsemen made their way down from the mountains, through meadows awakening to spring. The scenery at this time of the year would have been particularly striking. "In the spring," De Smet writes, this region "enchants the traveler who may happen to traverse it." It is "diversified with noble plains and enameled with flowers, whose various forms and colors" pre-

74. BJ, Coll. 1ac–4ac, No. 3ac, Joset account of Coeur d'Alenes. Letter of H.P., dated 21 May, in *Weekly Oregonian*, 12 June 1858.

sent the aspect almost of a "flowerbed." The view here can extend easily "over several days' journey." [75]

Coursing through small seas of camas flowers in Paradise Valley, the riders had reached the upper crossing of Hangman's Creek when they were challenged by a solitary warrior. Drawing rein, they recognized their fellow tribesman Basil San-ahn-ilo. In the name of Head Chief Vincent he forbade the group to proceed. Joset realized that his party was not alone. "Evidently my movements were watched; for the chief must have been more than 100 miles from the mission." He estimated that "the man had traveled nearly 24 hours as fast as his horse could carry him." Despite the chief's wishes, the three braves with Joset were for pushing ahead. But the Blackrobe felt the message to be "extraordinary." Never had a chief spoken to him so dictatorially. He told Basil: "go back; tell Vincent to come and explain himself; if he does not come the third day, I will go ahead." [76]

Patiently the four waited in camp. On one occasion, several wild Nez Percés appeared, riding up to the little band. Their conversation was of war. "We will not be able to bring the Coeur d'Alenes to take part with us against the Americans," one of the newcomers said. "The priest is the cause; it is for this that we wish to kill the priest." Joset apparently decided this was the time for a dramatic gesture. He approached them and cried out: "here I am! strike me." Then he held his crucifix high toward them: "behold my medicine! Possessed of this I do not fear you." Somewhat intimidated, the war band drew away.

Spurring south with Basil meanwhile, the head chief rode day and night. He arrived with a tale of Palouse and Nez Percé intrigue, of relations between these tribes and his own strained almost to the breaking point of war, of rumors about discontent among the Spokanes, of cattle stolen at Walla Walla, and Whites killed on their way to Colville. About one thing the chief was certain: "if the troops are coming to pass the river, I am sure the Nez Percés are going to direct them upon us." This is a significant statement, deserving to be remembered in view of subsequent ambiguous events.

Vincent protested that he had all he could do to restrain the excitable younger bucks from war. If Joset's companions continued south, they would certainly be ambushed in the Palouse country, in such a way as to cast suspicion on the Whites. The Blackrobe himself would probably be spared. But "they will kill thy companions, while hunting for the horses; they will noise about that they have been killed by Americans, and there will be no controlling the people." The Father might go alone, but would soon have to return without his horse.

75. Joset Narrative. CR, *1*, 377–78.
76. Joset Narrative; *LPT* (1901), p. 242 (dictatorially).

The scene is easy to visualize: Vincent, a celebrated orator and sage, with anxiety darkening the squared features one can study today in his portrait, and his admirer Father Joset, realizing that he could never find his way to the military outpost alone and reflecting sadly as he listened. "Well!" the priest conceded, "I listen to you, though I don't believe soldiers will come; anyhow should they come, as soon [as] you hear of their movement, do not fail to send me word; I want to meet the officer, to prevent trouble."

Travel-worn and worried, Joset returned to Sacred Heart. Here he dashed off a letter in his neat, level script to Father Congiato, due shortly from California for an official visitation of the missions. Already it was too late. His letter had to travel indirectly far north by Colville; several precious days were lost. Even as the Jesuit wrote, trouble brewed. The land of the Jesuit missions had become a giant powder keg.[77]

77. Joset Narrative. Vincent's 1891 portrait medallion is now in the Heye Foundation, Museum of the American Indian, New York City. J. Gilmary Shea, an early student of mission documents, has some details of the Nez Percés incident (involving Pend d'Oreilles) in his *History of the Catholic Church in the United States*, 4 (4 vols. New York, 1886–1892), 700.

6. Colonel Steptoe's Last Stand

THE STEPTOE EXPEDITION[1]

THE TROUBLE BEGAN down at the southwestern corner of the Interior. There the new Fort Walla Walla had been under construction during the past fall and winter. This installation was four days' journey out past the beginning of the Interior plains, and some miles to the west of the Hudson's Bay ruin of the same name. Isolated on the prairie it was something of a curiosity, so that a visiting friend of Brevet Captain Taylor took the trouble to sketch it at this time. (The captain himself was to fall in the coming Indian war.) The fort as pictured is feeble enough. Little more than an extensive parade

1. No real history of the 1858 war is available. Published sources include military correspondence and reports in *SED* and *HED* for 1858 and 1859; detailed in the Bibliography, below, they are here cited simply as army reports, sometimes with serial number or other identification. Similarly cited are Mullan's 1859 official *Topographical Memoir of Colonel Wright's Campaign*, and his volumes of the military road reports in *SED-HED*. The Joset Narrative is a unique item involving related documents (explained below, Chap. 7, n. 11). Besides manuscript and published documentation by Jesuits, Indian officials, and army officers, and Hudson's Bay or Canadian authorities, reminiscences exist of very unequal value by Whites such as Beall, O'Neil, Kenny, and Trimble, and by Indians such as Youmas and Stellam. Under this heading come the ethnological work of Teit and the untrustworthy *Ka-Mi-Akin* by Splawn. B. F. Manring has a small, jejune history, paraphrasing the more obvious sources and dressed with useful biographical detail: *Conquest of the Coeur d'Alenes, Spokanes, and Palouses* (Spokane, 1912). W. C. Brown attempts, from very late Indian reminiscence and claims, to tell *The Indian Side of the Story* (Spokane, 1961) in Washington Territory wars; the materials are often untrustworthy, and especially so for the 1858 war, but provide some useful detail (see esp. chaps. 16 to 20, 28). See also Jack Dozier's brief "The Coeur d'Alene Indians in the War of 1858" (part of a master's thesis), in *Idaho Yesterdays*, *5* (1961), 22–32. Short narrative accounts are available in Bancroft, *Washington*, pp. 178–200; Victor, *Early Wars*, pp. 424–500; Fuller, *Pacific Northwest*, pp. 243–60; and W. E. Rosebush, *Frontier Steel, the Men and Their Weapons* (Spokane, 1958), pp. 207–86. See also my "A Jesuit in the War against the Northern Indians," *RACHS*, *61* (1950), 9–54. I have edited Joset's main narrative as "Père Joset's Account of the Indian War of 1858," *PNWQ*, *38* (1947), 285–307, and have analyzed the Bancroft variant in "A Bancroft Library Manuscript on the 1858 Indian War," *OHQ*, *52* (1951), 54–57.

ground, it is vaguely defined out of the forlorn landscape by a circle of low-
lying cabins and barracks. The buildings huddle like a row of covered wagons expecting an attack. It hardly seems a fort at all.

Its garrison was unimpressive: two companies of infantry and four troops
of dragoons. But the *Weekly Oregonian* was hailing it as "probably the most
efficient command" in the Northwest. The compliment was premature. The
soldiers were raw recruits, badly housed and barely staving off famine. Congress had neglected to allot their pay, so there was a good deal of grumbling.
To increase their unease the Indians nearby were restive and prowling.

On the night of April 12 some fifteen or twenty Palouses raided the Walla
Walla Valley, driving off nearly two dozen head of cattle from Walter Davis'
herd. Since over half of these had been the property of the army commissary,
troopers hustled out next day in pursuit. They trailed the war party seventy
miles north to a crossing of the Snake River. It proved a futile gesture. The
Weekly Oregonian on the Coast duly reported the event under the inflamma-
tory headline "Another Indian Outbreak." The editors viewed the incident as
an initial maneuver in a new war by Kamiakin. Even in peacetime "the pilfering dispositions" of the Palouses had led Father De Smet to deal with them
warily. Now they had found a leader and a cause. Chief Tilcoax, whom Joset
terms "a refugee among the Peluses since the Cayuse war," was directing
their operations. His influence stemmed partly from his wealth in horses and
partly from his restless, driving hatred against the Whites.[2]

On the heels of the raid disquieting reports came from the Dalles Indian
agent about "the hostile Indians of the Palouse, Yakima, and other tribes." A
delegation from the hostiles had solicited an alliance from a friendly chief
sixty miles to the northeast. Two French Canadians on their way to Colville
had been killed.[3] By mid-April Colonel Steptoe, the commander at Fort
Walla Walla, had come to think "an expedition to the North advisable, if not
necessary." His intention was to provide a demonstration in force to overawe
unruly war factions and reassure the Colville miners. It would also be good
drill for the recruits after the long confinement of winter quarters. General
Clarke reports the march as designed to chastise bad Indians and restore calm
before things got worse.[4] Steptoe speaks especially of bothersome "Spokanes" near Colville.

On May 6 the Colonel led his little command north—two companies of infantry and three of dragoons, comprising 152 men under 5 officers, together

2. *Oregonian,* 24 April 1858. *Harper's New Monthly Magazine, 19* (1859), 135 (officer's 1858 comment on pay, food). CR, *2,* 561. Joset Narrative. Brown treats the Tilcoax (pronounced Tilch-ka-waikes) family at length in his chap. 7.

3. NA, IA, Oregon Sup., LR, Agent Dennison to Nesmith, 24 April 1858.

4. NA, EW, Army Commands, Dept. Pacific, Fort Walla Walla Letterbook, Steptoe
Report, April 17; also in *SED,* 35 Cong., 2 sess., 1 (1858); Clarke Report, 1 June, in
AGO, LR, P165.

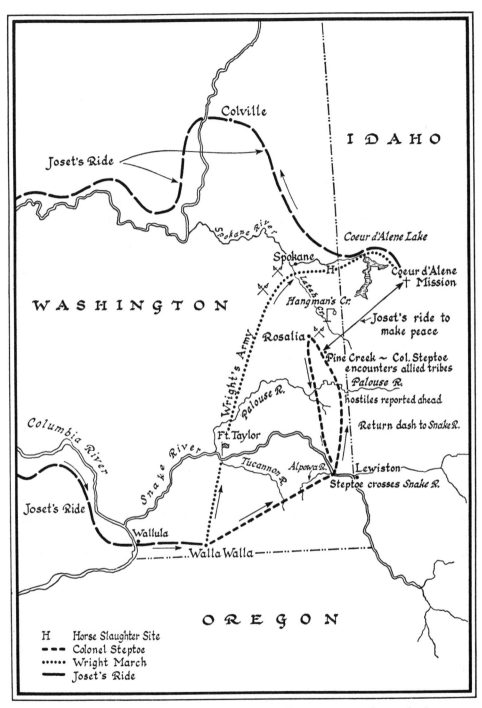

Colville

I D A H O

Joset's Ride

Spokane River

Coeur d'Alene Lake

Spokane H

Coeur d'Alene
+ Mission

Latah Cr.

W A S H I N G T O N

Hangman's Cr.

Joset's ride to
make peace

Rosalia

Pine Creek ~ Col. Steptoe
encounters allied tribes

Palouse R.

hostiles reported ahead

Palouse R.

Return dash to Snake R.

Wright's Army

Columbia River

Ft. Taylor

Snake River

Tucannon R.

Alpowa R.

Lewiston
Steptoe crosses Snake R.

Joset's Ride

Wallula

Walla Walla

O R E G O N

H   Horse Slaughter Site
- - -   Colonel Steptoe
...... Wright March
———   Joset's Ride

8. The War against the Northern Indians. Present state boundaries serve
as a background.

with a handful of civilian employees. After the defeat much would be made of Steptoe's "to say the least, imprudent act" in launching so negligible a force into the upper Interior. Most of his command, moreover, were "fresh recruits." A defect particularly singled out for adverse comment by the nation's military commander, Winfield Scott, was the deficiency of ammunition. The packmaster seems to have received only three mule loads from the fort's magazine. With forty rounds per man, Indian Superintendent Nesmith writes, Steptoe was "destitute of ammunition." [5]

Most scandalous of all to *post-factum* commentators, the dragoons were ordered to leave their sabers. Some commanders at this period believed that "there is no such thing as hand-to-hand combat with the Indians" for a force well equipped and led.[6] Anyway, one could look upon dragoons as mounted infantry of high mobility. They still kept infantry titles, practiced infantry drills, and were in transition from the title "company" to "troop." Nevertheless, they were expected to play the role of cavalry whenever necessary, and therefore the saber, for all its defects in fighting Indians, was a principal weapon. Nesmith believed the real explanation to be that Steptoe "certainly did not expect to fight"; when the battle came he would "avoid it as long as possible." But Steptoe had announced his readiness for a skirmish. He was prepared, so to speak, for a light rain but not for a flood. The Palouses were "feeble," and "the more powerful tribes" in the upper country were professing friendship.[7]

Steptoe's men were badly armed. The Indians had Hudson's Bay muskets of good range, as well as far-carrying rifles. Two out of three of Steptoe's dragoon companies, "more than half my command," depended largely on musketoons. Short and wide-mouthed, carrying a ball with three shot, having less than fifty yards' effective range, they were "almost useless." One dragoon company had rifles, but unfortunately they were Mississippi Jaegers, which loaded badly on horseback. Two mountain howitzers were proudly on display in the column. These were little guns borne by mules and assembled for battle on diminutive carriages; the Indians' smooth-bore muskets could outrange them. Even Father Joset noted that the troops were "miserably armed." [8]

5. Stevens Papers, Nesmith to Stevens, Salem, 20 August 1858 ("imprudent"). Joset Narrative. Kip, *Expedition*, p. 10 (recruits).

6. Eugene Bandel, *Frontier Life in the Army 1854–1861*, ed. R. P. Bieber (Glendale, Cal., 1932), p. 124. On Steptoe lack of sabers and ammunition, cf. Archer Corresp., 15 June 1858.

7. Nesmith to Stevens, above, n. 5. Kip, *Expedition*, p. 9 (last quots.).

8. Fort Walla Walla Letterbook, p. 37, Steptoe to Wright, 2 June; cf. two letters to Mackall, May 23, comprising Steptoe Report, pp. 34–35 (*SED*, pp. 346–49). Joset Narrative.

The march was uneventful enough for the fifty miles or more to the Snake crossing and for almost an equivalent distance beyond. This plains country is undulating and sometimes vaguely hilly, with bunch grass decorating the scene. The Colonel rode ahead, a southern aristocrat, elegant and slender and dark, with black hair, slightly staring eyes, and a full, pallid face—featureless except for his bushy pirate's mustache. A West Point graduate and a veteran of the Mexican War, he was no stranger to combat. Not anticipating trouble, he was informally dressed in civilian clothes and rode along with confident ease, a small riding whip in his hand. Just below the Snake he encountered some thirty Palouses said to be hostile. He was not disturbed when they fled. To ferry his troops across the Snake and to guide them to the Palouse encampments, he arranged for a Nez Percé ally.

This was Chief Tammutsa or Timothy, a former village chief who had risen to prominence a decade before through his connection with Dr. Whitman's mission. His Indians were to guide and scout for the command. They were Steptoe's only eyes and sense of direction for the country ahead. As the topographer Lieutenant Mullan confessed, all this country was "but little known" and the best map, that of the Stevens expedition, was not much use. Timothy's very presence was something of a bad omen. The command's half-breed guide had refused to go beyond the Snake, predicting a battle; Indians from this little village of thirteen lodges at the Snake were then persuaded to substitute.[9]

After the troops had been out for over a week, moving erratically about the countryside, rumors came that the Spokanes would dispute their passage. This seemed unlikely; no one gave it further thought. Yet by the time the troops went splashing across Pine Creek, an allied Indian camp of anything from five hundred to a thousand furiously angry braves had accumulated to their front. Indian women and children had been sent scurrying back to the safety of the central camp or off into the hills. The warriors had decorated themselves and their horses with elaborate patterns in war paint. All were properly accoutered in lucky charms and feathers and traditional symbols, and armed to the teeth.

The traditional exercises and functions, kept polished during the past years of buffalo fighting against the Blackfeet, were ready to go into smooth operation. After all these years of tension, if there had to be war, the northern Indians preferred to have it here. Steeled by war dances and harangues, they jogged their ponies in the direction of the troops. Where the soldiers' line of march dove through a little ravine, the warriors took up their positions.

9. Steptoe Report, 23 May, above, n. 8. Steptoe's appearance from J. G. Trimble reminiscence, in W. J. Trimble, "A Soldier of the Oregon Frontier," *OHQ*, *8* (1907), 46–47. Mullan, *Topographical Memoir*, p. 3.

There they set up an ambush. Toward it marched the little detachment of recruits. It was Sunday morning, May 16.

With startling suddenness, an hour before noontime, Colonel Steptoe encountered them—"all armed, painted, and defiant." As a colleague later described it, the Indians were "all painted and in their war dress, evidently meditating an attack." Captain Winder, second in command of the infantry, tried to estimate their numbers. "At first sight with my glass I could count but 70," he wrote just after the battle. Then a few of the colorful figures detached themselves, moving forward to parley; "in a few seconds as if by magic" a swarm of Indian warriors "appeared all around us, some 800, and in half an hour from 1,000 to 1,200, the Indians say 1,600 which may be true." Both men and horses were "painted and dressed in the most fantastic and savage style." Colonel Steptoe's professional eye also assessed them for his report: between 1,000 to 1,200 warriors, well mounted, most of them apparently carrying rifles. The two hostile masses briefly drifted toward each other, coming to a halt a hundred yards apart.[10]

The Indian Coalition: Confrontation

What had been happening just over the Colonel's horizon? Jesuit writings enable us to fashion a fairly detailed reconstruction. A "portion" of the Coeur d'Alenes, apparently under Chief Vincent, had been digging camas roots far to the south on Nez Percé territory. The place may well have been the camas ground described by Mullan twelve miles north of the Clearwater, far southwest of the mission. It measured some two miles by eight, "perfectly level, and enclosed on all sides by forests of pine." Here "a small creek or slough" ran, furnishing a seasonal encampment. "It is a great resort for all the Indians in this vicinity, principally the Nez Percés, Coeur d'Alenes, and sometimes Spokanes, it being a favorite racing grounds with all the Indians."

This Coeur d'Alene party was thunderstruck to learn that troops had finally crossed the Snake without sending notice. Nor were the soldiers on "the road for Colville, nor that for the Paloos country." Hastily the party decamped from Nez Percé land, sending word north to their main body in Spokane territory and to their allies. But "at once the Federals changed their line of march and came to the Indians' new camp." As the Indians maneuvered and turned, so did the menacing soldiers.[11]

10. Steptoe Report, above, n. 8 (first quot.); Nesmith to Stevens, above, n. 5. Kip, *Expedition*, p. 9. Teit and Ray are useful for decorations and war customs of our tribes. Captain (later General) Charles S. Winder, letter of 2 June 1858, as "Captain C. S. Winder's Account of a Battle with the Indians," ed. I. Ridgeway Trimble, *MHM*, 35 (1940), 57.
11. CR, 2, 750. Joset Narrative. *RR*, 1, ii, 533 (Mullan quots.)

Worse yet, Steptoe's guide, Chief Timothy, kept sending his braves toward them, taunting: "Coeur d'Alenes, your wives, your horses, your goods, shall very soon be ours." [12] Was this the malicious rivalry of an "American" and Protestant chief? Closer examination suggests a different motive. Steptoe meant to find Palouse miscreants on this trip to Colville. Timothy knew that a prime miscreant, perhaps the principal one, was Chief Tilcoax. Now at this time Timothy was enjoying a bitter personal feud with Tilcoax. Timothy himself would later cheerfully admit this to Fathers Joset and Cataldo. [13] Thus Timothy's private interests added a spice of zeal to his public efforts. It seems to have made him reckless. And this in turn played into the hands of the wily Tilcoax.

Tilcoax was also camped in the Nez Percé country. In fact, he was "in the neighborhood" of our Coeur d'Alene band. Perhaps the Palouse band of thirty or forty, sighted briefly by Steptoe below the Snake, were Tilcoax's men fleeing toward the Coeur d'Alene diggers. Tilcoax seems to have paralleled the Coeur d'Alene flight, in order to join the Palouse bands working in the Spokane country. Thus the soldiers may only have given an appearance of descending upon the retreating Coeur d'Alenes. Tilcoax may even have been deliberately confusing the two trails for them; after all, Vincent had predicted to Joset that the Palouse-Nez Percé war faction would direct the troops toward the Coeur d'Alenes. On the other hand, Timothy himself may understandably have been confused by the two small bands in flight.

Thus whatever blame can be attached to Timothy reveals itself at worst as a human thing, a heedless enthusiasm or irresponsibility. Something more can be said in his defense. He was a Nez Percé on Nez Percé land when the Coeur d'Alene band first fled. He was also a guide to the White soldiers who were his allies and the lords of the earth. He and they could wander as they pleased. Then, after they had gone so far out of the way in pursuit of Tilcoax, the road to Colville paradoxically did lie through Spokane land.

Why didn't Steptoe clear up the misunderstanding in his parleys with the hostiles? Why did he not explain to Father Joset on the battlefield, when the Indian grievance was exposed? Probably because he was in no position for candor. Aggressively he had pushed forward, eager for a small fight with some Palouses, only to find these Palouses engulfed in an ocean of hostile allies. Circumstances were hardly propitious for admitting his previous intentions. It was necessary for him to dissemble. He would simply insist that he

12. Joset Narrative. On Timothy see Drury, *Spalding*, pp. 213–14, 249, 344, 372, 415–16.

13. Marginal addition of Joset Narrative on OJ copy (1874 by Joset); see my edition, *PNWQ, 38,* 294. Cf. also Kamiakin and Coeur d'Alenes accusing Tilcoax, CR, 2, 751.

had been on his way to Colville all the time. That Steptoe wanted Tilcoax for stealing government stock and for killing Whites, Father Joset would learn only in November 1858 after all the battles of the year were over. "Colonel Steptoe never said anything of that sort to me," the priest wrote; "but if it was so, this would explain the whole puzzle." [14]

Nor should the language barrier between Timothy and the Coeur d'Alenes be forgotten. Although his bizarre message was probably meant for Tilcoax, it may well have been relayed and translated by that wily chief to apply to the Coeur d'Alenes. Some months after the battle, Joset heard the Coeur d'Alenes accuse Tilcoax "of having deceived them, by falsely reporting" the words of Timothy. De Smet also heard that Tilcoax's ally Kamiakin rebuked the Palouse chief for "this perfidy." [15] True, Timothy later admitted to the Jesuits that he had addressed such words to the Coeur d'Alenes; but this becomes understandable from the moment he saw the two tribes united in flight or in resistance. Tilcoax not only lied; he cleverly turned the lie into a real and desperate situation. The Coeur d'Alenes, caught out on the plains, notorious for their "quick temper," reacted predictably. "The stubborn and inexplicable march" of Steptoe "appeared to them hostile"; it seemed at last "to give the lie to all arguments of the more sensible men." [16]

The call now went out to all allies. Warriors came galloping from every quarter. Who were they, and where would they fight? De Smet describes the battle as taking place on Spokane land. But elsewhere he records that "the Spokan[e] Prairie is claimed by the Coeur d'Alene Indians." Governor Stevens during his explorations had noted this claim; he designated the general area of the coming battle as "Kamas Prairie of the Coeur d'Alene[s]." Except for this evidence, the fight must be placed in the territory of the more southerly, or Hangman's Creek, group of the Eastern Spokane tribe. Steptoe was still some distance south of any permanent Spokane settlements, however, and the ownership of the area may have been ambiguous. Perhaps it is best to say that it was Spokane land in which the Coeur d'Alenes held traditional or permissive rights.[17]

Populating the battlefield with the proper tribes and numbers is rather more difficult. The Indians were scattered and in motion much of the time. The observers were excited. Boiling dust and intervening hillocks obscured the action. Moreover, the Indian number, rapidly augmenting on both days of conflict, was still growing after the battle. Steptoe reports "ten or twelve

14. CR, *2*, 751.

15. Ibid.

16. Joset Narrative; CR, *2*, 749–50. Cf. Joset ethnological papers in OJ on temper.

17. CR, *2*, 750; *3*, 970. RR, *12*, i, 252, and folding map; cf. Ray, *PNWQ*, *27*, map on p. 116, with comment on p. 121.

hundred Indians." Joset on the night before the battle loosely calculates a thousand. De Smet notes that from 800 to 1,000 were allied just before the fighting. Lieutenant Kip retails the impression that "the hills around were covered" with Indians. The first newspaper report talks of 1,500. Lieutenant Gregg sets a more sober figure of 600 at the first encounter, rising to some 800 later. Captain Winder, writing expressly to correct newspaper talk and rumors, as noted above estimated the number at 800 initially, soon swelling to 1,000 or 1,200 and possibly to 1,600.[18]

No more than 150 of these could have been mustered by the small Coeur d'Alene tribe. It is unlikely that all the tribes known to the Whites as Spokanes could have contributed more than half again this number. Just after the battle, Lieutenant Mullan gathered from the Jesuits that there were some 130 Coeur d'Alenes "capable of bearing arms"; of these "about 90 actively engaged," the rest remaining "neutral." At the same time, Lieutenant Kip also talked with the Fathers. He puts the information less clearly; the Coeur d'Alenes muster no more than a hundred warriors, he says, the Spokanes about four times this number. Allowing for the Jesuit tendency at that moment to minimize the Coeur d'Alene participation and blame, and for the number of lodges reported by Stevens, the Coeur d'Alene number can be expanded slightly. On the other hand, 400 warriors is too large for the Spokane groups if we compare the relative size of the Spokane and Coeur d'Alene tribes. Did Kip misunderstand, or did the priests speak loosely of a capacity double that of the Coeur d'Alenes, or was Kip using "Spokane" to cover neighboring and similar bands?

About forty Kalispels seem to have been on hand, most of them related to the Spokane groups by marriage or descent. Walla Wallas "were at Colonel Steptoe's Battle," Wright states flatly; their number was large enough to contribute to Wright's anger against them in the subsequent peace talks. The Palouses were prominent. De Smet describes them as resembling the Nez Percés "in all respects"; since he numbers them at "scarce 300," they could have furnished anything from fifty warriors up. The Kettles were out in force; to judge from their later enthusiasm, the majority of their warriors was here. "The discontented portion of the Nez Percés" fought in this as in subsequent battles. Contributions came from distant tribes like the Okanogans and even the Thompsons. The Palouses at this time were harboring quite a few rogue Indians or patriots who had fled east when Fort Simcoe went up on Yakima land. Among these were the great Kamiakin "and a number of other Cayuse, Yakima, and Walla Walla refugees." Because of the Oblate Pandosy's

18. Steptoe Report, above, n. 8; Joset Narrative; CR, *2*, 731; Kip, *Expedition*, p. 10. Lt. Gregg to Vancouver friend, printed in *Weekly Oregonian*, 29 May 1858. Winder, *MHM*, *35*, 57.

influence for peace in 1856, some of them strongly resented missionaries.[19]

After the battle Steptoe, who held several talks with the chiefs and a long conversation with Father Joset, informed headquarters that about half the Spokanes, Coeur d'Alenes, and Flatheads were hostile, and nearly all the Palouses, part of the Yakimas, "and I think a small number of Nez Percés," together with units from various petty tribes. Agent Dennison at The Dalles, writing Nesmith after news of the defeat, said that the tribes involved were Palouses, Spokanes, Yakimas, Isle des Pierres (Sinkiuse-Columbias), Coeur d'Alenes, "and a few Flatheads." Perhaps for "Flatheads" should be understood such related tribes of the Flathead confederacy as the Kutenais and Kalispels.[20]

Father De Smet lists nine, possibly ten, tribes in the wider prewar coalition: Okanogans, Kalispels, Kutenais, Flatheads, Spokanes, Coeur d'Alenes, Kettles, Palouses, and Yakimas. Such an adventure would easily attract hotheaded individuals from yet other tribes. The Pend d'Oreille and Flathead tribes were to boast proudly before General Harney that they had never killed a White; despite this, a number of irresponsibles may have been present at the Steptoe fight. Since the war began so unexpectedly, almost by chance, the distant Flatheads as a tribe were probably spared the necessity of making a decision. Then, before the autumn campaign was launched by the army, the Jesuits had gained sufficient time to throw their influence onto the Flathead balance.[21]

Was Spokane Garry present? As a peace chief, an "American" Indian, and a neighbor of the battle area, he ought logically to have been there. Many decades later some Spokanes, the oldest of whom had been only a child during the war, spoke of Garry's presence from the beginning. But by this time the Spokane Garry myth had grown; even the old warriors were confused in their memories of important details. Garry's recent biographer assumes that he was on the battlefield as an active, even as the principal, peacemaker. He has Garry take Vincent to see Steptoe.[22]

19. See Coeur d'Alene and Spokane tribal estimates, pp. 180, 190, and Coeur d'Alenes at peace council below, p. 309. Kip, *Expedition*, p. 79. Mullan, *Topographical Memoir*, p. 38; on Nez Percés, p. 88, and above, pp. 177–78. Teit, BAE *Annual Report, 45*, 369 ("twoscore" Kalispel, a late tradition; Okanogans and Thompsons). NA, EW, AGO, LR, 290c, Wright to Mackall, 9 October 1858. CR, *3*, 991; cf. *2*, 455, 561; *2*, 748 (refugees).

20. Fort Walla Walla Letterbook, Steptoe to Mackall, 23 May. IA, Oreg. Sup., LR, Dennison to Nesmith, 24 April.

21. *SED*, 36 Cong., 1 sess., 2 (1858–59), Harney, 1 June 1859 report (here from NA, EW, AGO, 79-0; on Pend-Flathead claim). CR, *2*, 731 (here Kalispels probably include Pend d'Oreilles or upper Kalispels).

22. OH, No. 307, "Indian Account of Spokane Country," seven northeastern Spokanes through interpreter to W. S. Lewis (1916). Splawn's impression that he was at least in the Wright battles (*Ka-Mi-Akin*, pp. 98, 118) proves to be founded upon a misinterpretation of Kip (*Expedition*, p. 67). Jessett, *Spokan Garry*, pp. 137–38.

Yet contemporary accounts, always quick to record his overtures, omit his name. An unsigned letter of June 1 from Fort Dalles conveys information deriving from the Steptoe combatants then at Fort Walla Walla; "it was said that Kaniyaki was about but took no part in the fight—nor Spokan Garry, who is quite an important personage among the upper tribes." Was Garry also "about," and in the same remote fashion as Kamiakin? After the war Colonel Wright did not treat Garry as a hostile, the way he treated the Spokane chief Polatkin, nor even as a deserving friend. Agent Owen's diary reveals that Garry rode with him into Fort Colville on Saturday the fifteenth; indeed, he had stayed rather close to Owen during the preceding three weeks. There is no evidence that he traveled down for the Steptoe encounter the next day.

In a statement secured from him by Father Congiato two months after the Steptoe battle and carried south to the army by Father Ravalli, Garry claims: "I did my best to persuade my people not to shoot him; he goes to Colville, I said." His people wouldn't listen to him, the chief adds. Perhaps Garry in defending himself is speaking in a general way. All the evidence may be related and harmonized, together with Garry's ambiguous statement, if one assumes that he caught up with the action at the same time Kamiakin did: after the troops were cornered and surrounded on their hill. At the intertribal council held there, he could have made his plea against attacking and, like Kamiakin, have been overruled. Ever since the Spokane council of 1855 Garry gives the impression of having retreated into a frustrated and indecisive neutrality. Immediately after the battle he would speak of himself as "undecided," in fear of his life from the other Indians. Agent Owen then feared he would "make common cause with the enemy." [23]

The Spokane chief prominent as peacemaker that day was Sgalgalt. The Spokane chief most prominent in the attack on Steptoe and in the war was Polatkin. Polatkin spoke English well. He was the second most important chief of Garry's group, and his son was married to a daughter of the hostile Yakima leader Owhi. Lieutenant Kip makes the mistake once of calling Polatkin "the head chief of the Spokanes." Stevens refers to him during the 1855 crisis as "one of the principal chiefs of the Spokanes." Steptoe's packmaster Beall in his reminiscences recalls him as "war chief of the Spokanes." After Wright's campaign, when Polatkin came in peace, the Colonel unhesitatingly clapped him into irons as a war criminal. Later, at the peace conference with the Coeur d'Alenes, Polatkin signed as one of the important chiefs in the first treaty of surrender, and then again in the subsidiary treaty with the other

23. Owen, *Journals and Letters*, 1, 199 (15 May, Saturday); 2, 181 (16 July), report to Nesmith. Statement to Congiato in Congiato to Clarke, 3 August 1858, NA, EW, Army Commands, Dept. Pacific; also in *SED*, 35 Cong., 2 sess. (1858), 1. *Alta California*, 13 June 1858, Dalles letter of 1 June.

Spokanes. He was the only Spokane chief who refused to attend Agent
Owen's conciliatory council after the Steptoe defeat. When Owen sought
him out privately, he showed himself enthusiastic about the war; "he seemed
very sanguine of Exterminating the Soldiers" coming for the punitive campaign. Thus Polatkin seems to have played the role of war leader for the
Spokanes.[24]

Among the Coeur d'Alenes the elected head chief on the battlefield was
Vincent (Barsa to the Indian tongue) Xwipep; his Indian names were Barren
Earth and Old Man with a Staff. The medallion portrait of him in 1891, when
he was almost a hundred years old, shows a kindly man with small nose and
prominent chin. His lands were at present Hayden Lake, with a "sort of
claim to Lake Coeur d'Alene where the City of Coeur d'Alene now stands."
Vincent seems to have been the son of Martha, sister of the former head chief
Old Stellam.[25] Andrew Seltis, often mistaken for head chief, was rather a rising chief of great influence who was soon to supplant Vincent.[26]

Did the great Kamiakin direct the Steptoe encounter? This myth derives
from the pioneer Splawn, whose memoir on Kamiakin includes much dubious
romancing from Indian sources long after the event. Splawn has Kamiakin plan
the war like a general, drawing Steptoe across the Snake, alerting the tribes and
effecting their rendezvous, then directing the attack. Actually Kamiakin does
not seem to have been on the scene, or to have arrived until rather late in the
battle, or even to have influenced its course.

In his many conversations with Father De Smet five months after the war,
Kamiakin admitted a culpable participation but insisted he had only been "at
last drawn into the contest" after a dramatic council of all the chiefs. Had this
council occurred before or during Joset's peace efforts, Vincent and Joset
would have mentioned him among the instigators like Tilcoax or among the
peacemakers like Sgalgalt. Joset gives Kamiakin a prominent place throughout the war, but not here. The Jesuit is also clear as to the disposition of the
chiefs for peace, both on the night of the seventeenth and next morning. Such
a council as Kamiakin describes could only have assembled after the exciting

24. CR, *2*, 752 (Sgalgalt). Owen, *2*, 183; *1*, 158. Kip, *Expedition*, p. 95. *RR*, *12*, i, 224.
T. Beall Reminiscences (WU). Cf. Teit, BAE *Annual Report*, *45*, 378. Mullan 1860
Road Report, *HED*, p. 30.
25. On medallion see above, p. 198, n. 77. C. Wood, "Famous Indians," *Century
Magazine*, *46* (1893), 436–45. Basil Peone, "An Indian Herodotus," *Teepee* (Coeur
d'Alene domestic publication), *1* (1938), 7 (quot.). Occasional mention in Joset, De
Smet writings.
26. On Seltis see the Jesuit biography in *LPT* (1904), pp. 108–12. Frequent mention
in Jesuit MSS. Teit's informants erroneously make him 1858 head chief (pp. 128, 153);
Splawn has the same error for 1855 (*Ka-Mi-Akin*, p. 25). Portrait medallion of Seltis
in Heye Foundation, Museum of the American Indian, New York City.

chase and the cornering of the troops. Kamiakin seems to have been unavailable at first, or else events moved too rapidly and fortuitously for a time; perhaps he may even have held aloof from Tilcoax's unplanned, harebrained scheme until overwhelming success chanced to crown it. At the council, which must have been held after Steptoe was run to earth and it became possible once more to control events, Kamiakin was taunted or "upbraided" before the assembled chiefs for his caution. Then he, too, joined in.[27]

With both White and Indian military forces clarified, we may return to the disconcerted Steptoe facing the Indian horde. Colonel Steptoe managed to get two messages back to Grier whom he had left in command at Fort Walla Walla. One was not delivered at all. The other arrived too late to do any good. The Nez Percé who carried the first message must have ridden hard, for Steptoe started it off on May 15 and Grier relayed it to San Francisco on May 16. The Colonel was then comfortably settled on the Palouse River, only vaguely aware of some activity beyond his horizon.

He announces that "the Palouse are in front of us—we expect to come up to them today." He anticipates no difficulty. "They say that they will fight; I daresay they will, but I hope we shall be able to give them a good drubbing." No permanent peace can be had "until some of these people are overhauled." His preoccupation is to prevent "the growing disaffection of the Spokanes." The Nez Percé messenger added the information that ten Spokane chiefs "with their warriors have joined the Palouses and that they are determined to fight." In fact, wrote Grier to San Francisco, "if my information be correct, quite a number of the Spokanes are found with the Palouses." [28]

Steptoe's letter was not a call for help. As a matter of routine prudence, Steptoe ordered Grier to dispatch a solid detachment to the Snake, since he now expected a small skirmish instead of a few arrests. The Snake crossing was his Achilles' heel, so he wanted to have boats and provisions in readiness. Grier sent every man he could spare: 66 of the fort's garrison under Captain F. T. Dent, an officer whose remaining claim to fame is his status as the brother-in-law of Ulysses S. Grant. Fort Walla Walla was so stripped by this action that Grier could not even comply with an order to send a protective escort for Lieutenant Mullan's road-building gang. Ordinary business continued as usual; a handful of men, for example, was detached from Fort Dalles to Fort Walla Walla on the day of the battle.[29]

27. Kamiakin, in CR, *3*, 968–69; Splawn, p. 90. In 1928 Kamiakin's son denied that his father or his band took part in any phase of the Steptoe battle (Brown, *Indian Side*, p. 416).

28. NA, EW, Army Commands, Dept. Pacific, Steptoe to Grier, 15 May 1858; Grier to Mackall, 16 May.

29. Grier to Mackall, 16 May. YU, Fort Dalles, Post Orders 1856–63, 17 May 1858.

In his parleys with the hostile chiefs meanwhile, Colonel Steptoe achieved nothing. Head Chief Vincent indignantly demanded to know "what he meant by coming that way upon us?" The Colonel replied that he was merely passing through on his way to Colville. With closed faces the Indians hid their disbelief, pretending that he had not said something absurd. Joset was to remark that this was like going "from Paris through Berlin to Turin."[30] Steptoe blandly requested Spokane help in crossing the Spokane River farther up; the Indians refused. It was now uncomfortably clear to the Colonel that he would be lucky to get out of this without trouble. He warned his officers that a fight was imminent. Later, the Indians commented that Steptoe should have turned due south immediately, to demonstrate his good intentions. Instead, intent upon finding a suitable campsite, he closed up his train and forged ahead.

Approaching the Indian-held ravine, he shied sharply to the west and marched one mile to a small lake. The warriors by now exhibited open contempt. They paralleled the right flank of the march, flinging taunts and firing off their rifles. Winder reports how they charged "around us, yelling, whooping, shaking scalps and such things over their heads, looking like so many fiends." Throughout all this, the talks with Indian groups continued. At the lake there were further fruitless parleys. A Negro orderly of Lieutenant Gaston especially attracted attention: Indians curiously fingered his kinky hair, and the poor man muttered that he would not surrender his "wool" without a fight. At the lakeside the dragoons sat their mounts for three hours, immobile, until the setting sun dispersed the hostiles.[31]

The Indians had been in a bad temper. Why, then, had they postponed their attack? Partly because this was the Lord's day. The Indians called to the Whites that they would fight when Sunday was over. The action reads like a curious reflection of the medieval Truce of God. One author goes so far as to see in this "the simple Christianity" Garry had brought back from the Red River training, where Presbyterian elements in the Episcopalian formation induced a "Sabbatharism." In fact, the strict observance of Sunday derived rather from the Jesuit Reductions of Canada. The Iroquois had inculcated this particular practice among the Flatheads, for instance, long before Garry's time, indeed twenty years before the Jesuits arrived. Even on the dangerous buffalo hunts out on the Plains, the Flatheads had the "custom of never breaking camp on Sunday." A Hudson's Bay trader in the Oregon pre-

30. Joset Narrative; CR, 2, 750; Joset Papers, No. 70A, "History of Coeur d'Alene Indians."

31. Steptoe Report, above, n. 8; Mullan, *Topographical Memoir*. John O'Neil, "Recollections of a Soldier," *Indian Battles in the Inland Empire*, ed. E. F. Tannatt (Spokane, 1914), pp. 6–7 ("wool"). Winder, *MHM*, 35, 57.

missionary country of the '30s had already remarked how the tribes keep "Sunday inviolate," not even fishing or raising camp. Though he is unsympathetic to Catholics and Protestants alike, he tells how the story of the eighteenth-century Jesuit missionaries had filtered "to the remotest tribes," so that the Indians vaguely revered their memory as benefactors. The ubiquitous Iroquois and voyageur influence in the Northwest, strengthened by the converging influence of the Prophet Dance religion and Protestant teachings, explain the phenomenon that surprised Steptoe's men. The Jesuit missions and probably the Oblate missions insisted on such Sunday reverence; when Joset arrived on our battlefield, he reminded the tribes of this.

Another reason for the postponement of the attack on Steptoe was the vigorous resistance put up by Chief Vincent of the Coeur d'Alenes and Chief Sgalgalt of the Spokanes. From the time of the first parley, Vincent had moved through the Indian ranks, arguing and pleading. He hoped to restrain them from violence until Father Joset could arrive. With the Coeur d'Alenes and Spokanes milling about in uncertainty, the other tribesmen, and particularly the Palouses, were reluctant to begin the battle. Yet as fast as Vincent sent back one group of hotheads, "Telkawey [Tilcoax] and the Peluses were pushing" others to the fore. "The Coeur d'Alenes are very brave in words," they sneered, "like cowards and women."

Tilcoax was exultant; both his enemy Timothy and the White allies were in the power of the hostiles. He now had "just what he wanted, he who before and after this, did his utmost to raise enemies to the whites." All afternoon the nerve-wracking pattern of Palouse provocation and peace efforts was repeated. These were the savage but abortive feints recorded by Winder. Vincent and Sgalgalt only with the greatest difficulty persuaded the Indians to make camp that evening. Vincent was to complain to Father Joset "I had no rest the whole day; I feel very tired." He could do nothing more to hold in his warriors. The rest was up to Joset.[32]

A JESUIT ON THE BATTLEFIELD

Chief Vincent's desperate appeal was being raced back to Father Joset on Saturday, even before Steptoe was near the hostiles' ambush. Vincent's courier may have left sometime on Thursday; he reached the mission on Friday the 15th. His message was that troops were across the Snake, advancing

---

32. Joset Narrative (incl. Tilcoax episode). Jessett, *Garry*, p. 139 (Sabbatharism). On Sunday strictness see e.g. CR, *1*, 231, 289–90, 361–64. The Hudson's Bay man is John Dunn, *The Oregon Territory and the British North American Fur Trade with an Account of the Customs of the Principal Native Tribes on the Northern Continent* (Philadelphia, 1845), pp. 210, 235–36.

on the tribe and quite near. The Jesuit was needed as quickly as he could get there. This was not the only message to reach the mission that Saturday. Warriors on all sides were arming and leaving. Already the mission was in a turmoil, "an excitement you could hardly imagine."

The work for peace began on the spot. Joset hardly managed to restrain the braves working on the church from taking the warpath. He had the brothers destroy all powder at the mission. Then he set out "in an instant" and "in all haste." As he hurried away, he could see such male population as remained in the area, grim and "fully armed," speeding toward the field of action. Other tribes were pouring in from every side: "whether they were summoned or not is not known." The eagle wing and large feather, symbols of an Indian warrior in the Rocky Mountains, must have been ominously in evidence that day.[33]

For the trip across the lake Old Peter flatly refused the loan of his bark canoe. The mission normally owned a canoe, but Indian carelessness easily disposed of such things. To add to Joset's difficulty the waters were unusually high, the country was rough, and Vincent lay ninety miles to the south. It was evening of the next day, Sunday the sixteenth, before Joset could reach the warriors' camp at Sile. He found Chief Vincent thoroughly discouraged. The chief deposited the whole disheartening situation into his hands.[34]

Joset looked about him. Lieutenant Mullan, visiting the place just four months later, carefully describes it for us; "lodge poles of a large camp" were still standing lonely against the September sky. A favorite assembly camp of the tribes, it lay some distance northeast of the spot where Steptoe first encountered the Indians. It was "a broad prairie bottom," bounded on the south by a continuous line of prairie swells or hills, and on the west, about four or five miles off, by a similar line of hills but with an intervening screen of timber. In the distance to the north and east "high, frowning, pine clad mountains" could be seen. The camp had grass, wood, a small clump of cottonwoods, a sheltered situation and, as the main key to its popularity, ample water. Such a camp was usually circular, with the horses brought to the middle at dusk for night herding. Dancing and assemblage was at the center. If other tribes shared the same camp they did so according to a traditional scheme apparently based upon the geographical relation of each tribe to the other.

The braves by now were "indeed awfully excited." To Joset's mind it seemed already too late to calm them. But an effort had to be made. Gathering the chiefs and subchiefs "and a quantity of other Indians," the priest began his harangue. He explained the "principles of war." He stressed their ig-

33. Joset Narrative.
34. Ibid., *JMUS*, 2, 321 (carelessness over canoe).

norance of the actual motives of the White chief. He reminded them that this was Sunday, a day too holy for talk of war. "Whosoever kills by his private authority," he warned, "is a murderer; whosoever engages in battle without the order of his chief is guilty of all the evil which flows from it; it is the duty of the chief to examine when he has to wage war for his own defense." At dawn they were to prepare a horse for him. He would visit the White chief, first entering alone and later introducing them. They would see—all could be settled peaceably. Joset is not speaking here only to Coeur d'Alenes. The reputation of the Blackrobe was great over the whole region, so he had an audience composed of "the chiefs of the different tribes and a quantity" of their Indians. These chiefs heard him out carefully, and in the end "appeared well satisfied." [35]

With this the chiefs and more responsible warriors were quieted. But his exhortations produced "no or very little effect" on the young bucks. The scholastic rules for a just war hardly seemed to apply, in their individualistic political tradition. Joset did manage to gather the Catholic warriors for their customary evening prayers. Scarcely had the last Amen died upon the night air, when a "slave" of the Americans, a Nez Percé guide, arrived to repeat the boast of the day: "your lands, your women, are ours." By this time, the Coeur d'Alenes and others were identified in the eyes of Timothy's men as allies of Tilcoax. Joset told his people not to believe the Nez Percé. "No officer ever spoke that way, tomorrow I will ask the chief of the soldiers if he has said that."

Joset charged Chief Vincent with seeing that none of the war parties began hostilities in advance. All that early spring night war chants and weird yells resounded. In the traditional Coeur d'Alene repertoire there were special war dances for these occasions. They were not the simulated-battle or spirit-invocation dances that some tribes used. They were dances of incitement, a physically intense developing of emotional fervor. These dances were to be preserved by the tribe until the turn of the century, when changed circumstances induced the Jesuits to discourage them.[36]

What must have been Father Joset's thoughts that night? Only six miles away twinkled the bivouac fires of the troops—tired, tense men scattered about a swampy bottom land, each sleeping on his gun while a strong sentry guard listened nervously. The savage drumming and chanting carried clearly into the White camp. One soldier later recalled having been so unnerved that he couldn't bring himself to respond to his comrades' request to sing them the song *Arkansas Bay;* the Indians, he told them, had knocked all the music

---

35. Mullan, *Topographical Memoir,* p. 69; cf. Mullan map. Cf. Teit, BAE *Annual Report,* 45, 375, 155. Joset Narrative.

36. Ray, *Cultural Relations,* pp. 44–52; Teit, pp. 187 ff.

out of him. But these painted savages were Joset's children. He had baptized them, catechized them, gathered them so often into church, married them, and heard their individual confessions of sin such a countless number of times. Their very names he had bestowed, and had inscribed for them in the various church registers. He was part of them. Their battle panoply did not unnerve him.

All Coeur d'Alene warriors painted the face and body. Horses were painted, too, their manes and tails specially arranged. The Indians preferred white horses for battle, because they showed off colors to their best advantage. The common war dye was red, though other strong colors were used—blue, yellow, black, and even white. Weapons varied. They were frequently brightened with design and ornament: the circular shield of painted hide, the lances and spears, bows and arrows, or whatever took a fighter's fancy. War dress varied wildly. Some simply stripped to breechcloth and moccasins for full freedom of action. Each brave displayed an array of feathers, charms, luck pieces, scalps, and medicine case, whether on his shirt or shield or weapons or hair. Individuality was especially evident in the warrior's headdress, when it was not a plain leather band. Warbonnets were common, as well as horned headpieces and helmets contrived from large birds like the owl. Feathered streamers flashed out from hair or warbonnet. Arrayed in savage splendor, grimacing and cavorting in a simulated war frenzy to the throb of the war drum and the rasp of the notched stick, the Coeur d'Alene presented a different aspect than he did at devotions.[37]

Whatever the Jesuit's reflections on this paradox, they were rudely interrupted. A Kalispel named Ishequitsetias slipped from the American lines to Joset's tent to say the soldiers knew a priest was among the hostiles. The Kalispel had overheard a Palouse talking to the great chief of the Whites; the Palouse was describing how the Father brought a horse loaded with ammunition to the Coeur d'Alenes and urged them to "kill the Americans." There seems to have been a surprising amount of such intelligence work carried out under cover of being an Indian ally or visitor; the Americans probably had difficulty distinguishing one kind of Interior Indian from another.[38]

The seventeenth dawned—a day "of sorrowful memory" to Joset, and a day one army officer on the Coast was to describe as marking this month "a disastrous one for the army of the Pacific." It was not quite light as Joset got up and about. The Indians delayed in bringing his horse. This suggests that the war faction in the tribe, and perhaps Tilcoax, were at work. A pagan medicine man of the Spokanes, Tshequyseken, greeted Joset with the same news the priest had received from the Kalispel. The medicine man then cried out to

37. Teit, pp. 73–75, 117–18, 255–56, 354, 359.
38. Joset Narrative.

the assembled Indians: "do you see now the deceit of this people?" Joset commented that the Palouses and Timothy's men were each inventing slanders about the other's war camp. He was puzzled as to the reason, since he had no way of seeing that each side hoped to provoke a fight while its allies opportunely stood by to assist.

As the Jesuit rode out to hold his parley, a swirl of Indians swept behind him in pageantry of war paint, feathers, and lances. But the American camp "was empty; they had started early and were retreating." Official reports later did not put it quite that baldly. "A retrograde movement" toward the post, eight days distant, had been initiated before sunrise; since "no formal leave had been taken of the chiefs," the latter concluded that the White warriors were running away.[39]

"We went after them." A brisk gallop—not quite three miles but it seemed to Joset "a good while"—brought the enemy column into view. The long serpent of blue was winding and bobbing in the dim daylight along a little valley, two companies of cavalry in the van, another at the rear, and over a hundred pack horses as well as some twenty-five tense and subdued infantry strung in between. The Indian escort massed along the distant hills in the morning gloom, and moved their wiry ponies toward the rear of the American column.

Joset left the Indians, riding on alone to interview the commander, "whom there I heard to be Colonel Steptoe." He was surprised to find Steptoe knew his name, and he was pleased at the officer's display of southern courtesy. The present expedition, Steptoe explained, was in response to an appeal from Colville. Merely intending a personal reconnaissance, he had increased his military escort to pass through the ill-disposed Palouses. Joset remained suspicious, because Steptoe was so far "out of the way." The priest in turn explained the Indian panic, their indignation at the trespassing of the soldiers beyond the Snake, and the resolve of the allied tribes to massacre Lieutenant Mullan's surveying party. He apologized for the failure of his previous attempts to warn the authorities. He also "alluded to the report so injurious to his reputation" and to his Jesuit Order that he had supplied ammunition, a charge "too monstrous" to warrant a formal complaint.

Steptoe in turn protested the innocence of his own intentions. He would never have come north without first interviewing the Coeur d'Alene and Spokane chiefs, had he known all this. If the chiefs would ride up to Colville and then down the right bank of the Columbia so as to bypass both Palouses and Yakimas, he wanted a council with them at Fort Walla Walla. "Yesterday" he concluded, "I thought we were going to fight; I am happy to return without bloodshed." When Joset suggested an immediate interview with the dis-

39. SED, army reports; Kip, *Expedition*, p. 9; Joset Narrative.

turbed chiefs, the Colonel demurred. He could not stop "on account of the frightened [pack] animals." Joset suggested that "the talk may be done walking." Steptoe willingly agreed. Joset and Steptoe had talked a fairly long time by now. The various chiefs had scattered momentarily and were not easily available. Joset "could only find Vincent." He took the chief and some accessible subchiefs back to the Colonel.

It has been suggested that because Joset brought a Coeur d'Alene delegation to Steptoe, he was not speaking for all the chiefs. But Joset had talked last night with the chiefs of the several tribes. He is explicit that "all the other chiefs as well Coeur d'Alenes as Spokanes," with the exception of the Palouses, were now united behind him for peace. In a moment he would return to both the Spokane and the Coeur d'Alene chiefs. This is understandable. During the several peace efforts subsequent to the battle, as during the 1856 troubles, the Jesuits did not work for the mission tribes alone. Colonel Wright could therefore later condemn the attack by the various tribes on Steptoe as "contrary to the orders of their chiefs." [40]

In any case, no chief as strong and important as Vincent seems to have been on the field that morning. The other tribes may have been represented by men of lesser status in the group Joset brought to Steptoe; or the non-mission Indians may deliberately have hung back out of diffidence and suspicion, as they were to do again in September after their defeat by Colonel Wright. It is important to realize also that Joset had not been arranging a parley with the chiefs. He had been conducting his own interview and intervention. He now desired to associate a few chiefs in the last stage of his satisfactory visit, to witness and report on it, sealing it with a gesture of amity.

Steptoe spoke with Vincent "and gave him credit for the efforts he had made on the previous day to prevent the conflict." During this conversation a strange quarrel flared. Levi, one of Timothy's Nez Percé scouts, lashed his whip over the head chief's shoulders. As he did so he taunted him, presumably in Indian dialect: "proud man, why do you not fire?" Then turning upon one of Vincent's retinue, he accused this other Coeur d'Alene of having wanted to shoot a soldier. Timothy's men were apparently angry and frustrated. They could see their once-in-a-lifetime chance for spectacular revenge upon Tilcoax go a-glimmering. Chief Vincent bore the blow stoically: "hereafter you will be ashamed of having struck" a fellow Indian. The officers seem to have protested against the indignity suffered by Vincent, for the Nez Percé protested that he had only struck the chief's horse. Vincent replied: "it would be rather strange that my horse, which is very spirited, should not have made some movement if he had been struck." The affair came to noth-

40. Joset Narrative. See Steptoe Report, 23 and 29 May, above, n. 8, on this conversation. CR, 2, 752. NA, EW, AGO, LR, 290c, Wright to Mackall, 7 October 1858.

ing, but is a further revelation of the feeling among Steptoe's Nez Percé band.[41]

As chief and colonel were talking, Vincent's uncle rode up to interrupt with news that the Palouses were again agitating to open fire. Father Joset warned Steptoe. There were hasty expressions of full satisfaction on both sides and a handshake between the two chiefs White and Red. Then the Jesuit's party doubled back to "restrain the Spokanes and Coeur d'Alenes," whom they could better control. Ominously enough, Joset and Vincent met the main body massed and "coming on" warily. But the Indians received the news with "evident joy"; "you could see the faces clear up." Both the Spokanes and Coeur d'Alenes acquiesced. Subchief John Peter Kumpasket of the Coeur d'Alenes announced that the adventure was over. "We will each one go to his home."

Victor, a Coeur d'Alene headman, who was to fall in battle that day, spoke in the same vein. The crisis was past. Then an influential tribesman named Melkapsi sprang forward in a strange fury to slap the subchief's face. Headman Victor rounded upon Melkapsi, "severely" rebuking him. He received for his pains a blow from the culprit's whip handle. Instantly the two were locked in combat. The sturdy little priest threw himself between the warriors and tore them apart. Drawing Melkapsi aside, he calmed "the infuriated man." The explanation of Melkapsi's action was to emerge only after the coming battle. (Melkapsi was his family name; he may be the Leopold baptized by Father Point in 1842, or the younger man Antoninus.) [42]

Joset and two chiefs started for the war camp. Was the Jesuit naïve in leaving the field so early? He knew how excitable the young bucks could be. It would have been more prudent to wait a bit, delaying in the neighborhood to forestall fresh excitement. Joset's key virtue, however, was not prudence. He was an impulsive man. Besides, all his past experience in such tumults, as at the 1855 sack of Governor Stevens' wagons, betrayed him into the present overconfidence.

He returned to Sile, broadcast his good news to the boys and old men staying there, and retired to his tent. Perhaps he meant to rest. After all, he was no longer a young man. He had just gone through a tiring day and disturbed night. The Indians present eventually drifted away, most of them probably in Steptoe's direction, to gossip over this news. Joset had been in his tent for a

41. CR, *2*, 752. Joset Narrative.
42. Joset Narrative. OJ, "Liber baptizatorum." On the incident see also Father Weibel's much later marginal note to the Narrative MS, where Chief Stellam relays the story through his White friend M. M. Cowley. Joset was "fornito dalla natura di un grado non ordinario di robustezza e di forza," writes his friend Father Caruana (*LPT*, 1901, p. 187).

half hour to an hour when a messenger rode in announcing that the Indians had begun to fight the Whites.

THE STEPTOE DISASTER

Desperately Joset called for a fresh horse. None was to be had. As the distance "was about 15 miles, I could do nothing." Not until three in the afternoon did the camp Indians manage to secure for him a heavy wagon horse. He set off toward the battlefield, "with no prospect of getting there before dark." Soon he met an Indian returning from the scene of battle, who told the priest that "it was useless" for him to fatigue himself. By this time "the Indians are enraged at the death of their people, they will listen to no one."

Maddened to rage, there was no stopping them now. The two forces, locked in a running fight, had gone careening over the landscape. In what hidden ravine of that terrain the end would come, no one knew. Worn and weary, Joset returned to his tent, "the dagger in my heart." Surely his superiors would close the mission now. His rest that evening must have been even more troubled than on the previous night. The next morning he "stopped a moment to bury Zachary." This was Chief Vincent's brother-in-law, presumably carried in by friends during the night. Then "with the greatest sorrow" he headed his mount back toward the mission, heartsick though glad to leave "this place of horror." [43]

Only afterward, from conversations with his flock, could he piece together the details of the Steptoe Disaster. Melkapsi's outburst was explained. He seems to have been one of the Coeur d'Alenes previously won over by the Yakima chief Kamiakin. He planned to persuade the Indian leaders to retire to Vincent's private camp; there he meant to offer counsel of war which he was ashamed to give before the Father. The peace faction had frustrated this, and Melkapsi made a fool of himself in his temper. After Joset had gone, Melkapsi's relatives derided him. "What do you do? You maltreat your own people! If you wish to fight, behold your enemies." They pointed at Steptoe's troops. A few of the less stable braves, excited and confused by the kaleidoscopic events of the past few days, impulsively "revenged themselves in the Indian fashion by doing something foolish." One must remember how like children the Indians could be.

Paschal Stellam galloped off first, shooting in blind anger toward the soldiers, who were just beginning to ford a small stream. Paschal was a close friend of both Victor and Melkapsi. He had been particularly disturbed by the outburst between the two. He was a subchief whose clan lived near Spokane bridge; his personal property included "about 100 horses." Others fol-

43. Joset Narrative; CR, *2*, 753.

lowed Paschal's lead: Hilary Peenchi, Melkapsi, and "some other rash young people," less than a dozen in the first wave. Joset tells us that his "young men" fired on the soldiers first, but that only an "insignificant" few of the huge total were involved at this point. This demonstrative phase of the battle, with the troops stoically hurrying along without responding, lasted a long time. There were "only a handful of hotheads, and the troops did not return their fire until one of their number was struck."

Unfortunately the first fire of the troops brought down three of the most popular Coeur d'Alenes. These were James Nehlukteltshiye, "best of all Indians, beloved by all"; Zachary Natatkem, brother-in-law of the head chief; and Headman Victor Smena, who was mortally wounded. After these casualties "the rage of the Indians could not be restrained." Only now "did the engagement become serious." Chief Vincent himself later explained shamefacedly to Joset: "I had no intention to fight, but at seeing the corpse of my brother-in-law I lost my head." More Indians poured down, "then others and others," until the hills swarmed with howling warriors from a multiplicity of northern tribes.[44]

The harried troopers fought their way along as best they could, defending the lumbering, disintegrating pack trains. The action was taking place out in an anonymous tumble of rolling hillocks and ravines. A few months later the army caused a topographical memoir to be prepared on the war, complete with a map. It is painstakingly detailed, and moreover "examined and approved" by Steptoe, so a fairly precise picture can be formed of the Colonel's progress.[45] The column had cut back toward its previous day's line of march. Joset's conference had taken place during the next stage of the journey. Thereafter some of the Indians had dogged the steps of the troops for a distance. As the route was about to converge on Pine Creek itself, at a point where an intersecting canyon cut into the line of march, the first Indians struck.

Steptoe soon brought his men to higher ground on the left slope of his ravine. The Indians in turn rode up behind the marching column and down

44. Joset Narrative. On Stellam see OJ, "Stellame, the Death of an Indian chief." Bancroft, who makes poor use of the Joset information available to him, erroneously kills a "Jacques Zachary" (*Washington*, p. 181), and Splawn without citation repeats his error (*Ka-Mi-Akin*, p. 93). Cf. the accounts of the battle's opening by Steptoe and Gregg. Bancroft incorrectly has the Palouses begin the battle (*Washington*, p. 180); Splawn repeats him (*Ka-Mi-Akin*, p. 93). Contrast our account with that of Manring, *Conquest*, p. 97, on Coeur d'Alene deaths.

45. NA, EW, Army Commands, Dept. Pacific, LR, Mullan report, with map and Steptoe's approval. Rosebush reproduces the map as an overlay to a meticulous modern map, and tries to pinpoint each stage of the battle (*Frontier Steel*, p. 236). See Mullan, *Topographical Memoir*, passim.

both flanks, a tumble of painted wild men on nimble ponies. Shooting became
brisk and continuous, mostly from the Indian side, acrid powder fumes drifting in the morning air. Pack animals began to go down under the fire. The
plunging train was controlled only with difficulty.

The Indian strategy was to keep the soldiers on the run and "not to leave
them any rest to the Nez Percé [Snake] River." Detailed information on
their fighting techniques is not easy to come by. Father Mengarini offers an
eyewitness description. He is speaking especially of the neighboring Flathead
confederates who tutored so many Interior tribes in warfare on the buffalo
Plains. "An Indian battle consists of a multitude of single conflicts; there are
no ranks, no battalions, no united efforts; 'every man for himself' is the ruling
principle, and victory depends on personal bravery and good horsemanship."
Mengarini tells us that "there is no random shooting," but that each Indian
"always aims for the waist." The Interior Indians retreated when chased,
turning to charge again when pursuit slackened; thus their battles were a
highly mobile seesaw.[46]

Each tribe had its idiosyncrasies or specialties. The Kutenais, for example,
preferred a rather distant fire fight, reserving assaults for the three proud
warrior societies like the Crazy Dogs; these latter held back until a real crisis,
and were expected never to retreat.[47] The Coeur d'Alenes, like most of the
Interior tribes, did not have these societies, though they had adopted other
Plains techniques. The upper Interior Indians knew about ambush, choice of
terrain, dawn assault *en masse*, and rifle pits and similar defenses. In actual
battle, however, they tended to splinter into a swarm of individualistic and
fractional units. Their good luck superstitions, their wild undisciplined anger,
and the tendency of some tribes to turn war into a game of "counting coup"
all weighed against them.

On the soldiers' side, Steptoe's battle "was a series of gallant charges," with
the Indians closing in again and again. The dragoons were on the defensive.
Their maneuvers were largely dictated by the Indian pattern of attack. They
not only tried to screen the infantry and the pack train, but simultaneously
endeavored to seize a succession of strategic points to their front until the infantry could come up. It cannot be pretended that the soldiers were doing
well. On his return to Walla Walla from this engagement Steptoe would
praise the dragoons as valiant but condemn them for lack of proficiency; as
soon as he got back he set them hard at work drilling. White marksmanship

46. Joset Narrative (first quot.). Mengarini, *WL*, *18*, 146–48, describing a Flathead
battle of 1846 against Blackfeet.
47. H. H. Turney-High, *Ethnology of the Kutenai*, Amer. Anthrop. Assoc., Memoirs,
56 (Menasha, Wisc., 1941), pp. 162, 167.

was shameful. Steptoe says he could not keep his men from firing their limited ammunition "in the wildest manner."[48]

During this running phase of the battle, each side tried to outrace the other to better positions, as luck presented them, seeking the high ground above the enemy. Again and again the saberless cavalry groups charged the Indian formations. These in turn would break and scatter through the ravines of the undulating countryside, only to re-form swiftly for counterattack as soon as the charge ended. It was a hot and hard-breathing business—all flying hooves and shouted orders and stray shots nipping by. Dragoon horses wheeled and charged, raced and checked, as their handlers furiously hauled at them or spurred. The thin call of bugles cut through the air.

Occasionally there was clumsy hand-to-hand clashing. Cavalryman Victor De Moy, a former French army captain, swung his rifle like a sword, crying: "my God, for a saber!" The troopers later expressed admiration for the superb horsemanship of the Indians, who offered as target only an arm, a leg, a bit of painted face as they surged in or fled. For the dragoons the Colts were lifesavers. They were experimentally replacing the cumbersome foot-long dragoon pistol, a muzzle loader with a trigger pull so difficult as to render the weapon ineffective against fast-moving targets, and with a kick so formidable as to endanger the user.

Lieutenant Gregg's horsemen took the advance, Lieutenant Gaston and his men rode the hills to the left, and Captain Taylor's command protected the right. Sergeant Williams brought up the rear. Before the fight was over, all these leaders except Gregg would lie dead. When the Indians concentrated in some pines, the howitzer was unlimbered to slam a few shells there. Eventually the troops, untidily dispersed, paused on a convenient hill in order to rest and reassess the situation. Here Steptoe pulled his command together. The cavalry action had effectively kept the attackers off balance. Only one soldier was dead; others had been wounded. But the Indians seemed to be getting reinforcements. They were full of fight. Even more important, the troops had to reach water soon. Steptoe put his tightly compact column into motion, howitzers intermittently firing ahead, with Gregg's troops now covering the rear, Taylor and Gaston again shielding the flanks.

Gaston's death came first, and his troopers were rolled back in confusion upon the head of the column. There was a nasty moment or two before equilibrium was restored. Young Gaston was only a year out of West Point. Solemn, square-faced, with intense eyes and a strong jaw, he was slim, unusually

48. Steptoe Report, 23 May, above, n. 8. Kip, *Expedition*, p. 10 (quot.). Letter of Gregg to Vancouver friend, after battle, in *Weekly Oregonian*, 29 May 1858; cf. Gregg in *SED;* Mullan, *Topographical Memoir*, pp. 65–67.

tall, and handsome but with the shadow of tragedy over him. Because of a cancerous growth on his neck he had in recent months often expressed the wish to die in battle. He may therefore have been exposing himself the more recklessly. Lieutenant Kip, passing this way later in the year with Wright's command, sadly evoked his last meeting with Gaston "in his grey Cadet uniform" at West Point "full of life and spirits and bright anticipations of his future career." Though death may have been a mercy to him, the loss of a trained officer was a serious blow to the troops and an occasion of rising morale to the Indians.

Taylor fell shortly afterward, struck through the neck. Indians and Whites closed, in dismounted hand-to-hand combat, for possession of his mortally wounded body lying at the creekside. The troops barely recovered him. He was an uncomplicated man, small, sallow-faced, somewhat lantern-jawed, with fine mustachios, of erect carriage. A Kentuckian and a West Pointer, exacting and hot tempered, he was loved by his men. He proudly prefaced his surname with that of a celebrated relative, Oliver Hazard Perry. This day he would be long enough about dying to think upon his wife and two children, brought across the country and established only a few weeks ago at the bleak Walla Walla post. The deaths of Gaston and Taylor provoked a bizarre incident. One of the Nez Percé guides helping Steptoe called out to the Coeur d'Alenes: "courage! you have already killed two chiefs" of the Whites.[49]

In this kind of fight an Indian had several choices. He could try to shoot or unhorse his enemy; or slip around him to ride down the massed infantry; or try to keep the cavalry off balance until (as happened once on this day, but failed at the last moment) chance allowed a trap of converging braves to spring upon one large group of horsemen. In conversations after the battle, the Indians said they looked upon Steptoe's marching column as easy game once the horsemen could be neutralized.

Steptoe realized the danger. Eventually he would have to make a stand. Once he put his infantry into action, he could at least go down fighting with better odds in his favor. There was already far too little ammunition and far too many Indians. He hurried his men into the hills to the left, over onto a long ridge whose end or summit he determined to defend. His front now rested upon very high ground. Dropping before it was a long sloping descent to Pine Creek. The Colonel disposed his men in a circle around the brow of the slope. The animals he picketed at the center with the supplies. One howitzer stood to the north of the circle, guarding the length of ridge leading to their position. The other was at the south covering the creek below. These

49. Accounts of Joset (Indian quot.), Kip (quot.), Gregg, Steptoe, Mullan. Personal details partly from Trimble, *OHQ, 8,* 46; and Manring, *Conquest,* p. 103 and passim.

howitzers, badly manned all during the battle, provoked the laughter of the Indians. Before the battle, however, the sight of cannon on their lands had helped enrage the warriors.

The army immediately came under siege. Steptoe found the Spokanes and Coeur d'Alenes at his back, and the Palouses near the creek on his front. Whether by accident or design, these battle dispositions roughly correspond to the Rocky Mountain intertribal camp and to the relative geography of the tribes themselves. The Palouses were more to the south and west, the Spokanes to the north and east, and the Coeur d'Alenes on the eastern quarter of the circle.[50]

Did the Whites experience a feeling of *déjà vu* in all this? Major Haller, it will be recalled, had similarly been surrounded and cut off in 1855. Steptoe's command, however, was in a far worse position. In a huge circle on the lonely hilltop refuge, lying flat in the tall grass or in shallow trenches, the "exhausted" Whites fought desperately. They watched their ammunition dwindle to a few cartridges apiece. None of the bullets fired had much effect on the enemy. Whatever injury may have been done, Steptoe admits, was owing to the Colts used during cavalry rushes on the way here, "and to the few Sharpe's Carbines in possession of the Companies."

The fight continued now, he reports, "with unabated activity, the Indians occupying neighboring heights and working themselves along to pick off our men." While the action was fresh in his memory, Captain Winder was to describe how the Indians had "fought well." The running battle "beggars description, 1,000 of those infuriated devils" fiercely yelling and "charging in all directions." At the hill firing was "hot and heavy" for six hours, continuing thereafter steadily but less intensively.[51]

Standing on the battlefield even today, one easily recreates the aloneness experienced by this small detachment. Around them spread a bright, pleasant land, green and empty, utterly empty. The elevation was just sufficient to lift the soldiers' horizon to the vacant, rolling landscape, so as to emphasize the distance and the isolation. On the scene to map the ground four months later, Lieutenant Mullan recorded his view of "the high, pine clad spurs of the Bitter-root M[ountain]s" far off in the eastern distance, with other dim ranges to the south.

50. Mullan map, done some four months after the battle with the help of Indian combatants. Teit, BAE *Annual Report*, 45, 155, for intertribal camps.

51. Fort Walla Walla Letterbook, Steptoe to Wright, 2 June 1858. On the advantages of the Colt see Genl. Harney's report of February 1858, *Documents Relating to Col. S. Colt's Patent Extension* (Washington, D.C., 1858). *SED* army reports, especially Steptoe Report, 23 May, above, n. 8. Gregg letter of 29 May; Winder, *MHM*, 35, 57–58.

All that long spring afternoon and evening the men lay flattened along the crest of the butte, "while every hill around swarmed with their exulting enemies." Their thoughts could not have been pleasant "amid the howling of the Indians, the groans of the dying, and the whistling of bows and arrows." Steptoe says that the soldiers were downhearted and "not to be relied upon with confidence." A strange scene repeated itself in the White camp, unknown to Steptoe; toward evening the Colonel's Nez Percé guides again called to the attackers: "courage! the Americans can do no more." Were there Buffalo Nez Percés among Timothy's band that day who were proud of what their Red brothers were doing? Or is this more of Tilcoax's malicious translation? Or again, are these simply provocative taunts? [52]

Twice the warriors tried to overwhelm the White position by mass onslaught. Generally they crept about, probing and firing with patient cunning. They were not only growing more numerous, with the promise of swelling tomorrow to huge numbers; they were also far more dangerous. It had been difficult to load weapons on horseback, and the method used made the fire inaccurate and unstable. Now the Indians could take cover, prepare their weapons carefully, and fire from their preferred range of over a hundred yards. By tying bunch grass to their heads they wriggled unobserved into advantageous positions, close enough for their headlong charges. Even their arrows became more vicious. Bow and arrow in an Indian hand could be more effective than any muzzle loader. Arrow wounds in army campaigns carried a higher rate of death at this time than those of any other weapon. And an expert bowman could loose six arrows a minute; even the Colts did not entirely meet this challenge. [53]

There is yet another aspect to this kind of stationary fight. Governor Stevens in his general orders to the militia expressed it well some eighteen months before; his experience derived from his background as a professional soldier and from observation of the 1855 Indian war. In the Interior, "bold and repeated charges upon the enemy, even when the disparity of numbers is great, will alone lead to results," because "in all mere defensive contests with the Indians, whether behind breastworks or in the brush, an Indian is as good as a white man." In other words, the weakness of Indian cavalry, its undisciplined individualism, became a strength in the kind of foot battle now beginning to take shape, with its call for individual courage, cool steadiness, and

52. Joset Narrative (Indian quot.), Steptoe and Gregg accounts; Mullan, *Topographical Memoir* (and in NA, Army Commands), original sketch of battlefield with comments on terrain.

53. A. Hunt, *The Army of the Pacific* (Glendale, Cal., 1951), p. 268 (wounds report). Ewers, *Blackfeet*, pp. 141–42, and Harney, *Documents*, have pertinent comments on arrows.

marksmanship. Stevens had warned his troops: "few laurels can thus be won, and the result may be discreditable." [54]

One Coeur d'Alene veteran of the Steptoe siege, with a sense of humor and no experience in being shot at, Andrew Youmas by name, told a story against himself years later. "When we were fighting the soldiers, I hid behind some tall bunch grass; some soldiers must have spied me, for they kept shooting at me." But Andrew was not at all dismayed. "I kept a sharp lookout; for when they would point the gun toward the bunch grass behind where I was hidden, I watched the gun very closely, and when I see smoke coming out of the gun-barrel, I would duck to one side." As a result, he confesses, "they kept me ducking from left to right." He wryly comments, "how I was never hit was a puzzle, for many years afterwards I found out that the bullets had passed me a long time after the smoke came out of the gun." [55]

The Indians of this region did not usually sustain a fight after dark. They broke off the Steptoe battle just before sundown, at eight. Signal fires soon winked from eminences near the American position. One sergeant of dragoons recalls the spectacle of the surrounding hills as campfires flared on all sides. The command was "surrounded by an army of ferocious beasts, hungry after their prey, of Indians sufficiently numerous to relieve each other, and who had always means of procuring fresh horses," wrote Father Joset shortly after the battle; "it appeared impossible that the troops could escape." Not an officer of the American command, Steptoe says, "doubted that we would be overwhelmed with the first rush of the enemy" in the morning. Thoughts of torture ran through the Colonel's head.[56]

There must have been other thoughts, more shocking. This was not simply a case of a small detachment cut off from its fort. If Steptoe went down in defeat, so would Fort Walla Walla itself. The entire Interior would dissolve in war. The fort's garrison now lay scattered in three widely separate places; and it held only two to three weeks' provisions. Steptoe had taken three of his four dragoon companies north, reducing the fort's power largely to defensive infantry. He knew as well as any officer how ineffective were the "walk-a-heaps" against swiftly moving Indians. Less than a year ago, when his fort had counted among its personnel only one company of dragoons "a little more than half full," Steptoe had urgently drawn the attention of his superiors to this weakness; to forestall trouble, he had immediately required at least another company of dragoons. Now the very holding garrison left at Walla

54. MD, Genl. Orders No. 6, Headquarters, Fort Mason, Walla Walla Valley, 4 September 1856. In Field, *National Guard*, 2, 116–17. See also Joset's opinion and comment on it, in my "Père Joset's Account," *PNWQ*, 38, 298.

55. *Teepee*, 3 (1940), 10.

56. Joset Narrative; Steptoe reports.

Walla had again been split. Just yesterday, with Steptoe expecting a limited skirmish against Palouses, Grier had sent Dent's sixty-six men on the long jaunt to the Snake River. There would be some friendly Nez Percés in that area, though only a small minority could be counted upon as active allies. The combined American and Indian resources at the Snake would thus not amount to much more than Steptoe's own strength at the time of his defeat.

Little Fort Simcoe in the Yakima country was a negligible factor. It had all it could do at any time to defend itself, and was even "cut off in the winter" from communication with other posts "except at great risk"; this coming winter the new general was to order it closed. A month or so after the Steptoe battle friendly Indians revealed a project to attack and fire the Simcoe outpost.[57]

Neither Dent on his route nor Grier at his fort could know anything of Steptoe's problems until long after the battle was over. This was due to treachery among Steptoe's Indian allies. Wie-cat, "a notorious scoundrel," had carried Steptoe's second and last message down from the upper country. Wie-cat is probably the Indian courier in Winder's letter who arrived at Steptoe's lakeside camp at seven on Sunday evening during the height of the Indian demonstrations. He went down to Walla Walla but did not hand over the message, seeming to anticipate the "defeat and total destruction of Col[o-nel] Steptoe's command." Steptoe was thus cut off from help, and the split command in the south was kept from knowing that war had broken out. Worse yet, Wie-cat spent his time doing everything in his power to raise the valley Indians to attack the enfeebled Fort Walla Walla. Fortunately, Steptoe and Dent managed to get back before things came to a head. But the army was never to forgive Wie-cat, nor rest until it had hanged him to a pine tree during the coming fall.[58]

Back on the ridge the night was cheerless and dark. Steptoe perceived that he was helpless and would become more so with every delay. Yet he dared not move; even without ammunition his men could give a better account of themselves dying here than elsewhere. Apparently his officers argued him out of this opinion. The exultant Indians sensed the Colonel's plight. At midnight they rushed the White position. To their astonishment "they found it deserted." Steptoe had managed one of the cleverest retreats in Indian-fighting history. He and his officers in desperation had "determined to run the gaunt-

---

57. NA, EW, Army Commands, Dept. Pacific, LR, Steptoe to Mackall, 3 June 1857 (quot., provisions). Capt. Judah to Mackall, Fort Simcoe. Harney correspondence on Simcoe, in *SED*, 36 Cong., 1 sess., 2 (1858–59), pp. 94–96. On Fort Simcoe see below, Bib., Guie, Culverwell.

58. Adj. Genl., LR, Wright to Mackall, 9 October. Kip misled historians by sending Dent to rescue Steptoe (*Expedition*, p. 11).

let, so that if possible some might escape." Infantry mounted on pack mules, hooves silenced and light-colored horses blanketed, cannon spiked and cached, the dead decently buried, and with fifteen wounded lashed to their saddles—all crept away from their island of safety. In breath-holding silence they had filed through the careless, triumphant braves and slipped away into the night.

The escape route seems to have led down between the Coeur d'Alenes and Palouses. But the entire disposition of the attackers may have altered by this time. In a letter to Hoecken six days after the battle, Joset wrote that "the Spokanes retired to return next day with fresh animals." This may have resulted in a gap or two in the Indian cordon, despite all caution. Steptoe's Nez Percés probably discovered the opening and guided the troops through it and across the river; whether Timothy had a hand in this is still a matter of controversy. Once in the clear the soldiers kept their mounts to a gallop. By dawn they were at the Palouse River, by ten that night at the Snake crossing. Here the small band of allies among the Nez Percés protected them from the negligibly few hostiles pursuing.[59]

Captain Dent was on hand simply in accordance with the previous plan; there was no question of a military rescue. There was far less question of any return to the upper country, as Chief Lawyer of the friendly Nez Percés was boastfully urging. The military strength of Fort Walla Walla had marched out with Steptoe and was now returning with him. To the Colonel the Snake crossing was a humiliating exercise. He was in effect trapped north of the river, with no means of getting to the other side except through his band of Indian allies. Fortunately, these remained loyal and provided transport. Steptoe soon wrote to San Francisco urging that the first step in the counterattack must be a fort at the Snake. "Without the assistance of Timothy's Nez Percés" the crossing both coming and going would have been "utterly impossible." Even with his shaken force safely united within Fort Walla Walla, Steptoe did not feel secure. He feared an attack by the Indian hordes. All work on the fort's construction was stopped and a position of defense adopted. As the weeks passed with no report of the enemy crossing in their direction, Steptoe wrote San Francisco describing his preparations and requesting provisions.

Winder, who had won a captaincy for personal bravery in a military

59. *SED*, army reports, Gregg letter of 29 May (second quot.). Joset Narrative (other quots.). Teit's informants credit Nez Percés with finding a way out (BAE *Annual Report*, 45, 370). For Hoecken letter see below, p. 239, n. 78. Manring, *Conquest*, pp. 111–17. Winder, *MHM*, 35, 59. Brown's Indians offer several absurd recollections; Chief Joseph Seltis in 1936 even has Joset himself arrange the escape, approach the besieged troops under white flag to notify them, then go about distracting the other tribes by encouraging noisy celebrations (pp. 417–19).

shipwreck when only eight years out of West Point, was similarly unnerved. On June 2 he wrote of his experience to his brother-in-law Charles Key (whose father Francis Scott Key had composed the *Star Spangled Banner*). Winder confessed himself haunted by thoughts of death. He described the terrifying battle, noting that he had received Charles' own letter by courier during the initial hostile demonstrations. After the successful escape, "for two or three days" at Fort Walla Walla he had been hearing the echo of bullets all day. "We are in for a big Indian war." [60]

Despite the escape, the episode was a setback for the army of the United States. It merited the tag it won and kept: the Steptoe Disaster. A history of the United States cavalry published at the end of the Civil War chronicled the Disaster at length, characterizing it as "one of the most sad events that ever befell our cavalry."

Statistically the losses were not too high. The dragoons had been more numerous, exposed, and active; casualties were mainly among them. Company C lost their officer and two men dead with three wounded. In Company E the officer and sergeant were dead and seven men wounded. Company H counted two men dead and their sergeant missing. The infantry had three men wounded. This made a total of seven dead, six severely wounded, seven slightly wounded, and one temporarily missing. Three Indian allies had also been killed. Sergeant Ball, left behind in the confusion, made his way back several days later. The brave De Moy had a tragic end. Incapacitated by his wound and abandoned during the flight toward the Snake, he apparently wounded two of the Indians who found him, then shot himself. [61]

CRISIS AT THE MISSION

Why had the Indians refrained from pursuing? As a matter of fact, they had meant to pursue if the troops should somehow escape them, and "not to give them any rest" all the way to the Snake. To an Indian at war, however, killing was a subordinate objective. The warrior proved his bravery in battle, disconcerted his enemy and if possible counted coup on him, and above all seized the spoils of war as his triumphant reward. On Steptoe's ridge were rewards beyond the wildest dreams. The various bands gave up thought of pursuit, lest perhaps the "spoils should fall into other hands." Here were or-

60. Fort Walla Walla Letterbook, to Mackall, 23 May, 6 June. Cf. Winder letter, *MHM, 35*.

61. *SED*, army reports, casualty lists. A. G. Brackett, *History of the United States Cavalry from the Formation of the Federal Government to the 1st of June 1863* (New York, 1865), chap. 9, esp. p. 182. Fuller, *Pacific Northwest*, p. 249 and notes (on De Moy and others).

naments and saddles, "flour, bacon, sugar, and camp outfit, with about one hundred pack animals." The overjoyed Indians were to recount to Father Joset especially how the White warriors "had left all their horses and mules," the Indian idea of true wealth.

Indian triumph was complete. That the soldiers should retreat at all, Joset tells us, made them a laughingstock among the Coeur d'Alenes. De Smet was soon to describe the battle as "a victory for them and in their eyes a complete one, for they had not only driven off" the invader in "shameful flight" but had "captured his train and provisions." Among the victorious Indians the exact dimensions of the victory were understandably confused. Joset at first thought all the soldiers must have been killed. The Indians concluded that "thirty Americans," including three officers, had fallen. This would grow in the memories of the veterans, until fifty years later they could report to an inquiring ethnologist that they had "killed over half the command of 200 mounted men." [62]

In the White camp, conjecture as to losses was no more accurate. Steptoe's official report claimed that "the enemy acknowledge a loss of 9 killed and 40 or 50 wounded, many of them mortally; it is known to us that this is an underestimate, for one of the officers informs me that on a single spot where Lieutenants Gregg and Gaston met in a joint charge twelve dead Indians were counted." Father Joset ridiculed the soldiers who "were sure of having seen a dozen of Indians killed, and as many wounded." Given the quality of the soldiers, the nature of their weapons, the shortage of ammunition, and the frantic conditions of this running battle, it is surprising that the soldiers hit anyone at all. Lieutenant Kip was soon to remark on the Indian's cleverness in throwing himself to one side of his horse or in slipping under its neck; these erratic maneuvers must often have seemed to the excited Whites to be the result of direct hits.

Of the Coeur d'Alenes engaged only three fell. The Indians buried James on the field of battle. Joset interred Zachary's corpse at the Sile camp on the morning after the fight. Headman Victor, though badly wounded, lingered on until after Steptoe's escape. He died on the 18th. Since Joset buried him next day "in the cemetery" at the mission, the dying man's friends had probably carried him back. The Jesuit carefully inscribed all three in the mission burial records, with a notation as to circumstances and place of death.[63]

Even at the mission "it was none too safe." News of the victory preceded the arrival of Joset; it was abroad by the 18th. Upon learning that the lay

62. Joset Narrative; OJ, Sgt. Kenny, in W. P. Winans, "Stevens County" (typescript), p. 17 (spoils in detail). CR, 2, 731. Teit, BAE *Annual Report*, 45, 361.

63. OJ, "Liber defunctorum." Previous quotes from Steptoe Report, above, n. 8, and Joset Narrative.

brothers had destroyed the gunpowder, the Indians "were very angry." Some hotheads "proposed to plunder the Mission's house" but were eventually restrained by "sober minded" colleagues. The dead Zachary's widowed mother was fanning the embers of war into fiercer flame with her continual wailing and cries for vengeance. "Intoxicated with their first success, the Indians thought themselves invincible and able to meet the whole United States army."

The Coeur d'Alenes probably had made a ceremonial return into the mission camp. There was a traditional formula for this after a victory. Some distance from the assembly area, a gun would be fired four times to bring out the people as an escort. The solemn entry was made with faces blackened. Within two days there would be a scalp dance, lasting through four subsequent days and including appropriate re-enactments of high points in the battle. The war chiefs would then narrate the story of the battle, with each warrior who had distinguished himself standing forth proudly to recount his deed of valor. There would be much applause, drumming, and shouting. The women would make up a burlesque war party and execute a traditional war dance. We do not know whether the Coeur d'Alenes went through the full ceremony. They had refrained from scalping and therefore bore no scalp trophies—and they had to contend now with Father Joset.[64]

The day after the battle, as Lieutenant Mullan notes, Joset was already at work among his tribesmen. This may have begun at the Sile camp, which he left that same morning, or on the journey to the mission as he encountered bands of Coeur d'Alenes. He arrived sometime on the 19th, his burial register shows. A number of warriors had already returned.

One crisis needed immediate handling. Four White travelers in the neighborhood, perhaps miners, had been caught by the outbreak of the war. Joset was not yet back to give protection. A lay brother ran out to warn them, so they were able to stay out of sight. While the Indians were at the height of their jubilation on the 19th, one of the Whites left his three companions in hiding and from sheer hunger braved death by entering the mission grounds. A half-breed saved him from immediate death by insisting that he was a "Dane" rather than an "American." The man was indeed of foreign origin, with a Scandinavian name. Still, one Coeur d'Alene brave was barely able to restrain his battle fury. He begged that the stranger be removed from his presence before these passions should cause him to kill.

That same night one of the American's companions tried to reach the mission and in turn was "very near being killed." Adrian, one of the fire-eaters at the Steptoe battle who had been restored to his Christian senses by Father Joset, informed the newly arrived priest about it. The missioner managed to

64. Joset Narrative; CR, 2, 730. Teit, p. 189.

secrete both men in his house, keeping them there for two days. Eventually he induced an Indian named Bonaventure to spirit them east to the Flathead country.

The episode gives a precious glimpse of the work of the two lay brothers during the war. It was old Brother Francis, "running as fast as his age would permit through brushes and swamps," who first succeeded in warning the travelers. And the Irish "eloquence" of Brother McGean had done most to dissuade the Indians from harming them. Before leaving, the two strangers punctiliously drew up a testimonial of gratitude. "We [the] undersigned do here witness with thankfulness the exertions of the Fathers and Brothers of the Sacred Heart mission to save our lives and those of Mm. Daniel Miles and James Thomas, from the fury of some Indians who wanted to revenge on ourselves the death of their relatives killed in the affray with the U. S. troops on the 16th [for the 17th] of this month. Mm. Daniel Miles and James Thomas could not sign with us, being yet hidden in the Mountain[s], where we could not yet find them." The note, on paper from a stationery book, was dated May 21. The two signatures seem to read: Ludvig Nielson and Sorts Hotssjer. Shortly after it was written, Bonaventure and the two escaping Whites located their companions ten miles north of the mission, "feeding on grass." [65]

The record books of the mission church show some poignant entries at this time. The dead Zachary's wife Susannah was pregnant, for instance; she would bear a little Zachary for her slain husband three days before Colonel Wright crossed the Snake in his campaign of retribution. A daughter named Mary Magdalene had been born to Paschal Stellam, just two days before the attack on Steptoe precipitated by her father. The family's life would be disrupted by the coming war and then by Paschal's long term as hostage at Walla Walla. Subchief Seltis had a son baptized by Joset just at the end of the coming campaign. And even Melkapsi, the villain of the piece, was the father of a five-month-old child Athanasius by his wife Clara. These evidences of domesticity suggest the close, parochial bond between the priest and his flock, so casually glimpsed in such entries. [66]

Joset's work of pacification now began anew. Circulating among the exuberant warriors, who were "filled with pride" and glorying in their booty, he proceeded to give Zachary's mother a severe tongue lashing. He demanded of Chief Vincent what provocation he had received from the Whites. "None," replied the unhappy chief; "all the fault is on our side." Other Coeur d'Alenes

65. Joset Papers, No. 55, "Testimonial of Four Whites"; Joset Narrative, esp. BL version. This is not the Bonaventure Chinmitkasy in the peace conference of 1859 with General Harney. Joset Narrative has "Nelson."

66. OJ, "Liber baptizatorum," Sacred Heart Mission; this is Antoninus Melkapsi.

would have none of this. Ask the soldiers, they said, what we ever did to them to cause their invasion. But Joset pursued his point: why had they attacked after peace was settled? He insisted that "you are the murderers of your people, not the Americans."

Vincent answered: "it is true; I would rather die as the Americans, as our people are dead." Vincent knew that because war had broken out, he had failed in his function as head chief. "What will be the consequences?" he wondered. "Fools that we are, we always doubted the truth of what the Father told us; now we have it; the Americans do not want to fight us."

More inquiries and rebukes gradually helped to piece together a general picture of the conflict. The Christian background of the Indians showed to some advantage. Asked if they had taken scalps, they protested they had not, "with the exception of a small piece that had been taken by a half-fool." Had they been careful to bury the dead as their Christian teaching on the corporal works of mercy required? Yes, the women had done so for the enemy, but the pagan Palouses had opened the graves again at Sile. This explains why Lieutenant Mullan next September found that sun and rain "had bleached the whitened bones, which were scattered around," and that animals and birds had been at work. Subchief Anthony gave superficial burial to Lieutenant Gaston's body under some leaves. He meant to return for a proper burial but later could not find the body. Some Coeur d'Alenes seem to have found Sergeant Williams abandoned and in pain from his wound; they refused his plea to shoot him, and left a squaw to care for him until he died.

The priest "called together all the chiefs and men I could [and] explained to them the necessary consequences of their folly; they having shaken hands with the chief had, without provocation, attacked the Government forces." Somewhat subdued, the Coeur d'Alenes admitted that "the Father did not deceive us." They confessed that "we forced them to fight, we fired a long time before they answered our fire." [67]

Joset wasted little time in recrimination. He explained to them how "the Whites would never keep quiet until they got a fearful revenge." This theme he elaborated upon at some length: "you are bewailing the loss of three of your men; the whites would not be the least dismayed had they lost 3,000; should you have killed as many, immediately 30,000 others would come, and so on until not a single Coeur d'Alene would remain." He then showed them a map of the United States, "pointing to the little spot representing their country to let them understand how insignificant they were."

Having unsettled them, Joset delivered his most telling blow: "what shame that Christians should have behaved that way! The missionaries could not

67. Joset Narrative; Kip, *Expedition*, pp. 111 (Mullan), 95 (Anthony). O'Neil of Steptoe's command tells the Williams story in his reminiscences, though Kip has a less probable account (p. 11).

remain with such lawless people, etc." This threat had set the people weeping a decade ago, and it probably had a similar effect now. The Indians "expect to see themselves abandoned; I have told them positively we will go." Though this was the last thing Joset himself desired, he realized that his superior would indeed want to close the mission. Yet to quit the tribe now "would be to deliver them to the conceit of Kamiakin and to light, I think, a universal war throughout the whole country." [68]

Joset achieved his desired effect. "They manifested sorrow for the past, and promised to behave in future." He told them that he would ride to the White chief's land to "try to manage for peace." None of the Coeur d'Alenes had the courage to accompany him. Several feared for the priest's own life and tried to dissuade him. Spokane Garry was among these, either at the mission or shortly afterward in the Spokane country. Garry seems to have been overwhelmed at what had happened and appalled at what might yet come. He begged the priest: "don't go down; the Americans will hang you and then it will be impossible to control the people."

Joset considered the journey imperative. "If the war commences now, it is probable it will terminate only by the extermination of all these tribes, for their country is so difficult of access that it will be impossible that it continue without all these tribes, including the Blackfeet, taking part in it." He believed that "the war will cost thousands of lives, and all for an affair unpremeditated and for which the Indians feel much regret." A sense of tragedy colored his words: "God is my witness that I have done everything in my power to preserve peace." There was an added problem for himself and his Order. "I did not know whether my letter to Reverend Father Congiato had been received; if not, who could explain my presence among these savages?" [69]

REVERBERATIONS AND POST-MORTEMS

Few things illustrate so well the magnitude of the task facing the army (and therefore by indirection the need for, and the size of, the contribution by the Jesuits) than the manner in which the news passed to the Coast. The disaster had occurred on May 17. Fort Walla Walla heard only rumors of trouble until May 20, when the official account came in. Despite the urgency and the conviction that the tribes were about to descend on the fort, the Walla Walla courier could not get through to Fort Dalles until May 22. Five days had passed since the battle. Particulars were still not available until the second express rider came in on May 26.[70]

68. Joset Narrative.
69. Ibid.
70. NA, EW, Army Commands, Dept. Pacific, Jordan to Ingalls, Fort Dalles, 22 May; Ingalls to Casey, Fort Vancouver, 24 May.

These particulars, as reported by Agent Dennison at The Dalles to Superintendent Nesmith, were garbled. Steptoe's command had faced the Indians "and for a few moments each seemingly was waiting for the other to attack," until an "accidental discharge of a pistol" broke the spell. The Indians had then stood their ground, and had carried off Gaston's body. One thing came through clearly. "Colonel Steptoe says they were badly beaten and that the Indians fight like fiends and that his men fought bravely and behaved well." The Indians, though they lost "some 25 or 30" killed and as many wounded, had pursued Steptoe eighty-five miles to the Snake crossing. "I am of the opinion," Dennison concluded, "we are to have a general Indian war in the upper country." Among the several hundred miners assembled at The Dalles for the trek to the Fraser was one Herman Reinhart; "it made quite a stir among the miners," he tells us, to hear that all the tribes between them and the mines were at war, and that the Indians had killed sixty of Steptoe's soldiers.

From Fort Dalles Captain Jordan hastily relayed the news to the Coast. On May 24 his courier rode into Fort Vancouver with "the very melancholy intelligence from Fort Walla Walla." The "embodied Spokane, Palouse and Coeur d'Alene Indians, mustering some 1500 men" had butchered the American command; half the soldiers were lost. There was no way of getting word to army headquarters from the forest-locked coastal settlements. The mail steamer to San Francisco had already gone. Jordan's letter was therefore rushed north to Fort Steilacoom on Puget Sound. There Lieutenant Colonel Casey was ordered to see if he could send the reports by any other ship. Fort Vancouver told him that "we are in much grief, as well as excitement, on account of the disastrous news." Casey did manage to embark the information, with a covering letter of his own dated May 27.[71]

By June 1 General Clarke at San Francisco was reporting the receipt of "insistent rumors" of a defeat. Should they be confirmed, he told his superiors in Washington, he meant to hurry north to take charge in person. Unless there was speedy retaliation he feared "a general war, the end of which may be prolonged to a distant day and may be carried on only at very great expense." Confirmation soon arrived. The *Evening Bulletin* had released a rumor as early as May 26, "then and since poo-poohed by the wiseacres of the two antiquated morning papers in this city." This scoop was vindicated on the evening of Tuesday, June 8, when the steamer *Pacific* brought the Portland

71. Jordan to Ingalls, 22 May, above, n. 70; NA, IA, Oreg. Sup., LR, Dennison to Nesmith, 27 May. R. Glisan, *Journal of Army Life* (San Francisco, 1874), p. 401. NA, EW, Casey to Mackall, Fort Steilacoom, 27 May. H. F. Reinhart, *The Golden Frontier, the Recollections of Herman Francis Reinhart 1851–1869*, ed. D. B. Nunis, Jr. (Austin, 1962), pp. 113–14.

newspapers through the Golden Gate. By June 10, Editor Thomas King of the *Bulletin* was demanding from Clarke an official military clarification of the disaster. On June 13 the steamer *Columbia* carried into San Francisco the full news, including Steptoe's last information from "Father Joseph of the Coeur d'Alane mission." [72]

The Indian superintendent at Salem meanwhile had received word independently of Agent Dennison's letter. He immediately sent back a warning on May 28 to Lieutenant Mullan's road party operating out of Fort Dalles. Mullan's reaction was fretful anger over this "disastrous blow for me." He requested a military escort to enable him to push on with his work. But Steptoe confessed "that his whole command would not be sufficient to escort him through the Indian country with safety." Forced to return to The Dalles and disband all but a few of his unit, Mullan sent off a lengthy jeremiad to the superintendent and a letter to the secretary of War. He demanded: "in the name of the interests of thousands of a superior race how long shall these things Exist?" [73]

He also reported to San Francisco. General Clarke passed his letter on, commenting that "the presence of large bodies of troops" would be required to reopen the Indian country for Mullan's road; any peace must take into consideration "the acquisition therefore of the proprietorship of that and adjacent" Indian land. Mullan offered his own services, together with those of his topographer Kolecki, the artist Sohon (now civilian guide and interpreter), and some herders, for the coming campaign. Clarke gratefully accepted, because of the lieutenant's knowledge of the remote upper country. Mullan himself intended to continue his survey work and would carry his instruments and wagon along.[74]

Colonel Wright, commanding the Ninth Infantry at Fort Dalles, wrote on May 26 to San Francisco. "That all the Indians in that section of the country have combined for a general war, there is not a shadow of a doubt." They were "numerous, active, and perfectly acquainted with the topography of the country." He recommended a striking force of a thousand men so that an attack could be made "in two or three columns." This was the same number

72. NA, EW, Army Commands, Dept. Pacific, LR, King to Clarke, 10 June 1858. Clarke report on Steptoe, in *SED* (serial 975), army reports, p. 343. *Alta California*, 9, 10, 13 June 1858. *Daily Evening Bulletin*, 8, 10, 12 June 1858.

73. NA, IA, EW, Army Commands, Dept. Pacific, LR, Mullan to Nesmith, Dalles, 18 June. *Oregonian*, 6 June 1858 (Steptoe). Details of his movements in Mullan 1860 Road Report, *HED*, pp. 8-9.

74. Fort Dalles Letterbook (HL), Wright to Mullan, 14 July. OS, Mullan to Gov. G. Curry of Oregon, Olympia, 27 October 1858. NA, EW, AGO, LR, P165, Clarke notation on Mullan 1860 Road Report, San Francisco, 10 June.

Haller had requested, after his own defeat, to enter the Interior. Wright thought it would not be "prudent" to draw men from the posts east of the Cascades, since these were so small and since "there is much agitation among the friendly Indians" in the wake of the Steptoe battle. If the hostiles should influence the Indians on the Warm Springs reservation seventy miles to his south, no military force was at hand to hold them.[75]

The steamboat on the upper Columbia had unfortunately just gone over the Cascades rapids and was lost. Supplies at Walla Walla itself "are very limited." Wright anticipated "a protracted war." It must be prepared for "systematically, with an ample supply of the per-son-nel and materiel," to guard against failure. If the Mormon difficulties were over as was rumored, perhaps troops could be drawn from Utah. Colonel Steptoe also was to request a large body of troops, some five hundred men. Lieutenant Gregg would note in his report that "it will take one thousand men to go into the Spokane country." No one expected that any news would reach San Francisco before the 6th or even the 10th of June.[76]

On the Coast the story of the Steptoe Disaster swept like wildfire, slowly at first, then ever faster. From the Cascades to the Rockies the whole Pacific slope seemed about to be lit "in the lurid flames of war." [77] The newspapers contributed their note of hysteria. Under the headline "Indian War Recommenced," the _Weekly Oregonian_ at Salem on May 29 regaled its readers with a horror tale. Fifteen hundred "Spokanes, Pelouses, Flatheads, and Coeur d'Alene Indians" had killed "a large proportion" of Steptoe's expedition. The remainder of the army "may be able to reach Walla Walla in safety." The editor cautioned that the news might be exaggerated, since it had come in to Walla Walla "by friendly Indians only."

A "Later and Official" account was appended, reporting twenty-nine soldiers killed, wounded, and missing. Steptoe was back at Walla Walla "with the remnant of his command." The newspaper was "led to believe" that Steptoe had been "decoyed" by Kamiakin and by "the duplicity of friendly Indians in whom the officers of the regular army placed entirely too much confidence." Among the "six different tribes" in the battle, "the most formidable were the Flatheads, who are both numerous and powerful, and hitherto regarded as _friendly_." The editor reminded his readers that "the Indian character is universally false, deceptive and cruel." A letter from one of Steptoe's officers arrived as the paper was going to press; this supplied accurate information.

75. _SED_ (serial 975), Wright to Mackall, 26 May, and Fort Dalles Letterbook.
76. _SED_, army reports, Wright, Steptoe, and Gregg; also Gregg letter. _Oregonian_, 6 June 1858, letter and comment.
77. Mullan, _Topographical Memoir_, p. 631.

On June 6 the *Oregonian* carried rumors from The Dalles "that the Indians had crossed the Snake river in large bodies." According to a private letter printed in the newspaper, Steptoe believed that the attack had been deliberately planned. The paper wrung its editorial hands over the army's necessity of acting so tortuously from distant San Francisco; it recommended a separate military department temporarily for the coming campaign. An editorial of June 21 blamed the Indians as aggressors "without cause." The government "has been feeding, clothing, and feasting the Indians" for two years, with this sole result. Government officials "as a general thing protected and sympathized with the Indians, in place of whites," the only consequence being "murder, rapine, and destruction" as the Indians' "natural instincts and designs" break forth. "It is far cheaper to whip them at once and bring them into subjection" than to feed and fight them for years. "The time has come" to realize that war exists, "and has never ceased to exist" since 1848, between the Indians and Whites of the Northwest.

The bishop of Nesqually diocese also was worried. "Some of the Indian tribes have gone to war against the whites," he wrote to France on June 6; "we are very much afraid for our missions in the Rocky Mountains." Even the knowledgeable officials of the Hudson's Bay Company were cut off from their Interior post and could only await developments. Father Hoecken was the first outsider to get details of the war; these came in a long account dated May 24 from Joset, and reached the Flathead mission at the end of the first week in June.

With Agent Owen long fled from the country, Hoecken bethought himself of the troops concentrated in Utah for the Mormon War. He was particularly aware of their existence, because commissary agents had only recently been buying beef for them in the Bitterroot Valley. Translating Joset's French, he relayed the document through Dr. Garland Hunt, the agent for the Utes at Spanish Fork, to the Utah headquarters. Here General Albert Sidney Johnston passed it on to Washington, D.C., as coming from "a Catholic priest of great excellence of character." The general commented: "I do not doubt that the whole force has been destroyed; all the officers, I suppose, were killed in the first attack." [78]

The army's reaction was to be a military convulsion, a gathering of forces which ran from San Francisco to New York, from Newport to Utah and down to the Southwest deserts. The repercussions of the Steptoe Disaster echoed in the national capital. "Steptoe's defeat has made a great sensation

78. FL, *1858*, Répartition (in French), 6 June 1858. SED (serial 975), army reports, pp. 127–30, from Hoecken, 17 June 1858; Johnston to East, Camp Floyd in Utah, 29 July 1858. NA, EW, AGO, LR, P165, 17 April 1858 report on return from Flathead country beef contracting; cf. Owen, *Journals, 1,* 189–93.

here," Stevens gleefully noted. This was to be a turning point in army patience with the Indians: "the true mode of managing our Indians is generally acknowledged." He emphasized that "the news of Steptoe's defeat has made a very deep impression at the War Dep[artmen]t, and has shown that something was 'rotten in Denmark.' " As territorial delegate, Stevens was far from being disheartened: "the defeat of Steptoe, the discovery of rich gold fields, the rush of miners, and the rapid filling up of population will all help" induce Congress to pay the 1856 war debt.

In August Stevens sent word to Superintendent Nesmith that "the War Dep[artmen]t seem determined to prosecute the Indian war vigorously and are satisfied that it is a matter which should no longer be trifled with; the Secretary of War is giving his most earnest attention to it, and is now trying to make arrangements to despatch an additional Dragoon force." The president and the army officials at the capital intend to see the Indian rising "crushed out with a strong hand." Stevens himself was recommending to the army "a full regiment of mounted men" for the campaign, as well as a force of infantry.[79]

Harper's would receive the news in time for its August issue. "There is imminent danger of a general outbreak of hostilities among the Indians of the north," it told its readers. The author distorts the account, giving Steptoe four hundred men and increasing the number of Indians to fifteen hundred. He moves the battle over to the junction of the Snake and Columbia rivers. The *Harper's* casualty list stood at "fifty men." The attack came "while the troops were crossing the river." The command had "lost everything" except sixty pack mules, and had to "fall back with the utmost precipitation." Next month's issue returned to the subject of the Northwest war. "Official reports" were now at hand. "They confirm the previous account with the exception that our loss was greatly exaggerated." The editors quote Steptoe: "I fear that many lives will be lost before a satisfactory adjustment can be arrived at." The Indians had been "excited by rumors that the Government intends to take possession of their lands." [80]

In expecting a serious war, then, Father Joset had not been alone. Alarm reigned also in Canada. Toward the beginning of June, Dugald Mactavish, the Hudson's Bay agent at Fort Vancouver, relayed news of the defeat to Canada. From here it was forwarded to the Colonial Office for the attention of Sir Edward Bulwer-Lytton. Mactavish mistakenly located the battle at the Palouse Falls and identified the aggressors vaguely as "a number of Indians of the Spokane and other tribes." It was "impossible to say what steps the Gov-

79. Stevens Papers, to Yantis, 28 June; to Nesmith, 18 July, and again 3 August, all from Washington, D.C. Todd, *PNWQ, 31,* 442–45.

80. *Harper's New Monthly Magazine,* 17 (June–November 1858), 403, 545.

ernment will take to bring these Indians to their senses," he reflected; "but in the meantime it will not surprize me to learn that something has happened to the Company's Establishment at Colvil[l]e, where the natives for the last two or three years have been very troublesome and unmanageable." What was worse, a brigade had already left The Dalles under Chief Trader Blenkinsop for Fort Colville. No word had been received from him since May 2, when he had been crossing the Snake at the mouth of the Palouse.[81]

The responsible official in Canada in charge of North American operations, Governor Simpson, envisioned a serious war. "I presume," he wrote Mactavish, "the Americans will now declare 'war to the Knife' and not suspend hostilities until all the tribes are crushed beyond the power of giving further trouble to that country." He understood that there had been "considerable loss on both sides." The defeat now "is to be revenged by marching 1,000 men into that country." Simpson was of the opinion that "the natives must be driven to desperation, or else very confident of their resources, to judge by the determined stand they made at the Snake River against Colonel Steptoe." [82] In 1855 Governor Douglas had feared lest the Interior tribes' "spirit of mischief may spread into our own territory, and weak and defenseless as we are, we shall have to stand the brunt of an Indian War; we are unfortunately quite unprepared." At that time Douglas criticized the American manner of handling the Interior tribes; the troubles could only come from "some great mismanagement on the part of the American authorities." On July 29, 1858, a British representative was to visit the president of the United States concerning the problem of American miners at the Fraser. The president would soon send an agent to the Northwest, partly to promote good relations between Indians and Whites on both sides of the line.[83]

Less than a month after Steptoe's defeat, the Canadian Indians in the adjoining portion of the Interior finally "mustered under arms in a tumultuous manner, and threatened to make a clean sweep of the whole body of miners assembled there." The success of the Coeur d'Alenes and their allies encouraged the Canadian Indians on the Big Canyon, twenty miles up the Fraser River from Yale, to take the warpath. Miners were killed, sometimes suffering scalping or decapitation. Others were robbed or frightened into fleeing. The miners organized in three columns of 160 men and took the counter-offensive. Though they would claim a total of thirty Indians killed in the

81. BC, Record Office transcripts, H.B.C., F.O., *735-36*, 197-98, Mactavish to W. Smith, Vancouver, W. T., 3 June 1858, forwarded 3 August.

82. HB, D4, *54*, Simpson Corresp. out, Hudson's Bay House, Lachine, 30 July 1858.

83. BC, Napier to Earl of Malmesbury, Washington, D.C., 29 July 1858. F.O. 5, *617-63*, Douglas to Sec. State, Colonial Dept., Victoria, 8 November 1855; to Tolmie, 5 November.

fighting, the action amounted to no more than a demonstration of force which won a negotiated peace. By the time Governor Douglas could arrive with a naval vessel and a force of thirty-five men, the fighting was over. The Governor angrily protested against this autonomous waging of war; but the miners remained unimpressed.[84]

In the American Interior, however, circumstances would now conspire, and the Jesuits with them, to break the power of the Indian confederacy. The fires of war were not to rage on, nor to proceed unchecked into Canada. After a preliminary military action, they were to be stamped out at the Jesuit mission.

84. *Copies of Despatches from the Secretary of State for the Colonies*, doc. 4, Douglas to Lord Stanley, Victoria, 15 June 1858 (first quot.). BC, Vancouver Island Letters to the Secretary of State, No. 26. F. W. Howay et al., *British Columbia and the United States* (New Haven, 1942), p. 159. On Canadian Okanogans and the Steptoe war see below, p. 285.

7. The War against the Northern Indians

JOSET RIDES SOUTH

WITH ORDER RESTORED, Joset faced the problem of contacting the military at Walla Walla. There was less chance than ever of traveling through the Palouse land. He must circle far around the north, then down through the country of the Columbia tribes and the Yakimas. This would involve him in territory with which he was not too familiar. Prudence demanded that he go even farther out of his way, to the Kettle mission at Colville, for an Indian guide. Here, too, he could warn his Jesuit colleagues and the Hudson's Bay people that the Northern Indians had gone to war.[1]

Even the direct route from the mission to Walla Walla at this time, according to Father Ravalli, was one of "hardship and dangers." The country presented harsh and contradictory faces to the traveler. There were desert areas where one must know the watering spots, floodlands to maneuver across, and secret fords for the many rivers. This was the beginning of flood time in the Colville region. The tame streams of April would have already spilled over their beds "and assumed the appearance of large rivers and lakes, completely flooding all the lowlands." During this season it was sometimes hopeless to attempt the trip south from Colville toward civilization, unless one built a barge and floated downriver with one's horses.

Aside from such extraordinary obstacles, the trip itself was serious enough. "If only you knew what these journeys are," Joset writes, "you would readily persuade yourself that one doesn't undertake a single one of them without very urgent reasons." There were no "inns or bridges, nor highways, nothing except prairies, woods, swamps, and broad rivers." The preparations had to be painstaking; to forget anything essential meant serious embarrassment. The journey was wearing. "Ordinarily you start at sunrise and stop only at night," Joset says; "unless you have very urgent business, you go at a steady

1. The term Northern Indians here is historically and geographically correct; it is the most accurate of the titles generally used for this war, and Kip's war journal is so titled. But tidier minds prefer to restrict the term to the savage canoe Indians of the northwestern coast.

trot." On similar trips, he had sometimes been "awakened at two in the morning by my Indian" who then led him "at a gallop the whole day." [2]

As the priest headed out over the bleak, sandy plains of the Spokane country with their thin scattering of pines, he was anxiously preoccupied. Would he be an acceptable envoy, considering the charge that he had supplied the Indians with ammunition? He was not sure his letter to Congiato had been received. He feared that "most people would believe or feign to believe that slander." Besides, as he put it later, the troops with Steptoe "in their panic had seen so many things" that they "might have as well seen me, though I was more than 15 miles away." These fears were not unjustified. Army officers were even now seriously discussing Jesuit complicity in the attack.[3]

Long, difficult riding down the far bank of the Columbia took Joset to Wallula. There he parted with his Indian guide, who was probably reluctant to approach closer to the hostile Whites. The Jesuit struck east for the Walla Walla post "so as to say to the Colonel: 'if you think me guilty, here I am.'" But Steptoe was not the kind of man to entertain gossip. He received the priest royally, offering him the hospitality of the commander's table and sleeping quarters. Joset rested here at least a few days. His trip so far, to judge from records of travelers like Owen and from Joset's journey-map of 1849, must have taken about fifteen to twenty days by this route; the figures presume hard, driving travel.

Colonel Steptoe warned his guest "that the Officers below were very much incensed" against him. This was particularly true, he was told, of Captain Jordan at Fort Dalles. Characteristically, Joset "lost no time to go there." But his long-delayed letter to Congiato had come into the hands of Jordan himself; its alchemy transformed an enemy into an admirer. From now on, Joset would be accorded great respect "by all the officers to the General himself." The officers were eager for news from the hostile country. The missionary "explained everything" as seen from his vantage point.[4]

Joset then set out for Vancouver. He must have been impressed with the changes in the lower country, brought about by the mining boom. Already The Dalles was a port town. Proud little steamboats like the *Mountain Buck* carried passengers downriver in two days, with an intervening night at the Cascades; this cut a full day of travel. Joset took the less expensive route by land. Forty miles above Vancouver, near the Cascades village and fort, he encountered troops on the march heading for the hostile territory. A young officer, asking his name, volunteered that General Clarke was anxious to see him at Fort Vancouver. Not long afterward he reached Vancouver—a new

2. OJ, Ravalli, "Giorda"; De Smet, in CR, *1*, 380; Joset, in *JMUS*, 2, 319–21.
3. Joset Narrative.
4. Ibid.

fort, a frame cathedral, and a handful of houses scattered along the pine-wooded riverbank. Over a month had now passed since the Steptoe Disaster. Joset's reports had preceded him and gained some attention. Early in June the *Oregonian* had taken notice of the priest's opinions, received apparently through Steptoe or his men in a letter of June 3.

Probably the first man he contacted at Vancouver was his superior, Father Congiato, who had arrived shortly before. Congiato at this time was not a happy man. Rome had notified him, a month before the Steptoe Disaster, that California and Oregon were now separate missions. Congiato was ordered to terminate his affairs in the southern half of his previous jurisdiction, and go up to be superior-general of the Jesuits in the Northwest. This was a shock. He had been coping with the "truly miserable state of my health," having been released from all activity for the past three months to convalesce. Nevertheless, on May 28, a month after the news from Rome, he was steaming north on the four-day trip.

Thus he missed any early news from Joset. He landed at Fort Vancouver amidst the gold fever, just as a full-fledged crusade was being preached by local newspapers against his mission Indians. It may have taken the invalid some time to adjust to the situation. There was no possibility of contacting Joset or his colleagues in the upper country. Congiato did receive Joset's earlier warning letter and communicated it to the military. He also traveled toward the Interior as far as The Dalles, where he left the letter, or a copy, with Captain Jordan. This activity prepared the way for Joset's subsequent friendly reception.[5] Congiato thus found himself plunged into the heady atmosphere of war some time before the news could reach army headquarters in San Francisco.

He soon found the army eager to have Jesuit help. As early as June 10 General Clarke at San Francisco was advising his superiors that Jesuit missionaries should be used as a conciliatory force during the coming hostilities. "The Catholic Missions are in charge of men reverenced and enlightened, possessing great influence," he wrote; "I suggest that they may be introduced to advocate and promote the views of [the] Government in endeavors to pacify the Indians, should it adopt now or at [a] future day a system of negotiations with them or treat them at any time in a conciliatory manner."[6] Having spent more than a week attending to essentials, Clarke and his staff embarked on a little wooden steamer.

5. MJ, IX, AA, Congiato to ——, San Francisco, 18 April 1858 (Rome news, health). Joset Narrative. See J. W. Riordan, S.J., *The First Half Century of St. Ignatius Church and College* (San Francisco, 1905), pp. 89–90, on details of leaving; Riordan writes from documentation subsequently lost in 1906 earthquake and fire.

6. NA, EW, AGO, LR, 10 June.

He was at Vancouver on June 23. On June 25 he drafted a long letter to Father Joset. It was delivered next day; apparently Joset had just arrived at the fort. Then the General sent off an invitation to the superintendent of Indian Affairs to come up from Salem for a conference. He also made preparations to leave for Walla Walla within the week. Meanwhile, Captain Archer wrote home from Fort Simcoe, Clarke held "a grand consultation with Wright, Steptoe and others, but we are all in deep ignorance as to what is to be done." [7]

The settlers welcomed the aggressive Clarke as "not of the Wool-ly stripe of Indian fighters." Even Indian Superintendent Nesmith hailed this vigorous proponent of war. He wrote Stevens happily that the "Quasi peace" was over; "Clarke and the whole Military are now fully aroused, and they believe that there *'is a war.'* " [8] Then why did the General want so much to see Joset, the champion of peace? The answer is that Clarke's aggressiveness rose from his insecurity. Only swift, overwhelmingly victorious action could have lasting effect. Setbacks or delay would allow the Indians to consolidate. The White army labored under such disadvantages that a delayed war might easily become interminable. Clarke therefore pursued two parallel policies. On the one hand, he hoped that the Jesuits could induce the hostile Indians to surrender unconditionally; he seemed to fear that any offer of concessions would reveal to the Indians the weakness of the White position. At the same time he meant to conciliate all Indians not yet openly at war, and to strike a swift, decisive blow at intransigent hostiles.

Wherever possible, he explained, he would offer friendship and thus "paralize the hostile parties or factions," creating intertribal distrust so as to "prevent a general combination of various distinct" tribes. He had reason to believe, for example, that "a very large portion" of Yakimas might be induced to remain friendly. It is important to grasp the General's position here, since it relates directly to the nature of Joset's own contribution.

One tradition of coastal historiography misinterprets Clarke's first use of Joset as equivalently an abject surrender to the savage Indians. When the Coeur d'Alenes refused Clarke's golden offer, we seem to have a clear proof that they "denied having commissioned Joset to negotiate for a treaty." But the General's policy and the priest's mandate from the tribe are clear enough in the documents.[9]

7. NA, ibid., Clarke to Joset, 25 June, marked "delivered to him at Fort Vancouver June 26th"; also in *SED* (serial 975). IA, Oreg. Sup., LR, to Nesmith, Fort Yamhill, through asst. adj. genl., 26 June. Archer Corresp., to mother, 1 July 1858.

8. *Weekly Oregonian*, 3 and 17 July 1858. Stevens Papers, from Nesmith, 20 August (not pub. in Todd edition).

9. Clarke Report, 23 July, in NA, EW, AGO, LR; also in *SED* (serial 975), p. 349. Wright Report, 26 May in Fort Dalles Letterbook; also in *SED* (serial 975), pp. 350–51; Victor, *Early Wars*, p. 489 (last quot.); cf. Owen in episode below, p. 253.

For the interview with General Clarke, Joset went to the fort in company with the diocesan vicar general Father Brouillet. Brouillet, a valued friend of General Wool, was probably familiar with a number of officers. He was undoubtedly present also as a representative of Bishop Blanchet, whose headquarters were here at Vancouver. Although an exempt Order like the Jesuits operates under a separate chain of command reaching to Rome, it also works to some extent as part of the local diocesan mechanism. The Bishop had a direct interest in this mission problem. Joset and Congiato surely had visited and consulted with him already, as De Smet was to do when he came to the Northwest later that year for his own peace tour.

Brouillet and Joset were presented to General Clarke by his aide, Major Mackall. Joset told the General of the mitigating circumstances affecting the Coeur d'Alene attack, such as the deceitful war propaganda of the hostiles, the confusion as to Steptoe's real intentions, and the impulsive manner of the attack itself. Clarke professed himself satisfied with the repentance of the Coeur d'Alenes and with their past record of peace with the government. Nonetheless he sent severe terms through the priest.

The General proposed a council at Vancouver or some other fort. He insisted upon the right, rather than the privilege, of sending troops "when I please" through Indian lands, the right to construct the military road, and free passage for Whites "at all times" through Coeur d'Alene territory. In atonement for their "great crime" the Coeur d'Alenes must restore all government property and surrender the war criminals. No guarantees of life or liberty were offered. The tribe must expel from their country Kamiakin and similar outsiders hostile to the Whites: "I am going to make war on these people." Finally, troops were to be moved into Coeur d'Alene country. If all conditions were met, the troops would be friendly. In a letter of June 27 Clarke put all this formally. "And now sir, it only remains for me to thank you for your efforts in the cause of humanity, and to express my sincere wishes for your success in preserving a people among whom you have so long been a laborer." [10]

During this time Joset took to heart a suggestion made by Captain Jordan. He wrote up a brief account of the Steptoe episode, in the form of a report to Father Congiato, in French, dated June 27. Army officials had it translated and sent on to Washington, D.C., as part of their own report. This military version fills twenty closely written pages. Eventually it was incorporated into Lieutenant Mullan's published topographical report to the secretary of War. [11]

10. OJ, Clarke to Joset, 27 June (quots.); this probably sums up and formalizes the results of the recent interview. Joset Narrative for interview details.

11. This and several related manuscripts or published documents are cited in this book together as the Joset Narrative. The most elaborate account is in the Joset Papers, No. 67A, revised or recopied in other forms (Nos. 67B, 68A, 68B). My own edition

Joset had received the General's invitation on June 25 and had apparently visited him promptly that day or the next. Two military passes countersigned by Clarke were issued to Joset and Congiato on June 26; the passes protected "such Indians, Co[e]ur d'Alenes and Spokanes, as may come by invitation of Father Joseph a Catholic Priest" to visit any forces in the field or any post between their tribal country and Fort Vancouver. The following day Clarke wrote again, urging the Jesuits not to carry out their contemplated abandonment of the mission. He added that "your influence among these people may even now be for their good and you may yet be enabled to save them by remaining among them a little longer." Joset was touched by the gesture; he refers to it again in his later account of the war.[12]

But Clarke as a military realist also dispatched campaign instructions to Colonel Wright. In these he commented that the Catholic priests Congiato and Joset were on their way to the Coeur d'Alene country with authorization to send in Indians under the General's own safeguard. The peace feelers, however, were not to "embarrass" Wright's march against the tribe. If the Indians came to meet him in submission, all would be well. If not, a "vigorous war" would automatically ensue. Steptoe was to take friendly Nez Percés as allies, clothing them in uniforms "of the old pattern and condemned."

Having settled matters with the army, the two priests gave information to the general public, which was at that moment not particularly well disposed toward their mission Indians. This activity took the form of an interview with the editors of the *Weekly Oregonian,* a paper distinctly anti-Indian. The result appeared in print a week after Joset's visit to General Clarke. The paper noted that both priests were "just down from the remote northeastern Indian country." The substance of the interview was that miners and settlers would not be attacked by the tribes, but "that the Indians were determined to fight the soldiers whenever they came into their country, until the govern-

---

relates these (*PNWQ, 38*). A later version with important changes was gathered by Rowena Nichols for H. H. Bancroft and his ghost writer, F. F. Victor (now in BL; see my "Bancroft Library Manuscript," *OHQ, 52*). The translated version of the Jordan-inspired letter is in Mullan, *Topographical Memoir,* pp. 42–48, and in *SED* (serial 975), army reports, pp. 354–60. The English original, differing only slightly, is in NA, AGO, received 11 September. MJ has two French versions of 1858; their exact relation to the original French draft is unsure. The LC manuscript (Gregg Collection) is a copy of the original NA English. As a defensive answer to nativists, Congiato published a version in the San Francisco Catholic *Monitor,* 24 and 31 March 1860, today almost unobtainable (but see MJ). Some details cited under Joset Narrative are from his May 1858 letter to Hoecken and from De Smet's version of his story in 1858, CR, 2, 748–55.

12. Joset Papers, No. 56, Military Pass from Genl. Clarke, 26 June; No. 57, second pass differing slightly in form; No. 58, Clarke to Joset, Fort Vancouver, 27 June 1858. Joset Narrative.

ment of the United States fulfilled its treaty obligations." Very probably this
was not quite what the Jesuits said. There was no question of treaty obligations toward tribes like the Coeur d'Alenes, Spokanes, Kalispels, or Kettles,
while on the other hand the treaty tribes like the Palouses neither wanted a
treaty nor conceded that one really existed. At least the substance of the
story may be accepted: the Indians' quarrel was with the troops only, not
with transients or with the rare settler in the far Interior.

The assurance must have been given in answer to a question posed by the
newspapermen, since this worry had been aired in previous issues. Besides, a
rumor was in the papers from Indian sources that the Yakimas had battled a
party of sixty miners, killing a third of them, at a cost of two hundred warriors dead. Possibly the priests had said a word or two on the dangers of leaving the Flathead treaty commitments unfulfilled. One gathers from the report
that the two Jesuits candidly indicated the belligerent mood of their Indians.
The editor comments on all this: "from our knowledge of these missionaries,
we have no doubt but that they represented to us their honest convictions
and that they fully believe what they say." This somewhat reluctant endorse-
ment suggests that the editor is acknowledging but not publishing the Jesuits'
defense of the Indians. His own interpretation, added here, is that the Indians
would attack soldiers rather than miners simply because the abundant loot.
such as blankets and guns, attracted their lawless greed.[13]

Congiato and Joset now made their way toward the Interior. Congiato
does not impress one as a likely choice for peacemaker. He had no experience
as an Indian missionary; he did not understand the tribal languages; his character was not warm or sympathetic. Insofar as the situation called for firmness he was, for good or ill, possessed of that quality. He was eminently a
man of cold sense and vinegarish practicality—perhaps the worst man for this
project. On the other hand, his position as superior of all the Jesuits in the
Northwest counted for something in the Indians' eyes. And his very defects
may have provided the proper balance for the mercurial Joset.

AGENT OWEN VS. THE JESUITS

One other White in the Interior tried to work for peace. This was the
storekeeper John Owen, nominal Indian agent for a large tract of the upper
country, with the courtesy title of major. His career as agent had thus far
been undistinguished. He had little contact or influence with most tribes.
The trading post in the Bitterroot Valley absorbed his energy. But he was a
good man and did try to help the Indians. He was an anomaly, an improbable
mixture of roles—monopolist storekeeper, official representative of the gov-

13. *SED* (serial 975), pp. 361–64, 4 July. *Oregonian*, 3 July, 26 June 1858.

ernment, and an unwanted settler on 640 acres of Indian territory not yet yielded by the tribe.

Owen was aware of this last source of unpopularity; but he explained the Flatheads' opposition to settlement on their land in 1858 as "growing out in all probability of the Indians here belonging to the Catholic church." Forebodings of Indian trouble, revealed by his letters just before the war, may have unhinged a mind already none too stable. His troubles stemmed in part from alcoholism, a not unusual or incapacitating affliction on the American frontier, in part from a mind somewhat deranged. Father Vercruysse was of the opinion that a previous blow on the skull by a windmill had affected his reason, but that otherwise "he has a good heart."

A bearded, heavy man of medium height, just turned forty, Owen had fine features, florid complexion, and a strong voice. He was of sober mien, dignified, lethargic, and pleasant. The Jesuit Father Palladino remembers him as "of very loveable, kindly and generous character," esteemed by White and Indian alike, ready to interpose between hostile tribes to pacify them. The editor of his voluminous records has noted with bafflement the contrast between the jovial, baronial figure of the diaries and the truculent, querulous, "radically differing" Owen of the letters. The explanation seems to lie in the insanity which progressively blotted out his mind from about a decade after the 1858 war, eventuating in his legal commitment.

Although he was to malign the Jesuits in 1858 and impede their peace efforts, he was very friendly with them in his normal, nonconspiratorial mood. He visited various Fathers regularly, trusting himself and his Snake Indian wife to their doctoring, and sometimes taking comfort from their religious services. It is quite possible that they were his only really close friends. He often spoke of becoming a Catholic; and he finally did so, not long before his death.[14]

Despite Owen's shortcomings, Superintendent Nesmith now had to place absolute trust in the man. The only word from the hostile Interior, embarrassingly enough, was coming from the missioners Nesmith had so long and openly despised. After Joset's arrival at Walla Walla, Nesmith wrote a frantic letter to Owen, requesting him to discover what tribes had been involved in the Steptoe attack, how many, and for what reasons. He wanted a full report on the affair. He also desired Owen to conciliate the Flatheads. As for the hostiles, nothing should be done: they had to be punished.[15]

14. NA, IA, Wash. Sup., LR from Flathead district, Owen to Nesmith (first quot.). See above, Chap. 5, Pt. 3, for his forebodings as war approached. Owen, *Journals and Letters*, *1*, 10; *2*, 164; frequent visits, warm relations with Jesuits, e.g. in *1*, 104, 145, 155, 158, 173, 183, 197–99, 203; *2*, 32, 35, 41, 46–47, 50, 57, 64–65, 79, 87, 92, 105, 122, 131–32, 137. *JMUS*, *2*, 390–91 n. (Vercruysse, Congiato letters, 1860).

15. NA, IA, Wash. Sup., LS, Nesmith to Owen, Salem, 11 June (not published in Owen, *Journals*).

From his diaries and correspondence, and to some extent from the less reliable reminiscences of his assistant Frush a quarter-century later, Owen's progress can be followed closely. He had reached Fort Colville, still engaged in the complicated task of moving his stock and party south, out of the dangerous upper country. News of Sunday night's Steptoe Disaster was brought to the fort by a friendly Indian only on the following Wednesday night. Owen jotted down the "exciting news" of "troops in [the] country fighting." The women at Colville were "Scared to death." Owen moved his camp to the protection of a friendly chief. Not until Saturday, a week after the battle, did he learn from Spokane Garry of Steptoe's retreat. As yet there were no details, nor any concept of the magnitude of the Indian victory. But Owen abandoned his party to the care of the friendly chief, took five horses, and joined the safety of a Hudson's Bay party going to The Dalles "under the H. B. flag" with trader George Blenkinsop.[16]

There is a gap now in the agent's voluble diary and letters. Though a magpie for collecting bright trivia, he falls strangely silent. He had reached safety at The Dalles; perhaps he experienced some difficulty in explaining, even to himself, his swift exit from the upper country. Shame or reviving courage must have pushed him, within a month, to return to his post through the jaws of death. He had learned of Joset's mission of peace; could the upper country, then, be so bad? At Walla Walla with Colonel Steptoe, Owen discussed the widespread rumors about Joset supplying ammunition to the hostiles. The agent's subsequent references to Joset suggest that he was disconcerted at the priest's facile living in two mutually inimical worlds and perhaps a shade envious over the attention this drew.

On June 24 Owen is writing from Fort Walla Walla, vainly attempting to appease Superintendent Nesmith's thirst for official information. The agent has little to offer. News had come to him from Colville that "the whole country is up for War"; but "it appears that Father Joset" has seen Colonel Steptoe, and the Indians are ready "to play quits." Owen sensibly comments: "the truth of it I do not vouch for." [17]

The agent again prudently attached his pack train to the larger Hudson's Bay brigade leaving on July 4 for Colville under George Blenkinsop. They circled far around the country of the main hostiles. Owen's assistant Charles Frush recounts how they nevertheless encountered "sulky" Indians at the Snake, and had to frighten away seven or eight canoes of painted Yakimas by building their campfire high and yelling ferociously. Another assistant later wrote how a party of painted hostiles surrounded and terrified them at the mouth of the Spokane; the half-breed Antoine Plante persuaded the warriors

16. Owen, *Journals*, 1, 199–200 (diary).
17. NA, IA, Wash. Sup., Letters from Flathead-Blackfoot area, Owen to Nesmith, Walla Walla, 24 June (not published in Owen, *Journals*).

not to attack a Company brigade. At Fort Colville, to their horror, Owen's party discovered hundreds of hostile Indians carousing. The Americans found themselves "out of the frying pan into the fire."

Frush never forgot the scene. It was the most terrible experience he ever had with Indians. The war dance going on was primitive and frightening. Many braves were entirely naked, some painted half red and half black, some all white with red spots. They were chanting and leaping in a circle; an old hag sat at the center reciting deeds of valor, shaking swords and pistols, and urging the braves to surpass themselves in battle. A certain F. Perkins, a New York physician returning East from a visit to The Dalles, watched in dismay as a war party displayed Captain Taylor's bloody saddle, the warriors proclaiming their readiness to fight more of the White "women." Perkins says that there were noisy scalp dances every night, and that thirty Coeur d'Alenes with their head chief were occupying a room at the fort. Owen especially took to heart the current tale that a party of ninety miners had just been overwhelmed by Sinkiuse-Columbias; fifty were said to be dead, the remainder about to go down fighting in Yakima country.

The resident trader was George Blenkinsop, who for some months already had replaced the veteran Angus MacDonald. Refusing to be intimidated, Blenkinsop managed to maintain a semblance of authority. As long as Owen stayed at the fort, the trader shielded him. When a big Okanogan was making off with one of the agent's mules named Kitty, Blenkinsop retrieved it roughly and lectured the Indian on the respect due the Company's guests.[18]

Owen himself was unnerved. "I am safe only with an escort of friendly Indians to get out of the valley and even then not too safe; the war whoop is heard from one end of the valley to the other; Indians painted and looking more like demons than human beings are prowling about in squads, armed to the teeth." There could be no answer but violence. "*Never, never* until you have made a most serious demonstration on these Indians will peace and order reign." The agent had Garry and Sgalgalt to advise him, and a personal bodyguard of twenty braves he was paying as "allies."

His fright induced him to buy friends with a lavish hand. All the property brought from The Dalles he now "expended on the way for conciliatory

18. C. W. Frush, "A Trip from the Dalles of the Columbia, Oregon, to Fort Owen, Bitter Root Valley, Montana in the Spring of 1858," *CHSM, 2* (1896), 337–42 (written 1885). "Historical Sketch of Louis R. Maillet," by himself, *CHSM, 4* (1903), 212 (detail on Plante, a late reminiscence). On the Perkins scene see Kip, *Expedition*, pp. 43, 96; *SED*, 35 Cong., 2 sess., 32 (1858–59), p. 15 (from *Washington Union* of 31 October 1858). Frush puts MacDonald as protector here, but apparently by error; MacDonald is gone about a year (cf. HB, D5, *43*, Simpson Corresp. in, Mactavish to Simpson, 8 June 1857).

purposes." To one chief "I gave eight hundred pounds of beef, some flour and tobacco for his people; to others I have given tobacco and clothing only." Owen even drew on his private account at Colville. He offered the half-breed Montour $150 to $200 to run a message south, plus $100 expenses. "I feel myself far from safe but duty calls me." Yet "as Agent here I see no good I can do unless I am supported" by troops holding Colville.[19]

In such a frame of mind, what was he to make of the Jesuits, French Canadians, and Hudson's Bay officers—all of them serenely going about their respective affairs in the valley unimpeded? Owen suspected complicity. He queried the Indians and, not unexpectedly, got from a few the answers he wanted to hear. In his reports he accused all three bodies of men, though with a feeble qualification that he might be misinformed as to the Jesuits.

Owen talked to "the Coeur D'Aleine Chief with some ten" warriors, who were selling Steptoe horses. (Was this Vincent, or one of the war chiefs Melkapsi or Stellam?) These Coeur d'Alenes "deny having Sent" Father Joset on his mission, "and Want to Know Why he should Meddle with things that do Not Concern him." Owen therefore feared that the army might be deceived by the Jesuit's false claim; "there is No authority for it Whatever." But there was worse to tell Nesmith. "Serious charges are made voluntarily by some of the Coeur d'Alleine Indians against Father Joset; they told Mr. Chase [here] that he not only gave them ammunition but told them to have but one heart and that to fight." Owen modified the tale somewhat in an accompanying letter to the army. "This party of Coeur D'Alleines tell different tales; one voluntarily said that the Father not only furnished them ammunition but told them" to fight; "others deny the Fathers furnishing any ammunition at all."

The agent's own suspicions are undisguised. Joset's "sympathies for his Indian flock may lead him into error." After the Steptoe battle, when the Jesuit passed through Colville on his way to visit army authorities, Owen writes, he had "sneered at the idea of Col. Steptoe conquering the Indians[;] he says a thousand men can not subdue them[;] he says you may drive them from point to point but they can subsist themselves in the mountains and cut the troops off in detail," living on game. Owen was probably not misquoting

19. For Owen's movements and for the quotations here and on the following pages, see Owen to Nesmith (Steiniger's house, 11 July), to Steptoe (same, 12 July), to Nesmith (camp on Spokane River, 16 July), to same (Fort Owen, 18 September), all in Owen, *Journals, 2,* 175–86; 1860 quotation on pp. 233–34 (3 December, to Sup. Geary). A few quotations are from a rather different, unpublished version of the September 18 letter done on 20 September (NA, IA, Wash. Sup.). Frush material, as above, n. 18. Lansdale quotation from August 1 letter, in *SED,* 35 Cong., 2 sess., 1 (1858), p. 628. Owen May 31 letter to new superintendent is in *SED,* 36 Cong., 1 sess., 2 (1859), p. 791.

Joset. The priest's assessment of the military situation, in fact, was shared by
the leaders of the coming punitive campaign. Ironically, two years after the
war, Owen himself would similarly assess a renascent danger of war: "I have
no hesitation in saying that the United tribes of this M[ountain] locked Section Could Muster and put in the field ten thousand Warriors, Well
Mounted, Well Armed[,] inured to the Mountains etc. etc. [who] could
with all ease Subsist upon Game"; he concludes that "you have no conception
if War does break out of the Am[oun]t of blood and treasure it Would
cost."

From his frightened observations at Colville, Owen recommended "in
strong terms the removal of the Missions from the country" until after the
war. Both to Nesmith and to Steptoe he wrote: "no good has resulted from
their labors or the present state of affairs would not exist." As for the valley
Canadians, "I do firmly believe that if they do not urge the Indians to fight[,]
they will be in the ranks of the enemy when troops again make their appearance in the Country." It is "the wretched Canadians and half-breeds who I
sincerely believe are at the bottom of most of the disturbance."

The Hudson's Bay officers may or may not be giving the Indians ammunition: "I can't say." But these officials candidly admitted to Owen that a blanket refusal to sell any ammunition could be suicidal; and even if Colville
stopped sales without losing its neutral status, the Indians had only to go
thirty miles north to the Canadian post of Fort Fortynine. The Colville people do seem to have bought some Steptoe mules and horses, as a conciliatory
expedient. This was against general Company policy. Through Owen the
impression was soon abroad on the Coast that the Company traders "are encouraging the Indians in hostilities by purchasing the animals captured from
Steptoe, and are furnishing them with abundant supplies of ammunition."

On July 9 Owen hopefully assembled an informal powwow with some of
the hostiles at Colville. It lasted through the night into the dawn, and did
nothing to reassure the shaken agent. The Indians, impudently aggressive,
had the initiative. Owen announced a council to be held in a few days with
the Coeur d'Alenes, Spokanes, and San Poils. Since Garry and Sgalgalt cautioned him that it would be imprudent to venture onto Coeur d'Alene land,
Owen designated Spokane Falls in Garry's home territory as the council site.
An American official ought to have felt reasonably safe there if anywhere,
though Owen was dubious about even Garry's ability to escape the contagion
of his tribe's war fever.

After a week at Fort Colville, Owen's party slipped away from the Company's protection one dawn and made a dash for the farm of the Scotch squaw-
man Thomas Steiniger, thirty miles down the valley. They thus foiled an

attack the Indians planned, though pursuing braves managed to drive off one of the best horses in the train. The agent left Steiniger's on July 12 and held his council at the Falls four days later.

This proved to be the most harrowing experience of all. It was less a council than a badgering by the dangerous, triumphant warriors. Frush remembers it simply as their having been cornered by an intertribal war party. From the depths of gloom Agent Owen wrote another message for Nesmith. "I have just returned from one of the blackest councils, I think, that has ever been held on the Pacific slope." It had been a tumult of sound and fury. "Five hundred fighting men were present, elated with their recent success; the dragoon horses were prancing around all day: the scalp and war dance going on all night." The Indians made no secret of their opinion that Owen was Steptoe's "spy." They did not want him to go to the Flathead country, and darkly warned him against influencing the Flatheads "from making common cause" with them. Let more armies come: it will be an opportunity to capture more horses. Enemy "father and son will fall together."

The Indians seriously threatened to hold Owen hostage. "They have annoyed me and my party in every possible way except firing on us, and that has been threatened." He kept to his camp, constantly surrounded by his "few faithful" Indian allies. "I was in a delicate position; I never want to be in another such." His former friend, the Spokane chief Polatkin, would offer him only a safe conduct out of the country. The Coeur d'Alenes refused him any safe conduct at all; the chiefs said they themselves would do him no harm, "but that the Young Men were excited and beyond their control." This seems to have been the council in which the intimidated Garry, as Lieutenant Kip writes, "never said a word but merely looked on."

Owen's whole thought now was to get away. There was no going back. He could not hope to penetrate the Coeur d'Alene country ahead; "in fact my Spokan[e] friends advised me not to think of passing that way." Owen's entire contact with the Whites in the lower country for the rest of the war consisted in sending one set of letters south now by the half-breed Montour; the latter cleverly avoided the Indians trying to stop him but was never able to return and contact Owen. Agent Lansdale on the Coast was similarly unable to penetrate into the Interior, "as neither friendly Indians nor whites could be persuaded or hired to pass beyond those tribes well known to be friendly." Owen could exit in only one direction. He headed north and east.

Fear urged Owen's party on. They circled a discreet distance north around the Coeur d'Alene district. A war party of Kettles dogged their steps, eventually running off seven of their horses. At Pend d'Oreille Lake the Jesuit mission Kalispels took them in hand. Owen describes how the Indians aided and ferried them; Frush is grateful at their helping "very much." But Owen "was astonished myself to find they had so light a conception of the strength of the white man; they think the whole white tribe has already emigrated from the East to the West."

At the junction of the Flathead and Missoula rivers a band of "Mission Pend d'Oreilles" found them and supplied food. The Indians showed "delight" at this encounter because "they had feared" that hostiles had captured the party. At the Jesuit mission "we were met by the good fathers," who supplied them plentifully. "The genuine kindness, unsolicited, from these missionaries, I am sure the writer will ever gratefully remember." These grateful comments come from Frush. Owen refers as little as possible to the fear, the indignities, or the help he received.

The following May, when a new superintendent took office, Owen defended his rapid transit through and out of the hostile country. He says he left so hastily because he wanted to pacify the Flatheads before the hostiles could influence them; he implies that in this he was successful. By August 6 Owen was home within his solid, fortified post, bribing the adjacent Flatheads for their favor. Among other items, he gave them ammunition in quantity.

Owen's charges against the Hudson's Bay Company went from Steptoe to Vancouver, where they were handed to the chief trader Grahame on July 29. A reply came promptly next day. Grahame was notifying his Colville agent of the accusations but was confident they were groundless. He reviewed the Company's policy in the 1855 trouble: to restrict ammunition to a judicious amount, while avoiding the earlier mistake of cutting it off entirely. A trader on the spot had to use his common sense. Grahame followed this letter with one to Clarke on August 7, and also with an order to Fort Colville to stop all sale of ammunition and to surrender any stolen animals. (During the battles of the next month Colonel Wright captured a British musket of 1857 manufacture; President Buchanan's special representative to the Fraser troubles did not hesitate to include this in his report as an indication of the Company's guilt.)

None of these charges could have any effect at Colville, because the army first had to carry Grahame's letter north in the coming campaign! After the war, trader Blenkinsop attributed Owen's accusations to commercial avarice. To him, Owen was "another example of that dishonesty of character so peculiar to the American adventurers." Blenkinsop was the more disturbed because he had protected Owen's life from hostile Indians.[20]

20. Owen letters, as above, n. 19. Stevens Papers, Nesmith to Stevens; drawing from Owen charges, Salem, 20 August. NA, EW, Army Commands, Dept. Pacific, LR, Grahame to Mackall, Fort Vancouver, 30 July; Fort Walla Walla Letterbook, Steptoe to Mackall, 27 July, quoting Owen. HB, D5, *48*, Simpson Corresp. in, Ser. 1, from

Similarly, Steptoe received Owen's charges against the Jesuits about July 20. He informed the General at Vancouver, telling him that Owen "is decidedly of the opinion that the 'mission' should be discontinued in the Coeur d'Alene Country—if for no other reason than because it will be totally unproductive of good for some time to come and may be productive of much harm." Owen never went any further in investigating his suspicions of the Jesuits; he never apologized or retracted. His accusations, enlarged upon, were to live for years among the nativist element.

Superintendent Nesmith also relayed the agent's accusations to General Clarke, with the notation that Owen could be thoroughly relied upon. Nesmith had no more helpful suggestion to send back to Owen than that he should stay clear of hostile Indians. He urged him to keep friendly Indians from joining the hostiles; in a rush of economy on the other hand, alarmed at Owen's gifts or bribes, he cautioned him to make no promises he could not afford. As for the Jesuits, nothing should be done on unfounded suspicion. But "when you become satisfied that they are acting in bad faith, by inciting or encouraging the Indians in hostilities, you will order them out of the country at once." [21]

Owen could not have received these epistolary cautions, even had there been a way to send them. During the war he was everywhere but at his post. Two weeks after he reached the Bitterroot he traveled eastward onto the Great Plains. The excuse he offered Nesmith was that some Flatheads wished to be taken to see the annual distribution of Blackfoot annuities. Actually his party consisted of two Whites, his Iroquois interpreter, his favorite Flathead retainer, and a half-breed. During the time the army was fighting its battles, Agent Owen was traveling far east of Fort Benton, enjoying the company of Fathers Congiato and Hoecken as they located the new Blackfoot mission. Back at his post from September 10 to 20, but apparently uncomfortable at the lack of news about the war, he left for Utah. His excuse to Nesmith this time was that the Snakes required pacifying, and that he himself needed two plows from Salt Lake City. In fact he simply dropped south for "a pleasant

Blenkinsop, 25 February 1859; HB, A11, *71*, London Corresp. out, esp. Steptoe letter of 22 July, and No. 857, Grahame from Clarke, Fort Vancouver, 6 August; No. 858, reply of 7 August; No. 859, Grahame to Blenkinsop at Colville, same date; No. 860, Grahame report to Fort Victoria on Vancouver Island, same date; No. 893, Blenkinsop to Mactavish, 30 September. Buchanan's representative in *SED*, 35 Cong., 2 sess., 32 (1859), p. 14. *SED*, army reports, Grahame to Clarke and to Blenkinsop, both 7 August; Clarke to Grahame, 6 August, with excerpts from Owen letters.

21. Steptoe, in Fort Walla Walla Letterbook, 22 July. Nesmith reply to Owen summed up in Nesmith to Clarke, 2 August; full letter in *SED*, 35 Cong., 2 sess., 1 (1858), pp. 623–24. See NA, EW, Army Commands, Dept. Pacific, LR, to Clarke, 2 August, enclosing two Owen letters.

visit of a week" in Salt Lake City; here he called on Brigham Young. Four days after his return he again left, spending a month on the Plains near Fort Benton.[22]

Agent Owen's incapacity to accomplish anything among the hostiles, the desperate necessity of sheltering under Hudson's Bay protection in the Kettle country and under a band of Spokane allies even in Chief Garry's home district, his nervousness during brief stays in the Bitterroot—all add a dimension to our view of the Jesuit work for peace.

Fathers Joset and Congiato were in the heartland of the hostile tribes before Owen set about fearfully skirting their fringe. When the agent had given up all hope of peace, the two priests were pursuing their labors at tribal campfires. Long after he had dispatched his bitter letters and gained safety, they continued to travel around the remote war camps. Later, while Owen is recording an "agreeable" visit on the Plains, Joset will be making a final peace possible. When the peace treaties are being signed with the Spokanes and others, under Jesuit auspices, Agent Owen will be on his way to Utah.

THE FIRST JESUIT PEACE TOUR

The two priests had started out in a happy mood, feeling that Clarke's terms could be considered "glad tidings." As they headed toward The Dalles, they would have had company enough. This very week, the *Weekly Oregonian* reported, "large parties" of former California miners "are constantly arriving" at The Dalles; here they outfitted and pushed on, not permitting themselves to think long upon hostile Indians.[23] As many as a hundred miners were crowding aboard the little steamers for each trip, gladly paying for their accompanying animals an exorbitant five dollars apiece. Others were conveying their mules and wagons along the riverbanks on the route followed by Congiato and Joset. From The Dalles and Walla Walla the miners branched off on their own routes.

The two Jesuits did not arrive at the mission until July 16. This was the day of Owen's terrible council and frightened letter. The two were stunned to discover that the Coeur d'Alenes were "as yet under great excitement, and all their conversation was about war matters." They ferreted out the cause. The tribe had "resumed the war path," won over by the Machiavellian intrigue of Tilcoax's party and especially succumbing to that irresistible bribe, horses. Chief Stellam, in a later and somewhat dubious reminiscence, recalled

22. Owen, *Journals*, *1*, 201–08, diary entries; *2*, 183–86, September 18 letter. NA, IA, Wash. Sup., LR, Owen to Sup. Geary, 31 May 1859 (not in *Journals*, but in *SED*, serial 1023, pp. 791–92).

23. Joset Narrative. *Weekly Oregonian*, 3, 7, 24 July 1858.

how the Yakima chiefs Owhi and his son were bidding from one to three
horses per warrior according to the "fighting reputation of each." The chief
invidiously added that in joining the hostiles the Coeur d'Alenes nobly refused
a bribe, but that some Spokanes and others took it.

Congiato wrote to Clarke that the resurgent war fever was due above all to
Kamiakin, "who has been living, and still lives" among these crucial upper
tribes.[24] Joset found that the Spokanes had gone over, as had part of the
Kalispels. The Kettles would have followed, he believed, but for Chiefs Denis
Usinentutse and Theodosius Kolosasket. Denis is the "Zenemtietze" in Gibbs'
1853 Indian memoir for Stevens; the Kettles at that time had "no head chief
of note," but the Jesuit mission tended to elevate responsive chiefs like Denis
to effective authority.

It was heartening to find that about forty-five Coeur d'Alene warriors had
followed Vincent in remaining true to their promises. Vincent's party were
now almost outcasts as far as "a number of his people" were concerned. Here
we must take note of a fine point of Coeur d'Alene tribal legality, hitherto
neglected by Vincent. No one had the power to make peace until the relatives of the slain gave their consent. A storm of indignation had arisen from
the powerful kinfolk of the fallen when they discovered what the warriors
had promised to Father Joset after the Steptoe battle. The bereaved women
of the family (since Coeur d'Alene women were unusually influential in public affairs) may have been prominent in this protest. Now the priest returned
with Clarke's summary demands that war criminals be unconditionally surrendered. This sufficed to make the relatives veto the peace definitively. Lieutenant Kip, after talks with the Jesuits later that year, adverted to this odd
technicality. "It is a peculiarity, we are told, about these Indians that if any of
their number is killed his family have to decide the question whether or not
the tribe shall go to war; the chiefs have no voice in the matter; if the family
decide for war, all the warriors have to go, as those who refuse are outlawed." [25]

Father Joset and Chief Vincent might have carried the day despite all. So
complete had been the penitence of the tribe after Joset's previous confrontation, that Vincent had even forgotten this traditional rule. And when relatives had been raising "a great opposition," Joset had contrived to silence
them. What seems to have thrown the balance against peace now was

24. *SED* (serial 975), pp. 372–77, Congiato to Clarke, 3 August; this account of the
current peace tour supplements the Joset Narrative. Original report is in NA, EW,
Army Commands, Dept. Pacific, 3 August 1858, sent on to army headquarters 21 August.
Chief Stellam Reminiscence, "The Story of Stellam," Spokane *Review*, 6 October 1891.

25. CR, *2*, 754–55; Joset Narrative; Congiato Report, above, n. 24; Kip, *Expedition*,
p. 76. On Kettle chiefs see RR, *1*, ii, 413, and CR, *1*, 381, 357.

Clarke's stipulation that there must be unconditional surrender of "the authors of the battle with Colonel Steptoe without even their lives being promised them." To the Interior Indians, taught by experience, this could only mean death.[26] The Cayuse had surrendered a party of warriors in this fashion after their own war; the government had killed them. After the Cascades attack, nine Indians suspected of having fought were seized, tried, and promptly hanged. Following the 1856 war, the undefeated Yakimas would not deliver any of their fighters; but Stevens and the settlers still meant to catch and hang the war leaders despite the truce. Already the Whites had managed to hang several at Fort Steilacoom, especially Chief Leschi.

Numbers of other Indians in formal conflict with the Whites in the Northwest had been similarly treated. During the last war one Bistian (Sebastian?), for instance, was charged in court as "a party to the war now existing" and as having "communicated intelligence to the hostile Indians" about troop movements; seven of his colleagues were acquitted, but Bistian was hanged. In 1849 an outburst by the Snoqualmie Indians, largely consisting of an attack on the fur post Fort Nisqually, had led the Whites to hang both a chief and the brother of the head chief.[27]

To kill in the heat of battle was one thing. To prosecute criminal trials against enemy warriors afterward was quite another. The Interior Indian knew nothing about law courts or capital punishment. These things were strange and frightening. He could have understood fighting on until the scales were balanced, or perhaps exacting some alternative compensation. But this White way was iniquitous. When the tribesmen reflected further that the Whites had never yet won a war in the Interior, though they had blundered unhappily through protracted campaigns, and that they had just sustained the humiliating and total defeat of their professional warriors, the surrender demands could only appear perversely illogical.

Worse, the Indian war criminals or patriots had been killed in a very special way. They were hanged by the neck, convulsively leaping and pitching at the end of a heavy rope, with all the repulsive grimaces, distortions, and discolorations attending death by strangulation. It is unlikely that the Indians appreciated the difference between a sharp drop through a proper gallows, as happened amid solemn ceremonies after a court trial, and the equally popular lynching with its shattering horrors for the spectators. After this war Colonel Wright would hang his many Indian victims in the crudest fashion, on a handy tree limb, by kicking over a keg or wheeling away a gun limber. After

26. CR, *2*, 754, for quots.
27. MD, Proceedings of military commission at Camp Montgomery, W.T., 16 November 1855; in Field, *National Guard*, *2*, 54–55 (Bistian). Bancroft, *Washington*, pp. 13 (Nisqually), 174 (Leschi).

the Cascades fight in 1856 the local chief was hanged in a particularly messy performance. After vainly offering the army a ransom of ten horses and two squaws, this chief was hoisted by a rope over a tree branch; the dangling, struggling figure managed a defiant comment, and in the end had to be shot.

The Whites seemed obsessed with this form of punishment. Two years previously, a great war chief leading his braves in a daring attack upon a camp of the Ninth Infantry had been mortally wounded. Colonel Casey ordered him hanged immediately. A rope was knotted about the dying man's neck and a tree was being sought, when another attack forced the soldiers simply to shoot him in order to renew their own defense. So familiar were the Indians with this White compulsion, that in April 1854 the Snohomish had anticipated and appeased the Whites by voluntarily hanging in Seattle two of their own people guilty of killing a White man. The hanging of Leschi particularly struck the Indian imagination, so that by mid-1858 even friendly braves voiced their preference for death in battle.[28]

For the Coeur d'Alenes to surrender their community leaders or combat veterans to such a savage fate was as impossible as for White men to surrender their officers to the fiery stake of a Plains tribe. It was even more difficult for the primitive tribe, because their small communal society was more closely knit and familial. The result of Clarke's demands therefore was that the relatives of the fallen braves among the Coeur d'Alenes "pronounced obstinately against the peace." Their veto power was buttressed by an enormous advantage: a propaganda and human issue which could not but carry the day. At this time "the great majority" still wanted peace; but "they dared not go counter to an ancient usage and break with their brethren and friends."

The only counterbalance remaining to Joset was the threat of abandonment. Fearing this, Chief Vincent with his supporters braved the threats of their adversaries. They "forsook" the divided tribe and took their stand against war. Thus a good number of Coeur d'Alenes did not take part in the coming battle. Most of the others participated only halfheartedly. Vincent ceased his active work for peace; baffled and hurt he withdrew into himself. Several among the reluctant disciples of the war party, on the other hand, agitated openly for peace. Most of the Coeur d'Alenes were as confused and frightened as children, and as stubbornly bent on having their way. They threatened that if the Blackrobes left them, they would retaliate by throwing themselves unanimously and wholeheartedly into the war. The hard core of

28. Genl. P. H. Sheridan, *Personal Memoirs, 1* (2 vols. New York, 1888), 83–84 (keg) MD, Major Hayes to Gov. Stevens, Camp Puyallup, 29 February 1856; in Field, *National Guard, 2,* 66 (Casey). Bancroft, *Washington,* p. 94. Suckley Papers (YU), No. 21, anon. from Fort Steilacoom, 29 August 1858 (reaction on Leschi).

the war faction, however, "were so much incensed at the others that they promised, as soon as they should have done with the Americans, they would drive the Black gowns with all their followers from their country." "Nobody can tell," Congiato concluded in despair, "what they will do."

The two priests took infinite pains to canvass the tribe for opening wedges of peace. They found some individuals resolved to avoid the dilemma by fleeing into the mountains; yet at the same time these men spoke bravely of desiring another encounter with the soldiers. There was universal disgust at the conduct of the Palouses, who were regarded as the authors of all this misfortune. From later conversations with Joset and other Jesuits in the 1870s, Father Diomedi was to gather the impression that the priests "succeeded in keeping two-thirds of the whole tribe home and out of the battlefield," and that "only some wild young" bucks participated. The exaggeration suggests at least the underlying situation: a fanatic core dominating a majority which was susceptible to Jesuit influence.[29]

The two Jesuits concentrated upon the Coeur d'Alene, Spokane, and Kettle regions. Congiato especially reports having visited all the Spokane and Coeur d'Alene bands. They had to travel rapidly over a vast area, from band to band. Many bands were scattered, gathering food in preparation for the coming war. Some of the braves still retained their war regalia. "Day and night" the camps resounded with chants and uproar. Violent quarrels were in progress over army mules and horses. Both Jesuits spoke earnestly to the Indians, explaining "first, what the soldiers are; second, their peaceful and protecting mission; third, the difference which exists between soldiers and other citizens, or Americans, as they call them; and lastly, their number and power, the many and terrible means which they have at their command, in order to subdue their enemies and punish those who do wrong to them."

The Indian fervor "began to cool down wonderfully" as the two heaped their chilling eloquence upon it. They spoke to the Spokanes "several times and at different places." Having no Spokane mission, they could not use as leverage the threat of abandonment. But as with the Coeur d'Alenes, the Jesuits "did all we could to bring them to good sense." Probably the difficulties were the same among all the tribes. There would be a war party standing firmly for "war to the knife." Others would be astonished at Clarke's tone: "such is not the Indian fashion of making peace; we make peace with our enemies by forgiving each other the wrongs committed and by making to each mutual presents."[30] Government property, already sold several times

29. CR, 2, 754–55. Joset Narrative. Congiato Report. Cf. also Alexander Diomedi, S.J., *Sketches of Modern Indian Life* (Woodstock, Md., 1884), p. 76.

30. Joset and Congiato accounts. MJ, IX, AA, Congiato to De Smet, Fort Benton, 2 September 1858.

over, was so embroiled in tribal economic ethics that it could hardly be returned. Owing to their tribal structure, the Interior tribes would have had great difficulty anyway in arriving at a consensus.

On August 3 the war factions held a joint Coeur d'Alene–Spokane council. Its purpose seems to have been partly to offset the pacific effect of the Jesuits upon the two tribes, and partly to present through the Jesuits to General Clarke the rather stiff response of the war party. Only a few participants could be mustered, and their warlike sentiments "cannot be said to be the prevailing ones." The future lay with this faction, however, since the army's ultimatum left room for no other alternative. The leaders prepared letters for the military. All favored peace but on their own terms. Chief Polatkin of the Spokanes adopted a belligerent tone. He was willing to break off the war, in mutual peace; but "I will not deliver my neighbors" to White vengeance. Melkapsi of the Coeur d'Alenes included veiled threats, stressing the equality of Indian and White. He was not especially inclined to peace, though willing to hear the Whites. He felt that Clarke should come up to the Indian country for his peace parley. He particularly wanted nothing more to do with the treacherous Indian allies of the soldiers.

Spokane Garry was present, perhaps in a gallant effort to influence the war faction. Circumstances did not allow him to do much more than express sympathy for both sides. His approach resembled that used in his letters to Stevens during the previous war. He protested that he was a friend of the Whites and had tried to prevent his people from going to war; but he felt unable to meet the surrender terms. Garry urged Clarke especially to reconsider his demand for Indian culprits: "withdraw this one word," and peace can be made. He added the oblique threat that war might spread among other tribes like "the fire in a dry prairie."

Congiato took care privately to have "a long conversation with Spokane Gary." He reported that Garry "is strongly for peace, but he says he is for a general peace"; that is, the chief suggested a council between the Whites and all the tribes, to negotiate both about the war and about the murders and robberies. Viewed in the abstract, it was a sensible enough suggestion. It was also as much as he dared say; he could not hope to affect the present situation. Like most of Garry's performances, this was diplomatic and ultimately noncommittal. After the council, Congiato and Joset drafted their report on the peace tour, sending it together with the letters of the chiefs to General Clarke.[31]

At the Jesuit mission near Fort Colville the two priests found the bulk of the Kettles "more quiet," and in a general way opposed to war. However, some of the younger warriors were in a bellicose mood. The tribe, like those

31. Congiato Report, 3 August, with Indian letters.

around it, was being "much solicited to join the hostile Indians." [32] But Chiefs Denis and Theodosius continued to use their influence for peace here and among neighboring pagan bands. Ravalli as resident missioner contrived to keep the Kettles under some control. Kettle Falls was beginning to lose its status as the central fishery for the far-flung bands. New fisheries elsewhere accentuated the dispersal of the Indians, rendering their management by the Kettle missioners ever more difficult. Moreover, Indian contact with the Colville Whites was damaging; White vices had demoralized the tribe. Congiato therefore decided to suppress the mission. The White settlers in the area begged him not to do so until after the war. The Kettles were assuming a threatening attitude toward them, they said, and the Jesuits were the only restraining force. [33]

The Hudson's Bay establishment at Colville undoubtedly helped restrain these Indians. Blenkinsop had his hands full at the fort. Like his predecessor MacDonald he did what he could for local peace, but with necessary circumspection. In February of the following year he was to write: "for several months during the past year the Indians in our vicinity were in a most excited state, and assumed such a hostile position toward the settlers and miners in this quarter, that I was fearful for some time that the whole would have been swept away and ourselves in the general ruin." During the war, Blenkinsop says, "upwards of a dozen individuals have been saved by myself and Officers from massacre around this establishment." He asserts that "to us alone must be attributed the salvation of the settlers and miners in this valley."

Blenkinsop sees it as significant "that those Indians alone who resided at our Establishments were the *only* tribes who did not participate in the war." The trader may be excused for overstating his case, since he is angrily retorting to Owen's preposterous accusations. Besides, locked in his trading post and unable to communicate with Hudson's Bay superiors in any direction, he was probably not aware of the various efforts being made by the Jesuits. He does not even seem to know that the Kettles around the post had taken part in the battles of 1858. Throughout the war Colville remained notoriously the focal point of trouble. Blenkinsop does recall that an attempt to send out a brigade had to be abandoned because "on several occasions" the Indians employed had bolted in a body to fire on passing miners. [34]

In assessing the work of Congiato and Joset, one must always keep in mind how dangerous the country was. It was, in effect, closed to Whites. The Hudson's Bay's superiors in civilization could only hope that Blenkinsop had

32. BJ, Coll. 1ac–4ac, No. 3ac, later account by Joset, 29 May 1871.
33. Congiato Report. *JMUS*, 2, 337.
34. HB, D5, *48*, Simpson Corresp. in, from Blenkinsop, Fort Colville, 25 February 1859.

reached Colville; no news could come out of the upper country "until the Military shall have opened the communication." Mactavish, the trader at Vancouver, could not be induced to go to Colville: "I could not have moved about the Country, without some sort of escort." Only long after the peace treaties, in late February 1859, did Blenkinsop finally get word out, commenting that "the road between Fort Colville and the Dalles" had been "too dangerous to travel on account of the Indian outbreak." During this very peace tour by the two Jesuits, according to Lieutenant Kip, the tribes were burning "the entire plains from Walla Walla to the Snake River" in order to deprive the White soldiers of forage. Father Congiato realized that the upper country was completely cut off and had expressed his relief at getting through to the mission.[35]

Even friendly chiefs near the Whites were acting warily. Showaway, the chief of the Naches River band of Yakimas, was cold to overtures of friendship from the army. He announced that he probably would not fight; at the same time, he refused to help the Whites because his relatives were among the hostiles. Eventually he and a Dalles chief reluctantly promised to visit Fort Vancouver. Agent Lansdale, among the Indians near Fort Dalles, confiscated seven horses "sent by hostile Indians to the friendly Indians near this agency, for improper purposes." Distant tribes with no apparent connections in the Interior were also restless. The Salish tribe of Nooksacks at the top of the Coast, for instance, were angry at the miners' trail and ferry through their lands in 1858. Their open hostility cut local travel to a minimum for two years. Puget Sound was to remain unsafe for water travelers even in 1859. Not only were small parties in danger, but in February 1859 two schooners on their way to Port Townsend went down under the attacks of the canoe Indians.[36]

Most of the Interior tribes seem to have been affected to some degree by the unrest. The two Jesuits would have time to visit only those tribes closely identified with the Steptoe incident. Their stay at Colville was of necessity only "a short visit," though the local Jesuits continued to work there. The Palouses they bypassed, considering them either hopeless or a less promising field. As for the various tribes of the Flathead confederacy, the two could only relay to General Clarke the assurance of a missioner just down from the eastern country that these "are all peaceful." The brief span of time made it

35. Ibid., *47*, from Grahame, 20 September 1858; from Mactavish, 19 June 1858, from Blenkinsop, 25 February 1859. Kip, *Expedition*, p. 39.

36. NA, EW, Army Commands, Dept. Pacific, LR, Major Lugenbeel to Mackall, Fort Dalles, 22 July and 10 August; Lansdale to Clarke, White Salmon Agency, 24 September. M. W. Smith, "The Nooksack, the Chilliwack, and the Middle Fraser," *PNWQ, 41* (1950), 331; Bancroft, *Washington*, p. 212.

impossible to attempt any duplication of Ravalli's wide efforts among the more southern and westerly groupings in the previous war. There was so little time that when Congiato's first report reached Walla Walla, Wright was prepared to march. When the second report went south, the American army had already reached the Snake, had established its protective fort, and was about to cross the river in force.

How were priests' messages sent through? With all communication through the lower country broken, and intertribal tensions rife, Congiato had brought the experienced Ravalli down from the Kettle mission to run messages through the hostile territory. On one of these trips Ravalli took an Indian from the band of the Spokane chief Polatkin to Walla Walla; the poor fellow was to be hanged later for having helped precipitate the war by killing two Colville miners. It was probably Ravalli, rather than Joset, whom Lieutenant Kip saw on August 13 passing down through the temporary Fort Taylor on the Snake: "a Roman Catholic priest, who belongs to the Mission in the Coeur d'Alene mountains." Kip describes the Jesuit in his diary. "As the 'black robes' can pass to and fro uninjured among the different tribes, he was sent by General Clarke to the Spokanes and Coeur d'Alenes to announce to them the terms on which he would make peace with them." Kip was under the impression that the tribes had returned an "insulting answer" and that "the Indians were really for war and did not wish peace, but a war of extermination." [37]

Congiato, leaving Joset to influence the Coeur d'Alenes further if he could, set out on August 24 for the Flathead country. Another Jesuit, perhaps Menetrey, had already come down bringing news that the Flathead confederacy seemed "greatly displeased" over the Steptoe affair. Alexander of the Pend d'Oreilles was more positive. Not only would he refuse to join the hostiles, but he would kill any fugitive Coeur d'Alene or Spokane combatant who fled onto his land and compromised his people. During the tensions of the previous year, Congiato had taken Alexander to Fort Dalles for the express purpose of impressing him "with the greatness and power of our soldiers and our country." At Congiato's request, Steptoe himself had shown them the armaments. Alexander now announced that in view of what he had seen "he was not so foolish" as to risk a war with White warriors. This is an interesting example of Jesuit preventive work for peace. State and Indian officials had seen the necessity of something similar and had advocated a rather grandiose junket to the nation's capital, but bureaucratic clumsiness and expense proved too serious an obstacle. [38]

37. Kip, *Expedition*, p. 42.

38. Congiato Report; Joset Narrative. Cf. Stevens' plan to bring twenty chiefs to Washington on a budget of $30,000 (WU, to Mix, 17 February 1858; Todd, *PNWQ*, *31*, 430).

There would be no less than four Jesuit priests, counting Congiato, holding the Flatheads steady during the coming campaign. In the spring of 1858, for example, Menetrey made a long visit to the Kutenais, admitting thirty adults to baptism and hearing over five hundred confessions. In September Congiato was to leave the Flatheads, journeying out onto the Plains to find a suitable spot for the Blackfoot mission. He wrote Father De Smet from Fort Benton that "the Coeur d'Alenes have disgraced us; nothing in the world can excuse them." There still remained "twenty or thirty" warriors, he said, determined to fight. Yet "some good" had come of the peace tour. And the tribe as a whole were "greatly scared at the many things we told them" about the White soldiers. "They were much less excited than [they] were at first." As for Joset, "your Reverence cannot imagine how much he has suffered and is still suffering." Congiato told De Smet that after the Steptoe attack he had meant to abandon the tribe; Clarke had dissuaded him from this course at least until the peace tour failed or succeeded. Now, if the Coeur d'Alenes were to join in the coming hostilities, Congiato had left orders with Joset to break up the mission permanently and withdraw. Of course, the superior would expect Joset to interpret his orders in the light of changing circumstances.[39]

Clarke's demands had proved too onerous, and no time had been allowed to effect their modification. Still, a substantial portion of the Coeur d'Alene and Kettle tribes, as well as the Kalispels and other members of the Flathead confederacy and perhaps some of the Spokanes, had been induced to stay out of the war. The great majority of the Kalispels moved across the line into British Columbia or onto the buffalo Plains, to be as remote as possible from temptation; some would stay away as long as two years.[40] General Clarke found the news of the Flathead confederacy's continued neutrality "cheering." As for the other tribes, he reiterated his conditions stubbornly. "Less cannot be demanded or received." He expressed "more regret than surprise" at the Jesuits' efforts "kindly made, to avert war and the ruin of the people among whom you have been laboring." He concluded with "sincere thanks, sir, in the effort you have made in the cause of humanity, and an earnest wish that your visit to the Flatheads may confirm them in their present disposition, that your own mission may be successful, and your return in safety and health."

Lieutenant Mullan also lauded the peace effort of Joset and Congiato in his topographical report on the war. "They harangued early and late and long, 'til their weak voices were lost and drowned" in war cries, and until their motives were rendered suspect to the Indians. "Be it said to their credit, they did not even then desist, nor were they silent, but with their characteristic traits, they persevered to the end." After the Wright campaign, Mullan continued,

39. MJ, IX, AA, Congiato to De Smet, 2 September 1858. Cf. Palladino, *Indian and White*, p. 332, citing Fort Benton baptismal register on Congiato.
40. Teit, BAE *Annual Report*, 45, 371.

once again "the Jesuits reappeared, still active in their exertions," reminding the Indians of their crime and of its penalty.[41]

During all this time thousands of miners frantically attempted to make their way to the Fraser gold fields. They avoided the Pend d'Oreille mines. Generally they went up along the western fringe of the hostile country, in as military a posture as possible, maneuvering and fighting their way through. A number of them were killed, or robbed, or turned back. A party of 150 struck north from Walla Walla in early July; they lost a German who strayed from the main body, and near the Canadian border had 3 Californians killed and 3 wounded in a sustained fire-fight with the Okanogans; 500 Frenchmen, many of them veterans of the recent Crimean War, were reported as coming up from Sacramento, planning to push off from The Dalles in military companies. Toward the end of June a large party clashed with an Interior war band, losing 2 dead and 9 wounded, but claiming 13 Indians killed. On the very day Wright's army crossed the Snake, a party of miners were ambushed and robbed, four days out of Walla Walla.[42]

The express rider W. H. Pearson, just returned to Seattle from prospecting, contracted to take a party of 82 back through the Yakima country in mid-July. They were promptly stopped by 300 warriors under Owhi and Qualchin. More aggrieved than hostile, the Indians enumerated their complaints through Pearson, demanding to know if the Whites wanted peace or war. Then they offered to let the miners through if they in turn would deliver a letter from Qualchin to Fort Simcoe. Pearson agreed. He conveyed the message, and carried back the severe response it elicited. Meanwhile, his party went ahead, to be turned back two days later by an aggressive Indian force estimated at 800. In Washington, D.C., Stevens heard of this, and sent a documented account to the secretary of War. The Yakimas and the Indians of the upper country must be punished, he insisted; "their exemplary chastisement has become a matter of the first importance." [43]

41. Mullan, *Topographical Memoir*, p. 41; SED, army reports, Clarke to Congiato or Joset, 19 August.

42. HB, Blenkinsop letter of 25 February (Pend d'Oreille mines). Trimble, *Mining Advance*, pp. 34–35. Francis Wolf, in Winans, "Stevens County." NA, IA, Oreg. Sup., LR, Agent Dennison to Nesmith, Dalles, 28 June 1858 (June group). *Weekly Oregonian*, 24 July, 21, 28 August 1858. HB, D4, 55, Simpson Corresp. out, Ser. 1, 15 December 1858. Reinhart, *Recollections*, pp. 114–15 (Robinson's 175 lose 8 men). Archer Corresp., 8 and 15 June 1858. Archer and Major Lugenbeel at The Dalles rushed two companies to protect the relay station halfway to Simcoe; on the miners see letter of 1 July.

43. NA, EW, AGO, LR, 381S, Stevens to secretary of War, 15 September 1858, with clipping from *Democratic Standard* for 5 August, including letters. Trimble, p. 35. Fort Simcoe Letterbook (HL), 26 June 1858, on attack by Indians against party of 70 miners. Archer letter of 1 July on same attack (7 badly wounded, 6 dead).

MILITARY PREPARATIONS AND THEIR JESUIT DIMENSION

Throughout the Jesuit peace tour General Clarke prepared zealously for war. The General is "determined to *conquer a peace* with all the Indian tribes within his reach," reported the *Weekly Oregonian* with martial fervor, "and is now through the several military departments actively engaged in throwing forward troops and transporting supplies for an active campaign." His first problem was to find in these departments enough men to make an army. The tiny American military force lay scattered in small police parties over thousands of miles of western emptiness. The only serious concentration in the distant West was that gathered for the Mormon War. The troops on the Coast were dispersed over 1,500 miles.

Clarke had previously notified Washington that he had to withdraw men needed elsewhere, even at risk of endangering those posts, to put down this Northwest war. Already a shifting of troops was afoot. By the end of June Fort Dalles was accommodating 119 men, Fort Simcoe in the Yakima country 335, and Fort Walla Walla 611. Before the year was out the total of soldiers present would jump from under 1,600 to over 2,200.[44] To contrive such an effect with the army of that day could only mean that many a barrel bottom had been scraped. "All the disposable troops" in California had been rushed up to form at Fort Vancouver.

Lieutenant Kip, in the midst of this activity, describes how companies were "converging to the hostile country from every part of the Pacific coast, even from Fort Yuma on the far distant banks of the Colorado, and from San Diego on the borders of Mexico." Some of these came "from Posts at the South where they were really needed." One company of infantry was brought from little Fort Jones in northern California, one of artillery from Fort Umpqua in southern Oregon. On July 3 the steamer *Panama* was reported "at Vancouver with troops and about 500 miners." The *Weekly Oregonian* announced on this date that the steamer *Pacific* had been chartered to rush 500 troops from southern California; these were expected hourly and were "to be sent at a *Shanghai* pace into the Indian country."[45]

On July 2 a letter from Lieutenant Mullan told of the bustle at Fort Dalles, with couriers coming and going daily; four companies of artillery were about to leave for the Snake, and Clarke at Vancouver "will rush troops around as soon as possible." Kip's own company came up from San Bernardino by

44. *Weekly Oregonian*, 17 July 1858. R. C. Clark, "Military History of Oregon, 1849–1859," *OHQ*, *36* (1935), 37, 57–59, with chart.

45. Kip, *Expedition*, p. 12. NA, IA, Oreg. Sup., LR, John McCracken to Nesmith, Portland, 3 July (*Panama*). *Oregonian*, 3 July 1858.

steamer to San Francisco, arriving on June 12. They were not allowed to land at the city for fear of desertions. Instead, there was "a scene of confusion" as mules, cannon, ammunition, provisions, and "military stores of all kinds" were loaded from the wharf. There were in all three companies from the Third Artillery on the six-day trip from San Francisco north. Fort Vancouver proved to be not the dull, familiar post of 1855 but "lively as can be," with "constant drills going on, and nothing but hurry and preparation from morning to night" to the constant accompaniment of drum rattle and bugle call.[46]

Many of the troops called would be too late to see action. Many others would not even arrive; "400 recruits" were ordered to Vancouver from Newport Barracks in Kentucky. Stevens wrote from Washington to say that they would march on July 21; the civil contract for their sea transportation via South America had already been concluded. A week after Steptoe's return, Wright sent a suggestion to San Francisco that troops for this emergency might be spared from the Mormon War. On June 29 the War Department ordered the Utah army to detach the Sixth or Seventh regiment of infantry to Fort Walla Walla. On August 7 General Johnston selected the Sixth to hurry to San Francisco so as to approach Walla Walla via the ocean and river route. The overland path by Fort Hall was deemed too difficult; even in peacetime the direct Salt Lake City–Dalles march required sixty-one days, almost three times the duration of the New York–Panama–San Francisco trip by boat. The regiment got under way on August 21, pushing valiantly through snow-covered mountains to reach Benicia on San Francisco Bay by November 15. It was one of the longest continuous infantry marches in the history of the American frontier. But of course by then the war was over.

Even if the Sixth had gone the rest of the way to Vancouver and Walla Walla, the soldiers would have been in no condition to embark upon a campaign. And had they been able to do so, the descending winter would have made it impossible. By that time, too, the army regretted having withdrawn its troops from Fort Yuma in Arizona, the principal post of the Southwest. The Utah regiment was promptly turned around and marched down to those sandy wastes. Few episodes in the war so graphically illustrate the difficulties facing the American army in transporting its troops. Meanwhile, the seasoned Indian fighter General Harney was stopped halfway across the Plains on his march to the Mormon War. He was to return to New York and embark by water via Panama for Fort Vancouver, to take full command of the war. His arrival too was bound to be tardy.[47]

46. NA, IA, Oreg. Sup., LR, Mullan to Nesmith, 2 July. Kip, pp. 16, 18.

47. Wright Report, 26 May. Bandel, *Frontier Life in the Army*, p. 55. On Harney episode, see below, Chap. 8. Newport group mentioned in Stevens to Nesmith, 18 July

One of the young officers coming up from California had particular grounds for interest in Jesuit missionaries: Lieutenant Kip, son of the pioneer Episcopal bishop of California. Some thirteen years previously the elder Kip had published a volume on *The Early Jesuit Missions of North America.* The book had "met with a hearty reception" and a new edition was to appear in 1866. The bishop's introductory essay on the "touching and romantic" story of the Blackrobes with their "fearless devotedness and heroic self-sacrifice" was generous. It was, of course, tinged with the contemporary suspicion that there must be "something wrong in the whole system—some grievous errors mingled," especially to cause such a complete disappearance of the Order and its work.[48] The bishop was to write another book on the Jesuits in 1875. Young Lieutenant Kip would now meet real Jesuits, draw upon their fund of information about the Indian troubles, and write his own book.

The army was sluggishly gathering the raw materials for a war. Clarke was particularly exercised to collect six of the small mountain howitzers. Steptoe had already lost two; one was available at Walla Walla and another at Fort Dalles without a carriage. All available pack saddles and ammunition were prepared for trans-shipping 800 miles north: 500 rifled muskets, 50,000 rounds of ammunition, and 50 saddles with complete horse equipment were ready to go out of San Francisco Bay as early as June 10. One of the coastal carriers became involved in trouble at sea, failed to complete her voyage, and even had to jettison "a quantity" of these cartridges. They were replaced in a shipment of July 19. The artillery receipts alone bulked impressively.[49]

The source of all this muscle was Benicia in the bare hills across the bay from San Francisco—mostly an arsenal of deposit and repair, though it also made cartridges. At Fort Dalles on July 20 we find Captain Jordan passing along 12,000 rations of flour to Walla Walla, arranging for the purchase of horses in Oregon's Willamette Valley, and complaining that his contribution of 225 mules to the expedition left his own command deprived. Pork was a problem; it had to pass from New York through San Francisco and was subject to delays.[50]

The expense was appalling for those days. Even in peacetime, supplies reached distant posts only tardily and incompletely. Without considering the

(Todd, *PNWQ*, *31*, 445); their July 20 sea transport is among army contracts in *HED*, 35 Cong., 2 sess., 50 (1859), pp. 14–15; cf. also items on pp. 17, 18, 21.

48. W. I. Kip, *The Early Jesuit Missions in North America, Compiled and Translated from the Letters of the French Jesuits, with Notes* (Albany, N.Y., [1846], 1866), pp. xii, xiv.

49. Fort Dalles Papers (HL), Mackall to Callender, San Francisco; cf. other documents here on artillery. NA, EW, Army Commands, Dept. Pacific, LR, correspondence between Captain Callender at Benicia and Mackall, esp. 19 July, 10, 14, 15, 30 June.

50. NA, EW, Army Commands, Dept. Pacific, LR, Jordan to Mackall, Dalles, 20 July; cf. similar letters here.

difficulties of the wild Interior, building and repair costs on the Northwest Coast were higher than in any other military department during the decade of 1848–58. In 1856 chief topographer Cram reckoned costs as almost three times greater than in the nearby Department of the West, soaring higher in time of war. Troops took care therefore to come north, even in wartime, as simple passengers on the twice-monthly steamers, rather than incur the expense of a chartered ship. In 1855 it cost the army no less than $7,000 a day in direct expenses just to maintain a local war in Oregon involving 200 to 500 men, adding up to a grand total of $258,000. Just keeping a soldier in existence during peacetime in the Oregon country during this period—without counting the convulsions of transport, supplies, and motion incident to a war, and without counting guns, ammunition, building, and the like—consumed over $821 per man per year. Not only did expenses multiply in wartime, but prices went up. In helping to shorten the war, the Jesuit contribution thus had an economic as well as humanitarian aspect.[51]

The magnitude of the Jesuits' service must be measured basically in accordance with one's interpretation of the military factors. A common view of the war, for instance, is that Steptoe was defeated by musket-bearing Indians, but that Wright reversed the advantage and utterly crushed the tribes with Sharps rifles. If this is true, the Jesuit contribution was in facilitating an equitable and lasting peace. On the other hand, if Wright never really enjoyed an overwhelming weapon advantage or, more especially, if his campaign was essentially a failure, the role of the Jesuits becomes paramount.

Actually, the Jesuits were going to re-enter the war after Wright's army had exhausted its capacity for decisive action. Catching the Indians at an appropriately confused moment and the White commander in an eminently impotent and untenable situation, Joset then contrived to bring about a treaty with many of the central chiefs. This in turn dissipated the aggressive unity of the tribes and isolated the most hostile by a buffer zone. The army could get back to civilization safely and with honor. The way had thus been prepared for a subsequent more formal and positive consolidation of the peace by the Jesuits as a group. It would be folly to propose such a radical interpretation of the 1858 war simply to appease sectarian vanity; the traditional presentation leaves quite enough glory for Joset and his colleagues. This new explanation might well appall them; Joset and De Smet went out of their way to publish praises of Steptoe and Wright, and laid claim to nothing more than a minor, subsidiary role.

This interpretation requires a preliminary examination of the weapons used

51. Cram Report, *HED*, pp. 5, 7, 32. W. G. Ledbetter, "Military History of the Oregon Country 1804–1859," unpublished master's thesis (University of Oregon, [1935] 1940), p. 76. Clark, *OHQ*, *36*, 35–36. Bancroft, *Oregon*, *2*, 320–21.

by Colonel Wright. Lieutenant Kip attributed the success of Wright's battles to discipline and "to the long range rifles now first used by our troops." It was because the Indians "now for the first time" met the "long range rifles" that they were thrown into panic.[52] Outranged, overwhelmed by massive firepower, they were defeated before the battle could begin. The point is well taken, though it can be exaggerated. The Indians were well armed. Steptoe had remarked upon this; he was even under the impression that most were equipped with rifles. Joset emphasized that Kamiakin was anxious to win over mountain tribes like the Coeur d'Alenes and Kalispels precisely because they were better armed. The advantage of the Whites was more complex than Kip realized. The Whites had more and better rifles, as well as the Minié bullet. Above all, the impersonal and machine-like precision with which they deployed, and the advantage of surprise for their novel tactics, was effective.

The improved rifle, with its percussion cap and Minié ball, was one of the basic contributions of technology to war in the nineteenth century. It gave shape to the Civil War with its eventual trenches and new tactics. It may even be said to have ushered in the age of modern warfare. It was dependable and fast. A good man could get off two rounds per minute, a rare man three rounds. Above all, it greatly outranged the musket. The maximum range was over 1,000 yards; it could be used accurately at 400 to 600 yards, as against the musket range of 100 to 200 yards. The effective range (at which an equal number of attackers would be broken up) was from 200 to 250 yards. In practice this meant that enemies had to keep their distance, and that the old-time charge, whether by foot soldiers with bayonet, or by cavalry, or by Indians, was logically outmoded. It also meant that anyone not possessing a rifle, or as good a rifle as his opponent, was often out of the battle. Another factor was the vicious wound inflicted by the new bullet, which was not the old sphere but an elongated cone with a hollow base, that slipped easily into the muzzle and expanded to the rifling when fired. Contact with cartilage or bone spread it so as to give a dumdum effect. The full implications of the rifle were only to emerge during the Civil War. And it had some disadvantages also; Major Haller in his 1855 battles thought "the long range rifle is of little account" because of loading difficulties and continual fouling.

The question of the Sharps rifle in the coming campaign has been much agitated among historians, some attributing all the success to it, others denying it any serious role. Wright's command would carry three kinds of rifle. In 1855 the national armories had stopped making the smoothbores with their spherical shot; by the close of 1858 some 4,000 real rifles had come out of the Springfield and Harpers Ferry armories. At the same time the ancient muskets were converted by the insertion of a rifled tube; the inequality of

52. Kip, *Expedition*, pp. 56, 59.

length between the old outer barrel and the new inner tubing endowed this instrument with a dangerous kick, lessening its usefulness. Both the new and the remade rifles were muzzle loaders, involving a complicated ritual of preparation for every shot.

The Sharps, in contrast, was a single-shot breechloader, handy for dismounted cavalrymen but lacking the range and penetration of the other rifles. It was the first breechloader actually tested in American military service and adopted. A number of them went West with the first dragoons for experimental purposes, and had appeared in battle three years before. The present campaign would test the weapon further. Immediately following the defeat of the Coeur d'Alenes and their allies, the manufacturers were to incorporate Colonel Wright's success into their commercial advertising. "Principally armed with Sharps' Carbines," Wright's men killed or wounded fifty northern Indians, utterly routing the very warriors who "had previously defeated Colonel Steptoe's forces when armed with old muskets and carbines." [53] In the Mexican revolution of 1858 a thousand men with Sharps defeated the government forces, killing six hundred with only slight loss to themselves.

It is not accurate to claim the Sharps as Wright's chief armament. As Clarke prepared for war, a weapons report placed forty Sharps among the dragoons, ten to a company. Rifles and musketoons among them were about equal in number. Colt pistols were numerous, though the muzzle-loading cavalry pistol remained prominent. C company had thirty-nine of the latter, and I company five; H company held fifty-five, the only company in the territory without its authorized complement of Colts. But Steptoe's unfortunate command had carried some thirty Sharps and over a hundred Colts. Nor were the Indians who fought Steptoe and Wright completely unfamiliar with the Sharps; many thousands had already been sold to hunters and sportsmen.

Some five years before Steptoe's defeat, Lieutenant Saxton's branch of the Stevens exploration had even demonstrated the Sharps to intimidate the Interior Indians. The scene was the juncture of the Palouse and Snake rivers, the Indians a war party of fifty Palouses and Nez Percés. Saxton reported how they "were much astonished at the rapid shooting shown them with Sharpe's and Colt rifles, which made a very favorable impression in regard to their means of defence." In the Rogue River wars, as Captain Cram reports, some Indians fought with Sharps and Colts sold to them by greedy settlers.[54]

53. Sharps Rifle Co. catalogue (1859), p. 14, quoted in Rosebush, *Frontier Steel*, p. 304 (quot.). W. O. Smith, *The Sharps Rifle, Its History, Development and Operation* (New York, 1943), for background; our war is mentioned on p. 12. Haller quotation from Bischoff, "Yakima War," p. 86.

54. NA, EW, Army Commands, Dept. Pacific, LR, June 11 report to Mackall on arms of Washington Territory dragoons, with accompanying chart. *RR, 12,* i, 108. Cram Report, *HED,* p. 123. A letter from Victoria, B.C., reports a battle between 77

In preparing the militia campaign for 1856, Stevens' commissary general had particularly requested a hundred Sharps; only if these were unavailable did he want "the common U.S. Percussion rifles." Clarke did want to use the Sharps in this 1858 crisis; it might give an important margin of effectiveness in the fighting. There were none at Vancouver and only two in the Benicia arsenal, but a shipment of 340 was on the way from New York. Half of these were not expected for "a month or two"; the other half, complete with ammunition, arrived by clipper ship in San Francisco Bay not long after the news of Steptoe's defeat. These were neither unloaded nor examined but immediately dispatched to Vancouver. Word went ahead to the dragoon captains to expect them.[55] Yet future talk in the reports centers upon the rifled muskets, and there seems little doubt that the role of the Sharps was subordinate. The dragoon Sharps especially do not seem to have been used much in action; during the critical battles the dragoons entered as a classic shock force, apparently relying on sabers and pistols. The ninety-man rifle brigade in the campaign may have carried some Sharps.

Five hundred rifled muskets were rushed to the Northwest. They, too, came under the heading of long-range rifles. During the precampaign drills at Fort Dalles, Captain Keyes noted that they carried well for 200 to 600 yards; their long range "will in my opinion render the mountain howitzer worse than useless in the field." Wright reported after the battles that the Third Artillery battalion received these rifled muskets "at the moment of taking the field." They "have a long range, and shoot with great accuracy, but they have many defects, they are unnecessarily long, they have not sufficient weight of metal, the barrels are too thin to admit of their being converted into Rifles without danger of bursting—several have burst during the Campaign." In assessing the various weapons later, Wright particularly commended the standard rifle of his Ninth Infantry; this is the .58 calibre Mississippi Jaeger or Harpers Ferry, carried also by one of the dragoon companies in the Steptoe defeat. Wright insisted "that the *Rifle* of the 9th Infantry is the best arm I have ever seen in the hands of a foot soldier; it is of the right length and weight, and well suited for any field, particularly for the service in which the army is *habitually* employed: *Indian Wafare*." He had previously requested that the rifle brigade be allowed to keep their rifles and not be issued the new rifled muskets; his experiences now leave him convinced that his judgment was sound.[56]

---

miners, armed partly with 21 Sharps, and Washington Indians; the miners were forced to retreat to Fort Simcoe (*Daily Alta California*, 9 July 1858; cf. above, n. 43).

55. Arms report and letters in Callender-Mackall correspondence, above, n. 49, esp. 14, 15 June. Bischoff, "Yakima War," p. 264 (1856).

56. NA, EW, Army Commands, Dept. Pacific, LR, Keyes to Mackall, 5 July; NA, EW, AGO, 290c, Wright to Mackall, Camp near Fort Walla Walla, 8 October 1858.

However a battle is won, by rifle or tactics or chance, the war itself may still be lost. To evaluate the Jesuit contribution, therefore, one must also appraise General Clarke's campaign strategy. In this northern segment of his command he now controlled almost one-seventh of the whole American army, or over a sixth of its active forces in the field. Half of this, a thousand men, he planned to launch into the upper country. Major Garnett, the commander at Fort Simcoe, was to take 300 regulars north to the mouth of the Okanogan River. This would carry him through the country of the Yakimas and the petty Columbia tribes, putting him on the fringe of the Southern Okanogans. Somehow he was expected to discover and punish an Indian band that had attacked miners. Somehow also his thrust was supposed to drive all the hostiles of the region in toward the Spokane country. There might have been merit in such a plan, had Garnett been facing nineteenth-century White armies.

Wright was ordered to take his 700 men in a parallel direction, farther to the east, driving northeast to the Coeur d'Alene mission. There he meant to wheel them for a long march northwest to the fur post at Colville. Again, this was expected to drive the tribes on that side across Garnett's line of march. The Spokanes were to be left untouched at Wright's left on the march up. By concerted action the two converging columns could catch and destroy the combined Indian confederates in the open Spokane country. Garnett estimated Wright's maximum marching capacity as being only to Lake Coeur d'Alene, thence to Colville, then down to the junction of the Columbia and Spokane rivers, and finally back to Walla Walla. If all these points were to be touched the march had to be direct, or his supplies would fail.[57]

As the troops went north, Superintendent Nesmith confided frankly to Stevens: "I apprehend that the whole thing will be a failure and that the Indians will keep out of their way." Experience had demonstrated that the Indians had the choice of time and place, superior numbers, and a "vast number of fleet horses"; they "have in nearly every instance been victorious." In fact, Nesmith concludes, "a large force capable of chastising them is always adroitly eluded, while an inferior and weak one is invariably defeated."

Stevens had already perceived the problem clearly. Though he was professionally committed to a war policy and sanguine as to its success, he was a military man with experience in the region. His recommendations now to the army were that "the effective moving and striking force" must be a mounted regiment; infantry could assist only by garrisoning posts, establishing depots, and taking advanced positions. Even then, he foresaw that "all the fall and

---

The San Francisco *Daily Evening Bulletin* credited Wright's success to rifled muskets with Minié ball; a Portland correspondent especially emphasizes the "Minnie rifles" (14 September, 1 and 4 October 1858).

57. Fort Simcoe Letterbook, Garnett to Mackall, 17 July and 10 August 1858.

winter" would be required for the campaign. Despite such warnings, the army taking the field was to be essentially infantry, the "walk-a-heaps" so despised by mobile Indian warriors. The cavalry auxiliaries were tied to these infantry masses.[58]

Wright was undertaking a titanic game of hide-and-seek for which he was not equipped, a repetition of his 1855 fiasco. His campaign promised to be one of the most expensive and futile parades in American military history. The Whites could hardly hurt the Indians by conquering a piece of territory, since the tribes were essentially too scattered even in peacetime. Wright's army could not stay long anywhere without starving to death. Nor could another show of force by itself be expected to break the Indians' spirit. Indian warfare was essentially a matter of dispersed, and often guerrilla, operations. The warriors might easily move out of their own territory or back in, go to the Plains or retreat into the shaggy wilderness of Canada; they could even remain invisible within their particular territory. Wright knew all this from sad experience in the Interior. Two years earlier, Owen had feared the worst if the Americans managed to hold key areas of the lower Interior: even this would simply move the tribes of the Interior plains for a while into the mountains and the buffalo country.

Moreover, there were severe limitations on the action of the White army. They had no supply lines, merely a small post to cover the Snake crossing if they retreated. An expedition like this was expected to carry absolutely everything necessary for its existence and repair, down to the last button and horseshoe. It went off into the blue like some old sailing ship, not to be seen or even perhaps heard from for many weeks. Nor could Clarke afford to tie down for long in the Interior so much of the nation's military strength. A lengthy campaign could spell disaster elsewhere. After all, this decade of the '50s saw no less than 22 separate wars with Indian tribes. During the past year of 1857 alone, 37 expeditions had been dispatched into actual combat; 68 permanent and 70 temporary forts required garrisons. The small professional army simply had to be kept free and fluid. To achieve this in 1858, every regiment in the army was to average 1,234 miles of marching. Short wars and high mobility were a military necessity.

Major Garnett wrestled with the problem. He was no amateur. The son of a prominent Virginia family (his father represented that state through five terms in Congress), Garnett had been an instructor at West Point, won notice for his bravery in the Mexican War, served for two years as aide-de-camp to General Taylor, and put in two years in the Seminole campaign and then two more on the Texas frontier. A slightly built man, his small head framed neatly by a close-trimmed beard with mustache, the Major was

58. Stevens Papers, Nesmith to Stevens, 20 August (not pub. in Todd); Stevens to Nesmith, 3 August; Todd, *PNWQ, 31,* 445. *SED,* 35 Cong., 2 sess., 1 (1858), p. 572.

austere, aloof, and rather gloomy. Garnett now cautioned Clarke that Wright had to disguise the hugeness of his column from the Indians or else "they will simply retire and disperse before it as the[y] did in '56." He expressed the opinion that this kind of expedition was futile until the country "between us and the Blackfeet"—in other words all the Interior and mountain region—"shall become fettered with two or three strong Military posts." Only then can the Whites hold the Indians in subjection. Public opinion demands an expedition now, Garnett went on, so we shall have to give them one. But the Indians can refuse to fight the army. Garnett also suggested that his superiors enunciate a consistent policy for himself and Wright. What was the war's purpose? Somehow it should be made clear to the Indians that the Whites controlled events and could end the war on their own terms. His own contribution toward solving this latter problem was vague enough. He favored hanging Indians involved in the death of miners.[59]

The most prominent of Garnett's officers, Captain James Archer, was equally depressed at the inevitability of failure. Archer was a Princeton man, a lawyer who had distinguished himself for gallantry in the Mexican War, winning the rank of brevet major and a vote of thanks from the Maryland legislature. He had later re-enlisted as a captain, just in time to serve through Wright's clumsy marches and skirmishings of 1856. He was soon to succeed Garnett as commander at Fort Simcoe. A cold man, something of a martinet, he was an admirable soldier; his Civil War troops would come to love him and would dub him "The Little Game Cock." Archer now predicts: "Nothing will be accomplished by the expedition except a long march"; some comfort might be drawn from the circumstance that the march went "through some of the finest scenery in the world."

Garnett's subsidiary campaign proved in fact brief and ineffectual. Even in launching out into enemy country, Garnett was not sure of Wright's destination and route. Captain Archer chronicles the march in his letters home. This "expedition against the Northern Indians" headed north from the remote "Siberian Exile" of Fort Simcoe a few days after Wright's column moved out of Fort Walla Walla. Garnett's column totaled four infantry companies: 9 officers, 286 soldiers, 225 pack animals, and 50 civilian packers and herders. Since no dragoons were available, Garnett mounted ten infantry from each company as flankers for his footsoldiers, who were strung out in single file. The column carried provisions for fifty days, with a hundred rounds of ammunition per man. Officers bore rifles instead of swords and dressed in informal flannel shirts like the men. Garnett was "spoiling for a fight"; he was deter-

59. Owen, *Journals, 1,* 136 (Owen fears). Letter from Wright camp of 16 September by "Coeur d'Alene," in *Weekly Oregonian,* 25 September 1858 (barefoot). Garnett letter of 7 July, above, n. 57.

mined to exceed his orders by crossing the Columbia, if necessary, to find his battle. Soon he sent out a raiding party of fifteen mounted men; they surprised a little village, tying several inhabitants to trees to be shot. In the dawn rush into the village Lieutenant Allen was mortally wounded, almost certainly by his own excited men.

Garnett detached two scouting forces and smaller reconnaissance units. Lieutenant Crook, with 60 men on pack mules, persuaded a friendly chief to surrender five Indians for execution. One party pursued some Indian fishermen over the mountains; the Indians doubled back for more fishing before the troops caught up to resume the chase. Eventually Garnett's frustrated army hiked as far as the mouth of the Okanogan River. Low on supplies, their footgear dangerously worn, they were happy to receive news there of Wright's victory and head back to Fort Simcoe. "Major Garnett expects that we will be back at Simcoe by 20th Sept.," Archer writes; "we will not have a fight nor meet with any further successes; the remaining hostile Indians will avoid us." One terrible tragedy struck Garnett himself: "his wife died a few days before our return to Fort Simcoe and his son a few hours after his return"; this was his pretty bride of twenty months and son of nine months.

Archer takes as sober truth Wright's reports of a decisive victory against the confederated tribes. "Our column was not so successful as Col. Wright's," he says, "most of the Indians having fled over to that side of the Columbia." He can only conclude that Indian troubles are finished "for some years to come." But the Okanogans still remained as intransigently hostile as before. Less than two months after Garnett's campaign, Archer at Fort Simcoe felt it necessary to send thirty-nine troopers under Lieutenant Alexander galloping north "to attempt the capture of some hostile Indians and murderers of white men." Seventy-five miles out the patrol had to turn back, unable to reach the trouble spot 160 miles away; luckily, some friendly Indians helped them arrest five other Indians accused of killing Whites.

Even after the Colville area was fairly well pacified the following summer, with an army garrison to police the area, Agent Lansdale did not dare penetrate the Okanogan country. The tribe, reports Lansdale, had simply "secreted themselves from Major Garnett on his expedition." All through the year after Garnett's campaign, they continued to make "many attacks" upon passing miners. Clarke was forced to report to headquarters in the East that, despite Garnett's march of over five hundred miles, "the Indians would not meet him in battle." This, then, was Garnett's contribution to the war. There were no Jesuit missionaries nearby to give it further meaning.[60]

60. Archer Corresp., letters to mother, sister, Bob, from camps and Fort Simcoe, 2 August through 20 November. Cf. also letters and accounts in newspapers such as the *Alta California*, September 2, 10, 12; Crook's account in *General George Crook, His*

THE OPPOSING FORCES

Meanwhile, troops kept coming up by steamer to The Dalles. "The most unattractive" post on the Pacific in 1855 was now a pleasant little town, with a military fort vastly improved by buildings during the past year. This was the headquarters of the Ninth Infantry under Colonel Wright; it boasted a good band and some social life for the officers. There was a regular routine for the men going up to the war: dress parade at nine, drill a half hour later, target practice at noon, drill at five, and guard mount shortly afterward. Captain Keyes, in charge of the artillery companies, reported that "the men are now constantly engaged, drilling, firing at a mark, and estimating distances; in a few days they will be prepared for a fight." Artillery units, at that time thought of as essentially infantry, shared this training; only one company was allowed to serve the little smooth-bore howitzers carried by the expedition.

The more than twelve-day march from The Dalles to Fort Walla Walla further tried the troops. It was as "hot as the tropics" on those barren, sun-burnt plains.[61] At Fort Walla Walla, against a far backdrop of the Blue Mountains, the soldiers again sweated in the heat of the parade ground. Colonel Wright was on hand by the last week of July, to bend a severe eye upon these efforts. There were intricate maneuvers for the infantry, by which a marching column changed into a series of fighting ranks; this amounted to a kind of ballet in which any confusion spelled disaster. Even the manner of reloading by nine separate operations, standing calmly shoulder-to-shoulder, demanded long, careful practice. But Wright especially introduced intensive drills in Indian warfare. He had his own formula for fusing the foot with the horse into one fluid force.

The dragoons had their problems. Only two regiments of this cavalry ex-

———

Autobiography (Norman, Okla., 1960), pp. 64, 68 and passim; works of Guie and Culverwell in Bib., below. Our Archer letters are unpublished, but the earlier letters and the Civil War letters are edited by C. A. Porter Hopkins, with an introduction to Archer himself, in "A Marylander in the Mexican War, Some Letters of J. J. Archer," *MHM, 54* (1959), 408–22, and "The James J. Archer Letters, a Marylander in the Civil War," *MHM, 56* (1961), 125–49. *SED* (serial 975), p. 404, Clarke letter of 2 October. Lansdale Report, in *SED,* 36 Cong., 1 sess., 2 (1859), p. 778, 1 August 1859. Fuller, *Pacific Northwest,* p. 252 (fishers). Garnett's official reports are few and uninformative (*SED,* 35 Cong., 2 Sess., 1); he gives the Allen scout at the Yakima River (14–15 Aug.), the Crook scout up the Wenatchee River (21–24 Aug.), and an unproductive scout by 60 men (25–29 Aug.), with a total of ten Indians executed. He omits such affairs as Archer's 45-minute scout of the 16th, his three-day scout 20 miles above the Wenatchee, and Crook's 20-man exploration of the Columbia on the return march.

61. Kip, *Expedition,* pp. 24–25. NA, EW, Army Commands, Dept. Pacific, LR, Keyes to Mackall, Camp near Fort Dalles, 27 June.

isted. Service beyond the Rockies was considered so arduous as to bring extra pay. Though especially created for fighting Indians, the horsemen were not allowed to cut loose like the post-Civil War troopers. Even when not used as mounted infantry, they tended to function as an adjunct to the more important infantry body. The Interior country into which these few dragoon auxiliaries were headed was very hard on horses. On the peaceful jaunt of 1855, Stevens had been careful to take along a sizable herd. The commander at Fort Vancouver preferred to send up horses by water at least as far as Fort Dalles, on their way to Walla Walla, because a land journey could hurt the animals and frustrate plans involving their use.

Still, horseback was the only way to travel in the region. Joset tells us that "traveling on foot would be a singularity" and impractical; "you would merely use up your time and wear out your shoes; and afterward you would have much greater difficulty replacing your shoes than your horse." Wright's infantry force did not face a march in route step down a road, but a grim cross-wilderness hike. "You would meet with obstacles at almost every step, especially if you were surprised by bad weather." [62]

During these preparations the Hudson's Bay post at Vancouver experienced an unprecedented prosperity, happily supplying the army and assisting with the freighting. War may be, as General Sherman put it, hell. But not for local businessmen. Immediately upon Steptoe's defeat, the post had prepared for "large sales to the American troops for their new war." Mactavish and Grahame kept an informative flow of letters moving from Fort Vancouver; on July 30 Governor Simpson in Canada acknowledged the receipt of letters of "2, 3, 19, and 21 June." Simpson cautioned against allowing payment to be deferred by the military during these anticipated purchases; delayed accounts should be thoroughly certified to expedite future payment.

Mactavish gleefully reported to Simpson on June 19 as the troops arrived: "this expedition to the Spokanes is a grand thing for us all as it will put quite a lot of money into circulation, of which I hope we shall get a share; three companies of Soldiers came here from California last night, and some five or six more will accompany General Clarke." In good mercantile fashion he kept the higher administrators informed. Two days later he wrote that Clarke "is looked for daily at this garrison, and it is said, will immediately dispatch one thousand soldiers to the Spokane Country." On the 28th he announced that "General Clarke is now at the garrison; and as troops arrive from California, they are immediately sent on to the Dalles; it is supposed that the expedition-

62. NA, EW, Army Commands, Dept. Pacific, LR, Col. Morris to Mackall, Fort Vancouver, 18 April (horses). RJ, "Quelques remarques"; also in *JMUS,* 2, 319–20 (Joset).

ary force, in pursuit of the Spokane Indians, will cross the Snake River to-wards the close of next month." [63]

When General Harney arrived to replace Clarke, Simpson praised Mac-tavish for cultivating friendly relations with the new general for commercial motives. Simpson reported to London that "Military preparations on a grand scale are going forward" and that "it is proposed to march 1000 men into that country"; he remarked that the troops depended a great deal for their provisioning upon the Company. Much of this material had to be supplied on credit; later in the year the American secretary of War would return a favorable reply "respecting the claim of the Hudson's Bay Company for supplies furnished to the troops engaged in suppressing Indian hostility in Oregon and Washington." There were minor drawbacks incident to this commerce. "Recruits just out from New York have devastated our garden and orchard" during their brief stay. And Hudson's Bay pack trains, loaded with the annual supply of powder for Colville, had been immobilized.[64]

On the morning of August 7, with Fort Walla Walla securely garrisoned under Steptoe, an advance guard for the Wright expedition moved up to the Snake. At this crossing point it was swift, deep, and over 255 yards wide. In a gorge here the advance guard began to set up the depot Fort Taylor. The main body soon followed. The march up consumed two dusty, unpleasant days. The Indians had set afire "the entire plains from Walla Walla to the Snake river" in order to deprive the Whites of forage for their many hundreds of animals. Letters from soldiers speak graphically of a "lake of fire."

Field returns at the end of the campaign describe the bulk of Wright's army as 310 privates from the Third Artillery, 72 from the Ninth Infantry, and 123 First Dragoons. The more than 500 total was amply officered by a colonel, 2 majors, 6 captains, 15 lieutenants, 3 medical officers, 36 sergeants, and 29 corporals; 18 musicians went along, presumably as infantry drummers and dragoon buglers. "Altogether the Indians can have plenty of fighting to do if they want it." [65]

Fort Taylor, a small parallelogram of basalt rock with two towers, soon stood completed. A company of artillery acting as infantry remained here, fifty miles north of Fort Walla Walla. At 5 A.M. on August 25 the first units began crossing the Snake. Lieutenant Kip and official reports both list the column's strength as an "aggregate 570." This figure does not include the nu-

63. HB, D4, *54*, Simpson Corresp. out, Ser. 1, to Mactavish, 30 July 1858; *46*, letters in, 19, 21, 28 June 1858. On American war-profiteering see De Smet, in CR, *2*, 749.
64. HB, D4, *55*, Simpson Corresp. out, 2 February 1859; *78*, 2 August 1858; D5, *47*, letters in, 21 December, and 4 September 1858.
65. Kip, *Expedition*, p. 39 (first quot.). *Weekly Oregonian*, 28 August 1858, citing letters from camp. NA, EW, AGO, LR, 290c, November 30 field returns. Suckley Papers (YU), No. 21, from anon., Fort Steilacoom, 29 August (last quot.).

merous civilian employees. Lieutenant Mullan added his contingent of 30 Nez Percés in incongruous military blue, their alliance sealed by a war dance. The expedition carried along subsistence for 38 days, 800 "animals of all kinds," and "a very wholesome respect for the Indians who had so thoroughly defeated Steptoe's command." Camp talk centered on this supply tether for a month and a week, "during which time we must find and beat the enemy" in a country "almost unknown to us." [66]

Already there had been the disconcerting spectacle of a scorched-earth policy in the country below the Snake. Some shooting occurred at the river itself. And a vigorous personal combat in the water had engaged the energies of hotheaded Lieutenant Mullan against "an exceedingly athletic savage, the sight of whose proportions would have tempered most persons' valor with discretion." Wright's cumbersome array lumbered slowly toward the northern horizon—infantry, Indians, cavalry screen, mule train, spare horses and mules, beef cattle herd, and a rabble of some 100 civilian packers, herders, waggoners, and the like. At their head rode the unmartial but reassuring figure of Colonel Wright. He was a stolid, stern, and just Vermonter, with a hint of humor and humanity on his face and with combat experience in Seminole, Mexican, and Interior wars.

As the troops began their march, a prolonged summer storm had just cleared the air. Soon the heat would dry the ground, and the terrible dust would rise to obscure this grand cavalcade and call attention to its progress. On this farther side of the Snake again, as had been the case from Walla Walla to the river, the land had been deliberately burnt over.

Slowly the command toiled up the bluffs to the high tableland or grass plateau, which rolled to the Palouse and beyond that to the Spokane. Behind them, civilization and safety dropped rapidly from sight. Lieutenant Mullan was probably not alone in worrying about this unprotected rear; a general uprising behind them, "if once commenced, must end in our destruction." The Americans were marching toward the center of a multitribal powder keg. [67]

What awaited the troops beyond the desolate horizon? The confederated tribes, glorying in their past victories, had gathered for a great stand in the open. They had never felt anything but irritation for the blundering of the volunteer militia in previous wars, and the Steptoe fiasco convinced them that there was nothing to fear from the professional warriors. As with Steptoe,

66. Kip, *Expedition*, p. 51 (last quot.); Wright Report. Genl. (then Lieut.) M. R. Morgan, "Recollections of the Spokane Expedition," *Journal of the Military Service Institution of the United States*, 42 (1908), 492 ("respect" quot.).

67. Kip, *Expedition*, pp. 41, 51 (Mullan fight); Mullan letter to Mix, 5 September (quot.); *SED* (serial 974).

they hoped to draw off the few mounted men and engage them, leaving the despised infantry to be destroyed later at will. They meant to harry Wright's force, allowing it no time to reach any objective, dictating the terms of battle by striking first and decisively. They kept his army under observation from the moment it left Fort Walla Walla, making no secret of their close presence. Scouts brought back reports of the rich booty in horses, arms, and equipment being carried into the upper Interior by the White soldiers. Chief Stellam of the Coeur d'Alenes many years afterward remembered how "our hearts were overjoyed, because we thought it was all for us." [68]

Later in 1858 the secretary of War reported to the president that the Steptoe Disaster was "the signal for a general rising of the tribes, and an alliance was speedily formed between the powerful tribes of Spokanes and Coeur d'Alenes, together with many straggling warriors from amongst the Pelouses and other tribes." The historian Bancroft has Wright outnumber the Indians by "at least one or two hundred" men. But Lieutenant Kip estimates that the Indians "outnumbered us." And Wright reports 400 to 500 warriors on the plain, plus the "large numbers" in the wood. The Indian force for the second battle was to be somewhat bigger. Kip elsewhere brings the total down to 500; and a letter from Mullan after the first battle speaks of only 300 or 400 Indians. [69]

Less than half of the Coeur d'Alene warriors stayed out of the first battle but "did follow the Kalispels to the second battle." The Kalispels had recently debated "for several days" about joining as a tribe. The war party was unable to prevail, so the council broke up in anger. When a war dance was staged, very few braves joined in. One warrior named Xanewa eventually raised a party of about twenty-five; these were to fight against the army in both battles. As for the Pend d'Oreilles, a war party of a "very few" disassociated themselves from their tribe to join the hostiles. They fought under a famous war chief named Spotted Coyote. [70] Of the Walla Wallas, Wright says: "I know that many of them were opposed to me." In his angry council with them later, thirty or forty voluntarily stood forward as having taken part in the battles; allowing for the many absent or diffident braves, the full Walla Walla contingent must have been much larger. In his annual report for 1859 Agent Cain says that "many of the influential men" were prominent in the war and the Walla Walla tribe itself was hostile.

Kamiakin was on the battlefield with a large but indeterminate number of

68. CR, 2, 755 (De Smet-Joset on Indian reactions now, plans); Kip, *Expedition*, p. 86 and passim. Stellam Reminiscence.

69. SED (serial 975), p. 4. Bancroft, *Washington*, p. 187. Mullan letter of 5 September; Kip, *Expedition*, pp. 59, 64; Wright battle report of 2 September, SED (serial 975).

70. CR, 2, 755. Cf. Teit, BAE *Annual Report*, 45, 371.

Yakimas. Both Red and White evidence indicates that the Palouses were particularly prominent, rivaling the Spokanes or Coeur d'Alenes in size and importance. Cain has "nearly all" the tribe active in the war. The Kettles, too, were well represented; a considerable number of them would remain adamantly hostile long after the campaign, refusing all peace overtures. Individual Canadian Indians probably appeared on the battlefield. The usual Nez Percés were on hand.[71]

The Canadian Okanogans were repeatedly solicited to join the war. Head Chief Nicholas, a doughty old warrior, did sympathize with these friends and neighbors. Nevertheless, he stubbornly advocated peace, partly because this was a head chief's duty but also because the tribe inclined rather to lend their energies to the Thompsons in their war against the miners on the Fraser River. The miner Reinhart, who reached Fort Thompson at this time with a party of 300, particularly commends the policy of friendliness adopted by Chief Nicholas and by other Catholic Canadian tribes beyond; "the friendly Indians were all Catholics and had priests at the fort." A cognate tribe, the Southern Okanogans, well armed and somewhat larger than the combined Spokane tribes, were committed to the war. They had been active in the troubles of 1855–57. It was against their southernmost band that Garnett was driving. Wright, like Garnett, would find himself unable to do anything about them. It is almost certain that they had representatives on our battlefields.

At this time the Southern Okanogan chief Tonasket was trying to rouse the neighboring Nespelims and cognate San Poils against the Whites. Tonasket was not a chief but a kind of *condottiere* who headed, and perhaps originated, one of the four Southern Okanogan bands. A warrior of fame, he was a mean man who beat his wife and was disliked even by his own band. He had made a business of attacking miners, until one day he bluffed them into paying tribute to him as head chief of the Okanogans. From that day forward the Whites endowed him with tributes, gifts, the reputation of peacemaker, and the office of head chief. The Indians refused to admit this fraudulent latter function. But as in the case of the more legitimate Spokane Garry, White recognition tended to create a fiction which the Indians upon occasion found useful.

Splawn, who met Tonasket in 1861, says he had an unusually "fine-looking" face and was a "grand-looking fellow, big and strong," imposingly accoutered. He was a Catholic. Captain Archer, as head of the escort with the international boundary workers shortly after the present war, had "frequent" dealings with Tonasket. Archer says the chief "has great authority" over his

71. Quotes from NA, EW, AGO, LR, Wright to Mackall, 9 October 1858. Cain Report, in *SED*, 36 Cong., 1 sess., 2 (1859), pp. 782, 784.

Okanogans and "is a gentleman in comparison with the Simcoe Indians." Tonasket's tribe "are the most manly Indians I have ever seen and are said to be the best warriors in the two territories." The chief was to become an important cattleman before his death, which occurred in 1891 while he was returning home from the surgical removal of an eye.[72]

Between the Southern Okanogans and the Western Spokanes lived the San Poils. Gibbs listed them among the Spokanes while noting that the Okanogans also claimed them. Their country lay along the Columbia amid treeless deserts of great temperature ranges, extending over some 1,600 square miles of territory. They represented a cultural hangover from earlier days, with their anarchic lack of tribal development and deliberate policy of pacifism. Their sympathies lay with the embattled Spokanes; they had long been on good terms with both the Coeur d'Alenes and the Kalispels. It is indicative of how widely the war spirit had spread that both the Okanogans and the Spokanes tried to bring these pacifists into the war. Their chief Kolaskin especially gave ear to one of the important Spokane chiefs, probably Polatkin; but eventually he could not bring himself to fight.[73]

Other tribes were involved in the battles against Wright. This can be seen from the Colonel's peace talks with the Cayuses, with representatives from the Isle des Pierres or Sinkiuse-Columbia people, and with warriors from upper Interior tribes smaller than the Columbias or Kettles. Since the context of his activities excludes the better known groupings, these latter individuals must be from Lake bands, Nespelims, San Poils, or from trans-Columbia tribes like the Methows, Chelans, and Wenatchis. It is impossible to say how many of these were included among those other, smaller tribes represented at the peace.

Most of the Interior tribes, then, were to some degree implicated in the Garnett-Wright campaign. The Nez Percés were the only tribe who contributed bodies of fighters to both sides, perhaps more to the hostiles than to the Americans. Wright's treaty with the friendly Nez Percés provided for alliance and mutual aid. Whites like Lieutenant Mullan and General Clarke carelessly assumed that this treaty somehow ensured the good conduct of all the Nez Percé groupings. Head Chief Lawyer's association with the project may have misled them. But the active signers were relatively lesser chiefs. At least one of these, Three Feathers, was certainly against the Americans though he may not have fought.[74]

72. Teit, pp. 269 (Nicholas), 270–71. Cline, *Southern Okanagon*, pp. 83–84 (esp. Tonasket); Splawn, *Ka-Mi-Akin*, pp. 167–68; Reinhart, *Recollections*, p. 128; Brown, *Indian Side*, pp. 404–14 (eye); Archer Corresp., 7 September 1859.

73. V. F. Ray, *The Sanpoil and Nespelem: Salishan Peoples of Northeastern Washington* (Seattle, 1932), pp. 85, 109, esp. 115. Cf. Gibbs in *RR*, *1*, ii, 412, 414.

74. *SED* (serial 975), pp. 369–70 (treaty and allied documentation).

The aggregate of some 500 hostile confederates, an unusual number to be acting in concert when one considers the fragmented tribal situation of the Interior, represented only the enthusiastic first volunteers. More cautious or traditionally pacific tribesmen, not to mention those who had been persuaded by the Jesuits to refrain, might yet be swept into the alliance by news of a resounding victory. When the Coeur d'Alenes mingled with the soldiers during the later peace talks, they explained to Kip and his colleagues how an initial success would immediately have doubled the Indian numbers. Runners could then have gathered in even the most remotely distant tribes for a total annihilation of the Whites.

DAYS OF BATTLE

A year later Father De Smet traveled from Fort Walla Walla to the Spokane River along the route now being taken by the soldiers. His description of the countryside in the fall re-creates the contemporary scene for us. "The whole region is undulating and hilly, and though generally of a light soil, it is covered with a rich and nutritious grass, forming grazing fields where thousands of cattle might be easily raised; it is almost destitute of timber until you are within thirty miles of the Spokan[e] Prairie, where you find open woods and clusters of trees scattered far and wide." On these "continuous rolling plains," somewhat more level than the plains of Walla Walla, "wood is scarce" and "water fails in autumn."

Kip tells us the weather was hot and arid during the march, and unpleasantly sultry. Men easily grew exhausted. "Every little while one would fall out of the ranks," to be revived by the surgeon. Mullan records the route as "hot and dusty"; the men "suffered severely." Yet Wright was keeping to fairly easy country, avoiding the kind of terrain that had trapped Steptoe. Walking would in any case have been difficult; the weight of arms and equipment made it an ordeal. The soldier's canteen became the focus of his day. Unhappily the army was experimenting with rubber canteens in place of tin; Wright later confessed to his superiors that they proved "worthless." [75]

On the march shoes went to pieces, some of them after only three days. Wright was to enter "great complaint" concerning them. He estimated that a soldier would need new shoes every month of active duty if this quality were permitted. The simple problem of shoes limited Wright's movements considerably. On similar expeditions, after three months of chasing Indians, one's "shoes are absolutely worn out, and the best of mending will do no good." If

---

75. CR, 3, 970 (1859), 2, 746 (1861). Kip, *Expedition*, p. 78. NA, EW, AGO, LR, 290c, Wright to Mackall, Camp near Fort Walla Walla, 8 October 1858. Mullan, *Topographical Memoir*, p. 15.

this was true of good shoes, so that men were eventually reduced to going barefoot or to wearing makeshift moccasins of untanned hide, it is easy to imagine the Colonel's more serious plight.[76]

Wright moved his army slowly, averaging not much more than ten miles a day. Already he had changed his strategy. Beyond the Palouse River he found the country still without grass for the animals; it lay blackened and burnt to the far horizon, and promised to continue so to the north indefinitely. When Wright considered also "the lateness of the season," the problem of getting water, the fact that the Indians held the initiative, and the way the country favored ambush, he was uneasy. On the eve of the march he had written despondently: "from all that I can learn, we must not expect the enemy to meet us in pitched battle." The Indians will rely upon "a guerrilla warfare," upon the harshness of the countryside and season, and upon burning the grass so as to dismount the cavalry and destroy the pack train. If so, "serious consequences may follow." In that case the Colonel proposed to march to the Spokane River, kill his horses and mules, and walk home. At the Snake all vision of glory had faded completely. "For several days past the country north of us has been enveloped in flames." Without grass "it would be worse than madness to plunge into that barren waste, the inevitable result of which must be the sacrifice of men and animals." He conceded that failure would be "mortifying," but protested that he could not beat the elements.

Wright had seen the Steptoe Disaster write finis to an able career; he must have trembled for his own. One can imagine his relief when the Nez Percé scouts now announced that the hostiles had concentrated in the open, some twenty miles below the Spokane River. Wright therefore changed his strategy, away from the Coeur d'Alene objective. He meant to march directly north to strike the allies. His former plan had been fatuous, a counsel of despair; the present opportunity was golden. Wright was fearful, nevertheless, that the Indians were merely enticing him deeply into the country. He rested his army in successive camps as best he could. To guard against surprise he had the soldiers stand to arms every morning an hour before daylight. Horses were tethered at half length, reducing the area being defended at the camp.[77]

The countryside continually bore a gloomy and forbidding aspect. For long periods the soldiers tramped over burnt, ashy desolation. Everywhere there were "signs" of the omnipresent Red man. Soon a desultory exchange of fire broke out between sentinels and scouting hostiles. Four days out on the swelling grasslands, a few Indians appeared in the distance. As Wright's men camped later that afternoon, in a low-lying and badly chosen spot, the

76. Bandel, *Frontier Army*, p. 128 (last quot.).
77. Wright Report, 14, 19 August, *SED*, (Serial 975), pp. 383–84. Trimble reminiscence, *OHQ, 8*, tells of tethering, early rise.

warriors swept down on a hit-and-run raid. Some infantry moved against them, together with a squadron of dragoons. To the bugle call of Boots and Saddles, a lively but brief cavalry chase ensued. On the following day, the last day of August, the enemy again appeared in force, on the hills to the column's right, evoking alarm and scattered firing. The marching troops closed up nervously. Dragoons deployed as a protective screen.

All day the warriors kept increasing in numbers. In the late afternoon they cut off the overconfident little band of Nez Percé scouts and almost overwhelmed them; a dragoon force thundered to the rescue. This episode was followed by a "strong demonstration" against the supply train at the rear, carried on with annoying persistence. The rear guard formed a hollow square and, with infantry flankers, "handsomely dispersed" the attackers. "The grass was set on fire at many points," but luckily was too green at this place to burn as far as the troops. The soldiers later learned that these Indians were only scouts, sent out to lure them toward a field of battle already chosen by the tribes. The White command was proceeding by this time through a country less turbulently swelling and broken than before. There were scattered pines and "long skirts of timber." For three days the column had been able to glimpse the distant ridges of the Coeur d'Alene mountains far off in the hazy distance, and beyond them a faint view of the Rockies. The attitude of the Indian war parties made it obvious that battle was near.[78]

On the first day of September 1858 "at four beautiful lakes in the Spokane Plain, skirted by beautiful open pine forests," the army came upon the full Indian force spoiling for a fight. Many were in front of them, "defiant and insolent." The main body, they learned, lay just beyond. The two forces were now in the center of the Eastern Spokanes' territory, very close to the land of Garry's segment of that tribe, and southwest of the site of present Spokane city. De Smet characterizes these Spokane lands in general as "immense plains of light, dry and sandy soil, and thin forests of gum pines." Lieutenant Saxton, almost five years to the month before the battle, describes our particular region as boasting "beautiful, open pine forest" which was "interspersed with fine lakes and ponds."[79]

That morning Wright garrisoned his camp strongly, directing the bulk of his force against a distant high hill which seemed to be central to the Indians' defenses. This hill the United States Geographic Board was later to name Battle Butte. Grier took a column of dragoons around to intercept the Indians as they came down. Wright moved the main body of infantry more directly at

78. Wright Report, 31 August, *SED* (serial 975), p. 386 (attack quots.); Mullan Memoir, in *SED* (serial 984), p. 17 (fire, descriptive quots.).

79. Mullan Memoir, *SED*, p. 32 (first quot.). Wright Report, 2 September, *SED*, pp. 386–90. See Kip, *Expedition*, for details. CR, *1*, 379 (1842). *RR, 12*, i, 109 (1853); cf. p.252.

the hill. There was brisk fighting, the Indians soon retreating "pell-mell down the hill." An artillery company, acting in cooperation with a squadron of dragoons, secured the summit. From the top the troops had a splendid view of the country: four fine lakes just at their feet, "surrounded by rugged rocks" and fringed with pines, in a vast plain of "bare grassy hills, one succeeding another as far as the eye could reach" to the northeast, with a dim view of forested mountains in the distance.[80]

Lieutenant Kip was forcibly struck by the Indian panoply below him. "Every spot seemed alive with the wild warriors we had come so far to meet." To his amazed eye "they seemed to cover the country for two miles," thickly moving "in the pines on the edge of the lakes, in the ravines and gullies, and swarming over the plain." Unlike Steptoe, Kip estimated that their arms were Hudson's Bay muskets, together with bows and arrows and long lances. "Mounted on their fleet hardy horses, the crowd swayed back and forth, brandishing their weapons, shouting their war cries, and keeping up a song of defiance." The scene sparkled with movement and color. "They were all in the bravery of their war array, gaudily painted and decorated with their wild trappings; their plumes fluttered above them, while below skins and trinkets and all kinds of fantastic embellishments flaunted in the sunshine."

Their very horses were "arrayed in the most glaring finery; some were even painted, and with colors to form the greatest contrast, the white being smeared with crimson in fantastic figures, and the dark-colored streaked with white clay; beads and fringes of gaudy color were hanging from their bridles, while the plumes of eagles' feathers, interwoven with the mane and tail, fluttered as the breeze swept over them and completed their wild and fantastic appearance." The lieutenant stood there on his hilltop "in admiration" while through his head ran the lines:

> By heavens! it was a glorious sight to see
> The gay array of their wild chivalry.

Another observer was rather shaken by the sight: the Indians plunging and milling on the plain below seemed "like fiends incarnate." [81]

The Indians had probably not meant to hold this hill. Most were gathered on the plain, "showing no disposition to avoid a combat, and firmly maintaining their position at the base of the hill." Wright prepared to send his men down the hill and over the plain. A lake protected his left flank; but the pine forest on his right sheltered "large numbers" of Indians. He shifted his how-

80. Wright Report; "Coeur d'Alene" letter, *Weekly Oregonian*, 18 September 1858 (first quot.); Kip, *Expedition*, p. 55 (descriptive quots.). EW, C. B. Sloane, secretary of board, to J. Barry, June 1922 (name).

81. Kip, *Expedition;* "Coeur d'Alene" letter, *Weekly Oregonian*, 18 September 1858 (final quot.).

itzer to "a lower plateau" of the hill to achieve greater effect. The shells began to rise slow and high in their parabola toward the pine forest. Two companies of the artillery acting as infantry were shaken out into a skirmish line and sent down the hill, through the waiting dragoons on the slope, firing and loading with mechanical precision, driving the Indians before them onto the open plain.[82]

Two more companies of rifles, with a squadron of dragoons, advanced at a right angle like a long, thin, blue line into the pine woods. Their "spirited attack" met with "a vigorous resistance." But with help from both howitzer and Sharps they "dislodged the enemy and compelled them to take refuge on the hills." Amid a crash of musketry and shouting men, this action passed "beyond view," later to sweep around in an arc to emerge again on the plain, falling into line as the extended right wing of a united front.

From the hilltop one could see the companies moving down with enthusiasm and with "all the precision of a parade," opening fire at 600 yards and delivering it "steadily as they advanced." It was something of a pageant, the impersonal blue figures going through a drill, battle flags tossing, and officers urging them on. The heavy black powder of those days tended to settle heavily on the ground and to drift with any air current in streamers and soiled wreaths, blackening the soldiers as they fired.[83]

The Indians continued to fire and fall back, darting forward as opportunity offered, "with a quickness and irregularity which rendered it difficult to reach them." There seemed to be no order. "They were wheeling and dashing about, always on the run, apparently each fighting on his own account." The Whites could see, or thought they saw, "one Indian reel in his saddle and fall,—then, two or three,—then, half a dozen." Rifle balls frequently thumped upon Indian horses, causing them to spurt madly. As soon as a warrior fell, his companions galloped by and dragged him away.

According to Chief Stellam of the Coeur d'Alenes, reminiscing perhaps inaccurately thirty years later, the braves had begun their battle in roughly tribal grouping. The prominent figure at their right wing was Kamiakin with his Yakimas and Palouses. The Spokanes and other tribes had gathered particularly on the left. Among those in the center were the Coeur d'Alenes. The Pend d'Oreille war chief Spotted Coyote believed himself bulletproof; he rode the full length of the battle line twice, challenging the soldiers to kill him.[84]

---

82. Cf. Wright Report.

83. Kip, *Expedition*, p. 56 (quots.); Wright Report ("parade").

84. Kip, *Expedition*, pp. 56–57 (quots.); Stellam Reminiscence; Teit, BAE *Annual Report*, 45, 37 (Coyote). Stellam presents this and the following fight as a single action, as the Indians probably saw it; this makes it difficult to assign specific details in proper order.

But the battle was about to take a decisive turn. When the Indians had been herded onto the plain, the dragoons in a special drill led their horses through the infantry intervals, then mounted and charged "with lightning speed." Wright proclaims it "the most brilliant, gallant, and successful charge I have ever beheld." And indeed it must have seemed like something from a story book—the disciplined positioning as the wild, clear bugle calls rang out, the hard-riding line slowly rolling forward and gathering speed, and then the full thundering gallop in dust and heat, sabers glinting like flames in the sun. Even from his hilltop Lieutenant Kip could hear "the voice of Major Grier ringing over the plain as he shouted—'Charge the rascals!' and on the dragoons went at headlong speed." Lieutenant Davidson shot one warrior from his saddle; Lieutenant Gregg clove the skull of another. "We saw the flash of their sabers as they cut them down."

The horses were blown after a mile of this, and the Indians had slipped away easily into clumps of trees or places where the dragoon horses could not follow. The weary infantry line trudged up meanwhile as best it could, prepared to repeat the maneuver. But they did not advance far. For one thing, there were no more Indians in sight. For another, the men were "so totally exhausted that many had fallen out of the ranks." A band of venturesome braves remaining in the distance were scattered with a howitzer burst. The leader of the Kalispels, Xanewa, had died during the charge, run down by the dragoons. One dragoon caught him by the hair and threw him from his horse; others shot him while he lay on the ground. Either here or in the next battle, according to army sources, Spokane Garry lost two brothers.

A Kettle chief from near the Canadian border, who wished to observe the soldiers before committing himself to war, was appalled by the action at Four Lakes. Returning to his tribe, he assured them "he had seen the soldiers, but never wished to see them again." He advised his people always to seek friendship with the Whites. What especially impressed the chief were the long-range rifles and the steadfastness of the White soldiers.[85]

Wright now sounded recall. The weary men passed back through the litter of defeat. Around them lay a pathetic scattering of muskets, quivers, bows, blankets, and robes; riderless horses were "roaming about." White estimates now and later assessed the enemy dead at something under twenty, their wounded at something under fifty. The Nez Percé allies of the Whites had got out of control early in the fight and contributed little. Mullan "found their individuality developed so strongly that it was difficult for him to induce them to obey orders," so each Nez Percé fought "on his own responsi-

85. Wright Report; Kip, *Expedition*, pp. 57, 92–93 (Kettle); Teit, p. 371 (Xanewa; cf. Kip, *Expedition*, dead chief on p. 64). Jessett, *Spokan Garry*, p. 148 n.

bility." In the next battle therefore Wright used them "chiefly as spies and guides, as well as guards to the pack train." But in this present moment of glory they continued on for some eight or ten miles beyond the troops, coming back with "some scalps." [86]

The elated soldiers filed back into camp and stacked arms. Four hours had passed. It was time for lunch. There was, of course, no hope of pursuing the Indians. The men and particularly the tired horses needed several days' rest in camp. To judge from the lyrical effusion Wright now composed in lieu of a report, he was in a state of high euphoria. In his special commendations he even directed the attention of the War Department to the regimental assistant surgeon, who had stood by "ever ready to attend to his professional duties." The item reads oddly when one remembers that not a single White suffered even a wound in the action. Lieutenant Ransom became unhorsed, but the Nez Percé allies retrieved his animal from the hostiles. Lieutenant Pender's horse took a ball in the neck, not too badly.

The weather at this point "entirely changed, growing damp and cold." All the Indians seemed to have disappeared; the Nez Percé scouts were unable to locate them. Actually they were out gathering reinforcements (such as the peace party of the Coeur d'Alenes), and reassessing their tactics. They realized, as Joset remarks, that "it was not as at the first engagement"; the howitzer fire "crackling over their heads in all their ambuscades, then falling in the midst of their flight," had disheartened them. Instead of meeting the dragoons, as they had planned, they had been forced back by the implacable advance of the infantry who had come on like "bears," neither retiring to reload nor lessening their fire. When the dragoons finally appeared, they had poured out in a stunning, torrential shock. Wisely the Indians fled the field. They had sustained no great losses, and they had learned some important lessons.

From camp Lieutenant Mullan composed a long letter to the commissioner of Indian Affairs. Though he had just participated in a "memorable, never to be forgotten fight," Mullan's mood was sober, even despondent. "We are in the midst of another Indian war, fraught with what results, and of what duration the future alone must tell." The fighting thus far had left Mullan, a West Pointer and a man of experience in the Interior, "confident that the campaign in which we are now engaged cannot be completed this season." He excoriates Superintendent Nesmith: "where are his headquarters? in the southern portion of the Willamette valley, in a quiet, civilized spot, where Indians are not and war rages not, while hundreds of miles and thousands of Indians are left unvisited and unseen." Mullan complained that the superintendent had

86. Kip, *Expedition*, pp. 59–60, 44. Wright Report ("spies").

never seen a single one of the Indians the army was now fighting; he did concede that Nesmith's job was impossible for any man.[87]

Only on September 5 did Wright's command resume its march, skirting the large lake and finally emerging from the pine-covered region onto a vast prairie. Here they again encountered the tribes in force. Swinging along in the fresh morning air, the soldiers could see the enemy "collecting in large bodies on our right," paralleling the line of march for "some time" at a distance, "all the while increasing in numbers and becoming bolder." The Indians had chosen their terrain well. "The ground was so broken that dragoons could not operate effectively." The warriors concentrated in a pine woods on the right. As the White line of march closed in toward the woods, it became obvious that the enemy were preparing to attack.

Soon "they advanced in great force," firing the dry prairie both to the front of the troops and on the right flank. This was an unnerving tactic. With the wind "blowing high and against us," Kip says, "we were nearly enveloped by the flames." Great, choking billows of smoke boiled up to obscure the warriors as they slipped in under the farther range of the long rifles. Wright's advantage in fire power was seriously diminished. The Indians "poured in their fire." Wright, who was almost killed in this opening action, reacted with promptitude. He had his pack trains driven to a central position, "amidst the dust and smoke, and the noise and shouting of the Mexican muleteers," while two companies of foot and one of dragoons coolly formed a guard around them.[88]

The artist Sohon, who had been helping Mullan's road-building project and had followed the lieutenant on the campaign, chose this moment for his sketch of the day's battle. In the foreground he shows the frightened animals jammed together, necks tensed and heads lifted. Along the fringes of this confusion, bearded dragoon guards, or possibly civilian aides, are slouched in their saddles. On a slight rise in the middle distance Colonel Wright and his mounted regimental staff are busy; one officer seems about to ride away with orders. Filing into the middle distance from right and from left are single columns of infantry.

A long thin line of skirmishers, with considerable space between each soldier, is advancing toward the flames. In dust clouds to the left of them, the dragoons rapidly canter forward. Enormous volumes of smoke, very much like cloud formations, billow up all along the right and front, dwarfing the little figures in the advance. Along the fringes of the smoke one catches a hint of malicious flames. The country falls away in great undulating rolls. Beyond

87. Joset Narrative; Kip, *Expedition*, pp. 63, 85–86 (weather; bears). *SED*, 35 Cong., 2 sess., 1 (1858), pp. 629–35, Mullan letter, 5 August.

88. Kip, *Expedition*, pp. 63–64; Wright Report (ground broken).

the brow of one such roll, in a space blown free of smoke, can be seen a rabble of Indian warriors riding. The thin forest of pines is suggested, as are the distant mountains beyond them. Dashing along this uneven country the Indians achieved "feats of horsemanship which we have never seen equalled." Some riders threw their mounts down slopes of forty-five degree incline as headlong as though on level ground.[89]

Wright could do nothing where he was. He determined to charge his troops directly through the enveloping crescent of "roaring flames." Deploying three companies of artillery as skirmishers to his front and one company to his left flank, he sounded the advance. A rifle company and the howitzers gave direct support. "The firing now became brisk on all sides"; as "not a moment was to be lost," the entire command plunged through the blinding smoke and fire onto the hot, charred ground beyond. The timber in front of them "now swarmed with the red devils, bellowing and yelling like fiends from Hades." The foot went in after them, doggedly as though on drill, firing by volley. This phase of the battle soon developed into a continuous brawl, lasting almost seven hours and covering some fourteen miles of ground up to the Spokane River. "The enemy was braver and bolder than Indian enemies usually are, and only left the field from the most dire necessity."[90]

The Indians were not to be caught so easily as yesterday. Their fire plan having failed, they fought courageously, retreating cleverly whenever the Whites came too close. When reasonably large bodies of warriors collected at any point in the woods, Wright searched them out and flushed them with howitzer fire; he estimated that eight shells landed in the enemy's midst during the running battle. "Then the foot charged them again, driving them from cover to cover, from behind the trees and rocks, and through the ravines and cañons, until the woods for more than four miles, which lately seemed perfectly alive with their yelling and shouting, were entirely cleared." The scramble continued over rock formations and out onto the plain. Here yesterday's tactics were repeated: the dragoons sifted through the infantry intervals, then mounted and sounded the charge.

Yet the Indians continued to regroup in the woods "on every side." A company of infantry went to clear a hill on the right; two companies were thrust into the woods on the left where a "sharp contest" ensued. Eventually the column managed to re-form, with considerable bodies of troops acting as flankers. "Skirmishing continued all the way." By the end of the day the troops had marched twenty-five miles, "the last fourteen miles fighting all the way." Having filled their canteens in the morning, they had no other water

89. Ewers, *Sohon's Portraits*, reproduces scene. Kip, *Expedition*, p. 63 (quot.).

90. Wright Report; "Coeur d'Alene" letter, *Weekly Oregonian*, 18 September 1858 (final two quots.).

all day. The men were "entirely exhausted." They kept themselves going only by "the excitement of the contest." Finally, the declining sun in their eyes, they reached the Spokane River. Here Wright put his weary command into bivouac.[91]

At least some Indians did not retreat very far; the soldiers could see their campfires a few miles away. It had been a disconcerting battle. As before, not a single White man had been killed, though one was slightly wounded. Very few Indians had been hurt, so few that the Coeur d'Alenes apparently knew nothing of these rare casualties. De Smet would refer to the action of this day as "the second battle, if battle there was, for no lives were lost in it"; from the first "it was practically no fight, but a complete rout." Historians such as Bancroft, Victor, and Splawn err in reporting two Coeur d'Alene chiefs killed.

The tribes had learned for the second time that they should not compete on even terms with an equal body of infantry. They also learned more about howitzers. At one point, as soldiers raced to position a gun on a hill, the Indians assumed the crew were in flight and charged up behind them; the soldiers quickly reversed the howitzer, fired, and killed a number of horses and perhaps men. Later, Kamiakin "was knocked senseless by a limb that was broken off by a cannon shot." The most successful tactic used by the tribes in this second battle had been that of setting the grass afire. Many years later Chief Stellam took the credit for this idea. He added that the soldiers looked so formidable before the battle that the Indians remained "loath to commence the attack," even though "I swung myself from side to side of my horse almost in a frenzy." [92]

Wright had temporarily dissipated the Indians' will to fight. Routed in this set-piece battle, however, they merely fell back and disengaged. De Smet puts the Colonel's problem neatly. "Indian tactics render the ordinary method of warfare unavailing, and next to impracticable; the Indian is everywhere and nowhere at the same time." When the fortune of war turns against them, he says, they disappear, later regrouping elsewhere. The Indian has no towns to defend, lines of retreat to cover, or baggage train to manage. "The strategy of civilized nations is, therefore, of little use." [93] It will take the American military many years to absorb this lesson. In the spring of 1857 the war against the Cheyennes had gone along the same lines as this 1858 campaign.

91. Kip, *Expedition*, pp. 64–65; Wright Report.

92. Teit, BAE *Annual Report*, 45, 371–72 (howitzer); CR, 2, 755. Bancroft, *Washington*, p. 189; Victor, *Early Indian Wars*, p. 495; Splawn, *Ka-Mi-Akin*, p. 98. Stellam late Reminiscence (incl. Kamiakin; cf. Kip, *Expedition*, p. 66). Brown has "a few Coeur d'Alenes," perhaps four Spokanes, and four or five Palouses killed, with many wounded; demonstrable errors of detail in Brown's very late traditions add to one's skepticism over his face-saving Indian accounts of attitudes before the battle (*Indian Side*, chap. 19).

93. *LN*, 11 (1865), 63, De Smet to ——, Ghent, 1 January 1865.

Three hundred Cheyennes had marshaled to oppose the troops; a single cavalry charge scattered them. There followed the same complacent chase, the same inflated estimate of Indians killed, the same scattering of warriors in all directions. The Cheyennes had their camp burned and supplies destroyed. They assured their agent that the Whites had made a lasting impression on them. Yet their depredations continued as before.[94]

What, then, had Wright accomplished? He had been presented with the confederated tribes in one large body and had allowed them to disperse again. Almost no one had been hurt by his battles, though the bullets fell thick as rain. It had been all flags and sabers, foam-flecked horses and a confusion of musketry: the game of war with an illusion of danger, an illusion of dedication. The Colonel was at the end of his tether, on short supplies and with winter in the offing. Unlike Garnett, he had enjoyed a great stroke of luck. But Kamiakin and his war leaders would hardly repeat the mistake of presenting him with a united force in the open field. Wright had used up his resources in a grand, futile gesture. He was back where he had started in 1855—to marches on the empty plains. In short, he had lost the war.

This was not Wright's fault. His force was not mobile enough, fast enough, or enduring enough, nor was it skilled in guerrilla warfare. A new element was needed to bring meaning to Wright's situation and to precipitate a just and lasting peace. This element, in the upper country in 1858, happened to be the Jesuits.

94. L. R. Hafen and A. W. Hafen, eds., *Relations with the Indians of the Plains, 1857–1861, a Documentary Account of the Military Campaigns, and Negotiations of Indian Agents, with Reports and Journals*, Far West and Rockies Ser., 9 (Glendale, Cal., 1959), pp. 121–22, 165.

8. Peace Created and Consolidated

JOSET INVITES THE ARMY TO A TREATY

THE BATTLES OVER, the Indians lost heart for a time. Joset tells us that "they ran in every direction seeking hiding places in woods and mountains." Stellam wryly observes that Kamiakin "and his men joined the rout and made the best time of any of us in getting away from that fight." Spotted Coyote, despondently convinced that the Whites were superior in weapons, went home to his Pend d'Oreilles. The Yakimas "scattered here and there." The Kalispels struck out for Lake Pend d'Oreille. And the Coeur d'Alenes retreated into their own country.

Large Coeur d'Alene groups hid near the lakeside. Others went down to the St. Joe River. Still other Coeur d'Alenes fled up mountainsides or out onto their home plains. Ten days after the battle Agent Owen even reported a Coeur d'Alene band "in the vicinity of Hell Gate," presumably going onto the Montana plains. "A few," including Chiefs Vincent and Stellam, made their way back to the mission.[1]

Wright, meanwhile, loitered along the Spokane River for five days. The river here was fifty yards wide, lined with strips and forests of pine. Unable to cross it, he began moving upstream to the east along its lower bank. In a garbled account to an ethnologist fifty years later, some Indians described the tribes at this stage as going into a general council and then sending Garry to seek terms. Whatever truth may be in this, Garry did present himself at the White camp. It was only to justify his own conduct. "He had always been opposed to fighting," he said; but "the young men and many of the chiefs were against him, and he could not control them."

Colonel Wright handled the interview badly. He reprimanded the chief severely, demanding unconditional surrender. He ordered him to have the Spokane chiefs Moses and Big Star bring in their people. Wright also told Garry to pass the word to the other tribes that the army was invincible; all

---

1. Joset Narrative for most quotations (see above, p. 247, n. 11). Teit, BAE *Annual Report*, 45, 372 (Coyote). Stellam Reminiscence (quot.). Owen, *Journals and Letters*, 2, 186. Mullan, *Topographical Memoir*, p. 39 (last quot.).

Indians were to surrender unconditionally. His only concession was an amnesty for acts done during the campaign itself. The Indians knew that this meant hanging for at least some of them, and especially for the leaders of the Steptoe attack.

Garry was stunned by the reception. After the meeting he was too frightened ever to go back or to contact the soldiers. Next the Spokane chief Polatkin showed up with nine of his warriors. Wright promptly clapped him into irons and arrested one brave for trial; the rest he sent back with a message like that given to Garry. The following day at sunset the Colonel hanged Polatkin's companion. When Polatkin's sons appeared across the river, shouting for their father's return, an answering volley from the troops wounded one mortally and caught the other in the arm. The Spokane chief Big Star interviewed Wright independently of Garry but on the same day. Three days later, by proxy, he "surrendered" his small village—but he had been a friendly pro-American chief all along. The army by now had also discovered and burned a few food caches.[2]

Most eventful of all, the army had chanced to seize a herd of horses, estimated by Wright first as 800 and a month later as 1,000. To facilitate his march and to punish the Indian owners, Wright devoted two days to their systematic slaughter. Historians later claimed that this action unhorsed the Indians and ended the war. The Indian informants of the ethnologist Teit specifically unhorse the Spokanes and have them voluntarily surrender the herd. Bancroft distributes the loss more widely. The latest history of the Northwest conveys this same idea, as reinforcing Wright's victories.

Actually, almost all this herd belonged to one man, the Palouse Tilcoax. To own from 300 to 800 horses was to be a rich man, though some individuals owned more. Ironically, far from hurting the tribes militarily or economically, the destruction probably ensured a better market for horses this year with the Hudson's Bay Company. Horses were in great demand by Whites at the time, bringing from $40 to $100; Gibbs tells us that the tribes of the lower Interior were becoming "really wealthy" from such sales. The Interior was one of the most important Indian centers in America for the raising of horses.

It is probable that the hard winter a year before the Steptoe Disaster and the more severe winter just following the peace treaty caused far wider damage among the horse herds of the Interior Indians than Wright could ever do. The Hudson's Bay official Grahame reported how the first of these two winters "has caused great havoc among our horses at Colville, and also among

2. Wright Report; Mullan, *Topographical Memoir*; Kip, *Expedition*, esp. p. 67 (quots.); Teit, pp. 370–71. On Big Star, the Spokane Protestant mission, and his peace work in the Yakima war see e.g. Eells, *History of Indian Missions*, p. 236.

those of the Indians"; Blenkinsop at Colville wrote that the 1858–59 winter "has carried off the greater part of the Indians' horses." Even such losses could not dismount the Indians. What was the significance, then, in Wright's slaughter of Tilcoax's personal wealth? Father Joset explains it, from the Indian viewpoint. "The slaughter added not a little to the fright of the Indians," because a White chief who could despise and contemptuously destroy such considerable treasure must be a formidable man. Chief Stellam was to offer the same explanation many years later.[3]

It was at this moment, five days after the battle, that Joset sent out a feeler for peace from the Coeur d'Alene country. Thus far Wright had been having no success with his surrender program. Lieutenant Mullan records that Joset's message decided the Colonel as to his next move. What lay behind the priest's offer? Joset had prepared to abandon the tribe and take up work among the Blackfeet. During the five days after the battle, however, he saw his chance to save the Coeur d'Alene enterprise. As erstwhile combatants trickled back onto the mission grounds, rejoicing ensued among those of the peace faction who had not taken part in either battle. The hostiles returning here were only "some few," possibly those of the peace group who had fallen away at the time of the second engagement. Still caught up in the panic of defeat, they told Joset they wished to make peace. Head Chief Vincent acted as their spokesman. They begged the priest to see Colonel Wright and "plead for us."

Joset at first refused: "did I not tell you how it would be when the soldiers would come? You would not be advised by me in the beginning; now take the consequences." Determined that the lesson should be lasting, he scolded them: "you are too faithless: twice I exerted myself for you, and twice you have put me to shame; if you sincerely want peace, go yourself, I will give you a letter for your protection." Horrified, the warriors protested that they could never go themselves. All were for packing off into the mountains. "Such was the panic," Joset says, "that even the innocent ones wanted to run away: I had much to do to persuade them to remain at the Mission." Where, he asked them, "are all the brave men who went forth a few days ago to do battle?" None answered. "Send one who never fought," they suggested. Fi-

3. Joset Narrative (esp. for ownership). Stellam late Reminiscence; details in *SED* army reports, Wright and Mullan letters. OJ, Mullan to Joset, 10 September, on slaughter; cf. EW, Trimble to Hunt, 17 May (n.d., late reminiscence). HB, D5, *48*, Simpson Corresp. in, from Blenkinsop at Fort Colville, 25 February 1859 (market, winter); ibid., *43*, from Grahame, 25 March 1857. RR, *1*, ii, 404 (Gibbs, prices). G. B. Desmond, O.S.B., *Gambling Among the Yakimas* (Washington, D.C., 1952), pp. 19–20 (wealth in horses). Brown's Indian conversations in the 1930s give Tilcoax only half-interest in the herd, by marriage to the owner's widow (*Indian Side*, pp. 254–58, 263–66, 390–92). Bancroft, *Washington*, p. 191; D. O. Johansen and C. M. Gates, *Empire of the Columbia* (New York, 1957), p. 312.

nally an adherent of the peace party volunteered, Sebastian Xulxutrot. "I will carry the message to the white chief; I am not afraid, for I have done no wrong." [4]

Sebastian arrived at Wright's camp with Joset's letter during the second day of the horse slaughter. The Colonel immediately penned an answer in nervous, hurried script. Kind fortune had favored his command "beyond our most sanguine hopes." Two "severe" battles had killed or wounded many of the Indians including several chiefs. There must be "unqualified submission to my will," unconditional surrender before terms could be allowed, and "peace now and forever hereafter." Despite the rhetoric, one notices that terms were really offered. This was by no means a demand for unconditional surrender. Significantly absent is the one obstacle upon which the Jesuits' peace tour had shipwrecked. This is a crucial point in our story. It is indeed the turning point of the war.

General Clarke had been determined to punish the instigators of the Steptoe attack. This was the main purpose of the present war. He would yield on any other point, modify any other condition; but on this question of punishment he was adamant. On the other hand, the Indians correctly interpreted this to mean hanging for some of their tribesmen. The Indians would compromise on all points but *this:* they refused to turn over any of their relatives to be punished by the Whites. The deadlock was absolute.

Joset now offered a compromise. He agreed to find and gather the dispersed guerrilla fighters. He would persuade them to give back all the Steptoe booty available, to sign a treaty of submission and amity, to permit the Mullan road through their lands, and to surrender as temporary hostages the principal Steptoe criminals. For his part, Wright must guarantee that the lives of the criminals were to be spared, that they were to be not prisoners but hostages, and that no one at all would be punished. On this condition of guaranteeing the Indians' lives a meaningful treaty might be arranged.

General Clarke had specifically rejected Congiato's last-minute plea, and that of Spokane Garry, to make peace by this concession. What is more, the General had taken care to leave Wright no initiative on the point. He gave the Colonel written orders that the Steptoe criminals absolutely must be delivered for punishment. Indeed, Wright had no authority even to make a treaty; he could only arrange surrender terms as a basis for some future treaty.

Wright's yielding made nonsense out of Clarke's war. Clarke himself was to see it that way. The General could hardly quarrel with the stunning success Wright seemed to have gained; nor could he reprimand the returned hero just as the newspapers were hailing him and as authorities from the sec-

4. Joset Narrative.

retary of War down were preparing eulogies. (By February, Captain Archer writes from Fort Simcoe, rumor even had it "that Col. Wright will be made a Brigadier General and assigned to the command of this department.") But Clarke stuck to his guns in this at least; he repudiated Wright on the essential surrender issue. "Some of the stipulations made by Colonel Wright were in violation of the spirit of his instructions, and such as I cannot sanction," he reported; "the treaty will therefore be retained for transmittal at a later date." A week later he had to release the treaties to headquarters, still noting that on some points "I have been obliged to record my disapproval." This time he enters into specific detail: "the objections to the acceptance of the conditional surrender of prisoners are patent."

Clarke was shrewd enough not to disassociate himself from the triumph: "nevertheless enough has been done to secure the submission of the Indians and give security to the frontier, and though I feel obliged to note these departures from the spirit of my orders, I have no desire to magnify them into grave evils." His final comment on the surrender concession, however, is forthright; each sentence in it is placed as a separate paragraph, each a shot at Wright. "The 5th article in each of these treaties is disapproved in so far as it accepts a conditional surrender of those Indians guilty of commencing the attack on the troops. An unconditional surrender was demanded by me before the troops were sent into the field; less should not have been accepted. A surrender of the guilty conditioned on their immunity from punishment is futile. It is now too late to repair the error." [5]

None of this emerges very clearly from Wright's own reports, and therefore not at all from histories of the war. Wright sometimes speaks of offering the Indians their lives, sometimes of their having surrendered unconditionally. Even in the first case it is not easy to discern how great a gulf separates the immunities offered after the battles from those offered after receiving Joset's message. In his reports, the Colonel touches on the point briefly, and on the whole ambiguously. The Jesuits, on the other hand, emphasize it clearly. Joset knew that unless Wright agreed to let the Steptoe criminals go unpunished, his own precarious plans for peace were impossible. Indeed he sums up Wright's whole response in terms of this single condition: "no life will be taken." The priest then labored to convince his flock that "as far as life was concerned they had nothing to fear: that the Commander would never be false to his word." In discussing the peace problem shortly afterward, De Smet, who was to be involved in settling the 1858 troubles, also stressed the necessity of this condition, contrasting Wright's policy here to General Clarke's.

5. OJ, Wright to Joset, 10 September 1858. CR, 2, 754. *SED* (serial 975), army reports, esp. Clarke Report, 2 and 10 October, and letter to Wright, 4 July, pp. 363–64, 404–10. Archer Corresp., 17 February 1859.

A final question remains. Who suggested this sensible compromise between the traditional White demand for hanging and the Indian determination not to yield? This is not Wright's usual mode of thought. Indeed he hanged an Indian just before Joset's offer came, and he hanged many more as soon as he stopped dealing with tribes directly through Joset. It seems probable, then, that the Indian Sebastian brought the idea, and the arguments for it, to Wright's camp from Father Joset. Wright—at the end of his resources and reduced to conducting the kind of lonely promenade that had characterized his 1855 war—saw his chance to go home in an aura of victory, with a retrieved reputation and a formal peace treaty. He was willing to pay the price.

The Colonel prepared his report in high spirits. "I have this morning received a dispatch from Father Joset," he wrote; "the hostiles are *down* and suing for peace." This became the basis for an exaggerated news story in *Harper's*. Wright had refused peace to the Indians until they would surrender unconditionally, the magazine reported; to force such a surrender he had burned their grain fields and provisions. A generation later, some among the surviving old warriors evolved a myth of their own as to why the war ended. They said strong influence had been brought to bear on them by the priests and others, but their main reason was lack of ammunition with no way of replenishing the supply. They therefore held a council, debating whether to flee to the mountains to continue the war, to split into small parties for the same purpose, or to sue for peace.[6]

That a council took place after the battle, that alternatives to united action again in the field were mooted, and that some or all of the bands were low on ammunition—all this is plausible. But in later years the Indians had become so confused on the history of the battles that these details are no more trustworthy than the demonstrably untrue details which accompany them. The reminiscing Indians place the Steptoe battle very far from its real site, reckon the White dead at a hundred, and insist there were no Palouses present. Similarly, they garble the Wright campaign. They double both Wright's forces and the number of battles in Spokane lands; place the women and children in the war camp, surrender most of the chiefs through Garry just after the fighting, and also surrender their horses, thus being unable to reopen the war. There are gradations of credibility in kinds of Indian tradition, and the historian must pick his way carefully through them. In this council we seem to have a peripheral detail, exaggerated and then elevated to the status of a comforting myth; in short, it falls into the same category as the Whites' horse-slaughter episode.

There are extrinsic reasons for rejecting the tale. Abundant ammunition was available to the tribes both at a Canadian post thirty miles above Colville

6. Wright Report, 10 September, *SED*, p. 395. *Harper's New Monthly Magazine, 18* (1858-59), 113. Teit, BAE *Annual Report, 45,* 129, 370. Joset narrative. CR, *2, 754-55.*

and on the Plains. Colville alone had been forced to refuse sales, and that only recently. It was getting late for continued fighting anyway, and the horse and buffalo trade could easily supply the Indians for opening hostilities again next spring. Nor does the later tradition correspond with Joset's record of the hostiles' manner of flight. Equally important is Joset's account of how the tribes actually made peace.

The army soon sent word to the papers on the Coast, advancing the official story of a brilliant victory, noting that the Palouses and Spokanes had fled, and complacently rejoicing in the Coeur d'Alene surrender. If the overwhelming majority of hostiles was still at large, the report to the newspapers could at least take comfort that the Coeur d'Alenes "were our bravest enemies, and fought well." [7]

Colonel Wright did not waste any time. Before noon on that same day the troops broke camp and marched toward the forested mountains. It was to be a journey of several days. Before plunging into the forest, which had to be navigated over a choked and barely discernible Indian trail, the command abandoned its single wagon and the howitzer limber. Palouse Indians, for whom the war was not yet over, trailed the army and burned both wagon and limber. Meanwhile, Sebastian had delivered Wright's answer to Joset. He also brought a long message in a vigorous scrawl from Mullan. The lieutenant was "truly glad to know that you have not yet abandoned your mission, but like a kind father to ungrateful children that you are still endeavoring to bring them back." [8]

The missionary related the Colonel's terms to his Indians, including the special proviso that there would be no hangings. There was no assurance the tribe would accept such terms. After all, those at the mission were few in number and did not necessarily represent the sentiments of the tribe itself. Joset had been gambling that he could force the consent of the whole tribe. He proposed now to send his own terms to them. If they would come in "and submit to the terms proposed," the Jesuits would not abandon them for the Blackfeet. The warriors, scattered throughout the territory, were still confused and frightened. A strong tradition exists among present-day Coeur d'Alenes to the effect that their next stand was to be in the treacherous Fourth of July Canyon of their country. True or false, the Coeur d'Alenes certainly had a special knowledge of such defensive warfare, which employed stockades, trenches, pits, and loopholed breastworks or forts.

Head Chief Vincent had been unable to overcome the tribe's mistrust of the Whites. Perhaps the Jesuit ultimatum could do so. Joset immediately sent

---

7. Letter of 16 September by courier, "Coeur d'Alene," in *Weekly Oregonian*, 25 September 1858.
8. Joset Narrative. OJ, Mullan to Joset, 10 September.

Vincent to round up the braves and direct them to the mission. The head chief carried "a pass from the priest," as Lieutenant Kip noted, to protect him if he met soldiers. Vincent encountered the troops on the evening of September 11.[9]

One measure of the difficulty Wright would have experienced, had he attempted to continue his campaign, is Kip's description of the army's difficult progress through the Coeur d'Alene forest. Stevens had already referred to the trail here as "much obstructed by fallen timber, circuitous and bad." De Smet described making his way through it to the Coeur d'Alene mission, axe in hand, winding around "thousands of tree trunks, fallen on one another in confusion" and overgrown. The priest spoke of the Coeur d'Alene forests as "almost impenetrable," with trees in places so "prodigious" and numerous that, "as the rays of the sun cannot penetrate the dense mass," a kind of night reigns. He had difficulty distinguishing his companions a dozen feet away. Kip and his colleagues were traveling over its easier or western fringe, yet the troops had to fall into single file and stumble along laboriously. At the end of the first day the lieutenant recorded how "all day we have toiled along," through a country "difficult for a force to make its way" because "the forest [is] in its primeval state."

Next day saw a similar "very toilsome" struggle. "In some places the trail passed along the brink of precipices apparently a thousand feet in depth." So dense was the tangle of trees that detachments of pioneers had to stay in advance continually, chopping a path. Kip was moved to reflect upon the Coeur d'Alenes: "from their courage and the natural defences of their country, they can prove most dangerous enemies." Mullan soberly noted in his extensive topographical report on the war: "these mountain Indians, in their strong position, are well calculated to give us annoyance and trouble, and thus hold the key to one of the principal mountain passes." He recommended that in the future "they should be conciliated on just and equitable grounds." The forest became "more dense as we advanced," wrote Lieutenant Kip, "until we could see nothing about us but high hills and deep caverns, with thick woods covering all, through which we wound our way in a twilight gloom."

Wright himself, though noisily optimistic in every report after the first battle, describes the "trail which admitted only the passage of a single man or animal at a time." Moreover, "we found the trail infinitely worse" next day; "passing through a dense forest, with an impenetrable undergrowth of bushes on both sides, and an almost continuous obstruction from fallen trees, our progress was necessarily slow, having to halt frequently and cut away the logs before our animals could pass over." The total of 700 men and 800 ani-

9. Kip, *Expedition*, pp. 76, 79–80; Joset Narrative. On Coeur d'Alene defensive warfare see Teit, pp. 117–18.

mals stretched out in file "from six to eight miles," with no communication possible between head and rear of the column. Did Wright allow for an ambush anywhere on the march? Not in his present mood. "Nature," he announced, "had fortified either flank" by this very tangle.

One wonders at Wright's temerity. Had the Colonel thrust his army into the Coeur d'Alene wilderness uninvited, America might have witnessed a local version of the Braddock fiasco. And had the war continued, with the tribes rallying again to the confederated Indian cause, a Wright disaster might today be added to those of Haller and Steptoe. Wright had taken part in the Seminole War twenty years before, when a thousand warriors absorbed the energies of two-thirds of the regular army's regiments. Could he have forgotten its lessons so soon? But then, he was gambling on Father Joset's position as observer and strong man.[10]

Kip was struck by the natural beauty of the country. Buried in the mountains, centering on a great lake which he counted "one of the most beautiful I have ever seen," it was "a splendid country." In its beauty as a "Happy Hunting Ground," it offered the soldiers an insight into the Indian motives for fighting; "we cannot wonder that they are aroused." As the straggling troops came to their first glimpse of the mission about a quarter of a mile away on September 13, there lay behind them a trail of what Wright reports pompously as "slaughter and devastation." He refers mainly to whatever Indian provisions he had been able to lay his hands on, pathetic little caches of wheat, oats, vegetables, berries, and camas roots. "A blow has been struck which they will never forget." Determinedly he focuses his attention on such trivial triumphs.

The officers were impressed with the mission and charmed by Jesuit hospitality. A "wagonload of vegetables" was sent over to the soldiers the first evening, a service Kip records as having been continued daily, with the "luxuries" of milk and butter. The vegetables were especially useful in warding off scurvy. Lieutenant Morgan specifically recalls the "fresh potatoes, for which we were thankful." These gifts represented more than a hospitable *beau geste*. The soldiers were by now a sorry-looking lot, "almost barefoot." They were also on short rations, though Wright's reports admit only a "slight reduction." [11]

The most remarkable result of the wilderness encounter was the impact of

10. *RR, 12*, i, 366; cf. p. 56. *CR, 3*, 799; *2*, 567, 491; cf. *JMUS, 2*, 317–19 and n. Kip, *Expedition*, pp. 77–78. Mullan, *Topographical Memoir*, p. 51. Wright Report, 15 September, *SED*, pp. 396–97. General Sherman, in our next chapter, describes this country in similar exasperated vein.

11. Kip, *Expedition*, pp. 77–79. Wright Report, *SED*, pp. 396–97. Morgan, *Journal of Military Service Institution, 42*; "Coeur d'Alene" September 16 letter in *Weekly Oregonian* (rations, barefoot).

the Jesuits upon the hard-shelled American military. Captain E. D. Keyes, up from the San Francisco presidio to command the six companies of artillery serving as infantry, was never to forget the experience. Keyes was a vintage New Englander, who had previously been an instructor at West Point and aide-de-camp to Winfield Scott. "In Father Joset I found a cultivated gentleman in the prime of life," he says, "fit to adorn the most polished society in the world." The Captain was "unable to restrain my expressions of astonishment" that Joset had spent fourteen years "in the wilderness with the savages" here.

When Keyes asked the priest "if he had no longings for a better life and society," the Jesuit answered "no." Joset explained that "I am content and happy where I am; in your profession an outward obedience to orders is all that is required of you, but in the society to which I belong obedience must be internal and cheerful, and ready; I am happy, and have no desire to exchange situations with any person." Keyes was greatly intrigued by the priest. "Twice every day while I remained at the mission I had conversations with Father Joset, which increased my admiration for his character and my estimation of his self-denial." The talks affected the life of the future general profoundly: "it was primarily due to his influence that I enrolled myself, at a subsequent date, in the Roman Catholic Church." Many years later and far from the wilderness, the distinguished General Keyes was to confess in his autobiography that during these days of the Wright campaign, "by his explanations and revelations, Father Joset revealed to my mind vistas." [12]

Lieutenant Kip visited the mission with some brother officers, and was received "with great kindness and politeness" by Joset, Menetrey, and three lay brothers. Kip felt "no doubt but what the priests have had a most happy influence over" the Indians. He was impressed by the tribesmen themselves: no Indians "we have met have impressed us so favorably." Lieutenant Mullan waxed rhetorical after seeing again "the labors of that indefatigable band of Jesuit Fathers who, braving all dangers," had civilized the Indians and erected their "large and stately church." The Coeur d'Alenes he found "stunted and frightfully ugly," capable of becoming a "formidable enemy." [13]

Shortly after marching onto the mission flats and camping in the bowl of meadow land below the log buildings of the mission, Colonel Wright noted in a letter that "Father Joset has been extremely zealous and persevering in bringing in the hostiles; they are terribly frightened." Joset had continually to quiet their "alarm as to the fate which awaited them," despite the Colonel's promise of immunity. Some were already coming in by the night of the 14th.

12. E. D. Keyes, *Fifty Years' Observation of Men and Events, Civil and Military* (New York, 1884), p. 274.
13. Kip, *Expedition*, p. 79. Mullan, *Topographical Memoir*, p. 38.

On September 16 Wright sent a formal message from his headquarters to Joset, requesting him to soothe the Spokane chief Polatkin. Now that Wright glimpsed Coeur d'Alene and Spokane treaties in the offing, he changed tactics to suit his new strategy. He asked Joset to explain in some suitable way why he had kept the chief in irons. He also wished Joset to present the Colonel's reasons for having hung Polatkin's companion. The priest did so and, interceding for the chief, had him released. Polatkin went to the mission. Joset was later to exhibit the chief in the Spokane country as living proof of the army's mercy, so as to induce the Spokanes also to come in for a treaty.[14]

A penciled note of the same day suggested to Joset that final arrangements be made for a council on the morrow. Wright asked him to assure the Coeur d'Alenes, once again, that their hostages would incur no physical harm. The fate of the instigators of the Cayuse and Yakima wars, and of so many other hostile incidents, was not to fall upon Steptoe's principal attackers. Kip's diary reflects: "the priests will now be exceedingly helpful to us." Kip realized as clearly as Wright that "it will be through the agency and influence of their priests alone that we shall be able to reassure them and induce them to accede to the necessary terms."

Reassurance was doubly needed, for during the icy cold nights (the days were yet warm) Donati's comet streamed overhead in terrifying splendor, a phenomenon the tribesmen half connected with White men and howitzers and long-range rifles. Chief Vincent had returned on the 16th, disheartened, to tell Joset that the Indians were still afraid to come in. Joset sent him right out again. The priest's magic was slowly working. Small groups began edging closer and drifting in.[15]

As more and more Coeur d'Alenes arrived, the officers began to anticipate the end of the war. Captain Hardie requested a twenty-day leave of absence dating from the end of the campaign, to bring up his family from Benicia. Captain Keyes desired a transfer to the San Francisco presidio because "the climate of Washington Territory, in winter, is very hurtful to me." Assistant Surgeon Hammond wanted to go to San Diego, or else to San Francisco, or at least to Los Angeles; discretion forbade his divulging the reason, except to say that it was compelling. Other officers found their thoughts taking the same direction. Lieutenant Pender requested a two-month leave for urgent business in the East and for visiting; Smith had submitted an application previous to his, so Pender's had to wait. Captain Ord had anticipated his colleagues, his bid for leave having gone in from the temporary Fort Taylor; but just after

14. Wright Report, *SED*, pp. 396–97, for quotations. OJ, Wright to Joset, Camp near Sacred Heart Mission, 16 September. Joset Narrative.

15. OJ, Wright to Joset, second doc. of same place and date as above, n. 14. Kip, *Expedition*, pp. 80, 85–86.

the Coeur d'Alene Council he reinforced his request to visit his family in California. Lieutenant Gregg's permission would come through first, on October 2. While the officers constructed their several petitions, Mullan was holding talks with the Jesuits concerning puzzling sections of his planned road. Joset later collected much information for him and forwarded it.[16]

Eighty or ninety lodges were clustered about the meadow lands below the church by the evening of the 16th. The majority of the tribe had cautiously gathered during the past two days, trickling in at first, then appearing in larger and larger groups.

"BUT FOR THE PRIEST'S HELP"

At ten o'clock on the morning of the 17th the treaty council assembled in a "sylvan saloon," a bower of branches hastily thrown up in front of Wright's tent. (In describing a similar structure for an informal Yakima talk during the 1856 war, Captain Archer records that Wright "built a bower large enough for a circus.") About 150 chiefs and braves attended with their Blackrobes, Menetrey and Joset. Only six or eight were absent, among them notably Melkapsi. Head Chief Vincent was tribal spokesman, opening the council with a penitent speech. Joset acted as interpreter.

The terms were clear and reasonable. Steptoe plunder was to be restored. Steptoe war criminals who had struck the first blow, as well as one chief and four Indians, would accompany Wright back to Walla Walla with their families as temporary hostages. Whites and their troops were to have unmolested passage through Coeur d'Alene lands, and could make roads; hostile Indians were to be refused passage. Peace was to prevail between the former hostiles and the Nez Percés accompanying the army. The terms provided that a permanent treaty was to be drawn up later by the American government, embodying these terms and the White guarantees.

The important item is number five: the White guarantees. This is the longest of the seven articles. Here the army renounces vengeance. All Coeur d'Alenes who surrender, even those who initiated the Steptoe attack, "shall in nowise be injured"; the hostages will be safe and will return within a year.

16. NA, EW, Army Commands, Dept. Pacific, LR, Hardie to Mackall, Camp at Coeur d'Alene Mission, 15 September; Keyes to same, 15 September; Hammond to same, 25 September, from Camp near Steptoe's Battle Ground; Pender to same, mission camp, 15 September, with Steptoe note of conditional approval; Ord to same, from Camp Taylor on Snake, 19 August, and then from Camp on the Lhatta (Hangman's Creek), 24 September. Gregg Collection (LC), special orders No. 172, extending to 1 May 1859, the leave granted on 2 October 1858 by special order No. 158. Mullan 1860 Road Report, *HED*, p. 11.

Vincent and Seltis signed first, with Wright; the absent Melkapsi's name would later be inserted in the free space above the two chiefs, continuing there in publication. Below their names came the chiefs: Joseph, John Peter, and Peter Paulinus; twelve other subchiefs or principal men follow, like Bonaventure, Casimir, and Leo. The White officers signed as witnesses— Keyes, Grier, Kirkham, Dent, and eight more. These "Preliminary Articles of the Treaty of Peace and Friendship between the United States and the Coeur d'Alene Indians" having been duly signed, Joset concluded in his quaint English: "all is now truly rosy-tinted."

The Colonel was on thin ice in making such a treaty. This was not his duty or function. General Clarke had given him and Garnett some "formulas of agreement" to adapt as chance offered, which could "pave the way to more formal negotiations." But Wright had presented his treaty to the Indians as something more formal. He acted highhandedly, though sensibly enough in the circumstances. The Colonel was to take care when he reached The Dalles, however, to send copies both of his Nez Percé alliance and of his peace treaties to Superintendent Nesmith at Salem, soliciting his support. Wright confessed to Nesmith that "these Treaties are only preliminary, as I was not authorized to make any Treaty to be submitted to the action of the Senate." None of these treaties, it would seem, was ever formally ratified.[17]

Tension now relaxed at the mission. There was lively trading between the former enemies. To the Indians, "amazed" over the friendliness of the troops, Joset elucidated that they were lions in war and lambs in peace. The Coeur d'Alenes, with childlike simplicity, explained their ambitions and battle plans to the clusters of soldiers. Presumably the Jesuit Fathers and Brothers served as interpreters. Head Chief Vincent told the officers: "before, we knew you only by hearsay, and we hated you; now that we have seen you, we love you." The soldiers in their turn learned a thing or two about Indians. The myth of the stoic savage suffered especially during a touching scene, as a hostage parted from his relatives with great difficulty. Kip also watched "a number of women" at the mission "in great distress and weeping bitterly," some of them widows of the fallen braves and some of them related to the hostages. The tribe delivered six men as hostages: the three leaders of the Steptoe attack (Paschal, Hilary, and later Melkapsi) and three subchiefs, with their immediate families.[18]

17. The original manuscript treaty given the Indians is in Joset Papers, No. 66, twice endorsed by Colonel Wright. Cf. W. N. Bischoff S.J., and C. M. Gates, eds., "The Jesuits and the Coeur d'Alene Treaty of 1858," *PNWQ*, *34* (1943), 169–81. Joset Narrative; Kip, *Expedition*, pp. 83–85. NA, IA, Oreg. Sup., LR, Wright to Nesmith, 12 November 1858. Clarke Report, July 23, *SED* (serial 975), pp. 361, 370 ff. Treaty in *SED* (serial 1051), p. 89; none of the 1858 treaties are in the Kappler treaty collection. Archer Corresp., to mother, 4 July 1856.

18. Joset Narrative (incl. Vincent); Kip, *Expedition*, p. 85.

The troops broke camp at seven on the dark, cloudy morning after the council, heading through a light drizzle down the right bank of the Coeur d'Alene River. Before leaving, Wright penned a letter to Joset from his camp, enclosing a copy of the treaty for the head chief. He wished Joset to convey to the tribe the Colonel's pleasure "in seeing them come with all their people, promptly, and willingly." Closing "with high regard," he expressed his gratitude: "now my dear sir, I must thank you very sincerely for your zealous and persevering efforts in bringing about this accommodation, which has terminated so successfully." After this final salute to the Jesuit, the entire command again "plunged into the wilderness." It would be a rainy and unpleasant struggle through the forest ahead; but the Coeur d'Alenes helped them cross the deep, sixty-yard-wide river.[19]

Father Joset still had an important role to play. Polatkin had been allowed to sign the Coeur d'Alene treaty; he professed himself satisfied with the terms and promised to persuade his own people to come in. Joset now took him up around the northern end of the lake and into the Spokane country. Other Spokanes besides Polatkin had just participated in the Coeur d'Alene Council. One of them, Silimalxeltsin Spokane, with his family, was even added to the hostages. Most of the Spokanes, however, as well as a few diffident Coeur d'Alenes, had yet to be contacted. Joset and Polatkin labored to round up the Spokane chiefs and braves, as well as any available representatives from the other tribes involved in the war.

Considering the time at their disposal, less than five days, the results were impressive. The troops had swung in a huge circle down around the southern end of the lake and then out across the rolling Palouse hills, back toward their original line of march. By September 22 they came to rest on the stream thereafter significantly called Hangman's Creek, "at the place where it was afterwards crossed by the first Mullan's road." Here they found "that the head chiefs and warriors of the Spokanes had come in, accompanied by Father Joset."

Joset tells us he had "found the Indians rather eager to accompany me." Many Spokanes had already fled toward the buffalo country, but the leaders and the body of the tribe remained. Surprisingly, there were 107 Indians gathered at Joset's camp—Spokanes, Kalispels, Pend d'Oreilles, Kettles, Sinkiuse-Columbias, stray Coeur d'Alenes, and delegates from smaller tribes. The Jesuit had even succeeded in bringing in Kamiakin. Unfortunately, the great Yakima chief became nervous and fled just before the troops arrived. Head Chief Vincent of the Coeur d'Alenes was present again, as well as the Spokanes Polatkin, Big Star, and Sgalgalt. Joset tells us that "Spokan[e] Garry was there too, but afraid to present himself, because having been to the

19. OJ, Wright to Joset, Camp near Mission, 17 September. Kip, *Expedition*, p. 86 (last quot.). Mullan, *Topographical Memoir*, p. 51.

commander some time after the battle, he had gone away with the promise to return: but having heard of the arrest of Paulotken, he dared not stand to his word." Joset spoke of Garry's case to Wright, interceding for him. "The Colonel having said that he had nothing to fear, I presented him." [20]

Joset had to make a similar presentation for "the great boaster Melkapsi, who was as cowardly as his likes [are] used to be in such cases." The Coeur d'Alene Melkapsi had feared to attend the previous council with his own tribesmen. Wright reprimanded him. Melkapsi "arranged his head dress," rose to deliver a wary reply, and submitted. Joset "then explained to him" the treaty conditions. Others required intercession. "At the request of the Coeur d'Alenes I spoke in behalf of two brothers, Sons of a Palouses chief: the Colonel answered that they had nothing to fear provided they dwelled among the Coeur d'Alenes." While Joset was busy, the pro-Americans Big Star and Garry were sent to try their luck in bringing back Kamiakin or his brother Skloom; they had no success.

On the morning of September 23 the council opened, Wright reports, with "the whole Spokane nation." The Colonel enumerated their crimes, offered them "the same agreement as at the Mission," listened while the principal chiefs made conciliatory speeches, and proceeded to the formality of signing the prepared text. Included in the treaty articles was a recapitulation of item seven of the Coeur d'Alene treaty, guaranteeing the Steptoe attackers and other hostiles from all injury. Polatkin, Garry, and Sgalgalt, in that order, were first to sign, followed by thirty-two others. The two central tribes had now been formally conciliated. This would have to suffice.

The delegates of other tribes, or more properly the representative individuals gathered in passing by Joset, had no part in the treaty. Indeed, the Kalispels and others gathered here took care to proclaim their personal innocence; they conceded that "some of their young men had been in the fights." There were not enough representatives from any one of these distant tribes to justify formal, separate treaties. These tribes nevertheless got the protection and guarantees of the treaties indirectly. That is, they were loosely associated with the two agreements; their misdeeds were to be overlooked as long as their respective tribes abided by the general terms. [21]

There was no assurance, of course, that the other upper tribes would abide by any agreement. The war spirit still persisted. Colville remained as dangerous as ever it had been. Indians were attacking miners where they had at-

20. Joset Narrative (incl. first quot.); Kip, *Expedition*, p. 91 (second quot.); Wright Report (Spokanes fled), *SED*, p. 369.
21. Joset Narrative. Wright Report, 24 September, 2 October, *SED*, pp. 399, 407–08 (incl. Kalispels). Mullan Memoir, *SED*, p. 54. Kip, *Expedition*, p. 95 (Melkapsi actions in council). Treaty not in Kappler collection but in *SED* (serial 1051), pp. 90–91.

tacked them before. But on Joset's initiative and with his help, Wright had at least isolated the troublemakers farther to the south, interposing a fairly wide belt of neutralized tribes. There was no further necessity for showing the southernmost groups any mercy. From here on, the Colonel reverted to his policy of hanging.

Wright now "expressed his satisfaction" to Joset for all he had done. The officers agreed "that but for the priest's help the affair would never have been brought to so speedy a conclusion." A cavalry officer, E. O. C. Ord, was to write Indian Commissioner Denver four months later: "recently in the Spokane and Coeur d'Alene war, it was entirely due to the skilful management and persevering friendship of the Cath[oli]c Priests that the Indians were brought to submit to the terms imposed upon them." Joset says simply that, without Jesuit intervention, the Indians would have remained "invisible."

Wright concluded his official report with a recognition of these services. "I cannot close this communication without expressing my thanks to Father Joset, the superior of the Coeur d'Alene mission, for his zealous and unwearied exertions in bringing all these Indians to an understanding of their true position." He recorded how "for ten days and nights the Father has toiled incessantly and only left us this morning after witnessing the fruition of all his labors." The Spokanes were also grateful. Joset went to stay with them on a missionary excursion that winter and found them receptive. Something of the missionaries' role in the Wright war eventually filtered out to the newspapers in the wider world. The San Francisco *Herald* and the New York *Herald* reported how the battles left the Indians dispersed but by no means disposed to submit, their very fear ensuring that they would remain unavailable. It was now, the papers said, that the Jesuits redoubled their efforts to secure merciful conditions from the Whites and submission from the Indians.[22]

Before Joset left Wright's camp Chief Owhi, greatest of the Yakima war leaders after Kamiakin, rode in to ask for peace. The priest "was sent for to act as interpreter, and give his answers." Owhi, though much attracted to Catholicism and friendly with priests like the Oblate Pandosy and the Jesuit Ravalli, had never quite become a convert. Gibbs found him employing Catholic "forms" in 1853 and professing "to pray habitually." Lieutenant Mullan characterized him as "a large man" with "an open and benevolent face"—in all a "noble and generous Indian." He talked now with Wright through the mediation of Father Joset. Lieutenant Kip recorded the dialogue. Told he

22. Joset Narrative (esp. first two quots.). NA, IA, Oreg. Sup., Ord to Denver, 21 January 1859, as in Donnelly, "Liquor Traffic," p. 241. Wright Report. MJ, IX, Joset to De Smet, 27 April 1859 (Spokane excursion); cf. W. P. Schoenberg, S.J., *Chronicle of Catholic History of the Pacific Northwest* (Portland, Oreg., 1962), p. 43, No. 269, with refs. *Collection de précis historiques*, 7 (1859), 94 (quoting S.F. and N.Y. papers).

would hang immediately if his son Qualchin did not show up within four days, Owhi sank to the ground in fear. He took out a prayer book, distractedly leafed through it, and handed it to the Jesuit.

Chief Moses, of the Sinkiuse-Columbia tribe, is said to have been present posing as a Spokane; he rode off to warn Qualchin but failed to intercept him. It is also said that Kamiakin, anxious to see what the Whites would do, encouraged Qualchin to respond to Wright's call. Qualchin was a fire-breathing warrior, a name to conjure with, a killer of miners. On his arrival, Qualchin was hung. He died hard, cursing and pleading. About ten days later, on the march south toward a probable public hanging, Owhi himself was shot while escaping. In a poignant epilogue years afterward, Owhi's grandson, returning from exile after the Nez Percé war, made a sad pilgrimage with Chief Moses "to see the pine trees where they hung Qualchin." [23]

After Joset had gone, six or seven Walla Wallas from Kamiakin's camp came in to surrender. They claimed "that they had a letter from the priest, but it had been lost, and one of their number had gone back to look for it." Wright put two of them in irons as hostages; he promised not to hang them if the others brought in "their arms." A group of fifteen Palouses, who had fought under Kamiakin at the battle, later presented themselves. These men, says Joset, had been "emboldened by the mild treatment dealt to the Coeur d'Alenes and Spokanes." Wright arrested all fifteen. After an informal trial that evening he hanged six, taking the rest along in irons. These Indians were not covered by the priest's agreement with Wright. The Colonel was free now to confirm his appearance of victory with as many hangings as pleased him. Hangman's Creek, where Wright took leave of Joset, was only the beginning.[24]

This last Palouse band informed the Whites that Kamiakin had fled north. Owen was to note his passing through Flathead country. More precisely, as Father Hoecken soon reported, the chief had gone "with some of [his] people" to the Pend d'Oreille country. The Pend d'Oreilles did not welcome him, Hoecken said; they even quarreled with him and stole some of his horses. Kamiakin continued northeast therefore "towards the Coutonays; there Father Menetrey has seen him in a very hungry situation." This mission tribe likewise seems to have given him a poor reception. Some of his people went on over the Plains to hunt buffalo. Others came to the Kalispel mission of St. Ignatius; true to his promise of neutrality, however, Chief Alexander "has told them not to stay here." Father Hoecken gave the troublemakers

23. Kip, *Expedition*, pp. 100–01. *RR, 1*, ii, 411, 518 (Gibbs, Mullan). OH, Statement by Owhi in 1919, late reminiscence on Moses detail by grandson.
24. Kip, *Expedition*, p. 110; Joset Narrative (last quot.). Cf. Reminiscences of T. B. Beall, hangman for these episodes, in EW.

short shrift: "I for my part wished them out of the country." An unwelcome wanderer, Kamiakin and his diminished entourage sought hospitality with Chief Victor's camp when the Flatheads traveled far into eastern Montana for buffalo that winter. "No one feels for them: they merely live." The missionaries had taken a determined stand against Kamiakin for years now; the fallen leaders had fled to the wrong country.[25]

General Clarke and Colonel Wright wrote earnest letters begging the Jesuits not to abandon their Coeur d'Alene mission. These letters helped persuade the Fathers to remain. Lieutenant Mullan wrote Congiato from the mission on the day of the council. He asked "that you will be disposed to revoke your order regarding the breaking up of your mission among the Coeur d'Alenes and give them another trial." Mullan said he intended going to Washington, D.C., this winter and would "endeavor to use my best exertions on behalf of the missions and Indians" of the Rocky Mountains. The letter was long and eloquent, pleading the needs of the tribe and their changed dispositions.[26]

Joset piously attributed the happy outcome of the war to the tribe's devotion in having dedicated themselves to the Blessed Virgin. Had it not been for her protection, he was to write, "the year 1858 would have been the last of the mission, when deceived by false reports they attacked the government troops: it was the sure way to lose all and they lost nothing: and while the Fathers had resolved to abandon the place," the military dissuaded them, "saying that the Coeur d'Alenes could yet become good Indians." The Coeur d'Alenes at this time had also carried the army's mail to and from the lower country. They helped Mullan now as he prepared his topographical map of the Steptoe battlefield.[27]

Because the Jesuits "had a great deal to do to help [in] pacifying the Indians," Joset tells us, they "were much exposed to the revengeful dispositions of some of them on that account." This had not deterred "the exertions of the Fathers for the sake of humanity." Dark mutterings still circulated among the die-hard few. "Were the Black Gowns out of the country we would begin again." Trouble indeed was never far away in the years following the war. Many Coeur d'Alenes remained violently against the Mullan road. Since the army was determined to have it, Joset facilitated its peaceful building; at the

25. MJ, IX, AA, Hoecken to De Smet, St. Ignatius, 3 February 1859, when De Smet was in the Rockies looking for Kamiakin.

26. Joset Narrative. Mullan letter reproduced in *WL*, *17* (1888), 89, from San Francisco *Monitor* (of 1860?).

27. Joset Narrative. NA, EW, Army Commands, Dept. Pacific, LR, Mullan to Mackall, 9 October 1858, for Mullan progress. "Coeur d'Alene" letter in *Weekly Oregonian*, 25 September 1858, and Kip, *Expedition*, pp. 80, 109, on use of Coeur d'Alenes.

same time he was against its passage through the Coeur d'Alene heartland.

When Mullan's party appeared in Coeur d'Alene territory the summer after the treaty, the Indians "bitterly opposed" its work and threatened death to its leader. Mullan himself came up, was stopped by a "well mounted" band under Chief Peter Paulinus, was plied with questions, and had to stage an impromptu council. "They are wily fellows," he reported, "and great caution is necessary in all intercourse with them." During the winter after the war a strong faction tried to stop the party's use of Coeur d'Alene guides provided by Joset. In a stormy council the majority prevailed, however, keeping to the promises of their recent treaty. The Coeur d'Alene guide soon ran away: his brother had told him Mullan meant to hang him.

Mullan's comprehensive report on the road states that the Jesuit mission network "wield[s] an influence among the better portion" of the Indians of the Interior "such as no whites or government agents have ever been enabled to obtain." And for a pittance the Jesuits "actually take care of the Indians," while "thousands are squandered" with no result by the government. He sees their great influence as coming from "their lives [as] a voluntary offering," their "moral rectitude, zeal on behalf of the Indians," and their spiritual program.[28]

As for the Kettles up near Colville, the Jesuits at long last abandoned them. A certain control was retained. From another mission the Fathers continued to serve the tribe, and hope was held out for a possible return. Joset and Menetrey would in fact come up to reopen St. Paul's four years later. The fortuitous removal of the fisheries in 1858, at least as a favorite gathering place of the tribes, had made it difficult to control the scattered Kettles; but in the long run it reduced occasions of trouble.

Just after the closure the Kettle Chief Michael wrote a touching letter which is preserved at Paris. Addressed to the "Blackrobe head chief" at Rome, it apologizes for the poor showing the Kettles had made as Christians. The Kettle chief attributes their lapses to the bad example of the gold miners; "before the coming of the whites we were good, and happy." The letter was written by the chief himself ("the Blackrobe Joset had taught me to read and to write; he has also taught me French"). Michael was acting as a kind of lay missioner. He appealed for more priests: "our souls are as precious as those of the whites; Jesus Christ died for us as well."

The closing of the mission left Colville without any restraining influences except the Hudson's Bay post, so that even the experienced Company officials

28. BJ, Coll. 1ac–4ac, No. 3ac, Joset on Coeur d'Alenes, 29 May 1871 (first quot.). Joset Narrative. Mullan 1860 Road Report, *HED*, pp. 11, 14–18, 51–52, 95–100 (road episodes, M. on Jesuits); Mullan, *Topographical Memoir*, p. 38; cf. below, n. 88 and text. See Joset obituary in *LPT* (1902), Joset's peace "non senza pericolo della sua vita."

were worried. Grahame, their representative at Vancouver, pleaded with the army about "the necessity of sending troops to winter in the Colville valley and thereby afford protection." The army dismissed as impracticable the strenuous project of thrusting a command that far north so late in the season, and maintaining it through the winter. "Colville therefore is likely to be left to its fate until next summer, when a large force is to be sent thither." [29]

Colonel Wright meanwhile retraced his steps toward Fort Walla Walla. The weather turned decidedly cold, with hard rains and winds. Through this vile atmosphere, with all the little streams rising ominously, the troops made their chilly way south with as much speed as possible. Wright was extricating himself from the upper country in the nick of time. Had he remained much longer, he might have been in difficulties. While Wright reported that the days were warm enough, back at the mission "ice a quarter of an inch thick" was forming every night. On October 18 of that very year the veteran traveler De Smet, though familiar with the land and unencumbered by an army command, was immobilized at Lake Coeur d'Alene by snow storms. In November heavy ice would be floating in the rivers and the lake. De Smet was to report forty-three days and nights of snow at the Coeur d'Alene mission. The winter persisted almost until Easter; subsequently, flooded rivers caused poor fishing and much hunger for the Indians.

Lieutenant Sheridan in 1856 considered October already "late for operations," even in the more temperate lower Interior. Winter in fact had ended that 1856 campaign, with snow obscuring the trail back to safety and with the Indians long fled into the inaccessible Okanogan country. The Rains expedition had returned in October "severely frozen in the feet," men and animals in bad condition, the command "destitute of all the necessary means" for further campaigning. The present winter of 1858–59, as Hudson's Bay officials noted, was to be much more severe in the Interior. During the 1858 campaign also, the soldiers had seen little game—one bear and some prairie chickens and sage hens. Mullan, with a sanguine eye for settlers coming down his road, gives the general campaign weather as "mild and pleasant"; he does admit it rained during a fifth of the trip.

Steptoe had started for Colville but never arrived. Wright had started for Colville and was instead returning. Now the mission was leaving. The people of Colville, far away from the area pacified by Wright, were understandably chagrined. A group of miners galloped south in the "heavy rain storm" of September 27, overtaking the command. In view of Indian "depredations" at Colville, the settlers demanded "aid and protection." Okanogans and outlaws from other tribes were cutting off individuals in the upper country. The set-

29. FP, I, 5, 1 November 1858 (in French), copy sent by general to Association. HB, D5, 47, Simpson Corresp. in, from Grahame, 4 November 1858. *JMUS*, 2, 337.

tlers had prevailed on Father Ravalli there to send along a letter of his own to his friend Mullan. Mullan says "it set forth a fear of a general outbreak of the Indians among the miners and settlers of the valley, and represents an unpromising state of things among the people of that region." Wright had to admit to the miners that he could do nothing to help them.[30]

On the way south Wright assembled in council a "large number" of Palouses. He refused to give them a treaty, spoke angrily of hanging them all, promised death to any who ventured south of the Snake, and breathed threats of extermination should there be future trouble. Demanding that certain culprits stand forward, he acted again as judge and jury, promptly hanging one —as well as three others selected from his manacled prisoners—on a nearby tree. From the rest he took hostages.

At this camp he composed a detailed brief, listing all his arguments proving that "the war is closed." He had "signally defeated" the tribes "with a severe loss of chiefs and warriors," captured a thousand of their horses, destroyed "many barns" of grain as well as fields and caches, hanged culprits, retrieved the Steptoe howitzers, forced the delivery of the instigators of the Steptoe attack, borne away hostages for the good conduct of the tribes, restored both peace and property, secured safe passage of Whites, and so conducted the campaign that the Coeur d'Alenes, Spokanes, and Palouses became "entirely subdued and sued most abjectly for peace on any terms." The Colonel was soon to amplify this with the round statement that peace was fully established, the Colville troubles were negligible, and no need existed for army posts beyond Walla Walla.

At any rate, Wright's war was over. He headed his disheveled command back toward Walla Walla, leading them into the wooden fort on October 5. Here the inspector general of the army happened to be on hand, to review the heroes. Like a conquering Roman general, Wright brought along in his column thirty-three Indians—men, women, and children—of the Coeur d'Alene, Spokane, and Palouse tribes. These were the "hostages for the further good conduct of their respective tribes." The Colonel unloaded them without ceremony upon the fort commander. No one knew quite what to do with them. The commissary department was committed to supplying each of them during the coming year with camp equipment, one ration per day, and clothing. But the little necessities like tobacco were not provided. Superin-

30. CR, *2*, 759. Kip, *Expedition*, pp. 115 (weather), 121–22, 101, 110; unless there were two calls from Colville, Mullan and Kip supplement each other. Cram Report, *HED*, p. 95 (Rains); Wright Reports. Sheridan, *Memoirs*, pp. 54, 166–67. Mullan, *Topographical Memoir*, pp. 71, 75–76. For the milder weather in the lower country, especially the Yakima Valley, see Archer Corresp., e.g. letters of 20 November and 26 December 1858, 13 January, 1 February, 15 March 1859.

tendent Nesmith wrote to remedy the defect of tobacco. The exiles soon be-came miserable. Since they were willing hostages, under the most solemn im-munity, they were not confined.[31]

By prearrangement, Wright soon held his final council, this time with the Walla Wallas and Cayuses. He reprimanded them strongly. Wie-cat, the Steptoe messenger who tried to raise the tribe against the fort, was present. "I hung him forthwith." Three Walla Wallas, who pleaded guilty of killing Whites, shared the same fate. The entire tribe deserved hanging, Wright warned them, and if they again misbehaved, they would indeed be hanged. This wrote finis to the campaign.

The large army had been absent from Fort Walla Walla "sixty marching days," with rations for less than forty of these. None had died in battle, only one had been mildly wounded, two had succumbed to "poisonous roots" very early in the campaign. The main loss had been three horses and fifty mules. "That immense tract of splendid country over which we marched," Lieutenant Kip proudly announced, "is now opened to the white man." [32]

Huzzahs and Embarrassments

The newspapers made much of the campaign. Ten days after the first bat-tle the editors were in possession of sketchy details. The *Weekly Oregonian*, going to press on September 11, managed to insert a general description: "af-ter one charge by the troops," the Indians "appeared to be perfectly panic struck, and like craven cowards fled from the field." The paper did not doubt that "this victory will add more to the future safety of our citizens than any battle ever fought with the Indians in Oregon or Washington." Colonel Wright and his men would receive "the heartfelt plaudits of thousands of their countrymen, as well as that of the general government."

Particulars came in the next weekly issue under the headline "Brilliant En-gagement with the Hostile Northern Indians." The accurate details derive from an anonymous letter by one of the combat officers camped in the Coeur d'Alene country. Only the first battle is described, the account having been prepared on the eve of further fighting. Allowing for the time necessary to reach the Coast, the letter must have been carried down before the troops

31. Kip, *Expedition*, p. 116 (first quot.). NA, IA, Oreg. Sup., LR, to Nesmith from Lt. C. R. Woods in immediate charge of hostages, 14 October 1858 (quot.; 33 Indians). Wash. Sup., copies of LS, Letterbook of Nez Percé and Flathead areas, Nesmith to Craig, Salem, 24 October 1858, authorizing tobacco. NA, EW, AGO, LR, 290c, Wright to Mackall, Camp near Fort Walla Walla, 7 October; same to same, Camp on Umatilla River, 12 October (31 Indian hostages); same to same, itinerary, 6 October.

32. NA, EW, AGO, LR, 290c, Wright to Mackall, Camp near Fort Walla Walla, 9 October. Kip, *Expedition*, pp. 122 (days reckoned to 5 October), 127–28.

were anywhere near the mission. Perhaps Lieutenant Mullan, a personal friend of Father Joset, privately conveyed the letter through a Nez Percé ally, or by Joset's messenger for peace, Sebastian, or by another of Joset's Indians.

Next week's paper carried the headline "Two Other Battles Fought and Won! Indians Flying and Suing for Peace!! Suffering of Troops, etc." Like the previous dispatch, this was signed "Coeur d'Alene" and was datelined from the camp at Coeur d'Alene mission, September 16. Once again the story is accurately detailed. This time we learn that four Coeur d'Alenes had carried the message to the settlements. It seems improbable that Wright connived at this breach of professional ethics. The leakage of optimistic reports to the press nevertheless worked to his advantage; it also disposed the public to accept his later reports at face value.

Military headquarters below were disconcerted and annoyed at this publication of news from an anonymous officer. Major Grier had to write from camp at the Palouse River on September 30, solemnly assuring Vancouver headquarters that no soldier had sent anything out for publication. Lieutenant Kip must have been busily making notes all this while; he was to have his wonderfully detailed little book in hand at Fort Vancouver before the opening of December.[33]

More intriguing than the newspaper accounts are the official reports to the army. They exhibit heady enthusiasm and an appalling self-confidence. They seem a harbinger of the rhetoric for which American commanders were soon to demonstrate so awesome a talent in the opening phases of the Civil War. Wright's estimate of his own deeds was accepted completely by Secretary of War Floyd. In his published annual report for 1858 the Secretary congratulated General Clarke, who "with great promptness and a wise forecast" had "precipitated" his command "into the heart of the Indian country, where a powerful Indian force was assembled to meet him." Floyd remarked that "the campaign was prosecuted with great activity and vigor by Colonel Wright, of the 9th infantry, who gave battle to the Indians on several occasions, always routing them completely." As the Secretary saw it, the victory was straightforward, a prize of valor. "After beating their forces, capturing many prisoners, and destroying large amounts of property and laying waste their country, the Indians surrendered at will."

The next issue of the *American Almanac and Repository of Useful Knowledge* chronicled the battle as an important event. A *History of the United States Cavalry* published seven years after our war, in 1865, featured an imposing picture of Grier's charge at Four Lakes. Viewing the scene with imaginative freedom, the artist constructs in the foreground a first-class melee, Indians ferociously mixed with tight-jacketed dragoons; guidons wave bravely,

33. NA, Army Commands, Dept. Pacific, LR, Grier to Walker, 30 September.

and Wright's reserves maneuver at the rear; tipis frame the spirited action in the left foreground. The accompanying text tells how, after the horse slaughter, "without horses the Indians were powerless." Another imaginative drawing was devised for this battle, depicting Grier's men in full career across the plain, cutting down a horde of fanatic Indians.

In laudatory vein rivaling that of the Secretary of War, Winfield Scott, general-in-chief of all American armies, issued a proclamation on November 10. "Results so important, without the loss of a man or animal, gained over tribes brave, well armed, confident in themselves from a recent accidental success, and aided by the many difficulties presented by the country invaded, reflect high credit on all concerned." Historians have been content to repeat these encomiums. Bancroft is representative, seeing the campaign as a resounding success: "While Wright was thus sweeping from the earth these ill-fated aboriginals east of the Columbia, Garnett was doing no less in the Yakima country." [34]

What other influences had been available in that vast region during the troubles, to restrain or conciliate the Indians? It may be well to glance at the activities of the Indian service. The pathetic incapacity of this arm of the government lends emphasis to the Jesuit contribution. Neither superintendent nor agents were able to do anything; the situation was too remote, beyond all control. Major Owen had fussed very briefly in his passage through the Spokane country, and had broadcast his accusations. But general silence settled over the unified Indian service of Washington and Oregon at this critical juncture. Commissioner Mix, in the nation's capital, did not even know of the Steptoe attack until a steamer from California fortuitously arrived with newspapers from the Pacific coast.

The Commissioner was understandably embarrassed. He hurried a letter out to Nesmith immediately on July 3 inquiring after this "serious outbreak among the Indians of Washington Territory." His information, he drily commented, had not stemmed from an official source. If the news were true, Nesmith was to "use all available means at your disposal for such an emergency." Mix's advice was hardly helpful, since Nesmith had no means at all. Mix cheerfully urged the employment of these nonexistent means "to check at once the further spread of hostilities and to prevent the commission of outrages upon our citizens." This was a clarion call from a very uncertain trumpet. What is worse, it fell into a continuing abyss of silence.[35]

Months went by with no helpful word from the Northwest office or any

34. *SED* (serial 975), army reports, pp. 4 ff., 25. *American Almanac* (Boston, 1860), p. 383. Brackett, *History of Cavalry*, pp. 187 (picture), 191. Bancroft, *Washington*, pp. 193, 195–96. Second picture of charge in *Journal of the Military Service Institution of the United States*, 42 (1908), 485. Archer Corresp., 17 February 1859.

35. NA, IA, Oreg. Sup., LR, Mix to Nesmith, 3 July 1858.

of its dependencies. The latest intelligence on hand from Nesmith, ensconced amid the meager comforts of coastal civilization at Salem, was a set of financial estimates. This sort of record had been briskly passing back and forth over the heads of the unheeding Indians for some time, typical of the mindless activity that envelopes the meticulous, detached administrator on the vigil of any doomsday.

Finally on September 4, three and a half months after the Indian war had erupted, a tart reprimand issued from the nation's capital. In pained but august cadences it directed Nesmith's attention to the letter of July 3, enclosing another copy. It made a point of the fact that all its information thus far had come from unofficial rumors. It reflected that a second letter of August 4 had alluded to the strange silence. Yet "up to this time no information on the subject has been received from you, which has caused considerable embarrassment to the department." The Commissioner felt he had to "take this occasion to state that the Department expects you to Keep it advised ["regularly" is inserted, as an afterthought] of all matters pertaining to Indian Affairs within your Superintendency." [36]

Another letter went to Nesmith the same day, this time from Stevens. "I have learned this morning, that there is considerable dissatisfaction in the Dep[artmen]t in consequence of no reports having been received from you in relation to the recent outbreak." Happily, Stevens was at last in possession of a chatty letter from Nesmith; he intended to make "good use of it" for his friend, copying out extracts for general distribution. This letter unfortunately advanced no news beyond what Nesmith could extract from the newspapers and from Owen's one communication. The Indian Superintendent's contribution to the whole problem was a pious hope that troops and Indians would vigorously "fight it out."

Nesmith's major difficulty, aside from having no information, was the uncertain state of communications between West and East coasts. He wrote again to Mix on September 6, two days after Wright's last battle, regretting that his news of Steptoe's defeat had failed to reach Mix. Nesmith protested that his distance from the hostiles and lack of communication with the troops made it difficult to acquire news. He continued to be concerned about his budget; the Indians on this side of the Cascades would surely not join the hostile coalition "unless compelled to by reason of having their supplies of subsistence discontinued."

The same balance of contents may be observed in Nesmith's more private letter to Stevens. He frankly admits that the coastal Indian service is itself in the dark as to military and Indian doings, having "no important or definite

36. *Ibid.*, Nesmith estimate, 1 May 1858, and allied documents; Wash. Sup., letters from commissioner, to Nesmith, 4 September 1858.

news." He refers Stevens to the newspapers, and passes on a wild rumor that 125 miners have just been massacred. The one moment of passion that glints in the letter concerns the lack of provision for friendly treaty Indians. "For God's sake, Governor, try and get the Commissioner to forward all the annuity funds this fall." [37]

Nesmith wrote to Mix again on September 30, complaining about being blamed for sending no reports. "I have no agents residing among the hostile Indians" (wisely he neglects to chronicle the doings of Owen), nor any money to send someone five to six hundred miles into the Interior with the troops. At the same time he relayed news of Wright's activities during the first ten days of that month. As late as October 11, a note sent East by one of his Salem staff stiffly resented the complaints of Washington about Nesmith's "supposed failure" to report. [38]

Newspapers were calling attention to the embarrassing absence of the Indian service in connection with the war. During Wright's campaign in the north the New York *Tribune* loftily commented upon "the fact that nothing has been received from the Superintendent of Indian Affairs in Oregon and Washington Territories," so that the observer comes to believe "that some wrong exists which has wrought up the savages to the late hostile steps." The editor acidly concluded: "it is thought, in charity, that the Superintendents are among the Indians, seeking to restore pacific relations." The *Weekly Oregonian* for October 2 picked up the comment, adding its own jibes. It doubted that Nesmith "cares enough about the Indian war, its results or termination, to lose an hour's sleep, or devote an extra hour's labor to visit the hostile tribes within his superintendency." The editors accused the harried Superintendent of devoting himself instead to bad politics.

Nesmith was not completely inactive. He had gone up in the direction of Fort Dalles, and briefly entertained the notion of continuing as far as Fort Walla Walla. On November 1 he penned a few general remarks to the Commissioner. The Indians had given Wright "but feeble resistance"; up to twenty-five ringleaders had been hung or shot. It was rumored that "a few of

---

37. Stevens Papers, Nesmith to Stevens, 20 August 1858; Stevens to Nesmith, Boston, 4 September 1858; Nesmith to Stevens, 6 September; last two also in Todd edition, *PNWQ, 31,* 447. NA, IA, Oreg. Sup., reports and LS, Nesmith to Mix, 6 September; LR (from Oreg. Sup.), Nesmith to Mix, 6 September, annual report of Nesmith, 28 September, and of Lansdale, 1 August (cf. *RCIA*). Published official documentation is very unsatisfactory; in *RCIA* (1858) and *SED*, 35 Cong., 2 sess. (1858), 1; also in *HED*, 35 Cong., 2 sess., 2, same pagination, pp. 355–58, 566–635; see esp. Nesmith August report, pp. 571–75.

38. NA, IA, LR (from OS), Nesmith to Mix, 30 September; and Quincy Brooks (clerk writing in absence of Nesmith at Dalles) to Mix, 11 October; both letters also in Oreg. Sup., reports and LS.

the desperadoes" from different tribes were gathered at Colville, where they "still maintain a hostile attitude." Nesmith regretted that Wright failed to give the Colville Indians a specimen of White justice. In another display of administrative busy-ness, Owen's jurisdiction was extended in November to cover Agent Craig's Cayuses. At the same time Nesmith was authorized to send a special agent, presumably as an assistant for Owen, "among the Spokanes and tribes in their vicinity" at a thousand dollars a year if "the maintenance of peace requires it." [39]

Nothing came of all this agitation in the bureaucratic dovecotes, though later the next year a physician was to appear for a while in the upper country. Nevertheless, the whole episode had been a lesson to the Indian service. Nesmith sensibly put forth demands for three superintendents, one to manage the Oregon-Washington Interior. At the same time an investigating official from Washington, D.C., suggested at least two, one for the Interior. Stevens would urge the appointment of more agents, pointing out that there were now only three agents and two subagents for the entire wilderness territory. He desired separate agencies for the Flatheads, Nez Percés, and Yakimas, as well as one "for the remaining tribes East of the Cascades, consisting of the Spokanes, Coeur d'Alenes, and Pend d'Oreilles, Colvilles and Okenakains." [40]

Nesmith, despite his difficulties, did not hesitate to embark on a kind of feud with General Clarke's successor, William S. Harney, over opening the Interior to settlement. In December Nesmith was to confide to Clarke: "I have to regret that your successor has seen fit to adopt a policy marked by so wide a departure from what is at least due to courtesy, at the same time violative of the Acts of Congress in relation to our intercourse laws, and in utter disregard of the wishes of the Department and the rights of the Indians." Next spring Nesmith was replaced.[41]

Steptoe's career did not long survive the Indian war. He did stay on to help during the struggle. Captain Archer writes: "we think he has been badly treated by Genl. Clarke" in not receiving command of Garnett's column; leaving him at Fort Walla Walla "has done a great deal to confirm the first bad impression in the minds of the public." As soon as the fall campaign terminated and the army returned to Walla Walla, Steptoe left his regiment on

39. NA, IA, Oreg. Sup., reports and LS, Nesmith to Mix, Salem, 1 November 1858; LR, Grier to Nesmith, Fort Walla Walla, 28 October 1858. Wash. Sup., Mix to Nesmith, 17 and 18 November 1858.

40. Ibid. (Wash.), Mix to Geary, 9 April 1859; there is further documentation on physician, e.g. Mullan to Nesmith, Dalles, 2 July 1858, suggesting brother James for job. NA, IA, Special Files, No. 172, Mott to secretary of Interior, Washington, D.C., 22 November 1858 (incl. Nesmith suggestion). Stevens Papers, 10 January 1859 (not in Todd).

41. Oreg. Sup., reports and LS, Nesmith to Clarke, 13 December 1858. See WU, letter to Nesmith, 18 July; Todd, *PNWQ, 31,* 444, in opposition to Nesmith view on this.

October 10 to repair East. His sixty-day leave would soon become half a year, and then an additional year "for the benefit of his health." He left the Northwest on the same steamer as the stricken Major Garnett. On his arrival East he found himself the subject of a whispering campaign of "misrepresentations" reflecting alike upon his capacity and his courage. A reaction gripped military and civil authorities there against "the officers whose commands have led" to the Steptoe Disaster; Steptoe himself could hardly emerge unhurt. On December 4 he made formal demand that "a Court of Inquiry may be ordered to investigate the affair." He asserted that it would "give me the highest satisfaction to return at once to the De[partmen]t of Oregon" if necessary, to secure witnesses.[42]

A man deserving notice for his generous offer to negotiate peace was the former superintendent of Indian Affairs on the Coast, Anson Dart. Now resident on the Atlantic Coast, he learned of Steptoe's defeat two months after it occurred and immediately offered his services. He wrote first to President Buchanan with a view to "negotiating a settlement," and the next day in similar terms to the secretary of State. A month later we find that this offer had been referred to the Indian Department. Nothing came of it. Dart suggested that the government was too interested in an aggressive solution. In another message to Buchanan he protested that people familiar with the Northwest country cannot be true friends of the administration as long as "they advocate War measures in the settlement of Indian differences in that country." The gesture was generous. Distance and red tape brought it to nothing.[43]

ANOTHER JESUIT PEACE TOUR

Was the war really over as Colonel Wright proclaimed? Actually a beginning had been made, but much remained undone. To drive hostile Indians from a battlefield and to sign formal peace treaties did not constitute victory. The troops did not control the country. The tensions and injustices that were contributory causes of war had not been removed. Many of the Indians involved in the fighting had nothing to do with the peace. Given the tribal structure, few Indians would feel themselves bound just because others had signed a document.

The Hudson's Bay officials took a dim view of Wright's victories. Gover-

42. NA, EW, AGO, LR, 507S, Steptoe to adj. genl., Washington, D.C., 4 December 1858 ("misrepresentations"; final quot.); P165, Wright to same, Fort Dalles, 11 March 1859; S493, Steptoe to same, New York City, 2 December 1858; docs. of 4 May 1859 ("health") and 9 October 1861. Archer Corresp., "October" and 26 November 1858 (quot. in Archer sentence).

43. NA, IA, LR (from Oreg. Sup.), Dart to secretary of State, New York, 17 July 1858; to President, 16 July; to President, New York, 16 August.

nor Simpson in December 1858 wrote bluntly that "apprehensions are entertained for the safety of the establishment of Colville, owing to the disturbed state into which the Indians have been thrown by the abortive efforts of the U.S. troops to drive them into subjection." He hoped that Grahame's pleas at Fort Vancouver "may induce General Clarke to dispatch troops to the interior without delay." Two months later, though relieved that matters at Colville are somewhat better, Simpson still desired "that a sufficient military force may be forwarded to the disturbed districts, as soon as the season is sufficiently advanced to enable the troops to move from winter quarters."[44]

Superintendent Christopher Mott, an investigator for the federal Indian service, was not convinced of Wright's victory. "The latest intelligence from the Spokane Country," he reported, "is that the troops have met with some '*brilliant*' successes, and that the war is ended—*for the present*." At Fort Dalles, Mott observed the returning heroes of the campaign. He wrote the secretary of the Interior that he was amused "to hear their grandiloquent accounts of sanguinary battles and glorious victories won against an overwhelming foe—at the cost of ⸺ killed and *one* wounded." Mott observed that the people exhibited little "excitement or concern" for Wright's campaign. "But for the hanging operations" which had been projected on a generous and dramatic scale, "its results would not be properly appreciated." He felt that the hangings had probably subdued the tribes. Similarly Nesmith communicated to the commissioner his fears that Wright had been too sanguine in his attitude; with the troops withdrawn, hostilities could recommence.[45]

A message sent from the acting governor of Washington Territory to the legislative assembly in December expressed a skeptical view of the army's triumph. "It may however be doubted whether a permanent peace, such as shall from time to time render the life of a white man sacred, can be effected without a winter campaign, or the movement of troops at all seasons of the year through their country, and the establishment of permanent posts in their midst—in order that the savage foe may learn in winter, as well as in summer, the power of the military arm—and not to trust to the inclemency of the seasons to baffle its efforts, but be rendered subject to the authorities placed over him, and maintained in a condition in which he can do no harm."

Colonel J. Mansfield, the army's inspector general who arrived at Walla Walla in time to welcome the victorious Wright, wrote firmly to General Clarke: "Even if peace be made with all the tribes, I would not withdraw a single Company to any point below the Dalles this winter; I need not give

44. HB, D4, 55, Simpson Corresp. out, H. B. House, to J. Grahame, 15 December 1858; to Mactavish, 2 February.

45. NA, IA, Special Files, No. 172, Mott to secretary of Interior, Salem, 22 November 1858. LR (from Oreg. Sup.), Nesmith to Mix, 30 September.

you reasons for this." Two days later Wright's arrival in exuberant optimism moved Mansfield to modify his advice. He admitted in a second letter that there was "but one opinion here at Walla Walla as to the peace for a year at least if not permanently." For his part he will "simply say I would keep as large a force at this post as practicable, under the circumstances."

We have seen how Captain Archer at first took Wright's jubilant reports seriously. In an October letter he is developing an expansive view even of his own and Garnett's work. White troops had put in an appearance deep in Indian territory; "we took no hostages [substitute for a deleted "prisoners"] and killed but 10 Indians, but as far as we went our work was thorough, and peace established." But by November 2 he is contesting the received view of Wright's battle ("the opinion of all Col. Wright's officers, and of the people generally of Oregon and Washington Territories"): "which I hardly understand could have been a fight at all." Captain Keyes, who had been on Wright's expedition, was to complain that army officials at Vancouver scoffed at the too easily won victory.

In Washington, D.C., Stevens realized that something further was needed. Once more he urged upon the secretary of the Interior "the importance of bringing on a delegation of Indian Chiefs from Oregon and Washington, in order to impress them with the power and beneficence of the government and to diffuse through them among the Indian Tribes a disposition for peace and the arts and usages of civilized life." As far away as the Flathead country, Father Hoecken revealed in January that the Indians of the whole region were still upset, that "bad feelings and suspicions pervade the country," and that further work was needed to bring final peace.[46]

Father De Smet, involved deeply as a peace envoy later in 1858, wrote that the tribes "still retained their prejudices and their uneasiness and alarm which had to be dissipated, and there were false reports to be rectified; otherwise the war might soon break out afresh." Yet the Jesuit is equally insistent that Wright had turned the Indians against the war so completely that they "cannot even think of war any more." In context one realizes that the treaty conference as well as De Smet's own peace tour were necessary elements toward this effect.

The army was by no means disposed to rest upon Wright's achievements. After every man available had been committed to the Northwest campaign, the War Department found it was able to free General Harney, an experi-

46. Archer Corresp., "October," 2 November 1858. *Message and Correspondence*, pp. 55 ff. (8 December 1858). NA, EW, Army Commands, Dept. Pacific, Mansfield to Clarke, 2 October 1858; to same, 6 October. Stevens Papers, Stevens to secretary of Interior, 21 December 1858; also in Todd edition, *PNWQ, 31,* 459. Keyes, *Men and Events,* p. 288. MJ, IX, AA, Hoecken to De Smet, 25 January 1859.

enced Indian campaigner. Harney had won fame fighting the Seminoles, had subsequently commanded the American cavalry brilliantly for Scott in the Mexican War, and had campaigned against the Plains Indians, gaining a reputation especially for his victory over the Sioux. Almost sixty years old now, General Harney was a forthright, impetuous figure, with a soldierly face in an electric explosion of whiskers. He had been designated to conduct the Mormon War, but the campaign had proceeded without him when he was detained with the problems of Bloody Kansas. As the Mormon troubles subsided, Harney was intercepted a good distance across the Plains on his way to Utah. Brought back to New York, he embarked for the Northwest Indian war. His instructions were to set up a military department for the Northwest at Vancouver and fight to the end. Even as Wright was rejoicing over his Coeur d'Alene treaty, Stevens wrote from Washington to tell Nesmith that Harney "goes out determined to put the war through and to wage if necessary a winter campaign; he will be provided with everything which he desires."

Harney's party arrived in time to find the Wright victory being celebrated. They discounted what seemed obviously a pseudo-victory. The army would continue to maintain the huge concentration of nearly 2,000 troops in the Northwest, mostly in Washington Territory. A separate department was to be organized, with its own general and staff. A permanent fort was planted in the heart of the troubled area at Colville, that very winter and spring. Supply remained a problem; over half the ten companies at Walla Walla and Colville would not have enough clothing.[47]

On his arrival Harney found it necessary to write to eastern headquarters that "from all the information I have been able to obtain up to this time, I consider it essential and necessary that the force now here should not be diminished this winter, but that the steps which have been taken to subdue these Indians should be vigorously followed up." He was prepared to attempt a winter campaign. If that were not demanded, then at least "an imposing force should be marched through the country of the disaffected Indians, next spring and summer, to complete the impression already made and to satisfy them the troops had not left the Department." In fact some punitive columns were sent out into the Yakima country during the coming winter, without any real results. But no further expeditions were put in motion by the generals. Instead, another Jesuit was brought in and entrusted with the task of effecting a lasting settlement in the upper Interior.[48]

47. CR, 2, 743, 755; 4, 1571, Harney through aide Pleasonton to De Smet, 10 August 1858. Stevens Papers, to Nesmith, 10 September; Todd, p. 449. Clark, *OHQ*, *36*, 35, 37, 59.

48. *SED* (serial 1051), army reports; Harney Report, 24 October, p. 86 (quoted from NA original, AGO, LR). Bancroft, *Washington*, p. 198 (Yakima columns).

Before describing this major Jesuit undertaking, it may be interesting to see a similar though rather fruitless effort initiated by Wright. The only record of it is a later, hazy reminiscence by the man involved. This was W. T. Hamilton, an Englishman trading in the area, who seems to have been among the civilian employees on Wright's campaign. Shortly after the war ended, Hamilton was invited to a council of war at Fort Walla Walla. The officers discussed the possibility of an outbreak east of the Rockies, presumably in support of the Interior Indians. Hamilton supposedly was sent to discover their intentions and if possible to pacify them.

Accompanied by the half-breed Alexander McKay, he passed up through the Nez Percé country. The Indians here urged him to avoid the Coeur d'Alenes, describing them as "dangerous." Hamilton got rather a nasty reception from a huge band of Palouses; in parley he was able to conciliate them by showing his official papers. He traveled directly to the Coeur d'Alene mission, where he contacted Father Joset. On the strength of his letter from Wright, he was treated to a kind of council with the main chiefs in the priest's room. Father Joset displayed the letter and interpreted part of it to the chiefs. They were curious about the hostages at Walla Walla. Hamilton delivered himself of some bellicose generalities about Wright's readiness for peace or war. In his account he concedes that these statements were false but defends them as having "accomplished their object," making the Indians "uneasy."

As to his brief visit with the Flatheads farther east, Hamilton comments that they had resisted persistent efforts to involve them and had also held back "the majority of the Pend d'Oreilles." Once arrived on the Plains, he seems to have done very little. He did solicit Agent Vaughan's opinion, and met a few Blackfeet belonging to the friendly band of Little Dog. In general, he might have saved himself this trip by asking Congiato what he had discovered during his recent lengthy stay in the Blackfoot country, preparing for the new mission. Hamilton says that as he slipped back through the Spokane country, he could hear the war drums plainly at night. The whole story is narrated in terms so pompous and inflated, and with such errors of detail, as to make it difficult to accept. Still, for what it is worth, it may echo a courageous attempt at a peace tour.[49]

The Jesuit peace tour was to be more formal and sustained. Its central figure is Father De Smet. General Harney on his way to the Mormon War had the secretary of War induce De Smet to accompany him, technically as chaplain to the Utah army but in reality to conciliate Indians along the line of march. The priest received his formal designation as chaplain on the very day

---

49. W. T. Hamilton, "A Trader's Expedition among the Indians from Walla Walla to the Blackfeet Nation and Return in the Year 1858," *CHSM, 3* (1900), 33–123.

of the Steptoe Disaster far away in the Oregon country. De Smet at this time
was a white-haired man of almost 60. His biographer and editor, Hiram Chittenden, not a Catholic and indeed inclined to think of Jesuits as narrow in
character and training, emphasizes De Smet's unusually wide range of sympathy, his mild, benevolent, yet commanding presence. There was something
about him that was "august"; yet "he was of a genial and buoyant temperament, fond of jest and merriment, and humorously disposed."

"Installed" in the seventh regiment at Fort Leavenworth with a courteous
little ceremony by Harney, De Smet started over the Plains on June 1. Once,
when a band of Arapahoes attacked a Pawnee camp, he hurried to stop the
fighting but arrived too late; he did baptize 200 of the Pawnee children there.
Sioux and Cheyennes claimed his attention in small conferences along the remaining route. Five hundred miles out, at the South Fork of the Platte and
long before the Utah Indians were reached, orders arrived to return home,
the Mormon troubles being under control. De Smet went back to St. Louis.
Almost immediately Harney and the secretary of War were telegraphing him
to come and help in the Oregon Indian war. "There is no one," wrote the
General, "whose aid could be more valuable than yours."

De Smet took the only practical way of getting to the Northwest with
some speed. Rushing by railroad to New York, a thousand miles away, he
embarked with Harney's military party on the steamer *Star of the West* for
the long voyage to the Isthmus of Panama. The little steamer was crowded
with 640 passengers, mostly gold seekers for the Fraser mines. Its voyage was
beset by "squalls and small tempests." On the Pacific side of the Isthmus the
gold fever was even more virulent. De Smet and his military companions now
had 1,300 fellow travelers "busy stowing themselves away the best they can
in the interior and the deck of the great steamship." The better part of October was consumed in the long voyage up the South and North American
coasts, "shut up in a ship" with a mass of adventurers of "all nations on earth,
all with their morals infected with the yellow (or golden) fever, and who
think, speak and dream of nothing but of mines of gold." San Francisco was a
transit point. Harney, with his staff and De Smet, landed here on October 16
from their steamer *John L. Stephens*. To De Smet, the city seemed like a
strange "modern Babel," its 60,000 people bemusing both eye and ear with
international "uproar and movement." Here Harney was able to talk with
General Clarke and learn that the war was over.

Large crowds milled at the wharf as their ship stood out through the
Golden Gate on October 20 for the final leg of the voyage. On October 23
they passed over the bar of the Columbia River. "By the steamer of October
24th," reported the Hudson's Bay man at Vancouver, "Gen[era]l Harney
arrived at the garrison here" to command the new department; an army of

500 men was at the fort to receive him. De Smet found Vancouver impressive: "some hundred houses," the new army fort, a small frame cathedral for the Catholics—"the most flourishing of the towns on the Columbia."

The Northwest itself had greatly changed. "The savages, formerly so numerous along the coast and the river, have almost entirely disappeared." Pushed back or hidden away on the reservations, they were declining into "drink, misery and diseases," while the Whites became ever stronger. De Smet and Harney docked at Vancouver just in time to mingle with Wright's returned heroes. Harney and Clarke had already agreed to keep the forces now serving in Washington and Oregon as a garrison for the new Oregon department.[50]

De Smet was ordered to make an extensive reconnaissance and at the same time consolidate the peace by personal visitation to the tribes who loved him so well. Harney explained his project in a report to the East. The Jesuit was going to the Indians of the upper country "for the purpose of observing their disposition and to counsel them to observe most faithfully all the conditions they have promised to fulfill towards the Gov[ernmen]t and its citizens."

Harney's instructions to De Smet anticipate "the happiest results from your presence." He directs that "every facility shall be furnished you" to accomplish the journey. De Smet should impress upon the Indians the need of living up to their promises, and urge them to surrender men like Kamiakin and Skloom, who are reported to be among the Flatheads. He is to inform the chiefs that the troops do not mean to go away. If the peace terms are not observed, the soldiers will "most assuredly be placed upon their trail in the spring, with instructions to give no quarter." On the other hand, the government is prepared to be generous to a fallen foe.

Harney ordered De Smet to remain in communication with his headquarters as he proceeded on his "holy mission of charity." Post Commanders were

50. CR, *2*, 717 ff., esp. pp. 735–40; *1*, 13, 108–14. *JMUS, 3*, 72–73, with doc. Harney Correspondence, in *HED*, 36 Cong., 1 sess., 65 (1858), pp. 84 ff., and *SED*, 36 Cong., 1 sess., 2 (1858–59), 91 ff., esp. orders, letters of 19, 24 October. Riordan, *First Half Century*, pp. 91–92. HB, D5, 47, 4 November. MJ has original documentation for this episode, such as the September 7 telegram from the secretary of War and many writings of De Smet (e.g. long account to provincial in IX, C3, 351–73 and passim to 393, done 1 November 1859, and Linton Album in IX, C7). BJ has a journal of the trip, Cartons Deynoodt, Box 26, and an account by Cataldo ca. 1876, an itinerary, etc. CR has military documentation, *4*, 1569 ff. De Smet's work is treated in Reavis' biography of Harney (see below, Bib.), but by way of panegyric and with nothing useful to our purpose. A brief and incomplete account of our pacification appears in the otherwise commendable monograph by W. P. Donnelly, S.J., "Father Pierre-Jean De Smet: United States Ambassador to the Indians," U.S. Catholic Historical Society, *Historical Records and Studies, 24* (1934), 7–142.

told to provide "guides, interpreters, escorts, and animals" and to facilitate the project in every way. De Smet himself describes his mission as "removing the Indian prejudices, soothing their inquietude and alarm, and correcting or rather refuting the false rumors which are generally spread after a war, and which otherwise might be the cause of its renewal." [51]

The purpose of De Smet's tour was also described by the General's aide, who transmitted Harney's orders. By Wright's campaign "submission had been conquered, but the embittered feelings of the two races, excited by war, still existed, and it remained for you to supply that which was wanting to the sword; it was necessary to exercise the strong faith which the Red man possessed in your purity and holiness of character." This officer, dragoon Captain (later General) Alfred Pleasonton, was deeply impressed by De Smet. Even during the early stage of their friendship, as Pleasonton communicated Harney's orders for the Interior tour, he added a private note that "I shall always look back upon the agreeable moments we have spent together as among the most pleasant of my life." [52]

De Smet to the North

The veteran peacemaker climbed into the saddle on October 29 and started out alone on his hazardous six-month journey—a round trip of considerably over 1,600 difficult miles. Aged now, and grown somewhat stout, he found the trip painful. The sturdy frame, Congiato noticed, had so weakened as "no longer to be able to stand much strain." De Smet was experienced enough to know what such a winter trip involved. Beyond the merely physical pain, there was the unpopularity he might court among his Indian friends by appearing as mediator. "My position humanly speaking will be unpleasant." Still, his Indians who "have been enticed" into war needed his help. [53]

A few days after the priest's departure, General Harney, on November 5, sent a second long report to the East. Nothing had changed regarding the Indians since his last report; but he now feels easier in his mind about con-

51. Harney Corresp. (NA and *SED*), letters of 5 November and ff. CR, *4*, 1571–72, Harney through aide Pleasonton to De Smet, Fort Vancouver, 28 October 1858 (also in NA and in *SED*, serial 1024). Fort Dalles Papers, special order No. 4 on De Smet, 28 October 1858; De Smet's own copy in CR, *4*, 1573; NA army copy with Harney letter, n. 52, below.

52. CR, *4*, 1571, 1581, Pleasonton to De Smet, Fort Vancouver, 28 October 1858, 9 November 1859; *2*, 763.

53. BJ, De Smet, I–V, No. 5, from New York, 19 September 1858; Coll. 1ac–4ac, No. 3ac, Joset to Cooseman, ca. 1877, on motive and travel difficulties. RJ, MSax, II, 3, Congiato to general (in Italian), Fort Vancouver, 20 May 1859.

trolling them, and he composes a little disquisition concerning tribal structure in the Interior. Its context reflects the many conversations with De Smet. The General concludes by describing the Jesuit's peace tour, enclosing copies of the pertinent orders. As for military force, Harney plans a post for the protection of emigrants at Fort Boise, to be supplied from Walla Walla; he would like a similar establishment at Fort Hall. "As soon as the season will permit, I shall establish a Garrison of at least four companies in the vicinity of Colville" to check the activities of "the Indian tribes who were so lately hostile." His fort projects were vetoed back East on grounds of economy. He stubbornly persisted with the important Colville plan, under the guise of providing a depot for the boundary survey.[54]

Two days after his arrival Harney invited settlement near the military posts, in effect opening the whole Interior. With fears of Indian trouble still brooding, writes Agent Dennison from The Dalles, this created "quite a stir." Superintendent Nesmith, fearing war, promptly protested against the order as "contrary to law and void." Nesmith got small comfort from his friend Stevens, who admonished him in a letter of January 4: "I consider Harney's order a wise, beneficial and statesmanlike order and shall stand by it, whatever the consequences."

Very early in November, Harney had a talk with the federal Indian investigator Mott. The General proposed his military fort at Colville, with Agent Cain stationed there to oversee Indian affairs. Mott reported to his superiors that nothing could be done until spring, and meanwhile "the mere ipse dixit of a military commander" had thrown the Interior open. This was "directly in the teeth of solemn assurances made by us," in a council at The Dalles not long after Wright's return, with the Nez Percés, Cayuses, Klickitats, and lesser tribes. This new order "must serve to weaken their confidence in the promises and good faith of the Government."[55]

De Smet meanwhile made his way upriver, enjoying the wild "beauty and magnificence" of the autumn countryside. At the Cascades stood a bustling village. Farther east, The Dalles had suddenly become a city "with upward of 100 houses, some of which are of stone"; farms clustered nearby, and there was a larger fort. Whites were greedily eyeing the undulating, grassy country that stretched 175 miles toward Fort Walla Walla. A military ambulance

54. SED (serial 1051), Harney Report, 5 November; NA, EW, AGO, LR, 072.

55. Nesmith Papers (OH), to Mix, 19 November 1859, including excerpt from letter of Grier to Nesmith, 28 October 1858, and enclosing Harney order of 31 October 1858. NA, IA, Oreg. Sup., LR, Dennison to Nesmith, 18 November 1858, with copy of Harney order; Special Files, No. 172, Mott to secretary of Interior, 22 November. Stevens Papers, to Nesmith, 4 January 1859 (not in Todd).

conveyed the Jesuit to Walla Walla in a comfortable eight-day journey. Here De Smet had the pleasure of encountering Father Congiato.[56]

Congiato had been moving about the upper country ever since the beginning of his own peace tour last June. He was to write next month, perhaps in jest, that many believed him dead. In a trip "very full of dangers," he told a friend, he had made his way "as far as the Missouri River," traversing four thousand miles of territory. "When I consider the poor condition of my health, the roughness of the country through which I travelled, the many privations to which one who travels in a wild country like this is naturally subject, I am astonished at myself; and the 4,000 miles ride, through mountains, woods, plains, rivers and deserts, appears to me like a dream rather than a reality."

He could thank God that it had all been "very successful." In addition to "several other good things done, I sucçeeded in opening a new mission among the Blackfeet Indians." Congiato now interrupted his trip to spend three days with De Smet at Fort Walla Walla. He prepared him for his tour with up-to-the-minute information. Congiato shared General Harney's worry about the tribes; he remarked in a report to Rome: "though the war may be over and peace concluded, Father De Smet will do great good by this trip." De Smet for his part acquired "reassuring news from him concerning the dispositions of the savages." Ravalli was also traveling to the Coast with Congiato; he could give De Smet all the news from Colville.[57]

Upon their arrival at Vancouver, Congiato and Ravalli visited General Harney. Ravalli had left the Kettle country only two weeks before. Since Harney complained on November 5 that "nothing has been heard from Colville" for some time, he must have welcomed Ravalli's news. The Jesuit went so far as to vouch for the Kettle tribe as "peaceful and quiet." He and Congiato had "resided for some months past" in the upper country, continuing their previous work to keep the Kettle groups under control. They felt that conditions were now "quiet and satisfactory." Humanitarian motives may have inclined both priests to color the general picture favorably; the main purpose of their visit to the General was to plead that the hostages be sent home, as being no longer necessary to guarantee peace. On the other hand, the work of Congiato and Ravalli, if successful, would explain why De Smet did not bother to include the Colville region in his own peace tour. General Harney was particularly pleased that the Jesuit superior put "all his

56. CR, 2, 742–43.
57. *Pittsburgh Catholic*, (1 March 1859), p. 2, Congiato to ——, in San Francisco (first printed there in *Monitor*) from Portland, Oreg., 29 November 1858; he arrived at the Coast "some three or four days ago." RJ, MSax, II, 3, Champoeg, 10 December 1858 (in Italian). CR, 2, 744.

establishments at my disposition" to implement any policies regarding the Indians.[58]

Congiato soon went on to Champoeg, in Oregon, where on December 10 he composed a painstaking, lengthy account of the entire war to send on to Rome. He made plans to return to the upper country as soon as the rigors of winter had passed. On the Coast he was pleased to note that the peace services of the Jesuits had won them friends. In tangential ways the war had effected "a great deal of good to the Catholic cause in this country, and the conduct of the Catholic missionaries during the war has dissipated a good many prejudices from the minds of many, both white and savages." Congiato told Rome that whereas he had feared the Jesuit work would be ruined by the war, as was that of the Oblates by the war of 1855, things turned out quite the opposite. The Jesuits were currently held in "high esteem as much by the whites as by the Indians themselves." The newspapers, too, had picked up the story. The Jesuit general wrote to France that the papers "had made known the happy issue of the mediation by our Fathers to effect a pacification of the Indian tribes in revolt against the Americans."

Despite his bad health, Congiato was to stay on the frontier and especially in the upper Indian country until November of 1860, except for a brief, four-month trip earlier in the latter year. His health then forced him to retire to San Francisco permanently, though technically he continued for some time to be head of the separate Oregon mission. On his last trip south he would bring out with him Father Hoecken, whose health was impaired by wilderness rigors.[59]

At Walla Walla, Father De Smet found the Indian hostages camped near the fort and thoroughly unhappy. The commander liked them; he was doing all he could to help them. But he had no authority to allow the one thing they particularly desired: to go home. The hostage families were both surprised and "delighted" to meet the greatest of the Blackrobes so unexpectedly, after eleven years of absence. De Smet learned "with pleasure" that all of them, especially the Coeur d'Alenes, had gained the good will of the officers and soldiers at the fort by their Christian conduct. They had continued their communal prayers morning and evening. The soldiers used to gather about, as had those at the treaty grounds, "fond of enjoying this edifying spectacle." A captain told De Smet he would "never forget the deep impression which the piety of these poor savages had made upon him."

58. *SED* (serial 1051), Harney Reports, 5, 27 November; from NA, EW originals in AGO, LR, 072 and 74–0.

59. Congiato letter in *Pittsburgh Catholic* (first quot.); 10 December, Congiato letter to Rome, n. 57, above. FP, I, 5, Jesuit general to Association (in French), 25 April 1859. Riordan, *First Half Century*, pp. 94, 96.

De Smet felt it lay within the meaning of his orders to release the prisoners. They could at least assuage their home-sickness by a winter's stay in the north. They might also be considered as guides. In any case, they would be a dramatic illustration of the army's good will. Congiato could ask Harney's permission meanwhile; if the General refused, the hostages promised to return to the fort with De Smet in the spring. There was no question of delaying at Walla Walla until authorization could come up from the Coast; winter was setting in, threatening to close the upper country or at least to increase the difficulty of access. Only the Palouses could afford to stay an extra week or so and then return home, their country being much more accessible. The Walla Walla commandant happily concurred in all this, received the Indians' pledge to return, "seconded by the Rev[eren]d Father De S[met]," and wrote immediately to headquarters for formal permission.[60]

Leaving the fort on October 13, the Jesuit's party made rapid time. At the Snake "a numerous camp" of Palouses "received us with kindness and eagerly aided us in getting across." In camp that night a "large number" of Palouses came for a visit. They were "hungry for news, in the critical situation in which they were with regard to the whites," being "among the principal instigators of the warfare on the whites." De Smet "found them very attentive to my advice." He also gave them some religious instruction. As the hostages traveled toward their homes, "they showed me unceasing signs of gratitude."

During the "beautiful and agreeable" weather which surprisingly prevailed, and especially during the long evenings around the campfire, "the Indians loved to relate to me with touching simplicity the principal things that had happened since I left them, such as the death of their chiefs etc." De Smet himself was an enthusiastic conversationalist with Indians and "did not lack interesting things to tell them." Arriving at Lake Coeur d'Alene on October 18, the party was welcomed "with the liveliest cordiality" by the Indian families camped there. The return of the Spokane and Coeur d'Alene prisoners "heightened the universal joy still further."

At this point winter descended ferociously. De Smet was to be snowbound at the mission with his colleagues for some months. Fathers Gazzoli, Vercruysse, and Joset were there to tell him at length how the Indian mind "becomes uneasy, gloomy and apprehensive" as the White frontier draws closer, plunging them "into a state of entire hopelessness." De Smet could see that "it

60. Fort Walla Walla Letterbook, commandant (unsigned) to Pleasonton, 13 November 1858. CR, 2, 744. Harney permission to Congiato was reported East in his November 27 letter. Joset Papers, No. 65, Captain Kirkham to Joset, from Fort Walla Walla, 13 November 1858, notifying him of the release. Joset Narrative. See also BJ, Coll. 1ac-4ac, No. 2ac, Cataldo description; No. 3ac, Joset to Cooseman (both ca. 1877); Joset Narrative.

will not be easy to preach resignation to them." He had already received a letter from Chief Michael of the Kettles, begging him to come and help them as he had before. It was at this time that De Smet conceived the idea of bringing a delegation of chiefs from the various tribes down to Vancouver.[61]

He composed a report to Harney on December 9, passing along the information collected from Indians and missioners in the north and outlining his project. Runners conveyed this to Vancouver by the end of the month. Harney returned a favorable answer. He would "see them and explain to them the intentions of the government." The army would underwrite the expenses of the journey. But De Smet must come down "as early in the spring as practicable," lest Harney or his troops be suddenly called off to some new military emergency. Indian wars were breaking out with distressing frequency. Colonel Sumner had taken the field against the Kiowas that July, and a small gold rush during the fall had stirred up the Colorado tribes. A serious Navajo war erupted in September and continued through November. A Mojave outbreak in October was to last into the next year. The Mescalero Apaches were about to become troublesome, and risings were anticipated in several other places. Worse, the Mormon pot was bubbling again. The army had to keep a garrison of 2,000 to 3,000 men alert in Utah all through 1858 and 1859. As late as March 1859 and again in August a real Mormon war was barely averted.[62]

The affirmative response eventually reached De Smet by March of the next year at St. Ignatius mission, having been delayed "owing to the deep snows and the impracticableness of the mountain passes." At Christmas in the Coeur d'Alene mission church De Smet chanted the midnight Mass, the Indians intoning the Gloria, Credo, and assorted hymns in their own language. He found the episode deeply moving. He had also baptized a small namesake on November 21: "ego Petrus Joannes De Smet baptizavi Petrum Joannem."

De Smet did not labor alone on his peace tour. The Indians were scattered; getting in touch with them required the help of the other Jesuits. He was soon formally to record his "indebtedness to all the Fathers and Brothers" of the mission for "the efficacious aid which they rendered me toward fulfilling the special mission" of the army. Father Hoecken sent a letter down to the Sacred Heart mission urging De Smet to come up among the Flathead confederacy and allay the "bad feelings and suspicions of the Indians." On February 18 Joset conducted De Smet east for the rendezvous with Hoecken on the Clark Fork River. Traveling over snow and ice and visiting as many camps as possible, the two priests were out no less than twenty-five days on this stage

61. CR, 2, 745–46, 758 (quots.).
62. OJ, "Liber baptizatorum" of Sacred Heart mission. CR, 3, 966; 4, 1574; 2, 761. Furniss, *Mormon Conflict*, pp. 185–86, 205, 217, 224; Hafen, *Indians of the Plains 1857–1861*, p. 159.

of the peace tour. Winter was still very much with them. "Ice, snow, rain and winds impeded very much our course, in our frail canoes of bark." The Indians were at winter camps in the forests and along the waterways "where they lived by the chase and fishing." [63]

Everywhere the Indians received the two Jesuits with eagerness, hearing De Smet carefully. They attended also to the religious instructions. De Smet was heartened by his reception: "the country, I have reason to believe, will remain quiet." At St. Ignatius he worked with the Kalispels and Pend d'Oreilles. Hoecken had broadcast news of the great Blackrobe's coming. Even the Kutenais, "having heard of my arrival, had travelled many days' journey through the snow to shake hands with me, to bid me welcome, and manifest their filial affections." De Smet also "crossed deep snow a distance of seventy miles" to visit with the Flatheads in their home valley to the south of the mission. He was able to assure them that Rome intended to reopen their own mission again.[64]

The first phase of De Smet's tour was completed. He could write soon to St. Louis that "in my several visits" to the various tribes, the Indians had received him with "every demonstration of sincere and filial joy." He ventured to say "that my presence among them has been of some advantage to them, both in a religious and secular point of view." He had encouraged the Indians "to maintain the conditions of the treaty of peace with the Government," and he had baptized over a hundred infants as well as "a large number of adults." According to his report to Harney, he had "held frequent conversations with the chieftains" of the Spokanes, the Coeur d'Alenes, the Kettles, and the Kalispels. The Flatheads, Pend d'Oreilles, Kutenais, and Palouses should, of course, be added. The hostile Yakima leaders had not yet been contacted.

There were shadows in this picture. A "small portion" of the Kettles remained unconvinced and badly disposed, as did some of the Kalispels. In general, though, De Smet felt he had succeeded "in removing many doubts and prejudices against the intentions of the Government, and against the whites generally, which were lurking in the minds of a great number of the most influential Indians." [65]

Bringing in the Chiefs

There remained only De Smet's final project of bringing the chiefs down. Delegates were offered by almost all the important tribes of the upper country. They included Head Chief Alexander Man without a Horse of the Pend

63. MJ, IX, AA, Hoecken to De Smet, 25 January 1859; CR, 2, 764; 4, 1581.

64. MJ, IX, C4, St. Ignatius, De Smet to St. Louis superior, 2 April 1859. CR, 2, 765; 3, 967, May 25 report; *SED* (serial 1051), pp. 141–43, also has May 25 report.

65. CR, 2, 766 (November 10); 3, 967. May 25 report.

d'Oreilles; Head Chief Victor Happy Man of the Kalispels; Head Chief Denis Thunders Robe of the Kettles; the Coeur d'Alenes, Chief Andrew Seltis and Subchief Bonaventure, elected to replace the disgraced Head Chief Vincent; Head Chief Garry of the Eastern Spokanes; Subchiefs Adolph Red Feather and Francis the Iroquois, replacing the seriously ill Head Chief Victor of the Flatheads; and, after some hesitation, the Yakima chiefs so central to the confederation of hostiles: Skloom and Kamiakin.

The Kutenais, who had come so far to visit with De Smet, sent no delegates. Perhaps this was because of their alienation from all things American ever since the Stevens treaty of 1855; or perhaps they felt they had demonstrated their neutrality sufficiently by deliberate withdrawal into Canada at the beginning of the war. Nor would there be representatives from the lesser tribes farther to the west, especially the still hostile Okanogans, the Central and Western Spokanes, the San Poils, and the Columbias. The reason for this omission seems to have been Harney's recent letter ordering De Smet to return as soon as possible; delivered in March, it allowed De Smet and his Jesuit colleagues no time to extend their activities into the corner of the Interior. Besides, Congiato and Ravalli had effected something there already.

De Smet had not conceived his idea of a council with Harney until after his talks with the Palouses and Spokanes during the journey north from Walla Walla. He did try now to contact the Palouse chief Tilcoax. But Tilcoax seems to have taken refuge "among the Buffalo Nez Percés" out on the Plains. As the principal target of Colonel Steptoe's expedition, Tilcoax had been an enemy of the Whites too long and too intensely to entertain any great expectations of their mercy. De Smet was to report that "from all I can learn, he has been the prime mover" in the Steptoe and Wright wars; this was owing not to any great influence but to his persistence. He had been "unceasing in his endeavors to create bitter feelings against the whites" at every opportunity. The loss of almost a thousand of his horses to Wright must have been a heavy blow to his financial status; the manner of their slaughter, brutal and vindictive to the Indian mind, could not have endeared the military to him. Tilcoax therefore disappeared from sight. Sometime during the next decade or so he is said to have been killed by Bannocks.[66]

Kamiakin's brother Skloom was sick and almost blind, able at this time to travel only "by small journeys." Skloom promised De Smet that, if he came out of his present sickness alive, he would join the chiefs at Vancouver "in the course of the summer." Kamiakin was at first understandably nervous about the army. The great chief was no stranger to Catholic priests, Jesuit or Oblate. Gibbs in his inquiries for Stevens, for example, found Kamiakin in 1853 at the Oblate mission "much under the influence of the missionaries,

66. CR, *3*, 967–70; Joset Narrative (Tilcoax death). Family tradition has him later return from his flight of 1858, soon dying a natural death (Brown, *Indian Side*, p. 392).

with whom he lives altogether." He had "adopted some of the forms of Catholicism" but "refuses to be baptised, because he would be compelled to put away his surplus wives, of whom he has several." We know that he often advised other Indians to become Catholics, and he sought Father Pandosy's advice in his affairs. Stevens had been impressed with Kamiakin's imposing presence and personality, which seemed to combine the qualities of the grizzly bear and the panther. He was kingly, controlled, and intelligent. Gibbs describes the chief as "a large, gloomy-looking Indian, with a very long and strongly-marked face, slovenly in dress, but said to be generous and honest." De Smet came to respect and admire Kamiakin during this peace tour. The priest must have been unimpressed by whatever remained of the chief's Catholic sympathies, since he regarded both Kamiakin and the backsliding Spokane Garry as "still pagans, though their children have been baptized."

De Smet held a number of earnest talks with the Yakima chief and with his brother Skloom during the whole stay among the Flathead confederacy "in February, March, and April." He explained Harney's desire for peace, the determination to protect Whites everywhere, and the General's generosity toward defeated enemies. The two chiefs "invariably listened with attention and respect" to the Blackrobe. Kamiakin made "open avowal of all he had done in his wars" against the Whites, particularly in the Steptoe Disaster and the Wright campaign. He claimed to have advised his people against joining in the troubles of 1858, but to have been "at last drawn into the contest by the most opprobrious language the deceitful Telxawey [Tilcoax] upbraided him with in full council" of the several tribes. Kamiakin protested, too, that he had restrained his people as much as possible from attacking any White travelers. At this point in the project the two Yakima chiefs did not yet feel prepared to accompany De Smet to Vancouver.[67]

The various chiefs were now "in readiness for the long journey as soon as the snow would have sufficiently disappeared." Joset had written to say that the Kettle head chief, Denis, was waiting at Sacred Heart. The Coeur d'Alene tribe were also gathered there, to prepare during Lent for the coming Easter. Gazzoli wrote on April 10 that he was collecting chiefs for the visit south. Head Chief Vincent wanted to go down, but Gazzoli believed "he will hardly be" a true representative of the tribe. Since Vincent had shown himself lacking the prestige to command Coeur d'Alene obedience, Gazzoli had the tribe elect other delegates.[68]

At this critical juncture a familiar face put in an appearance. We last saw

67. CR, *3*, 968–69. RR, *1*, ii, 407, 410–11 (Gibbs). Bischoff, "Yakima War," pp. 12–13, with Oblate docs. cited.

68. MJ, IX, De Smetiana, from Joset, 27 April 1859; ibid., AA, from Gazzoli, 10 April; both from Coeur d'Alene mission.

Agent Owen wandering on the Plains, then visiting in Utah, and in November journeying again to Fort Benton. He had returned to his trading post on December 1. There he meant to remain only a few months, until the first hint of spring would allow him to start for the Coast. With De Smet operating in the mountains, Owen bestirred himself to send a report of his own to Nesmith on February 2. As he often did, he stopped by at St. Ignatius mission, six days after Joset and De Smet had finally arrived there. Owen stayed at the mission almost two weeks. Since the passage to the lower country would not be open for a month yet, he had ample time to brood over De Smet's successfully completed peace tour.

Even now, he might have saved face by associating himself with De Smet's project. As agent for at least some of these tribes, Owen had reason, and perhaps even some right, to participate in it. But a self-destructive impulse recurrently impelled the man to overreach himself. A characteristic aspect of his life is the headlong charge onto some untenable ground, followed by an embarrassing retreat over a field littered with his recriminations, defensive expostulations, and small lies. As a flaw of character, it was not the worst a good man might suffer. On this occasion, however, it was to prove for the Jesuits a serious nuisance.

Owen coolly informed De Smet that he himself was in possession of orders for an undertaking precisely similar. He explained that these came from Superintendent Nesmith and the government investigator Mott; De Smet at first seems to have understood him to say Mix, the national commissioner. Owen left De Smet in no doubt that the entire project was now removed into his own hands; the priest was not in any way to be associated.

The agent, as his subsequent letters show, was lying—he held no such commission. Nor had Nesmith, to whose authorization Owen would henceforth appeal, conceived such a project. De Smet did not know this. The priest could still have stood firmly upon his military orders from the general commanding this department. He could also have pointed out that his own project was fully organized. At least he might have demanded some share in its direction.

Whatever De Smet's faults were, his makeup contained no trace of pettiness. He promptly and cheerfully handed everything over to Owen. Neither now nor later would the Jesuit allow himself to take part in the acrimonious controversy which was to result between army and Indian officials. "I persuaded the Indians that as Major Owen had received orders from the highest authority [Mix], he superseded me, and they should look upon him as their principal leader in this expedition, while I would follow on with them as far as practicable and [as far as] I would be allowed."

Embarrassingly enough, Owen had no outfit or provisions for the trip. De

Smet therefore "lodged the chiefs in my own tent and provided them with all necessary supplies" during the month's journey to Walla Walla. The chiefs rendezvoused at the mission, leaving with De Smet on April 16. Two days later they reached Owen's camp, and the combined parties prepared to break trail down the snow-clogged passages to the Sacred Heart mission, where more chiefs were waiting.[69]

Along the route, Kamiakin and his family were camped to await De Smet for another talk. Kamiakin finally expressed his willingness to go down if the priest could lend him a horse in good condition for the trip. De Smet was moved. "The sight of Kamiakin's children, the poverty and misery in which I found them plunged, drew abundant tears from my eyes; Kamiakin, the once powerful chieftain, who possessed thousands of horses and a large number of cattle, has lost all, and is now reduced to the most abject poverty." Though De Smet had no horse to spare, he determined to send one back later on.

As soon as Chief Garry joined the party in the Spokane country, the priest "entreated him, for the sake of Kamiakin and his poor children, to send him a horse and an invitation to come on and to accompany the other chiefs." This would be Kamiakin's "best opportunity to present himself before the general and superintendent, in order to expose his case to them and obtain rest and peace." Garry agreed, and Kamiakin was soon a member of the party.

De Smet "had daily conversations with him until he reached Walla Walla." Kamiakin thus came to place "implicit confidence in the generosity of the general." De Smet for his part came to believe in the sincerity of Kamiakin's "repeated declarations" that he would never fight the Whites again. "My candid impression is, should Kamiakin be allowed to return soon, pardoned and free, to his country, it will have the happiest and most salutary effect among the upper Indian tribes, and facilitate greatly all future transactions and views of [the] Government in their regard." De Smet told the army that "the Indians are anxiously awaiting the result; I pray that it may terminate favorably with Kamiakin." [70]

Owen, meanwhile, found himself in something of a predicament. What had seemed in the Bitterroot Valley like an opportunity to seize credit for himself now began to look like a possibility of trouble. Would Nesmith welcome all these chiefs? Though De Smet had been astonishingly gracious in turning over the project, the army might prove suspicious. It would be well to have

69. *SED* (serial 1023), pp. 791–92, Owen to Geary, 31 May 1859. NA, Wash. Sup., LR, Flathead-Blackfoot district, full report on movements and episode (not in Owen, *Journals and Letters*). *SED* (serial 1024) and NA, EW, AGO, 79-0, Harney Report, 1 June, on incident. CR, *3*, 967–68, De Smet report to Harney, 28 May, corrected slightly from NA original. Owen diary, in *Journals, 1*, 208–11; *2*, 190–91, letter to Geary, 2 June 1859. See also CR, *2*, 765–67.

70. CR, *3*, 969.

some documentation waiting at Walla Walla. Owen went into camp south of the Spokane River and hurriedly sent a letter to the superintendent on May 7. "Kamiakin the Yakima chief has today voluntarily surrendered to me as a Civil officer of the U. S. Gov[ernmen]t; I have made him no promises whatever but would like under the circumstances to be able to guarantee him a safe convoy to the lower country in company with some other Chiefs that are with Me, and back again to his own people." A querulous note enters the letter. Since the chief desired a fair talk with General Harney, Owen complained, "I could not under the circumstances refuse to take him into my camp."

Having thus detached himself from any responsibility for this most notorious of the hostiles, Owen attempted to explain the coming of the other chiefs. They "are anxious to visit you in person[,] and thinking much good might result from it, I gave them without orders my permission; I sincerely hope you may take a favorable view of the matter and forward me orders to carry out their wishes." Later on in this message he takes occasion to mention casually that Father De Smet "is with me on his way to Vancouver," from what seems to have been some kind of winter tour among the Indians on behalf of General Harney. Owen coolly qualifies this reference to De Smet's undertaking: "the nature of which I do not know." In his diary for the journey down, he has the minuscule entry: "the Rev[erend] father De Smet is travelling." [71]

The difficulties of the weather and of the early spring terrain, the problems involved in gathering the chiefs along the route, and Owen's reluctance to decamp for Walla Walla until his letter could be in Nesmith's hands all combined to keep the little party on the road almost a month. Rivers were high and the snow was deep. "We suffered much and ran many dangers on the route." At one stage ten days were spent cutting through a tangle of fallen trees laden with snow; several horses perished here. The little party finally entered Fort Walla Walla on May 13.

Owen halted the party. To protect himself, he had decided to wait here until definite authorization from Nesmith could arrive. The delay proved unfortunate. De Smet left shortly, being under orders to put in as prompt an appearance as possible at Vancouver. Removed from the Jesuit's influence, Kamiakin could see what Owen was up to. The chief had many sources of information among the half-breeds, and as the days drew on he assessed the situation accurately, slipped from the fort, and fled forever back to his secure refuge in the expanses of forest and plain.

This news was going to come as something of a shock to the General. Har-

---

71. NA, Wash. Sup., LR, Flathead-Blackfoot district, Owen to Nesmith, Camp on Spokane River, 7 May 1859 (not published in Owen, *Journals*).

ney had received word of Kamiakin's presence a week after the party's arrival at Walla Walla. The General of course was pleased and excited. During
the week of his arrival at Vancouver he had expressed his conviction to eastern headquarters that Wright's victory might be made lasting if Kamiakin
and Skloom were properly managed. Now his enthusiasm for De Smet's feat
reveals itself in the report he immediately sent east. De Smet had just brought
down "the noted chieftains Kamiakin and Schloom, the leaders of the late
war." They "have been induced to offer themselves to my disposition." Harney promises that "a special report will be submitted on this subject." What a
coup for the new general: the surrender of Kamiakin, elusive red ghost of the
Interior wars! But there was to be no further report. Harney was furious at
the result of Owen's "officious interference." [72]

De Smet may have stayed with Owen at Walla Walla for about a week. We
find him at Vancouver composing his formal report on May 25. It is difficult
to say where Superintendent Nesmith was during all this time. Officially he
had already left office, but his replacement seems not to have arrived. He may
have been anywhere in the large Indian jurisdiction, tidying up affairs in
preparation for his successor. Did he eventually send some belated authorization to Owen? The agent's ample documentation and the manuscripts of the
Indian service do not reveal it. De Smet's departure now put Owen between
two fires. He did not want to go down to Vancouver without a document;
yet if he waited longer, De Smet's arrival without the chiefs was sure to un-
leash the anger of the military at Vancouver and eventually at Fort Walla
Walla. He could afford to give De Smet a head start, since the newly inaugurated steamboat service would get him from Walla Walla to The Dalles in
two days.

From The Dalles, Father Congiato soon wrote to De Smet, informing him
that Owen had reached that place by steamer with Chiefs Alexander and
Adolph. The other chiefs were following overland. Kamiakin had fled, re-
portedly when other Indians told him he would be hanged. Congiato urged
De Smet: "try, for God's sake, to calm the General." He felt that "the less
noise is made on that disagreeable business the better [it] is; the people speak
here against the interference of Major Owen in that affair, and say that had
the thing been left in your hands there would have been no difficulty in
bringing Kamayaken down." [73] At Vancouver on May 28 the Indians were
all present for their visit with General Harney.

72. CR, *3*, 967 (weather problems), and Harney Report, 1 June. Owen diary (diary
entries cease from 7 May on Spokane River until April 1860), in *Journals, 1*. Harney,
May 21 letter, in *SED*, 36 Cong., 1 sess., 65 (1858), p. 139; June 1 letter on pp. 140–41.
SED 35 Cong., 2 sess., 1 (1858), pp. 413–14, Harney Report, 29 October.
73. MJ, IX, AA, 751, Congiato to De Smet, Dalles, 24 May (?).

On this date, too, the army informed Owen in clear, chill tones that it did not mean to tolerate his interference. The first letter in the interchange is from Harney to Owen. The General "desires to know by what authority you have taken charge," sowing "doubt and confusion" among the Indians. Owen returns an answer immediately to the note, affecting to be "startled and surprised at its singular manner." He rejects the General's right to take such a tone. He himself is only acting under the orders of the Indian Department. He holds "documents in my possession that show my authority." He regrets any confusion and doubt sown, and would like an interview at the General's convenience. This missive drew a sharp rejoinder from Harney, still on the same day, acknowledging receipt and protesting stiffly that "it is not a satisfactory answer to his question of this morning." For the future, "the General further directs, you will not in any way interfere with the Indian chiefs now at this Post, so long as they are under his charge." Harney wrote De Smet this day that Owen was "not to interfere in any way"; he asked De Smet "to inform the Indians of this." [74]

Harney's council with the chiefs "produced most happy results on both sides." There seems to have been a renewal of the peace treaty, perhaps verbally. The Indians particularly expressed their willingness to accept a reservation. Harney assured them he was satisfied with Kamiakin; they were to convey this to the Yakima chief. De Smet then took the chiefs to Salem to present them to the superintendent of Indian Affairs. At the expense of the army, the chiefs were granted a tour of several weeks through the Oregon coastal towns, with presents for all. De Smet wrote: "the poor Indians can make nothing or very little" out of the industrial establishments, steam engines, printing shops, and the like. But they were vastly impressed with the chained wretches in the prison cells at Portland. They asked many questions about prisons and chains. [75]

At one point in this tour a settler named Robbins invited De Smet and his Indian party "to my house to dinner and afterward had their photos taken— Father De Smet writing their names." A fascinating picture resulted. All the chiefs wear expressions of suitably grim, almost dour, solemnity. Their hair

74. NA, EW, AGO, LR, 79-0, Pleasonton for Harney to Owen, Fort Vancouver, 28 May 1859; Owen to Pleasonton, same place and date; Pleasonton reply, same place and date. Copies of this correspondence from Nesmith's office are in IA, Wash. Sup., LR, from Flathead-Blackfoot district. CR, 4, 1574–75, Pleasonton to De Smet, 28 May 1859. Owen to Pleasonton, same date (in Owen, *Journals*, 2, 190).

75. CR, 2, 766–67, De Smet to superior in St. Louis, 10 November; 18 May here is incorrect for the interview, as is 19 May in *JMUS*, 2, 74. Harney Report, 1 June. De Smet's letter seems to have Nesmith present; either he refers carelessly to a separate interview that same day or soon after at Salem as in Linton Album. Geary Report, 1 September 1859, in *SED*, 36 Cong., 1 sess., 2 (1859), p. 748.

hangs long in Indian style. Seltis is partly wrapped in his blanket. All have been incongruously buttoned into White clothes, with Francis the Iroquois boasting a rather elaborate necktie.

Seated in the front row are the formidable looking Kalispel Victor; then the Pend d'Oreille Alexander with lighter visage and dignified, hooded eyes; the Flathead Adolph, presenting a rough-hewn, unyielding face; and the Coeur d'Alene Seltis, handsome and a shade insouciant. Standing at the back, with Father De Smet's bulk sandwiched in between, are the Kettle Denis, rugged but somehow diffident; the small and sad-looking Coeur d'Alene Bonaventure; and the large, open-faced Iroquois Francis. They all look vaguely uneasy at this first confrontation with the White man's camera.

After extensive touring of the tiny towns in the coastal forests, the chiefs returned in June to their respective tribes, bearing presents from the General and the Superintendent. "They returned to their own country contented and happy and well determined to keep at peace with the whites." Each probably had, as did Victor Happy Man, a document formally recognizing him a friendly chief.[76]

Spokane Garry is not in the photograph. He had White friends on the Coast and may have visited with them. Perhaps he disdained the role of mere tourist borne by his less sophisticated colleagues. Nesmith, Geary, Harney, and De Smet vouch, however, for his presence. Garry may have felt uneasy about this voyage south. Previously, a month after De Smet had gone from Sacred Heart mission to St. Ignatius, while local Jesuits were canvassing the Kettles, Spokanes, and Coeur d'Alenes, Garry had written a special message to General Harney. He said that all the Spokanes were ready to sell their lands, to permit roads, and to allow soldiers; he recommended that the Spokanes be put on a reservation. He also offered apologies: "my horses have given out, and it is so late in the spring I will have to return home to attend to my Crops, or I would go and see you." Should Harney turn up at Walla Walla this spring, the chief said, Agent Cain would send a message north and Garry would go down for a visit. Harney passed this letter from "one of the principal chiefs of the Spokane Indians" to his superiors back East.[77]

76. G. Collier Robbins to John R. McBride (first territorial congressman from Idaho), 25 February 1899, Spokane *Spokesman-Review*, 12 February 1939; CR, 2, 766 (two original positives, chiefs changing positions, in OJ, PA, Whitman College museum, and MJ), 768 (last quot.). Teit, BAE *Annual Report*, 45, 377 (Victor's doc.).

77. Nez Percé–Flathead Letterbook (NA, IA, Wash. Sup., LS), Nesmith to Mix, Salem, 6 June 1859; CR, 2, 766, 775; cf. 3, 969 (Garry part of delegation). HED, 36 Cong., 1 sess., 65 (1858), p. 121; cf. p. 149 (Garry's letter above from NA original, AGO, LR, Harney Report, 28 March); see also Harney Report, 1 June. Geary Report, September 1859, *SED*, p. 756.

Agent Owen, having emerged badly from his battle with the military, prepared to return to his mountains. Before leaving, he composed a letter for Nesmith's successor as superintendent, Reverend E. R. Geary. Again he put forth his story of how the group of chiefs had desired to go to the settlements, and how he had given them his permission. Kamiakin had surrendered "under the influence of Spokane Garry." Still at Salem two days later, Owen sent Superintendent Geary a copy of his correspondence with Harney, justifying his own course of action. Owen's fantasy of a previous commission from Nesmith had by now assumed larger dimensions. He appeals to "the fact that My party was organised and on the March," at the request of the chiefs themselves, even "before it was known that the Rev[eren]d Father De Smet was in the country." Though the General had warned the agent away from the delegation, "I feel myself moral[l]y bound" for their safe return. He reasserts his position that the chiefs had expressed their desire to go on their mission to the Coast before De Smet arrived. "My conscience acquits me." The rest he leaves in Geary's hands. Having done his best to reanimate jurisdictional jealousies and to ensure a bitter battle of wills, Owen thoughtfully expresses his hope that the Indian service and the army will not come into conflict.[78]

A few days later Nesmith wrote to the national commissioner, Mix, as a final favor for Owen. He reported that his colleague's presence was necessary in the Flathead country to preserve good will. He described the mission of the chiefs, with no mention of De Smet. Nesmith himself was going with Owen to Vancouver in a day or two, he said, to help pacify the chiefs. Geary, the new superintendent, naturally accepted Owen's story and gave the agent his official backing. The chiefs had come as a "deputation to this Office," he asserted; consequently they "will return under your care to their own country." General Harney refused to accept either the premise or the conclusion. Geary also instructed Owen to win over the Indians, but with economy because appropriations would probably be "greatly cut" for the next fiscal year.

A subsequent letter particularly desired Owen to restrain the Snakes and Bannocks "in their aggressive and predatory habits" and to inhibit certain other "aggressions." Geary had to contend with other crises. Among the lower tribes, outside the zone of Jesuit peace activity, Agent Cain was reporting disaffection. Geary told him to conciliate the tribes; should they ally for war, the military would descend upon them. The Nez Percés were bedeviled by rumors that soldiers were coming to hang some of their chiefs and to impose the White will. The Cayuses and Walla Wallas still remained dis-

78. Owen to Geary, 31 May, as above, n. 69; to same, Salem, 2 June (Owen, *Journals*, 2, 190–91).

affected. Shortly after De Smet's success with the upper tribes, all but fifty Walla Wallas abandoned their own country, following a war leader up the Columbia, where they reveled in whiskey and war talk.[79]

We hear from Owen again later in the year. In early October he writes nervously that "I find things not as quiet as I could wish in this particular district." Three months after his return with De Smet and the chiefs, when two of the agent's close friends had apparently been ejected by the tribe, Owen is protesting to Father Menetrey: "I am by the U. S. Gov[ernmen]t Supposed to be the person in charge of this district and I do Most Solem[n]ly protest against your having any talks With the Indians relative to their tribal relations With the Gov[ernmen]t." A year later Owen reports anxiously that "the Flatheads who repulsed the overtures of Kamiakin in '58" might join neighboring hostiles now, having "Sympathies in common with their Red Brethren." Two years after the war he will charge Father Menetrey with inciting the Pend d'Oreille chief to burn the house of the settler Louis Brown. Congiato will write to De Smet in despair: "the Major is becoming very troublesome to the Fathers and has taken to write [*sic*] letters full of vague imputations." By this time, Congiato believed that "it would be a great benefit to the poor Flatheads if this miserable agent were removed at once." [80]

Harney had sent the Owen correspondence to his superiors, "showing the course I pursued with him." He added a special commendation for De Smet. "It gives me great pleasure to commend to the General-in-chief, the able and efficient services the Reverend Father De Smet has rendered." He was particularly taken with the Jesuit's report, which he calls to the attention of army headquarters at some length. "From what I have seen of the Indian affairs of this department," he concludes, "the missionaries among them possess a power of the greatest consequence in their proper government, and one which cannot be acquired by any other influence. They control the Indian by training his superstitions and fears to revere the religion they possess, by associating the benefits they confer with the guardianship and protection of the Great Spirit of the whites. The history of the Indian race on this conti-

79. Nez Percé-Flathead Letterbook, Nesmith June 6 letter; Geary to Owen, Salem, 12 and 13 June; Geary to Cain, 18 and 21 July. Also NA, IA, Wash. Sup., LR, Flathead-Blackfoot employees, Owen to Geary, 10 October 1859. Of this Owen correspondence, only the final letter is published in Owen, *Journals*, 2, 195–96. *SED*, 36 Cong., 1 sess., 2 (1859), pp. 781–83, Cain letter of 2 August 1859.

80. MJ, IX, AA, Congiato to De Smet, 4 February 1860. *JMUS*, 2, 390–91 n. *WL*, 17 (1888), 88, excerpt from San Francisco *Monitor* (early 1860) replying to Owen in Portland *Daily News*. Owen quotes from letter to Menetrey, 12 October 1859, and to Geary, 3 December 1860, in *Journals*, 2, 196, 233; first quotation from 10 October 1859 letter.

nent has shown that the missionaries succeeded where the soldier and civilian have failed; it would be well for us to profit by the lesson its experience teaches." To this end the General urges that the reservation plan incorporated by De Smet in the report be studied and adopted.[81]

DE SMET'S SECOND TOUR: PEACE CONSOLIDATED

De Smet's peace tour was not completely finished. In a more leisurely fashion he was to take the Indians back to their tribes, then continue out through the tribes of the Plains. His new orders from the army, after declaring that he had "accomplished in highly satisfactory manner the important duties confided to his Charge" during the past winter, authorized him to pass again through the upper country, "Visiting the Various Indian Tribes of the Interior." Post commanders were to "afford every facility and assistance" to the priest "in his mission of peace to the unfortunate race, whose Confidence he has always most generously maintained." He was about to make his way to St. Louis "through the different tribes of the Interior" so as to confirm them "in their good disposition towards the whites." The journey was meant to supplement the priest's "labors of the past winter requiring such self-denial and resolution" and "so signally productive of good will and confidence" among the Indians.[82]

De Smet left the Coast with the chiefs on June 15. Owen probably went along; De Smet was not the kind of man to interpret Harney's instructions as excluding the agent from traveling back with the party. If Owen came, discretion would forbid De Smet from including this in his report. The agent omits all mention of the priest; he reports to Geary that the delegation "to Salem resulted in Much good," and that he returned with the chiefs.

De Smet stayed for three days at the Coeur d'Alene mission in early July. He then accompanied Father Congiato to St. Ignatius and later to Fort Benton on the Plains. He held several conferences "of a peaceful and religious nature" with 200 lodges of Gros Ventres and various Blackfeet. On the Plains he visited among the Sioux, Crows, Arikaras, Mandans, Minitaris, Assiniboines, and others. "I always stopped a day or two with them." All had long been friendly to the Jesuits; they listened to De Smet "with the utmost attention." Along the way he baptized 900 children. He planned to visit the Comanches, but his six horses gave out.

81. Harney Reports, 1, 3 June, NA, EW, AGO, 79-o, 80-o; also in *SED* (serial 1024), pp. 98–99, 103–04.

82. NA, EW, Quartermaster Genl., special orders No. 59, Fort Vancouver, 1 June 1859. Fort Dalles Papers, departmental orders file, local copy. CR, 4, 1581–82, De Smet's own copy; detailed instructions and comment of Harney through Pleasonton in June 1 letter, pp. 1577–78, and in NA, AGO, 78-o, and *SED* (serial 1024).

Having arrived in St. Louis, he submitted a meticulous expense account to the army, including such items as twenty dollars for tobacco to Indians east and west of the mountains. The gratitude of the military followed him. Harney's aide Pleasonton wrote: "the victory is yours and the general will take great pleasure in recording your success at the War Department." The army officials, like so many other officers in the past and to come, had been impressed by De Smet. "We all miss you so much; I have not met an officer of your acquaintance who has not expressed great regret at your departure, and we all feel indebted to you for the good understanding between the poor Indians and the whites at this time." [83]

Later in 1859 Harney was to write to his military superiors: "I would again call the attention of the Government to the important services the Reverend Father De Smet has rendered in the past year; my reports of his good offices during his term of duty with this Command characterize the merit of his success in establishing peace and confidence between the whites and the different tribes of Indians who were so lately hostile." Harney remarks on the priest's last "remarkable journey from the shores of the Pacific to Saint Louis." He concludes: "the extraordinary influence which this benevolent and charitable ecclesiastic exercises over the vast tribes in the interior is suggestive of the great benefits to be attained in the encouragement of the Missionaries among them." Newspapers like the New York *Herald* and the New York *Freeman's Journal* picked up the story, praising the work of both Joset and De Smet. When the Sioux massacres erupted three years later, the secretary of the Interior and the commissioner of Indian Affairs again turned to De Smet, sending him on the first of several peace missions to the hostile Sioux, including his celebrated and very dangerous penetration into Sitting Bull's war camp of 3,000 hostiles.[84]

The figure of De Smet rather overshadows the work of his Jesuit colleagues on this peace tour. However, we have seen his admission of indebtedness to them, and the activity of several priests. In the second phase of the tour, during De Smet's trip back to St. Louis, Father Congiato particularly helped by making a renewed search for Kamiakin. After the Yakima's escape

---

83. *SED* (serial 1051), pp. 184–86, and NA, EW, AGO, LR, 80-0, De Smet Report, 5 October. Quartermaster Genl., De Smet to assist. adj. genl., St. Louis, 12 October 1859 (accounts, approved and forwarded); same to same, 29 October (resignation, final accounting; annotated). CR, *2*, 769, 775–76; *4*, 1580–81, Pleasonton to De Smet, 9 November 1859.

84. *SED* and NA, Harney Report, 12 November. Newspapers in *Collection de précis historiques*, 7 (1859), 93–95; *Freeman's Journal* (15 September 1860), "The Late Troubles in Oregon," On Sioux missions see, for example, Stanley Vestal, *Sitting Bull, Champion of the Sioux, a Biography* (Norman, Okla., 1957), chap. 15, "The Blackrobe Makes Peace"; and *JMUS*, *3*, 66–79, "Peace Envoy to the Western Tribes."

Congiato had told De Smet: "assure the General that we will try hard to persuade Kamayaken to give himself up and come down with some of the Fathers: but you must insist" on written safeguards for his life and liberty. On two occasions, when Joset had brought Kamiakin to the Spokane camp for Wright, and when De Smet had persuaded him to join the delegation to Harney, the chief had fled at the eleventh hour. There was to be no third chance. Congiato's search was in vain.

Kamiakin apparently stayed briefly in Canada and then spent some time on the Plains. In 1860 Agent Lansdale sought him out in Yakima country, to persuade him to assume the position of Yakima head chief, arranged for in the first Walla Walla Council. This would amount to acceptance of the 1855 treaty, so Kamiakin refused. Long after his return, when an agent sought to relieve Kamiakin's poverty and gain his cooperation with a payment of 600 blankets due from the treaty of 1855, the chief contemptuously rejected any gift from the Americans. But at least one thing the Jesuits gained for him from the government: from mid-1859 he no longer had the status of a hostile.[85]

Father Congiato kept in touch with the army at Vancouver, solidifying the peace as best he could. He and the diocesan vicar general dined with the military at Vancouver in the fall of 1859, for example, with Congiato intending to return to the mountains in the spring. Father Joset also continued his work for peace along with his apostolic activities. While Congiato and Hoecken inaugurated serious missionary work among the Blackfeet, Joset struck out in the other direction and began the Jesuit evangelization of the Spokanes early in 1859. Among the Coeur d'Alenes he presided over the growth of a strong government under Seltis.

Seltis had been elected shortly after the events of this chapter, in an unprecedented move, to succeed Vincent as acting head chief. When actually promulgating decisions, Seltis shrewdly associated himself with Vincent, even many years later when the *de jure* head chief was simply an aged relic. Seltis seldom took a really important step in tribal government without consulting also the superior of the mission. Every Sunday he called a tribal council at the Sacred Heart mission, where he patched up feuds and incipient quarrels. He frequently acted as lay preacher in the villages. Eventually he even organized the tribal police into an effective disciplinary force.

Thus he was the first chief in the history of the tribe who exercised real

85. MJ, IX, AA, No. 751, Congiato to De Smet, Dalles, 24 May 1859. W. P. Winans MS cited in Fuller, *Pacific Northwest*, p. 374 (blankets). See also Splawn, *Ka-Mi-Akin*, p. 121 (dubious story of later movements and return); and the interview with Kamiakin by the plainsman Sherwood, in Simms Papers (WP), to Winans, 14 September 1872. Bischoff, "Yakima War," p. 310 (Lansdale).

authority, so that the tribe became a proper community capable of being controlled. Equally important, he brought the Jesuits' influence for peace directly into the tribal councils from now until his death in 1902. Seltis is credited with preventing war several times. He became celebrated as one of the great chiefs of the Northwest, and even managed eventually to bring about an era of relative friendliness and good relations locally between Indian and White. It was through him that the Jesuits consolidated the effects of their labors for peace and forestalled, for the trying times to come, the probability of other angry uprisings.

Keeping the peace would never be easy. The bishop of Washington Territory in 1859 could only say: "one hopes that this peace will be lasting." He is happy to add that "despite the war between the whites and Indians last year the missions are in a prospering condition; since last autumn peace reigns everywhere in that country, thanks to the influence of the missionaries over the Indians." General Harney gave the Jesuits a final and lasting token of the army's gratitude, a vehicle to be used at the Jesuit mission which was being opened on the Plains. Governor Meagher of Montana admired it in 1866, describing it as a "commodious ambulance of rather an elegant air and finish." [86]

Before De Smet could glimpse the sprawling waterfront of old St. Louis, 2,000 settlers had taken advantage of Harney's opening of the Interior. They poured into the Walla Walla and Umatilla valleys. A boom town named Steptoe City was soon mushrooming near the fort. Renamed Walla Walla, it remained for over twenty years the most populous city in Washington Territory. Ratification of the Indian treaties had now become both a necessity and a foregone conclusion; Congress attended to this in 1859.

That spring also troops came up to found Harney Depot (later Fort Colville), fourteen miles from the Hudson's Bay post, in "a position favorable to the restraint and control of our own Indians as well as those of British Columbia who cross over our border." The Boundary Committee, seriously at work now, used this as its base; a moving escort of three companies under Captain Archer meanwhile guarded them in the Okanogan Valley. The Kettles called upon the Colville depot, to pay their respects. And the first government benefits arrived. Major Lugenbeel, post commander and official Indian agent as well, "purchased and distributed as presents to the Palouse, Spokane, Coeur d'Alene, Pend d'Oreille, Colville [Kettle], Lake, and Sans Poils bands of Indians" 75 plugs of tobacco, 16 boxes of matches, 9 pipes, and an

86. FL, *1858*, Répartition, Bishop Blanchet (Nesqually) to Association (in French), 19 June 1859; also in SA, with related documents. Caruana to provincial, *LPT*, n.v. (1904), 108–12 (details on Seltis). *LN*, 7 (1870), 194, Governor T. F. Meagher of Montana to De Smet, 15 December 1866.

axe. Superintendent Geary promised food supplies in order to help the Indians in the Colville area through a bad winter. Agent Lansdale, however, like De Smet at the conclusion of his peace tour, reported in August 1859 that some of the tribes around Colville were still openly hostile, as were also the Okanogans.[87]

The Mullan road had cracked the wilderness shell at both ends. Steamboats came all the way up to Fort Benton on its east and to Fort Walla Walla on its west. It was a dangerous road, soon overgrown and replaced by other modes of travel. But it lasted long enough to serve as a practicable passage in opening the upper country for settlement. At one point the Indians and Jesuits protested Mullan's choice of route; this put the visionary engineer at loggerheads briefly with the missionaries, and gave Owen yet another chance to damn the Jesuits.[88] Within a year a special body of troops was marching from the Missouri headwaters to Walla Walla, to reinforce the area and to prove the road was sound. One of their number, Lieutenant Kautz, met Fathers Congiato and Hoecken near Fort Benton. Falling into lengthy conversation with them, he found the two "very pleasant" and picked up "considerable news" of the region, especially concerning the late war. Farther down the road, the troops encountered "a large body of Coeur d'Alene Indians going over to the buffalo country." At the mission itself the soldiers were "highly grateful" to behold the peaceful scene of enclosed fields and stately church. Father Ravalli furnished them with "some fine vegetables" here.[89]

Miners now ranged through all the nooks and crannies of the upper country. Indeed they infested much of the Indian West; in 1859 a hundred thousand miners converged on the Cheyenne-Arapaho country during the Pike's Peak boom, triggering Indian risings. In 1860 the richest discovery ever made in the Northwest was heralded from the Nez Percé reservation itself, and new miners tumbled in by the thousands. Neither dragoons nor Indians nor agents could stop them. In June a city ominously sprang up on Nez Percé territory to become the river port of Lewiston. Other towns followed in Washington, Idaho, and Montana. This was to be one of the great mining

87. *SED* (serial 1024) and NA, AGO, LR 92-0, Harney Report, 20 July, referring to order No. 36 of 14 April (first quot.). Nez Percé-Flathead Letterbook, Geary to Lugenbeel, 12 October 1859, thinking of sending 5,000 pounds of flour. Simms Papers, bill for 1859, second and third quarters (presents). Another boundary depot in Pend d'Oreille country, April 1859, is in Owen, *Journals, 1,* 212. *SED,* 36 Cong., sess. 2 (1859), p. 778 (Lansdale). Archer Corresp., 24 April 1859 (moving escort).

88. NA, IA, Wash. Sup., LS, Geary to Owen, Owen to Geary, Owen to Menetrey, Chase to Owen (all October); esp. Geary to Mullan, Portland, 1 December. Echoes in Portland *Daily News* with San Francisco *Monitor* reply, in *WL, 17* (1888), 88.

89. M. F. Schmitt, ed., "From Missouri to Oregon in 1860, the Diary of August V. Kautz," *PNWQ,* 37 (1946), 216, 226, 229.

booms of all time. By 1867, less than a decade after the Steptoe Disaster, the mines on the American side alone had yielded 140 million dollars, with remote Montana and Idaho the largest producers. This was surplus wealth, and it attracted the services and aids of civilization.

Unlike so many frontiers, this one changed overnight. Hamlets expanded into cities. Farms appeared everywhere. Wharves and steamboats, mills and wagon transport, lawyers and all the impedimenta of White life were soon on hand. The Indians were stunned. Jostled and overrun, submerged and contemned, they began to take fire. Superintendent Geary in his report of 1860 fearfully expected another Interior war. The Sioux troubles and the Blackfeet troubles and the Nez Percé troubles were on their way. They would arrive in a world far different from that of the Interior wars which had taken place so short a time before. The world was changing, and war was changing.

Near the end of 1860 the first of the Southern states seceded. The Civil War years that followed were a turning point both for America and for many of the figures in the Jesuit-Indian story. The military record of those years, too, demonstrates that the men who fought so indecisively against the Northwest tribes were competent enough at their trade. Jordan, who got Joset to write his valuable narrative, became chief of staff to Confederate General Beauregard. De Smet's friend Pleasonton led his cavalry through a roll call of great battles, and commanded all the Union cavalry at Gettysburg. Garnett organized the Virginia Confederates into an army and served as adjutant general to Lee. Crook, Garnett's right hand in the Okanogan campaign, was a brilliant cavalry general; after the war he became one of the greatest Indian fighters in Western history. Mackall, Clarke's aide and a friend to Jesuit peace efforts, was chief of staff to the Confederate general Joseph Johnston. Albert S. Johnston, who relayed Father Hoecken's notice of the Steptoe Disaster, became a famed Confederate general.

And what of the young officers who put their signatures to the Coeur d'Alene treaty? General Ord fought Jeb Stuart, commanded the left wing of the Army of Tennessee, served on Grant's staff, and assisted at Lee's surrender. General Tyler was badly wounded at Cold Harbor; at Gettysburg he commanded the reserve artillery. Pender, who nearly lost his life grappling with an Indian in the Spokane Plains battle, shortly became the youngest major general on the Confederate side; at Gettysburg he drove the Federals off Seminary Ridge, losing his life. Confederate General Winder was killed in midcareer. General Dent became aide to Grant and military governor of the conquered Confederate capital. Hardie rose from a combat general to be inspector general of the army. Morgan, who had been impressed with the Jesuits at the Coeur d'Alene mission and had shot the escaping Owhi, became a Confederate general; later he would publish his memories of the Coeur d'Alene–Spokane War.

General Keyes, Joset's convert during the 1858 treaty preparations, won a commendation at Bull Run and commanded the Fourth army corps in the peninsula campaign. General Smith became Halleck's chief of cavalry and then a dependable troubleshooter with a record of victories. Steptoe was a dying man; but the hero Wright became general in charge of the Department of the Pacific. Harney, unjustly suspected of southern sympathies, was left on the war's periphery but raised to major general. Phil Sheridan, the bullet-headed, hard-eyed little man who had never quite been able to catch the Interior Indians in 1855, hurried East to become the terror of the Confederate cavalry and a legend in his own day.

Old General Wool, veteran of the War of 1812, captured Norfolk and suppressed the New York draft riots. General Rains, of the 1856 Yakima fiasco, headed the Confederate torpedo bureau. General I. I. Stevens died dramatically, rallying his men to the attack during a wild, driving thunderstorm in the retreat from Second Bull Run. The ranks of the generals were swelled by men like Ingalls, Grier, Mansfield, Lyon, Dandy, Archer, Gregg, Alvord (later paymaster general of the army), and, of course, McClellan. And even that seedy lieutenant, the haunted figure with an air of failure which hung on him like an ill-fitting suit of clothes, who had taught Lieutenant Mullan to play poker during the *longueurs* of barrack life at Fort Vancouver but lost $200 doing so—even he was to go on to save the Union as general of the armies, Ulysses S. Grant.

Later on in life, after a career as consul in Austria, the distinguished General Gregg took the trouble to have the War Department prepare a special copy of Father Joset's narrative of the 1858 war for him. He kept other reports and mementoes of the Steptoe action among his papers. Fifty years after the Coeur d'Alene war the old General writes of how he often visits the graves of the officers Gaston and Taylor at West Point, thinking upon "the thrilling events of that fateful 17th of May 1858." For that was where the young Gregg had faced death, as the bugle notes slashed sharply across the fall air, when all the world was young.[90]

The actors seem almost to have changed plays. When America awoke after her nightmare of blood, it was into a modern technological age. Somewhere deep within her being, the machinery of social evolution had accelerated. Its hum was now discernible, though the visible parts for a brief time might look familiar. The first of the industrial wars had been fought, technocracy was loose, and the world would never be innocent again. Somewhere during that war too many Rubicons were crossed, too many Romes had burned.

90. Gregg Collection, 2. Manring, *Conquest*, p. 261 (Gregg letter).

9. Drums along the Rockies (1877)

Deadly Peace[1]

AFTER THE WAR of 1858 the Interior knew twenty years of peace. It was an uneasy peace. Indian and White clashed regularly all along the southern periphery. An unending series of bloody incidents left its debris: burning farms, wrecked stagecoaches, and corpses of mutilated miners. In a single massacre in 1865 fifty (perhaps a hundred) Chinese lost their scalps. That same year eight men grimly fought off 150 Indians for four hours. Travel out of The Dalles to Fort Boise was perilous, as was the road south to California. Bands previously regarded with amused contempt, like the Diggers, suddenly transformed themselves into warrior prodigies. Troops dissipated their effectiveness in futile chases, inconclusive skirmishes, and embarrassing failures.

From 1863 to 1868 soldiers like Crook and Connor slowly reduced the violence to manageable proportions. By this time the toll of Whites killed over the past thirty years, outside of battle and in Oregon state alone, amounted to over a thousand. Then in 1872, as settlers breathed more easily, came the shocking Modoc war. In the labyrinthine lava beds near the Oregon-California border fifty Modocs kept a thousand soldiers at bay, until lack of ammunition forced the Indians to surrender. The army suffered 120 casualties and lost their departmental commander, General Edward Canby.

Blood also flowed freely on the Plains forming the eastern border of the Interior tribes. The Blackfeet fought and raided with desperate ferocity. Even the Jesuit mission among the Blackfeet was not quite safe. In 1865 an army of 800 regulars and 500 volunteers took the field against them. In 1870

1. Besides the manuscript sources, the main published works on the Nez Percé War (see below, Bib.) are the several titles of Haines, McWhorter, Howard-McGrath, and, more recently, Beal and Josephy. Materials by participants include the writings of Generals Howard, Gibbon, and Sherman, Agent Ronan, Bishop O'Connor, and Fathers Palladino, Diomedi, and Cataldo; official documentation is in *HED, RCIA*, and *RBIC*. For the present chapter see also my "Coeur d'Alene Diplomacy in the Nez Percé War of 1877," *RACHS, 63* (1952), 37–60; and "The Jesuits, the Northern Indians, and the Nez Percé War of 1877," *PNWQ, 42* (1951), 40–76.

another army of 400 met them in a terrible battle that cost the tribe 173 warriors dead and 100 captured. But by 1873 the Blackfeet were again slashing out on raids. In eastern Montana the Crows talked of friendship but took scalps as opportunity offered.

The Sioux kept southwestern Montana and the wider Plains in turmoil throughout the '60s and the '70s. Sully fought them on the Yellowstone in 1864, Connor on the Powder River in 1865, Stanley and Custer during the railroad survey of 1872. So serious had the Sioux situation become by 1876 that the government issued an ultimatum. The result was a memorable war, with chiefs like Sitting Bull and Crazy Horse facing generals like Gibbon, Crook, Terry, and Miles. Its most remembered episode took place in 1876 on the Montana prairies where the Flathead confederates hunted: Custer's Last Stand.

The Interior tribes were not insulated from these shocks of war. On each occasion a wave of rumor and excitement swept from the Cascades to the Plains. In 1861 war talk grew loud in the lower Interior; troops rode out from Fort Walla Walla to discipline the Cayuses. That same year miners and Indians clashed near the mouth of the Pend d'Oreille River, three Whites being killed and five Indians. Captain Archer took sixty soldiers from Fort Colville to investigate; he found himself opposed by a war party of fifty, but conciliated the chiefs. In 1862 Fort Lapwai went up in the heart of Nez Percé territory to forestall trouble there. Crisis succeeded crisis among the Flathead confederates during the decade leading to the Nez Percé war. In 1865 the Okanogans acted badly, stealing and threatening with "overbearing talk."

The Spokanes were troublesome in 1866. Much of this was highhanded mischief but dangerous considering their brooding angers. In 1870 Spokane Garry made a speech complaining that the Whites "are going to rob us" of the land, "as they have done with the Yakamas, Nezpercies and other Indians." And "I won't stand it, I won't submit like those others, I want enough room to raise my children." Garry "would sooner be dead than not have what land belongs to us." He was willing to settle for a large region; but "we don't want to be driven like horses" to a small reservation.[2]

The Colville area remained sensitive. As early as 1862 the superintendent of Indian Affairs commented on the appreciable loss of Indian land here to settlers, the absence of government aid, and the distances isolating the agent at the fort. In 1871 an uprising threatened. Camps buzzed with rumors that the

---

2. Simms papers, settler at farm at Semilkiman Forks to Simms, 13 October 1865 (Okanogan quot.); A. R. Booth to Agent G. A. Paige, White Bluffs, 23 July 1866 (Spokanes); cf. P. Norris to Simms, Willow Springs, 30 May 1866, and James Monahan to Paige, 18 April 1865; Winans Collection, Journal, May 1870, speech of "Geary." Archer Corresp., to mother, 14 April 1861.

troops planned to withdraw. Most of the Kettles, Okanogans, Spokanes, and San Poils believed this. Now they could dispossess the settlers. "They made no effort to conceal their intentions." They even boasted of their plans to "many settlers." The Catholic and Protestant Spokanes actually stopped feuding and joined in an amicable council of war. Chief Garry led the aggressive faction favoring forcible ousting of the settlers. Some Okanogans were eager to fight the Colville garrison. The fort, concluded Agent Winans, "is our only security against an Indian war." When a cavalry troop passed that way, the tribes in angry panic assumed that they had come to drive out the Indians.

The plainsman Fred Sherwood made a tour of nearby camps, "quieted their fears, [and] settled some differences between themselves and their white neighbors." The Colville agent remonstrated with the Department of the Interior against continuing the project of removing the Kettles, Spokanes, Okanogans, and Pend d'Oreilles. There were simply not enough troops. Since these tribes could field at least seven hundred well-armed warriors, it was "madness to tempt them to hostility." He reported the Jesuit influence as the main restraining force for peace.[3]

The Jesuit mission of St. Francis Regis near Colville served, among other Indians, over six hundred Kettles; these were scattered along the east bank of the Columbia from the Spokane River to Canada. A separate Jesuit staff took care of the White settlement near the fort. Sisters of Charity taught and nursed. There was a central Indian complex consisting of a church, a school, thirty-nine farms, and eighty-five houses. Now the government planned to take it all away. In March 1876 the Indians sent a petition to the secretary of the Interior, with six pages of names including those of Jesuit witnesses. A government commission planned to investigate these complaints but was cut off in the lower Interior by the Nez Percé war. The commission's instructions admitted that the proposed Kettle reserve was "too barren and mountainous to afford any facilities for agriculture"; still, the Indians were remaining on their former homelands illegally and were liable to eviction.[4]

The situation was general. In 1872 Inspector General Ludington summed up the anger of the Coeur d'Alenes and Spokanes: to move them means "re-

3. Winans Collection, Journal, p. 156 (1871), Winans to McKenny, 31 May and 31 December 1871. *RCIA* (1871), p. 294, Winans Report, 21 September (Spokanes); (1873), p. 362 (Simms). NA, IA, Wash. Sup., Simms Report, 21 May 1878 (last quot.). Cf. the Sherwood peacemaking, Federal Records Center, Seattle, Record Group 75, box 17, Simms to commissioner, 30 April 1873.

4. NA, IA, Letterbooks, *136*, 145 ff., Acting Commissioner S. A. Galpin to Inspector E. C. Watkins, 7 May 1877. LR, Wash. Sup., Colville Indians' petition, 8 March 1876; agency report, 31 January, with farm statistics. Cf. *RCIA* (1875), p. 362. *RBIC* (1877) has color map of 1877 reservations, frontispiece.

sistance and bloodshed." There were treaty talks in 1873 with tribes like the Kettles and Coeur d'Alenes. In 1874, hearing that more soldiers were being posted to the north, thirteen chiefs from the Kettles, Spokanes, and Okanogans sent an angry letter to President Grant: "give Soldiers to Indians who are on the war path." In 1876 the Jesuit general described, from his missionary reports, how the Indians were recoiling before the White advance; they "are withdrawing into the mountain area and are burying themselves in the vast solitudes." Settlement threatened even the solitudes.

Agent Medary of the Flatheads warned in 1876: "it is a well-known fact that many of the Nez Percés, Colvilles, Callispells, Spokanes, Coeur d'Alenes, etc., who were defeated by Colonel Wright in 1858, would at once resume hostilities if they could succeed in uniting with other tribes; at least efforts have been made to this end." As early as 1867, contemplating Nez Percé trouble, Governor Ballard of Idaho assumed that a general rising was imminent. The disturbed neighboring tribes could not be held down; he listed the Kutenais, Pend d'Oreilles, Coeur d'Alenes, Flatheads, Spokanes, Palouses, Blackfeet, Bannocks, and Snakes.

In 1877 the experienced agent A. J. Cain underlined this same peril in a communication to the Board of Indian Commissioners. The upper Interior tribes were upset and dangerous, he wrote; none would surrender any land except by force. They were fully aware of the processes by which even reservation lands were ultimately taken. "I am convinced that unless some legislation is had to protect the Indians alluded to, trouble of a very serious character must occur before the expiration of another year, which will require a large military force to adjust." Like the Jesuits, Cain feared that "an indiscriminate war" would result in the Indians' "speedy extermination, contrary to all the dictates of humanity." [5]

The commissions sent to investigate Nez Percé recalcitrants were involved in this larger pattern. The Lapwai council commissioners in the fall of 1876 had instructions to conduct similar councils among "the Coeur d'Alenes in Northern Idaho, the Spokanes, Pend d'Oreilles, and Kootenays, also the Colville Indians, with a view of settling certain difficulties that have arisen from their not being on lands set apart for them." But winter closed off the upper Interior: "we should have been detained in the Colville country for the winter."

A subsequent commission in the spring of 1877 was directed to proceed from the Nez Percé Council to the upper Interior, especially along the Columbia River and in northern Idaho. Here "bands of roving Indians" were a

5. Kulzer Collection (WP), chiefs to Grant, 3 March 1874. FP, I, 5, general to Association (in French), January 1876. *RBIC* (1877), p. 90, 12 December 1877. *RCIA* (1867), p. 246; (1872), p. 343; (1876), p. 89.

"source of annoyance and danger." General Sherman, commander of America's armies, on a tour through the upper Interior during the last stage of the 1877 war, was aware of the larger pattern. "All these [tribes] were agitated by the recent Nez Percé outbreak," he said in his report, "for they are of the same type and class, are intermarried, and have common grievances." [6]

Historians of the war have conceived of it as occurring almost in a vacuum. The mass of combat documentation and the large body of warrior reminiscences culled by later friends of the Nez Percés create an illusion. One sees two powers, Nez Percé and American, locked in mortal combat on a vast and lonely arena, with no force at hand capable of tipping the balance. From this angle of vision the history of the two combatants has been well written. What is lacking is an awareness of the sullen Indian world to which the action relates. This world must be seen in the dimension of its stormy past. And it must be viewed with an understanding of the religious influences involved. The Nez Percé war came as an episode in a multitribal pattern of hostility. It might easily have become a spontaneous conflagration over all the upper country. A number of factors converged to ensure that it did not. Principal among these was the swift, decisive intervention of the Jesuits and of the Indians they influenced.

THE NEW NORTHWEST OF 1877

De Smet says in 1872: "today the country is filled with settlements of the whites." In 1876 the Jesuit general describes how the "very great number of whites" here "build towns where there had only been wilderness a few years before." In that same year the governor of Washington Territory estimated his population at 45,000. The metropolis of the Northwest lay on the coastal section of Oregon state, across the Columbia River from Fort Vancouver. This was Portland, in 1877 boasting 8,000 people, sixteen churches, fifteen newspapers, twenty schools, a theatre, industry, and an unusually handsome cemetery. Portland was the point of departure for Walla Walla and the Interior.[7]

As for the Interior, only six years after De Smet had returned home from his 1859 peace tour an enterprising author was able to compile a two-hundred

6. *RBIC* (1877), pp. 48–49, report of civil and military commission to Washington Territory. Galpin's instructions to Watkins, 7 May 1877, above, n. 4. *Reports of Inspection Made in the Summer of 1877 by Generals P. H. Sheridan and W. T. Sherman of Country North of the Union Pacific Railroad* (Washington, D.C., 1878), p. 47 (Sherman report of 23 September 1877).

7. BJ, coll. 1ac–4ac, 1ac, 18 March 1872. FL, *1876*, fasc. Grandes Congrégations, 14 December 1876. WS, Ferry miscellany, Gov. Ferry to Rand, McNally and Co., 22 August 1876.

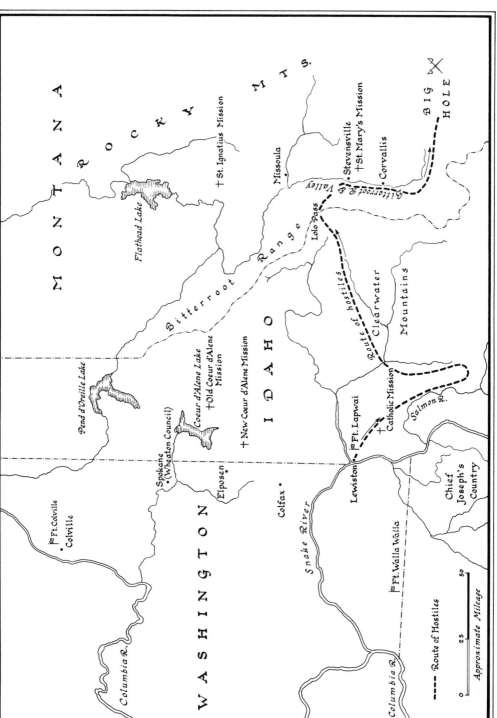

9. The 1877 Troubles.

page *General Directory and Business Guide of the Principal Towns East of the Cascade Mountains.* These little towns already fitted into a map of territories—Washington, Idaho, and Montana—resembling our present states. The population tended to cluster along the bottom of the Interior, with a few hamlets and farms probing north like cautious outriders. Another line of settlement ranged along the eastern flank of the Flathead confederacy, with villages and farms dotting the Bitterroot Valley itself.

Few of these towns amounted to much. As the governor of Montana wrote De Smet, "every collection of log huts is called a city in this ambitious country." The main towns of Washington Territory were Seattle and Walla Walla with 2,500 people each, Olympia with 2,000, and Port Townsend and Vancouver with 800 each. During the war General Sherman found Helena to be a place of three to four thousand people, as comfortable as any town in Iowa; but most settlements in western Montana were unimpressive hamlets, little atolls in a sea of surrounding Indians. All northern Idaho was one huge county, with perhaps a thousand voters scattered in its depths. Similarly Stevens county, covering much of the upper Interior from the Columbia River clear to the Idaho line, held only 350 settlers.[8]

Sherman's party passed through the Flathead, Coeur d'Alene, and Spokane territories and down to Walla Walla during the Nez Percé war, leaving us a valuable description. The Flathead country struck the General as "so large and the people so scattered, that concert of action is difficult if not impossible." Moving west, "for a thousand miles we had not seen an orchard or a fruit tree." Only within thirty miles of Walla Walla could they feel themselves to be in "settled country." Here they rejoiced to see farmhouses and "began to realize we were 'out of the woods.'" They looked back upon the Coeur d'Alene country in particular as "that wilderness." Even the Mullan road, so useful ten or twenty years ago, was overgrown—"a mere pack-trail now," its bridges all down and the way *"very much* obstructed."

It required eleven days to struggle from Missoula in the Flathead country to Spokane Bridge on the farther edge of Coeur d'Alene territory. Sherman comments ruefully that an army officer had made his way by sea from Washington, D.C., to Fort Vancouver via South America in exactly the same time— "yet we thought we had traveled very rapidly." He emphasizes the wildness of the area. Farmers and ranchers were too far apart "here as in Montana" and were encumbered with livestock; they "cannot collect for offense or defense." The military post at Colville was too remote; another was needed at

8. *LN*, 7 (1870), 187, Governor Meagher to De Smet, 1866. Washington population figures in Ferry to Rand-McNally, above, n. 7; cf. also Bancroft, *Washington*, and his *History of Oregon*, passim, under towns, and L. M. McKenney, *Business Directory of the Pacific States and Territories for 1878* (San Francisco, 1878).

Lake Coeur d'Alene. Sherman predicted Indian troubles for years to come from Fort Colville to Fort Boise, especially along the Rockies.[9]

Commercial railroad plans occasioned a revealing report on the Interior in 1879. The county east of Walla Walla County already had 3,800 settlers by mid-1876, and 200 more by mid-1878. In the five years before 1877 the whole far side of Washington Territory up to the Spokane region grew from ninety-nine homesteads to 301, and from 283 preemption land claims to 758.[10] Spokane Falls in 1874 boasted a population of five families. Some distance upstream, at the edge of the Coeur d'Alene country, was a companion settlement, Spokane Bridge, comprising a trading store, a stable, a rickety bridge and a couple of houses, all built of logs. South toward Walla Walla, little settlements were tucked away at odd points like Hangman's Creek, Pine Creek, and the Palouse River.

These settlers, remarked Sherman's aide, "have but one mind, that the Indians are a lazy, thieving set of vagabonds, that ought to be exterminated." Joset put the same idea into an article published in 1882. "There is no sympathy lost between the whites and the Indians"; if the Jesuits were to confine their work exclusively to the Indians, the settlers would despise the priests. A commission sent to investigate Indian grievances in 1873 noted how the people of Idaho "have the general dislike to Indians that is felt to some extent all over the west." [11]

In this riot of expansion and Indian resentment the role of the army was not a happy one. The great armies of the Civil War, over a million men at the close of hostilities, had melted away. Economy measures had long ago cut the remnant ruthlessly to a total of 25,000. The actual number available for Indian fighting was far less; among these the ten cavalry regiments bore the brunt. Yet there was so much more to do now. The number of little forts had increased, outposts of outposts. On the Plains the Indian wars demanded a series of strong posts. Indeed the fortifications of Montana were almost exclusively arranged against the foe to the east, so that the Nez Percé invasion, far at the back, was to come as a doubly bitter blow.

In the Interior there were new forts at Lapwai in the Nez Percé country, at Boise in the Snake country, and at Colville in the Kettle-Okanogan country; a post was projected for Missoula in the Bitterroot. Garrisons here were small, averaging perhaps 150. The Department of the Columbia at the time of the Nez Percé war was commanded by General Howard in Portland. It was

9. *Reports of Inspection,* pp. 41–45, 48, 55, 89, 91–94.

10. Henry Villard report, "Two Railroad Reports on Northwest Resources," *PNWQ,* 37 (1946), 180–84. Cf. Anon., *Settlers' Guide to Homes in the Northwest, Being a Hand-Book of Spokane Falls* (Spokane Falls, 1885), esp. p. 29.

11. *Reports of Inspection,* p. 48. Joset, "Washington Territory, Then and Now" (letter of June 1882), *WL, 12* (1883), 174. *RCIA* (1873), p. 157.

one of three segments of the Division of the Pacific, with headquarters at San Francisco under General Irvin McDowell, the first commander of the Army of the Potomac in the Civil War. But the Flathead and Montana country fell under the district commander, Colonel (or General) Gibbon, as part of the Department of Dakota.

The religious scene, too, had grown more complex. By 1874 Idaho Whites had fifteen Protestant churches, and in Montana there were Methodist, Presbyterian, and Episcopalian establishments. Catholicism also had increased its strength. The diocesan map, redrawn, included a vicariate of Idaho (which held part of Montana) and one of Montana. During the war each of these happened to be without a local incumbent, administered therefore respectively from remote Portland and even more distant Omaha. The Idaho vicariate had only four or sometimes two diocesan priests, so that the ten Jesuit missioners had to assume much of the parochial and circuit work. Montana was in a still more primitive condition ecclesiastically.

In 1878 Archbishop Blanchet prepared a sweeping overview of the Northwest area, excluding that part of Montana beyond the Divide but including British Columbia with its 20,000 Catholic Indians. He listed 80 priests, 115 churches or chapels, 176 nuns, 4 orphanages, 6 hospitals, 20 academies for girls, and 4 high schools for boys. Washington Territory had 10 diocesan clergy and 5 religious (Oblate and Jesuit), 23 churches or chapels, 17 stations, 59 nuns, 5 institutions of charity, a college and some schools, 2 Indian schools, and 10,000 to 12,000 Catholics both Indian and White. Idaho had 10 regular and 3 diocesan priests, with 14 churches or chapels, 2 hospitals, 3 convents, 3 schools, and 4 Jesuit missions, for a Catholic population of 3,000 Whites and 2,650 Indians.[12]

The Jesuit mission chain had expanded. It ran from the Yakimas in the southwest to the Blackfeet on the Plains. Some 20 priests and 20 brothers served it; only half these priests were healthy and really active on the Indian missions. The network comprised 7 missions, some at distances of 300 miles from one another. The Yakima mission alone served an area between the Klickitats and the Okanogans, 200 by 60 miles, comprising 14 tribes. Distributed among the several Jesuit missions of the Interior were 6,000 to 7,000 Catholic Indians, excluding nominal Catholics among the nomadic tribes of the Montana Plains.

12. *AFQ, 1* (1879), 279 ff. See statistics in FL, *1876–78*, fascicules Etats Unis, Grandes Congrégations, Rome-Jésuites, and Propagande. Similar statistics in FP, I, 5, esp. "Etat des recettes et dépenses." Ecclesiastical color map of area in *MC, 9*, supplement (1877). See also CR, *3*, 804–05 (1836), and details in Schoenberg chronology, Bradley-Kelly, and Palladino. Superintendent Geary in 1860 lists 7,000 Indians for Oregon state and 31,000 for Washington Territory; of this 38,000 total, 24,000 were in the Interior.

The figures represent a widespread Interior flock, including over 2,000 in the northwestern or Colville region, 2,000 among the Flathead confederacy, 400 Coeur d'Alenes, several hundred Kutenais beyond the Canadian line, and 500 Indians at the Yakima mission. The San Poils and smaller tribes had 229 Catholics, the Spokanes 300 (230 upper Spokanes, 60 lower), the Southern Okanogans 107, the Kettles 606, the Nez Percés from 200 to 300.

There were also Catholic Indians not under Jesuit care; their tribes lay rather outside the Interior as defined in this book, but they were susceptible to the influence of their own priests during the coming war. Among these the Umatilla mission of St. Ann stands out. Abandoned by the Oblates, it was reopened by the diocesan priest Adolph Vermeersch in 1865; Father Bertram Orth succeeded him, eight years later, and Father Louis Conrardy from 1875. But the man most influential with the Catholic Indians was their missionary of over a decade ago, the diocesan priest Toussaint Mesplié. A jovial, stocky little man, he had won many converts here, including the Cayuse chief "and his numerous relatives." In 1877 there were 837 Catholic Umatillas and Walla Wallas. Mesplié, working with Father Andrew Poulin, also had 400 converts among the Snakes. His main work had long been among the Whites of Idaho. When the war broke out, he was army chaplain at Fort Boise, away on leave at Washington, D.C.; in July the army was to send him among the excited Umatillas to dissuade them from going to war.

Each Jesuit mission and dependent station had its own inner history over the past two decades. Thus the diocese reopened the Yakima mission in 1867, a decade after the wars had closed it, and in 1870 transferred it to the Jesuits. The Blackfoot mission, abandoned during the war of 1866, reopened in 1874. After several false starts, the Kettle area developed prosperously from 1873 at St. Francis Regis, halfway between the old mission and Colville. "Many other tribes" were begging for Blackrobes, but the general at Rome refused to extend the labors of his overworked group any further. Conversions among the Interior Indians were continuing apace. All this added up to a potential Jesuit influence for peace far beyond that of 1856 or 1858.[13]

13. FL, *1875*, "Etat des recettes et dépenses"; letter of general, 30 December 1873; *1876*, "Etats Unis"; *1877*, "Etats Unis." FP, I, 5, general to Association, 5 February 1872, 6 April 1870. Grassi letter, *AFL*, *41* (1869), 384, on sick Jesuits. CR, *4*, 1300 ff., figures for San Poils to Nez Percés. WS, report of Joseph Oppenheimer on Colville agency (number of Catholic Umatillas, Walla Wallas), 12 July 1877. On Mesplié see esp. Davenport, *OHQ*, *8*, 112; Bradley-Kelly, *Boise Diocese*, pp. 82, 101–02, 97, 107–09. A statistical and descriptive survey of all the Jesuit network four years after the war is "The Missions of the Rocky Mountains in 1881," *WL*, *11* (1882), 43–56. See also the MS record books and varied statistics in OJ. On the influence of the veteran diocesan missioner A. J. Croquet among the Grande Ronde Indians, see *HED*, 45 Cong., 2 sess. (1877–78), 1, Pt. 5, *1*, 565.

Protestant missioners had returned to the Interior by the opening of the 1870s. The Reverend James Wilbur, a Methodist, had been among the Yakimas even in the 1860s, and the Reverend Mr. Spalding had returned among the Nez Percés briefly in 1862–65. By 1877 a zealous Methodist group flourished among the Yakimas. The Presbyterians had three solid missions, two among the Nez Percés and one with the Spokanes; Lapwai officially listed 200 members, Kamiah 470, and the Spokanes 429.

Christian expansion among the Interior Indians was paralleled by a revival of the Dreamer religion. A messianic form of the old Ghost Dance faith, it swept through the mass of non-Christian Indians, especially along the Columbia River and in Nez Percé territory. It taught a mystic identification of the Indian with his tribal land. Though borrowing elements from Catholics, Protestants and Mormons, it abhorred agriculture and White civilization as an offense against nature. Particularly attractive to the Indians was its ritual, emphasizing révivalistic ceremony and personal testimonies and accompanied by an almost continuous drumming. Father Grassi in his winter circuit of 1877 beyond the Colville area found the Dreamers very active. Early that year ex-agent Cain informed General Howard that the cult had become the exponent of tribal traditions for the Columbia and Snake River bands and for many on the Nez Percé and Umatilla reservations, whatever their other religious affiliations. The pioneer Splawn asserts that the Dreamer cult dominated the San Poils and Palouses. Father Joset says "the great majority" of the Nez Percés were Dreamers, or "drummers" as they were commonly called.[14]

Until 1870 missionary and government activity followed independent lines. In that year the lines converged. The rising tide of public criticism made it impossible to continue as before. A congressional committee had just excoriated the Indian service as the most corrupt branch of the government. The commissioner of Indian Affairs estimated that the preceding forty years cost the government a public charge of a half billion dollars for Indian wars, an average of twelve and a half million every year. A million dollars had been spent for every Indian killed. In fact, the Indian wars had already cost more than all the country's foreign wars combined. To appease the general outcry, President Grant appointed a permanent advisory committee of citizens called the Board of Indian Commissioners.

In 1870 Grant also inaugurated his Peace Policy. The Policy sweepingly reorganized the agencies, placing them directly under missionary control. So

14. *RBIC* (1877), p. 73, for Presbyterian numbers. Cf. Drury, *Spalding,* pp. 407–08, and revival background passim; also his *Cowley,* e.g., pp. 129, 105 ff., 116 ff., 52 ff., 93. *WL,* 7 (1878), 174, Grassi letter of 23 April 1878. NA, IA, LR (from Idaho Sup.), Cain to General Howard, 5 May 1877. Joset Papers, No. 105 ("la grande majorité" of Nez Percés). Splawn, *Ka-Mi-Akin,* pp. 392 ff.; also K. McBeth, *Nez Perces Since Lewis and Clark* (New York, 1908), chap. 5, "The Great Revival."

arbitrarily did it divide them among the denominations that the Catholics got not the expected half but a mere seven out of eighty-eight. This put 90,000 Catholic Indians under agents or missionaries chosen by Protestant mission boards, leaving only 17,000 of the flock under Catholics. Other causes contributed to turn the Peace Policy into a disaster. A principal cause was the determination of many agents to Americanize the Indians in language, dress, concepts, and manner of life.

The Methodist Yakima agent, the Reverend Mr. Wilbur, in a statement to the government near the end of 1876, grimly urged the use of force to this end. He believed the Indian should be compelled immediately to give up hunting and to come onto one of three main reserves. Malcontents who objected should be exiled far away. Chiefs should be deposed and "tribal relationships should be broken up." The Presbyterian agent J. B. Monteith (a layman) had similar recommendations for his Nez Percés. Monteith wished them to cut their hair like Whites, adopt White table manners and dress, and converse in English. In opposition to the early ministers like Spalding, he even objected to the Bible in the Nez Percé language. The Reverend H. T. Cowley among the Spokanes (not an agent) went so far as to oppose smoking tobacco, a blow to ceremonial and social life. Like Wilbur, Monteith anticipated no trouble with the Nez Percés over removal. Active dissenters under Chief Joseph "could not raise over sixty to sixty-five fighting men." On the other hand, he believed that some show of force would be necessary to overawe the dissidents. "Nothing but force will get these Indians to cultivating the soil." [15]

Prominent among the causes contributing to the failure of the Peace Policy was its bizarre interpretation by a number of non-Catholic agents. These individuals, drawn from the groups most affected by neo-nativism, saw the Policy as furnishing a governmentally established religion for each reservation. Catholicism particularly was to be outlawed, by force if necessary. Catholic Indians were prevented both from leaving the reservation to worship and from worshiping on it. Agents like Wilbur and Monteith appear to have devoted more effort to warding off the antichrist than to improving their own religious and humanitarian facilities.

15. *RBIC* (1876), pp. 40–41 (Rev. J. H. Wilbur's Statement and John B. Monteith's Statement); see also pp. 84 (the Congregational Statement), 74 (the Presbyterian), 88 (the dissent of Rev. Eells). Drury, *Cowley,* p. 158. On Protestantism as an acculturative agent among the Nez Percés see also Robert F. Berkhofer, "Protestants, Pagans, and Sequences among the North American Indians, 1760–1860," *Ethnohistory, 10* (1963), 201–32; his *Salvation and the Savage: An Analysis of Protestant Missions and American Indian Response, 1787–1862* (Lexington, Ky., 1965); and Whitner's work, cited below, n. 16.

Monteith was upset when Cataldo defied his prohibition against Catholics' worshiping, even in the open air. "Have I the right, this being a Protestant Agency and Mission," Monteith expostulated to the commissioner, "to exercise such control over the morals of this people as will enable me to prohibit the teaching of the Catholic faith or the holding [of] Catholic service among [them], even though the Indians desire it and clamor for it?" Advised by the commissioner that his position was illegal, the agent was even more upset. The Yakima agent Wilbur, who kept Father Caruana on the outer fringe of that reservation, joined Monteith in protesting against the commissioner's decision. The Methodist minister serving the Northwest as superintendent backed his two agents, declaring the commissioner's ruling itself illegal.

Behind this phenomenon of bigotry lay the startling increase of Catholic immigration, with its attendant problems. There were now almost as many Catholics in the United States as there were Negroes. Many Protestants mistrusted what seemed to be the coming of a monolithic, persecuting agency. The preceding decade had witnessed a number of ultramontane extravagances in the Catholic world, little calculated to reassure the Protestant mind. The defensive reactions of a newly aroused Catholicism here and abroad were often unduly provocative. Moreover, the censures of the Syllabus in 1864 and the definition of papal infallibility at the Vatican Council of 1870 had triggered widespread antagonism. Hosts of Protestants and Catholics dedicated themselves now to a polemical crusade, while the drums on both sides beat No Quarter.

Another element was present. American Protestantism in the '70s, reeling under the assaults of skepticism, the New Science, and changing social patterns, was rallying in an evangelical revival. This in turn released a wave of combative energy with which to meet the Catholic enemy. Unpalatable though it is to modern taste, this aggressiveness does imply an honorable concern, an underlying humanism. And the fanatic taint affected only a minority of non-Catholics.

In the coastal portion of the Pacific Northwest all this tumult led to some understandably passionate effusions by ministerial bodies. One outburst called attention to the Romanist infiltration into the highest places: the government meant to turn Protestant schools and churches "into horse stables and public brothels by handing the Indian Department over to the Romish Church." An Oregon religious committee, including ex-Superintendent Geary and a number of legislators, proclaimed at this time: "Protestanism will triumph against Congress and Rome." An influential segment of the Northwest population was convinced both of "the hellish hate of Romanism against Protestants and Americans" and of Jesuit responsibility for the past wars. This bitter atmosphere of accusation and recrimination brooded over the Nez Percé tribe during the months before the war.[16]

There was a third agent in the Interior, the Catholic J. A. Simms. (We shall meet Ronan, the Catholic Flathead agent, in the next chapter.) Simms resided at Fort Colville, as yet without helpers or staff. The Protestant portion of the Spokanes in his agency had a mission and school under Cowley. The minister describes Simms as "an educated gentleman, in no way bigoted in his religious views." Each of the three agents had a vague jurisdiction extending over many other tribes. The main body of the Coeur d'Alenes, for example, on the restricted reserve recently established from their ancestral lands by executive order, were often considered to fall under Monteith, while their western fringe came under Simms.[17]

The local Jesuits mistrusted the Peace Policy in principle. None of them took the compromising position of agent, though the Oblate Father Chirouse did so on the Coast. Giorda as superior of all the missions wrote to Father Brouillet at the incipient Bureau of Catholic Indian Missions in the nation's capital: "Please Knock Down the present christian-antichristian Indian policy: it is a disgrace for any Church to meddle in such work." His successor, Father Cataldo, superior during the Nez Percé war, recommended to Congressman Fenn of Idaho that the Indian agencies be given to the army, because the present system was both unconstitutional and in practice "does a

16. ABFM, ABC, 18, 4, 1, 2, Nos. 129, 157. See other letters and manifestoes here, and the *Pacific Christian Advocate*, e.g. 25 September 1869. Nez Percé Agency Letterbook (OU, Pendleton microfilm), Monteith to commissioner, 5 May 1873. CR, 4, 1302–03 (Caruana). Splawn devotes chap. 42, "A Great Indian Agent," to a sympathetic, candid biography of Wilbur. On the Peace Policy itself see P. J. Rahill, *The Catholic Indian Missions and Grant's Peace Policy 1870–1884* (Washington, D.C., 1953), e.g. chap. 5 on 1877; and L. B. Priest, *Uncle Sam's Stepchildren, the Reformation of United States Indian Policy 1865–1877* (Newark, N.J., 1942), chap. 3. For the phenomenon of anti-Catholicism and of acculturation in the Policy see R. L. Whitner, "The Methodist Episcopal Church and Grant's Peace Policy: A Study of the Methodist Agencies, 1870–1882," unpublished doctoral dissertation (University of Minnesota, 1959); and especially his "Grant's Indian Peace Policy on the Yakima Reservation, 1870–1882," *PNWQ*, 50 (1959), 135–42. One recent interpreter challenges "the accepted view," and unabashedly defends the Policy as both practical and a "phase of a Protestant movement for the assimilation of Indians" to the White, Christian society; he has it founder largely due to Catholic obstructionism (H. E. Fritz, *The Movement for Indian Assimilation, 1860–1890* [Philadelphia, 1963], esp. chap. 4; cf. pp. 19, 85–86, 102–03, 135, and passim).

17. H. T. Cowley, Reminiscences (WU), for quotation. Cf. Simms' letter of welcome to Cowley, 11 December 1874, Federal Records Center, Seattle, Rec. Group 75, box 17. The Colville agents, after seven military commanders from Lugenbeel to Houston (1859–68), were J. C. Parker (1868–69), E. Y. Chase (1869–70), G. W. Harvey (1870–71), W. P. Winans (*in loco*, 1870–72), and J. A. Simms (1872 ff.). Special Agent George Paige served in the mid-'60s (died 1868).

great deal of harm to religion." And sad experience caused Father Palladino to write in 1873 that as agent he preferred an honest, liberal-minded Protestant to a poor Catholic.[18]

These religious tensions, culminating especially on the Nez Percé reservation in a four-cornered squabbling between the Catholics, Presbyterians, Dreamers, and Methodists, were an important element in confusing the Indians on the eve of the Nez Percé war. Catholics and Dreamers tended to ally at least in their common regard for tribalism and the old ways.

FATHER CATALDO IN THE NEZ PERCÉ CALDRON

Many things argued against a Nez Percé war. The Nez Percés had so long sheltered a Protestant mission and flock that coastal Americans tended to think of the tribe itself as Presbyterian. The Presbyterian group possessed good seasonal farms, worked industriously at them as well as at odd jobs for Whites, and found time for food-gathering and hunting. Many of this group favored American dress and speech. They had a long history of schooling. Some of their camps flew American flags. They were situated fairly close to the troop concentration at Fort Walla Walla, and a new military fort stood at their own center where upper and lower Nez Percés divided. White settlement, especially at the river port of Lewiston, had taken root on their lands. When the war did come, in fact, it broke out in an almost accidental, haphazard way. It affected only a segment of the tribe. And it was more in the nature of a flight than an Indian war. Chief Michael's Kutenais had thus fled to Canada in 1855, as had the defeated Blackfeet in 1870 and the thousand Sioux under Sitting Bull early in 1877.

By the same token there was as much reason to expect an Indian war from the Nez Percés as from any tribe in the Interior. They had much the same grievances as the Flatheads or Coeur d'Alenes, much the same proud background of Plains warfare, much the same feeling of betrayal after long efforts to accept the Whites, much the same anger because their land was being wrested from them and overrun by Whites. From 1860 to the eve of the Nez Percé war, the tribe lost 33 victims to White brutality; they in turn killed 4 Whites. In 1863, the year Congress created Idaho Territory, the government in one breath-taking council swept away the entire Nez Percé reservation, except for a ludicrously small plot in its north. The chiefs holding land within that plot signed the treaty; the two-thirds whose lands lay outside (except for Timothy) rejected it.

18. CM, Giorda to Brouillet, 25 February 1876; Cataldo to Fenn, 12 December 1876; Palladino to Brouillet, 9 November 1873. See also Rahill, *Peace Policy*, p. 100.

The antitreaty faction then coalesced. Basically they were the old nucleus of pagan, buffalo-hunting dissidents, with a penumbra of new-found allies. Their leader was to be Chief Joseph, a strikingly handsome man, the very image of the romantic's noble Indian. His small village of perhaps sixty braves stood not far from the meeting place of the Washington, Idaho, and Oregon boundaries. His land ran far south into Oregon, especially in the rich grasslands and pine forests of the Wallowa Valley. Joseph's father had been one of the first two converts of the Presbyterian mission, a staunch Christian and an ally of the Whites until the loss of his lands induced a reversal of both loyalties.

The federal government, becoming cognizant of Nez Percé complaints, investigated. It honorably returned the Wallowa to the Indians in 1873. Local settlers forced a reconsideration; in 1875 the Wallowa was declared open to homesteading. Tension accumulated. The Whites harassed the Nez Percés and called for militia to protect themselves from retaliation. An ultimatum went out: come onto the reservation by April 1877. The desperate Indians begged for one last council at Lapwai. This fateful council was scheduled for the first days of May.

Meanwhile, the Jesuit mission expansion had reached the Nez Percés by 1866–67. In such a time of crisis, however, confusion and apathy slowly demoralized the few Nez Percé Catholics. In 1870 Father Cataldo had to employ the Jesuit device of temporary abandonment. The Catholic chiefs made determined efforts to regain their mission. In the spring of 1871 Cataldo returned to a very different situation. The Catholic group in the years before the war proved to be loyal and durable. Within six months their numbers rose from twenty to over ninety. By the time Chief Joseph's war broke, Cataldo had assembled a solid nucleus of perhaps two to three hundred Nez Percé Catholics centering on a log settlement eight miles from Lapwai, in a valley of the Craig Mountains.

It is difficult to say precisely how large the Catholic body was. Monteith, in April 1877, admitted to only forty "heads of families" being Catholic. Timothy, leader of the Nez Percé Methodists, asserted in a public letter that the Catholics now outnumbered the Presbyterians because Monteith had alienated so many. Territorial Delegate Stephen Fenn of Idaho, a Protestant familiar with the Lewiston area but a foe of Monteith, told Congress at this time that the Catholics were "the most numerous denomination of Christians located on the reservation and of those who lived without its limits." One set of Catholic records running from late 1868 to 1875 among the Nez Percés listed 295 baptisms, 189 adult conversions, 50 marriages, and 27 funerals. A descriptive survey of the mission four years after the war set the census at

400 Catholics, 500 Protestants, and 1,100 pagans, commenting that the recent war "destroyed the fairest prospects of this Mission." [19]

Something about Father Cataldo won the attention of the pagan majority. They listened so closely and courteously to him, as he traveled from camp to camp, that he became convinced the whole tribe was on the eve of conversion. Cataldo may have been too sanguine, but the reaction of the pagans gives a measure of the man and indicates something of his influence among the nontreaties. He was not the only Jesuit here—from 1875 Father Anthony Morvillo and a coadjutor brother helped. But Cataldo was the heart of the mission.

Joseph Cataldo (1837–1928) had been teaching at the Collegio Massimo in Palermo when Garibaldi's revolution exiled the Jesuits from the Kingdom of the Two Sicilies. Volunteering for the Rocky Mountain mission, he completed his studies at Louvain in Belgium, then at Boston for six months, and finally at Santa Clara College in California, where he also taught briefly. From 1865 to 1928 he was active as a missionary in Idaho, Washington, Montana, Oregon, Wyoming, and Alaska. Cataldo mastered twenty languages, European and primitive. For an unusually long time (1877–1893) he was superior-general of the mission network. In Idaho the town of Cataldo is named after him; in Washington civic organizations in 1936 erected a granite shaft in his honor near Spokane.

Though sickly all his life and badly tubercular when he arrived in the Northwest, Cataldo developed through physical hardship an unusually durable physique. Lean and weatherbeaten, he went by the Indian name Dried Salmon. His outstanding quality was a resilient toughness of spirit and body. His allied defect seems to have been an insensitivity, somewhat masked by his regard for the forms of courtesy. His reaction to nativist attacks by Monteith reveals a strain of pettiness. A combative note recurs in his writings, perhaps not inappropriate to those hard times but jarring to modern sensibilities.

Cataldo may be summed up as a soldierly figure. He had the dedication, the drive, and the executive ability denied Joset and De Smet; conversely, he

19. NA, IA, LR (from Idaho Sup.), notarized statement of Timothy, with similar document from another Indian, enclosures in Fenn to commissioner, 7 April 1877; Monteith to commissioner, 23 April 1877. FL, *1876*, fasc. Etats Unis, Idaho vicariate. Fenn's speech of 2 May is also abridged in *ACIM*, 2 (1878), cf. p. 41. Dreamer incident in *AFL*, 45 (1873), 358 (Cataldo letter to De Smet, April). Bischoff, *Jesuits in Old Oregon*, pp. 141–48. OJ, see Cataldo Papers, esp. codex "Sketch on the Nez Percé Indians," "History of the Nez Percé Mission," "Short Sketch on the Nez Percés Indians Catholic Mission" (similarly titled Cataldo MSS are cited below); see also the mission diary, "Historia domus missionis Sti. Josephi apud Slickpoo, Idaho." "Missions in 1881," *WL*, *11*, 52 (last quot.).

lacked their deeper humanity. A number of his colleagues remembered him as
hard on himself and hard on others, a man easier to admire than to like. He
was a steely person, never intimidated, seldom incautious, ascetic, devout,
sure-footed, with a surface geniality above a flinty substructure. He was a
good man to have on one's side but a very uncomfortable superior to serve
under. Writing in January 1872, the Jesuit general at Rome was impressed by
the "tireless zeal" of Cataldo; he remarked that the Nez Percé mission "promises already the most valuable results." [20]

Five months before the Nez Percé war, after a group conversion of Nez
Percés at Captain John Creek, Father Cataldo rode on with his Indian escort
for a long-promised "friendly visit" to Chief Joseph's camp eight miles away.
Such visits among the nontreaties were usual; they prepared the way for later
conversions. Joseph's people were "very friendly towards the Catholic priest,
and received him with great courtesy." Both Joseph and his brother Ollikut
discussed the possibility of conversion. Preoccupied with the loss of the Wallowa, "they would listen to his exhortation, but they were not just then disposed to become Catholics; they said they would see about it when the question about their land was settled." This promise immediately precipitated a
violent protest by a Dreamer group present in Joseph's camp.

With the topic of religion adequately covered, Chief Joseph sought to
elicit the Blackrobe's opinion on the Wallowa injustice. Joseph's brother
Ollikut particularly delivered himself of a long address on the subject. Ollikut
was the band's war chief and the idol of the young braves. A federal investigating committee at this time describes him in impressive terms. Joseph's
"younger brother, in whose ability he evidently confides—putting him forward much of the time as his advocate—is two inches taller than himself,
equally well formed, quite as animated, and perhaps more impassioned in

20. FP, I, 5, general to Association (in French), 17 January 1873. G. F. Weibel, S.J.,
has a eulogistic biography, *Rev. Joseph M. Cataldo, S.J., A Short Sketch of a Wonderful
Career* (Spokane, 1928, revised from article of same title in Gonzaga University *Quarterly, 16,* 1928); published serially also in *Salem Catholic Monthly, 1* (1928), No. 5,
9–12, 18–23; No. 6, 11–15, 21–22; No. 7, 11–15, 19–20. Bradley-Kelly devotes a chapter
to his life, in *Boise Diocese,* pp. 145–58. OJ has valuable MSS, including a typescript
biography by L. E. Crosby, "Kuailks Metatcopum, Being a Series of Interviews with
Father Cataldo" (later published in pamphlet form: Wallace, Idaho, Press-Times
Press, 1925); Italian translation by C. Testore, *Kuahilks Metatcopnim, le memorie di un
vestenera* (Venice, 1935). Unpublished typescript in OJ, C. A. Hawkins, "Father Cataldo S.J." (2 vols. 1930, "personally read and revised by Father Cataldo"). G. Giardina, *Il
P[adre] Cataldo S. J. apostolo dei pellirosse* (Palermo, 1928, 1932). Joseph Giorda, S.J.,
"Il Missionario gesuita tra i selvaggi naso-forati," *Museo delle missioni cattoliche, 15*
(1872), 593–603. Brief biographies in *DAB, Catholic Encyclopedia,* and *Enciclopedia
cattolica.* My interpretation of character is also influenced by conversations twenty
years ago with elderly Jesuits who had served under Cataldo.

speech, though possibly inferior in judgement." Cataldo tells how Ollikut now reviewed for him the government's misdeeds against the various tribes, emphasizing the many Sioux victories over the Whites, and "of course exaggerating everything in their own favor." Ollikut warned that his people would fight.

To all this the Father answered that he was not prepared to give his opinion, as he had come on an exclusively spiritual mission and had nothing to do with the government or with land questions. In all his actions and writings, this neutrality was Cataldo's inflexible position, both with White men and Red. Caught between two fires, he walked with the utmost care. On the one hand, his own Catholic Nez Percés were passionately antitreaty; on the other, Monteith and the ministers scanned every word or action for confirmation of their conviction that he was conspiring with the nontreaties. Chief Joseph was pleased with the priest's answer. Up to that point Joseph had secretly "thought I was sent by the government." The chief gave Cataldo a "sumptuous" feast, and a night's hospitality in his camp.

Cataldo departed, "cheered by the hope of future conversions." He had the impression that Joseph's people were intrigued by Catholicism but too disturbed at the moment to consider any great change. Other Nez Percés had given him much the same answer. "We want to be practical Catholics" if converted, their argument ran; "but we cannot be practical Catholics on account of our difficulty with the government; what good would it be if we are now baptized and the next day we fight the government?" Cataldo optimistically believed that the issues would soon sort themselves out.[21]

Writing to the Bureau of Catholic Indian Missions, Cataldo explained his habit of avoiding even the shadow of politics. "I came to the Indians to Christianize them and have replied nothing to their questions relative to the government, to the troops, to their land; I always said that I knew nothing of these things but only religion." When Congressional Delegate Fenn requested Cataldo's opinion in connection with his own work in Congress on the Wallowa problem, the priest answered in a similar vein. "It is my practice never to interfere at all in such matters." As a private citizen he rather thought that White settlement should be postponed ten to fifteen years until the Indians could select and secure their own claims. But he would not publicly put forward any opinion. "The least thing we say, sometimes unintentionally, is interpreted in a wrong way by our friends at the Agency."[22]

21. CM, Cataldo to Brouillet, 10 July 1877. Supplementary details in OJ, Cataldo, "History," pp. 95–97; "Short Sketch," p. 13; Crosby, "Interviews with Cataldo," pp. 11, 13. RBIC (1877), p. 44 (Ollikut description); cf. Helen Howard and D. L. McGrath, *War Chief Joseph* (Caldwell, Idaho, 1946), p. 144.

22. NA, IA, LR (from Idaho Sup.), Cataldo to Brouillet, 7 March 1877, enclosure in Fenn to commissioner, 7 April. CM, Cataldo to Fenn, 12 December 1877.

Even qualified neutrality offends men at either extreme of a given position. To the friendless underdog, seeking only his own rights, it can be a sustaining force. Not to oppose the Indians openly, when almost everyone else was doing so, almost surely provided them with some indirect moral support. Cataldo did express himself against Indian violence in this case, and during the war he was to oppose Joseph from the start. However, he felt he could not lend his priestly authority and influence to the treaty injustice any more than he could give it to the antitreaty violence.

Had this been a Catholic tribe and had the local atmosphere been less charged with misunderstanding, Cataldo would have been able to undertake a more active role on behalf of the Indians, as did his fellow missionaries in the Flathead country. As it was, Monteith already accused the priest of having "kept the Spokan[e] Indians from going into council" with him concerning their lands. He also blamed Cataldo for the Coeur d'Alene hostility against him during his 1873 negotiations in the north. "Yet far from preventing the Indians to make the treaty," Cataldo protested, "I help[ed] these gentlemen to do so." Even Father Brouillet's visit to the Northwest in 1874 elicited a dark response from Monteith: "I suppose he has come to assist in creating trouble among the Indians; he is the same that was accused of complicity in the massacre of Dr. Whitman and family." [23]

Unhappily, when Cataldo visited the Umatillas to preside over a group conversion of about twenty Indians, Joseph's brother Ollikut chanced to be holding a council of war with the tribe. Monteith protested. He probed and prodded among the Nez Percés until he found one willing to confirm his own worst fears. In February 1877 he sent a seven-page letter to the Indian Bureau, informing them how "priest Cataldo" was preventing Joseph's band from coming on the reservation; a reliable source, the niece of the Indian Jesse, had exposed the Jesuit's attempt to influence Joseph. According to this source, Cataldo had told Joseph that the treaty plan was not backed by the government but was simply an expedient to secure federal money.

The Jesuit plot went deeper than this. Monteith declared that in a council held a short time before with the Indians and Captain Perry, one of Joseph's own men had confessed. This Indian revealed how "the priest and Catholic Indians told them that if they came on the reserve, they would all freeze, as there was no wood on the Lapwai for them." Determined to make this a principal subject at the council, Monteith challenged Chief Joseph with the revelation. The chief's first reaction was surprise: "who told you that?" Joseph then refused to honor the subject with further comment. The agent took this

23. Cataldo letter of March 7, above, n. 22. CM, Cataldo to Brouillet, 17 April 1877 (incl. Monteith accusation) and 19 April. Lapwai Agency Letters (IHS), Monteith to Rev. J. C. Lowrie, 14 October 1874 (on Brouillet).

as further proof. He put Joseph's question to the malicious informant, who answered (Monteith underlines this): "*I will tell;* it was the same person." Chief Joseph's patience was exhausted: "immediately Joseph punched the young man." Captain David Perry, the Lapwai commandant, accepted this episode as proof of Cataldo's complicity.[24] Perry warned the Indians against the priest's lies.

Three months before the war Cataldo wrote Brouillet how Monteith everywhere "repeats that I have prevented the Indians from coming onto the reservation and he believes that I am opposed to the government." By the following month the agent's accusations had appeared in the local paper, along with a counterattack by the congressional delegate Fenn. The editor of the *Teller* speaks of "the character Cataldo has established for peace, obedience to the law, and general probity in all his dealings with whites or Indians." He adds that "Chief Joseph was in town this week and we conversed with him through an interpreter and he declares unqualifiedly that Cataldo has never by word or deed tried to persuade him not to go upon the reservation."

Monteith could hardly have chosen a less opportune time for his disturbing accusations. He was already as busy as a juggler, tending to a series of bitter quarrels. Both the Methodist and the Catholic Indians had filed charges of prejudice against him. Presbyterian coreligionists were still sniping at him in the aftermath of his struggle against Spalding. The Lewiston townspeople were upset by his apparent inability to control the Indian situation. A number of individuals, whom he dismissed as land speculators and liquor sellers, were enthusiastically feuding with him. And the Indian Bureau was preparing to mount a formal investigation on charges of peculation and fraud. Just at the time he required all his energies for the Wallowa problem, Monteith had provided his enemies with a victim to defend, a human figure more appealing and exploitable than the abstract issues. Like many frontier controversies, this one was larger than life. And one hesitates to absolve Cataldo of all blame; he was not without his own prejudices and angularity.[25]

One of the principal leaders endowed with the prestige and personality required to lead the nontreaties into war was Ollikut. Over him Cataldo had special influence. In April young Ollikut sought out the priest at the Catholic

24. NA, IA, LR (from Wash. Sup.), Monteith to commissioner, 2 February 1877; this long letter of seven pages is permanently misfiled under the Washington superintendency.

25. NA, Cataldo March 7 letter, above, n. 22. Lewiston *Teller*, 28 April 1877, with Monteith February 28 letter in full, synopsis of Fenn attack, editorial comment. See also Fenn speech to House of Representatives, above, n. 19. Editor Alonzo Leland, *Teller*, issues e.g. of 4 and 18 August 1877. NA, IA, Letterbook, *136*, 252, transmitting charges against Monteith, 21 June; LR (from Idaho Sup.), Monteith to commissioner, 30 April 1877.

mission. He told him he was a "Catholic at heart and if peace was established he would become a Catholic at once with some of their relatives and friends." He particularly desired again some advice from Cataldo "concerning the Wallowa trouble." In giving his reply, the Jesuit was firm on the subject of keeping the peace. Beyond that he could offer no solution. He told Ollikut: "do what you think is best, provided that everything is done peacefully; for my part I would like to see you all near this mission." Ollikut seemed persuaded. "He promised to act peacefully, and try to have the others do likewise." He also said that "when the trouble was over, he would settle down and become a Catholic." Thus Cataldo was unworried on the eve of the last Lapwai council.[26]

Monteith conveyed to Chief Joseph the federal government's determination to have him on the reservation by April 1. Joseph appealed this decision to General O. O. Howard, commander of the Department of the Columbia. Howard sent his aide Lieutenant Boyle, who had a long conversation with Joseph's representative Ollikut. The General himself left Portland on April 16, to hold a conference with Ollikut's party three days later at Fort Walla Walla. Howard was involved in the Nez Percé problem because the army was under instructions to assist Monteith in the removal. His talks now with Ollikut culminated in an agreement to meet the dissident chiefs in the great council at Lapwai in twelve days.

Howard was an unusual man. A gallant if controversial general in the Civil War, he commanded Sherman's right wing on the march to the sea. At Fair Oaks he won the Medal of Honor and lost an arm. He was intensely, even painfully, religious; known as the Bible General, he was to gain some reputation as a lay preacher. The wife of an army surgeon, herself a devout Protestant, describes him in 1875 as unpopular with his officers "owing to his ferocious religion." She admires Howard's intelligence and eloquence but confesses that "he is one of those unfortunate Christians who continually gives outsiders a chance" to mock. An "ordained preacher," Howard "preaches and leads meetings on all occasions—on street corners, steamboats, etc."; he will preach at Lapwai during our council. Stern and somewhat remote behind his bushy white beard, he resembled a latter-day prophet. Recently he had successfully carried through a presidential peace mission to the warring Apaches and had led an expedition against Sitting Bull. Later he was to become superintendent of West Point.

General Howard sent word to Father Cataldo inviting him to the council. Afterward, when the General arrived in Nez Percé territory for the council, he paid a visit to Cataldo's mission. It stood midway up a choice valley, Howard writes, "a nicely constructed church holding perhaps two hundred peo-

26. Cataldo, "History of Nez Percé Mission," p. 98; "Short Sketch," pp. 13–14. Bradley-Kelly incorrectly has Joseph visit Cataldo (*Boise Diocese*, p. 153).

ple," with "a small village of log houses" for those Indians resident and farming. "But as is often the case there is considerable controversy, above and beneath the surface, between the followers of the Mission and the Protestants." Howard himself was a partisan of Monteith's plans for the Indians. He had already studied Monteith's accusations against Cataldo. He knew, too, as exagent Cain was to remind him in a letter two days later, that "the dif[f]erence in religious sentiments—Catholicism and Protestantism"—followed the division of treaty and nontreaty "to a considerable extent." In fact, Howard would not have consulted Cataldo at all except for Monteith's accusations of covert opposition. "This explains my interview with the priest."

The General reported how Cataldo "denied to me a desire to hinder the Government plans." Howard was not satisfied. He protested to Cataldo that "sometimes 'neutrality' was, in my judgment, equivalent to positive opposition." He urged the priest to use his position to persuade the nontreaty Indians to yield. Then "I invited him to be present at the Councils, and I believe that after this I had the cooperation of the Father and most of his people." General Howard had a bluff and overriding approach to these problems. It is improbable that he listened as closely as he lectured. Neither Cataldo nor the Catholic Nez Percés had changed their positions, nor did they budge from them later.

Next day the council assembled at the "most frontier of posts," Fort Lapwai. "Bright sunshine" lit up the "rolling hills and gorgeous mountains," General Howard says, as the Indians made their ceremonial entrance, chanting in a sad, searching, defiant wail. A striking feature of these councils was the physical "difference of appearance" among the Indian factions. "The Treaty Indians nearly all wore shirts, pants, and coats," had their hair cut relatively short, and eschewed paint. The nontreaties "were very Indian looking indeed" in clothing, hair, and ornament. Father Cataldo rode up from his mission and "opened the exercise by a short and extempore prayer in Nez Percé"; many years later the participant Yellow Wolf recalled this as a "prayer talk." There was to be a series of meetings between May 3 and 15. The talks centered in a hospital tent in front of a garrison building, with flaps raised so that the massed Indians outside could participate.[27]

During the council several Dreamers visited with Catholic leaders, seeking

27. Quotes from NA, IA, LR (from Idaho Sup.), Cain to Howard, 5 May, Howard May 2 report; *HED*, 45 Cong., 2 sess., 1 (1878), Pt. 2, *1*, 592. See also O. O. Howard, *Nez Perce Joseph: An Account of His . . . War, His Pursuit and Capture* (Boston, 1881), p. 53 (council opening). L. V. McWhorter, *Yellow Wolf: His Own Story* (Caldwell, Idaho, 1940), p. 37. Howard's preaching is from letters of 1875 and 1877, in E. M. and J. A. Fitzgerald, *An Army Doctor's Wife on the Frontier, Letters from Alaska and the Far West, 1874–1878*, ed. Abe Laufe (Pittsburgh, 1962), pp. 140, 251; see passim on the council, life at Fort Lapwai, and different appearance of nontreaties (p. 220).

a united front for the removal of Monteith and for the retention of a large reservation. The Catholic Nez Percés were disturbed by rumors that Howard harbored some plan against the Catholic Indians. Meanwhile Cataldo himself followed the arguments of the council closely but abstained from active participation. He had already attended all the councils held at Lapwai; there was little he could contribute to this one.

During a previous council Captain Perry had privately consulted him as to "whether he thought there would be war." Cataldo had inclined to believe there would not, "but realizing the prevalent unrest said he recommended a much larger force at Fort Lapwai, for the moral effect and for use in case of emergency." Perry laughed at him, boasting that he "had 300 soldiers, sufficient to take care of the Indians if they resorted to arms."

During the present council the accusations against Cataldo were again aired. "All were asked about the charges against me." Only one Indian, the young man who had slandered him during the council with Perry, spoke up. This time he vaguely blamed some Catholics. Questioned closely, he admitted that the priest had not been involved. Pressed by Cataldo to name the Catholics, he could not remember. There was some muttering in the council against the youth, and two Indians delivered short speeches on the subject. Finally the culprit protested: "I never mentioned the priest." A Catholic Indian "got up and rebuked Monteith for writing a lie on the priest." Cataldo now intervened, explaining that he was satisfied. General Howard publicly promised for the second time to incorporate into his official report a vindication of the priest's reputation. Cataldo did not entirely trust the General; he asked his friend Father Brouillet at Washington to "let me know what kind of report they make."

The council itself was a failure. During one angry interchange, Howard arrested the main Indian spokesman and clapped him in the guardhouse. He concluded with an ultimatum: come onto the reservation peacefully within thirty days or be driven there by force. None of the chiefs was quite prepared for open resistance. Helpless, they yielded. There was even a good deal of premature "rejoicing over the peaceful outcome." Cataldo candidly tells us that "I never knew nor even suspected that the Nez Percés would ever dare oppose the U. S. Army." Joseph himself bowed to the inevitable. Cataldo's friend Ollikut firmly put his influence behind Joseph and peace. There must already have been a small war faction, however; and certainly an alienation of spirit existed which boded ill for the future.[28]

28. CM, Cataldo to Brouillet, 10 July (Dreamers solicit Catholics); to same in Latin, 8 May (rumor; charges in council). Hawkins-Cataldo, "Cataldo," 2, 60 (Perry boast). Cataldo Papers, public address of Cataldo at Lewiston jubilee banquet in his honor, 20 February 1928.

WAR ON THE COEUR D'ALENE DOORSTEP

A few days before the war broke, Father Cataldo rode north for a routine administrative meeting at the Sacred Heart mission. The Coeur d'Alenes were now "the best among the Rocky Mountain tribes" of the Jesuits. Solidly organized under the able Head Chief Seltis and policed by a militia of forty braves called Soldiers of the Sacred Heart, they supported themselves with abundant harvests and livestock. General Sherman commends their "considerable progress as farmers and rough mechanics"; some even "had money out at interest." In 1876, as the buffalo culture collapsed in a welter of battles on the Plains, the Jesuits had persuaded the Coeur d'Alenes to renounce the annual hunt forever. On the international scene the tribe had even offered warriors to Pope Pius IX for his struggle with the *Risorgimento;* the Pope returned a gracious answer. Yet the tribal life was essentially intact: the Coeur d'Alenes were still Indian in dress, language, social and political organization, customs, and law—a remote little Indian nation. The resident missioners were Joset and Diomedi; Joset appears in General Sherman's report of 1877 as "well and favorably known to the United States authorities for thirty years." [29]

Most important to the Coeur d'Alenes was the shifting of their entire mission center far to the south. The new site was a long way below the lake or the traditional village places. It was a camas prairie, an important tribal summer encampment with the descriptive name of Nilgwalko, or Spring in the Timber. Accessible to visitors on all sides, it had been a cosmopolitan gathering spot as well. Down here all the buildings and farms would have to be started over again. Transition to an agricultural economy had, however, reached the point where a large expanse of rich land must be utilized; and this land had to be taken before more settlers arrived. The new site was also necessary for supplies and for marketing the farm surplus.

On February 1877 the Coeur d'Alenes formally voted to move. Later, as enthusiasm or energies waned, Father Diomedi spirited their beloved statues and church furnishings to temporary buildings in the south. The war would catch the Coeur d'Alenes suspended in mid-move, most of them at the new site but many still up at the old mission. The removal also put the tribe close to the borders of Nez Percé territory to the south, and to the borders of the troublesome Palouse Indians just to the southwest. The Coeur d'Alenes were thus more vulnerable to Nez Percé solicitation to enter the war. And since their difficult mountain country lay at their back, they were defensively as

29. Joset Papers, ethnological treatises; *Reports of Inspection,* p. 93; *RCIA* (1872), p. 342.

strong as ever. Being only sixty miles above Lewiston made them, from a White point of view, uncomfortably close to the upper fringe of isolated settlements. On the other hand, they were ideally situated to act in the cause of peace.

Coeur d'Alene grievances identified them closely with the Indian world, as did their dislike of Americans. An executive order in 1867 had designated a large reserve for them out of their former lands; they refused to remain within it. An 1873 commission raised a furor trying to negotiate a return to the reservation boundaries. Another federal commission had been unable to reach their territory in 1877 during its tour. In May 1877 the government was sending yet another commission because few of the Coeur d'Alenes were within the 1873 limits. Worse, the government had stripped the tribe of valuable lands without paying the promised indemnity. Nor was this all. Officials had already betrayed their enthusiasm for removing the Coeur d'Alenes altogether from their strikingly beautiful mountain country onto the bleak and sterile moonscapes of the Colville reserve. Father Giorda noted that if this move were attempted, it "would create an immense dissatisfaction" among the tribe.[30]

Father Diomedi records that the Coeur d'Alenes had lost all confidence in White men's justice. Fenn, in a speech at Washington before the House of Representatives in May 1878, could refer to their stoic silence in the face of "white settlers occupying a large portion of the country formerly occupied by them." With such grievances festering, every unpleasant incident became an invitation to violence. During some difficulties between the Coeur d'Alenes and the White courts in 1876, for instance, Agent Simms cautioned the commissioner of Indian Affairs that the Coeur d'Alenes "are a very excitable people, and the Chief [Seltis] referred to is one of the Most intelligent and influential in this section of the country; unless some steps are taken to pacify them they may seek redress in their own way and cause serious trouble." On that occasion, the Jesuits interpreted the Coeur d'Alene complaint and facilitated a settlement.

The tribe had no effective agent. Monteith was technically agent for the Idaho segment, but they treated him with cold contempt. One hundred and fifty Coeur d'Alenes, severed by the Idaho line, belonged under Simms at Fort Colville. His control over them was as tenuous as that of Monteith. In June 1876 Lieutenant Boyle, reporting on the Interior Indians, wrote that Simms

30. On Nilgwalko see Ray, *PNWQ*, 27, 131, No. 21 and map. Giorda narrative of war in OJ, "A Blessing in Disguise" (last quot.). Cf. also Jack Dozier, "Coeur d'Alene Country: The Creation of the Coeur d'Alene Reservation in North Idaho," *Idaho Yesterdays*, 6, no. 3 (1962), 2–7.

has "very little" influence over any of the tribes, since they were so impossibly scattered. Visiting even those tribes closer than the Coeur d'Alenes, Boyle "found there was very little affinity between them and their Agent." One report to the commissioner of Indian Affairs lists the Coeur d'Alenes as "not under an agency." [31]

But these were common problems. One sustained them as part of life. The mission diary for 1877 says only: "we went from Christmas to Lent without any important event." The tribe had put up a rude convent for the nuns who were coming to open a school, and had organized a supporting farm. Now they settled down to digging camas roots in the late spring months. With them in the field was a multitude of guests—Palouses, Nez Percés, Spokanes, and others. On Thursday, May 31, the Indians celebrated Corpus Christi, the great mid-year feast for Catholic Indians of the Interior. Simms reports of the Kettle mission to the north: "more than a thousand Indians were recently in attendance at the Catholic Mission near here during the festival of Corpus Christi." A similar number, if Catholic Indian guests are included, probably gathered at the Coeur d'Alene mission at the same time.[32]

Father Giorda, the superior of the mission network, left the Kettle mission with Father Tosi as early as May 23, to prepare a formal consultation with his advisers. He planned to hold it at the older Sacred Heart site in mid-June to consider the common problems of the missions. Consequently, Father Cataldo was sitting with his colleagues Giorda, Joset, and Diomedi on Saturday, June 16, when news came of the war. The consulters had just finished discussing financial support for the nuns who were to teach at the proposed school and had taken up the problems involved in Coeur d'Alene removal, when "an Indian entered the room with the mail."

Two letters were important. One informed Giorda that Cataldo replaced him as superior of all the missions. The other letter was from General Howard. Carried up by special express from Lewiston, it announced the outbreak of war and urgently recalled Cataldo to the Nez Percé country. As an old man Cataldo recalled this dramatic moment: "on one side was the war, and on the other side the superiorship and my duties to all; poor Father Cataldo!" He appointed Giorda local superior of the Coeur d'Alene mission, with young Diomedi in charge of temporalities. Then he began his long work of touring

31. Diomedi, *Sketches of Indian Life*, pp. 78–79. Fenn speech, *ACIM*, 2, 37. NA, IA, LR (from Wash Sup.), Simms to commissioner, 30 July 1876; Lt. Wm. Boyle report on Colville agency, 3 June 1876. *RCIA* (1876), p. 210 (no agency).

32. Diomedi Papers (OJ), "Historia domus S. Cordis Jesu." Simms Report, 31 May 1871. On school see Sister M. Caron, superior-general, Montreal, to Coeur d'Alenes, 16 February 1877, ibid., in "Short Notice" and "Sketch of Sacred Heart Mission."

the tribes, calming both Whites and Indians and collating for publication the reports of other Jesuit workers for peace.[33]

What had happened in the south? Joseph's band had prepared to come onto the reservation at last. They and other nontreaties gathered their stock and moved close to the reservation limits. Then, on June 13 and 14, three young braves staged a murder raid along the Salmon River, killing four Whites and wounding another, apparently attempting to force a war. This coup was followed by a wider raid, involving a war party of twenty-one Nez Percés. Some fourteen or fifteen Whites were killed; others barely escaped. Terror seized the countryside. The only atrocity of the war occurred now. The father of a family was killed, his wife repeatedly assaulted, the daughter's tongue partially cut out, and the little boy's head crushed between the knees of a warrior. Indian custom made the Nez Percés, as a whole, responsible for all the evil. Joseph, more familiar with the White mind, tried in vain to reassure his people. The whole band fled to a hideout in White Bird Canyon in the south. They counted perhaps 150 men capable of bearing arms, a number soon augmented by almost another hundred.

With all the confidence of a Custer or Steptoe, General Howard rushed 99 men in hard pursuit. The Nez Percés ambushed them and wiped out a third of the command, with only two Indians wounded. On June 23 Howard himself took the field with 227 troops. After costly skirmishes, he increased his force to 400 soldiers plus 180 civilian scouts and packers. The Indians pinned down and besieged this army for a day and a half, killing 15 and wounding 25. Tiring of the sport and with four Indians dead, the Nez Percés withdrew. Burdened with 2,000 horses and 550 noncombatants, they set out over the long Lolo trail directly toward the Bitterroot Valley of the Flatheads.

The General telegraphed ahead to Montana to arrange an interception. He himself planned to march, not in pursuit of the hostiles, but directly north. He meant to overawe the Coeur d'Alenes and other tribes before they could rise, to reassure the settlers, and to forestall any circling back over the Mullan road. Befuddled by disturbances of the Nez Percé rear guard, however, and fearful of leaving the settlements open to attack in the south, he later decided to follow close on Joseph's trail. An auxiliary force under General Wheaton, already on his way to Idaho, was ordered to carry out the northern march. By the last week of July, when Howard's command set out over the Lolo trail, the Nez Percés were already in the Bitterroot.

With Howard leaving, Lewiston held by only a small garrison, and Wheaton not yet present, the upper Interior was left to its own turmoil. The

33. Diomedi Papers, "Sketch of Sacred Heart Mission" (quot.); see also Hawkins-Cataldo, "Cataldo," 2, 78; Giorda, "Blessing," p. 1; "Diary of St. Francis Regis Mission at Colville 1870–1892," under May. Crosby, "Interviews with Cataldo," p. 14 (last quot.).

danger here was twofold. First, settlers or Indians might precipitate trouble out of panic or malice. And secondly, segments of the Indian world, excited by Joseph's triumphs and exacerbated by their long-standing grievances, might explode into sympathetic violence. To each of these problems the Jesuit mission network addressed itself.

Nez Percés and Coeur d'Alenes being contiguous, the little settlements and isolated farms between the two tribes were particularly frightened. Suppose the hostiles chose to come north, the most obvious route of escape? Pine Creek was the settlement closest to the new mission center in Coeur d'Alene territory. Gripped by fear, "a great many" settlers here were packing and fleeing to Walla Walla, eighty miles southwest. In Paradise Valley, twenty-five miles from the new Coeur d'Alene center, settlers were frantically throwing up stockades. Newspaper stories reflected and increased this excitement. The Lewiston *Teller,* amid a page full of harrowing detail about Nez Percé violence, had a dispatch datelined June 17 at four o'clock: "Joseph's command will be augmented by several hundred fighting men from the different bands who have hitherto been considered friendly."

Lewistonites could not feel too secure, with their town on Nez Percé tribal land, with the Coeur d'Alene center only a leisurely two days' ride north, and with the Palouses and other tribes at their elbow. Many people believed the Coeur d'Alenes had already gone to war. The Walla Walla *Union* describes public reaction in the upper Interior during the week after the Jesuits received news of the war. "Rumor filled the air during the week with reports that the Co[e]ur d'Alene Indians had joined Joseph's band of outlaws; that they numbered several hundred warriors; and that they were marching down from Hangman's Creek, killing and destroying as they came."

One F. M. Dougherty broadcast the news that fifty Coeur d'Alenes had deserted Chief Seltis and gone to war. Another citizen, George Popham, after sundry harrowing experiences including capture by Nez Percé hostiles, entered into circumstantial detail. He informed the *Teller* that "runners had been sent to Palouse, Spokane, Columbia River, and Umatilla tribes who would join them, and that they could capture the whole country." The Nez Percés expected to seize Lewiston itself and all the Interior within two months, Popham claimed, "and then they would have a good time." Father Mesplié was credited with predicting a sympathetic rising by the Coeur d'Alenes, Spokanes, Columbias, Kettles "and their allies," Umatillas, Yakimas, Flatheads, and other tribes, to a total of 10,000 warriors; "the greater number will join the hostiles." The settlers, alarmed by such reports, "on the ragged edge of suspense," and disturbed over "the fact of the known treachery of the Indian character," condemned "applying the Bible to the Indian question."

They demanded extermination of the hostiles. Ever-widening ripples of rumor spread out; from Philadelphia they sped to Europe "by Anglo-American Cables."

Cataldo, however, was already at work, sending authoritative information to the newspapers. Having inquired into the disposition of the Coeur d'Alenes, he wrote a letter from the old mission to the Lewiston *Teller*. "A letter from Father Cataldo says the Indians are all quiet up on Hangman['s] Creek, although a good many of the Nez Percés and Palouses are there, messenger just through in two days." The editors were not entirely reassured, because of recent Nez Percé triumphs. "What effect this victory of the Indians [White Bird Canyon] may have upon those now friendly, remains to be seen." [34] Cataldo had left the old mission on the 18th, arriving at the new Nilgwalko center next day. He paused to investigate for himself the mood of the great multitude of Indians gathered there. The Coeur d'Alenes and their various guests—Palouses, Nez Percés, Spokanes, and others—"flocked around the Church" at his arrival. Some Whites came in at the same time with news that "all the settlers had fled panic-stricken to Colfax."

The county seat for its region, Colfax was a little clump of houses and trees fitted into a deep canyon. The few inhabitants had dug rifle pits, welcomed the refugee auxiliaries, and looked to their arms. One farmer fled into town in such a hurry that, when his hat blew off, he wouldn't stop his wagon to retrieve it. Cataldo decided to have the Indians draw up testimonials of friendship; these he endorsed and sent by two Coeur d'Alenes to Colfax. Head Chief Seltis composed a formal little note. "I the undersigned testify that all my Indians the Coeur d'Alenes are always friendly disposed towards the whites, and we will help them as much as we can, if any help should be necessary here round." Since the unruly Palouses were also feared, Cataldo's second testimonial came from John Tla[?], a chief of the Palouses, advising that "my heart is good." The third letter was from the Palouse chief Ususpa Euin, head of the Almotu band, apparently one of the six main divisions of the Palouses; these people were located on the north bank of the Snake, thirty miles above the mouth of the Palouse River. He says they had joined the Coeur d'Alenes only for gathering camas. These testimonials were published in the *Walla Walla Union* four days later, the editor commenting that Father Cataldo "is a very trustworthy man." [35]

34. OJ, Wm. Brewer to Joset, Pine Creek, 30 June 1877 (Pine Creek quot.). *Teller*, 23, 24 June, 7, 21 July, 11 August 1877. Walla Walla *Union*, 23 June 1877. Helena *Independent*, 5 July, communication of 26 June 1877 (Mesplié). At Fort Lapwai itself, compare the fears of a general rising by the northern Indians as late as 11 July, against the contrary picture by 18 July (Fitzgerald, *Army Wife's Letters*, pp. 271, 280).

35. Giorda, "Blessing," with copies of letters from chiefs.

From the new mission Cataldo "started immediately for Lewiston with Barthelmy, one of the Co[e]ur d'Alen[e] chiefs, assuring everyone on the road of the peaceful disposition of the Catholic Indians." In the wake of his reassurances new rumors sprang up. A letter from the Palouse City settlers to Cataldo dated June 20 gave "the latest" news: the White Bird battle "will sum up in killed about 100 Men, Mostly soldiers—it would seem that the soldiers have been whipped every fight from the first." Cataldo brought the Coeur d'Alene chief into Lewiston to testify to his tribe's disposition. He then set out for the Nez Percé mission.[36]

THE WHITE WORLD: PANIC AND THE READY TRIGGER

For the next critical week, Coeur d'Alene affairs were in the hands of Joseph Giorda. Of a noble Piedmontese family, Giorda had completed his theological studies with unusual distinction, had done some pastoral work in the wilds of Corsica, and had then settled into a seminary teaching career. Hardly a year after his coming to the Rocky Mountains, he had been named superior of the network (1862–66). He guided its rapid expansion to eight mission centers, and has therefore been called the second founder of the Rocky Mountain missions. Though drafted again as superior in 1869, in 1877 apoplexy made necessary his replacement by Cataldo. Five years later he died. Wherever he went, honors accrued. He managed to elude a bishopric; Pius IX forebore to command acceptance only because he was "deeply moved" by Giorda's "unique modesty" in the manner of refusal. In 1866 the first territorial legislature of Montana elected him chaplain and would not listen to his refusals.

The Indians called him, because of his outstanding physical feature, Round Head. His photograph shows a face kindly and candid, though drawn, with eyes masked by illness. Agent Owen, in the Bitterroot, describes him in 1863 as "quite a young Man and a very Zealous Jesuit; I find him very pleasant." He could preach fairly well in six Indian languages, including Nez Percé, Flathead, and Blackfoot. His main defect as an administrator was his excessive kindness. Now fifty-four years old, he had had wide experience with both Indians and Whites. The Helena *Daily Herald* was soon to speak at length in his obituary of his intellectual gifts, kindliness, and the "fatherly interest he displayed to everyone who approached him" whether Catholic or Protestant. As intermediary between Indian and White during the critical days of the Nez Percé war, a better man could hardly have been chosen.[37] His assistant

36. OJ, Palouse City settlers to Cataldo, 20 June 1877. Giorda.
37. OJ, menologies and biographical sketches by contemporaries, including Joset, "Sketch of Joseph Giorda," in Joset Papers, No. 86, and Ravalli, "Account of Labors

Paschal Tosi had been in the Rockies for over a decade, mostly in the Kettle-Okanogan region; he was later to become founder and superior of the Jesuit Alaskan missions, an authority in Alaskan linguistics, and first prefect apostolic of Alaska.

When the first excitement died down, Giorda and Tosi on June 26 left for Portland to receive the nuns coming to teach the Coeur d'Alenes. Before leaving, Giorda sent a letter of reassurance to General Howard.[38] The burden of peace in the Coeur d'Alene area then fell on Joset. Joset's work, which is fairly well documented, suggests something of what other Jesuits must have been doing in their respective missions. Joset was unable during part of this time to move about because of a leg injury.

Giorda says that Joset had already been kept busy "going round the settlements to reassure the minds of the settlers, and writing continually to everyone that danger was not from these Indians." He ruefully adds: "still, incredible to say, news were spread by frightened brains that the Priest had told them that the Co[e]ur d'Alen[e]s could no more be trusted, that Seltish had given them notice that he could no more control his young men." There was continual wrestling with the dark force of rumor. "The Priests would write to every post office words of peace and assurance, but bad news would find more ready believers than truth." [39]

In one episode, Joset was troubled as to how Nez Percé guests of the Coeur d'Alenes might return to Lapwai without dangerous incident. He wrote to nearby Pine Creek to arrange for White companions during their trip through the settlements. William Brewer replied on June 26 "in behalf of the citizens of this Place." He says "we are prepared to furnish a Small Escort to go along with Such peaceable Indians as may wish to return to Lapuai[,] and will by so doing guaranty their safety while travelling Home; should this Proposition meet with your views I will thank you to send word when they wish to go, also about what Number there is willing to go[;] you know about how many are gone north."

On June 30 the Pine Creek people thanked Joset for his latest "Kind note." They tell how "a great many of these people have left for Walla Walla on account of fear of Indian's Trouble." A week later, acknowledging "your favour of yesterday," Brewer says that "some of the Men have gone to bring

---

of Giorda," in Ravalli Papers. See also Bischoff summary in *Jesuits in Oregon*, p. 222; Palladino, *Indian and White*, passim; A. P. Casagrandi, S.J., *De claris sodalibus provinciae taurinensis societatis Jesu commentarii* (Turin, 1906), pp. 105–16. Owen, *Journals and Letters, 1*, 283.

38. Joset papers, No. 85, diary of the 1877 war, 26 June. PA, Book of Records of Letters sent (with diary), 3, 6 June (for July?).

39. OJ, Brewer to Joset, Pine Creek, 7 July. Giorda, "Blessing," pp. 6–7.

back their families." [40] The Jesuit kept in touch with James Ewart, the spokesman for the people of Colfax. Through Ewart he refuted the rumor that "the Spokanes had taken arms" and plundered the store at Spokane Bridge: Spokane Garry had been at the new Coeur d'Alene mission on July 2 "and reported everything quiet." Joset says Garry's information was confirmed by a message from Agent Simms. "My impression is that the Indians from whom we might have feared mischief are Scared themselves at least as much as the Settlers." Ewart, in replying, conveyed the gratitude of the Colfax people. "I am glad of the information you Send me; it enables me to contradict Successfully the most absurd and improbable rumors." Though the townspeople were holding up bravely, he said, "we Sometimes See and hear lots of Panic Stricken Stories and People." He asks Joset to send anything further "that will allay public excitement." [41]

The Jesuits maintained communication with Agent Simms at Colville by Indian messenger. On June 29, for example, Simms conveyed to the priest a request from General Howard for information. Howard and Indian Inspector Watkins had directed Simms "to send a messenger to the Coeur d'Alenes and to communicate with the Fathers at the Mission in order to find out the disposition of the Coeur d'Alenes in regard to the outbreak, among the hostile Nez Percés, and whether they could be relied upon as remaining friendly." Simms says "it would be gratifying to the Inspector and to General Howard to have some expression from the Chiefs, and the opinion of the Fathers at the Mission." The agent "would be glad to have Seltise or Stillam" return with the Indian messenger, "so they could report in person on the condition of affairs in their section."

Simms also passes on to Father Joset his own instructions from Watkins and Howard "to Cooperate with the Fathers and endeavor to Maintain our present friendly relations with the Indians in this part of the Country." The agent wrote again on the next day, this time to the absent Father Giorda, thanking him for previous reassurances and "the Message from Seltis." He asks: "please give me all the information you can in regard to matters in your section; there are constant rumors here about disaffected Indians between the Snake river and the Spokane, and the people at the Fall[s] and Spokane Bridge seem to be uneasy." He passes on a rumor that "one or two persons have been Killed Near Pine Creek, and that there is a party of Palouses on the Spokane who are supposed not to be very friendly." Any available information "will be thankfully received." [42]

40. OJ, Brewer to Joset, 26, 30 June, 7 July; Joset to James Ewart, Hangman's Creek, 4 July.
41. OJ, Joset to Ewart, 4 July; Ewart to Joset, Colfax, 5 July.
42. OJ, Simms to Giorda, 30 June, and to Joset, 29 June.

Time and again the settlers oscillated between confidence and fright. On July 7 the Lewiston *Teller* reported that four hundred warriors were menacing settlers on the north side of the lower Spokane, breaking down fences and plundering houses. "A Flathead Indian has been there and told them that the Flatheads would join them against the whites." On July 21 "Fred Sherwood, the renowned expressman," reported "much interest among the Indians north, by the movement of Joseph," and uneasiness in the Colville Valley settlements. Small raiding parties were abroad. These bands apparently had no connection with the hostile Nez Percés, but their horse stealing and plundering of abandoned homes in the upper Interior added to the widespread distrust felt toward all the Indians. Disquieting reports were also being received from the south, about the Bannocks at Fort Hall and the Paiutes.[43]

Captain J. M. Greenstreet, of the local farmers' militia known as the Palouse Rangers, appealed on July 27 to the "Priest at Hangman Mission," authorizing him to issue passes to friendly Indians in order to guarantee their safety while "traversing the trails." He promised to "take care that all friendly Indians shall be treated in the most courteous manner by anyone whom I may send out, and would request that you make all your Indians acquainted with our friendly intentions." On July 28 the Pine Creek settlers again thanked Joset for his news. They tell how "petty thieving from the Houses still continues." As late as August 25 William Ewing, county commissioner and a resident at Palouse Bridge, informed the Lewiston *Teller* that some Indians here were hostile, while many others were becoming increasingly so because of the mistrustful attitude of the Whites.

During the course of the war the Coeur d'Alenes actively kept in touch with Joseph's movements, and with every stir of news in Indian circles. Chief Stellam used to ride as spokesman to the settlers of Spokane Bridge with much of this news. A pioneer was to recall that, even when the information seemed hardly credible, it usually turned out to be correct. "The Coeur d'Alenes who were friendly gave us information from two to three days in advance of our own despatch riders; in this way we were able to keep in touch with the operations of the Indians." Coeur d'Alene messengers traveled out from the mission also to other settlements.[44]

At Palouse City their coming can be seen through the eyes of the Whites. The farmers had gathered to organize a defensive militia. The Indians interrupted the meeting; consequently they appear in its minutes. As discussion

43. *Teller*, 7, 28 July 1878. OJ, Brewer to Joset, 23 July. Bancroft, *Washington*, p. 517, on south.

44. OJ, Greenstreet to Joset, Palouse City, 27 July; Brewer to Joset, Pine Creek, 28 July. *Teller*, 25 August 1875. N. W. Durham, *History of the City of Spokane and Spokane County, Washington*, 1 (3 vols. Spokane, 1912), 355 (last quot.).

was going forward, a Mr. Hughes ushered in "two of the Sons of the Cordolain Indian Louie[,] Son of the Chief and a nephew of another Chief[,] bearing friendly communications from their tribe and Chief; the Indian Andrew made a speech to the audience which was interpreted by Mr. Powers." Andrew said the Indians "were very sorry that the whites had left their homes, it looked as if the whites distrusted them but he declared that they wished to live in peace with the whites [and] that they would fight for them and that if the Nez Percés should attack us they would fight them." Andrew explained how the Indians had posted guards to patrol all abandoned property for its protection.

The assembly "voted them thanks and gave them three hearty cheers." They passed "a resolution to make the Indians a nice present of blankets and Tobacco." Then they returned to the business of forming a militia against the Indians, electing officers, and in general preparing for war. It is no wonder that General Howard, by the end of July, was fretting about these militia groups: "as I think they might drive the Indians into hostilities." [45]

Other expressions of thanks came from the Whites. The Colfax population, a miscellany of settlers and refugees from miles around, were greatly relieved by Cataldo's first letter. Through the priest's Indian messengers they sent back a formal "vote of thanks." It expressed "our appreciation of the good will manifested by the Northern tribes generally, and especially the Coeur d'Alenes"; 101 "citizens of Colfax and vicinity" in Washington Territory signed it. A committee headed by a Mr. Gilbert brought a similar testimonial to the Coeur d'Alene mission from the "citizens of Pine Creek and surrounding country" in Idaho. They "feel thankful to you for all your Kindness towards us during the present excitement." They prudently assured the Coeur d'Alenes that they had really fled from fear of "other Indians." They told them a petition was going to the government "to grant you good title to your land, that you may lead a quiet and peaceful life—and we are willing to do anything in our power to promote the peace and happiness of you Coeur d'Alenes." Ninety Idaho settlers signed the document. These testimonials were ceremoniously interpreted into Coeur d'Alene in the mission chapel. [46]

The Coeur d'Alenes went to extraordinary lengths to demonstrate their neutrality. The Jesuits prevailed upon them from the beginning to protect and care for the settlers' abandoned farms. The Soldiers of the Sacred Heart, in details of twelve, regularly made the rounds of these scattered homesteads "twice a day, morning and evening." Partly they were patrolling the region

45. WS, docs. on organizing Palouse Rangers, esp. report of 26 June (?). NA, EW, consol. Nez Percés file, AGO, Howard to Indian commissioner, 30 July.

46. OJ, vote of thanks, Colfax; copy and details in Giorda, "Blessings"; cf. Bischoff, *Jesuits*, p. 138. Pine Creek vote in Giorda and in *CD Docs.*, Pt. 1, pp. 18–19.

to keep off "bad Indians" who were tempted to plunder. Giorda admits that there was "reason to fear" that less disciplined individuals among the tribes "would pilfer the abandoned houses." But the Coeur d'Alenes went further. Many of the homesteads, as Giorda explains, "had no fence yet; of course the cattle loose would have destroyed every field in a single night." The Coeur d'Alenes took care at each place "to feed the domestic animals left behind," and to see that existing fences "were kept repaired and the gates shut." Giorda comments that "by Seltis' action a number of families have been saved from inevitable ruin." More than thirty of the Indian soldiers participated in this labor, taking up their duties from the very beginning of the White exodus. On June 23 the Walla Walla *Union* related how a Coeur d'Alene messenger arrived at Colfax on the 20th, urging the settlers to return and explaining how the Indians "had been herding the stocks off the crops for them." [47]

This dramatic demonstration of good will broke through the suspicions of the settlers and touched their hearts. The people of Pine Creek even sent the tribe an invitation to a feast on the 4th of July. Seltis accepted, asking only that no whiskey be served to his Indians. The Lewiston *Teller* reported this incident under the heading "Good Feeling": "The settlers in Pine Creek, in consideration of the good services of the Coeur d'Alenes in protecting their property when abandoned upon news of the Nez Percés, sent to Sultis and his men an invitation to a Fourth of July dinner to be given by the settlers." Unfortunately the feast was never held. Too many Whites doubted the dispositions of the Coeur d'Alenes. As Father Giorda put it: "some could not believe that Catholic Priests and Indians could be sincere." The settlers still felt safer with all Indians at a distance. At other places in the Interior, in fact, preparations by the Indians themselves to celebrate the Fourth were construed by Whites "as a preparation for war." [48]

Nine years later the citizens of Whitman County, the county comprising most of the settled country affected by the Coeur d'Alene action, referred in a public document to this protection "in both life and property." Seltis replied, giving his motives: "the care we gave the whites and their property during the Nez Percé War, was due to the excellent instructions which the Catholic church and its pastors gave us from the time they first came among us; should it have occurred before we knew anything about religion or the teachings of the Catholic church, we are sure that we would have been numbered among the hostiles." At that same time the editor of the Spokane Falls *Review* commented: "well might the people of Pine Creek and others feel thankful to

47. Giorda; Diomedi, *Sketches*, p. 75; Cataldo, Lewiston speech (in. n. 28, above); Walla Walla *Union*, 23 June 1877.

48. *Teller*, 7 July 1877; Giorda; Diomedi, *Sketches*, pp. 74–75. Agent Milroy Letterbook (WU), fol. 74–75, report of 2 July 1877 (last quot.).

Seltis, for to one who knows the ways of the Indian it is evident that he and his people saved this country from devastation." Agent Waters of the Coeur d'Alenes similarly recalled how the Whites had "cause to remember the friendship of the Coeur d'Alenes during the Nez Percé war and the good influence of the Fathers with these Indians." [49]

THE INDIAN WORLD: INTRIGUE AND NEZ PERCÉ INSTIGATION

All this was only part of the Coeur d'Alene role in the war. Catholic and Protestant missionary sources indicate widespread soliciting by Nez Percés and others. General Sherman, too, was to report that the Nez Percés "made every effort to draw in the Spokanes, Coeur d'Alenes, and Flatheads." There was some substance to the settlers' suspicions that conspiracy was abroad. The Coeur d'Alenes were a special target for those Nez Percés openly or secretly hostile. The two tribes shared a long border; the recent movement south had brought the Coeur d'Alenes even closer. [50]

Quite apart from accessibility, the Coeur d'Alene area was strategically important; the Nez Percés could easily double back through it from the far Bitterroot, as Howard expected them to do. Any hostility here would give the soldiers an embarrassingly unmanageable second front. The lands of the Coeur d'Alenes and Flathead confederates combined were a maze, in which military operations could become almost hopeless. Moreover, a number of paths here led straight into the refuge of Canada. And finally, Coeur d'Alenes had traveled and fought along with Nez Percés and Flatheads on the annual war-cum-hunt, as had the various Kettle, Spokane, and other bands.

When the war began, the Coeur d'Alenes were not alone on their camas fields at the new mission site. Observing the Interior tradition of hospitality, they were host to a number of other tribes. Although many such Indians would have come anyway, their numbers this year were unusually large. The Whites had encroached on native camas fields elsewhere; their hogs rooted up the little plant; their neat farms discouraged the undisciplined Indian presence. For the camas season was a time of fun—of races, trading between the tribes, socializing, bravado, and feasting. Such summer encampments were a remarkable riot of games and pleasure. Horse racing was the main sport. Amid a city of tents disparate crowds of Indians pursued their several diversions.

49. *CD Docs.*, Pt. 1, Art. 6, pp. 5 (Seltis), 14–15 (Waters); Spokane Falls *Review*, 24 April 1886; cf. the Farmington, Washington, *Post*, 10 April 1886, and the Murray, Idaho, *Coeur d'Alene Sun*, 6 April 1886.

50. A Protestant source is Rev. M. Eells at S'Kohomish agency, *RBIC* (1877), p. 87, on Protestant Spokanes, Nez Percés, and Yakimas. Jesuits like Cataldo, Palladino, and Giorda will be cited. Sherman quotation from September 23 letter to secretary of War, in *Reports of Inspection* (see above, n. 6), p. 48.

An early trader described such a congregation in the Yakima Valley. "We visited every street, alley, hole and corner of the camp," he says. "Here was gambling, there scalp-dancing, laughter in one place, mourning in another; crowds were passing to and fro, whooping, yelling, dancing, drumming, singing." The camp was a kaleidoscope of "flags flying, horses neighing, dogs howling, chained bears [and] tied wolves grunting and growling, all pell mell amongst the tents."

Of all the tribes west of the Flathead confederates, the Coeur d'Alenes had "preserved a greater amount of independence." Because of this, ever since 1873 "the other tribes come in great number in the months of June and July" to the Coeur d'Alene camas fields. The visitors were precisely those braves most attached to the traditional wild ways. They were not Catholics, although Catholic tribes and lodges were among them. Dreamers were prominent. Drunkennness was common, of course, with the accompanying danger of murder and mutilation.

Joset describes the gathering of 1877 in a letter dated July 4 to Agent Simms; Giorda adds some details. The tribes especially represented were the Nez Percés, Spokanes, Palouses, and Isle des Pierres or Sinkiuse-Columbias, along with lodges from other tribes. Normally welcomed by the Coeur d'Alenes, these ever-increasing "crowds" had for three years past "much bothered" the more disciplined Coeur d'Alenes. Seltis was a strong chief with real tribal power; he laid down conditions now for the visitors.

"He wanted his church respected: no gambling, no drinking would be suffered near it." The Dreamers were not allowed to hold their noisy services at the chapel grounds. The chief's prohibition on gambling at first seems short-sighted; gambling was an intregal part of Indian social life, of their games, and of their status system. During these gatherings, however, public gambling of a sustained nature formed part of a more vicious, larger pattern which the missionaries could not tolerate. Even when it was not compulsive, it proved an easy door to violence, licentiousness, and dangerous drunkenness.

The other tribes were not prepared to discard these amenities, or indeed to accept any restrictions. Seltis warned Father Joset in 1877 that the visitors were bent on coming and enjoying themselves in the old way. The Coeur d'Alene soldier band was prepared to fight them. "There will certainly be bloodshed." At this point three influential Spokanes intervened—Chief Nchigaskwe, Antoine Plante, and William Tion. They effected a compromise. Those who desired uninhibited revel would remove about nine miles to the west. This was a summer camp and fishing place of the Coeur d'Alenes called Elposen (*nlpo'sentsen*) near the beginnings of Hangman's Creek, just over the line in Washington Territory at present Tekoa. Those who favored a more modified and orderly convention were to gather in the mission area. Still, the situation was unpleasant and tense. So many foreigners flocked to the pleasure camp from all sides that they "were thinking of laying down the law" to their Coeur d'Alene hosts. At this time and under these strained circumstances, the startling announcement of war raced through the camps in mid-June.

The malcontents left no doubt as to where their own sympathies lay. They exulted in the outbreak of violence. Immediately they demanded a statement of policy from Seltis. Twenty years before he would have been powerless. Portions of his tribe would have ridden off, as they did in the war of 1858. Now Seltis could challenge the dissidents. "We are the friends of the whites," he answered the Elposen group; "we will have nothing to do with the murderers." Firmly he ordered all those openly hostile and residing near the church to leave. Frustrated, many Nez Percé braves and their sympathizers rode off. In their anger they burned and plundered as they left. Others simply fled to the powerful protection of the gamblers' camp. The Soldiers of the Sacred Heart followed in hot pursuit of the destroyers. They did not catch them, but at least they diverted them from damaging severely the settlers' abandoned farms.[51]

Seltis meanwhile was in constant communication with the Fathers at the upper mission. Around June 21 two Nez Percé emissaries visited Chief Seltis and Chief Garry of the Spokanes. Both chiefs declined their offers of war. These Nez Percés may not have been connected with Joseph's band; one must not think of the Nez Percés or Palouses as a people organized under a government like the Whites, acting as a unit or under a hierarchy of command. Native patriots flourished on all sides, even among Nez Percé bands that were as a whole peaceful.

This war stratum, represented in disparate bands of Nez Percés, determined to resort to direct methods. They could depend upon the Palouses to precipitate some action in the Coeur d'Alene environs and thus bring on war. In short, they hoped to duplicate what had happened in Joseph's own case, thus stampeding the excitable Indians and Whites of the North into a similar course of action. The instigator was the powerful subchief Husishusiskute or Hushhushcute (Baldhead). He hoped "to oblige the Colvilles, the Kalispels, the Spokanes, and the Coeur d'Alenes to join in the war." He could not operate easily in the upper region without the aid of the Coeur d'Alenes and the tribes they influenced. He could not do so at all, should the Coeur d'Alenes

51. OJ, Joset to Behrens and Epewa (in French), summer 1877; Joset to Simms, 4 July 1877. Details in Giorda, Diomedi. Bancroft, *Native Races*, *1*, 280–81 (Yakima Valley scene). Ray, *PNWQ*, 27, 132, and Teit, BAE *Annual Report*, 45, 38 (more on Elposen).

support the Whites. In view of Seltis' declared attitude, Hushhushcute would have to work through a fifth column of agents in the gamblers' camp at Elposen.[52]

Hushhushcute, unctuous and sly, was one of the most important figures in the antitreaty party. General Howard considered him as important as Joseph and White Bird. Because of his eloquence he was chosen as supporting speaker to Chief Toohoolhoolzote at the last Lapwai council. His arrival there with his followers gave renewed courage to the antitreaties. Howard so mistrusted Hushhushcute that he refused to give him the papers of protection granted to other Nez Percés after the council. Hushhushcute took part in the fighting, unfortunately killing three of his own men, under the misapprehension that they were scouts of the Whites. When Joseph rode off to surrender at the end of the war with only an honor guard of four braves, Hushhushcute walked beside his horse, talking to the chief. He was a Palouse, not a Nez Percé, though De Smet and others treated the Palouses simply as a band of the Nez Percés. Whites spoke of Hushhushcute as a chief; but this new Tilcoax was really an important advisory leader or subchief to Red Echo's Wawawai band on the west bank of the Snake in southeastern Washington Territory. His importance lay rather in himself than in any formal office. A priest or medicine man of the Dreamer sect, he was popular with the people.

Hushhushcute's campaign had opened with preliminary propaganda. Shortly after the Coeur d'Alenes learned of the war, "Skwelkeel or his brother came here and told the Nez Percés who were camped with the Coeur d'Alenes: don't remain here; the Coeur d'Alenes will be droven [sic] from the country with their priests." This had been a standard taunt from Indians committed to the "American religion." Joset comments that it was "a story which I hear constantly repeated, the more than thirty years." Giorda admits it was cleverly "calculated to turn the good feelings of our Catholic Indians." The Palouses and Spokanes "firmly believed" the tale; they "immediately" moved north.[53]

On June 21 the Spokane chief Sgalgalt, the veteran of the 1858 war and now a Catholic, dictated a long letter to Father Giorda, to be sent to General Howard. "My Church" was his dearest possession; he had "no idea of fighting"; and he was restraining his Spokanes "from stealing from the deserted houses of the settlers; you tell them to come back to their homes." Sgalgalt

52. Cataldo, Lewiston speech (see above, n. 28), quotation. Cataldo, "Sketch on Nez Percés Indians," pp. 75–76. On Hushhushcute see Howard and McGrath, *War Chief Joseph*, pp. 107–08, 111, 114, 122, 129, 282; L. V. McWhorter, *Hear Me, My Chiefs! Nez Perce History and Legend* (Caldwell, Idaho, 1952), pp. 171–72, 273, 313, 482, 533; Howard Report, 22 May, in NA, IA, LR, Idaho.

53. OJ, Joset to Simms, 4 July, and Giorda, "Blessing," for quotations.

pointed out that he was taking the first step toward peace; he urged the General to meet him halfway. "I promised Col[onel] Wright not to fight anymore, and I shall never more take up arms." He meant to leave for salmon fishing on the Spokane River, "and there I shall keep quiet." One thing bothered him. "Did you say, that all the Catholics will be driven away of their lands?" Giorda affixed his name as witness; "this is the substance of what this chief" wants put into English.

With it went a letter from Seltis to Howard: "the Palouse Indians were quiet here amongst us digging camash as of old; now a report came of late telling them to run away from amongst us, because the soldiers would come and drive all Catholic Indians away." Seltis says hopefully, "I do not believe such stories." The other Indians however were disturbed. "I told them repeatedly not to believe such stories; but their chief Ususkein wanted to move off, so did Three Feathers." As for the Coeur d'Alenes, "we stay quiet at our usual place and want to give no trouble to any white man whom we hold as friends." Three Feathers or Metot Waptus was an important Nez Percé chief and warrior who had represented his disaffected band in the recent Lapwai Council.

These disturbances came in the opening days of the war, when the panic of the settlers was at its worst. The letters from the chiefs, along with those of Father Cataldo, allowed Indian Inspector Watkins at Fort Lapwai to despatch corrections of previous, exaggerated reports. On June 27, for instance, Watkins telegraphed: "messengers from Spokans, *Coeur d'Alenes* and Other Tribes North report Indians quiet but Whites apprehensive." Father Giorda now gathered his confused flock around the chapel for a program of devotions. This occupied their emotions and minds during the crisis, and afforded them spiritual resources with which to meet it. "Strong in their faith, they appealed to the Sacred Heart of Jesus[,] and Mary: their arms were their fervent prayers." Even as "they were all engaged in public devotions to the Sacred Heart, another thunderbolt struck the country with terror, and again scattered the white folks in every direction." Hushhushcute's followers had taken direct action. The time was June 23, the day after General Howard took the field with his 500 men.[54]

The house diary of the Coeur d'Alene mission records that two young braves, "sons of the Nez Percé Etelschen" from a "small band of Indians on the Snake river," rode triumphantly into the Elposen tent-town. They brought along a captured horse and a tale of battle; they had killed one of

54. Giorda Papers (OJ), Chief Sgalgalt to Howard, Desmetsville, Hangman's Creek, 21 June. Seltis to Howard, copy in Giorda, "Blessing." On Three Feathers see Howard and McGrath, p. 71; McWhorter, *Hear Me, My Chiefs*, p. 563. NA, IA, LR (from Idaho Sup.), Watkins telegram, 27 June.

two White aggressors in a running gunfight. After causing a sensation at Elposen the two bucks withdrew to their father's lodge among some camas diggers, five or eight miles south of the Hangman's Creek chapel.

The Coeur d'Alenes in general disbelieved the boast of the two Nez Percés. But they could not afford to ignore the possibility of its truth. Trivial to a White mind, the incident was of overriding importance to an Indian. According to tribal ethics, such a killing by guests on Coeur d'Alene land automatically involved the entire tribe in the war. As Joset presently put it in a letter to a friend: it was "a violation of the territory of the Coeur d'Alenes, to whom Pine Creek belonged, the equivalent of a declaration of war." A similar, deliberate killing had almost caused the war of 1858 to begin weeks earlier than it did. And other killings had turned the reluctant Nez Percés to the 1877 war. The instigators of the present trouble, says Father Giorda, "thought that as this murder was committed on what all Indians considered Coeur d'Alene land, it would in Indian policy be an act of hostility on their part against the whites; had the Coeur d'Alenes looked upon it indifferently it would have been taken as a sign that they were at heart with the rebels." Given the circumstances, Joset agrees, "it is hardly possible to doubt that this killing was a first trial," to test the Coeur d'Alenes. Had they taken no action, "all the country would have been delivered" to the war factions.

Chief Konmoss, whose camp harbored the two men, did not delay. By seven o'clock that same evening he had found Father Giorda, dictated the following letter, and sent it by runner to the settlements. "Konmoss, a Coeur d'Alene chief sends word that two Indians from between Palouse and Nez Percés [Snake] River came to his camp telling that they have been attacked and shot at by two white men; then one Indian . . . killed one of the Americans between Pine Creek and Smith's old place; the Indian had the American's horse." This Coeur d'Alene messenger, a Soldier of the Sacred Heart, spent the night "with some whites" searching for the supposed victim. He came back to the chapel with reassuring news that "nobody was found missing, no runaway had made his appearance."

Next day, June 24, Seltis confiscated the stolen horse from the Nez Percés at Elposen, returning it to Pine Creek under care of the Indian Charles Louis. With it he sent a letter. "Seltish sends back this horse—the Coeur d'Alenes took him from an Indian of the Snake river—the Coeur d'Alenes know the owner, and call him Asquire[?]—They know his horse—three days ago the owner was absent making shingles; the fear is the owner was robbed and killed; the thief says he murdered the white man." [55]

55. Joset Diary or Chronology (OJ), 23 through 30 June; Giorda, "Blessing"; OJ, Joset to Behrens (in French), summer 1877; Joset to Simms, 4 July; Giorda "Blessing," incl. copy of letters from Chiefs Seltis and Konmoss. *CD Docs.*, Pt. 1, pp. 18–21 (Giorda).

This stirred a sensation. The horse "had been lent to an old man," an inoffensive pioneer named John Ritchie living in the foothills "a few miles from the Chapel" at Hangman's Creek. Charles Louis rode out with two Whites to Ritchie's cabin. They found him murdered, "shot on his bed." The pendulum of the settlers' emotions swung from terror to anger and back again. "A great panic prevailed over all the country." Seltis realized this was a challenge to his peace policy. He ordered the several Coeur d'Alene families living in the area of Elposen, as well as stray Coeur d'Alenes there, to join the tribe at the mission immediately. The revelers at Elposen became "afraid both of the Americans and of the Coeur d'Alenes." They "dispersed in every direction"; by the evening of June 25 "nobody was left." Some of the Nez Percé troublemakers, pretending to be friendly, drifted back to the mission along with those Coeur d'Alenes who had been near Elposen. The murderer and his group galloped off in hasty flight.

The Coeur d'Alene Charles Louis brought back a message from Pine Creek meanwhile, requesting identification of the culprit. Seltis dictated a reply through Giorda. "When I heard of the fighting of Joseph's band I told my children to be quiet and friendly to the whites; but after the lamentable murder of Mr. Ritchie I still more exhort them to walk straight and Kindly to the Americans." He promised the settlers: "now I the chief with several Coeur d'Alenes come to pay you a friendly visit on the part of my people." Because of the tension between the Coeur d'Alenes and the Elposen group, Coeur d'Alenes with business away from the mission were carrying arms; "but should you think it advisable for us to go around without guns, let us Know it." The chief admitted that his tribe knew the father of the two murderers, "a good old man." The sons were "wild" and not amenable to their father's control. He added that the Indians under his charge would carry "a paper along to show what they are." [56]

True to his word, the head chief "with some twenty other chiefs and headmen" mounted and rode down on June 24 to the village on Pine Creek. The settlers had shut themselves up in a temporary log fort. They were in no mood to receive Indian visitors. Some even believed that the Indians were on a reconnaissance mission, preparing for a surprise attack. "All this sincere demonstration of friendship," laments Giorda, "did not seem to allay the apprehensions of the citizens, bewildered with fear." Hurt and more than a little angry, the chiefs rode back to their Blackrobes.

Giorda and Tosi, distressed by the reports of their Indians, traveled over to Pine Creek the next day. They found the settlers badly in need of reassurance. Rumor had it that General Howard's courier Craig, running military messages from Fort Lapwai to Fort Colville, had been killed at the Coeur

56. Joset Diary, 24 and 25 June. Giorda "Blessing," incl. Chief Seltis letter, 25 June.

d'Alene camp and that two Whites had been ordered out of Coeur d'Alene territory. The two priests refuted the story. They also wrote to tell the General that his messenger had enjoyed the mission hospitality and had started off for Fort Colville in good health.

At Hangman's Creek trouble was brewing. The Colfax settlers sent two of their men, Ewart and Baker, to demand Coeur d'Alene help in tracking down the murderers of Ritchie. It was a touchy situation, and the Whites were not being tactful. Robert Ewart gave Joset a long letter from James, the elder Ewart. "At present the Indians but a short distance from us have taken up arms, and have murdered Men, Women and Children in cold blood," it proclaimed. Now "a portion of this hostile tribe of Indians have in passing through our Community and in Close proximity to the Mission, Murdered a peaceable and unoffending Citizen, and as we understand boasted of it in the Camp of the Co[e]ur d'Alenes."

The Whites admitted they had no idea "where to look for the Murderers." If the Coeur d'Alenes knew, "we expect them to bring them to us." A threat followed: "If they cannot do this, We will have to do it ourselves; and in the present excited condition of the Public Mind many Innocent persons may suffer and much property may be destroyed." There was more in the same vein. "The people demand this and are in a condition to enforce it," so that "we have all we can do to restrain the citizens from going into your Country and forcibly taking the Murderers from their tribe." Ewart closed on a more pacific note. "Will you if you please interpret this to the Chief . . . and tell him that I send this as a Friend and to prevent the Commencement of a War which would ruin the Country." In this way "much bloodshed may be prevented."

The mission Indians protested that the killers "were certainly not among the Coeur d'Alenes [and] most probably not among the Spokanes of Gerry." The Indians here already "had ordered them off their country." Again the missionaries interceded to effect a compromise. After long deliberation the Coeur d'Alene chiefs on June 28 finally supplied Ewart and Baker with two guides to help them search. They strongly advised the Whites to hold a parley with the Spokane chiefs before searching Spokane lands. They also reminded the two men that not all the tribes were friendly. Nor was the Coeur d'Alene ascendancy over neighboring tribes based on larger numbers: the Coeur d'Alenes "ought to be cautious, being as they were in face of a large hostile camp—which critical situation was appreciated by few cold headed whites."

Independently, the Coeur d'Alenes were keeping close watch. Friday morning their scouts brought reports of fresh horse tracks "appearing towards the eastern mountains." Next day the plot broke. Hostile Nez Percés, in communication with Joseph's warriors, had remained among the Coeur d'Alenes. Apparently discouraged by the consistent opposition of Seltis, they had made off on the evening of June 28. "After these Nez Percés were gone," Joset's diary records, "the old crippled Chief (father of the murderer) indignant of having been left alone accused them and said that the murderer had been in their lodges at night." Thus "it seems while they were playing friends, they were acting as spies; there remains here only Three Feathers and those Nez Percés who never joined the other [Elposen] camp, but were all the time quiet with the Coeur d'Alenes." On July 2 Inspector Watkins could telegraph to the commissioner: "Northern Indians Quiet." [57]

Father Cataldo was proud of the way the Coeur d'Alenes had handled the Nez Percé war faction. On July 10 he wrote about it to Father Brouillet in Washington, and promised to have Joset draw up an account. Joset did so, supplying other details of the mission tribes in the war; his account of October 12, 1877 appeared in German in the St. Louis *Katholischen Missionen* and probably in other Catholic journals now equally obscure.

During all this time the Coeur d'Alenes kept in touch with the Jesuits in the Bitterroot, informing them of the movements of unfriendly bands. The Coeur d'Alenes were careful about the very appearance of neutrality. "A camp of Nez Percés, after claiming to be at peace with the whites," asked to come to live at the mission. Seltis refused them, citing his promises to the settlers. The suspect band moved on. These successive refusals and ejections probably led to that accumulation of Nez Percés up across the Spokane River which was so to disturb the local Whites.

Trivial incidents continued to agitate the settlers in the Coeur d'Alene area, and to revive their aggressive attitude toward the Indians. On July 21 some Pine Creek men went over to the Coeur d'Alene camp and stole a horse. Brewer later wrote to apologize: they had thought they were recovering a horse stolen previously from a Mr. Smith of Silver Creek. Besides, "during the same night old man Price's house was broken into and plundered; among other things taken, the inside works of his clock were taken out and carried away." The Pine Creek settlers were brooding over these wrongs. "Now all we want," they wrote to Father Joset, "is to find the parties that did this." Had the priest "any suggestions to make?" [58]

As late as July 21 the Lewiston *Teller* says "nearly all the settlers of this

57. Giorda, "Blessing." Joset Diary, 27–29 June. OJ, J. Ewart to Joset, Colfax, 27 June. NA, IA, Idaho Sup., telegram of 2 July, Lapwai.

58. CM, Cataldo to Brouillet, 10 July. Joset account of 12 October, in *Die katholischen Missionen, illustrirte Monatschrift,* 6 (1878), 42–43. NA, EW, consol. Nez Percé file (AGO), Agent Ronan report to Governor Potts, 17 July (Bitterroot contact, Seltis quot.). OJ, Wm. Brewer to Joset, Pine Creek, 23 July.

place have either been compelled to fort up in stockades or abandon the country." But when Giorda returned from Portland on July 20, passing through the communities of Colfax and Pine Creek, then out over Coeur d'Alene lands to Colville, "with two Sisters of Charity for this last place," fear began to yield to shame. The nuns' presence "seemed to inspire courage in weak men's hearts, and made them believe that the Priest would not expose two young Sisters to dangers, if he knew that there was any apprehension."

The impression persisted that some Coeur d'Alenes had joined Joseph. The historian Bancroft was to assess their number at "twenty or more Coeur d'Alenes, thirsting for the excitement of war." A more recent historian of the war cautiously places "a few Coeur d'Alenes" with Joseph. A writer sympathetic with the Coeur d'Alene mission allows "only a few irresponsible members of the Coeur d'Alene tribe." Even General Howard's aide-de-camp, Thomas A. Sutherland, asserts that "there were eight or ten Umatillas and as many Spokanes and Coeur d'Alenes" in the Clearwater battle. But in fact not a single Coeur d'Alene participated. All the early missionaries without exception are explicit and insistent on this point.[59]

Father Giorda emphasized the particular significance of Seltis. "The Spokanes, Palouses, and other tribes were intently looking at Seltish ready to follow him, so great is his influence, owing to his upright and gentle but firm government of his people; had he but raised one finger, had he not constantly sent words of peace to the whites around and Indians abroad, we should have had another large conflagration of another war; the country would have been left deserted." Chief Joseph later told Howard's aide Sutherland, during a conversation on the upper Missouri, that had he been more successful on the Clearwater the Indians all the way "to the Spokane country would have joined him, and the remnant of Soldiers been annihilated." But success in battle had only been one element of the story. "The splendid behavior of the Coeur d'Alenes," as Giorda put it, "has undoubtedly been the means of averting another Indian war."[60]

ECHOES TO THE NORTH AND WEST

The Coeur d'Alenes have been a window on the Interior world. There is no similar body of documentation for other tribes, except for the Flathead confederates. At Fort Colville Agent Simms did maintain contact with the nearby Kettle mission. Two weeks after the war began, Simms reported to

59. Giorda, "Blessing." Bancroft, *Washington*, p. 505. Howard and McGrath, *Joseph*, p. 171. E. R. Cody, *History of the Coeur d'Alene Mission of the Sacred Heart* (pamphlet; Caldwell, Idaho, 1930), p. 37. T. A. Sutherland, *Howard's Campaign against the Nez Perce Indians* (Portland, Oreg., 1878), p. 8. Cf. Splawn, *Ka-Mi-Akin*, pp. 470–76.
60. Sutherland, *Howard's Campaign*, p. 8. Giorda, "Blessing."

the national commissioner how the hostilities have "caused great uneasiness throughout this section of country, partly in consequence of the unsettled condition of affairs among our Indians." Watkins had ordered Simms to make a tour through the several tribes and "in short to do everything in my power to prevent disaffection among all the Indians under my charge." By the time the agent came to write a report, he was inclined to think that his tribes would not rise; on the other hand he recommended giving them presents "to tranquilize them."

Two weeks before the war General Howard had sent Major Towler north to explain to the Kettles and their neighbors that Howard's movements in the lower Interior were not directed against them. This was "to prevent the Indians in that direction from being induced under a panic, that had already begun among them, from joining malcontents" among the lower tribes. Even before the war Simms had been convinced that the precarious peace in his district was preserved by the Kettle mission. This local Jesuit intervention continued all through the war, though its details are now obscure. Thus a letter from Father Gazzoli to Bishop Blanchet, preserved quite by chance, tells something of his work for peace among the Spokanes and others during the war. This information was republished in papers like the Walla Walla *Statesman* and the Portland *Catholic Sentinel*. Gazzoli's obituary notice in the Colfax *Palouse Gazette*, less than five years after the war, asserts that he "more than once prevailed upon the Indians to abandon contemplated raids against the whites," thus "preventing bloodshed." [61]

Chief Moses may have made some attempt to control the Columbia tribes. Early in the war he sent a message to the Colville commander that he meant to keep peace, and "that under no circumstances would he make war against the whites." Moreover, "he would be responsible that the Columbia River Indians did not disturb the whites." This contemporary document finds some support in the memoirs of the pioneer settler Splawn. Nez Percé emissaries, he says, were continually trying to draw the Columbia Indians into the war. As Chief Joseph's band gained stature through victories, Indians from all sides began moving toward the camp of Moses. Their temper was ugly. Some passed over Splawn's own range, "committing depredations such as burning our houses and corrals and driving off the saddle horses and killing cattle." For a month "everything indicated an Indian uprising." The Indian camps soon spread ominously several miles along the Columbia River.

Splawn and a friend went to talk peace with Moses. On this trip they

61. NA, IA, LR (from Wash. Sup.), Simms to commissioner, 29 June, incl. quotation from Watkins to Simms of 27 June. LR (from Idaho Sup.), Howard to assistant adj. general in San Francisco, 22 May 1877 (Towler). *RCIA* (1875), p. 362 (Simms on Jesuits). Colfax, W.T., *Palouse Gazette*, 23 June 1882; Portland, Oreg., *Catholic Sentinel*, 19 July 1877, reprinting Walla Walla *Statesman*, later correcting it.

counted 190 lodges at one camp; they heard of a Chelan encampment of 200 lodges nearby and an Okanogan–San Poil grouping of 150 lodges. Moses himself was surrounded by 200 lodges. The numbers here seem to be exaggerated, but the picture is clear. Splawn felt sure that the chief's purpose was to control these Indians, and that he was able to do so. Other evidence suggests that Moses and his band became unfriendly as the war progressed.[62]

Further trouble threatened along the Spokane River. As soon as the killings began to the south, certain Nez Percé bands fled north. Most were probably anxious to avoid involvement, but there were troublemakers among them. And their prevailing mood of betrayal and resentment promised future trouble. Military officials at first suspected that they represented a deliberate maneuver by a wing of the hostiles. These bands were of no considerable size, but the Nez Percés and Palouses ejected by Seltis swelled their numbers. Agent Simms informed the commissioner of Indian Affairs that the latter groups amounted to 200 to 300 from both tribes. Such a concentration of potential hostiles, in an area with only a few resident families, was bound to cause worry; "suspicion and alarm" were abroad. Indian agitators were working to stir up both visiting and local Indians. Even the most innocent among them might kill cattle or steal, being now without food.

Two weeks after the outbreak of war a call came from the Spokane Bridge postmaster and a neighbor "to the Captain here [at Fort Colville], to send Some Soldiers to the Bridge for the protection of the Citizens." The commander believed that matters were not "sufficiently serious yet awhile to do so." On July 9 military authorities wired Washington, D.C., that the "situation on the Spokane [is] threatening"; there was "ample reason for General Howard's application for more troops." As Joseph left Idaho by the Lolo trail, a confidential report from A. J. Carr to the governor of Washington Territory, dated July 29, asserted that "the danger now is in the Spokan[e] country." [63]

Agent Simms sent beef and flour to the troublesome and hungry visitors, hoping to forestall violence. He also hired one Thomas Flett to keep their every movement under observation. As late as July 16 the agent believed that "these Indians should be closely watched." The fort commander soon

62. WS, Indian Affairs, Col. Grover commanding Fort Walla Walla to Governor Ferry (citing letter from Colville commander), 23 July 1877. Splawn, *Ka-Mi-Akin*, pp. 339–40. See also below, pp. 416, 418.

63. NA, IA, LR (from Wash. Sup.), Simms to commissioner, 16 July; ibid., LR (from Idaho Sup.), McDowell to adj. genl., telegram from San Francisco, 18 June; sec. War to sec. Interior, forwarding S.F. military information, 9 July. NA, EW, consol. file, Howard to McDowell, Fort Lapwai, 16 June; Keeler to McDowell, Lewiston, 5 July. OJ, Simms to Joset, Colville, 29 June. Cf. Durham, *Spokane*, 1, 350–51. WS, Carr to governor, Dayton, W.T., 29 July.

assumed the task of maintaining the surveillance. Simms delivered to their chiefs and headmen eight hundred pounds of flour, seven hundred of beef, and five of tobacco. He had nothing further to give. To his distress, the agglomeration of Indians "continually" received "accessions to their numbers, supposed to come from the hostile camps."

The settlers at both the bridge and the falls were most uneasy. A promotional booklet about Spokane Falls a few years later, anxious to dissipate any apprehension concerning Indians, conceded nevertheless that the weeks from June 27 to August 10 of 1877 were "a season of intense anxiety for the safety of the whole upper country, and many removed to Walla Walla." It was "the most trying period in the history of our settlement"; the Falls people remained and "braved it through." At one point settlers and refugee farmers barricaded themselves on an island in the river. For ten nights during that time, several dozen Indians howled and cavorted about a smudge fire.

Pioneers later recalled that individual Spokanes reassured the settlers. Spokane Garry seems to have done his best to control Indians amenable to his influence, and to notify the Whites of their disposition. Undoubtedly the Reverend Mr. Cowley, who had been working with some of the bands for three years, had a peaceful influence upon his own group of Protestant Spokanes. He bravely went out to parley with the Spokane medicine man who had come to talk with the frightened settlers at Spokane Falls. Another Cowley (no relation), the postmaster at Spokane Bridge, sent Father Cataldo information on the local Indians; Cataldo had the letter published in the *Teller* of July 14.

An examination of the manuscript account books of the Spokane Bridge store reveals no lag in sales at this time; perhaps fright stimulated the appetite. One pioneer called "all the old Indians to my store" to intimidate them with the prospect of troops marching from Fort Colville. On August 2 another plea for help came from Spokane Falls, demanding arms for thirty refugee families. A reminiscence recalls the Spokane Indians sending a message of reassurance to the Reverend Mr. Cowley; the description indicates that this came from the common intertribal encampment down at the new Coeur d'Alene mission.[64]

The Jesuits closely observed the Spokane situation, especially through their Catholic Spokanes. An influential chief at this time was the half-breed Antoine Plante. In earlier days considered something of a White man and in demand as a guide, Plante seems to have retreated more deeply into the Indian

64. NA, IA, LR (from Wash. Sup.), Simms to commissioner, 16 and 22 July. *Settlers' Guide*, p. 29. OH, Nez Percé War folder (clippings), J. N. Glover Reminiscence (Indians to store); cf. Rev. H. T. Cowley interview. Drury, *Cowley*, pp. 159–61. OJ, Spokane Bridge store account books.

community as the gap between the two peoples widened. One hears him spoken of now as a chief, "the chief," and even once as "head chief." He kept the Jesuits at the several missions informed of dispositions in the Spokane region. When disaffected Nez Percés and the Spokanes held a council in mid-July on Hangman's Creek, for instance, "the chief of the Spokanes, a half-breed by the name of Antoine Point [Plante], will come to St. Ignatius after the talk with news of conclusions." The Flathead agent near St. Ignatius was to pass the information on to Governor Potts of Montana. "Antoine Point is a Christian and opposed to war," the agent writes, "but will report the action of the Council to the Fathers."

Elsewhere in the Interior there were similar scenes of flight by settlers, Indians secretively sullen or triumphantly insolent, and farmers organizing their pathetic little militia bodies. The latter bombarded the governors of their respective territories with petitions for rifles; some desired books of instruction on elementary military drill and tactics, the better to fight Indians. A place like Klickitat County, for example, experienced the expected "intense excitement," the wholesale abandonment of homes, the construction of amateur fortifications, the quartering of refugee families in the stronger settlements, and the "friendly Indian here and there" warning a favored family. Everywhere, "we are destitute of arms." Indians in the Interior tended to respond to this panic with malicious mischief, possibly half playful but as dangerous as a spark in a powder storeroom. One day they asserted that they were friendly, the next they warned that they would die fighting rather than accept a reservation. In the Yakima country twenty braves abused an isolated settler, wrecked his furniture and provisions, but eventually allowed him to escape; fifteen mounted Indians pursued and "nearly surround[ed]" six ranchmen.[65]

The Reverend Mr. Wilbur at his agency among the Yakimas did his best to calm both Indians and Whites. General Howard requested him to use his influence, and regarded him as important in preserving the peace there. In late July Agent Wilbur undertook a trip to the Sinkiuse-Columbia Indians 150 miles north, to investigate rumors of hostility. He found that "the excitement through the white Settlements near these Indians visited was quite as high as I have ever known Indian excitement." After reassuring the Whites, Wilbur had talks with Chief Moses and his Indians. About the Indians in his vicinity generally, the minister asserted that "not a man has gone to the hostile band or Sympathized with them."

65. NA, EW, consol. Nez Percés file, Agent Ronan to Governor Potts, 14 July; see also Potts' appeals for help, passim. WS, Ferry Misc. and Indian Affairs, for telegrams, letters, vouchers and other documentation of Washington Territory panic; esp. E. Richardson to Governor Ferry, Goldendale, 9 July (quots.), and Dalles telegram, 1 July ("destitute"). IHS, Territorial Executive Papers, file 5, 1, Military Records, and esp. 5, 3, Nez Percé War (panic and militia documentation).

Other officials did their bit for peace. On June 20 Governor Brayman of Idaho sent a Boise citizen named Logan to investigate the dispositions of the Bannocks. Logan reported that hostile Nez Percés had come and gone without winning allies. The governor invited the Bannock chiefs to his executive chambers for a lengthy interview. From this meeting it seemed that the chiefs favored peace, but that circumstances might dictate their ultimate policy; the more northerly Indians like the Coeur d'Alenes would probably join the war.[66]

FATHER CATALDO, PEACEMAKER

In attempting to cover a fragmented situation, we have lost sight of Father Cataldo. For a moment the settlers did also. Conflicting rumors arose following his brief stay with the Coeur d'Alenes and his passage through Lewiston. Some people charged that "he had run away from the war." Others claimed that the Coeur d'Alenes held him prisoner; D. S. Bowman and James Tilton bravely rode out to the mission to check. But Cataldo was busy in the cause of peace. At Fort Lapwai he joined with Father Morvillo; Morvillo, isolated at the mission of the Nez Percés and insecure in his grasp of their language, had just come up to the fort "to inquire as to the rumors of war." With Morvillo and Gazzoli, Cataldo pressed on for the Nez Percé camps.[67]

They found their Nez Percés confused and angered. The Catholic Indians were caught between the fires of two hatreds, Indian and White both eyeing them with suspicion. The priests gathered their people around the mission, to remain under Jesuit direction through the coming months of the war. Under their guidance the Catholic warriors refrained from joining the hostilities. One must remember that these Catholic Indians were nontreaty, enemies of the Americanized "short hair" Nez Percés. Their grievances were as great as those of Joseph's band; they had relatives riding with Joseph; and the hostiles were waging an excitingly successful war. During the course of the war a few braves from the Catholic group weakened and went to join the fighting; but this happened only under severe provocation. Some Catholic women were with Joseph from the beginning; they had little choice in the matter, having to accompany their families.

66. NA, IA, LR (from Wash. Sup.), McDowell telegram for Howard to Wilbur, San Francisco, 21 May 1877; two other telegrams showing work for peace by Wilbur with Wheaton; Wilbur to commissioner, 28 July. Ibid., Idaho Sup., Howard to adj. genl. at S.F., Wallula, 24 April 1877, Wilbur's influence on eve of war; contemporary news clipping (Brayman contribution); cf. also Idaho City *Idaho World*, 3 August 1877. Cf. praise of Monteith and Wilbur in *HED* (serial 1794), pp. 117, 477, 592, 598.

67. Hawkins-Cataldo, "Cataldo," 2, 79. Durham, *Spokane*, 1, 631 (prisoner episode).

Knowing the sympathies of his people, Cataldo tried to prevent their act-ing as scouts. Agent Monteith had called for scouts to help Howard track the fleeing hostiles. Some Catholic braves volunteered immediately. Cataldo knew that a number of these men had relatives among the hostiles, while the others sympathized with their general position. There was a good chance that such scouts would mislead the troops or decoy them into ambush. The results could prove fatal for the whole community of Catholic Nez Percés. Treach-ery from the Catholic camp would bring hysterical retaliation.

"I wrote Gen[eral] Howard to make him acquainted with the fact" of their relationship, Cataldo tells Brouillet. The Jesuit emphasized that no overt reason existed to suspect the volunteers; but it would require extraordinary qualities for an Indian in such a position to remain faithful. However sincere, his loyalty might waver when he saw a brother or a friend killed. "Some of these scouts," accepted for service by Howard anyway, were "near relatives of the warriors," Cataldo later wrote; nevertheless "they all proved faithful."

There was one sad defection. "After the first battle" some scouts did not return, apparently having been taken prisoner by the hostiles. "The father of one of the missing men obtained permission from the military authorities to go and look for his son." Meanwhile the missing scouts were on their way back. "The poor man went straight to Joseph's camp to inquire about his boy and ask for his release; he was told that the boy was not there, and that he himself ought to remain and fight with his relatives." The father succumbed to their arguments and to his general sympathies, "and was killed in the next encounter, the only Indian then killed." This resulted in further tragedy. "When the news of his death reached his son, the latter immediately ran to Joseph's camp and joined his forces." [68]

Oddly enough, a number of Whites "repeatedly asserted that Chief Joseph and his people were Catholics." Others condemned all the scouts, including the Catholics, as spies and traitors. Others again claimed that the Catholic Nez Percés had joined the hostile band. When news of the outbreak reached Washington, D.C., Father Brouillet worried lest Monteith's charges of Catho-lic plotting gain support. He wrote to ask Cataldo if the Catholic Nez Percés were among the hostiles. Actually only four Catholic warriors seem to have joined Joseph, including the father we met above. Cataldo mentions one of these, a Catholic "who was such only by name," in a letter of July 10.

The issue, so trivial to modern ears, was important to Cataldo. The attitude of settlers and authorities toward the Catholic Nez Percé body rested upon it, as did the fears of some concerning Jesuit treason. With the passing of years, the matter was to turn into one of sectarian pride. In his later years

68. CM, Cataldo to Brouillet, 10 July 1877. Cataldo, "History of the Nez Percé Mis-sion"; cf. OJ, note thirty years later, Cataldo to O'Sullivan, on a scout pension.

Cataldo noted rather smugly that a number of Protestant Indians fought among the hostiles. Some Catholic commentators much later, in their zeal to reduce Catholic participation in the war, denied that any Catholics joined the hostiles. Ironically, in the later reversal of viewpoint which romanticized the Indian, participation in the war became a badge of honor.[69]

The same day that Giorda and Tosi left the Coeur d'Alene country, Cataldo attended yet another Indian council at Fort Lapwai. The Lewiston *Teller* reported on it. "Many Catholic Indians were present at the council; also Father Cataldo, as well as the Presbyterians and some Methodists." The newspaper described how Cataldo "addressed them" with a speech in their language urging them to remain peaceful. But Cataldo could not stay down here near the Craig Mountains with Father Morvillo. He was no longer simply a Nez Percé missionary; he had become the superior of the whole network. His responsibilities ran to the Canadian line and to the Cascades; for that matter, they ran out onto the Great Plains of Montana, though distance prohibited any personal effort there. This trip deep into the Nez Percé country was only the first of his famous rides of 1877.

When he began his tour through the various tribes, he found that "many Indians, well disposed, were undecided for peace or war because they feared injury or death at the hands of those who insisted that they join Joseph." The Blackrobe was often able to tip the balance against such a war faction. In some places adventurous individuals had already set out to join the war; Cataldo managed to have these warriors recalled. "I called on some of the other tribes, and was able to get their warriors to come back, so that others did not league against the whites."

His major efforts, to judge from a close reading of his recollections, were confined to the area between the Coeur d'Alene mission and the Nez Percé mission. Here he journeyed tirelessly to supply counter propaganda for peace among Indians and Whites. Hydra-headed rumor required continual "pacifying them and assuring them that there was no war." Cataldo also made trips to "the Spokanes, Colvilles, Kalispells, and Coeur d'Alenes, sending couriers when he could not go personally, and writing letters when he could do neither." Whatever tribe or band he visited, he "never failed to secure a promise of neutrality or better."[70]

69. Cataldo, "Nez Percé Indians," p. 71 (first quot.). Editorial comment in Walla Walla *Union*, reprinted in Lewiston, *Teller*, 4 August 1877 (spies). CM, Cataldo to Brouillet, 10 July. See OJ, "Historia domus Sti. Josephi," 13 June ("scarcely any Catholics," not contemporary notation); Palladino, *Indian and White*, p. 350 (one woman, on Cataldo's authority); Bischoff, *Jesuits*, p. 147 (four). Hawkins-Cataldo, "Cataldo," *1*, 73 ("only a few" women); Weibel, *Cataldo*, p. 20 ("a few women").

70. *Teller*, 30 June 1877. Hawkins-Cataldo, *2*, 78–80; Crosby, "Interviews," p. 14; and Cataldo speech (above, n. 28), pp. 4–5.

Cataldo's work among the Whites is reflected in the newspapers of the region. For example, on June 23 the Portland *Weekly Oregonian* carries a reassuring report from him. The files of the Lewiston *Teller* contain many a Cataldo item. On June 21 "Cataldo came to town with a subchief of the Coeur d'Alenes" and gave assurances that the tribe was friendly. A Cataldo notice of June 26 admitted that the important Nez Percés, Three Feathers and Peopeomoxmox, were living with the Coeur d'Alenes; he explained that they were staying until the war excitement cooled and not, as some were saying, for purposes of sedition. In the July 7 edition of the *Teller*, Cataldo quashed a rumor that "all the tribes" of the north had met in a council in which "all proposed to join against the whites." A June 23 item illustrates what he had to contend with. "When our extra [appeared] containing the information from Father Cataldo," one confused settler "went to the Paradise Valley settlers reporting the reverse of the statement of Cataldo's letter." This "alarmed them much, and then he left himself for Walla Walla."

Cataldo's services were widely recognized both during the war and afterward. The Colfax "Vote of Thanks" was later published in the Walla Walla *Union*. Delegate Fenn, during a report in Congress six months after the war, publicly praised the priest:

> As soon as the Nez Percés commenced hostilities, and the situation was fully appreciated by the military authorities, Father Cataldo and Mr. Craig were especially deputed by them, with the acquiescence of Agent Monteith and Inspector Watkins, to visit the Spokanes and other northern and western tribes and endeavor to restrain them from yielding to the appeals of the emissaries of the hostile Nez Percés and unite their fortunes with them, by which one thousand warriors would be added to their force.

In context, Fenn is defending both Cataldo and Craig from the attacks of Monteith, so he is probably hewing fairly closely to the substantial facts rather than laying himself open to denials. "The danger was imminent, the situation critical"; but the two men, "with their powerful influence, by their protestations and appeals restrained the passions of the Indians and averted the danger."

Even General Howard, though he had little sympathy for priests, recognized his debt to Cataldo. A decade after the war he wrote offering his thanks. "I am deeply grateful to you for your work with the Indians during my campaign." A half century after the war, on the occasion of Cataldo's seventy-fifth anniversary as a Jesuit, the War Department sent official thanks to the jubilarian through Secretary of War Dwight Davis for "his valuable assistance to General Howard and General Wheaton" in the war of 1877.

President Coolidge similarly offered "congratulations" and "all praise" for the "part you played as peacemaker between the Indians and the whites in 1877." An editorial in the Spokane *Spokesman Review* on the occasion told the inhabitants of this main town of the Interior: "so long as history endures, the name of Father Cataldo will be written upon its pages." He had been "an instrumentality of peace in the troubled years of warring clash between the Red men and the white invaders." The paper felt that "Spokane honors itself in doing him honor." At the civic reception, "the largest non-sectarian affair of its kind ever held here," the leading citizens praised the man "who did much to prevent it [the Nez Percé war] from becoming a general war." Cataldo even won a modest place in the history books. "The controlling influence," says Fuller in a standard modern history, "proved to be Father Cataldo"; the priest "travelled through the country for two months after the outbreak urging the Indians to remain quiet." [71]

Cataldo's insistence that "the greater part of the honor must go to my older companions in the missionary field" is paradoxical. Each in his own locality had done as much as Cataldo, and sometimes more. To some degree, Cataldo had been only their spokesman. For certain of these men there is little or no documentation—Caruana, who worked among the Yakimas; Guidi, with the Kettles; Morvillo, with the Nez Percés; or Imoda, out among the Blackfeet. In the case of others, like Giorda and Joset, ample evidence has survived. Even without considering the story of the Flathead confederacy, one sees that there is substance behind Cataldo's claim: "but for the Catholic Indian Missions the Nez Percés war of 1877 would have become a general war of all the northwestern Indians." [72] The upper Interior had been spared the anguish of even subsidiary Indian uprisings. The peace and continued progress of the scattered central-northwest hamlets had been secured.

71. OJ, General Howard to Cataldo, Headquarters at Portland, 12 January 1888. Fenn speech, *ACIM*, 2, 42. Congratulatory messages, Gonzaga University *Quarterly*, *16* (1928), 152–57. Fuller, *History of Pacific Northwest*, p. 273; cf. his *Inland Empire of the Pacific Northwest*, 3 (3 vols. Spokane, 1928), 49; 2, 107. Spokane *Spokesman-Review*, 14 March 1877. Colfax vote in n. 46, above.

72. Cataldo speech (above, n. 28), and Cataldo, "Sketch on Nez Percé Indians," pp. 77–78, for quotations.

10. Meeting of Eagles: Joseph's Hostiles in Montana

THE JESUITS AND THE WHEATON COUNCIL

THE UPPER INTERIOR during the war had seen a series of local troubles, with a common background of grievances. The work of the Jesuits for peace now culminated in a gathering of all the tribes into one great council. The last of the grand peace councils in the Interior, it stands as a final chapter in the long story of conflict there between Red man and White. It closes the story of the western tribes in the 1877 troubles, and introduces that of the Nez Percé hostiles in Flathead territory.

What De Smet's tour did in 1859, the Wheaton Council was to attempt in 1877. As the threat of open war subsided, firm support had to be given to the new orientation toward peace. In a personal encounter, with formal reassurances and almost liturgical solemnities, the foundations of peace were to be diplomatically reinforced. The place chosen was central to all the upper tribes, without being too close to the military establishment at Colville. It was not inconveniently far off the route of the Wheaton column, which had been instructed to travel north through Coeur d'Alene country, turning toward Montana at the Sacred Heart mission. This was the hamlet of Spokane. Although not a dozen families lived in the village or vicinity, this nucleus sufficed to place the spot on the White map as a center of reference and, for travelers, as an oasis of primitive amenities. Ironically enough, Spokane intruded into the heartland of a tribe who had been previously the best friends of the Americans in all the upper country; it even preempted a favorite fishing spot at the falls, hard by a large permanent Indian village.

A council had been scheduled just before the war. It was to have been akin to the Lapwai council, dictating terms to the Indians, rebuking the restiveness of the tribes, and demanding that they move onto two consolidated, bleak reservations. Like the Lapwai conference, it was to have taken place at the local garrison. In the manuscript house diary of St. Francis Regis mission near Colville two consecutive entries reveal something of the federal government's about-face. The first reads: "June 17, Received word of a general council to be held on the 27 of this month at Colvil[le] for the purpose of assigning a personal locality to the Indians that belong to this Agency." With maddening lack of detail, the second entry follows immediately. "4 August, Joseph's band revolted which brought a delay, today finally arrived a letter from the Inspector announcing the Meeting should take place the 10th of August at the Spokan[e] falls or Spokan[e] Bridge." [1]

Government planning had veered away from the concept of two great reservations. After the trouble with one small band of Nez Percés, with the concomitant ugly fright from neighboring tribes, few planners would want to be associated with such a potential disaster. Nor could a council be attempted with only a single garrison to control it; an army would have to be sent. The timing of the council, too, is significant. By then the hostiles had passed the Bitterroot, thus negating any danger of return via the Mullan road or of linking with the upper Interior tribes. But the army had to consolidate its advantage. Joseph was fighting in Montana. Two days before the date set for the council, the Nez Percés would inflict upon the American army at Big Hole one of the more serious defeats in its Indian-fighting career. Nothing had yet broken the long series of Nez Percé victories; nothing would, for weeks to come. And the restlessness and grievances of the Interior tribes remained. The council would now complete and officially ratify the peace efforts of the Jesuits and of the mission tribes in this area. With Jesuit help, it would lay the ghosts of possible misunderstanding.

General Wheaton's march to the north, and the council in which it ended, came about as part of Howard's grand strategy. Howard "originally intended" to march over the Mullan road in Coeur d'Alene territory so as to "make a demonstration to intimidate the Northern Indians, as well as to head off Joseph should he turn northward." When the situation continued tense around the new Sacred Heart mission on Hangman's Creek, Howard persisted in this original strategy, with one modification. He proposed to make short work of Joseph somewhere in Idaho; then "I shall proceed against the Indians collecting and threatening on Hangman's Creek, near the Spokane." As the war progressed along somewhat different lines, Howard still kept a nervous eye cocked toward the north.

The Indian service, too, was concerned. The Lapwai council and the Nez Percé war had merely interrupted a proposed show of strength in the north. On July 20, with the war more than a month old, Indian Inspector Watkins explained to the national commissioner how he and General Howard had intended "going, with sufficient force to enforce instructions, to have a talk

1. OJ, St. Francis Regis House Diary, 1870-92, 17 June and 4 August. On the council see my "The Jesuits and the Spokane Council of 1877," *PHR, 31* (1952), 65-73.

with the Spokanes, Cuoer d'Alanes [sic], Colvilles and others." En route, the outbreak changed their plans. Now, "unless we go soon, I fear a more general uprising."

During the opening week of war Howard optimistically scheduled the council for June 29. Watkins directed Agent Simms to send messages to all the tribes involved. Subsequent cancellation of these plans left Simms brooding over the forty-dollar expense incurred; if he attempted a private peace circuit of the Indian camps, as Watkins suggested, the agent feared these expenses would swell to the appalling sum of two hundred dollars.[2]

Howard prudently abandoned his plan of leading the main army north, and instead followed doggedly over the Lolo trail. He surrendered the northern portion of the campaign to a relieving force, which was being hurried to Lewiston under General Frank Wheaton. A cavalry officer in the Indian wars of the '50s, Wheaton's bravery and skill in the early battles of the Civil War had jumped him to major general. He led the sixth corps at Fredericksburg, Gettysburg, and through the Wilderness; it was he who rushed back to save the nation's capital from Jubal Early's raid. His exploits won him public honors and a permanent brevet as major general. He had gained further experience recently as the field commander of the Modoc War. Serving as colonel now, he was soon to rise in rank to regular general and become a departmental commander.

Wheaton's troops were slow in arriving. Coming from South Carolina via San Francisco and reaching Lewiston on July 29, they "at once proceeded" into Coeur d'Alene country. Meanwhile the upper country had only a token company of cavalry holding Fort Colville. As the settlers objected in a petition of June 25, this lone post was too small, too distant, and too isolated by poor communications to have any effect away from its immediate neighborhood. Yet, badly as Howard needed Colville's troop for his pursuit of Joseph, he dared not withdraw it, "on account of the restlessness of the numerous bands

2. HED (serial 1794), 45 Cong., 2 sess. (1878), 1, Pt. 2, *1*, 614 (first quot.). This *HED* reference will hereafter be cited only by serial number. NA, IA, LR (from Idaho Sup.), Howard through McDowell telegram to Sherman, S.F., 19 June 1877; McDowell telegram to adj. genl. at Washington, D.C., 19 July; Watkins to commissioner, Lapwai, 2 July. LR (from Wash. Sup.), Simms to commissioner, 29 June, and quoting Watkins orders of 13 June. Correspondence in the Colville Agency documents, Federal Record Center, Seattle, includes (1) Watkins to Simms, 13 June 1877, announcing council to settle reservations on Wednesday the 27th; (2) same to same, 20 June 1877, postponing it because of the Nez Percé outbreak, and urging cooperation with Jesuits; (3) same to same, 27 July, announcing council at Falls soon, with double purpose of pacification and acceptable reservations; (4) expenses of council, 14 September 1877 (all in Record Group 75, box 1).

of Indians in its vicinity." Howard also left behind him a small reserve force at Lewiston under General Sully.

In his field order of July 23, Howard instructed Wheaton's force to travel up to the Sacred Heart mission via the Hangman's Creek area of the Coeur d'Alene territory; to cooperate with Howard's column; to overawe malcontent tribes or distract them from joining Joseph; to engage the Nez Percé hostiles should they swing back through "the Coeur d'Alene country"; to quiet the settlers; and to cooperate with officials of the Department of the Interior in arbitrating disputes between the settlers and the Indian tribes. Wheaton was to "exercise the greatest caution in the anticipation and the prevention of complications tending to cause an increase of allies either direct or indirect to those Indians now actually at war." Should any delay in his marching schedule become necessary, it must take place "as far northward (near the Coeur d'Alene country) as possible."

A newspaper interpretation of the time softens, for the comfort of its readers, the elements involved in Wheaton's march. The "principal object in passing through that country is to make personal inspection of the character and disposition of the Indians." The editor continues: "it is also thought the marching of a large force of troops through there will have a very beneficial effect on the Indians; most of them are peaceably disposed towards the whites, while some of them are restless and inclined to be turbulent." Father Cataldo is more specific: "there was danger of a coalization of many Idaho and Washington Indian tribes to join the war." To prevent this, "Wheaton came with some companies to Spokane Fall[s] to hold an Indian council." [3]

All the upper tribes were involved. The army was particularly worried about three general groupings, however: the various tribes in the Colville region, the disparate Spokane River tribes, and the Coeur d'Alenes. Cataldo describes the council as designed "to see that neither Coeur d'Alenes, nor Spokanes, nor Colville Indians would join the Nez Percé war." Wheaton especially "begged F[ather] Joset to come with some of his Coeur d'Alene Chiefs." The Lewiston *Teller* reported the council as "embracing the Coeur d'Alenes, Spokanes, and some other bands; Sherwood says that the different bands of Indians will demand a large area of the country as a reservation, which if not granted may produce trouble." Near the end of July Inspector Watkins directed Simms to bring "the representative men of the extreme

3. Quotations from *HED* (serial 1794), pp. 72, 125, 590, 641, including Howard's general field order No. 3 of 23 July, his letter of 1 September, and Genl. McDowell's report of 17 October from San Francisco on troop movements. *Weekly Oregonian*, 30 July 1877; Lewiston *Teller*, 4 August 1877. OJ, Cataldo, "Historical Sketches: Joseph Joset."

Northern tribes" to the council. Watkins himself sent special invitations to Seltis of the Coeur d'Alenes, Garry of the Spokanes, and Moses of the Columbias. If the council did nothing else, General Howard felt, it would preoccupy "at least a thousand malcontents" at a critical moment.[4]

Agent Simms spent weeks in the expensive business of facilitating the passage of Indian delegations. "Including supplies issued to Indians, traveling expenses of Agent and Interpreter, express to chiefs and headmen to convene at council," as well as for goods from Walla Walla and the rental of office, council room, and storage room at the settlement from September 1 to October 31—the costs ran to a thousand dollars. Pay vouchers and agency reports break down these figures. The triple rental was $90, supplies during the council $222, traveling and incidentals $50. Thomas Flett got $10 for conveying a message ninety-five miles "to the Pend d'Oreille Indians Notifying them to meet in Council." One Ignace drew $20 for the longer but less complicated trip of two hundred miles, from Colville out over Okanogan and San Poil lands. A voucher drawn during the early days of preparation allowed $10 "for ferriage across the Columbia River of Okinagen Chief Tonasket and three other Indians with horses while en route."

Even minute expenditures reveal something of the council's assembling. The day it opened, a draft for $62 included the item "6 meals for U. S. Ind[ian] Agent and Interpreter on 9th and 10th July 1877 while enroute to attend [the] Ind[ian] Council at Spokane Falls, at 50 cts. per meal" and $2 for forage. A similar bill marks the return to Fort Colville after the council. A picture of the preparation also emerges from the charges for board "while looking after Nez Percé and Palouse Indians Camped on Spokane river from July 8th to July 16th, 1877, seven days at $1.00 per day." Though present at the council, Simms seems to have contributed little beyond its organizing. "Agent Simms has had nothing to do with [it]," wrote Watkins to Howard in annoyance, "and has done *nothing;* [I] am inclined to think he will have to be replaced by a more energetic man." [5]

On August 3 Inspector Watkins and Brevet Captain Melville Wilkinson rode out of Lewiston to join Wheaton's column. Wilkinson was aide-de-camp to Howard; as the General's personal representative, he was to have full powers at the coming council. Wilkinson could embarrass people with his religiosity. The wife of a fellow officer describes one impromptu perform-

4. Cataldo Papers; *Teller*, 11 August 1877; NA, EW, consol. Nez Percé file (AGO), Watkins to commissioner, 30 July. Howard in *HED* (serial 1794), p. 314.

5. NA, IA, LR (from Wash. Sup.), estimate of funds, third-fourth quarters, Colville Agency 1877; reports on supplies for council. Simms papers, voucher for third quarter 1877, vouchers for Eneas, Flett, and Tonasket bills (with provisional first date of council in mind); bills for 10, 20–21 August. *HED* (serial 1794), p. 642 (Watkins to Howard, 18 August).

ance aboard a steamer, in which "he wrung his hands and wept" and told "how he had found his saviour etc.," to the point of being "ridiculous." He "leads religious meetings" but less effectively than General Howard. A capable man for all that, he had won his brevet for gallantry in Civil War battles like Antietam. Wilkinson was to be breveted major for his activity in the Nez Percé fighting of early July. On August 6 he and Watkins left the troops again and went "riding over the mountains to the Lower Coeur d'Alene mission, where we met Fathers Cataldo and Joset; the Chief of the Coeur d'Alenes, Selties, arrives at the mission one hour after us."

A formal little conference or council was held with the important men of the tribe the next day in the Hangman's Creek chapel. Here Watkins thanked the Coeur d'Alenes "heartily" for their cooperation. He issued another, more personal invitation for the tribe to come "to the council at Spokane Bridge" (for Spokane Falls). To gain their good will from the start, Watkins guaranteed the Coeur d'Alene lands in the name of the president. He wished the Coeur d'Alenes to go to the council "not to treat of lands, but simply as an example" to the other Indians.

Captain Wilkinson in his report afterward tells how "this visit settles the question, an important one just now to this section, as to the friendliness of these Indians." The Captain was intrigued to hear that the Coeur d'Alenes had cared for the homes of the settlers. With careful skepticism he later investigated. "These facts were afterwards verified by the testimony of the settlers themselves." As for the specter of Coeur d'Alenes assisting the Nez Percé hostiles, Wilkinson was able to tell Howard: "Selties gave us assurances that he would, with his people, do all in his power to prevent re-enforcements for Joseph."

The Coeur d'Alene deputation, the two officials, and the Jesuits traveled west to rejoin the column at Hangman's Creek. Here a number of settlers presented themselves, boldly petitioning for some of the Coeur d'Alene timberland. White squatters were stealing these lands on a large scale; in 1873 a federal commission had met the problem by simply stripping the tribe of many valuable tracts. Inspector Watkins heard out the petitioners, and "firmly" rebuffed them.

General Wheaton had previously written the governor of Washington Territory on July 30, arranging to rally the several militias from the neighboring countryside to rendezvous with his troops at Pine Creek on the way north. Still nervous about the northern Indians, the General preferred to have "our whole force" on hand when meeting the Indians at Spokane Falls. The settlers however did not honor their military commitments.[6]

6. Wilkinson report to Howard, 5 November 1877, *HED*, pp. 643 ff. Giorda, "Biessings" (quots. on council). Fitzgerald, *Army Wife's Letters*, p. 141 (Wilkinson relig-

The council "was set for the 10th inst.," the day of Wheaton's arrival "at the Spokane lower Falls." Wheaton says that only five people were settled here. Describing the site later, Cataldo did not conceive of the several families as constituting a town. There was "no town, and no begin[n]ing or idea of a town: we were all camped on the gravel where is now Riverside Ave[nue and Howard Street]." General Sherman, passing this way some weeks after the council, is more generous. Spokane Falls is a "small village with a saw-mill and the usual store and post office." He is unenthusiastic about its prospects.[7]

The council did not open on August 10. The Coeur d'Alenes "were the only Indians that kept the day assigned." Some of the bands summoned had been two hundred miles west of Fort Colville and could not reach Spokane Falls easily; others were restive and uncooperative. By Sunday many still were absent, though the important chiefs were on hand. Spokane Garry put in a tardy appearance, writes Wilkinson, "but is offish and does not receive us at all kindly."

A penciled note from Inspector Watkins to Joset advised the priest that the council would open on Monday, if possible. It actually got under way on Wednesday the fifteenth. The delay was designed to allow Chief Moses of the Sinkiuse-Columbias to arrive; but Moses rejected both the council and its reservation plan. The extra days of waiting, General Wheaton says, did give "the best-disposed Indians of influence an opportunity to bring disaffected Indians, particularly the Spokane tribe, to a more correct understanding of the government requirements."

Wheaton's August 10 report speaks of meeting with delegates from "some nine thousand" Indians. Wilkinson's report lists 2,767 Indians represented. This "grand council" involved all the northern Indians west of the Flathead confederacy except the recusant band of Moses. The official report has Seltis head the list of chiefs present, followed by two of his subchiefs. There are also three chiefs of the upper Spokanes, two from the "Falls Band Spokanes" including Garry, five from the lower (Central and Western) Spokanes, two from the lower Pend d'Oreilles or Kalispels, one representative from the Dreamer sect, and two Palouse chiefs.[8]

iosity). WS, Indian Affairs, note added by Wheaton on letter from Mr. Claywood (?) to Governor Ferry, Colfax, 30 July. OJ has documentation on the 1873 land seizure and related land troubles.

7. *Teller*, 18 August 1877 (first quot.). OJ, Cataldo, "Historical Sketches," p. 6; cf. his MS "Notes on the Nez Percé Indian Mission," p. 13. *Reports of Inspection*, p. 94.

8. OJ, Wheaton to Joset, August 1877. Giorda, "Blessings," p. 6 (first quot.). *HED* (serial 1794), p. 643, Wilkinson report, and p. 653, Wheaton to Howard, Spokane Falls, 18 August; cf. p. 644; p. 652, Wheaton August 10 Report (9,000 Indians; Moses perhaps uninformed); *Settlers' Guide*, pp. 29–30. On council's division of Spokanes into upper and lower see above, p. 178, n. 34.

This roll call of chiefs is incomplete; disbursements of beef, flour, and tobacco betray the presence of other Indians. The Okanogans were represented by Chief Tonasket with thirty-one men. Three bands of Kettles are recorded, with twenty representatives. In one list five Kettle groups appear, three Palouse, three Pend d'Oreille, and so on. Garry was accompanied by forty tribesmen, a large group since this was his home ground. Chief Sgalgalt and a retinue of nine represented the Little Spokane band. Three Mountains with two of his followers appeared for the Hangman's Creek Spokanes. There were three chiefs from the Western Spokanes, each with eleven men.

The final statistics in Wilkinson's report name the leading chiefs present, each simply with the number of Indians under his control. Thus Seltis and Subchief Stellam appear for 450 Coeur d'Alenes, Garry for 160 Falls Band Spokanes, the Catholics Baptiste Peone and Sgalgalt for 383 Spokanes, Victor and Semo (Simon) for 250 Kalispels, Tonasket for 170 Okanogans, and Three Mountains for 40 Spokanes. There were also 318 Western Spokanes, 60 Colville band Kalispels, 200 Dreamers (probably of the Columbia tribes), 50 Palouses, and 680 Kettles.

Cornelius, a Protestant from the more westerly Spokane groupings, opened the first day with a prayer; he exhibited a testimonial from the Reverend Mr. Eells as to his people's friendly dispositions. Seltis delivered the first formal speech. He ended the parleys of the second day with an elaborate "good talk." During the council Seltis also "made several very good speeches in which he said what he had already done for the whites, and that, if he were forced to go to the war, he would take part with the U. S. soldiers; hence he exhorted all the Indians present to follow his example, because the white soldiers were the best friends of the Indians." To give solidarity to the chief's personal influence, "all the other Catholic Chiefs expressed themselves in like manner." Seltis was followed by the Catholic Tonasket, who spoke formally for both his Okanogans and the Kettles.

Cataldo opened the second day with a prayer. Later in the session he was to give an extended speech. "Father Cataldo, at the earnest solicitation of the inspector, then gave the Indians excellent instruction, especially in the direction of the cultivation of the soil, the sin of sloth, the necessity of giving the inspector a decided answer." The Reverend Mr. Cowley, Presbyterian minister among the Spokanes, followed him. Cowley "warmly indorsed what Father Cataldo had said, adding some other practical thoughts," Wilkinson reports. On the third day the opening prayer was given by Elder Havermale, "resident Methodist clergyman at Spokane Falls" settlement. Cowley offered the closing prayer of the council. Agreements were duly signed by the Coeur d'Alenes, Okanogans, Spokanes, Kettles, San Poils, Lakes, western bands of the Kalispels, and the Palouses.

Chief Garry proved sullen and ill-disposed. He appealed to ancient Indian superstitions and in general made a poor impression. When offered the choice between a reservation and citizenship like the White settlers, Wheaton says, Garry preferred the latter. In this, however, the chief was registering a protest. Garry seems to have been caught pathetically between present realities and his past dreams of progress through friendship with the Americans. As a result, he provided no leadership during the council. He did speak up on the first day, determined to retain his tribal land. By the second day he found himself isolated. Refusing to speak, he lost power even to obstruct. By the third day the official report pictures him as silent and (expressive addition to the language) "grum." He was the only chief who refused to sign the agreements, and had to be given an ultimatum with an attached time limit.

Garry, in fact, was growing desperate. Shortly afterward, when Sherman came through the Spokane country, the chief rode all night to intercept him. He related the troubles of his people to the General at length and intensely. Sherman comments: "his language was that of despair, not defiance." Garry even put aside his long-held religious antipathies and begged "to have the Coeur d'Alenes united with his people." Sherman conceded that "there was too much truth" in the chief's woes and accusations; but he could offer no help, and for that matter no advice except to take up heavy farming. A year and a half later General Howard came up with Governor Ferry and some troops for a series of conferences with the northern Indians; in the Spokane country he was displeased by the "growling of Spokane Garry who would agree to nothing."

Chief Moses also was recalcitrant. Immediately following the Wheaton Council he spoke his feelings openly to Watkins' messenger Sherwood. Some of the Indians in his neighborhood, together with stray Palouse and Nez Percé braves, showed their resentment by burning the grass, pilfering all the houses they came upon, and killing cattle. Sherwood met these marauders shortly after the council. (Moses occasioned a small war scare in 1878; as a result Fort Simcoe was strengthened and Moses himself arrested.)[9]

At the termination of the council General Wheaton, in his report to Howard from the "Camp at Spokane Falls," singled out the Coeur d'Alenes for special praise. He described how they "protected valuable property at abandoned ranches" on their own initiative. And he gave them "special credit

9. Simms Papers, lists for council at Spokane Falls, 31 December 1877. OJ, Cataldo, "Notes on the Sketch of the Nez Percé Indian Mission," p. 14 (Indian speeches). Howard-Ferry report in Fields, *National Guard,* 4, 314. *HED* (serial 1794), pp. 644–47, Wilkinson report on council, with Indian agreements attached; pp. 649–50, J. F. Sherwood to Watkins, 4 September, and excerpt of Rev. Mr. Cowley letter (on Moses). *Reports of Inspection,* pp. 95–96.

for their efforts to keep other Indians quiet during Joseph's outbreak."

There had been three Jesuits at the council: Fathers Cataldo, Joset, and Giorda. "The army officers thanked the Fathers," Cataldo says, "and especially Father Joset for the good accomplished." As a special courtesy, Wheaton lodged the priests in his headquarters tent during the council. Giorda, in his account of the council, tells how Wheaton, Watkins, and Wilkinson "paid very complimentary praises to Seltish and the Coeur d'Alenes, and reassured them again of their lands." The three Jesuits "were treated with the greatest courtesy by General Wheaton, whose hospitality and kindness they will never forget, as well as the regards of all the officers of the troops." Giorda at first suspected that their effusions were conventional politeness or "flatteries to the face"; but the officers meeting in conference in Wheaton's tent on the 19th "were overheard by one of the Priests" in a neighboring tent, expressing the sentiments again "though not Catholics."

As a pledge of loyalty, the northern Indians turned over eight prisoners at the falls, describing them as "Nez Percés and bad Indians." Unfriendly bands who gathered in the vicinity to foil the council were frightened away. This episode may be related to a very late reminiscence by Cataldo, though it is difficult to place such stories exactly. Cataldo tells us that "there were seven Indians who were responsible for the death of a few white people." Without the knowledge of their own chiefs, who "were our best friends," these seven irresponsible warriors had decided "to kill a few men and it would result in an attack by the white men," with subsequent open war. Learning of the plot, Cataldo "and the captain of the troops sent here by the government" revealed it in a meeting with the chiefs. With the plot exposed, "inside of a few hours the various Indian tribes that were located here had vanished; it was many months before they came back to this district." Wilkinson's report tells of four nontreaty Nez Percés putting in an appearance and being clapped into irons.[10]

The troops remained at the council ground until the Indian delegations dispersed. Wheaton had received an order on the evening of August 16, from General Howard in the Bitterroot, "halting my further advance." The presence of the little army did not satisfy the farmers of the upper country. "Of course every settler," wrote Wheaton in frustration, "would like to have a military post very near his ranch." The Spokane Falls settlers especially petitioned for protection.

The army had independently decided that the northern country demanded

10. *HED* (serial 1794), p. 653 (Wheaton Report, 18 August). Cataldo, "Historical Sketches," p. 5. Weibel, *Cataldo*, p. 21. Giorda, "Blessing," pp. 7–8. *Teller*, 1 September 1877 (first quot. on bad Indians); Cataldo late reminiscences in OJ clipping, 13 March 1928.

special care. A separate military district was decreed on August 27, covering the upper Interior from the Cascades over through central and northern Idaho. Wheaton commanded it from headquarters at Fort Lapwai, under Howard at Fort Vancouver near Portland. He kept five companies at Lapwai, left two in camp through the winter at Spokane Falls, sent two others to Mount Idaho, and kept the one-company outpost at Colville. With the coming of spring Fort Coeur d'Alene was established some distance to the east of Spokane Falls, on Coeur d'Alene land. The Spokane–Coeur d'Alene area was now safe for towns. By 1879 Spokane Falls had a population of 150; three years later it had grown to 500, and the arrival of the Northern Pacific Railway opened an era of swift expansion.

The major part of Wheaton's command returned down through Lewiston and took up quarters at Fort Lapwai by September. The *Teller* was not impressed with their work. Arguing from the premise that Watkins had no money, presents, or authority for definite commitments, the paper concluded: "from all we can gather" about the Great Council, "it amounted to nothing." The *Teller* did concede that the military "all seem remarkedly well pleased with the country north of this place." In view of the council's aftermath, Cataldo could write: "after that great council, all were tranquilized, both whites and Indians." Inspector Watkins and Howard's representative Wilkinson, upon their return to Lewiston, drew up a formal testimonial of gratitude to Seltis and his Coeur d'Alenes; they praised their "loyalty" and their "great" influence used "to maintain peaceful relations between the whites and Indians." Forty Pine Creek settlers also signed. Seltis returned a lengthy, courteous answer.

Next year, when the tribe requested formal title to the reservation they held only under presidential executive order, their services in the recent war were cited. "The pittance they would be thus granted would but illy recompense them for the noble and patriotic part they took in suppressing a coalition of Indian tribes under Chief Joseph, in the recent Nez Percés campaign." [11]

Western Montana, 1877: Stage and Cast

Joseph had been steadily making his way over the Lolo trail. He was to erupt into the heartland of two thousand Flathead confederates, themselves

11. Wheaton Report, 18 August. *Teller*, 1 September 1877. *CD Docs.*, pp. 18 ff. (testimonial, Seltis reply). *RBIC* (1878), p. 114 (last quot.). *HED* (serial 1794), pp. 114, 641–42, General McDowell report of 17 October; petition for garrison by Spokane settlers and 87 others, 25 June; new petition, 30 July. *AFQ*, October 1878, pp. 218–21 (Seltis to Watkins, n.d.; Watkins to Seltis, 30 August; Pine Creek citizens to Jesuits and Coeur d'Alenes, 19 June). Testimonial of 25 August republished in Spokane Falls *Review*, 24 April 1886.

long simmering over White injustices. The main body of the confederacy had a seventy-acre reservation centering upon St. Ignatius mission in the upper valley. This area was still wild; the tribes roamed at great distances beyond the reservation, much as they always had.

St. Mary's mission stood among the Flatheads proper, in the lower or Bitterroot Valley, now "well settled up with ranches and farms" strewn here and there over its capacious expanse. At the north of the valley stood the proud little hamlet village of Missoula, described by Bishop O'Connor in his visit during the 1877 summer as "the last outpost of civilization in the Northwest" for travelers coming from the east. General Sherman, arriving just after the Nez Percé passage, described it: "as new as pine boards fresh from the mill," yet "already a fair-sized town." His aide portrayed it as "a brisk little place," over 300 in population, situated on the river bank, boasting a weekly paper, a bank, taverns, and several stores. It also displayed a flour mill, hotels, churches, schools, saw mills, and a bridge.[12]

Halfway up the Bitterroot Valley to the south, close to St. Mary's, stood little Stevensville, consisting of perhaps 150 people. These Bitterroot beginnings were isolated. The valley's agricultural resources had induced men to leap over rougher country to attain it. To the east, two days of violent stagecoach travel away, lay the more considerable village of Deer Lodge. Two days beyond was the even larger town of Helena.

Until the very month of the war there were no soldiers at all in western Montana. Though Montana Territory was a country of many battles, including the Custer Massacre the preceding year, military resources were few. A single regiment garrisoned the territory; even its strength had diminished from 1,000 to a mere 300, and half of these were away fighting. There were also four companies of cavalry, but almost all had just been ordered down the Yellowstone River for campaigning. Worse, the Montana garrisons were located far away at the east of that expansive territory, and scattered into five different posts hundreds of miles apart, designed to guard against tribes like the Sioux.

Presiding over the posts was General John Gibbon, another Civil War general with permanent brevet serving as colonel, who like Wheaton would again rise in rank to become a regular general and a departmental com-

12. Genl. John Gibbon, "The Pursuit of 'Joseph'," *American Catholic Quarterly Review,* 4 (1879), 326 (first quot.). Bishop James O'Connor, letter of 13 December 1879, Omaha, published in French, *AFL,* 52 (1880), 201–32; quotation here from English original published subsequently without date, "The Flathead Indians," *RACHS, 3* (1888–91), 87. *Reports of Inspection,* pp. 43, 88. M. D. Beal's *"I Will Fight No More Forever," Chief Joseph and the Nez Perce War* (Seattle, 1963), the ablest history of the war to date, treats the Bitterroot phase in a disappointingly jejune fashion (pp. 91–106).

mander. At this moment of crisis he was "absolutely without cavalry" to
meet the Nez Percés; he could gather an infantry army of perhaps 100 men
out of a potential 150. He had the further disadvantage of being stationed at
Fort Shaw, far beyond the Sun River.

At Missoula, by merest chance, there existed the germ of a military garrison. The Flathead agent had warned the government in 1876 that "this is a
central point for the Indians" of both Interior and Plains to rendezvous or to
pass, "and the least protected in the territory." Later, a casual decision by the
army sent Captain C. C. Rawn, a Civil War combat veteran, with one company of infantry to start building Fort Missoula. The date was June 1877,
and the forlorn detachment might better be said to have walked into a trap.
Rawn got his men into camp, threw up some temporary sheds, and then sat
helplessly through the last half of June as daily rains postponed construction
work. The captain noted the "dread" of the Nez Percés, which sent the
populace "stampeding from the valley." As a pathetic gesture of assistance,
the army stripped Fort Ellis in order to send a second small company to the
Missoula campsite. The hostiles had destroyed better forces in Idaho.[13]

The Whites here were disturbed not only by the military vacuum but also,
and worse, by the presence of the Flathead confederates. Here, if anywhere,
Joseph's Nez Percés could feel totally secure. The confederates were his people's constant allies, and through intermarriage they had become something
of a kindred race. As early as 1835 the great Presbyterian missionary Whitman remarked that the two were "almost one people"; he commented that
"the Flatheads and Napiersas marry and mingle together so much that their
interest is the same, and they join together in their wars with the Blackfeet."
In subsequent years any number of observers noted the same fact. "Proximity, constant intercourse, not less than common interests and common dangers," says the Flathead missioner Palladino, made the two tribes "allies and
friends from time immemorial." More than this, "they also intermarried," so
that at any given time a number of Nez Percés would be living as Flatheads
and being absorbed into the tribe. In 1877 the superior at St. Mary's regards
the two tribes as "to some extent kith and kin by intermarriage."

The Flathead agent, Peter Ronan, similarly reported in 1877 that the Nez
Percés were so mixed into both Flathead and confederated tribes as to make
them all "related and intermarried to a great extent." The territorial secretary, James Mills, sent by the governor in late June 1877 to assess the Bitterroot situation, concluded that "one half the Indians called Flatheads and Pend

13. *Reports of Inspection*, p. 34. A. E. Rothermich, ed., "Early Days at Fort Missoula,"
Frontier and Midland, 16 (1936), 225–26 (quots. from Rawn to adj. genl. at Fort Shaw,
3 July). T. E. Blades and J. W. Wike, "Fort Missoula," *Military Affairs, 13* (1949), 29–
36. *HED* (serial 1794), p. 11.

d'Oreilles are Nez Percés or intermarried until the name is only a distinction." Bishop O'Connor, in the Bitterroot at the same time, tells how the several confederated tribes were "the most intimate friends and allies of the Nez Percés," so that it was generally expected that the confederacy would be "the first to join them in their rising." Even the chief currently recognized by the federal government as head of the Flatheads proper was himself half Nez Percé and half Snake.[14]

Besides this absorption of Nez Percés by the confederates, there was also a close fusion between the distinct bands of Nez Percés and Flathead confederates for the annual hunt, trade, and war. Thus in May 1877 just before the war, a large party of mixed Flatheads and Nez Percés came back from buffalo hunting to the Bitterroot, camping for ten days at Missoula; "the two bands carried out a sort of gala program." Some of the wilder pagan Nez Percé groups annually resided in the Bitterroot for a short period of time. Owen had grumbled about them just after the 1858 war; in 1873 Agent Daniel Shanahan filed a complaint against the "large and uncontrolled band of Nez Percés which camp in and around Missoula every spring," buying whiskey and creating an environment dangerous to peace. As early as 1875, therefore, the settlers feared the Flatheads would make common cause with the unhappy nontreaty Nez Percés. As the Nez Percé situation grew tense in 1877, Flathead Agent Medary protested against the presence of the buffalo Nez Percés in the Bitterroot; he demanded they be sent back to their own country. The Jesuits had nursed these pagan bands in the Bitterroot during epidemics, and had gained at least their respect.[15]

Great chiefs of the Nez Percés, like Looking Glass and Eagle From the Light, were long-time hunting comrades of the confederates. During the war itself the Bitterroot settlers were much disturbed that Chief Eagle From the Light remained among the Flatheads. He had always been the most stubborn of the Nez Percé dissidents. He had been a prominent leader of the Nez Percés opposed to the 1855 treaty; because of his opposition, troops had been brought to the council ground. He was one of the leaders fighting Stevens in the battle which ended the second council of Walla Walla. In 1859 he was the one chief Agent Cain had been unable to reassure concerning government intentions. In 1863 he was one of the four big chiefs seceding from the united

14. Young, *OHQ*, 27, 249 (Whitman). Owen reflects this hunt-trade fusion, *Journals and Letters*, e.g. 1 (1854), 69, 83, 89–90. Palladino, *Indian and White*, p. 8. NA, EW, consol. Nez Percé file, Ronan mid-July report; report to Governor Potts by Secretary Mills, 3 July. Bishop James O'Connor, *AFL*, p. 231. NA, IA, Montana Sup., Medary to commissioner, 8 December 1876 (Chief Arlee origins).

15. Will Cave, *Nez Percé Indian War of 1877 and Battle of Big Hole* (Missoula, 1926), pp. 4–5 (first quot.). *RCIA* (1873), p. 250; (1875), p. 305. NA, IA, Montana Sup., Medary to commissioner, 19 February 1877.

Nez Percés to become nontreaty. And when Chief Joseph's hostiles crossed into the Bitterroot in 1877, according to McWhorter's informants, their first camp was to be among the lodges of Left Hand, a brother or relative of Eagle From the Light.

At the upper mission of St. Ignatius the staff in 1877 consisted of Fathers Leopold Van Gorp and Joseph Bandini together with four lay brothers; the Sisters of Providence conducted the mission school for Indian girls. Van Gorp, a Belgian with a decade of experience in the Northwest, had been superior here from 1875; he was later to become superior-general of the network for eight years.

Bishop James O'Connor of Omaha, on a visit to eastern Montana which fell within his Nebraska vicariate, paid a tourist's visit also to the western part just as the war broke out. He describes how "the mountain labyrinth that extended for hundreds of miles on all'sides of us made me, at least, feel completely shut out from the world beyond"; the scenery would "rival the Jungfrau or the Matterhorn." The St. Ignatius mission valley itself was a scene "of surpassing beauty and grandeur, stretching away for forty miles to Flathead Lake." It was "inclosed on the south by a chain of mountains that rise as abruptly as a wall to a height of 10,000 feet above the plain," covered "with perpetual snow." The buildings of the Reduction were "dwarfed into toys by the mighty mountains that overshadow them."

The Indian houses and tents were arranged to face the large, modern church. This was the spiritual center for 1,200 resident and nomadic confederates, excluding the 500 at St. Mary's in the south. Bishop O'Connor found the Indians leading their timeless Indian life, dressed in Indian fashion, and with the interior of their cabins arranged exactly as an Indian tipi. War and the buffalo hunt were still annual occupations. Numbers of Indians cultivated small grain crops, however, and raised cattle or horses. "They say they do not want Government support, and they cannot abide the sight of an agent." At their printing press Salish books were being run off. A rather elaborate spiritual regime governed the daily life of those Indians currently resident.[16]

In 1869 Agent McCauley had reported how the St. Ignatius mission Jesuits, "poor and unaided," had been "priest, physician and benefactor to these

16. O. W. Holmes, ed., "James A. Garfield's Diary of a Trip to Montana in 1872," *Frontier and Midland*, 15 (1934–35), reprint as Sources of Northwest History, No. 21, p. 8 (hunting comrades). On Eagle see e.g. Haines, *Nez Percés*, pp. 126, 129, 137, 146, 184; Cain Report, 2 August 1859, *SED* (serial 1023), p. 783; NA, IA, Montana Sup. MSS, incl. Mills report. McWhorter, *Hear Me, My Chiefs*, pp. 358, 360, has the Bitterroot Nez Percés of Poker Joe and Tom Hill join the hostiles. O'Connor, *RACHS*, 3, 92–94, 99; on O'Connor's vicariate, and the complicated ecclesiastical history of Montana east of the Divide, see H. W. Casper, S.J., *History of the Catholic Church in Nebraska: The Church on the Northern Plains, 1838–1874*, (Milwaukee, 1960), chap. 11.

tribes," without "fee or reward" and without aid beyond the "miserable pittance" once given for a few months to help their large school. Agent Ronan's wife says in her memoirs that a series of agents had left a trail of "everlasting trouble, of misappropriation of Indian and Government property, and of constant court proceedings." For three years prior to the war, Bishop O'Connor records, government funds promised to the Flatheads had not gone beyond the agent's own pocket. In June, the very month the war began, the Jesuits finally managed to secure a really fine agent for their people. This was Peter Ronan, undersheriff of the largest county in Montana, who was to remain on the scene for the next sixteen years out of a genuine regard for these Indians. Thrust suddenly into a war situation, without any previous experience, Ronan could do little more for peace than cooperate with the missionaries.[17]

The Whites called all 2,000 confederates Flatheads. Indeed the Flatheads of Bishop O'Connor's report in 1877 are precisely the confederates of the upper valley. Technically, the name belonged rather to the Bitterroot group. De Smet described the new St. Mary's in the Bitterroot as twenty miles from its earlier site. In his 1863 visit he had found the Indians putting up a church, with another already built for Canadian settlers thirty miles below. The new mission centered on a neat little wooden church, with buildings and shops and barns arranged around a small enclosure. The Indian economy was much like that in the north; in 1868 Special Agent McCormick described the "fine farms" where the Bitterroot Flatheads were "raising wheat, barley, potatoes, cattle and horses."

The Jesuit priests down here were Fathers Ravalli and D'Aste. During the war months Ravalli was "partially paralyzed" and generally confined to his bed. Yet he was alert of mind and active in the affairs of the mission. The Bitterroot settlers would long remember the "great debt which western Montana owes" to Ravalli, "the one man who more than all others" kept the Bitterroot peaceful. Without his influence in 1877 the Nez Percé passage "would have been a very different story," one which "would be indelibly stamped in blood upon the pages of western Montana's history."

The more active work of pacification in the Bitterroot would have to be

17. *RCIA* (1869), pp. 294 (27 September 1877). Mrs. Ronan, "Memoirs," p. 246. NA, IA, Letterbooks, *136*, 71–72, commissioner to Ronan and to Medary, 13 April, 11 May; Montana Sup., docs. on Medary resignation and Ronan arrival etc. (April–July 1877); cf. *Weekly Missoulian* (June 1877), passim. W. L. Davis, S.J., *A History of St. Ignatius Mission* (Spokane, 1954), p. 40. The government agents here after Lansdale and Owen were C. H. Hutchins from 1862, Augustus Chapman in 1866, J. W. Wells to 1868 (suicide), M. McCauley in 1868–69 (suspended), Major A. S. Galbreath in 1869–70, C. S. Jones in 1870–72 (suspended), Major Daniel Shanahan (to 1875), and Medary to 1877 (suspended, replaced by Ronan).

done by Ravalli's superior Jerome D'Aste. A native of Genoa, displaced by the revolution of 1848, he had studied mathematics at the University of Paris before coming to the Rocky Mountain mission a decade ago. At that time Agent Owen appraised him as a "very intelligent Gent." His later photograph shows a slight, white-haired man, with a strong face, rather contained and reflective. Father Lawrence Palladino, a Flathead missioner stationed among the Whites at Helena during the war, underlines the important role played by D'Aste in the Nez Percé troubles. "Father D'Aste was in charge when the rebel Nez Percés invaded the valley, and in the common opinion of the people in that section his influence with the whites and the Indians, together with his tact, prudent counsel, and his prayers, had much to do with the maintenance of order and peace." [18]

Four main chiefs enter the story. Successor to the great Head Chief Victor in the Bitterroot was his son, the warrior Charlo (Charles Louis) or Little Claw of a Grizzly. Long experience with the treachery of federal representatives had marked the chief's character; his countenance wore a "habitual expression of stubborn pride and gloom." Though a good Catholic, he refused to allow his children to attend the Fathers' trade school because they had introduced the acculturatively significant policy of cutting the boys' long hair. His friend Father Palladino describes him as "a man of quiet, yet firm disposition, a thorough Indian, and a true representative type of his race." Stubborn and strong, his repugnance for White deceit had "resulted in a deep aversion to adopt, or have any of his tribe follow, the ways and customs of the whites."

About five years previously, in one of the many efforts to maneuver Charlo's Flatheads out of the Bitterroot, the federal government had arbitrarily established a puppet regime for those few Flatheads who would agree to remove to the north. This was headed by the usurper Chief Arlee (Henri) or Red Night. To him the government gave its bounty as head chief. Bishop O'Connor, writing in 1877, considered Arlee "a noble-looking man." He says that "obesity had taken all the grace from his figure, but I thought I had never seen a finer head or face than his; I could hardly take my eyes off him." In character Palladino describes Arlee as "a man of rather difficult disposition to treat." Agent Medary in December 1876 characterized him as a "*chronic grumbler*," unpopular with the tribe. Charlo never spoke to him or recognized his presence. But Arlee did have a small Flathead following. And the government had chosen him because of his wider influence "with the roving

18. CR, *3*, 796. *RCIA* (1868), p. 212. P. Ronan (then agent), *Historical Sketch of the Flathead Nation to 1890*, p. 55 (paralyzed). A. L. Stone (*Missoulian* editor), *Following Old Trails* (Missoula, 1913), p. 13 (latter quotes on Ravalli). Owen, *Journals*, *2*, 145. Palladino, *Indian and White* (1922 ed.), p. 72.

Indians from Idaho," presumably his tribesmen among the Snakes and Nez Percés.

Among the Pend d'Oreilles, old Alexander's successor was Michael or Plenty Grizzly Bear. He struck the Bishop as a good man but feeble. Michael seems to have lost much control over his tribe, because he lived at the agency twenty miles away from his people at the mission. By default the real control tended to fall to Andrew (André or Antelé), a respected leader who had declined the chiefainship just before Michael accepted. During the war, however, Michael would again take hold and come into prominence.[19]

The fourth of the great chiefs was Ignatius or Ignace (Aeneas to the Whites), heading the Kutenais. In 1877 he was a "tall, handsome, clean, commanding" figure. Bishop O'Connor describes him as a noble-looking Indian, standing six feet in his moccasins. Many Kutenais were somewhat removed from the problems of the other tribes and were out of sympathy with Joseph's revolt, but they were the wildest of all the confederates, the least amenable to discipline of any kind, and the most likely to erupt into violence. All were Plains hunters. Actually, St. Ignatius mission cared for three groups of Kutenais. One was permanently in America, one permanently in Canada, and the third based in Canada but wandering for long periods of time in America. Father Grassi says the first was located 65 miles from the mission, the second 250 miles, and the third 128.[20]

THE FLATHEADS AT THE EDGE OF WAR

All the confederate tribes nursed serious grievances against the government. The complaints of the Bitterroot Flatheads were particularly spectacular. Under the terms of the 1855 treaty, the government claimed a span of territory running through two degrees of latitude. Now with the great Bitterroot leader dead, federal authorities were trying to eject the tribe from the valley itself, the last foothold in their former homeland. When the tension became intolerable, General Alfred Sully with the help of the priests at both missions arranged a provisional agreement in 1869.

Two years later President Grant ordered the tribe's removal from the valley, by force if necessary, and opened it to settlement. The Jesuits tried to prevent war and save some of the Indians' territory by having them take up individual homesteads of 160 acres. The moment failed because of a legal

19. Palladino, pp. 64–65. O'Connor, *RACHS, 3,* 104–05. NA, IA, Montana Sup., Medary to commissioner, 8 September 1876. Mrs. Ronan, "Memoirs," p. 315. Davis, *Mission,* 74–81 for background.

20. Mrs. Ronan, p. 16 (first quot.). Turney-High, *Kutenais,* pp. 21–22 (sympathies) *AFL, 45* (1873), 362, Grassi letter, 14 December 1872.

technicality. As a compromise, the Fathers even induced the tribe to agree to a withdrawal to the north, keeping the letter of the presidential order without ceding their rights under the 1855 treaty. But the government refused to compromise; consequently the Flatheads would not budge from their valley.

In 1872 Congress sent James Garfield, House minority leader and chairman of the Committee on Appropriations, to break the impasse. Cynically, the future president of the United States forged Charlo's signature to an agreement. He cheerfully announced that this device would force the Flatheads to submit. At the time there were 450 Whites in the Bitterroot Valley. Insisting that Charlo had actually signed the treaty, they clamored aggressively for the tribe's removal. Feeling ran high on both sides.

In the next year, the Shanahan report remarked with some astonishment upon the Flathead Indians' bitterness and their lack of understanding with respect to the Hell Gate Treaty of 1855. "They made many complaints," and "said they have been promised much but got little." They were especially angry over the misuse of the treaty clause about the two valleys. "They dwelt much on the eleventh article of the treaty, which they seemed to think guaranteed them a right to the Bitterroot Valley." Shanahan "fully explained" the government's views to them. With a complacency recalling Governor Stevens' own, he goes on: "and besides explaining it through my own interpreter, Rev. Father D'Aste did so in such an effectual manner that they were all convinced of its true meaning." [21]

Meanwhile, the government commitments under both treaties (1855 and 1869), wrote De Smet in 1871, "have remained unfulfilled." In 1874 the Pend d'Oreille head chief, in a sworn statement, deposed that nothing had been done to fulfill the promises of 1855, except for the provision of a miller. About this time the government offered a niggardly subsidy to help their school. The one importunate request of the Indians to the agency itself proved to be a mistake. During a severe winter they begged four bolts of cloth for the children; for these the dishonest agent entered a bill with the government for over $1,500. Perhaps some light may be thrown upon such conditions by the annual report of the commissioner of Indian Affairs for 1872. He wrote candidly that the American tribes had to be "reduced to the condition of suppliants for charity" before the Whites could be safe. With gruesome piety he detected "something that savors of providential mercy in the rapidity with which their fate advances upon them," swallowing them up before they can have a chance to fight back. Jonathan Swift could not have said it better.[22]

21. MSS originals of Garfield treaty presented to Indians, 27 August 1872, and Shanahan report, in OJ. Davis, *Mission*, chap. 6.

22. BJ, Coll. 1ab–14ab, under 12ab, 10 May 1871 (De Smet). MH, 970.3 F61, "Statement of Michel" before O. Pichette, Justice of the Peace, 2 May 1874. Davis, *Mission*,

On the eve of the Nez Percé war, then, the Flathead confederates' grievances resembled those of the Nez Percés, even to a Wallowa of their own. But the injustices to the Flatheads were more extensive and long standing. For over a decade, consequently, the confederates had been moving closer to war. In 1865 Agent Owen noticed how the Flatheads, "once proverbial for their honesty," were becoming sly and thievish. "They require rigid and great punishment which will fall upon them Ere they least Expect it; the old Chiefs can do nothing with them; the young Men are growing heedless and will Not listen to the Councils of their Sages."

Two years later the confederates shared in the disturbances that swept the lower Interior and the Plains. Stealing and vandalism broke out in their territory; crops were fired and four prospectors killed. Owen hurried to confer with the superior-general, Father Giorda, "relative to the present alarming reports that are circulating around." Settlers were demanding arms from the government. The Indian superintendent soon proposed a treaty that would thrust 200 Whites out of Flathead lands. But the Whites indignantly memorialized Congress and forced his retreat. In March 1868 and again in February 1869 Giorda expressed his conviction that tension between Whites and Flatheads "cannot last any longer without bringing a clashing." He felt it "high time for [the] Government to put an end to the question of the Land, and give sufficient protection to both the whites and the Indians."

Another crisis occurred in 1872. A militia of a hundred men formed in the Bitterroot; muskets were rushed to them. The politician Garfield, busily pushing through his solution to the Flathead dilemma, dismissed the excitement as instigated by commercial interests. In that year, too, the former chairman of the Board of Indian Commissioners recorded the board's indignation over the government's obstinate resolve to seize the Flathead homeland; he thought the tribe "was justified in combining" for a defensive war. In 1874 the confederates appealed to the Montana territorial delegate in Congress for a new agent, to be selected with the help of Jesuit advice. Chief Michael formally requested a federal investigator. A covering letter from a settler added: "we are anticipating Indian trouble soon, and now is the time to stop it." [23]

In the year preceding the Nez Percé outbreak, Agent Medary reports, there was talk of a threatened "wholesale slaughter of the people of Montana." The superior of the mission network, Father Giorda, sent an unusual

---

pp. 40 (cloth), 69. *RCIA* (1872), p. 397. Cf. a different and more tentative "providential" theory in CR, *3*, 1195–97, and an intriguing variant by Bancroft in his *Oregon*, *2*, 379.

23. Owen, *Journals*, *1*, 333; *2*, 68. Bancroft, *Washington*, pp. 706–07. OJ, Giorda letters of 9 March 1868 and 11 February 1869. Garfield, *Diary*, pp. 6–7. Davis, *Mission*, p. 77, letter of 13 August, Wm. Welsh to Owen. MH, Chief Michael statement, 2 May; T. J. Demers to territorial delegate, M. Maginnis, 2 May.

message to President Grant in February 1876. He meant it to be private and
an urgent warning. "From information which I cannot altogether disregard, I
learn that the Flathead Indians in Bitter Root, Montana, are restless and may,
if driven to the wall, go and join the hostile tribes on the plains." Knowing
"how reticent the Indians are when they want to do some mischief," Giorda
was uneasy to find them sullenly secretive. The Jesuits and the chiefs eventually managed to control this situation.

A few months later, the Sioux massacre of Custer exhilarated the confederates. The Flathead agent reported that "nearly all the young Indians had
become insolent in their bearing and openly bragged of their ability to whip
the whites." He told how "the inhabitants of the surrounding country have
been for years apprehensive of an Indian war, and the greatest alarm prevailed after the news of the Custer calamity that these Indians would form a
combination with the non-treaty Nez Percés and others to make war."

This situation grew so ugly by December 1876, only six months before the
Nez Percé war, that Agent Medary had to call upon the troops for "immediate aid." The tempo of open insult had increased. Some of the angrier chiefs
had held a council and voted in a general way for violence, or at least for
forcibly ousting the agent. Medary felt unhappy that he had no stockade in
which to seek refuge. He wired General Gibbon at Fort Shaw for soldiers "*at
once.*" With all Montana Territory to control, Gibbon could spare only
twenty men and an officer. These duly arrived. The situation now took an
unexpected turn. Instead of going on the warpath, the confederate Indians
presented their case before a grand jury. One can detect the Jesuit hand in
this. The disconcerted agent entered into frantic correspondence with the attorney general of the United States. Meanwhile, General Gibbon grimly kept
the soldiers ready in the Bitterroot; they stayed until early March, just three
months before the Nez Percé war.[24]

As the soldiers returned to Fort Ellis, the Indian service was casting about
for a more competent agent to handle such crises. "For years," wrote the national commissioner in exasperation, "this agency has been a source of uneasiness." These flare-ups prior to the Nez Percé War allowed the Jesuits to
build up a sustained psychological advantage. Each crisis, successfully met,
furnished precedents and experience for the next. Arguments could be
elaborated upon again and again, points driven home with stubborn persistence, concern for the true interests of the Indians amply demonstrated, and a

24. CM, Giorda to President Grant, 21 February 1876. *RCIA* (1876), p. 98, September
1876; NA, IA, Montana Sup., Medary to Gibbon, 7 December 1876; Medary report of
July 1876; Gibbon to Medary, Fort Shaw, 21 December; Medary to U.S. attorney
general, 3 January 1877; cf. summons from U.S. marshal to Medary, April 1877. Gibbon
Report, 18 October 1877, in *HED* (serial 1794), pp. 520–21.

general mood developed that would be favorable for Jesuit intervention in the Nez Percé troubles. All this is important, Father Palladino writes, because in 1877 the Nez Percés, "as is well known, sought first to tempt and then intimidate the Flatheads into rebellion." [25]

The Flatheads in both valleys, then, had an accumulation of reasons for fighting. They had been goaded to the breaking point and faced no real obstacle to military success in western Montana. Only one factor remains to be considered. Because the confederates ultimately did not fight, historians of the Nez Percé War tend to assume that they were a peaceful tribe, no match for the Nez Percés. Their narratives introduce the Nez Percés into the Bitterroot in a phenomenally peaceful manner, pass them casually south through the valley, and resume the real story of the war a few days later beyond the valley. This is owing to the apparent absence of documentation.

Besides, it has been easy to think of the Flatheads simply in terms of Charlo's tribe and to regard them as an isolated pocket of somnolent and pacific mission Indians. That such a tribe could have made demands upon Joseph or have been of value to him as allies seemed improbable. [26] But the evidence, which on this point is more ample for the Flatheads than for any other Interior tribe, resoundingly shows their warlike character. Bravery in battle was the hallmark of this "chivalry of the mountains." Such testimonials precede the coming of the Blackrobes and were still being produced right up to the month of the war itself.

In 1868, a decade before the war, Special Agent W. J. Cullen had reported to the commissioner of Indian Affairs that the Flatheads were "still a very brave and warlike people, whose enmity is not to be scorned." War dances kept the memory of the annual victories green among all the confederate tribes. In 1872 Garfield attended one of these among the Bitterroot Flatheads, noting the "heroic recitals" of Flathead triumphs over Sioux, Crows, and Snakes. "These customs," he wrote, "are very effective in keeping up the pride and warlike spirit of the tribe." (Garfield resented their close attachment to the Jesuits and hoped that removal to a reservation would "help emancipate them from the undue influence of the Jesuits.") In 1877, at the northern mission, Bishop O'Connor commented on Flathead bravery. "The most warlike perhaps of all Rocky Mountain tribes, the piety of the Flatheads has not diminished their bravery, for since their conversion as well as before, they have been more than a match for their neighbors, the Sioux and

25. CM, commissioner to BIA, encl. in letter of 28 March 1877. Palladino, *Indian and White*, pp. 49, 349.

26. Haines, *Nez Percés*, p. 249. Howard and McGrath, *War Chief Joseph*, pp. 202, 204, 195. Cave, *Nez Percé Indian War*, p. 12, incorporating Duncan MacDonald. Cf. Teit, BAE *Annual Report*, 45, 372–73, on hopes of Flathead help.

the Blackfeet." To a man, the Flathead confederates were professional buffalo hunters and warriors. All the confederates, concludes Curtis in his monumental survey of the Indians of our region, "were reckless fighters when aroused."²⁷

Even those who worked farms at either mission were unable to dispense with the military buffalo hunt. The ethnologist who has most carefully studied Charlo's Bitterroot Flatheads characterizes them as nomadic or semimigratory. For as long as eight months each year they roamed the dangerous Plains, especially on the Musselshell and the Yellowstone. Their enemies the Blackfeet indeed considered them simply a Plains tribe. No Indian-White war in the Northwest was so costly in human life as the never-ending wars of the confederates on the Plains. Twenty-five men were lost in an 1860 encounter with the Assiniboines for example, five in an 1869 clash with Blackfeet on the Sun River, and eighteen "of their best men" in a fight with the Sioux in 1871. Sitting Bull fought one of his most famous battles against the Flatheads. Here he counted the bravest of all his life's thirty coups, and later in the battle was scarred for life. Here, too, half a dozen good Sioux lost their lives.

White men, and occasionally Jesuits, rode with the tribe to these fights. Such yearly battles continued even after Joseph's band went into exile. Year after year men like Owen and the several Flathead agents, as well as the Jesuits, recorded triumphs and disasters of the war as the Flatheads migrated back into the valley. Warriors from other tribes continually replaced the dead, thus changing the composition of the Flathead group. As early as 1849 some Jesuits complained that the pure Flatheads were dying off. This proved only an illusion; the Flatheads had long been fluidly composed. The process of replacement among the Flatheads was sufficiently slow that it did not affect the substantial portion of the tribe at any given time, or diminish the celebrated Flathead *élan.*²⁸

Flathead victories over their far more numerous Plains enemies, says the standard ethnological study of the Flatheads, "must be ascribed to greater cleverness and military sagacity, the greater resourcefulness and 'push' of the Flathead over the stolid Blackfeet." This opinion, interestingly enough, derives not from Salish affiliates but from the testimony of their enemies like the Crows and from their non-Salish friends, the Nez Percés. War to the Flat-

27. *RCIA* (1868), p. 220; (1875), cf. pp. 304–05. Garfield, *Diary*, p. 9. O'Connor, *RACHS, 3*, 97. E. S. Curtis, *The North American Indian*, ed. F. W. Hodge, 7, (20 vols. Seattle, Wash., Cambridge, Mass., and Norwood, Mass., 1907–30), p. 52.

28. Turney-High, *Flatheads*, p. 116. Ewers, *Blackfeet*, p. 14. Cf. Bancroft, *Native Races, 1*, 290–91, 268; Palladino, *Indian and White*, p. 49; Gibbs on heroism, above, Chap. 3. *RCIA* (1869), p. 297, Major Galbreath report of 6 September; (1871), p. 426, Agent Jones report of 1 September (Sioux fight). Vestal, *Sitting Bull*, chap. 17, "The Fight with the Flatheads." On the Flatheads as a Plains tribe, see above, p. 91, n. 72.

heads was "the greatest sport of all able-bodied men." The tribe even developed "an intelligence system," infiltrating enemy camps with Flathead spies. But their forte was direct, simple bravery. The Kutenais, cleverer at preparing a battle, admitted that the Bitterroot Flatheads were better warriors in action, "fine men and marvelously fine fighters." An advantage over other Plain tribes was the deadly Flathead marksmanship, developed by the hunting of small game at long range in the mountains during a part of every year.

In the lower valley serious battles in and before 1871, together with a preoccupation to save their valley by demonstrating agricultural competence, seem to have led the Bitterroot Flatheads to neglect the Plains for several seasons. Economic necessity in 1877 forced them to return to the Plains again regularly. The other confederates continued to ride off even during these exceptional years.

It is ironical that the question of Flathead warrior qualities should ever arise in relation to the Nez Percés. The Nez Percés as a group recognized that the Bitterroot Flatheads were better than themselves at the military game of hunting on the Plains. The dressing of buffalo skins, indeed, was the one aspect of material culture in which the Flatheads excelled the Nez Percés. Because of this superiority on the Plains many, perhaps most, Nez Percés preferred to let the Flatheads do the hunting; the Nez Percés could then buy from the Flathead surplus in Flathead country without the trouble of going to fight the Blackfeet. When the Flatheads came home, the Nez Percés made their way up to the Bitterroot in great numbers for a trading rendezvous and feasting. In short, "the Flathead traded articles involving danger for those involving skill" from the Nez Percés. This assertion requires a careful distinction between those Nez Percés who went regularly to buffalo and those who only occasionally indulged, but the comparison is nevertheless illuminating.[29]

This Flathead psychology is as important a background to the war as is the Flathead terrain. The number of warriors among the confederates is also pertinent. To go north into Canada from the Lolo trail involved passage through a warrior force larger than Joseph's band. At the end of 1876 the Flathead agent, Medary, in his census of tribes actually resident on the agency in the northern valley, listed 161 Kutenai males, 402 Pend d'Oreille males, and 41 Bitterroot Flathead males who had moved up onto the reserve —in all a total of 604 resident males. This does not include the wilder, wandering bands cared for by the Jesuit missions among the confederates, nor the main body of Bitterroot Flatheads.

A circumstance sometimes cited to support the thesis of Flathead ineffectu-

29. Turney-High, *Flatheads,* pp. 61–62, 116, 136–37, and *Kutenais,* p. 167 (quots.). Ewers, *Sohon's Portraits,* p. 17. Cf. McWhorter, *Hear Me, My Chiefs,* p. 567. *RCIA* (1875), pp. 304–05 (hunt declines). Garfield, *Diary,* p. 9. O'Connor, *RACHS, 3,* 97.

ality was their lack of ammunition in 1877. Father D'Aste says of the Bitterroot Flatheads: "they had only a few old guns, and scarcely any ammunition." But he is overstating the facts to make a point. Authorities had closed
off the sale of ammunition at the beginning of the crisis. There is no doubt
that sufficient ammunition and guns were on hand to sustain a brisk action.
Had the Flatheads joined the Whites, further ammunition would immediately
have been supplied. Had they taken matters into their own hands, they could
have purchased it in the valley in quantities, as did the Nez Percés during
their passage. And immediately following the war, still without sufficient
ammunition to sustain a half year's hunt on the Plains, the confederates managed to make do with what they had kept on hand. Ronan wrote at the time
that he feared the Flathead hunters would "use force" on the merchants to
supplement their supply.[30]

TERROR IN THE BITTERROOT: POLICY OF THE CONFEDERATES

Understanding this background, one is more prepared for the scare head-
lines in the contemporary newspapers which promised dire catastrophe. The
San Francisco *Chronicle* announced prominently:

> THE FLATHEADS PREPARING TO JOIN
> THE NEZ PERCÉS IN THEIR WAR
> ON THE WHITES

The Cincinnati *Weekly Star* has the Nez Percés preparing "to clean out Bitter Root Valley," with the Flatheads scheduled to join them in the war by
July 1. The *Teller* quotes the Nez Percé James Reuben as saying "that the
Crows are more friendly with these hostiles and will join them against the
whites, and so will some of the Flatheads." That the Flatheads, in whole or
in part, would join the Nez Percés was widely believed in Montana, especially in the Bitterroot Valley.[31]

When the Jesuits had succeeded in reassuring many settlers, Chauncey Barbour, *Weekly Missoulian* editor, warned Governor Benjamin Potts against

30. *RCIA* (1876), p. 88. OJ, Jerome D'Aste, "The Nez Percé War," written up
fifteen years later from wartime notes, to serve as source material. Ammunition just after
war: see NA, IA, *Letterbooks*, *136*, 457, commissioner to Ronan, 3 August, citing
congressional resolution of previous 5 August; Montana Sup., Ronan to commissioner,
20 August; Palladino to Ronan (forwarded to commissioner), Deer Lodge, 15 August;
D'Aste to Ronan and forwarded, Stevensville, 18 August; Ronan to commissioner (incl.
Palladino and D'Aste letters), 1 October.

31 San Francisco *Chronicle*, 30 June; Cincinnati *Weekly Star*, 5 July; *Teller*, 4 August. Cf. Agent Ronan statistics for 1877, in *HED* (serial 1800), 45 Cong., 2 sess. (1878-
79), 1, Pt. 5, 530–33; and in the annual FL and FP census MSS.

"some of our papers who are trying to persuade themselves that the Flatheads and the Pen[d] d'Oreilles will not make war on the whites—that the Catholic religion has the effect of making them lamb-like; there are some who affect to believe that Charlot will not lie." Father D'Aste in a convoluted sentence conveys the popular mood. "The idea that the Flat Heads who had been so much abused and were dissatisfied with the Gen[eral] Garfield treatise might avail themselves of the chance to revenge themselves and might join the Nez Percés at their passage by the valley, and thus be masters of the valley, excited considerably the minds of the settlers." The Whites "were watching closely," and "freely expressed" their suspicions. As a result "there were therefore bad feelings and mutual fears between the two races."

On Saturday night, June 23, the last day of Bishop O'Connor's visit at the upper mission, news of the Nez Percé war came to St. Ignatius "direct by special runners sent to our Indians from the lower country," perhaps from Cataldo. The cónfederates disclaimed prior knowledge of a war. The Bishop felt that "the news was evidently as unexpected as it was unwelcome to the chiefs and others who heard it; they said little, but looked very thoughtful and even sad; their manner more than their words satisfied me that the Flatheads had had no knowledge of an intended outbreak by their friends and allies."

The Bishop used his influence among these primitive people to persuade them toward peace. He made "particular inquiries to ascertain the actual dispositions of the Catholic Indians, fearing much that they might be drawn into making common cause with the Nez Percés." Before leaving the mission he "saw the chiefs and other leaders of the tribe, spoke to them words of peace, and directed them to follow in everything the counsels and advice of the Fathers." With Father Bandini serving as his interpreter, he secured from the confederate tribes at the upper mission a promise not to join the revolt. Returning to Missoula on Sunday, June 24, Bishop O'Connor was able to reassure frightened settlers making their way into town. On his journey back to Omaha he also sent "a lengthy dispatch to the New York *Herald,* with the intention of forestalling rumors." [32]

But the Bishop had not seen all the settlers. "Quite an excitement gripped the entire Bitterroot Valley." The majority of White farmers fled along the valley to Stevensville, seeking the meager protection of the crumbling adobe walls surrounding the old trading post of Fort Owen. In their panic they freely expressed hatred and suspicion of the Flatheads—"in [the] presence of

32. Barbour to Gov. Potts, Missoula, 15 July, in P. C. Phillips, ed., " 'The Battle of the Big Hole': An Episode in the Nez Perce War," *Frontier and Midland,* 9 (1929), reprint as Sources of Northwest History, No. 8, pp. 8–9. D'Aste, "Nez Percé War." O'Connor, *RACHS,* 3, 108–10; Palladino, *Indian and White,* pp. 49, 348 ff.

half Breeds who would repeat their conversations to the Indians." Father D'Aste rode down and "tried to calm the agitation among the settlers," as Cataldo was doing in another corner of the theater of war. The Bitterroot people were far from grateful. They refused to give any credit to D'Aste's account of the Flatheads' peaceful dispositions. Someone argued that D'Aste himself was "with the Indians against the whites." A suggestion was even voiced that the mission be set on fire.

Eventually the settlers tired of confinement and returned home, only to flee again a week later as fresh rumors arose of approaching Nez Percés. This time the excitement was intense. Ravalli's friend the Reverend Daniel Tuttle, the pioneer bishop of the Episcopalian church in the Northwest, later recalled that only women and children had heard his sermon on July 1 in Stevensville, because all the men of the area were alerted.

A report dealing with this second panic derives from the governor's secretary. Governor Benjamin Franklin Potts had a wealth of practical military experience behind him, and he prepared to draw upon it. Unlike his counterpart in Washington Territory, who had been a political general on the home front during the Civil War, Potts had risen in combat to be a major general in Sherman's fighting army. A tall man, huge and energetic, he was respected for his good judgment. On June 22 he decided to send his secretary, James Mills, to assess the Bitterroot situation. Mills' report of July 1 was not reassuring. Excitement in the valley "amounted to a panic." At Missoula itself brooding worry prevailed. Nearly all the valley's settlers were sheltering again at Fort Owen. Less than ten effective rifles could be found.[33]

Dismaying rumors circulated. Various Indians were quoted or misquoted with devastating effect. A Nez Percé boasted that his tribe would raid the valley. "A friendly Flathead privately warned some of his intimate friends among the whites of impending danger; the Flatheads began to act differently, to become reserved in their talk but evincing a jubilant spirit." The Nez Percé chief Eagle From the Light intimated that his band of thirty lodges was leaving the Bitterroot to join the war but would return in equally combative mood; on June 22 he was reported heading for Idaho on the Lolo Pass "in great haste." At about this time the Flatheads also began to disappear. By June 28 "no Indians were to be seen in the valley." Indians from St. Ignatius mission spoke of a small Pend d'Oreille outbreak. Other Indians had heard that the Sioux and Crows were sealing a mutual peace so as to turn upon the Whites. Nez Percé envoys were said to be among the Crows. The half-breed Duncan MacDonald claimed that "preparations had long been progressing for an alliance of all the Indians to fight the whites." MacDonald

33. D'Aste (all quots.). NA (see below, n. 34), Mills letter of 1 July; Bishop D. Tuttle, "Early History of the Episcopal Church in Montana," p. 319; cf. also Tuttle visit to St. Ignatius in Ravalli Papers, St. Mary's mission chronology, June.

also said Chiefs Arlee and Michael feared "that they could not control their men."

Mills judged that a general outbreak had been in the wind, but that Joseph's war came too suddenly to allow any wider movement to mature. He estimated the absent band of Charlo at 200 warriors, in 75 to 90 lodges. The Pend d'Oreille chief Michael had 240 in 60 lodges near St. Ignatius mission. Chief Arlee had 15 to 20 removed Flathead lodges on the reservation; "they have been very surly since the soldiers came" to build Fort Missoula. Chief Ignace at Flathead Lake had 40 lodges of Kutenais.

To oppose all this the Whites could muster very little. An amateur militia company had organized at Stevensville halfway down the Bitterroot, and another at Missoula. Similar posses, ineffectual in battle and too distant to arrive in time, were gathering at places like Butte and Deer Lodge. Blockhouse refuges were soon to go up. A hundred stand of arms were to reach Missoula in a few days. At least a hundred cavalrymen were needed. Talking with the most experienced frontiersmen, Mills could only conclude that the situation was grave.[34]

Governor Potts wired the army the same day that "Charlos, Flathead chief, controlling two hundred fighting Indians, has disappeared from Bitter Root Valley, probably to join Joseph's Band." The Governor shrewdly noted that the settlers' "dread" of the Flatheads was such as to be in itself "very favorable to the spread of the present hostilities." Meanwhile, where had Charlo gone? The army soon learned that he was encamped on the Big Hole near French Gulch, southwest of the Bitterroot. On July 3 the San Francisco headquarters, casting about for some explanation, informed the Department of the Columbia that Charlo was "seeking safety from Joseph's Band, who threatens to Kill them unless they join him."

Even before receiving Mills' report, the Governor had got in touch with Agent Ronan on June 29 to request "that you, with some of your most influential Fathers, seek out the Flathead Indians." Together they were to hold a peace conference and also secure information as to Flathead dispositions. It required nearly five days for this urgent message to make its way from Helena over to Missoula. Captain Rawn turned up at Ronan's agency on the same day as the letter, equally anxious about the confederates' intentions. The two men, working through Father Van Gorp the superior of St. Ignatius and his assistant Father Bandini, arranged for a council on July 6 with the Indians of the upper valley.[35]

34. NA, IA, Montana Sup., Governor Potts to sec. of Interior, 22 June; to same, 3 July, encl. Mills report.

35. NA, EW, consol. Nez Percé War file (AGO), Genl. McDowell at S.F. to Sherman, enclosing Potts telegram, Helena, 1 July; McDowell telegram to Howard, 3 July. NA, IA, Montana Sup., Potts telegram to Ronan, 29 June (cf. Ronan to commissioner, 11 July, and Ronan nine-page reply to Potts).

At this council the several tribes elucidated the position they were to hold for the rest of the war. It was a species of neutrality, one not easy for the White men to grasp. The Indians gave formal and unqualified assurance of their commitment to the White cause, or so Agent Ronan understood. But this alliance was seriously qualified. They would join the Whites in fighting against the Nez Percés only if the latter attacked settlers on Flathead territory. When the Captain requested scouts to watch the passes, the Flatheads showed reluctance. They did assure Captain Rawn that they would let him know when the Nez Percés approached. There was some confused talk of payment at this point. The chiefs may have used Rawn's inability to pay as a pretext for refusing regular scouting duty; yet they offered more limited but still considerable services without payment. They seemed determined to preserve meticulous neutrality, as long as their territory was not violated by untoward acts on the part of the invaders. Chief Arlee also complained to the Whites because some settlers kept saying he meant to lead his people to join the hostiles.

The Captain and the Agent then prepared to conduct a similar council with the Bitterroot Flatheads below. This visit appears in the Jesuit house diary. They "came up to find out the mind and dispositions of our Indians about the troubles below in the Nez Percé country." At St. Mary's church on Sunday, July 8, they met Charlo after Mass. The superior, Father D'Aste, "arranged preliminaries for our talk with the chief." At the council Charlo proved cordial enough. He explained that the recent mysterious Flathead movements were connected with their return from camas and fishing activities to the harvesting of crops. Twenty lodges were at present encamped near Missoula, the others being on their way north.

Charlo delivered himself of a ringing address stating his friendship for the Whites. "I am my father's son," he proclaimed. He guaranteed protection to the Whites on his lands. He would inform them by runner of all dangers, and he committed himself to their defense. But he reminded the Whites sternly that the Nez Percés were his friends. For many years now the Nez Percés had fought beside the Flatheads against the Blackfeet. "I cannot send my young men out to make war on the Nez Percés." Should the invaders "molest his people," Red or White, or commit some provocation in Flathead territory, then the Flatheads would fight.

Charlo also complained that the soldiers had assaulted an innocent camp of the Nez Percés, killing a chief whose wife was a Flathead. His reference is almost certainly to the outrageous attack on the peaceful camp of his friend Looking Glass in Idaho, an attack which brought that great war leader into the hostiles. (Charlo had tried to contain the emotion aroused; he sent runners to the various Indian camps, to argue that the attack had only been an error. Unfortunately the Whites had believed these Flathead runners to be hostiles, because a captured member of Joseph's band told them so.) Charlo revealed to the Whites news brought in by his runners about some Cayuses near Fort Hall. He was also trying to discover Joseph's current whereabouts, keeping the passes under observation.

Captain Rawn duly reported Charlo's policy to his military superiors at Fort Shaw on July 12. If the Nez Percés came peacefully, the chief would be neither for nor against them; and he would not help the Whites beyond the gathering of information. What was the result of these councils? Ronan hoped for the best. But he realized the limitations of the several chiefs' power. After all, even Chief Joseph had stood for peace. Ronan feared that the young men would get out of control when the Nez Percés were passing, "as there are restless and adventurous spirits among the Indians as well as whites, who would be only too glad for an opportunity for plunder and rapine." The Jesuits, too, were anxious about this element of unpredictability.

Before the councils the *Weekly Missoulian* editor wrote to tell Governor Potts that the Pend d'Oreille head chief and Head Chief Arlee believed the young men of both tribes would join in hostilities "as soon as the Nez Percés should reach Bitter Root Valley." [36] The editor was expressing the threat rather too vigorously, as MacDonald had done. Still, it remained a constant danger. Thus there were grounds for the Governor's telegraph to the President on July 13: "the situation is critical." He asked President Hayes for "authority to raise five hundred volunteers to meet the Indians as soon as they reach our Border." He maintained pressure on the War Department for troops to be sent to the Bitterroot. Soothing answers marched back to him.

Meanwhile, the Jesuit mission offered practical assistance. "The mission-police placed themselves at the agent's service," reported Ronan, "and received orders from their chiefs to immediately arrest and incarcerate in the Indian jail any disaffected reservation Indian who might attempt to join the hostiles." The grim jail building at the mission and the long tradition of its communal use under Jesuit guidance were a persuasive antidote to the war spirit. "This prompt action had a salutary effect upon the malcontents, and we had no occasion to arrest anyone."

The presence of Chief Eagle From the Light remained a continuing source of uneasiness. Head Chief Michael of the Pend d'Oreilles brought the Nez Percé chief to visit Ronan. He explained that eleven Nez Percé lodges had decided to stay at the mission, "desirous to keep out of trouble and to encamp somewhere out of danger." The Catholic chiefs, realizing that this would

36. NA, EW, consol. file, Ronan to Potts, 10 July (councils). Ravalli Papers, St. Mary's mission chronology, 8 July; D'Aste, "Nez Percé War." Rothermich, *Frontier and Midland, 16,* 226. Barbour to Potts, Missoula, 29 June, in Phillips, *Battle,* p. 4.

arouse foolish suspicions, wished to register the plan openly with the agent. Ronan was dubious. He told the chiefs that "I saw a letter from Coeur d'Alean, which stated that a camp of Nez Percés, also claiming to be at peace with the whites, requested the same permission in that country" recently and were refused. The agent sent the chiefs to ask at the fort. Ultimately, Eagle From the Light neglected to pursue the matter.

An ominous note was the arrival of a Blackfoot chief among the confederates on July 13. They were feasting him, disguising his presence as a pleasure visit. Actually the Blackfeet were angry at the Whites; they were soliciting the Flatheads to a rising. The Flatheads refused to commit themselves to war, and stubbornly repeated their position of neutrality. The Blackfeet threatened to consider the Flatheads common enemies with the Whites against the Red men. The Blackfeet were not alone in expressing displeasure at the Flathead stand. In another letter to the Governor on July 15 after the councils, the *Weekly Missoulian* editor entered strong complaint. "I am prepared to say that the men who declare that no part of the Flatheads or Pen[d] d'Oreilles will join in the war offer an insult to common intelligence."

Charlo, however, was keeping his promises. As the Nez Percés approached the valley the chief dispatched a picked warrior band under his own son, Ronan reports, to help the Whites observe and control the situation. Head chiefs Arlee, Michael, and Ignace "all lent their aid." Thus the entire confederacy of 2,000 Indians cooperated to preserve the integrity of the confederate territory. The agent tells also how the chiefs "so well managed to keep their young men in subjugation, that I can venture to say, without fear of contradiction, that up to the present date, not a single Indian of the above mentioned tribes are in the hostile Camp." This success, he says, reflects the efforts of the Jesuit mentors at their respective missions.[37]

In the third week of July word again swept through the valley that the Nez Percés were approaching. "Another general stampede" to Fort Owen began, as well as a frantic last-minute building of blockhouses. "By July 23 with the Nez Percés but a few miles away," Father D'Aste tells us, "the excitement grew wilder, [and] every movement of the Flat Heads was watched and suspected." This reached ludicrous proportions. "Were an Indian seen running horseback he was surely a messenger between the Flat Heads and the Nez Percés; even a Government official sent a message to the Governor from

37. NA, EW, consol. file, Potts telegram to president, Helena, 13 July; reply from sec. of War; headquarters Missouri division, Chicago, to asst. adj. genl., Washington, D.C., 19 July (Gibbon orders). Ronan report to Potts, 17 July, forwarded to Dept. Interior, forwarded to army (Eagle From Light episode, Blackfeet); other Potts telegrams here. NA, IA, Montana Sup., letters from War Dept. on Potts' requests for troops; Gibbon reply of 22 July. Barbour, 15 July, see above, n. 32. Ronan report, 13 August 1877 (police), in *HED* (serial 1800), No. 1, Pt. 5, *1*, 532.

Missoula, announcing that Charlo (who was quiet cutting hay on his ranch) had gone with his warriors . . . to join the Nez Percés." Yet by this time the Flathead chiefs had long made it clear to the Nez Percé hostiles themselves "that if in passing through the Bitter Root" Joseph's people betrayed Flathead hospitality, the confederates "would join in the pursuit of him." [38]

Though the Flatheads wished to facilitate the Nez Percé passage onward to some other land, the Whites were not prepared to compromise. Governor Potts telegraphed San Francisco on July 23 that the Nez Percés "profess to want to pass peaceably." In answer came the army's order: Stop them. Potts telegraphed in frustration that he was powerless to do so. He had not even been able to raise a militia capable of opposing Joseph. Missoula mustered sixty-four settlers; Stevensville down by St. Mary's, thirty-eight; and four other little hamlets about thirty apiece. The best the Governor could really do was provide arms for the protection of homes. Meanwhile, the Whites were busily opening loopholes in the walls of Fort Owen. Farther south in the valley at Corvallis, and beyond that at Hamilton, little forts were being thrown up. "In these forts the settlers imprisoned themselves, waiting for the Nez Percés who were still a good way distant." [39]

The Nez Percé Invasion

The army was not entirely inactive. Information was being collated by telegraph on the probable disposition of tribes like the Snakes and Crows. Howard's army was embarking at the beginning of the rugged, hundred-mile Lolo trail, just as Joseph reached the Bitterroot at the other end. Following the Lolo was not easy or pleasant for a modern army; Sherman describes it in his 1877 report as "one of the worst *trails* for man and beast on this continent." General Gibbon would not begin his own march from Fort Shaw in eastern Montana for two weeks. But Howard had telegraphed ahead to Captain Rawn at his Missoula fort-building site, urging him to stop the hostiles.

Leaving fewer than ten soldiers behind him, Rawn took his thirty infantrymen and five officers out of the Bitterroot on July 25 into the lateral Lolo canyon. At its head he set up an unimpressive log breastwork three feet high. With him came some 150 undisciplined volunteers, about two-thirds of them from the Stevensville refugees and the rest from Missoula. The approaching enemy had the advantage in numbers, fighting ability, and, as events proved, choice of strategic position. The hostiles could have swept away this rabble before them. They had already disposed of more formidable forces.

38. D'Aste, "Nez Percé War." O'Connor, *RACHS*, 3, 108–09 (last quot.).

39. NA, EW, consol. file, Potts telegram to McDowell; reply and counterreply. D'Aste (last quot.).

It has been said that the Nez Percés sent scouts at this point to the Flatheads again, to argue against their neutrality. Rebuffed, they tried then to negotiate with Rawn for free passage through the Bitterroot peacefully. When
the civilian volunteers learned of the Nez Percé offer, they began to desert in
great numbers; at the time of the crisis, fewer than two dozen remained to
help Rawn's tiny force in a suicide stand. Battle seemed imminent. But on the
fourth day after Rawn's arrival the entire band of 700 Indians with their
2,000 horses outflanked the White position, slipping high along the side of the
hill. Undoubtedly relieved to find himself alive, the Captain abandoned "Fort
Fizzle" and returned to his fort site. Wisely he made no further effort to interfere with the passage of the Indians.[40]

So astounding was this outcome, when the hostiles could have destroyed
the soldiers as they had done in Idaho, that one historian of the war has even
suggested treason on the part of Rawn. The real reason was that the Nez
Percés had too much to contend with already without arousing the confederates. And the confederates were on close guard. D'Aste tells about one important group. At the urging of "half-breeds," some fifteen Flatheads had
joined Rawn's force. Partly because of White suspicion and perhaps equally
because of their neutral stand, they carried "neither arms nor ammunition."
Mills speaks of these Flatheads in a dispatch of July 29 to General McDowell.
The Nez Percé hostiles, in their later reminiscences to McWhorter, described them as wearing white flags of truce on their heads. These Flathead
observers, D'Aste says, told Rawn the Nez Percés could outflank him; "he
smiled at the idea." Actually, Rawn was safe enough. If the hostiles in passing
above the troops opened "a murderous fire," as they had done "in another
similar circumstance in Idaho," D'Aste notes, then the Flatheads and "other
Indians, Kalispelim, Kooteneys, and Pend d'Oreilles" would soon be arrayed
against them.

Now the hostiles could rest at long last, and resupply in the Bitterroot before resuming their weary journey. Shortly after Rawn was bypassed, a Flathead delegation called upon the triumphant hostiles. The Nez Percé Chief
Yellow Bull in a later reminiscence laconically describes their visit: "a camp
of Flatheads came to us and talked." They probably spelled out again their

40. Besides the standard accounts such as Haines, Bancroft, McWhorter (incl.
treason), and Howard and McGrath (esp. pp. 198, 195, for late conference with Flatheads), see D'Aste account on the Rawn episode; Ravalli Papers, St. Mary's mission
chronology; Rawn to *Teller* of 4 August 1877; Bishop O'Connor talk with Captain
Logan, *RACHS*, 3, 110; and the materials in Rothermich, *Frontier and Midland, 16.*
NA, EW, consol. file (AGO), and IA, Montana Sup., has informative official correspondence. Official reports sometimes differ in detail: Howard and McGrath, *War
Chief Joseph*, gives Rawn 25 men, Sherman 40, Gibbon 32, Rawn himself 30.

implacable determination to ensure a peaceful passage by the Nez Percés.[41]

From the very late reminiscences of Nez Percé braves can any light be thrown on this moment in their war? Unfortunately, the Indians who survived thirty years or more after the Nez Percé War already had memories distorted by half a lifetime of defeats and shocks. Feuds within and without the tribe had given way to the neurotically factional mentality of the reservation Indian. Romanticizing by later Whites was also well developed, with its impact upon the Nez Percé's image of himself. The aging warriors seem therefore to have clung to a substantial outline history of their war, the picture of a peaceful people who wished in 1877 merely to pass by in quiet dignity, a great people, master of its fate, contriving its epic passage without much relation to neighboring tribes.

They seem indisposed to dwell on the Bitterroot episode. They do not deny the elements of the story given here. They simply diminish or forget them, a normal reaction to less pleasant circumstances. Thus one informant contents himself with saying of the Bitterroot Flatheads: "we had no help from any of them during the war." A Nez Percé chief protests: "it is all a lie about them helping us in any way"; he rightly dismisses as untrue the story that a Flathead war dance frightened the Nez Percés from attacking the Whites. One laconic but very significant admission comes from this same chief: the Flatheads "did try to keep us from further fighting."

The Bitterroot settlers were now in "the greatest excitement." Numbers believed that the Flatheads had at last broken out. "The Father to avoid any imprudent move on either side," says D'Aste, "told the Indians to come to camp around the Mission and thus take away any pretext on the part of the whites to suspect them." The St. Mary's house diary tells how "all the Indians and half-breed[s] gathered together by the Mission." It also repeats some of the confused news apparently being brought back by the absconding volunteers. The diary notes that the Nez Percés had gone into camp near "Rob Carleton's place."

The Nez Percés lay at the northern end of the Bitterroot Valley. They had to make a final, agonized decision: should they go out of the Bitterroot directly north through the confederate lands—either into Canada only 240 miles away or out onto the Plains by the Kutenai trail? These were the easiest and most secure routes open to them, devoid of settlements and very difficult for an army. Directly east was the Hell Gate passage onto the Plains; but a large settlement stood here—as well as the troublesome little force of Rawn, the hostile Blackfeet beyond, and inevitably more soldiers. They might also

41. McWhorter, *Hear Me, My Chiefs*, p. 353. D'Aste, "Nez Percé War." NA, EW, consol. file, Mills telegram, 29 July. Curtis, *North American Indian, 8*, 166 (Yellow Bull).

go south through the frightened, more scattered settlers. In that direction they could either double back to the Salmon River and the Snake country or else go over the mountains east toward the country of the friendly Crows. Many, perhaps most, simply wanted to reach the buffalo herds, believing pursuit was outdistanced.

What was the Flathead preference in all this? McWhorter, though dependent upon very late reminiscences by Nez Percé veterans, came fairly close to stating it. "There is strong evidence that before leaving Idaho the Nez Percés had assurance from the Bitterroot Selish of safe-conduct through their domain and, even more, that runners would pilot them to the buffalo country over trails unknown to the Whites and free of soldiers; the refugees bitterly realized the false nature of this pledge when they reached the outlet of the Lolo Pass." The ethnologist Teit collected some earlier reminiscences from Salish informants. These, too, explain the circuitous southern route as resulting from a failure to win allies, despite their efforts to do so. Joseph should have "from the beginning gone straight north" through the Coeur d'Alene lands, said these Salish, and then either to the west or east of the Rockies; in this way "he could easily have escaped to the Canadian side." The Nez Percés went east and then south by east because they expected "some of the Flathead, Shoshoni [Snakes], and Crow would join" as allies.

McWhorter's informants tell us the hostiles had now come to mistrust the intentions of the confederates. Looking Glass, who wished to go to the Crow country, argued that the Lolo incident showed the confederates to be on the side of the Whites. He warned that in going north the Nez Percés might have to fight their way through the St. Ignatius country. He and his adherents won over the other Indians in this critical first conference in the Bitterroot. Next morning the Nez Percé band turned south. Looking Glass was now their dominant war leader, a *primus inter pares* of the chiefs.[42]

That same morning of July 29, halfway along the valley at St. Mary's mission, the Flatheads who had assembled the previous day were still waiting. "After a short and early service in the church," the body of the tribe disposed themselves to observe and control the passage. The citizens of nearby Stevensville were naturally disturbed. They were almost defenseless. "Some prominent citizens," D'Aste records, "came to the Father's house, and had a talk with the leading Indians, consulting together about the plan it would be more prudent to follow; again Charlo spoke in the same way as he did before."

During this meeting or council, while Charlo was advising the Whites, a

42. McWhorter, *Hear Me, My Chiefs*, pp. 353, 358 n.; Teit, BAE *Annual Report, 45*, 372–73. Ravalli Papers, St. Mary's chronology.

Flathead runner came in. This was Pierish, really a Nez Percé chief residing with the Flatheads. In a few days General Gibbon would highhandedly arrest and imprison Pierish at Stevensville, presumably for collaboration. The chief was now carrying a message from the hostiles. "On the part of the Nez Percés chiefs," says D'Aste, he "invited Charlot to visit them." The Flathead chief, "true to his character, answered proudly: that he had nothing to say to those chiefs, that he was sorry they had not minded him when he told them the way to go to Buffalo by the Kooteneys country which was almost unsettled by whites, and not to come to Bitter Root, causing trouble between Indians and whites; and now he wanted them to pass through the valley as fast as possible." Charlo added "that it was more wise for the hostiles to come up by the West side of the river, where there were then only a few settlers."

Once again the Flathead chief delivered his warning. "I heard that the Nez Percés called and killed some of their friends in Idaho; tell them that we will be watching them, ready to protect ourselves in case of any wrong done by their people." That account was committed to writing somewhat later; the house diary of the mission says only that "Charlot went to meet them with his men armed and ordered them to come by the other side." Perhaps this meeting occurred after Charlo's rhetorical address.

The Nez Percés did stay on the west side of the river, which was running very high.[43] But a "good many of the Nez Percés rode well armed to Stevensville" on July 30 and 31 to buy provisions. Mission business seems to have gone on much as usual; on July 29, for example, Father D'Aste joined the Indians Martin and Mary in marriage.

It would have been at this time that the dramatic confrontation took place between Charlo and his Nez Percé friend Looking Glass. Charlo had already refused "an interview" to Joseph. Now the war chief Looking Glass (Wind Storm, to the Indians) came up to the mission with a very large body of braves. He was six feet tall, a strong man about 45 years old, with a wide, flat face; brass rings hung from his ears, feathers from his hair, and a tin mirror from his scalplock. He found the Flatheads drawn up about the mission stoically, their guns conspicuously in view. The Nez Percé, who as principal war leader currently held the destinies of the tribe, approached the silent Charlo and proffered his hand in friendly greeting. It was a cruel moment. The Flathead chief rebuffed the gesture of friendship. The occasion, solemn and formal, called for a strong demonstration of the neutrality he had proclaimed. "My hand is clean," he told Looking Glass, "and I cannot extend it

43. D'Aste. Ravalli Papers, St. Mary's chronology. Gibbon in *HED* (serial 1794), p. 549.

to hands stained with the blood of white people: we have always been friends, but not in this circumstance." This was Charlo's last sight of his friend. Looking Glass later fell in battle.[44]

The Nez Percés showed no disposition to hurry through the valley. They realized that here they were safe for a while. After purchasing what they needed from the storekeepers, they chatted with some of the settlers. It was a time for resting, traveling with prudent slowness, and storing up strength. Their activities were extraordinarily law-abiding. Within two days they paid more than a thousand dollars in cash for their purchases. Yet the situation was not without danger. Buffalo Indians were not easily restrained, nor very susceptible to any kind of tribal discipline. Irresponsible or drunken Nez Percés could still cause trouble if not very closely watched.

On the second day of enthusiastic trading such trouble seemed imminent. "Some unprincipled men sold the Indians whiskey," Father D'Aste says; "there were about 15 of them drunk." Each of these Nez Percés, armed, exhilarated, and released from his inhibitions, was like a spark flying about in a powder magazine. Had some quarrel led to shooting, D'Aste comments, "a good many people" might have died. Considering the Flathead warnings and commitment, the Nez Percé leaders could not tolerate such an eventuality. "Fortunately one or two of the chiefs drove the drunken people to their camp across the river," so the peace was not broken. Looking Glass himself seems to have been one of these chiefs.

Flathead observers were also on the scene. These were probably, as in the Coeur d'Alene situation, members of the honored Soldiers band. One crisis was settled by "an old warrior" of the tribe. The Jesuits pointed him out, six years after the war, to the congressional investigators, Senator Vest and Representative Maginnis. They explained how he "had drawn his revolver and protected the wife of the blacksmith at Stevensville from outrage at the hands of the Nez Percés."

Minor disorders, thievery and destruction here and there, could not be entirely prevented. A Methodist minister, the Reverend W. A. Hall, describes some of this in a letter printed on August 17 in the *Weekly Missoulian*. "Mr. Landrum's house was pillaged about $5 worth, and several houses were broken into above this place." At Joe Blodgett's place, the Reverend Mr. Hall adds, "household goods and a large quantity of provisions were stolen, his

44. D'Aste; OJ, codex, "Liber matrimoniorum in missione S. Mariae Selicorum ab anno 1866 ad annum 1894," pp. 41–42. The Looking Glass visit is told by several Jesuits, esp. in Cataldo, "Sketch on the Nez Percé Indians," p. 75 (quot.), Joset Papers, Joset letter to Epewa, summer 1877 (Joset assumed the leader was Joseph); and Palladino, *Indian and White*, pp. 65, 349. See also the Joset account of it written 12 October 1877 and published in *Die katholischen Missionen*, 6 (1878), 43. The chief was the son of old Chief Looking Glass of the 1855 Walla Walla Council.

harness cut all to pieces and about fifteen head of horses taken; Alex Stewart had several head of cattle shot by the invaders." In two other cases a false impression was conveyed by buffalo Nez Percés who reclaimed materials previously cached.[45]

Farther south in the valley at Corvallis, where the women and children were shut up in a sod fort, the Nez Percés displayed childish pleasure at the fright they were causing. They seemed to feel that it compensated for the discomfiture they had suffered while cut off in the Lolo canyon. They were angry at the refusal to trade here and threatened to burn down the storekeeper's house. "Although some of the more desperate ones urged extreme measures," says General Gibbon, who arrived soon after, "they were dissuaded by the more moderate."

The only malicious damage of any seriousness occurred in the last home at the very end of the valley, as the invaders were leaving. Some later historians have minimized this as trivial. In the light of what has already been seen, however, the affair sheds further light on Flathead–Nez Percé relations. Hall's letter says simply that "M. M. Lockwood's house was broken open and everything demolished except the stove." Gibbon, who reached the scene just after the Indians had left, describes it more closely. He found the house "a perfect wreck." Trunks were broken, "furniture, crockery, and everything perishable" was smashed and strewn about.

He particularly comments on the vindictive nature of the damage. And he remarks, significantly: "the Indians appear to have been kept under pretty good control whilst in the lower valley"; he thinks that the last of the departing Indians could not resist this final outburst to show their true feelings. Nez Percé survivors in Canada after the war blamed the episode upon the disorderly band of Chief Toohoolhoolzote. They recalled that Chief Looking Glass was angry upon learning of it and made the pillagers leave three horses at the place as payment. Father Palladino records that the isolated house lay beyond the area kept under surveillance by Flathead braves. The Bitterroot had been kept safe.[46]

The peaceful passage of the Nez Percés was so extraordinary that, as memory of events faded or was contained locally, Joseph's people received sole credit for the achievement. The legend of the chivalrous Nez Percés flourished, as had so many legends among Whites or even among ex-combatant Indians after the 1858 war. The Nez Percés should be honored

---

45. D'Aste; cf. *Teller*, 18, 25 August 1877. P. Ronan, *Flathead Nation*, p. 65 (blacksmith wife), drawing also on report of congressional delegates; Palladino, p. 349. Hall letter, *Missoulian*, 17 August 1877. McWhorter, *Hear Me, My Chiefs*, p. 360. Cf. Beal, "*I Will Fight No More Forever*," pp. 105–06.

46. Gibbon, *American Catholic Quarterly Review*, 4, 326–28; Hall letter, *Missoulian*, 17 August. McWhorter, *Hear Me, My Chiefs*, p. 361; Palladino, p. 350.

for their restraint. But this did not derive from gratuitous good will alone. Perhaps the hostiles might have spared Rawn's little force anyway. Then again, perhaps they might have destroyed Rawn and vented their displeasure in the valley. Nothing in Indian character, or in the Idaho phase of the war, or in the warriors' mode of action after leaving the Bitterroot, rules out such violence. However, one factor made a peaceful passage through the valley imperative, whatever the sentiments of chivalry also present: the stubborn attitude of conditional neutrality on the part of the 2,000 Flathead confederates.

Agent Ronan proudly reported to Washington how Charlo "called all his men around him and warned the Nez Percés that if an outrage against the whites or a theft was committed by them in the Bitter Root Valley, that he would immediately fall upon them with his warriors; Joseph's band heeded Charlo's warning and not a single outrage was committed." Both in the valley and outside, newspapers hailed the Flatheads for having "told the hostiles that if they turned loose around here, that they the Flatheads would fight with the whites, not otherwise." A few years after the war Senator Vest's report similarly praised the Flatheads.

The Bitterroot citizens showed their gratitude openly. Just after the passage of the Nez Percés, they prepared a huge feast for the Flatheads to be held on August 7. Citizens contributed beef, sugar, flour, and other substantial offerings. This was meant "as a mark of appreciation for their fidelity and friendship to the whites, notwithstanding the unkind way they had been treated by them, previous [to] the coming of the hostile[s]."

The Whites recognized also that Jesuit influence lay behind the Flathead attitude. "Thanks to the activity of the chiefs, to the religious and moral influence of the fathers in charge of St. Ignatius and St. Mary's missions, and to the good sense of the Indians themselves," Agent Ronan says in another report, "the white settlers of the Bitter Root Valley owe their preservation of life and property." As to the problem of young Flathead warriors wanting to join their Nez Percé friends: "I am firmly of the opinion, that if it was not for the activity displayed by the chiefs, head men and Jesuit Fathers at the Missions of St. Ignatius and St. Mary['s] it would be a matter of impossibility to restrain some of the wild and thoughtless youths of the tribes." [47]

GENERAL GIBBON AND THE JESUITS: THE FINAL SCENE

Where had the army been during all these alarums? General John Gibbon was busily concentrating men from scattered posts into a rendezvous at Fort

47. Quotes from NA, IA, Montana Sup., Ronan to commissioner, 1 October 1877; *Teller*, 25 August 1877; D'Aste; cf. Ravalli Papers, St. Mary's chronology, under 7 August. *RCIA* (1877), Ronan report of 13 August, and Ronan report excerpt in NA, EW, consol. file, 25 August, from sec. Interior to sec. War.

Shaw. Gibbon, whose spare, soldierly face displayed a fashionable Napoleon III goatee-cum-mustache, was an experienced commander. He had served in the ancient Seminole wars and in the older West, and then taught for five years at West Point. Later he won fame as general of the Iron Brigade in the Civil War. He was division commander through the heavy fighting of the Wilderness, corps commander in the final operations against Lee, and a commissioner for Lee's surrender. Scarred by two wounds and rich in reputation, Gibbon came West again to serve as colonel in the last great Indian wars. Commander of all the garrisons in Montana Territory, his best efforts still could not muster a force much larger than that which Perry had led to disaster in the first battle of the Nez Percé War.

General Howard was still toiling over the Lolo trail, to an orchestration of jeers from newspapermen throughout the country. General Sherman, stung, defended his subordinates. "Our little army is overworked" and doing as well as can be expected. Divisional headquarters at San Francisco also lost patience with "the abuse from the hounds and whores of the press." Sherman prodded Howard by telegram and received a snappish reply. General Wheaton, meanwhile, was taking his army up through the Coeur d'Alene country. Sherman did his patient best not to interfere with the field commanders. "Too many heads," he confided to the secretary of War, "are worse than *one*." By a bizarre turn of circumstance Sherman and his party, sightseeing in Yellowstone Park, narrowly missed contact with the hostiles and possible capture.[48]

On July 28, the day Rawn failed to stop the Nez Percés at Fort Fizzle, Gibbon was able to lead an inadequate little column of seventy-six infantry under seven officers out of Fort Shaw toward Missoula, 150 miles distant over the mountains. Troubles, especially with heavily packed mules, kept them from progressing more than twenty-five miles the first two days. Picking up reinforcements and some cavalry as they went, they reached Missoula late on the afternoon of August 3. Far from being able to intercept the hostiles, Gibbon found them long gone to the south, out of the valley. His own men became now, like Howard's, a pursuit force. Gibbon added Captain Rawn's unit to his own, as well as a few citizen volunteers.

His first preoccupation, however, was to secure Flathead help. "Immediately on my arrival I sent a messenger to Charlot inviting him to come and see me." Next morning the chief came in. He conferred with the General through an interpreter. Gibbon demanded that the Flatheads single out Nez Percé spies in the valley and seize them. But Charlo, whom the general describes as a "quiet, pleasant-faced Indian" of few words, spoke "to the point." He and his people were neutral. He "firmly declined to do what I wished."

48. R. G. Athearn, *William Tecumseh Sherman and the Settlement of the West* (Norman, Okla., 1956), pp. 317–18. D'Aste; Ravalli Papers, St. Mary's chronology.

Father D'Aste explains that Charlo refused precisely on the grounds that the hostile Nez Percés had kept their part of the bargain. The chief even told Gibbon "he thought it would not be right for him to give scouts." In reporting this incident, the journalists at the Lewiston *Teller* managed to confuse the issue: "Charlos declines to lend his warriors to Gen[eral] Gibbon, and will fight the Nez Percés on his own account."

Gibbon now had a total force of about 160 regulars. Even this was gathered, he complains in his report, only by "stripping every post in the district [of Montana] to the very lowest point compatible with the care of public property." By a forced march on August 4, his troops pushed south twenty-five miles along the valley to Stevensville, reaching there in the dark. On the way the General noted Fort Owen, "a stockade, inside of which were huddled a promiscuous crowd of men, women, and children, who in fear and trembling had sought safety there from anticipated hostilities." Preceding the troops into Stevensville, Gibbon immediately had himself guided out to St. Mary's mission. "I was hospitably received by the priest in charge, and sat in his room till the arrival of the command." He especially desired to see Father Ravalli, "having heard so much of him." [49]

The General was brought into the sick priest's tiny room. "Here, propped up in bed, and *reading medicine* by the light of a dim lamp, was a charming old Frenchman, who with a skullcap on his head and a pair of glasses on his nose, received me with all the cordiality of a past age." Gibbon found himself "much attracted by the charms of his conversation, and sat talking to him for some time" as the night wore on. When Gibbon asked him if he were not tired of the life after thirty-five years with the Interior tribes, Ravalli replied that it was his ambition to stay here until he could lay his bones among the Indians. Gibbon with grim humor reflected that, in quite another way, he himself might soon be laying his bones among the Indians.

But the General had not come for philosophical interchanges. The amenities over, he began to inquire about more practical matters. Ravalli was by no means isolated in his room; he managed an intensely active life in it as physician, adviser, and spiritual guide—a phenomenon Senator Vest would comment upon during his stay at St. Mary's six years later. The Jesuit was able to furnish Gibbon "a great deal of information in regard to the Nez Percés, who had remained in this vicinity for some days." Many of them were buffalo hunters, so the priest was long familiar with their strength and capacities.

"How many troops" did the General have, asked Ravalli? Gibbon instinctively concealed the weakness of his force: "about 200." "Ah," said the old

49. D'Aste; Gibbon, *American Catholic Quarterly Review*, 4, 323–24; Gibbon Report, 18 October, *HED* (serial 1794), pp. 522–23; *Teller*, 18 August 1877.

man, "you *must* not attack them, you have not enough." He pointed out: "they are splendid shots, are well armed, have plenty of ammunition, and have at least two hundred and sixty warriors." To his chagrin, Gibbon soon discovered this was true. During the coming battle he was to note particularly that "with very few exceptions the command did not contain any such marksmen as these Nez Percés." The General incorporated Father Ravalli's information into his report of September 2, as the "best estimate of their strength." He gives this generically as deriving from Bitterroot inhabitants, but uses the priest's words.

The Nez Percé hostiles had traveled some distance to the east and south of the Bitterroot. They were still deep in the tumble of Rocky Mountain ranges, traveling slowly at some twelve miles a day, apparently feeling fairly secure. Gibbon pushed after them as fast as he could, frustrated because haste was of the utmost importance; he was "utterly unable to make *any* thing move faster than a sloth" in this rugged region. Mountain succeeded mountain, each one seeming higher than the last. Gibbon had to contend with loose, shifting trail beds and with badly choked timber areas. He describes in awe how

> the heavily-wooded mountain peaks towered one above the other, culminating in one whose rocky gorges, bare of timber, were filled with immense glaciers, the smooth glassy surfaces of which glistened in the rays of the setting sun, presenting to the eye an arctic scene in strong contrast with that which immediately surrounded us; on one side of us, stretching eastward as far as the eye could reach, was one continuous mass of timbered hills, with one isolated bare peak rising above the whole.

The General caught up with the Nez Percés at Big Hole basin. This was a lovely, crescent-shaped valley sixty miles long, nearly 7,000 feet up in the mountains. In an open meadow by the Big Hole stream the Indians had settled down for a lengthy stay, apparently intending to rest well and prepare an impressive entrance into the Crow country. Gibbon disposed his forces, crept up on their camp, and in the chill of dawn made his sudden charge. In this attack he had every advantage, including surprise. After an initial melee, however, devastating counterfire halted the troops. A nightmare battle developed in the village, five hours of no-quarter fighting during which nearly half the White officers were killed or wounded. Finally the warriors forced the soldiers to withdraw from the village to a small pine woods. Here Gibbon found himself encircled and penned in, somewhat after the fashion of his predecessors Steptoe, Haller, and Custer.

He was cut off from his pack train, ammunition, medical supplies, artillery, and water. "To retreat was out of the question," he writes; "*there was no place to retreat to.*" The officers did their best to restrain the men from panicky firing, so as to conserve ammunition. Log breastworks swiftly went up and trenches were dug. But the Indians had sustained too much punishment in the first shock of battle. They did not charge the position. All day long they kept the troops pinned down with accurate rifle fire, occasionally hitting a soldier imprudent enough to show himself. The body of the tribe meanwhile extricated itself and made off. Gibbon could do nothing at all for his wounded. A moment of desperation for the troops came when the Indians sent fire sweeping over the grass toward the dry brush and timber of their refuge. Luckily the wind died before the sparse grass could carry the flames all the way.

That night the soldiers shivered in the mountain cold, not daring to build a fire, expecting a final and overwhelming rush by the Indians at dawn. A number of citizen volunteers managed to sneak out quietly and run away. Gibbon himself sent two hardier civilians into the dark and through the Indian lines with a plea for help. Unhappily his messages both to General Terry and to Governor Potts ultimately went by telegraph to the Governor alone, giving rise to the impression that they were not authentic; the newspapers compounded the confusion by predating their version a week.

Near midnight the Nez Percé rear guard, having sent their noncombatants a good distance away, were ready to break off battle to join the fleeing tribe. The Whites were in no condition to follow next morning. Couriers from General Howard made contact that day, and by sundown Gibbon's own pack train came in. The little army had improvised a meal of horse-meat and buried its dead. Casualties amounted to 40 per cent of the command, including General Gibbon; 31 officers and men died in the brief battle and 43 were wounded. From Indian bodies the Whites estimated enemy losses at 89; probably most of these were noncombatants killed in the first rush.

General Phil Sheridan was appalled at the carnage. As head of the Division of the Missouri (containing Terry's department and therefore Gibbon's district), he was familiar enough with the Sioux and Cheyenne wars; but he characterized the Big Hole battle in his 1877 report as "one of the most desperate engagements on record." The Congressional Medal of Honor, the nation's highest military decoration, was awarded to no less than seven men for their individual gallantry in this battle.[50]

50. Gibbon, *Catholic Quarterly*, 4, 324–25, 329–30, 337, 339. See Gibbon Report, *HED* (serial 1794), pp. 68–71 (2 September), 501–05, 520–23 (18 October); Sheridan Report, *HED* (serial 1794), p. 57. Indian reminiscence in Curtis, *North American Indian*, 8, 167, gives 74 killed, 33 of them men (cf. McWhorter informants, in *Hear Me, My Chiefs*, passim). Beal devotes a chapter to casualties and general evaluations of the battle; he has 29 regulars dead and 40 wounded, plus 5 civilians dead and 4 wounded; of the Indians perhaps 30 were men, including a dozen good warriors ("*I Will Fight No More Forever*," chap. 12).

At this point the Jesuits, in the person of Father Palladino, reappear briefly. Howard had combined with fifty of Gibbon's survivors to continue on for the next stage of the pursuit. The wounded, including Gibbon, were loaded onto springless wagons to be trundled off to Deer Lodge, some ninety miles of rough roadless prairie distant. "The horrors of that march for those having wounds cannot easily be imagined"; the Indians seem to have used "a flat nosed explosive bullet in their Winchesters which made a frightful wound." After twelve or fifteen miles of such travel, "our hearts were gladdened by the appearance of a great crowd of ambulances, wagons, buggies, etc., loaded with all sorts of necessities and luxuries," sent out by the people of Deer Lodge, Butte, and Helena.

The pastor at Helena was the Jesuit Lawrence Palladino, a naïve but open-hearted man who had served from 1867 to 1873 as missionary at the upper Flathead mission. Within an hour of hearing Gibbon's call for help on August 11 he and two hospital nuns, Sister Benedicta and Sister Mary Liguori, "were on their way to the battlefield." A citizen's relief committee supplied transportation; an army major acted as escort. They were not the only party to meet Gibbon's shattered command but they could offer organized professional aid. There were Catholic hospitals conducted by nuns at Missoula, Helena, and Deer Lodge. Gibbon was "highly pleased" to find such help at hand. Preparations were made for moving the wounded to St. Joseph's hospital at Deer Lodge.

Father Palladino had seen "the horrors of war on a much larger scale indeed" at the terrible battle of Solferino in Italy in 1859, where over 27,000 men were killed or wounded. But he felt that Gibbon's wounded had gone through a special suffering of their own "here in the wilderness, amid bleak prairies and desolate woods, a hundred and more miles away from civilization," without adequate medical attention.

The hospital Sisters from Helena came over to assist those at the Deer Lodge hospital. Two diocesan priests also served in the town, Father Remigius De Ryckere and his assistant Father Andrew Poulin. The latter was an "enormously large" Canadian weighing nearly 300 pounds—but an agile administrator withal, and a cool head in emergencies. He tells in a letter of August 15 how "we are expecting the wounded Friday at the hospital." [51]

General Sherman visited the wounded about two weeks after their arrival. He describes Deer Lodge as "quite a pretty little town" in the middle of a

51. Gibbon, pp. 343–44 (trip). NYPL, Indian file, Homer Coon Recollections (bullet). Palladino, *Indian and White*, pp. 350–52 (aid quots.). Poulin Papers (PA), folder 1, No. 110, to archbishop, 15 August 1877; there is a biography of Poulin in Bradley-Kelly, *Boise Diocese*, chap. 4. On Palladino (1837–1927) see *DAB*; also biog. in Bischoff, *Jesuits*, p. 228. On wounded see also Howard's surgeon in Fitzgerald, *Army Wife's Letters*, p. 304.

valley. "On the edge of the town, upon the plateau, is a good stone Catholic church, with a hospital behind; this is a good two-story frame house, well arranged, clean, and well furnished; indeed, as good a hospital as can be found anywhere, in charge of six Sisters of Charity." Sherman talked to each of the patients, to satisfy himself that they were properly cared for. The General's aide, Colonel Orlando Metcalfe Poe (himself a distinguished general in Sherman's Civil War army), recounts how "the most seriously wounded" had been brought to the hospital, to be given "kindly care and attention" by the nuns and the two doctors there. "Most of the wounds were severe."

At this time Palladino "heard it said by General Gibbon himself, and several others of his command, that if the Indians had followed up the advantage which they gained in the beginning of the bloody struggle, his whole force would have been annihilated, just as the year previously Custer's command had been wiped out by the Sioux." [52]

The Nez Percés meanwhile continued their anabasis, proceeding tenaciously south to the battle of Camas Meadows, then west and north to the battle of Canyon Creek, and finally due north to the final battle of Bear Paw Mountain and the pathetic surrender on October 5, just short of the Canadian line. After they had passed out of Flathead territory, they again began to loot, steal stock, and even murder. Reminiscing at a much later date, some Nez Percés explained this conduct as an aftermath of the Big Hole battle, which was fought in Flathead country: the Nez Percés considered the presence of civilian volunteers from the Bitterroot at the Big Hole battle a betrayal. [53]

General Samuel Sturgis set a trap in the upper Yellowstone, ironically enough with the reorganized Seventh Cavalry of the dead Custer. Sturgis was a veteran of the Mexican War, the Indian wars of the '50s and (as a general) the Civil War. After having engaged the Plains tribes during his postwar service in the active rank of colonel, he could hardly have anticipated any difficulty in stopping the Nez Percé band. But the latter cleverly bypassed him. Sturgis had to add his 300 men and their Crow allies to the army units chasing Joseph from the rear.

Still another force of 600 soldiers from Fort Keogh, with Cheyenne auxiliaries, were converging on the hostiles. These were led by the impetuous Nelson Miles, a Civil War brevet general and holder of the Medal of Honor for bravery. As a colonel again, he had recently distinguished himself in Plains warfare. He was to rise once more to be general, and commander of all

52. *Reports of Inspection*, pp. 42, 87–88. Palladino, *Indian and White* (1922 ed.), p. 411; quoted more briefly in 1st edn., p. 350. Beal, *"I Will Fight No More Forever,"* pp. 131–34, on the individual injuries being treated.

53. McWhorter informants, in *Hear Me, My Chiefs*, p. 407

the American armies at the time of the Spanish-American War. Miles, determined to win glory by capturing Joseph, made an historic forced march of 160 miles to intercept the hostiles. All he really managed to do, however, was hold them for the final battles. In his own first assault on the Nez Percé village, despite the advantage of surprise, Miles lost twenty-four soldiers killed and forty-two wounded. Finally, on October 4, in cold and snowy weather, Joseph surrendered to the combined White forces on generous terms. The terms went unhonored.

The war had involved three separate military divisions. It drew troops from Alaska to Arizona. It challenged the talents of nine excellent Civil War generals, five of them taking armies into the field. Howard's own army had pursued the Nez Percés for 75 days, over 1,500 miles. For every Indian engaged, the Whites spent over a thousand dollars. They met the motley little band in eighteen major and minor battles. Of the thousands of soldiers involved, 127 were killed and 147 wounded; 50 civilians died. Of the Nez Percés, 151 braves and civilians fell; 88 more were wounded. Perhaps a hundred escaped into Canada or into the hands of inimical Blackfeet. In November 1877 the 400 surviving hostiles—men, women, and children—were hustled off to Fort Leavenworth in Kansas, on their way to exile in Oklahoma.

The Whites with unconscious arrogance soon decided they had faced a military genius, a "Red Napoleon." Howard, Miles, Shields, and even Sherman wrote in this admiring vein. We now know that Joseph was not a war chief or warrior; he was a peace chief and civilian leader, though he could also fight on occasion. The Nez Percé achievement upon close analysis proves to be a communal thing: the traditional loose union of war chiefs, employing the traditional guerrilla tactics of the buffalo-hunting Interior tribes. A similar band of buffalo Okanogans, Kutenais, Coeur d'Alenes, or Flatheads, operating in the same country in 1877 and with similar goals, would have given a like account of themselves.

For all its romance and for all the damage it caused, the Nez Percé trouble was not a full-fledged war. A modern historian correctly characterizes it as only a "desperate and unreasonable, though brilliant," adventure, "akin to such episodes as that of Geronimo." The real war had been the 1858 rising, "intrinsically more important than the better known outbreak of Chief Joseph"; 1858 had been "an effort to stay the white advance of like nature with the efforts of Pontiac, Tecumseh, and Black Horse." As the Jesuits and their tribes helped extinguish a war in 1858, so they helped channel and contain a potential war among the many Northwest tribes in 1877.[54]

Now the army was fully determined to fetter the troublesome upper Inte-

54. Trimble, *Mining Advance*, p. 37 n. (quot.); Kip, *Expedition*, p. 92, also cites the parallel of Tecumseh. See also Merle Wells, "Nez Percés and their War," *PNWQ*, *55*,

rior. Fort Coeur d'Alene went up at the head of Coeur d'Alene Lake, on the traditional land of the Coeur d'Alene head chief. Sherman himself chose it for its strategic advantages. It stood, his report says, in "the heart of the wilderness"; at the same time it was "the most delightful site for a military post that heart can desire." Seven years after the war, the army's Fort Colville moved south to the junction of the Columbia and Spokane rivers. Renamed Fort Spokane, it was strategically situated near the borders of several tribes— Kettles, San Poils, Columbias, and Western Spokanes. More significantly, the new departmental commander, General Nelson Miles, shifted the whole military center of gravity toward the upper Interior. "Forts Walla Walla, Spokane, and Coeur d'Alene have been made the principal posts of this department, where troops are stationed for immediate use in the sections of the country most liable to Indian hostility." Fort Vancouver diminished in importance, functioning as a reserve depot.

At last Major Garnett's vision of 1858 was a reality: a chain of military forts across the mountainous upper Interior, beginning near Colville and ending at Missoula, drawing support from the posts like Walla Walla, Lapwai, and Boise. In Montana the scare of 1876–77 also led to a demand for garrisons; four large forts, including Fort Missoula, went up in the strategic heartland of the Montana tribes. In 1877 Sherman ordered Fort Missoula itself enlarged to four times its original capacity.[55]

POSTSCRIPT TO A WAR

The heart of Father Cataldo followed his Nez Percés. As superior-general of the missions he offered the Jesuit services for the remote Indian Territory exile. Ecclesiastical authorities thought it best to refuse. Many of Joseph's band on their bleak wasteland "were in a brief period stricken down with disease, and died outside the pale of the Church." Survivors were eventually allowed to return to the Northwest; but out of fear of legal prosecution and private vengeance in Idaho they were settled on the Colville reservation in Washington.

"Some of the warriors returned unobserved," Father Cataldo says, "to their own folks and land." The majority of Nez Percés, who had no part in the war, were nevertheless profoundly shaken by it. "Those poor people were so irritated against the whites," Cataldo adds, "that they hated any-

(1964), 35–37, which, however, rather overstates the thesis of the Nez Percé movement as a migration rather than a war.

55. *Reports of Inspection*, pp. 95–96. Sherman report (through aide, General Tidball) on Northwest journey, 27 October 1883, in Fields, *National Guard*, 4, 325; Miles report, 2 October 1884, ibid., p. 324. Terry report, 12 November 1877, HED (serial 1794), p. 518.

thing coming from the whites, even religion." As a result "all our hopes of converting the whole tribe were shattered," though "some few were converted."

A postscript comes from the private journal of a Jesuit residing in the Midwest, two years after the war. In 1879 Father Paul Ponziglione of the Missouri Jesuits visited the Nez Percés on the arid Indian Territory by the Arkansas River. Ponziglione, a wiry little man, fearless and optimistic, was the son of an Italian count. While a teacher at the Jesuit college of Genoa in 1848 he had been arrested and abused by Sardinian revolutionists. He knew what it meant to be thrust into exile. Ponziglione worked as a missionary among the Osages and other tribes. His missionary circuit included bands of Catholic Chippewas, Foxes, and Kaws. The Arapahoes and Cheyennes held him in high esteem. In 1879 he was visiting the numerous Catholic Poncas on their reservation some fifteen miles east of Joseph's band.

In his subsequent conversations with the exiled Nez Percés, Ponziglione received the exaggerated impression that, before the war, the whole band had determined to become Catholics. This probably reflects their innate courtesy, as well as their respect for the Blackrobes. It may also reflect the hopes entertained by Cataldo. But now the few active Catholics among them, apparently the same women spoken of by Cataldo, were fearful of demonstrating any sympathy for the White man. "The few that are Catholic are so timid that they do not dare show themselves for what they are; if you ask them whether they are Roman Catholics, first they may answer yes, then after a while if you ask them the same question they will answer no." The significant point is reached when one pins them down to a positive answer. "If you ask them in what religion they believe, they will answer, 'we believe in Cataldo's teaching and that is the only teaching we wish to have.'"

The Jesuit also records an interview he had at this time with Chief Joseph. "Their great Chief Joseph is a very nice man, yet he too is afraid of the Government Agent and when I asked him whether he was a Roman Catholic he replied that he had no religion of any kind." Ponziglione pursued the matter further. "When I asked whether he knew Father Cataldo, 'yes,' he replied, 'Cataldo is my friend, he is a good man, all my people love him, and I would wish very much to see him once more.'"[56]

Back in the Bitterroot the Flathead trials continued. A fearful government refused to add to the confederates' ammunition, pitifully inadequate for the long winter hunt. As Flathead angers rose, Father Van Gorp took Ronan to intercede personally with General Sherman, who was passing through Mis-

56. OJ, Cataldo, "Short Sketch on the Nez Percé Indian Mission," p. 14; "History of the Nez Percé Mission," pp. 10, 104–05. Ponziglione Journal (MJ), quoted in *JMUS*, 2, 562–63; on the exile see J. S. Clark, "Nez Percés in Exile," *PNWQ*, 36 (1945), 213–32.

soula. The commander of the armies, after his talk with this "most intelligent priest," persuaded the War Department to relent. "From personal observation," he reported, "I think the Flathead Indians behaved so well in the Nez Percés war, that we can safely allow them to purchase" ammunition, though only for muzzle loaders.[57]

The Pend d'Oreilles became a little wild immediately after the Nez Percé passage. One Otto Zugbaum, recently returned from Horse Plains to Missoula, reported indignantly that the tribe "have repeatedly threatened to drive all the settlers from Horse Plains; and that they have been unusually insolent of late, killing hogs, pasturing stock in fields, and shooting arrows into stock." Mr. Zugbaum conveyed his own sentiments in a burst of apoplectic prose: "they have a big brave on after the easy passage of the Nez Percés through this part of the country, and will certainly go on the warpath unless these savages are made a frightful example of the fruits of Indian depravity." Charges were eventually entered with the Fort Missoula commandant against the tribe. The Jesuits and Agent Ronan arranged a formal conference between the settlers and Subchief Simon of the Pend d'Oreilles, to be held at Christmas.

But no one really trusted the confederates. Less than a year after the Nez Percé war, Father D'Aste notes in his diary (July 17, 1878): "the Indian excitement is increasing—people are running away again." A band of rogue Nez Percés was on the rampage in Flathead country. Adventurers from stray bands of the Nez Percés, Sioux, and Blackfeet had been raiding out of Canada over the northern plains of Montana. Now a group of fugitive Nez Percés, excited by the Bannock War, were heading south to Snake country. Perhaps, as their leader Yellow Wolf explained in his reminiscences years later, they only wanted to return to their homeland and were betrayed by circumstances into incidental looting and killing. At any rate, they acted badly while passing through Flathead territory. The Flatheads, consistent with the policy they had enunciated the previous summer, actively helped the White pursuers. A patrol of fifteen cavalrymen with Flathead aid chased the marauders for several days, finishing with a battle in which six Nez Percés died and three fell wounded; the pursuit involved a round trip of 450 miles.

In 1878 the Sioux were keeping parts of Montana in turmoil. The great Sitting Bull was still a refugee in Canada, giving hospitality to Nez Percés who had escaped during the last battle of their own war. The Nez Percé saga deeply stirred Sitting Bull. At this time both Canadian and American authori-

57. *Missoulian*, 7 September 1877. *Reports of Inspection*, p. 44. NA, IA, Montana Sup., D'Aste to Ronan, 20 September; Ronan reply, 21 September; Ronan to Delegate Maginnis, 20 September; War Dept. to Interior Dept., quoting Sherman and concurring, 31 October.

ties desired the Sioux chief to return peacefully across the border. He seems to have been preparing for any eventuality by seeking war alliances with Montana tribes. The confederates wanted no part of this. To Sitting Bull's offer, Chief Michael returned the proud answer that from childhood he had known the Sioux only as enemies; if Sitting Bull came near Flathead country, his Pend d'Oreilles would fight. The incident was the occasion for an informal council with the agent on July 14.[58]

Trouble was not always thus contained. In the south another hopeless war broke out in 1878. It involved 1,500 to 2,000 Indians, mostly Bannocks but including hundreds of Snakes and numbers of Umatillas. Though the excitement roused by the Nez Percé revolt was not the real cause of the Bannock War, it was an important condition, or immediate occasion. Out on the Plains that same year, the Cheyennes under Dull Knife staged their pathetic "return" to Montana from the Oklahoma reserve, fighting off the armies which nipped at their flanks, until the Whites closed in with Gatling guns to effect a near annihilation. In 1879 the Utes rose in Colorado. In the 1880s came the Apache troubles, lasting until their exile to Florida. And in 1890, when the Indians attempted to create a hopeful new religion of their own, the Whites drowned it in blood at the Ghost Dance massacre of the Sioux.

But all this was postscript. The real Indian wars were over in 1877. The buffalo were gone. The Indians now receded onto their faction-torn reservations. White men flowed from the east like a prodigious sea in the '80s, submerging the old West. The ubiquitous steel railroad lines, fanning out farther and farther, channeled the flood into the utmost corners. The Indians had no choice; they adapted to the White world or did not survive. At best they could huddle on their reservations, under the eyes of the government agent. Should resistance threaten, there were jails and sheriffs, soldiers and hangmen.

When Sherman passed through Flathead lands again, only six years after the Nez Percé War, he came by railroad. His companions on the train chanced to include Chief Tonasket of the Okanogans and Chief Moses of the Columbias, returning from signing a land agreement in Washington, D.C., and the Catholic bishop. The General's party, like any tourists, visited the colorful Jesuit missions. But a more significant sight was the steamboat plying the waters of Lake Coeur d'Alene, or the bustling city of 3,000 people at Spokane Falls, Jewel City of the Pacific. In a promotional booklet the citizenry here proclaimed itself to be "of a very highly intellectual and moral character,"

58. OJ, D'Aste "Diary, 1878–1880," 17 July 1878; Blades and Wike, *Military Affairs,* 13, 35. *Weekly Missoulian,* 17 August 1877 (Zugbaum). NA, IA, Montana Sup., Ronan to commissioner, 10 December 1877 (Pend d'Oreille council). Phillips, *Battle,* doc. on pp. 19–20 (Sioux proposal); cf. Vestal, *Sitting Bull,* pp. 214–15; Bancroft, *Washington,* p. 718. Beal has a sympathetic account of Yellow Wolf's violent return (*"I Will Fight No More Forever,"* pp. 280–81).

committed to "intellectual culture." Their brochure asks the rhetorical question: "have you any Indians, and are they troublesome?" It returns the reassuring answer: "only a few and they are not troublesome; all of them will soon be removed to reservations remote from us." [59]

On the ride to the Jewel City, the General's party noted a huge pile of bones, still drying naked in the sun from Colonel Wright's horse-slaughter in the 1858 war. It loomed there, a symbol of some murdered body buried deep within the national memory. Under the autumn sky it gleamed whitely like a ghost for an uneasy conscience.

59. *Settlers' Guide*, pp. 58, 63.

BIBLIOGRAPHY

I. ARCHIVES AND MANUSCRIPT COLLECTIONS

A number of promising archives and depositories eventually yielded nothing, and so are not included in this list—for example, the Ludwig-Missionsverein in Munich, the Jesuit holdings in Switzerland, and the headquarters of the adjutant general at the army's Presidio in San Francisco.

UNITED STATES

WASHINGTON, D.C.

BUREAU OF AMERICAN ETHNOLOGY
Especially photographs of Indians, delegations.

BUREAU OF CATHOLIC INDIAN MISSIONS
Correspondence of Northwest mission personnel and agents, including Medary, Giorda, Brouillet, and Cataldo. Nez Percé collection.

LIBRARY OF CONGRESS, MANUSCRIPT DIVISION
General D. M. Gregg Collection, including Joset account. McClellan Papers, including Gibbs Report.

NATIONAL ARCHIVES
Department of the Interior, Bureau of Indian Affairs (record group 75):
1. Letters received, 1830–80. Reports, telegrams, correspondence, forwarded communications, letters of Jesuits, chiefs, soldiers, etc., from Oregon

Superintendency (1842–80), Washington Superintendency (1853–80), Idaho Superintendency (1863–80), Montana Superintendency (1864–80).
2. Letters sent by commissioner.
3. Oregon Superintendency, letters sent and received, financial records, field records, reports, claims, treaty proceedings.
4. Washington Superintendency, same.
5. Idaho Superintendency, same.
6. Montana Superintendency, same.
7. Special Files, Nos. 157, 172, 173.
8. Special Cases.
9. Records, Board of Indian Commissioners, tray 43.
10. Ratified Treaties, 1854–55.
Department of War (Early Wars Branch):
1. Office of the Secretary of War (record group 107), correspondence received and sent.

2. Adjutant General's Office (record group 94). Especially correspondence and reports from every level of command in war. Most of our National Archives war documents come from here, from No. 3, below, or, for 1877, from No. 7, below.
3. U.S. Army Commands (record group 98). The Eleventh military department, or the Pacific and Columbia departments, are especially pertinent, including post reports, quartermaster and arsenal records, letterbooks of Fort Walla Walla and of Fort Vancouver.
4. Quartermaster General, Consolidated File (record group 92), including De Smet accounts.
5. Headquarters of the Army (record group 108). Letters, orders, records, telegrams.
6. Record groups 159 (office of Inspector General), and 77 (Chief of Engineers, Topographical Department).
7. Consolidated File, Nez Percé War. Brings together the manuscripts from the several military departments and sections bearing on this war.

Still Pictures Branch (record group 111). All sketches, photographs, and pictures in any division of the National Archives, including forts, commanders, Indian chiefs.

Cartographic Division. All maps from any division of the National Archives. See especially the two fine maps of the U.S. northwestern boundary survey (filed under 1846 treaty, record group 76); J. Alden sketches; plots of Hudson's Bay claims at Colville, with mission;

tribal and reservation land limits and conflicts.

Department of State, General Records: territorial papers (record group 59).

N.B.: Each of the above divisions is a complex of manuscript collections in itself, requiring much time and patience to peruse. Less important but still occasionally useful are the General Land Office (record group 49), the U.S. Senate Records (record group 46) for ratified treaties and 1877 petitions, and Secretary of the Interior for territorial papers before 1873 (record group 48).

SMITHSONIAN INSTITUTION, NATURAL HISTORY BUILDING
Suckley Papers, especially daily Journal of 1853, notebooks, field books.

BALTIMORE, MD.

MARYLAND HISTORICAL SOCIETY
Archer Collection: weekly letters home, 1856–61, from infantry officer James Archer.

BERKELEY, CAL.

UNIVERSITY OF CALIFORNIA, BANCROFT LIBRARY
Joset account of 1858 war. Rowena Nichols notes on Indian Affairs. Pioneer diaries such as the P. W. Crawford Narrative. Reminiscences such as those of Superintendent Nesmith and Major Haller. Background materials on Interior wars and development. Mullan maps.

BOISE, IDAHO

IDAHO STATE HISTORICAL MUSEUM
Includes Idaho territorial archives and gubernatorial correspondence. Especially useful are the

Nez Percé Agency Letterbooks in 6 volumes, 1871–76, 1880–83. Territorial Executive Papers, especially military records, 1865–76, and Indian Affairs. Military records of the Nez Percé War.

CAMBRIDGE, MASS.

HARVARD UNIVERSITY, HOUGHTON LIBRARY
Archives of the American Board of Commissioners for Foreign Missions, 45 stack sections on deposit. A considerable body of correspondence from and about the Interior missions, especially for the earlier period; no Cowley or Monteith material. Letters and reports of missionaries, with many references to Indians, Catholics, Jesuits by Protestant correspondents.

EUGENE, OREG.

UNIVERSITY OF OREGON, LIBRARY, SPECIAL COLLECTIONS
Croke letters; Cayuse-Yakima-Rogue River War papers; Rev. A. M. McClain notes on Nez Percés; G. W. Jewett papers on same; Umatilla County Library microfilm of Nez Percé agency letterbook, 1871–79. Pioneer diaries and Superintendent Palmer papers are disappointing for our purposes.

HELENA, MONT.

HISTORICAL SOCIETY OF MONTANA
Includes territorial archives and historical society manuscript materials. See especially Hutchins Papers; Statement of Chief Michel, 1875; Samuel Johns collection of historical reminiscences; Owen Papers; newspaper files.

NEW HAVEN, CONN.

YALE UNIVERSITY, LIBRARY, WESTERN AMERICANA ROOM
In Coe and Miller Collections, especially Suckley Papers; Evans 1853 diary; Lansdale larger and smaller diaries; Fort Simcoe daily report book, 1858–59; Fort Dalles post orders, 1856–63. Collection of Governor Stevens Correspondence. Acting Governor Mason Correspondence. Collections of mission correspondence by the Whitmans, Spaldings, Lewes, etc. Owen letters.

NEW YORK, N.Y.

AMERICAN GEOGRAPHICAL SOCIETY
Maps.

MUSEUM OF THE AMERICAN INDIAN, HEYE FOUNDATION
Medallion busts of Head Chiefs Vincent, Seltis.

NEW YORK PUBLIC LIBRARY, MANUSCRIPT DIVISION
U.S. Boundaries, Northwest Boundary Survey, 1857–69: George Gibbs notes on Interior, with McMurtrie-Sohon drawings. Homer Coon recollections (photostat).

OLYMPIA, WASH.

WASHINGTON STATE ARCHIVES
Governor Ferry Papers, especially Militia and Miscellany. Indian Affairs. The official correspondence is incomplete before 1870, but especially useful on the 1877 troubles as reflected over eastern Washington.

WASHINGTON STATE LIBRARY
The governor's letterbooks of 1853–55, the official letterbooks, the territorial secretary's papers, and the military correspondence

surprisingly have nothing directly concerning our theme. The interviews and reminiscences gathered by the state Pioneer project illumine the Interior scene and confirm previous impressions.

PORTLAND, OREG.

CATHOLIC CHANCERY,
ARCHDIOCESAN ARCHIVES
Mesplié Papers. Poulin Papers. Episcopal letterbooks, diary notes. Statistics. A wealth of ecclesiastical background is here, and some useful mission data.

OREGON HISTORICAL SOCIETY
J. W. Nesmith Papers especially. Folders of reminiscences by Indians and Whites. Clippings. Some promising collections— such as of Gibbs, Lane, Superintendent Geary, and political figures—offer little or nothing for our purpose.

PULLMAN, WASH.

STATE COLLEGE OF WASHINGTON,
LIBRARY, MANUSCRIPTS
Valuable for official documentation on the Colville area. See the thousand Simms Papers, including censuses, correspondence, statistics, finances. Similar rich material also in the Winans Collection. Items of use in collections of Kuykendall, Kulzner, Presbyterian missionaries. The enormous but well-catalogued McWhorter papers have useful Indian reminiscence and notes.

ST. LOUIS, MO.

MISSOURI PROVINCE ARCHIVES
OF THE SOCIETY OF JESUS
(ST. LOUIS UNIVERSITY,
PIUS XII LIBRARY)
Particularly useful for the huge

collection of De Smet correspondence and related materials, much of it in letterbooks. There are almost 100 pages of Joset correspondence, mostly among the De Smet papers, as well as items by Congiato and others. Notable also are the Point materials and Kuppens, and Ponziglione items. The collection is more useful for the period before 1860, and is especially important for the earliest years of the Rocky Mountain mission.

ST. LOUIS UNIVERSITY, ARCHIVES
De Smet's Linton Album is a valuable record of itinerary and personal data, sometimes a kind of diary or memoir.

SALEM, OREG.

OREGON STATE ARCHIVES
Papers of the Territorial Government; see especially 193, 7653, 7681, 8894, 8899, 10,850, 12,005. Newspaper files. Military records, 1851–59.

SAN FRANCISCO, CAL.

UNIVERSITY OF SAN FRANCISCO,
ARCHIVES
Mengarini, copy of Italian original Memorie (1848). J. O'Sullivan Papers. Croke collection in photostat (see Dublin below, p. 466). Catalogues for Pacific Coast, including Interior.

SAN MARINO, CAL.

HUNTINGTON LIBRARY
Fort Dalles Letterbook. Fort Dalles Papers. Suckley Correspondence. Military departmental orders, including De Smet's. Fort Simcoe Letterbook. E. Holbrook Journal. The almost 200,000 pieces on the Pacific Steamship line are

not yet organized for investigation.

SEATTLE, WASH.

CATHOLIC CHANCERY,
ARCHDIOCESAN ARCHIVES
Episcopal letterbooks, including correspondence with Jesuits, statistics. Journal de l'évêque. Dellanoy copies of Brouillet letters.

FEDERAL RECORDS CENTER,
GENERAL SERVICES ADMINISTRATION
Record group 75 consists of a hundred cubic feet of Colville Indian Agency documentation, 1865–1943. See especially boxes 1, 2, and 19, and on the Coeur d'Alene Tribe boxes 17 and 28. The Simms letters are particularly good.

UNIVERSITY OF WASHINGTON LIBRARY, PACIFIC NORTHWEST
MANUSCRIPTS
The Stevens Collection, in 56 folders, containing over 1,000 letters, plus other pieces, is particularly useful. Some collections, such as the Governor Ferry Papers and the Swan carton, are disappointing for our subject. The collections of Huggins and of Indian superintendents Milroy and Kendall supply background, as do the reminiscences of Delegate W. H. Wallace, Rev. H. T. Cowley, J. T. Dane, and others.

SPOKANE, WASH.

EASTERN WASHINGTON STATE
HISTORICAL SOCIETY
Reminiscence and auxiliary late documentation on the Interior wars. A similar though less directly pertinent collection is at the Washington State Historical Society, Tacoma.

OREGON PROVINCE ARCHIVES
OF THE SOCIETY OF JESUS
(GONZAGA UNIVERSITY,
CROSBY LIBRARY)
Central depository of Pacific Northwest Jesuit materials. This remarkable assemblage of diaries, mission records, Indian materials, treaties, memoirs, correspondence, reports, and the like was carefully sifted for material relevant to our book over a period of three years. The 400 boxes of Northwest Mission Papers, with 35,000 items, comprise the section of the archives most useful for our theme. Especially pertinent are the administrative and historical documentation for the several missions, including house diaries, baptismal and burial records, and mission histories. Collections under the names of individuals, such as the Joset Papers, the Cataldo Papers, the Giorda Papers, and the De Smet Papers, also stand out.

SPOKANE PUBLIC LIBRARY,
MANUSCRIPTS
A small collection of background materials, including letters of Stevens, Monteith, De Smet.

TACOMA, WASH.

ARCHIVES, MILITARY DEPARTMENT,
WASHINGTON STATE (CAMP
MURRAY, AT TILLICUM)
Washington territorial military records, some 15,000 documents. Militia and military correspondence, muster rolls, orders, reports, etc., through all our Interior wars, 1855–80.

WASHINGTON STATE
HISTORICAL SOCIETY
Reminiscence (including Spokane Garry's daughter), Skoko-

mish Agency account book 1869–78, clippings, journals.

CANADA

MONTREAL

COLLÈGE STE. MARIE, ARCHIVES
Memoirs of Nicholas Point (No. 4073); Point sketch book.

OTTAWA

SCOLASTICAT ST.-JOSEPH,
ARCHIVES DESCHATELETS
Chirouse letters (microfilm in Spokane, Oregon, Jesuit Archives).

VICTORIA, B.C.

PROVINCIAL ARCHIVES OF BRITISH COLUMBIA
Especially volumes of record office transcripts, including Hudson's Bay reports. J. R. Anderson memoirs. Vancouver Island letters to the secretary of state.

EUROPE

BRUSSELS

ARCHIVES DE LA PROVINCE
(JÉSUITE) BELGE DU NORD
Cartons Deynoodt, 1–35. Fardes Deynoodt, A–Z. De Smet, 1–4. Collection 1ab–14ab. Collection 1ac–14ac. A great collection of De Smet materials, including also letters of Joset, Gazzoli, Caruana, and others.

COURFAIVRE, SWITZERLAND

JOSET FAMILY PAPERS
Letters and information in possession of Joset's family, especially Sœur Martens Joset; family data from communal archives. Some copies now deposited at Univer-

sity of San Francisco archives, others in Oregon Jesuit microfilms at Spokane.

DUBLIN

ALL HALLOWS SEMINARY
Croke Papers (now available in University of San Francisco photostat collection).

FRIBOURG, SWITZERLAND

ARCHIVES DE LA SOCIÉTÉ
POUR LA PROPAGATION
DE LA FOI DE LYON
Boxes of documents according to year, 1840–80. Includes voluminous correspondence, mission statistics, Indian Affairs, from the Northwest and Rome. The business accounts, a separate section, are not directly useful. The researcher must keep in mind the shifting ecclesiastical jurisdictions, looking under the several dioceses, vicariates, and Orders, and for letters from Rome or the Catholic Indian mission bureau.

STAATSARCHIV (ARCHIVES
CANTONALES)
Collection Gremaud, No. 28.

LONDON

HUDSON'S BAY COMPANY
ARCHIVES
Simpson Correspondence, books outward, Ser. 1 and 2. Same, books inward. London Correspondence. Annals. Includes correspondence of all kinds with officials in Pacific Northwest.

LYONS

ARCHIVES DE NOTRE DAME
DE LYS [JESUIT]
De Smet letters, fasc. 49 (microfilm in Spokane, Oreg., Jesuit Archives)

ARCHIVES DE LA PROVINCE
(JÉSUITE) DE LYON
Documents divers sur les missions
étrangères, XII (microfilm in
Spokane, Oreg., Jesuit Archives).

MAASTRICHT, HOLLAND

ARCHIVUM PROVINCIAE
GERMANIAE INFERIORIS,
SOCIETATIS IESU
Pertinent manuscripts are surely
here, but a visit indicates they will
not be available for a long time,
until the archives are organized.

PARIS

ARCHIVES DE LA SOCIÉTÉ
POUR LA PROPAGATION
DE LA FOI DE PARIS
F 70–71, F 99a–b, F 102, F 110–
111, I 5–6. Especially reports of
Jesuit generals, statistics, Oblate
and diocesan information, letters
on wars.

ROME

ARCHIVIO DELLA S. CONGREGAZIONE
'DE PROPAGANDA FIDE'
Background materials; nothing di-
rectly on our wars, little on the
Indians, in official episcopal cor-
respondence to 1864.

ARCHIVIO DELLA CONGREGAZIONE
DEI MISSIONARI OBLATI
DI MARIA IMMACOLATA
Especially letters section of Ob-
late reports and correspondence:

Pandosy, Durieu, Chirouse, Ricard, etc. Mazenod correspondence has been consolidated apart
in connection with his canoni-
zation cause.

ARCHIVUM HISTORICUM SOCIETATIS
JESU
This is the central Jesuit archives
at the Roman headquarters.
Rocky Mountain mission manuscripts from our period are consolidated under the file Missio
montium saxosarum in two divisions: I, 1840–51; II, 1852–84. Letters and reports are here in Latin
and modern languages from De
Smet, Congiato, Joset, Gazzoli,
Hoecken, Point, and others. Valuable comments on wars and Indian
problems; ethnohistorical materials; statistics, etc. Cf. also generals' letters outward and Missouri manuscripts.

TURIN

ARCHIVIO DELLA PROVINCIA
TORINESE DELLA COMPAGNIA
DI GESÙ
Catalogues. Manuscript materials
have largely been moved to Rome.

VIENNA

ERZBISCHÖFLICHES ORDINARIAT,
LEOPOLDINEN-STIFTUNG
Jesuit and De Smet materials;
nothing directly concerning our
major theme.

II. PUBLISHED MATERIALS

This is primarily a listing of works cited, to which is added a scattering of standard and background works. A few items cited in the notes, whose connection
with our themes is especially tenuous or accidental, are not included. Other titles,
such as Catlin and Schoolcraft or the rich travel literature including Lewis and
Clark, are omitted for brevity. Domestic Jesuit journals, like *Woodstock Letters*
or *Letters and Notices*, are a storehouse of missionary letters and recollections;
only an example or two are provided here.

Though the resulting bibliography is representative enough, it may easily be enlarged by consulting the usual bibliographical guides for regional, religious, and Indian history. Current Jesuit bibliography is supplied in the Roman journal *Archivum historicum societatis Iesu.*

GOVERNMENT DOCUMENTS AND PUBLICATIONS

Each year during our period a small library of source materials bearing upon the themes of this book issued from the government press. Besides the formal messages or summaries of officials from the president down to the commissioner of Indian Affairs, there were regional and minutely local reports; this is especially true for the Indian service and the army. Volumes of field reports, correspondence, and the like are involved from men like Wright, Steptoe, Harney, De Smet, Wheaton, Howard, Clarke, Wool, Congiato, and Joset. Whole books and sets of books, as well as shorter monographs, were also produced, such as the reports of Mullan and Cram or the railroad surveys of teams of men under Stevens. The following items are a selection of the more important material in these collections.

Bureau of the Census, *Historical Statistics of the U.S., 1789–1945,* Washington, D.C., 1949.

Congress

Serials 758, 791, 992, 33 Cong., 1 sess. (1853–54), House Exec. Doc. 129; 2 sess. (1853–54), Sen. Exec. Doc. 78 and House Exec. Doc. 91; cf. 36 Cong., 1 sess. (1859), House Exec. Doc. 56. See Stevens, *Railroad Reports,* below, p. 488.

Serial 819, 34 Cong., 1 sess. (1855), Sen. Exec. Doc. 26. Yakima war correspondence, reports.

Serial 822, 34 Cong., 1 sess. (1856), Sen. Exec. Doc. 66. Yakima war documents.

Serial 858, 34 Cong., 1 sess. (1856), House Exec. Doc. 93. Yakima war documents.

Serial 859, 34 Cong., 1 sess. (1856), House Exec. Doc. 118. Yakima war documents.

Serial 876, 34 Cong., 3 sess. (1856–57), House Exec. Doc. 5 (cf. serial 894). Yakima war documents.

Serial 881, 34 Cong., 3 sess. (1857), Sen. Exec. Doc. 41. Yakima war documents.

Serial 906, 34 Cong., 3 sess. (1854), House Exec. Doc. 76. Alvord report; Yakima war.

Serial 929, 35 Cong., 1 sess. (1857), Senate Exec. Doc. 40 (cf. House Exec. Docs. 38–39, serial 955). See Browne, *Indian War,* below, p. 472.

Serial 975, 35 Cong., 2 sess. (1858), Sen. Exec. Doc. 1 (also serial 998, House Exec. Doc. 1). Steptoe war documents—including Wright, Clarke, etc.—correspondence, treaties, Joset, Hoecken, and Congiato accounts, Wright war.

Serial 984, 35 Cong., 2 sess. (1859), Sen. Exec. Doc. 32. Includes Joset account, Mullan Memoir. See Mullan, *Topographical Memoir,* below, p. 483.

Serial 1006, 35 Cong., 2 sess. (1859), House Exec. Doc. 50. Troop movements.

Serial 1014, 35 Cong., 2 sess. (1855), House Exec. Doc. 114. See Cram, below, p. 474.

Serial 1024, 36 Cong., 2 sess. (1858–59), Sen. Exec. Doc. 2. Military correspondence, 1858 war, including De Smet, Harney.

Serial 1051, 36 Cong., 1 sess. (1858), House Exec. Doc. 65. Military, Indian correspondence, reports of 1858 war, treaties.

Serial 1079, 36 Cong., 2 sess. (1860), Sen. Exec. Doc. 1. Military, and northern Indians.

Serial 1097, 36 Cong., 2 sess. (1860), House Exec. Doc. 29. Cf. serial 1099, House Exec. Doc. 44. Early Mullan Military and Road Report.

Serial 1149, 37 Cong., 3 sess. (1863), Sen. Exec. Doc. 43. Later Mullan Road Report. See Mullan, *Report on Construction*, below, p. 483.

Serial 1674, 44 Cong., 1 sess. (1875), House Exec. Doc. 1. Nez Percé problems.

Serial 1780, 45 Cong., 2 sess. (1878), Sen. Exec. Doc. 14. Nez Percé war documents.

Serial 1794, 45 Cong., 2 sess. (1878), House Exec. Doc. 1. Nez Percé war documents, including Sherman, Wheaton, Howard, McDowell, Gibbon, Rawn, Terry, etc., Wheaton Council.

Cram. See below, p. 474.

Department of the Interior, *Annual Reports of the Board of Indian Commissioners*, 1869–80.

Department of the Interior, Office of Indian Affairs, *Annual Reports of the Commissioner of Indian Affairs*, 1849–80. Published simultaneously in *House Executive Documents* and in *Senate Executive Documents* to 1858, then in the latter to 1861 and in the former to 1880. There is also an independent Department of the Interior edition from 1854, used for quotations in our chapters. Congressional serial numbers for the other editions are: 449 and 463 (year 1844), 470 and 480 (1845), 493 and 497 (1846), 503 and 515 (1847), 537 (1848), 550 and 570 (1849), 587 and 595 (1850), 613 and 636 (1851), 658 and 673 (1852), 690 and 710 (1853), 746 and 777 (1854), 810 and 840 (1855), 875 and 893 (1856), 919 and 942 (1857), 974 and 997 (1858), 1023 (1859), 1078 (1860), 1117 (1861), 1157 (1862), 1182 (1863), 1220 (1864), 1248 (1865), 1284 (1866), 1326 (1867), 1366 (1868), 1414 (1869), 1449 (1870), 1565 (1871), 1560 (1872), 1601 (1873), 1639 (1874), 1680 (1875), 1749 (1876), 1800 (1877), 1850 (1878), 1910 (1879), 1959 (1880), Cf. War Department, below.

Handbook of American Indians North of Mexico. See below, p. 478.

Handbook of Federal Indian Law. See below, p. 478.

Indian Affairs, Laws and Treaties. See below, p. 479.

Mullan. See below, p. 483.

Reports of Inspection, 1877. See Sherman, below, p. 486.

Smithsonian Institution. Miscellaneous Publications; BAE *Reports, Bulletins.*

Stevens, I. I. See below, p. 488.

Swanton, John R. See below, p. 489.

U.S. Geographical and Geological Survey of the Rocky Mountain Region, ed. J. W. Powell. See Gibbs, "Tribes of Western Washington," below, p. 477.

War Department. Department (or Bureau) of Indian Affairs, *Annual Reports*, 1825–48. Cf. Department of Interior, above.

BOOKS AND ARTICLES

Albright, George L., *Official Explorations for Pacific Railroads*, [*1853–1855*], University of California, Publications in History, 11, Berkeley, 1921.

Arnold, Royall Ross, *Indian Wars of Idaho*, Caldwell, Idaho, 1932.

Athearn, Robert G., *William Tecumseh Sherman and the Settlement of the West*, Norman, Okla., 1956.

Atkinson, G., "Diary of Rev. George H. Atkinson D.D., 1847–1858," ed. E. Ruth Rockwood, *OHQ, 40* (1939), 52–63, 168–87, 265–82, 345–61.

Avery, M. W., "The W. Park Winans Manuscripts" [with life], *PNWQ, 47* (1956), 15–20.

Bagley, Clarence B., *Early Catholic Missions in Old Oregon*, 2 vols. Seattle, 1932.

Baker, P. E., *The Forgotten Kutenai, a Study of the Kutenai Indians, Bonner's Ferry, Idaho, Creston, British Columbia, Canada, and Other Areas Where the Kutenai Are Located*, Boise, 1955.

Bancroft, H. H., *History of British Columbia, 1792–1877*, in *Works, 32*, San Francisco, 1877.

——— *History of the Northwest Coast, 1543–1846*, in *Works, 27–28*. 2 vols. San Francisco, 1884.

——— *History of Oregon, 1834–1888*, in *Works, 29–30*, 2 vols. San Francisco, 1886–88.

——— *History of Washington, Idaho, and Montana, 1845–1889*, in *Works, 31*, San Francisco, 1890.

——— *The Native Races of the Pacific States*, in *Works, 1–5*, 5 vols. San Francisco, 1874–83.

——— *Works*, 39 vols. San Francisco, 1874–91.

Bandel, Eugene, *Frontier Life in the Army 1854–1861*, ed. R. P. Bieber, Southwest Historical Series, 2, Glendale, Cal., 1932.

Barnum, F. A. (S.J.), "The Last of the Old Indian Missionaries, Father Joseph Joset, a Sketch from Notes Gleaned from the Missionary," *WL, 30* (1901), 202–14.

Barry, J. N., "Early Oregon Forts, a Chronological List," *OHQ, 46* (1945), 99–133.

Beal, Merrill D., *"I Will Fight No More Forever." Chief Joseph and the Nez Perce War*, Seattle, 1963.

——— and M. W. Wells, *History of Idaho*, 3 vols. New York, 1959.

Beall, Thomas, "Pioneer Reminiscences," *WHQ, 8* (1913), 83–90.

——— [Reminiscences], Lewiston *Teller*, 14 March 1884.

——— and J. E. Smith, [Reminiscences], Spokane *Spokesman-Review*, 24 September 1916.

Beaver, Herbert, "Experiences of a Chaplain at Fort Vancouver, 1836–1838," ed. R. C. Clark, *OHQ, 39* (1938), 22–38.

——— *Reports and Letters of Herbert Beaver, 1836–1838, Chaplain to the Hudson's Bay Company and Missionary to the Indians at Fort Vancouver*, ed. T. E. Jessett, Portland, Oreg., 1959.

Beers, Henry P., "The Army and the Oregon Trail to 1846," *PNWQ, 28* (1937), 335–62.

——— *The Western Military Frontier 1815–1846*, Philadelphia, 1935.

Beeson, John, *A Plea for the Indians; with Facts and Features of the Late War in Oregon*, New York, [1857] 1858.

Begg, Alexander, *History of British Columbia from its Earliest Discovery to the Present Time*, Toronto, 1894.

Belknap, George P., *"Authentic Account of the Murder of Dr. Whitman:* The

History of a Pamphlet," *Papers of the Bibliographical Society of America, 55* (1961), 319–46.
Bemis, S. F., "Captain John Mullan and the Engineers' Frontier," *WHQ, 14* (1923), 201–05.
Berkhofer, Robert F., "Protestants, Pagans, and Sequences among the North American Indians, 1760–1860," *Ethnohistory, 10* (1963), 201–32.
—— *Salvation and the Savage: An Analysis of Protestant Missions and American Indian Response, 1787–1862,* Lexington, Ky., 1965.
Berreman, Joel V., *Tribal Distribution in Oregon,* Amer. Anthrop. Assoc., Memoirs, 47, Menasha, Wisc., 1937.
Billington, Ray Allen, *The Protestant Crusade 1800–1860, a Study in the Origins of American Nativism,* New York, 1938.
Bischoff, William N. (S.J.), "Documents: Yakima Campaign," *Mid-America, 31* (1949), 170–208.
—— *The Jesuits in Old Oregon, a Sketch of Jesuit Activities in the Pacific Northwest, 1840–1940,* Caldwell, Idaho, 1945.
—— "The Yakima Campaign of 1856," *Mid-America, 31* (1949), 163–69.
—— "The Yakima Indian War, 1855–1856, a Problem in Research," *PNWQ, 41* (1950), 162–69.
—— See Bischoff, "Yakima Indian War," below, p. 492.
—— and C. M. Gates, "The Jesuits and the Coeur d'Alene Treaty of 1858," *PNWQ, 34* (1943), 169–81.
Blades, T. E., and J. W. Wike, "Fort Missoula," *Military Affairs, 13* (1949), 29–36.
Blanchet, F. N., *Historical Sketches of the Catholic Church in Oregon,* Portland, Oreg., 1878.
—— et al., *Notices and Voyages of the Famed Quebec Mission to the Pacific Northwest, Being the Correspondence, Notices, etc., of Fathers Blanchet and Demers, Together with Those of Fathers Bolduc and Langlois . . . 1838 to 1847 . . . ,* ed. Carl Landerholm, Portland, Oreg., 1956.
—— and J. B. A. Brouillet, *Early Catholic Missions in Oregon during the First Forty Years (1838–1878)—Blanchet. Also Authentic Account of the Murder of Dr. Whitman and Other Missionaries by the Cayuse Indians of Oregon in 1847—Brouillet,* ed. Clarence B. Bagley, Seattle, 1932.
Blue, G. V., "Green's Missionary Report on Oregon," *OHQ, 30* (1929), 259–71.
Bolduc, J. B. Z., *Mission de la Colombie, deuxième lettre et journal,* Quebec, 1845.
Boyd, J. H., "Reminiscences of Joseph H. Boyd, an Argonaut of 1857," ed. W. S. Lewis, *WHQ, 15* (1904), 243–62.
Brackett, A. G., *History of the United States Cavalry from the Formation of the Federal Government to the 1st of June 1863,* New York, 1865.
Bradley, Cyprian (O.S.B.), and Edward J. Kelly, *History of the Diocese of Boise 1863–1952,* Boise, 1953.
Bradley, James H. (Lieutenant), "Affairs at Fort Benton from 1831 to 1869 from Lieutenant Bradley's Journal," *CHSM, 3* (1900), 201–87.
Briley, Ann, "Hiram F. Smith, First Settler of Okanogan County," *PNWQ, 43* (1952), 226–33.
Brimlow, George F., *The Bannock War of 1878,* Caldwell, Idaho, 1938.
Brosnan, C. J., *History of the State of Idaho,* rev. ed. New York, 1918.

Brouillet, J. B. A., *The Bureau of Catholic Indian Missions—the Work of the Decade Ending December 31, 1883*, Washington, D.C., 1883.

Brown, F. R., *History of the 9th U.S. Infantry*, Chicago, 1909.

Brown, William Compton, *The Indian Side of the Story, Being a Concourse of Presentations Historical and Biographical in Character Relating to the Indian Wars and to the Treatment Accorded to the Indians, in Washington Territory East of the Cascade Mountains during the Period from 1853 to 1889 . . .*, Spokane, 1961.

Browne, J. Ross, *Indian War in Oregon and Washington Territories*, Washington, D.C., 1858. Published as congressional serial 929; see Government Documents, above, p. 468.

—— et al., *Resources of the Pacific Slope, Statistical and Descriptive Summary of the Mines and Minerals, Climate, Topography, Agriculture, Commerce, Manufactures, and Miscellaneous Productions of the States and Territories West of the Rocky Mountains*, New York, 1869.

Buck, Amos, "Review of the Battle of the Big Hole," *CHSM*, 7 (1910), 117–30.

Bureau of Catholic Indian Missions, *Status of the Catholic Indian Missions in the United States, 1876*, Baltimore, 1876.

Burlingame, Merrill G., "The Influence of the Military in the Building of Montana," *PNWQ*, 29 (1938), 135–50.

—— "The Military-Indian Frontier in Montana, 1860–1890," *University of Iowa Studies in the Social Sciences*, 10 (1938), 59–69.

—— *The Montana Frontier*, Helena, Mont., 1942.

—— K. Ross O'Toole, et al., *A History of Montana*, 3 vols. New York, 1958.

Burns, Robert Ignatius (S.J.), "A Bancroft Library Manuscript on the 1858 War," *OHQ*, 52 (1951), 54–57.

—— "Coeur d'Alene Diplomacy in the Nez Percé War of 1877," *RACHS*, 63 (1952), 37–60.

—— "Descriptive Calendar of the Joset Papers," *PNWQ*, 38 (1947), 307–14.

—— "Drums along the Rockies: Father Joseph Joset," in J. P. Leary (S.J.), ed., *I Lift My Lamp: Jesuits in America* (Westminster, Md., 1955), pp. 175–92.

—— *Indians and Whites in the Pacific Northwest. Jesuit Contributions to Peace, 1850–1880*, pamphlet, San Francisco, 1961.

—— "A Jesuit at the Hell Gate Treaty of 1855," *Mid-America*, 34 (1952), 87–114.

—— "A Jesuit in the War against the Northern Indians," *RACHS*, 61 (1950), 9–54.

—— "The Jesuits and the Spokane Council of 1877," *PHR*, 21 (1952), 65–73.

—— "The Jesuits, the Northern Indians, and the Nez Percé War of 1877," *PNWQ*, 42 (1951), 40–76.

—— "Père Joset's Account of the Indian War of 1858," *PNWQ*, 38 (1947), 285–307.

Bushnell, David I., *Drawings by George Gibbs in the Far Northwest, 1849–1851*, Smithsonian Miscellaneous Collections 97, No. 8, Washington, D.C., 1939.

Business Directory of the Pacific States and Territories for 1878, Containing Names, Business, and Address of Merchants, Manufacturers, and Professional Men, County, City, State, Territorial, and Federal Officers, and Notaries Public, of the Principal Towns of California, Nevada, Oregon, Washington,

Utah, Montana, Idaho, Arizona and British Columbia, Together with a Sketch of the Different Towns . . . Over 30,000 Names, San Francisco, 1878.

Carey, C. H., *A General History of Oregon Prior to 1861*, 2 vols. paginated as one, Portland, Oreg., 1935-36.

Carpenter, John A., *Sword and Olive Branch, Oliver Otis Howard*, Pittsburgh, 1964.

Caruana, G. M. (S.J.), "Lettera del P. G. M. Caruana al R. P. Provinciale," *LPT*, n.v. (1904), 108-12.

———— "Necrologio: Padre Giuseppe Joset," *LPT*, n.v. (1900), 185-89.

Casagrandi, A. P. (S.J.), *De claris sodalibus provinciae taurinensis societatis Jesu commentarii*, Turin, 1906.

Casper, H. W. (S.J.), *History of the Catholic Church in Nebraska: The Church on the Northern Plains, 1838-1874*, Milwaukee, 1960.

Cataldo, J. M. (S.J.), "Sketch of the Nez Percés Indians," *WL, 9* (1880), 43-50, 109-18, 191-99; *10* (1881), 71-77, 198-204.

———— See Crosby, below; Hawkins, below, p. 492.

Catalogus sociorum et officiorum provinciae taurinens[is] dispersae societatis Iesu, Rome, Nice, Marseilles. Published annually.

Catholic Encyclopedia, 15 vols. New York, 1907-12 (esp. articles on individual Jesuits, tribes, dioceses, Bureau of Catholic Indian missions).

Cave, W., *Nez Percé Indian War of 1877 and Battle of the Big Hole*, pamphlet, Missoula, Mont., 1926.

Chadwick, S. J., "Colonel Steptoe's Battle," *WHQ, 2* (1907-08), 333-43.

Chalmers, Harvey, *The Last Stand of the Nez Perce: Destruction of a People*, New York, 1963.

Chittenden, H. M., *Fur Trade of the Far West: A History of the Pioneer Trading Posts and Early Fur Companies of the Missouri Valley and Rocky Mountains, and of the Inland Commerce with Santa Fe*, 3 vols. New York, 1903.

———— and A. T. Richardson. See De Smet, *Life, Letters, and Travels*, below.

Clark, J. Stanley, "The Nez Percés in Exile," *PNWQ, 36* (1945), 213-32.

Clark, Robert C., "Military History of Oregon, 1849-1859," *OHQ, 36* (1935), 14-59.

Cline, Walter, et al., *The Sinkaietk or Southern Okanagon of Washington*, ed. Leslie Spier, Amer. Anthrop. Assoc., General Series in Anthropology, 2, Menasha, Wisc., 1938.

Coan, Charles F., "The Adoption of the Reservation Policy in the Pacific Northwest, 1853-1855," *OHQ, 23* (1922), 1-38.

———— See below, p. 492.

Cody, E. R., *History of the Coeur d'Alene Mission of the Sacred Heart*, pamphlet, Caldwell, Idaho, 1930.

Coe, H. C., "An Indian Agent's Experience in the War of 1866," *OHQ, 14* (1913), 65-67.

Copies of Despatches from the Secretary of State for the Colonies to the Governor of British Columbia, Pt. 1 of Papers Relative to the Affairs of British Columbia, London, 1859.

Cowan, Mrs. George, "Reminiscences of Pioneer Life," *CHSM, 4* (1903), 156-87.

Cox, Ross, *The Columbia River; or, Scenes and Adventures during a Residence of Six Years on the Western Side of the Rocky Mountains among Various Tribes of Indians Hitherto Unknown,* ed. E. I. and J. R. Stewart, American Exploration and Travel Series, 24, Norman, Okla., 1957.

Cram, T. J. (Captain), *Topographical Memoir of the Department of the Pacific,* Washington, D.C., 1859. Published as congressional serial 1014; see Government Documents, above, p. 468.

Cronin, Kay, *Cross in the Wilderness* [Oblates], Vancouver, 1960.

Crook, George (General), *General George Crook, His Autobiography,* Norman, Okla., 1960.

Crosby, L. E., *Kuailks Metatcopun (Black Robe Three Times Broken),* Wallace, Idaho, 1925. (For typescript original, which is used in citations, see below, p. 492). Italian trans. C. Testore, *Kuahilks Metatcopnim, le memorie di un vestenera,* Venice, 1935.

Cross, Osborne (Major), and George Gibbs, *The March of the Mounted Riflemen, First United States Military Expedition to Travel the Full Length of the Oregon Trail from Fort Leavenworth to Fort Vancouver, May to October 1849,* ed. Raymond W. Settle, Northwest Historical Series, 3, Glendale, Cal., 1940.

Culverwell, Albert, "Stronghold in the Yakima Country: Fort Simcoe and the Indian War, 1856–59," *PNWQ, 46* (1955), 46–51. Pamphlet reprint (centennial brochure), modified, Olympia, Wash., 1956.

Cullum, George W., *Biographical Register of the Officers and Graduates of the U.S. Military Academy at West Point . . . ,* 4 vols. New York, Boston, 1891–1901.

Curtis, Edward S., *The North American Indian, Being a Series of Volumes Picturing and Describing the Indians of the United States and Alaska,* ed. Frederick W. Hodge, 20 vols. Seattle, Cambridge, Mass., and Norwood, Mass., 1907–30.

Davenport, T. W., "Recollections of an Indian Agent," *OHQ, 8* (1907), 1–41, 95–128, 231–64, 353–74.

Davis, David B., "Some Themes of Counter-Subversion: An Analysis of Anti-Masonic, Anti-Catholic, and Anti-Mormon Literature," *MVHR, 47* (1960), 205–24.

Davis, William Lyle (S.J.), *A History of St. Ignatius Mission,* Spokane, 1954.

──── "Peter John De Smet: The Journey of 1840," *PNWQ, 35* (1944), 29–43, 121–42.

──── "Peter John De Smet, Missionary to the Potawatomi, 1837–1840," *PNWQ, 33* (1942), 123–52.

──── "P. J. De Smet, the Years of Preparation, 1801–1837," *PNWQ, 32* (1941), 167–96.

──── See below, p. 492.

Demers, Modeste, *Notice sur l'établissement de la province ecclésiastique de l'Orégon, précédée de quelques renseignements sur le Canada,* Brussels, 1867.

Denig, E. T., *Five Indian Tribes of the Upper Missouri, Sioux, Arickaras, Assiniboines, Crees, Crows,* ed. J. C. Ewers, Norman, Okla., 1961.

De Smet, Pierre Jean (S.J.), *Letters and Sketches: With a Narrative of a Year's Residence among the Indian Tribes of the Rocky Mountains,* Philadelphia, 1843. (Also Dutch, German, Italian, and 6 French editions; reprint in Thwaites, *Early Western Travels,* see below).

──── *Life, Letters, and Travels of Father Pierre-Jean De Smet, S.J., 1801–*

1873, Missionary Labors and Adventures among the Wild Tribes of the North American Indians, Embracing Minute Description of their Manners, Customs, Games, Modes of Warfare and Torture . . . , ed. H. M. Chittenden and A. T. Richardson, 4 vols. New York, 1905.

────── *New Indian Sketches,* New York, 1865, 1885.

────── *Oregon Missions and Travels over the Rocky Mountains, in 1845–46,* New York, 1847. (Also a Flemish and 2 French editions; reprint in Thwaites, *Early Western Travels,* see below).

────── *Western Missions and Missionaries: A Series of Letters,* New York, 1863. (French and later English editions).

Desmond, G. B. (O.S.B.), *Gambling among the Yakimas,* Washington, D.C., 1952.

"Despatches." See "Copies," above.

Deutsch, H. J., "The Evolution of the International Boundary in the Inland Empire of the Pacific Northwest," *PNWQ, 51* (1960), 63–79.

────── "The Evolution of Territorial and State Boundaries in the Inland Empire of the Pacific Northwest," *PNWQ, 51* (1960), 115–31.

────── "Indian and White in the Inland Empire, the Contest for the Land, 1880–1912," *PNWQ, 47* (1956), 44–51.

Deynoodt, François (S.J.), *Le Révérend Père P. J. De Smet de la Compagnie de Jésus, missionnaire belge aux Etats Unis,* Brussels, 1878.

Dictionary of American Biography, 21 vols. with supplements, New York, 1937–45 (including Jesuits such as De Smet, Menetrey, Mengarini, Palladino, Ravalli).

Diomedi, A. (S.J.), *Sketches of Modern Indian Life,* Woodstock, Md., 1884. Written 1879; first published in *WL, 22* (1893), 231–56, 353–78; *23* (1894), 23–40.

Donnelly, J. P. (S.J.). See below, p. 492.

Donnelly, W. P. (S.J.), "Father Pierre-Jean De Smet: United States Ambassador to the Indians," *Historical Records and Studies, 24* (1934), 7–142.

────── "Nineteenth Century Jesuit Reductions in the United States," *Mid-America, 17* (1935), 69–83.

Downey, Fairfax, *Indian Wars of the United States Army, 1776–1865,* New York, 1963.

Dozier, Jack, "Coeur d'Alene Country: The Creation of the Coeur d'Alene Reservation in North Idaho," *Idaho Yesterdays, 6,* no. 3 (1962), 2–7.

────── "The Coeur d'Alene Indians in the War of 1858," *Idaho Yesterdays, 5,* no. 3 (1961), 22–32.

Driver, Harold E., *Indians of North America,* Chicago, 1961.

Drury, Clifford M., *Elkanah and Mary Walker, Pioneers among the Spokanes,* Caldwell, Idaho, 1940.

────── *Henry Harmon Spalding, Pioneer of Old Oregon,* Caldwell, Idaho, 1936.

────── *Marcus Whitman, Pioneer and Martyr,* Caldwell, Idaho, 1937.

────── *A Tepee in His Front Yard, a Biography of H. T. Cowley One of the Four Founders of the City of Spokane,* Portland, Oreg., 1949.

────── See Spalding, *Diaries,* below, and Whitman, *First White Women,* below.

DuBois, C. A., *The 1870 Ghost Dance,* University of California, Anthropological Records, 3, Berkeley, 1939.

Duflot de Mofras, Eugène (Count), *Exploration du territoire de l'Orégon, des Cal-*

ifornies et de la mer vermeille pendant trois années 1840, 1841 et 1843, 2 vols. Paris, 1844. Eng. trans. M. E. Wilbur, *Duflot de Mofras' Travels on the Pacific Coast,* Santa Ana, Cal., 1937.

―――― "Extract from Exploration of the Oregon Territory, the Californias, and the Gulf of California, Undertaken during the Years 1840, 1841, and 1842," trans.-ed. N. B. Pipes, *OHQ, 26* (1925), 151–90.

Duignan, Peter, "Early Jesuit Missionaries: A Suggestion for Further Study," *American Anthropologist, 60* (1958), 725–32.

Dunn, Jacob P., *Massacres of the Mountains, a History of the Indian Wars of the Far West, 1815–1875,* New York, [1886] 1958.

Dunn, John, *The Oregon Territory and the British North American Fur Trade with an Account of the Customs of the Principal Native Tribes on the Northern Continent,* Philadelphia, 1845.

Durham, N. W., *History of the City of Spokane and Spokane County, Washington,* 3 vols. Spokane, 1912.

Durkin, J. T. (S.J.), *General Sherman's Son,* New York, 1959.

Edwards, Jonathan, *History of Spokane County, State of Washington,* Spokane, 1909.

Eells, Reverend Myron, *History of Indian Missions on the Pacific Coast, Oregon, Washington and Idaho,* Philadelphia, 1882.

Elliott, T. C., "In the Land of the Kootenai," *OHQ, 27* (1926), 279–91.

―――― "The Mullan Road: Its Local History and Significance," *WHQ, 14* (1923), 206–09.

―――― "Religion among the Flatheads," *OHQ, 37* (1936), 1–8.

―――― "Steptoe Butte and Steptoe Battle-field," *WHQ, 18* (1927), 243–53.

Elsensohn, Sister M. A. (O.S.B.), *Pioneer Days in Idaho County,* 2 vols. Caldwell, Idaho, 1947–51.

Ewers, J. C., *The Blackfeet, Raiders of the Northwestern Plains,* Civilization of the American Indian, 49, Norman, Okla., 1958.

―――― *Gustavus Sohon's Portraits of the Flathead and Pend d'Oreille Indians 1854,* Smithsonian Miscellaneous Collections, 110, No. 7, Washington, D.C., 1948.

―――― *The Horse in Blackfoot Indian Culture, with Comparative Material from Other Western Tribes,* Smithsonian Institution, BAE *Bulletin, 159,* Washington, D.C., 1955.

―――― "Iroquois Indians in the Far West," *Montana, The Magazine of Western History, 13,* no. 2 (1963), 2–10.

―――― See Denig, above.

"Extract from a Letter of a Rocky Mountain Jesuit Missionary," *Indian Sentinel,* unnumbered 1st Ser. [5] (1906), 31.

Farrow, E. S., *Mountain Scouting, a Handbook for Officers and Soldiers on the Frontiers,* New York, 1881.

Fee, Chester, *Chief Joseph: The Biography of a Great Indian,* New York, 1936.

Field. See below, p. 492.

Fitzgerald, E. M. and J. A., *An Army Doctor's Wife on the Frontier, Letters from Alaska and the Far West, 1874–1878,* ed. Abe Lauf, Pittsburgh, 1962.

Flannery, Regina, *The Gros Ventres of Montana,* Catholic University of America, Anthropological Series, 15, Washington, D.C., 1953.

Flathead tribe, *Our Friends the Coeur d'Aleine Indians,* comp. Louis Palladino (S.J.), pamphlet, St. Ignatius Mission, 1886.

Forbis, Richard G., "The Flathead Apostasy, an Interpretation," *Montana, The Magazine of Western History, 1,* no. 4 (1951), 35–40.

Foreman, Grant, *The Last Trek of the Indians,* Chicago, 1946.

Fritz, Henry E., *The Movement for Indian Assimilation, 1860–1890,* Philadelphia, 1963.

Frush, Charles W., "A Trip from The Dalles of the Columbia, Oregon, to Fort Owen, Bitter Root Valley, Montana, in the Spring of 1858," *CHSM, 2* (1896), 337–42.

Fuller, G. W., *A History of the Pacific Northwest,* 2d rev. ed. New York, 1938.

———— *The Inland Empire of the Pacific Northwest,* 3 vols. Spokane, 1928.

Furniss, N., *The Mormon Conflict, 1850–1859,* New Haven, 1960.

Galbraith, John S., *The Hudson's Bay Company as an Imperial Factor, 1821–1861,* Berkeley, 1957.

[Galpin, C.], "Father De Smet's Sioux Peace Mission of 1868 and the Journal of John Galpin," ed. G. G. Garraghan (S.J.), *Mid-America, 2* (1930), 141–63.

Garfield, James, "James A. Garfield's Diary of a Trip to Montana in 1872," ed. O. W. Holmes, *Frontier and Midland, 15* (1934–35), 159–68. Published separately as Historical Reprints, Sources of Northwest History, 21.

———— "Peregrinations of a Politician, James A. Garfield's Diary of a Trip to Montana in 1872," ed. O. W. Holmes, *Montana, The Magazine of Western History, 6,* no. 4 (1956), 34–45.

Garraghan, G. J. (S.J.), *Chapters in Frontier History, Research Studies in the Making of the West,* Milwaukee, 1934.

———— *The Jesuits in the Middle United States,* 3 vols. New York, 1938.

———— "Nicolas Point, Jesuit Missionary in Montana of the Forties," in *The Trans-Mississippi West, Papers Read at a Conference Held at the University of Colorado, June 18–June 21, 1929,* ed. J. F. Willard and C. B. Goodykoontz (Boulder, Colo., 1930), pp. 43–63.

———— See Galpin, above, and Point, below.

Gates, C. M., ed., "Defending Puget Sound [Notes and Documents]," *PNWQ, 36* (1945), 68–78.

———— ed., *Messages of the Governors of the Territory of Washington to the Legislative Assembly, 1854–1889,* University of Washington, Publications in the Social Sciences, 12, Seattle, 1940.

———— See Bischoff, "The Jesuits and the Coeur d'Alene Treaty," above, and Johansen, below.

Giardina, G., *Il P. Cataldo S.J. apostolo dei pellirosse,* Palermo, 1928 and 1932.

Gibbon, John (General), "The Pursuit of 'Joseph,'" *American Catholic Quarterly Review, 4* (1879), 317–44.

Gibbs, George, "Pacific Northwest Letters of George Gibbs," ed. Vernon Carstensen, *OHQ, 54* (1953), 190–239.

———— "Tribes of Western Washington and Northwestern Oregon Published with Extensive Vocabularies," in W. H. Dall, *Tribes of the Extreme Northwest,* Contributions to North American Ethnology, 1, for U.S. Geographical and Geological Survey of the Rocky Mountain Region, J. W. Powell, director (Washington, D.C., 1877), pp. 163–361.

—— See Bushnell, above.

—— et al., "Report on the Indian Tribes of the Territory of Washington" [1854], in Secretary of War, *Reports of Explorations, 1*, 400–49, below.

Giorda, Joseph (S.J.), "Il Missionario gesuita tra i selvaggi naso-forati," *Museo delle missioni cattoliche, 15* (1872), 593–603.

Glisan, Rodney, *Journal of Army Life*, San Francisco, 1874.

Glueck, Alvin C., "Imperial Protection for the Trading Interests of the Hudson's Bay Company, 1857–1861," *Canadian Historical Review, 37* (1956), 119–40.

Goetzman, W. H., *Army Exploration in the American West, 1803–1863*, New Haven, 1959.

Grassi, Urban (S.J.), [account of Yakima War, 1855], *MC, 12* (1880), 14–16.

—— 1869 letter, *MC, 5* (1873), 220.

Guibert, Joseph de, *The Jesuits, Their Spiritual Doctrine and Practice, a Historical Study*, trans. W. J. Young, Loyola University, Institute of Jesuit Sources, 1, Chicago, 1964.

Guie, Heister D., *Bugles in the Valley, Garnett's Fort Simcoe*, Yakima, Wash., 1956.

Gunther, Erna, "The Indian Background of Washington History," *PNWQ, 50* (1941), 189–202.

Hakola, John W., ed., *Frontier Omnibus*, Missoula, 1962. Reprints the *Frontier and Midland* articles, above by Garfield, and below by Mengarini, Mullan, Partoll, and Phillips.

Hafen, LeRoy R. and Ann W., eds., *Relations with the Indians of the Plains, 1857–1861. A Documentary Account of the Military Campaigns, and Negotiations of Indian Agents, with Reports and Journals of P. G. Lowe, R. M. Peck, J. E. B. Stuart, S. D. Sturgis, and Other Official Papers*, Far West and Rockies Historical Series, 9, Glendale, Cal., 1959.

—— *The Utah Expedition, 1857–1858: A Documentary Account of the United States Military Movement under Colonel Albert Sidney Johnston, and the Resistance by Brigham Young and the Mormon Nauvoo Legion*, Far West and Rockies Historical Series, 8, Glendale, Cal., 1958.

Haines, Francis, "Chief Joseph and the Nez Percé Warriors," *PNWQ, 45* (1954), 1–7.

—— "The Nez Percé Tribe Versus the United States," *Idaho Yesterdays, 8*, no. 1 (1964), 18–25.

—— *The Nez Percés, Tribesmen of the Columbia Plateau*, Civilization of the American Indian, 42, Norman, Okla., 1955.

—— *Red Eagles of the Northwest, the Story of Chief Joseph and His People*, Portland, Oreg., 1939.

Hamilton, J. M., *From Wilderness to Statehood, a History of Montana, 1805–1900*, Portland, Oreg., 1957.

Hamilton, William T., "A Trader's Expedition among the Indians from Walla Walla to the Blackfeet Nation and Return in the Year 1858," *CHSM, 3* (1900), 33–123.

Handbook of American Indians North of Mexico, ed. F. W. Hodge, BAE *Bulletin, 30*, 2 vols. Washington, D.C., 1907–10.

Handbook of Federal Indian Law with Reference Tables and Index, comp. F. S. Cohen, Washington, D.C., 1942.

Hanks, L. M. and J. R., *Tribe under Trust, a Study of the Blackfoot Reserve of Alberta*, Toronto, 1950.

Harmon, G. D., *Sixty Years of Indian Affairs, Political, Economic, and Diplomatic, 1789–1850*, Chapel Hill, N.C., 1941.

Harney, M. P. (S.J.), *The Jesuits in History, the Society of Jesus through Four Centuries*, Chicago, [1941] 1962.

Harney, W. S. (General), et al., *Documents Relating to Col. S. Colt's Patent Extension*, Washington, D.C., 1858.

Harrison, Michael, "Chief Charlot's Battle with Bureaucracy," *Montana, The Magazine of Western History, 10* (1960), 27–33.

Hawkins-Cataldo. See below, p. 492.

Hawley, J. H., *History of Idaho*, 2 vols. Chicago, 1920.

Heitman, F. B., *Historical Register and Dictionary of the United States Army, 1789–1903*, 2 vols. Washington, D.C., 1903.

Henderson, Palmer, "The Flathead Indians, a Visit to Their Agency and to the St. Ignatius Mission," *The Northwest, 8* (1890), 1–3.

Hickey, E. J., *The Society for the Propagation of the Faith, Its Foundation, Organization and Success (1822–1922)*, Washington, D.C., 1922.

Hill, W. H., [obituary of A. Hoecken], *WL, 26* (1897), 364–68.

Hines, Clarence, "Indian Agent's Letter Book," *OHQ, 39* (1938), 6–15.

Hines, H. K., *Missionary History of the Northwest*, Portland, Oreg., 1899.

Hodge. See *Handbook of American Indians*, above.

Holmes, O. W. See Garfield, above.

Hoopes, Alban W., *Indian Affairs and Their Administration with Special Reference to the Far West, 1849–1860*, Philadelphia, 1932.

Howard, Addison, "Captain John Mullan," *WHQ, 25* (1934), 185–202.

Howard, H. E., and D. L. McGrath, *War Chief Joseph*, Caldwell, Idaho, 1946.

Howard, O. O. (General), *Nez Perce Joseph: An Account of His Ancestors, His Lands, His Confederates, His Enemies, His Murders, His War, His Pursuit and Capture*, Boston, 1881.

Howay, F. W., et al., *British Columbia and the United States*, New Haven, 1942.

Hughes, Thomas A. (S.J.), *History of the Society of Jesus in North America, Colonial and Federal*, 4 vols. New York, 1907–17.

Hulbert, A. B. and D. P., eds., *The Oregon Crusade, across Land and Sea to Oregon*, Overland to the Pacific, 5, Colorado Springs, 1935.

Hunt, Aurora, *The Army of the Pacific. Its Operations in California, Texas, Arizona, New Mexico, Utah, Nevada, Oregon, Washington, Plains Region, Mexico, etc. 1860–1866*, Glendale, Cal., 1951.

Hunter, George, *Reminiscences of an Old Timer, a Recital of the Actual Events, Incidents, Trials, Hardships, Vicissitudes, Adventures, Perils, and Escapes of a Pioneer, Hunter, Miner, and Scout of the Pacific Northwest . . .*, San Francisco, 1887.

Hussey, J. A., *The History of Fort Vancouver and Its Physical Structure*, Tacoma, 1957.

Indian Affairs, Laws and Treaties, comp.-ed. Charles J. Kappler, 5 vols. Washington, D.C., 1903–41.

Jackson, W. T., "Indian Affairs and Politics in Idaho Territory, 1863–1870," *PNWQ, 14* (1945), 311–25.

Jenness, Diamond, *The Indians of Canada*, 5th ed., National Museum of Canada, Bulletin 65, Anthropological Series, 15, Ottawa, 1960.

Jessett, Thomas E., *Chief Spokan Garry, 1811–1892, Christian, Statesman, and Friend of the White Man*, Minneapolis, 1960.

—— "The Origins of the Episcopal Church in the Pacific Northwest," *OHQ, 48* (1947), 225–44, 287–308.

—— "The Origins of the Episcopal Church in Western Washington," *PNWQ, 37* (1946), 303–12.

—— See Beaver, *Reports*, above.

Johannsen, Robert W., *Frontier Politics and Sectional Conflict, the Pacific Northwest on the Eve of the Civil War*, Seattle, 1955.

Johansen, D. O., and Charles M. Gates, *Empire of the Columbia: A History of the Pacific Northwest*, New York, 1957.

—— See Newell, below.

Joseph, Chief, "An Indian's Views of Indian Affairs," *North American Review, 128* (1879), 412–33.

Josephy, Alvin M., *The Patriot Chiefs, a Chronicle of American Indian Leadership*, New York, 1961.

Joset, Joseph (S.J.), [account of 1858 war], San Francisco *Monitor*, 24 and 31 March 1860.

—— *L'Histoire de la mission de Colvil[l]e, d'après les notes de P. Joset*, pamphlet, n.p., n.d.

—— "Washington Territory, Then and Now," *WL, 12* (1883), 172–80.

—— See Burns, "Père Joset's Account," above.

Journal of the Council of Washington Territory. See *Journal of the House*, below

Journal of the House of Representatives of the Washington Territory: Sixth Session of the Legislative Assembly, 1858, Olympia, Wash., 1859.

Jung, A. M., *Jesuit Missions among the American Tribes of the Rocky Mountain Indians*, pamphlet, Spokane, 1925.

Kappler. See *Indian Affairs*, above.

Kautz, A. V. (Lieutenant), "From Missouri to Oregon in 1860, the Diary of August V. Kautz," ed. Martin F. Schmitt, *PNWQ, 37* (1946), 193–230.

Kelley, John F., "The Steptoe Disaster," *Pacific Northwesterner, 1* (1956–57), 9–16.

Kenny, Michael, [Military reminiscences], Spokane *Spokesman-Review*, 12 May 1901.

Keyes, E. D. (General), *Fifty Years' Observation of Men and Events, Civil and Military*, New York, 1884.

Kip, Lawrence (Lieutenant), *Army Life on the Pacific: A Journal of the Expedition against the Northern Indians, the Tribes of the Coeur d'Alenes, Spokans, and Pelouzes, in the Summer of 1858*, New York, 1859. Reprinted in *The Magazine of History*, Extra No. 30, New York, 1914.

—— *The Indian Council in the Valley of the Walla Walla*, San Francisco, 1855; reprinted Tarrytown, N.Y., 1915; also reprinted as *The Indian Council at Walla Walla, May and June 1855, a Journal*, University of Oregon, Contributions of the Department of Economics and History, Sources of the History of Oregon, 1, Eugene, Oreg., 1897.

Kip, W. I., *The Early Jesuit Missions in North America, Compiled and Translated from the Letters of the French Jesuits, with Notes*, Albany, N.Y., [1846] 1866.

Knuth, Priscilla, "Nativism in Oregon," *Reed College Bulletin, 24* (1946), 1–25
——— "Oregon Know Nothing Pamphlet Illustrates Early Politics," *OHQ, 54* (1953), 40–53.
Kroeber, A. L., *Cultural and Natural Areas of Native North America,* Berkeley, 1939.
Kuppens, F. X. (S.J.), "Thomas Francis Meagher, Montana Pioneer," ["Stray Leaves from the Diary and Musings" of Kuppens], *Mid-America, 14* (1931–32), 127–40.
Lamirande, Emilien (O.M.I.), "L'Implantation de l'église catholique en Colombie Britannique, 1838–1848," *Revue de l'université d'Ottawa, 28* (1958), 213–25, 323–63, 453–89.
——— "Projet de fondation oblate en Californie (1849–1853), un chapitre des relations entre Jésuites et Oblats en Orégon," *Etudes oblates, 22* (1963), 1–38.
Laveille, Eugène (S.J.), *Le Père De Smet, apôtre des Peaux-Rouges (1801–1873),* 4th ed., Museum lessianum, section missiologique, 9, Louvain, [1913] 1928. Eng. trans. Marian Lindsay, *The Life of Father De Smet, S.J. (1801–1873),* New York, 1915.
Ledbetter. See below, p. 492.
Lent, D. Geneva, *West of the Mountains. James Sinclair* [1806–56] *and the Hudson's Bay Company,* Seattle, 1963.
Lever, W. H., *An Illustrated History of Whitman County, State of Washington,* n.p., 1901.
Lewis, A. B., *Tribes of the Columbia Valley and the Coast of Washington and Oregon,* Amer. Anthrop. Assoc., Memoirs, 1, Lancaster, Pa., 1906.
Lewis, B. R., *Small Arms and Ammunition in the United States Service,* Smithsonian Miscellaneous Collections, 129, Washington, D.C., 1956.
Lewis, W. S., *The Case of Spokane Garry, Being a Brief Statement of the Principal Facts Connected with His Career* . . . , Spokane, 1917; issued as Spokane Historical Society *Bulletin, 1* (1917), 1–68.
Liljeblad, Sven, *The Indians of Idaho,* pamphlet, Idaho Historical Society series, 3, Boise, 1960. Reprint from *Idaho Yesterdays, 4,* no. 3 (1960), 22–28.
——— See below, p. 492 f.
Logan, David, "22 Letters of David Logan, Pioneer Oregon Lawyer," ed. H. E. Pratt, *OHQ, 44* (1943), 253–85.
Lownsdale, D. H., "Letter by Daniel H. Lownsdale to Samuel R. Thurston, First Territorial Delegate from Oregon to Congress," *OHQ, 14* (1913), 211–49.
Lyman, W. D., *History of Old Walla Walla County, Embracing Walla Walla, Columbia, Garfield and Asotin Counties,* 2 vols. Chicago, 1918.
Lyons, Sister M. Letitia (S.H.N.), *Francis Norbert Blanchet and the Founding of the Oregon Missions, 1838–1848,* Washington, D.C., 1940.
McBeth, K. C., *The Nez Perces since Lewis and Clark,* New York, 1908.
McDonnell, Anne, and J. B. Ritch, eds., "The Fort Benton Journal, 1854–1856," *CHSM, 10* (1940), 1–99.
McElroy, H. L., "Mercurial Military, a Study of the Central Montana Frontier Indian Policy," *Montana, The Magazine of Western History, 4* (1954), 9–23.
McKenney. See *Business Directory.*
MacLeod, W. C., *The American Indian Frontier,* History of Civilization series, 40, New York, 1928.

McLoughlin, John, *The Letters of John McLoughlin from Fort Vancouver to the Governor and Committee,* ed. E. E. Rich, Toronto, 1941.

McNamee, Sister M. Dominica (S.N.D. de N.), *Willamette Interlude,* Palo Alto, Cal., 1960.

McWhorter, L. V., *Hear Me, My Chiefs! Nez Perce History and Legend,* Caldwell, Idaho, 1952.

────── *Yellow Wolf: His Own Story,* Caldwell, Idaho, 1940.

Maillet, Louis, "Historical Sketch of Louis R. Maillet," *CHSM, 4* (1903), 197–228

Mallett, Edward (Major), "The Origin of the Flathead Mission of the Rocky Mountains," *RACHS, 2* (1889), 174–205.

Malouf, Carling, "Early Kutenai History," *Montana, The Magazine of Western History, 2,* no. 2 (1952), 5–9.

Manring, B. F., *The Conquest of the Coeur d'Alenes, Spokanes, and Palouses, the Expeditions of Colonels E. J. Steptoe and George Wright against the "Northern Indians" in 1858,* Spokane, 1912.

Mansfield, J. K. (Colonel), *Mansfield on the Condition of the Western Forts 1853–54,* ed. R. W. Frazer, Norman, Okla., 1963.

Manypenny, George M., *Our Indian Wards,* Cincinnati, 1880.

Marie Antoinette, Mother (F.C.S.P.), *The Institute of Providence: History of the Daughters of Charity Servants of the Poor Known as the Sisters of Providence, 5* vols. Providence, R.I., 1937–49.

Masterson, J. R., "The Records of the Washington Superintendency of Indian Affairs, 1853–1874," *PNWQ, 37* (1946), 31–57.

Meagher, T. F. (Governor), [1866 letter to De Smet], *LN, 7* (1870), 187–201.

Mengarini, Gregory (S.J.), "The Rocky Mountains, the Memoirs of Fr. Gregory Mengarini," *WL, 17* (1888), 298–309; *18* (1889), 25–43, 142–52. Also published as "Father Mengarini's Narrative of the Rockies," ed. A. J. Partoll, *Frontier and Midland, 18* (1938), 192–202, 258–66; and separately as Historical Reprints, Sources of Northwest History, *25.*

────── "Indians of Oregon," *Journal of the Anthropological Institute of New York, 1* (1871–72), 81–88.

Merk, Frederick, *Manifest Destiny and Mission in American History a Reinterpretation,* New York, 1963.

────── See Simpson, below.

[Mesplié, Toussaint], Interview-report on Mesplié, Fort Boise military chaplain, *Army and Navy Journal,* 6 April 1878.

Message and Correspondence. See Stevens, *Message,* below.

Missioni della provincia torinese della Compagnia di Gesù nelle montagne rocciose dell' America settentrionale, lettere dei pp. missionari, Turin, 1887.

"The Missions of the Rocky Mountains in 1881," *WL, 11* (1882), 43–56.

Mofras. See Duflot, above.

Monti, A. (S.J.), *La Compagnia di Gesù nel territorio della provincia torinese, 5* vols. Chieri, Italy, 1914–1920.

Mooney, James, "The Ghost Dance Religion and the Sioux Outbreak of 1890," *BAE Report, 14* (1892–93), Pt. 2, 641–1110.

────── "Mengarini," *Catholic Encyclopedia, 10,* 188–89.

Morgan, M. R. (General), "Recollections of the Spokane Expedition," *Journal of the Military Service Institution of the United States, 42* (1908), 489–96.

Morice, A. G. (O.M.I.), *Dictionnaire historique des canadiens et des métis français de l'ouest*, Quebec, 1908.

———— *Histoire de l'église catholique dans l'ouest canadien du Lac Supérieur au Pacifique*, 4 vols. Montreal, 1921–23.

Mullan, John (Captain) "Journal from Fort Dalles O. T. to Fort Wallah Wallah W. T. July 1858," ed. Pal Clarke, *Frontier and Midland*, *12* (1932), 368–75. Published separately as Historical Reprints, Sources of Northwest History, 18.

———— *Miners and Travelers' Guide to Oregon, Washington, Idaho, Montana, Wyoming, and Colorado, Via the Missouri and Columbia Rivers, Accompanied by a General Map of the Mineral Region of the Northern Sections of the Rocky Mountains*, New York, 1865.

———— *Report on the Construction of a Military Road from Fort Walla Walla to Fort Benton*, Washington, D.C., 1863. Published as congressional series 1149; see Government Documents, above, p. 469 (cf. earlier report, serial 1097).

———— "Report on the Indian Tribes in the Eastern Portion of Washington Territory, 1853," in Secretary of War, *Reports of Explorations*, *1*, 437–41, below.

———— *Topographical Memoir of Colonel Wright's Campaign*, Washington, D.C., 1859. Published as congressional serial 984; see Government Documents, above, p. 468.

Muratori, L. A., *Il Cristianesimo felice*, Venice, 1743.

———— *A Relation of the Missions of Paraguay. Written Originally in Italian by Mr. Muratori and Now Done into English from the French Translation*, London, 1759.

Murdock, George P., *Ethnographic Bibliography of North America*, 3d ed. New Haven, 1960.

Murray, K. A., *The Modocs and Their War*, Norman, Okla., 1959.

Nedry, H. S., ed., "Willamette Valley in 1859, the Diary of a Tour," *OHQ*, *46* (1945), 235–54.

Neil, W. N., "The Territorial Governor as Indian Superintendent in the Trans-Mississippi West," *MVHR*, *43* (1956–57), 213–37.

Neilson, Jean C., "Donald McKenzie in the Snake Country," *PNWQ*, *31* (1940), 161–79.

Newell, Robert, *Robert Newell's Memoranda: Travles in the Territory of Missourie; Travle to the Kayuse War; Together with a Report on the Indians South of the Columbia River*, ed. D. O. Johansen, Portland, Oreg., 1959.

Nichols, M. Leona, *The Mantle of Elias: The Story of Fathers Blanchet and Demers in Early Oregon*, Portland, Oreg., 1941.

Notice sur le territoire et la mission de l'Orégon, tirée des Mélanges religieux, Montreal, 1845.

Notizie storiche e descrittive delle missioni della provincia torinese della Compagnia di Gesù nell' America del Nord, 2 vols. Turin, 1898.

O'Connor, James (Bishop), "The Flathead Indians," *Records of the American Catholic Historical Society of Philadelphia*, *3* (1888–91), 85–110. French translation of this original version of 1879 is earlier in the *APF*, *52* (1880), 201–32.

Ogden, Peter Skene, *Traits of Indian Life and Character*, San Francisco, 1933.

O'Hara, Edwin V., *Pioneer Catholic History of Oregon*, Portland, Oreg., 1911; Paterson, N.J., 1939.

Oliphant, J. Orin, "Old Fort Colville," *WHQ*, *16* (1925), 29–48.

O'Neil, John, [Military reminiscences], Spokane *Spokesman-Review*, 2 April 1906.
—— "Recollections of a Soldier," in E. F. Tannatt, comp., *Indian Battles in the Inland Empire* (Spokane, 1914), pp. 6–7.
Ormsby, M. A., *British Columbia: A History*, Vancouver, 1959.
Ortolan, Théophile (O.M.I.), *Les Oblats de Marie Immaculée durant le premier siècle de leur existence*, 4 vols. Paris, 1914–32.
Otto, Jos. A. (S.J.), *Gründung der neuen Jesuitenmission durch General Pater Johann Philipp Roothaan*, Freiburg-im-Breisgau, 1939.
Overmeyer, P. H., "George B. McClellan and the Pacific Northwest," *PNWQ, 32* (1941), 3–60.
Owen, Homer L., "Nesmith: Pioneer Judge, Legislator, Farmer, Soldier, Senator and Congressman," *Reed College Bulletin, 28* (1950), 139–76.
Owen, John, *The Journals and Letters of Major John Owen, Pioneer of the Northwest 1850–1871, Embracing His Purchase of St. Mary's Mission; the Building of Fort Owen; His Travels; His Relation with the Indians; His Work for the Government; and His Activities as a Western Empire Builder for Twenty Years*, ed. Seymour Dunbar and P. C. Phillips, 2 vols. Helena, Mont., 1927.
Owens, George, *A General Directory and Business Guide of the Principal Towns East of the Cascade Mountains For the Year 1865: Including Valuable Historical and Statistical Information; Together with a Map of Boise Basin, Embracing a Portion of Ada, Owyhee, and Alturas Counties*, San Francisco, 1865.
Palladino, Lawrence B. (S.J.), *Anthony Ravalli, a Memoir*, Helena, Mont., 1884.
—— *Education for the Indian*, New York, 1892.
—— "Historical Notes on the Flathead," *Indian Sentinel, 1* (1919), 6–16.
—— *Indian and White in the Northwest; or, a History of Catholicity in Montana*, Baltimore, 1894; also Lancaster, Pa., 1893; inferior rev. ed. 1922.
—— "Noted Indians," *Indian Sentinel, 1* (1919), 19–25.
—— See Flathead tribe, above.
Pandosy, Charles (O.M.I.), "Pacification de l'Orégon" [letter of 24 June 1858], *Missions de la congrégation des missionnaires oblats de Marie Immaculée, 1* (1862), 112–20.
Papers Relating to Affairs of British Columbia. See *Copies of Despatches*, above.
Partoll, Albert J., "Angus McDonald, Frontier Fur Trader," *PNWQ, 42* (1951), 138–46.
—— "Fort Connah: A Frontier Trading Post, 1847–1871," *PNWQ, 30* (1939), 399–415.
—— ed., "The Blackfoot Indian Peace Council," *Frontier and Midland, 17* (1937), 199–207. Published separately as Historical Reprints, Sources of Northwest History, 3.
—— ed., "The Flathead Indian Treaty Council of 1855," *PNWQ, 29* (1938), 283–314.
—— See Mengarini, "Narrative of the Rockies," above.
Pastells, Pablo (S.J.), *Historia de la Compañía de Jesús en la provincia de Paraguay*, 5 vols. Madrid, 1912–33.
Paul, R. W., *Mining Frontiers of the Far West, 1848–1880*, New York, 1963.
Peone, Basil, "An Indian Herodotus," *Teepee* (Coeur d'Alene domestic pub.), *1* (1938), 7.
Pfülf, Otto (S.J.), *Die Anfänge der deutschen Provinz der neu erstandenen Gesell-*

schaft Jesu und ihr Wirken in der Schweiz, 1805–1847, Freiburg-im-Breisgau, 1922.

Phillips, Paul Crisler, *The Fur Trade*, 2 vols. Norman, Okla., 1961.

—— "Jesuit Missionaries as Doctors," in his *Medicine in the Making of Montana*, Missoula, 1962.

—— ed., " 'The Battle of the Big Hole': An Episode in the Nez Perce War," *Frontier and Midland, 10* (1929), 63–80. Published separately as Historical Reprints, Sources of Northwest History, 8.

—— See also Owen, above; Stuart, Walker, Work, below.

Poe, O. M. See Sherman, *Reports of Inspection*, below.

Point, Nicholas (S.J.), "An Early Missouri River Journal," ed. G. J. Garraghan (S.J.), *Mid-America, 13* (1930–31), 236–54.

—— "Recollections of the Rocky Mountains," *WL, 11* (1882), 298–321; *12* (1883), 3–22, 133–53, 261–68; *13* (1884), 3–13.

Pouliot, Léon (S.J.), "Le Père Nicolas Point (1799–1868): Collaborateur du P. De Smet dans les Montagnes Rocheuses et missionnaire en Ontario," *Rapport de la Société canadienne d'histoire de l'église catholique, 3* (1936–37), 20–30.

Priest, L. B., *Uncle Sam's Stepchildren: The Reformation of United States Indian Policy, 1865–1887*, Newark, N.J., 1942.

Pritchett, J. P., *The Red River Valley 1811–1849, a Regional Study*, New Haven, 1942.

Prosch, Thomas W., "The Indian War of 1858," *WHQ, 2* (1908), 237–40.

—— "The Military Roads of Washington Territory," *WHQ, 2* (1908), 118–26.

—— "The United States Army in Washington Territory," *WHQ, 2* (1908), 28–32.

Prucha, F. P. (S.J.), *American Indian Policy in the Formative Years, the Indian Trade and Intercourse Acts, 1790–1834*, Cambridge, Mass., 1962.

—— *A Guide to the Military Posts of the United States, 1789–1895*, Madison, Wisc., 1964.

—— "Indian Removal and the Great American Desert," *Indiana Magazine of History, 59* (1963), 298–322.

Quebec Mission. See Blanchet, above.

Rahill, Peter J., *The Catholic Indian Missions and Grant's Peace Policy, 1870–1884*, Catholic University of America, Studies in American History, 41, Washington, D.C., 1953.

Railroad Reports. See Stevens, below.

Rappagliosi, Carlo and Agnes, *Memorie del P. Filippo Rappagliosi d. C. di G., missionario apostolico nelle montagne rocciose*, Rome, 1879.

Ray, Verne F., *Cultural Relations in the Plateau of Northwestern America*, Southwest Museum, Publications of the F. W. Hodge Fund, 3, Los Angeles, 1939.

—— "Native Villages and Groupings of the Columbia Basin," *PNWQ, 27* (1936), 99–152.

—— *Plateau*, Culture Element Distributions, 22; University of California, Anthropological Records, 8; Berkeley, 1942.

—— *The Sanpoil and Nespelem: Salishan Peoples of Northeastern Washington*, University of Washington, Publications in Anthropology, 5, Seattle, 1932.

Reavis, L. A., *The Life and Military Services of General William Sibley Harney*, St. Louis, 1878.

Redfield, F. M., "Reminiscences [and letters] of Francis M. Redfield [Nez Percé subagent during]: Chief Joseph's War," *PNWQ*, 27 (1936), 66–76.

Reichard, G. A., *An Analysis of Coeur d'Alene Indian Myths*, American Folklore Society, Memoirs, 41, Philadelphia, 1947.

Reinhart, H. F., *The Golden Frontier, the Recollections of Herman Francis Reinhart, 1851–1869*, ed. D. B. Nunis, Jr., Austin, 1962.

Relander, Click, *Drummers and Dreamers*, Caldwell, Idaho, 1956.

Reports of Explorations. See Secretary of War, below.

Reports of Inspection. See Sherman, below.

Rich, E. E., *The Hudson's Bay Company*, 3 vols. to date, Publications of the Hudson's Bay Record Society, 22, London, 1958–61.

Riordan, Joseph W. (S.J.), *The First Half Century of St. Ignatius Church and College*, San Francisco, 1905.

Robinson, W. B., "Frontier Architecture" [Coeur d'Alene mission], *Idaho Yesterdays, 3*, no. 4 (1959), 2–6.

Roe, Frank G., *The Indian and the Horse*, Norman, Okla., 1955.

Ronan, Peter (Agent), *Historical Sketch of the Flathead Indian Nation from the Year 1813 to 1890*, Helena, Mont., 1890.

Ronan, Mary C. (Mrs. Peter). See below, p. 493.

Rosebush, W. E., *American Firearms and the Changing Frontier*, Spokane, 1962.

––––– *Frontier Steel, the Men and Their Weapons*, Spokane, 1958.

Ross, Alexander, *The Fur Hunters of the Far West*, ed. Kenneth A. Spaulding, Norman, Okla., 1956.

Rothensteiner, John, *History of the Archdiocese of St. Louis in Its Various Stages of Development from 1673 to 1928*, 2 vols. St. Louis, 1928.

Rothermich, A. E., ed., "Early Days at Fort Missoula," *Frontier and Midland, 16* (1936), 225–35. Reprinted separately as Historical Reprints, Sources of Northwest History, 23.

Royce, C. C., "Indian Land Cessions in the United States," BAE *Report, 18* (1896–97), Pt. 2, 521–997.

Schaeffer, Claude, "The First Jesuit Mission to the Flatheads, 1840–1850, a Study in Culture Conflicts," *PNWQ, 28* (1937), 227–50.

Schiach, W. S., H. B. Averill, et al., *An Illustrated History of North Idaho Embracing Nez Perces, Idaho, Latah, Kootenai, and Shoshone Counties, State of Idaho*, Spokane, 1903.

Schmeckebier, Lawrence F., *The Office of Indian Affairs: Its History, Activities and Organization*, Service Monographs of the U.S. Government, Institute for Government Research, 48, Baltimore, 1927.

Schmidlin, Joseph, *Catholic Mission History*, ed. Matthias Braun, Techny, Ill., 1933.

Schoenberg, W. P. (S.J.), *A Chronicle of the Catholic History of the Pacific Northwest, 1743–1960*, Portland, Oreg., 1962.

––––– "Historic St. Peter's Mission: Landmark of the Jesuits and the Ursulines among the Blackfeet," *Montana, The Magazine of Western History, 11*, no. 1 (1961), 68–85.

––––– *Jesuits in Montana*, pamphlet, Portland, Oreg., 1960.

––––– *Jesuits in Oregon, 1844–1959*, pamphlet, Portland, Oreg., 1959.

––––– *Jesuit Mission Presses in the Pacific Northwest, a History and Bibliography of Imprints, 1876–1899*, Portland, Oreg., 1957.

Scott, H. W., *History of the Oregon Country*, 6 vols. Cambridge, Mass., 1924.

Scott, Leslie M., "Indian Diseases as Aids to Pacific Northwest Settlement," *OHQ*, 29 (1928), 144–61.

Secretary of War, *Reports of Explorations and Surveys to Ascertain the Most Practicable and Economical Route for a Railroad from the Mississippi River to the Pacific Ocean, Made under the Direction of the Secretary of War, in 1853–5*, 12 vols. in 13, Washington, D.C., 1855–60. Published as congressional serials, several numbers; see Government Documents, above, p. 469.

Settle, Raymond W. See Cross, above.

Settlers' Guide to Homes in the Northwest, Being a Hand-Book of Spokane Falls, W.T., the Queen City of the Pacific, Its Matchless Water Power and Advantages as a Commercial Center, Spokane Falls, 1885.

Shaver, F. A., et al., *An Illustrated History of Southeastern Washington Including Walla Walla, Columbia, Garfield and Asotin Counties*, Spokane, 1906.

Shea, J. Gilmary, *History of the Catholic Church in the United States*, 4 vols. New York, 1886–92.

—— *History of the Catholic Missions among the Indian Tribes of the United States, 1529–1854*, New York, [1855] 1881.

Sheridan, P. H. (General), *Personal Memoirs of P. H. Sheridan*, 2 vols. New York, 1888.

Sherman, Thomas E. (S.J.), "Across the Continent," Pt. 3, *WL*, 11 (1882), 141–63. Memoir by General Sherman's son, mostly copied from his 1877 diary.

Sherman, William T., by aide O. M. Poe, *Reports of Inspection Made in the Summer of 1877 by Generals P. H. Sheridan and W. T. Sherman of Country North of the Union Pacific Railroad*, Washington, D.C., 1878.

Simpson, George, *Fur Trade and Empire: George Simpson's Journal . . . 1824–1825*, ed. Frederick Merk, Harvard Historical Studies, 31, Cambridge, Mass., 1931.

Smart, W. B., "Oregon and the Mormon Problem," *Reed College Bulletin*, 26 (1948), 41–62.

Smead, W. H. (Flathead agent), *Land of the Flatheads, a Sketch of the Flathead Reservation, Montana, Its Past and Present, Its Hopes and Possibilities for the Future*, St. Paul, Minn., 1905.

Smith, Alan H., "The Indians of Washington," *Research Studies of the State College of Washington*, 21 (1953), 85–113.

—— *The Puyullup-Nisqually*, Columbia University, Contributions to Anthropology, 32, New York, 1940.

Smith, M. W., "The Nooksack, the Chilliwack, and the Middle Fraser," *PNWQ*, 41 (1950), 330–41.

Smith, Winston O., *The Sharps Rifle, Its History, Development and Operation*, New York, 1943.

Snowden, C. A., *History of Washington, the Rise and Progress of an American State*, 4 vols. New York, 1909.

Spalding, H. H., *The Diaries and Letters of Henry H. Spalding and Asa Bowen Smith Relating to the Nez Percé Mission, 1838–1842*, ed. C. M. Drury, Northwest Historical Series, 4, Glendale, Cal., 1958.

—— "A Letter by Henry H. Spalding from the Rocky Mountains," ed. J. Orin Oliphant, *OHQ*, 51 (1950), 127–33.

Spier, Leslie, *The Prophet Dance of the Northwest and Its Derivatives; the Source of the Ghost Dance*, Amer. Anthrop. Assoc., General Series in Anthropology, 1, Menasha, Wisc., 1935.

———— *Tribal Distribution in Washington*, Amer. Anthrop. Assoc., General Series in Anthropology, 3, Menasha, Wisc., 1936.

———— See Cline, above.

Spinden, H. J., *The Nez Percé Indians*, Amer. Anthrop. Assoc., Memoirs, 2, Lancaster, Pa., 1903.

Splawn, A. J., *Ka-Mi-Akin, The Last Hero of the Yakimas*, Portland, Oreg., 1917, 1944.

Steele, R. F., et al., *History of Stevens, Ferry, Okanogan, and Chelan Counties State of Washington*, Spokane, 1904.

Stellam, Chief, "The Story of Stellam," Spokane *Review*, 6 October 1891.

Stevens, Hazard, *The Life of Isaac Ingalls Stevens by His Son*, 2 vols. Boston, 1901.

Stevens, Isaac Ingalls, *Address on the Northwest, Before the American Geographical and Statistical Society, Delivered at New York, December 2, 1858*. Washington, D.C., 1858.

———— "Letters of Governor Isaac I. Stevens, 1857–1858," ed. Ronald Todd, *PNWQ, 31* (1940), 403–59.

———— *Message of the Governor of Washington Territory; also the Correspondence with the Secretary of War, Major General Wool, the Officers of the Regular Army, and of the Volunteer Service of Washington Territory*, Olympia, Wash., 1857.

———— *Narrative and Final Report of Explorations for a Route for a Pacific Railroad, near the Forty-Seventh and Forty-Ninth Parallels of North Latitude from St. Paul to Puget Sound*, Washington, D.C., 1860. See Secretary of War, *Reports of Explorations* (incl. as *12*, Pt. 1), above.

———— *Report of Explorations for a Route for the Pacific Railroad near the Forty-Seventh and Forty-Ninth Parallels of North Latitude, from St. Paul to Puget Sound*, Washington, D.C., 1855. See Secretary of War, *Reports of Explorations* (incl. in *1*), above.

Steward, J. H., *Basin-Plateau Aboriginal Socio-Political Groups*, BAE *Bulletin, 120*, Washington, D.C., 1938.

Stewart, E. I., *Washington, Northwest Frontier*, 4 vols. New York, 1957.

Stone, A. L., *Following Old Trails*, Missoula, Mont., 1913.

Stork, B. C., *Pioneer Days in Montana*, New York, 1952.

Strachan, John, **Blazing the Mullan Trail. Connecting the Headwaters of the** *Missouri and the Columbia Rivers and Locating the Great Overland Highway to the Pacific Northwest, by John Strachan (a member of the Pioneer Expedition)*, Rockford, Ill., [1860–61] 1952.

Strong, William, "Knickerbocker Views of the Oregon Country: Judge William Strong's Narrative," ed. W. D. Strong, *OHQ, 62* (1961), 57–87.

Stuart, Granville, *Forty Years on the Frontier as Seen in the Journals and Reminiscences of Granville Stuart, Gold-Miner, Trader, Rancher and Politician*, ed. P. C. Phillips, 2 vols. Cleveland, 1925.

Sullivan, Sister M. Louise (O.P.), *Eugene Casimer Chirouse O.M.I. and the Indians of Washington*, Seattle, 1932.

Sutherland, T. A., *Howard's Campaign against the Nez Percé Indians, 1877*, Portland, Oreg., 1878.

Swan, J. G., *The Northwest Coast; or, Three Years' Residence in Washington Territory*, New York, 1857.
Swanton, John R., *The Indian Tribes of North America*, BAE *Bulletin, 145,* Washington, D.C., 1952.
Tebble, J. W., and K. Jennison, *The American Indian Wars*, New York, ca. 1960.
Teit, James, "The Salishan Tribes of the Western Plateaus," ed. Franz Boas, BAE *Report, 45,* (1927–28), 23–396.
Terrell, John U., *Black Robe, the Life of Pierre-Jean De Smet, Missionary, Explorer, Pioneer*, Garden City, N.Y., 1964.
Thibodo, A. J., "Diary of Dr. Augustine J. Thibodo of the Northwest Exploring Expedition, 1859," ed. H. S. Brode, *PNWQ, 31* (1940), 287–347.
Thompson, D., "Discovery of the Source of the Columbia River," ed. T. C. Elliott, *OHQ, 26* (1927), 23–49.
Thwaites, Reuben G., ed., *Early Western Travels*, 32 vols. Cleveland, 1904–07.
———— ed., *The Jesuit Relations and Allied Documents; Travels and Explorations of the Jesuit Missionaries in New France, 1610–1791,* 73 vols. Cleveland, 1896–1901.
Todd, Ronald. See Stevens, "Letters," above.
Tolmie, W. F., *The Journals of William Fraser Tolmie, Physician and Fur Trader*, Vancouver, B.C., 1963.
Trenholm, V. C., and Maurine Carley, *The Shoshonis: Sentinels of the Rockies*, Civilization of the American Indian, 74, Norman, Okla., 1964.
Treutlein, T. H., "The Jesuit Missionary in the Role of Physician," *Mid-America, 22* (1940), 120–41.
"La Tribù dei Cuori di Lesina," in *Notizie storiche e descrittive, 2,* 8–34, above.
Trimble, J., and August Wolf, "Where the Steptoe Expedition Made Its Last Stand," *Journal of the Military Service Institution of the United States, 42* (1908), 498–501.
Trimble, William J., *The Mining Advance into the Inland Empire, a Comparative Study of the Beginnings of the Mining Industry in Idaho and Montana, Eastern Washington and Oregon, and the Southern Interior of British Columbia, and of Institutions and Laws Based on That Industry*, University of Wisconsin, Bulletin 638, Madison, Wisc., 1914.
———— "A Soldier of the Oregon Frontier," *OHQ, 8* (1907), 42–50.
Tschan, Francis J., "The Catholic Church in the United States, 1852–1868: A Survey," *RACHS, 58* (1947), 123–32, 182–88; *59* (1948), 35–43, 77–119, 223–40.
Tuohy, R., "Horseshoes and Handstones, the Meeting of History and Prehistory at the Old Mission of the Sacred Heart," *Idaho Yesterdays, 2,* no. 2 (1958), 20–27.
Turney-High, H. H., *Ethnology of the Kutenai*, Amer. Anthrop. Assoc., Memoirs, 56, Menasha, Wisc., 1941.
———— *The Flathead Indians of Montana*, Amer. Anthrop. Assoc., Memoirs, 48, Menasha, Wisc., 1937
———— *The Practice of Primitive War, a Study in Comparative Sociology*, University of Montana, Publications in Social Sciences, 2, Missoula, 1942.
Tuttle, Daniel S. (Bishop), "Early History of the Episcopal Church in Montana," *CHSM, 5* (1904), 289–324.
———— *Reminiscences of a Missionary Bishop*, New York, 1906.
"L'Ultimo degli antichi missionari degli Indiani," *LPT*, n.v. (1902), 242.

Underhill, Ruth M., *Red Man's America, a History of Indians in the United States*, Chicago, 1960.

Van der Heyden, J., "Monsignor Adrian J. Croquet, Indian Missionary (1812–1902) and Some of His Letters," *RACHS, 16* (1905), 121–61, 268–95, 456–62; *17* (1906), 86–96, 220–42, 267–88.

Van Ree, L. (S.J.), "The Spokane Indians," *WL, 18* (1889), 354–64.

Vestal, Stanley, *Sitting Bull, Champion of the Sioux, a Biography*, Norman, Okla., 1957.

Victor, Frances Fuller, *The Early Indian Wars of Oregon Compiled from the Oregon Archives and Other Original Sources, with Muster Rolls*, Salem, Oreg., 1894.

Villard, Henry, "Two Railroad Reports on Northwest Resources," *PNWQ, 37* (1946), 175–91.

"A Visit to a Famous Mission," Baltimore *Catholic Mirror*, 14 April 1888.

Waggett, G. M. (O.M.I.), "The Oblates of Mary Immaculate in the Pacific Northwest of U.S.A.," *Etudes oblates, 6* (1947), 7–88.

———— "The Oblates of Mary Immaculate in the Pacific Northwest, 1847–1878," *RACHS, 63* (1952), 177–87; *64* (1953), 72–93, 166–82.

Walker, E., "The Oregon Missions as Shown in the Walker Letters, 1839–1851," ed. Paul C. Phillips, *Frontier and Midland, 11* (1930), 74–89. Published separately as Historical Reprints, Sources of Northwest History, 13.

Weibel, G. F. (S.J.), *Rev. Joseph M. Cataldo, S.J., a Short Sketch of a Wonderful Career*, Spokane, 1928. Revised from an article of the same title in Gonzaga University *Quarterly, 16* (1928); also in *Salem Catholic Monthly, 1* (1928), No. 5, 9–12, 18–23; No. 6, 11–15, 21–22; No. 7, 11–15, 19–20.

Weinberg, A. K., *Manifest Destiny, a Study of Nationalist Expansion in American History*, Baltimore, 1935.

Weisel, George F., *Men and Trade on the Northwest Frontier, as Shown by the Fort Owen Ledger*, Montana State University, Studies 2, Missoula, Mont., 1955.

Wells, Merle W., "The Nez Percés and Their War," *PNWQ, 55* (1964), 35–37.

White, M. C., "Saleesh House, the First Trading Post among the Flathead," *PNWQ, 33* (1942), 251–63.

Whiting, J. S., *Forts of the State of Washington, a Record of Military and Semi-Military Establishments Designated as Forts from May 29, 1792 to November 15, 1951*, Seattle, Wash.

Whitman, Marcus, "Journal and Report by Dr. Marcus Whitman of His Tour of Exploration with Rev. Samuel Parker in 1835 beyond the Rocky Mountains," ed. F. G. Young, *OHQ, 28* (1927), 239–57.

Whitman, Narcissa, et al., *First White Women over the Rockies. Diaries, Letters, and Biographical Sketches of the Six Women of the Oregon Mission Who Made the Overland Journey in 1836 and 1838*, ed. C. M. Drury, Northwest Historical Series, 6, 7, 2 vols. Glendale, Cal., 1963.

Whitner, R. L., "Grant's Indian Peace Policy on the Yakima Reservation, 1870–1882," *PNWQ, 50* (1959), 135–42.

———— See below, p. 493.

Winder, C. S., "Captain C. S. Winder's Account of a Battle with the Indians," ed. I. Ridgeway Trimble, *MHM, 35* (1940), 56–59.

Winther, O. O., *The Great Northwest, a History*, New York, 1947.

—— *The Old Oregon Country, a History of Frontier Trade, Transportation and Travel*, Stanford, 1950.

Wolf. See Trimble, above.

Wood, Charles E. S., "Famous Indians," *Century Magazine, 46* (1893), 436–45.

Woody, F. H. (Judge), "A Sketch of the Early History of Western Montana ·Written in 1876 and 1877," *CHSM, 2* (1896), 88–106.

Work, John, *The Journal of John Work, a Chief-Trader in the Hudson's Bay Co., during His Expedition from Vancouver to the Flatheads and Blackfeet of the Pacific Northwest*, ed. W. S. Lewis and P. C. Phillips, Early Western Journals, 1, Cleveland, 1923.

NEWSPAPERS

CATHOLIC AND PROTESTANT

Baltimore *Catholic Mirror*, 1850–1908.

Boston *Missionary Herald*, American Board of Commissioners for Foreign Missions (Presbyterian-Congregationalist), 1805 et seq.

Denver *Colorado Catholic*, 1884–99.

New York Evangelist, 1830–1902.

New York *Freeman's Journal and Catholic Register*, 1840–1911.

Pittsburgh Catholic, 1844 et seq.

Portland, Oreg., *Catholic Sentinel*, 1870 et seq.

Portland, Oreg., *Pacific Christian Advocate* (Methodist), 1855–1940.

San Francisco *Monitor* (Catholic), 1858 et seq.

Tualatin Plains *Oregon American and Evangelical Unionist*, 1848–49.

SECULAR

Cincinnati *Star*, 1872–80.

Colfax, Wash., *Palouse Gazette*, 1877 et seq.

Colville, Wash., *Examiner*, 1907 et seq.

Farmington, Wash., *Post*, 1929 et seq.

Helena, Mont., *Independent*, 1874 et seq.

Idaho City *Idaho World*, 1863–1919.

—— *Signal*, 1872–74.

Lewiston, Idaho, *Teller*, 1876–1910.

Missoula, Mont., *Daily Missoulian*, 1888 et seq.

—— *Gazette*, 1888–92.

—— *Weekly Missoulian*, 1873–1910.

Murray, Idaho, *Coeur d'Alene Sun*, 1884–1913.

Portland, Oreg., *Daily News*, 1883–88.

—— *Weekly Oregonian*, 1850–1922.

San Francisco *Alta California* (title varies), 1849–91.

—— *Chronicle*, 1865 et seq.

—— *Evening Bulletin*, 1855–1929.

Spokane (Falls) *Review*. See *Spokesman-Review*, below.

—— *Spokesman-Review*, 1883 et seq.

Wallace, Idaho, *Press-Times*, 1906 et seq.

Walla Walla *Statesman*, 1861–1910.

—— *Union*, 1869 et seq.

Domestic Journals (Privately Distributed)
  Lettere edificante della provincia torinese della Compagnia di Gesù (Turin Jesuits, Turin), *1* (1883).
  Letters and Notices on Subjects Appertaining to the Society of Jesus (English Jesuits, Roehampton), *1* (1862).
  Teepee (Indian, Coeur d'Alene Reservation, Idaho), *1* (1938).
  Woodstock Letters, a Record of Current Events and Historical Notes Connected with the Colleges and Missions of the Society of Jesus (American Jesuits, Woodstock, Md.), *1* (1872).

III. UNPUBLISHED DISSERTATIONS, THESES, AND TYPESCRIPTS

Besson, P. (O.M.I.), *Un Missionnaire d'autrefois, Monseigneur Paul Durieu O.M.I.* (mimeographed), [France], 1962.
Bischoff, William N. (S.J.), "The Yakima Indian War: 1855–1856," doctoral dissertation, Loyola University of Chicago, 1950.
Coan, Charles F., "Federal Indian Policy in the Pacific Northwest, 1849–1870," doctoral dissertation, University of California, 1920.
Crosby, L. E., "Kuailks Metatcopun," interviews with Father Cataldo, typescript, ca. 1925, Oregon Province Archives of the Society of Jesus. See Crosby, above, p. 474.
Davis, William Lyle (S.J.), "Mission St. Anne of the Cayuse Indians, 1847–1848," doctoral dissertation, University of California, 1943.
Donnelly, J. P. (S.J.), "The Liquor Traffic among the Aborigines of the New Northwest, 1800–1860," doctoral dissertation, St. Louis University, 1940.
Duggar, Sister Anna Clare (F.C.S.P.), "Catholic Institutions of the Walla Walla Valley," master's thesis, Seattle University, 1953.
Field, Virgil F. (Colonel), "Index to Washington Territorial Records" (mimeographed), Camp Murray, Tacoma, 1960.
——— "The Official History of the Washington National Guard" (mimeographed), 4 vols. to date, Camp Murray, Tacoma, 1961.
Forbis, Richard G., "Religious Acculturation of the Flathead Indians of Montana," master's thesis, Montana State University, 1950.
Garretson, Charles E., *A History of the Washington Superintendency of Indian Affairs, 1853–65,* master's thesis, University of Washington, 1962.
Gibson, George D., "Jesuit Education of the Indians of New France, 1611–1658," doctoral dissertation, University of California, 1939.
Hawkins, C. A. (rev. by Father Cataldo), "Father Cataldo S.J.," 2 vols. typescript, 1930, Oregon Province Archives of the Society of Jesus.
Hinton, H. P., "The Military Career of John Ellis Wool, 1812–1863," doctoral dissertation, University of Wisconsin, 1960.
Ledbetter, W. G., "Military History of the Oregon Country, 1804–1859," master's thesis, University of Oregon, [1935] 1940.
Liljeblad, Sven, "The Indians of Idaho in Transition," typescript book, 1960, on deposit in Idaho Historical Society, Boise.
——— "Indian Peoples in Idaho," typescript book, 1957, on deposit in Idaho Historical Society, Boise.

Loehr, N. P. (S.J.), "Federal Relations with the Jesuit Osage Mission, 1847–1870," master's thesis, St. Louis University, 1940.

Malan, Vernon D., "Language and Social Change among the Flathead Indians," master's thesis, Montana State University, 1948.

Morrow, Sister M. Claver (F.C.S.P.), "Bishop A. M. A. Blanchet and the Oblates of Mary Immaculate," master's thesis, Seattle University, 1956.

Nowland, Sister M. Julice (S.S.N.D.), "United States Government Relations with the Catholic Indian Missions of the Trans-Mississippi West, 1803–1882," master's thesis, St. Louis University, 1940.

Oviatt, Alton B., "The Movement for a Northern Trail: The Mullan Road, 1859–1869," doctoral dissertation, University of California, 1947.

Ronan, Mary C. (Mrs. Peter), "Memoirs of a Frontierswoman," ed. Margaret Ronan, master's thesis, Montana State University, 1932.

Thomas, Sister Marian Josephine (S.H.N.), "Abbé Jean Baptiste Abraham Brouillet, First Vicar General of the Diocese of Seattle," master's thesis, Seattle University, 1950.

Waltmann, H. G., "The Interior Department, War Department, and Indian Policy, 1865–1887," doctoral dissertation, University of Nebraska, 1962.

White, Sister M. Afra (S.C.L.), "Catholic Indian Missionary Influence in the Development of Catholic Education in Montana, 1840–1903," doctoral dissertation, St. Louis University, 1940.

Whitner, R. L., "The Methodist Episcopal Church and Grant's Peace Policy: A Study of Methodist Agencies, 1870–1882," doctoral dissertation, University of Minnesota, 1959.

INDEX